Japanese/Korean Linguistics

Volume 13

Japanese/Korean Linguistics

Volume 13

edited by

Mutsuko Endo Hudson
Sun-Ah Jun
Peter Sells
Patricia M. Clancy
Shoichi Iwasaki
Sung-Ock Sohn

Published for the
Stanford Linguistics Association by

CSLI
PUBLICATIONS
Center for the Study of Language and Information
STANFORD, CALIFORNIA

Center for the Study of Language and Information
Leland Stanford Junior University
Printed in the United States
12 11 10 09 08   1 2 3 4 5

Library of Congress Cataloging-in-Publication Data

Conference on Japanese/Korean Linguistics (1st : 1989 : University of Southern California)

Japanese/Korean Linguistics / edited by Hajime Hoji.

Volume 13 / edited by Mutsuko Endo Hudson, Sun-Ah Jun, Peter Sells, Patricia M. Clancy, Shoichi Iwasaki and Sung-Ock Sohn.

p.   cm.

Includes bibliographical references and index.
ISBN-13: 978-1-57586-517-1
ISBN-10: 1-57586-517-3
ISBN-13: 978-1-57586-518-8 (pbk.)
ISBN-10: 1-57586-518-1 (pbk.)

1. Japanese language—Congresses. 2. Korean language—Congresses. 3. Japanese language—Grammar, Comparative—Korean—Congresses. 4. Korean language—Grammar, Comparative—Japanese—Congresses. 5. Linguistics—Congresses. I. Hoji, Hajime. II. Stanford Linguistics Association. III. Center for the Study of Language and Information (U.S.) IV. Title.
PL503.C6 1989
495.6–dc20   90-2550
CIP

∞ The acid-free paper used in this book meets the minimum requirements of the American National Standard for Information Sciences—Permanence of Paper for Printed Library Materials, ANSI Z39.48-1984.

For a list of volumes in this series, along with a cumulative table of contents, please visit
http://cslipublications.stanford.edu/site/JAKO.html

CSLI was founded in 1983 by researchers from Stanford University, SRI International, and Xerox PARC to further the research and development of integrated theories of language, information, and computation. CSLI headquarters and CSLI Publications are located on the campus of Stanford University.

CSLI Publications reports new developments in the study of language, information, and computation. Please visit our web site at
http://cslipublications.stanford.edu/
for comments on this and other titles, as well as for changes and corrections by the authors, editors, and publisher.

Contents

Part II
Morphology, Morphosyntax and Syntax

Part IV
Grammaticalization and Functional Grammar

Part V
Pragmatics, Discourse and Sociolinguistics

Contributors

CHAE, HEE-RAHK: Department of Linguistics and Cognitive Science, Hankuk University of Foreign Studies, Yongin, Kyunggi, 449-791, Korea
hrchae@hufs.ac.kr

CHO, YOUNG-MEE YU: Department of Asian Languages, Rutgers University, New Brunswick, NJ 08901-1164, USA
yucho@rci.rutgers.edu

CHOI , YOUNGJU: Department of Linguistics, University of Illinois at Urbana-Champaign, Urbana, Illinois 61821, USA
ychoi1@uiuc.edu

CHUNG, DAEHO: Division of English Language and Culture, Hanyang University, Ansan, Gyeonggi-do, 426-796, Korea
cdaeho@hanyang.ac.kr

COOK, HARUKO MINEGISHI: Department of East Asian Languages and Literatures, University of Hawai'i at Manoa, Honolulu, Hawaii 96822, USA
hkcook@hawaii.edu

DAVIS, STUART: Department of Linguistics, Indiana University, Bloomington, Indiana 47405, USA
davis@indiana.edu

FRELLESVIG, BJARKE: Oriental Institute, University of Oxford, Oxford OX1 2LE, UK
bjarke.frellesvig@hertford.oxford.ac.uk

HAN, CHUNG-HYE: Department of Linguistics, Simon Fraser University, Burnaby, BC V5A 1S6, Canada
chunghye@sfu.ca

HARA, YURIE: Department of Linguistics, Kyoto University, Kyoto, 606-8501, Japan
yhara@ling.bun.kyoto-u.ac.jp

HAYASHISHITA, J.-R.: Department of Languages and Cultures, University of Otago, Dunedin, New Zealand
j-r.hayashishita@stonebow.otago.ac.nz

HISAGI, MIWAKO: Research Laboratory of Electronics-Speech Communication Group, Massachusetts Institute of Technology at Cambridge, Massachusetts 02139-4307, USA
mhisagi@hotmail.com

HOJI, HAJIME: Department of Linguistics, University of Southern California, Los Angeles, California 90089-1693, USA
hoji@usc.edu

JUN, SUN-AH: Department of Linguistics, University of California at Los Angeles, Los Angeles, California, 90095-1543, USA
jun@humnet.ucla.edu

KAWAHARA, SHIGETO: Department of Linguistics, Rutgers University, New Brunswick, NJ 08901-1108, USA
kawahara@rci.rutgers.edu

KIM, CHONGHYUCK: Department of English Language and Literature, National University of Singapore, 119077, Singapore
ellkc@nus.edu.sg

KIM, HAEYEON: Department of English, Chung-Ang University, Seoul, 156-756, Korea
haeykim@cau.ac.kr

KIM, HEESOOK: Department of English Education, Korea National University of Education (KNUE), Chongju City, Choongbuk Province, 363-791, Korea
hskim@cc.knue.ac.kr

KIM, JONG-BOK: School of English, Kyung Hee University, Seoul, 130-701, Korea
jongbok@khu.ac.kr

KIM, MEESOOK: Department of English Language and Literature, Sangji University, Wonju, Gangwondo, 220-702, Korea
meesook@sangji.ac.kr

KIM, MINJOO: Department of English, Texas Tech University, Lubbock, Texas 79409-3091, USA
min-joo.kim@ttu.edu

KIM, MINJU: Department of Modern Languages, Claremont McKenna College, Claremont, California 91711-6400, USA
minju.kim@claremontmckenna.edu

KO, HEEJEONG: Department of Linguistics, Seoul National University, Seoul, 151-748, Korea
heejeong@alum.mit.edu

KOIKE, CHISATO: Department of Modern Languages and Literatures, California State University, Los Angeles, Los Angeles, California 90032-8112, USA
chisatok@ucla.edu

LEE, CHUNGMIN: Department of Linguistics, Seoul National University, Seoul, 151-742, Korea
clee@snu.ac.kr

LIDZ, JEFFREY: Department of Linguistics, University of Maryland, College Park, MD 20742, USA
jlidz@umd.edu

MA, CHUNHUA: Department of English, Yanbian University of Science and Technology, Yanji City, Jilin Province, 1333000, China
hisgrace04@gmail.com

MOON, EUN-JOO: Center for Educational Development, Daejeon University, Daejeon, 305-762, Korea
ejm1002@gmail.com

MUSOLINO, JULIEN: Department of Speech and Hearing Sciences, Indiana University, Bloomington, IN 47405-7002, USA
musolino@indiana.edu

NARUOKA, KEIKO: Department of English, Japan Women's University, Tokyo, 112-8681, Japan
knaruoka@gmail.com

NISHI, KANAE: Sr. Research Associate, Boys Town National Research Hospital, Omaha, NE 68131, USA
nishik@boystown.org

OKADA, JUDY: Department of Asian Languages and Literature, University of Washington, Seattle, Washington 98195-3521, USA
jokada@u.washington.edu

OKAMOTO, SHIGEKO: Cowell Faculty Services, University of California at Santa Cruz, Santa Cruz, CA 95064, USA
sokamoto@ucsc.edu

OSHIMA, DAVID: International Student Center, Ibaraki University, Mito, 310-8512, Japan
oshima@mx.ibaraki.ac.jp

PARK, CHONGWON: Department of Writing Studies, University of Minnesota, Duluth, Minnesota 55812, USA
chongwon.park@gmail.com

RHEE, SEONGHA: English Linguistics Department, Hankuk University of Foreign Studies, Seoul, 130-791, Korea
srhee@hufs.ac.kr

SAIKI, MARIKO: International Student Center, Kanazawa University, Kakuma, Kanazawa, 920-1192, Japan
saiki@kenroku.kanazawa-u.ac.jp

SATO, SHIE: Independent scholar, 35 Winston Ave, Palmerston North, New Zealand
sophiesato@xtra.co.nz

SATO, YUTAKA: Division of Languages, College of Liberal Arts, International Christian University, Mitaka-shi, Tokyo, 181-8585, Japan
yutaka@icu.ac.jp

SELLS, PETER: Department of Linguistics, SOAS, London WC1H 0XG, United Kingdom
ps58@soas.ac.uk

SHIN, SEUNG-HOON: School of English Language and Literature, Yeungnam University, Gyeongsangbuk-do, 712-749, Korea
sshin@yumail.ac.kr

SON, MINJEONG: CASTL/Dept. of Linguistics, University of Tromsø at Tromsø, N-9073, Norway
minjeong.son@hum.uit.no

STRANGE, WINIFRED: Ph.D. Program in Speech-Language-Hearing Sciences, The City University of New York-Graduate Center, New York, NY 10016, USA
wstrange@gc.cuny.edu

TSUJIMURA, NATSUKO: Department of East Asian Languages and Cultures, Indiana University, Bloomington, Indiana 47405, USA
tsujimur@indiana.edu

VANCE, TIMOTHY J.: Department of East Asian Studies, University of Arizona, Tucson, Arizona 85721-0105, USA
vancet@email.arizona.edu

WESCOAT, MICHAEL T.: Department of Linguistics , University of California at Davis, Davis, California 95616, USA
wescoat@cruzio.com

WHITMAN, JOHN: Department of Linguistics, Cornell University, Ithaca, New York 14753-4701, USA
jbw2@cornell.edu

YIM, YOUNG-CHEOL: Department of Japanese, Chung-Ang University, Seoul, 156-756, Korea
yim1120@cau.ac.kr

YOON, JAMES: Dept of Linguistics, University of Illinois, Urbana-Champaign, USA
jyoon@uiuc.edu

YOSHIDA, NINA AZUMI: Department of Asian Languages and Cultures, University of California at Los Angeles, Los Angeles, California 90095-1540, USA
nyoshida@ucla.edu

Preface

The annual Japanese/Korean Linguistics (JK) Conference is an international forum for presenting innovative research work in Japanese and Korean linguistics, facilitating efforts to deepen our understanding of these languages that have striking typological similarities. It also provides opportunities for well-established scholars, young scholars, and students of Japanese and Korean linguistics to interact and exchange research results and ideas.

The papers presented at JK13 cover a wide range of areas, including phonetics, phonology, morphology, syntax, semantics, pragmatics, discourse analysis, historical linguistics, sociolinguistics, and psycholinguistics. Abstracts were refereed, and the selection process was rigorous. Out of the 141 abstracts submitted, 33 were selected for presentation in addition to the two keynote and seven invited presentations.

Part I

Historical Linguistics, Phonetics and Phonology

Preservation of Lexical Prominence in Vocative Chant

YOUNG-MEE YU CHO
RUTGERS UNIVERSITY

MARIKO SAIKI
KANAZAWA UNIVERSITY

1. Introduction

Vocative chant[1] refers to tunes for calling people, often from a distance. Important cross-linguistic generalizations are beginning to emerge with regard to the nature of the tunes and the role of prominence in the association of lexical stress/tone with the melody in vocative chant.

The first generalization concerns the musical aspect; i.e., vocative chant is associated with melody, or pitches specifiable on the musical score; as Bolinger (via Ladd 1978: 525) states, "the level pitches of stylized intonation must have some connection to music." More specifically, Gardiner (via Ladd 1978: 525) finds "a 'hierarchy of melodic forms' from the least for-

[1] What is called 'vocative chant' in Liberman 1975 and Leben 1976 is also known as the 'calling contour' of Gibbon 1976, the 'stylized fall (associated with routineness)'of Ladd 1978, 1996, 'the chanted call' of Hayes and Lahiri 1992 and Gussenhoven 1993.

malized (normal speech intonation) to the most formalized (accompanied singing)".[2]

The second generalization concerns the interface between music and language; there is a strong tendency to preserve underlying lexical prominence in vocative chant, whether the prominence is derived by the foot structure or tonal structure. For instance, Koizumi (1994b), upon observation of *warabe-uta* (game songs for children) in Japanese, points out that "in order to see the nature of the correspondence between the words and the melody in Japanese folk songs, one needs to pay attention to not only the falls but also the rises of the lexical pitch" (i.e., the presence and absence of lexical tones as well as the location of the accent).

In this paper, we will review past research on the vocative chant in European languages where more research has been focused and provide an Optimality-theoretic analysis of Korean and Japanese vocative chant.

2. Vocative Chant in European Languages

In English the accentual H tone (H*) is associated with the most salient syllable in the metrical structure (1).

(1) Vocative Chant in English

Ábernàthy   Pámela   Ábernathy dèar

The tone realization of English can be summarized as follows (Hayes and Lahiri 1992): a) H* is associated with the main stress (with the strong foot), b) M is associated with the secondary stress (with the next strong foot), c) If there is no secondary stress, M falls on the final syllable, and d) Tone spreads to right. Quite interestingly, the only difference between English and Dutch is that in Dutch the last syllable always has a separate pitch level (a boundary tone) (Gussenhoven 1993).

On the other hand, in languages such as Hungarian and French, which do not have any lexical stress, the H tone occurs in a fixed location as in (2). Just as the regular intonational phonology is determined by predictable phrasal mechanisms, the association of the vocative melody is determined by edge-alignment (e.g. associating HM from the right-edge).

```
(2) a. Hungarian:  Anna]    Katalin]  or  Katalin]
                   |  |     | | |         \/  |
                   H  M     L H M         H   M
```

[2]Gardiner lists talking blues performers, street vendors, auctioneers, newspaper headline callers, and train conductors on some sort of gradual scale in between.

```
b. French :    Monique]   Ja-acques]     Anne-Marie]
                |   |        |  |          |       |  |
                H  M         H M           L       H M
```

In addition to the data on stress languages, it is quite instructive to see how vocative chant is realized in a pitch-accent language such as Serbo-Croatian (Inkelas and Zec 1988). As shown in (3), the melody is (L)H*M, and the association proceeds from the right-edge. Any underlying H is preserved by linking it with the accented H* of the vocative melody. Rightward spread of H to any toneless moras and default L insertion produce the surface structure.

(3) Serbo-Croatian (Inkelas and Zec 1988)

```
Underlying                          Surface
Gospodjice    Slobodane     →      Gospodjice    Slobodane
 |               \ /               \  |  /  |      |   \/  |
II*               H*                  H     M      L    H  M
```

In all of the above languages, we observe that underlying lexical prominence in vocative chant is preserved whether the prominence is derived by the foot structure or tonal structure. On the other hand, when the languages have no underlying prominence, a completely predictable melody is assigned to segments.

3. Vocative Chant in Korean

Vocative chant in Korean and its relevance in identifying lexical prominence were first discussed by Ko (1999). Quite interestingly, she derives the differences between Standard Korean and Chonnam in terms of lexical prespecification. Korean vocative chant is realized on the sequence of a name (which is usually disyllabic) and a vocative suffix (*-a* after a consonant-final name and *–ya* after a vowel-final name). The same melody is repeated on the word, *nolca* ('let's play!").

(4) Korean Vocative Chant

Segments: Name-suffix,   nol-ca   'Name, let's play!'
Melody: **M H M**   **MHM**

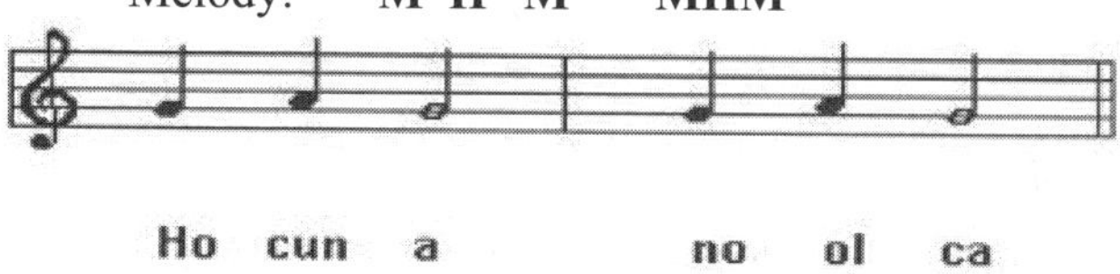

Whereas all names in Standard Korean are realized as **MHM**, names in Chonnam are divided into two groups—one with the **H** tone on the second syllable and the other with the **H** tone on the initial syllable (Ko 1999).

(5) Chonnam: **H*** on the initial or second syllable, **M** on the vocative suffix

a. (M)HM: ən-suk-a myəŋ-cun-a ɨ n-a-ya saŋ-wən-a himyəŋ-a

b. H* M: yəŋ-sən-a hyən-c^həl-a sən-suk-a ho-cun-a cɛ-hun-a

The second class involves lexical pre-specification; unlike the unmarked case, the lexical H is preserved by the association of the ***H** from the vocative melody. Contrary to Ko's analysis, we assume that the vocative melody is **HM** and is right-aligned, as shown in (6). Default **M** is assigned to the syllables other than the last two syllables.

(6) Unmarked Names

Align **HM** to the right edge of a name

```
acəs'i]      tulumi-ya]      c^holoŋc^holoŋpitnali-ya]
| | |         \ /  | |         \ \  | /  / / | |
MHM           M   H M               M        H M
```

This edge-alignment is best seen in non-disyllabic names. Regardless of the number of syllables in a name or the presence or the absence of the vocative suffix, the association is always from the right edge, with the penultimate **H**, followed by **M** on the final syllable. When a name is not long enough to accommodate **HM**, there is lengthening, and when there are more than two syllables, all syllables other than the last two are assigned **M**. This fact argues for the position that there is no underlying accentual marking in Standard Korean.

The contrast in the tone-melody association between Standard Korean on the one hand, and such pitch-accent systems as Kyungsang on the other hand, is quite remarkable. As shown in (7), the three tone classes exhibit an expected three way distinction in South Kyungsang, as discussed in Cho (2002) in detail.

(7) Vocative Chant in South KS (p.c. Y-H Cho)

a. MHM: ho-cun-a cɛ-hun-a pyəŋ-c^həl-a ɨ n-a-ya

b. H*M: yəŋ-sən-a hyən-c^həl-a sən-suk-a myəŋ-cun-a

c. HHM: saŋ-wən-a hi-myəŋ-a kuk-wən-a saŋ-kɨ n-a

```
e. g.   ho-cun-a]     yəŋ-sən-a]     saŋ-wən-a]
        |  |  |       |      |        \  /  |
        M  H  M       H*     M         H*   M
```

An Optimality-Theoretic account for Korean vocative chant (with the **HM** melody specification) calls for the ranking: **Max-IO (Lexical Tone)** >> **Align-R, Default Tone Assignment**.

Dialectal differences follow from underlying tone specifications with the same ranking. When there is no underlying tone, **MHM** surfaces (all names in Standard Korean, and default names in other dialects). In initially-prominent names, the **H*M** melody emerges. Doubly-accented names in Kyungsang surface as **HHM**, again preserving the underlying accent.

The comparison in (8) illustrates how the best candidate emerges in each type of name in Kyungsang.

(8) Kyungsang Vocative Chant

a. Atonic Names

/ho-cun-a/	**MAX-IO**	**Align-R**	**Default Tone**
☞ ho-cun-a] | | | **M H M**			
[ho-cun-a | \ / **H M**	*!	*	*
[ho-cun-a | | | **H M M**		*!	

b. Accented Names

H* | /sən-suk-a/	**MAX-IO**	**Align-R**	**Default Tone**
☞ H* | sən-suk-a] | | | **H M M**		*	
H* | sən-suk-a] | | | **M H M**	*!		
H* | [sən-suk-a | | **H M**		*!	*!

c. Doubly-Accented Names

H* / \ /saŋ-wən-a/	**MAX-IO**	**Align-R**	**Default Tone**
☞ H* / \ saŋ-wən-a] \ / | **H** **M**			
H* / \ saŋ-wən-a] | | | **M H M**	*!		
H* / \ [saŋ-wən-a | | **H M**	*!	*	*

In (8a), the **HM** melody is assigned from right-to-left, while the initial syllable is marked M by default. On the other hand, the underlying accent, whether singly or doubly-linked, should surface as **H** to satisfy the highest ranked constraint, **MAX-IO**, as shown in (8b) and (8c).

In sum, we see a systematic relationship between the musical melody and linguistic specification in Korean.

4. Vocative Chant in Japanese

In most unmarked cases, segments for vocative chant in Japanese consist of a name, or a sequence of a name and a vocative suffix (usually *-tyaN* or –*kuN,* and sometimes *–saN*), followed by the word *asobo* or *asobimasyo* ('let's play!'). Then, an answer to this invitation may follow in the form of either *hai* ('yes') or (*mata*) *atode* ('later').

(9) Person 1: Name (+vocative suffix), asobo/asobimasyo 'let's play'!

Person 2: Hai! / (Mata) Atode! 'Yes! /Later!'

The melody associated with the chant is perceived with the three tunes that we describe as **L**, **M,** and **H** in bold face below. They should be interpreted so that there is a minor interval by three degrees between **L** and **M**, and a major interval by two degrees between **M** and **H**. Thus, for example,

L, M, and **H** designate the musical tunes that correspond to the notes E, G, and A on the major scale in Western music.

In our study, we collected data from native speakers of the Tokyo dialect and the Fukui dialect, a well-known dialect due to its total lack of distinctive pitch. We have discovered that Tokyo speakers are divided into two groups with regard to the vocative melody they produce. In one group (Tokyo 1), the vocative tunes reflect highs and lows of the lexical pitch, while in the other (Tokyo 2) the melody is independent of linguistic specifications. Fukui speakers show the same chanting pattern as the Tokyo 2 speakers.

In Tokyo 1 vocative chant, if we take 3-mora names, for example, the unaccented names (LHH+H) and the accented names (HLL+L) are chanted to the tunes **LMH** and **H*MH**, respectively, as shown in (10). Note that in both cases *asobo* ('let's play!') is sung to the melody **LMH**.

```
(10) Mayumi-tyaN   asobo    vs.   Máriko-tyaN   asobo
      |  \ /   |    | | |          |   \/   |    | | |
      L  M     H    L M H          H*  M    H    L M H
```

The table in (11) shows the comparison between the lexical pitch specification and the chanting tunes for unaccented and initially or medially accented 2, 3, and 4-mora names with a vocative suffix.

(11)

	Speech	Vocative chant
Unaccented 2-μ names	Koga +saN L H + H	Koga +saN **L M +H**
Initially Accented 2-μ names	Maki +tyaN H*L + L	Maki +tyaN **H*M +H**
Unaccented 3-μ names	Mayumi +tyaN L H H + H	Mayumi +tyaN **L M M +H**
Initially Accented 3-μ names	Mariko +tyaN H*L L + L	Mariko+tyaN **H*MM +H**
Unaccented 4-μ names	KeNichi +kuN LHHH + H	KeNichi +kuN **LMMM +H**
Initially Accented 4-μ names	KeNsuke +kuN H*LLL + L	KeNsuke +kuN **H*MMM +H**
4-μ names with accent on 2nd μ	Hidetoshi +kuN L H*L L +L	Hidetoshi +kuN **MH*MM +H**
4-μ names with accent on 3rd μ	Midoriko +tyaN L H H*L +L	Midoriko +tyaN **MHH*M +H** or **HHH*M +H** or **LMH*M +H**

The following regularities are observed in (11). First, the L and H in unaccented names occur as **L** and **M**, respectively. Second, the initial H and the other lexical pitches in initially accented names are realized as **H** and **M**, respectively. Third, in medially accented names, the accented μ (H*) is realized as **H**. Finally, all through the data, the vocative suffix and the penultimate μ are assigned the **H** and **M** tunes respectively, regardless of the kind of lexical pitches they bear. It is obvious that the pitches lexically specified are faithfully reflected in the tunes in Tokyo 1 vocative melody.

An OT account for Tokyo 1 vocative chant is given in (12). The two highest ranked constraints ensure that underlying tones surface faithfully to satisfy the vocative template, **MH**, except for atonic words as in (12a). The direction of association is from the right edge (**Align-R**), and as in ordinary speech, the initial mora is linked to **L** as long as higher ranked constraints are satisfied. In non-initial positions, the default tone is **M**. The variation in (12c) is not addressed in this paper, although it may be possible to derive it by the interaction among **H*L**, **Finalμ-H, Agree, *Contour,** and **Default-M**.

(12) Tokyo 1 Vocative Chant

Max-IO(H), Max-(MH) >> Align-R, Initialμ-L >> Default-M >>
….. H*L, Finalμ-H, Agree, *Contour

a. Atonic Words

/Koga+saN/	**Max-IO**	**Max-(MH)**	**Align-R**	**Initial**	**Default-M**

☞ Koga+saN
   | | |
  L M H
					*

Koga+saN | \ / **L H**		*!			*
Koga+saN | | | **H M H**				*!	*
Koga+saN \/ | **M H**				*!	
Koga+saN | | | **M H M**			*!	*	

b. Words with Initial Accent

H* | /Mariko+tyaN/	**Max-IO**	**Max-(MH)**	**Align-R**	**Initial**	**Default-M**

☞ Mariko+tyaN
    | \/ |
   H M   H
				*	

Mariko+tyaN | \ / | **L M H**	*!				*
Mariko+tyaN \\|/ | **M H**	*!			*	
Mariko+tyaN | \ | / **H M**			*!	*	
Mariko+tyaN \/ \ / **H M**		*!	*	*	

c. Word with Medial Accent (Variation observed)

<table>
<tr><th>H*
|
/Midoriko+tyaN/</th><th>Max IO</th><th>Max-(MH)</th><th>Align-R</th><th>Initial</th><th>Default-M</th><th>Agree</th></tr>
<tr><td>☞ Midoriko+tyaN
| \/ | |
M H M   H</td><td></td><td></td><td></td><td>*</td><td>*</td><td>***</td></tr>
<tr><td>☞ Midoriko+tyaN
\/ | | |
M HM   H</td><td></td><td></td><td></td><td>*</td><td>*</td><td>**</td></tr>
<tr><td>☞ Midoriko+tyaN
| | | | | |
LHMH   H</td><td></td><td></td><td></td><td></td><td>*</td><td>***</td></tr>
<tr><td>Midoriko+tyaN
| \| | /
L   M</td><td>*!</td><td>*!</td><td>*</td><td></td><td>*</td><td>*</td></tr>
<tr><td>Midoriko+tyaN
\|/ | |
H   M   H</td><td></td><td>*!</td><td>*</td><td>*</td><td></td><td></td></tr>
</table>

Unlike Tokyo 1, Tokyo 2-Fukui vocative chant disregards lexical pitch distinction. Here, all names with a vocative suffix are realized as **HMH**. Compare (13) with (10).

(13) Mayumi-tyaN asobo vs. Máriko-tyaN asobo
| \ / | | | | | \/ | | | |
H M H H M H   **H* M H H M H**

Moreover, in Tokyo 2-Fukui vocative chant, the **HMH** melody is repeated for all segments that appear in the chant. In addition, there is systematic variation in melody association as in 'KeNichi+kuN' (1. HMMM+H, 2. HHMM+H, 3. HHHM+H). The outputs can be obtained if we assume logically possible multiple linkings of the first two tunes of the **HMH** melody. The association of the **HMH** chanting tunes with the segments is again from right to left. Since the chanting of Fukui speakers is not constrained linguistically, it automatically takes up the melody determined by music. Likewise, Tokyo 2 vocative chant allows music to take over linguistic specifications. In other words, melody overrides lexical pitch specification. Moreover, we observe similar cases in other kinds of chant in Japanese. For example, in a counting chant (*ichi, nii, san,…*'one, two, three,…'), numbers are invariably chanted to the **HM** melody up to ten, thus ignoring the lexical pitches, while afterwards, chanting tunes reflect the lexical pitches assigned to the number words. Also, in the Japanese teasing chant (*Mityatta. Mityatta. Sensei-ni itte-yaroo* 'I saw it. I saw it. I'll tell the teacher!'), **HM** is repeated throughout the segments.

Finally, not only the two kinds of vocative chant we have been discussing, but also the other chants mentioned above are associated with the melody tune of **L**, **M,** and/or **H**. Part of the explanation is found in Koizumi's (1994a) claim that these three tunes form a tetra cord in traditional Japanese folk music.[3]

5. Conclusion

We conclude that cross-linguistic realization of stylized intonation is shown to be a function of the prosodic structure of the word. In other words, vocative chant can be used as a window through which one can investigate the nature of the prosodic structure of a language. As in stress languages, vocative chant preserves lexical specifications of prominence in pitch-accent languages such as Serbo-Croatian, Kyungsang Korean, and Japanese, except for those cases when music overrides language in Japanese.

In our future research, we hope to elucidate the link between language and music in the spirit of the Generative Theory of Music of Lerdahl and Jackendoff (1983), where grammaticality is assumed to interact in intricate ways with both the well-formedness of the structure and the preference rules the theory of music provides.

[3]The Japanese folk scale is shown below, of which the second tetra cord consists of EGA (LMH). Nettl (via Lerdahl and Jackendoff 1983:292) also observes wide-spread use of these three tunes in a children's teasing chant.

References

Cho, Y-M. 2002. Syllable Weight and Tone in Korean. *Japanese and Korean Linguistics* 12: 104-116.

Gibbon, D. 1976. *Perspectives of Intonation Analysis*. Bern: Lang.

Gussenhoven, C. 1993. The Dutch Foot and the Chanted Call. *Journal of Linguistics* 29: 37-63.

Hayes, B. and A. Lahiri. 1992. Durationally Specified Intonation in English and Bengali. *Proceedings of the 1990 Wenner-Gren Center Conference on Music, Language, Speech, and Brain*, eds. R. Carlson, L. Nord and J. Sundberg, 78-91.

Inkelas, S. and D. Zec. 1988. Serbo-Croatian Pitch Accent. *Language* 64.2: 227-48.

Ko, E.-S. 1999. Interaction of Tone and Stress in Seoul and Chonnam Korean. *WCCFL* 246-259.

Koizumi, F. 1994a. *Nihon-no Oto* [Sounds of Japan]. Heibonsya Library 71. Tokyo: Heibonsya.

Koizumi, F. 1994b. *Ongaku-no Kongen-ni Aru Mono* [What Underlies Music]. Heibonsya Library 57. Tokyo: Heibonsya.

Ladd, D. R. 1978. Stylized Intonation. *Language* 54.3: 517-39.

Ladd, D. R. 1996. *Intonational Phonology*. Cambridge: Cambridge University Press.

Leben. W. 1976. The Tones in English Intonation. *Linguistic Analysis* 2: 69-107.

Lerdahl F. and R. Jackendoff. 1983. *A Generative Theory of Tonal Music*. Cambridge: MIT Press.

Liberman, M. 1975. *The Intonational System of English.* Doctoral Dissertation, MIT.

McCarthy, J. and A. Prince. 1993. Prosodic Morphology I. Rutgers University Optimality Archive.

Prince, A. and P. Smolensky. 1993. Optimality Theory: Constraint Interaction in Generative Grammar. Rutgers University Optimality Archive.

The Japanese/Korean Vowel Correspondences

BJARKE FRELLESVIG
University of Oxford

JOHN WHITMAN
Cornell University

1. Introduction

Korean and Japanese share cognate vocabulary, at least some of it the result of contact. Recent advances in the reconstruction of the vowel system of Proto-Japanese (including Ryûkyûan) enable us to clarify and distinguish the vowel correspondences that hold for later loan vocabulary as well as earlier cognate material. Various types of evidence point to a PJ system of seven vowels, including two mid vowels, **e* and **o*, which rose in most positions to merge with **i* and **u* in main island varieties; and a high central vowel **ɨ*, which merged with the ancestor of Old Japanese *o*. Evidence for the latter comes from variable outcomes in contractions with **i*. The seven vowel system for Japanese is reconstructed entirely on Japanese-internal grounds (primarily internal reconstruction and dialect comparison), but it turns out to have interesting consequences for the comparative study of Japanese and Korean.

The paper is organized as follows: Section 2 presents our reconstruction of the vowels of Proto-Japanese based on internal criteria. Section 3 focuses on the comparative consequences of this reconstruction, addresses the issue of dating cognate vocabulary, and proposes a new view of the pre-Middle Korean vowel system.

2. The Vowels of Proto-Japanese

In this section we motivate the reconstruction of short vowels for Proto-Japanese in (1), following Frellesvig and Whitman (forthcoming a, b).

(1) **i* **ɨ* **u*
**e* **ə* **o*
**a*

The correspondences between the PJ vowels we reconstruct and the vowels and postconsonantal diphthongs of OJ are shown in (2a).[1] Until recently, a four vowel hypothesis (4VH) has been dominant, holding that PJ had only four primary vowels (e.g. Miller 1967, Ohno 1977, Matsumoto 1974, 1984, Whitman 1985), /*i, *a, *u, *ə/, reflected as OJ /i, a, u, o/. (2b) gives the correspondences between the PJ four vowel system and OJ.

(2) a. Seven vowel hypothesis (7VH)

PJ	OJ
**i*	*i*
**e*	*i, ye*
**a*	*a*
**o*	*u, wo*
**u*	*u*
**ɨ*	*o*
**ə*	*o*

Pre-OJ	OJ
**ui*	*wi*
**ɨi*	*wi*
**ai*	*e*
**əi*	*e*
**ii*	*ye*
**ia*	*ye*
**iə*	*ye*
**uɨ*	*wo*
**ua*	*wo*
**uə*	*wo*

b. Four vowel hypothesis (4VH)

PJ	OJ
**i*	*i*
**a*	*a*
**u*	*u*
**ə*	*o*

Pre-OJ	OJ
**ui*	*wi*
**əi*	*wi*
**ai*	*e*
**ia*	*ye*
**iə*	*ye*
**uə*	*wo*
**ua*	*wo*

[1] We phonemicize the '*kô/otsu rui*' syllables as exemplified in the following, with /Cwi/ for Ci_2, /Cwo/ for Co_1, /Cye/ for Ce_1, and /Ce/ for Ce_2 (aligning Ce_2 with neutral *Ce*): mi_1 /mi/ 'three', *ti* /ti/ 'thousand', mi_2 /mwi/ 'body'; ko_1 /kwo/ 'child', *po* /po/ 'ear (of grain)', ko_2 /ko/ 'this'; me_1 /mye/ 'woman', *te* /te/ 'hand', me_2 /me/ 'eye'.

The 4VH claims that the OJ nuclei *wi, e, ye,* and *wo* are **all** secondary, resulting from contractions of vowel sequences as in (3):

(3) a.	*ui > wi	_*waku-iratukwo_ 'young-honored.male' > _wakwiratukwo_
	*əi > wi	_*əpə-isi_ 'big-stone' > _opwisi_ Proper name
	*əi > e	_*tənə-iri_ 'palace-enter' > _toneri_ 'palaceservant'
	*ai > e	_*taka-iti_ 'high-market' > _taketi_ Proper name
b.	*uə > wo	_situ-ori_ 'native.weaving-weave' ~ _sitwori_ 'type of cloth'
	*ua > wo	_*kazu-ap-_ 'number-join' > _kazwope-_ 'count'
	*ia > ye	_*saki-ari_ 'bloom-is' > _sakyeri_ 'is blooming'
	*iə > ye	_*pi-əki_ 'sun-put' > _pyeki_ Proper name

So-called 'apophonic nouns' give further support for the secondary origin of the nuclei *wi* and *e* (but not *ye* and *wo*):

(4)	freestanding form	compound form
wi ~ u	*mwi* 'body'	*mu-kapari* 'hostage' ('body-substitute')
wi ~ o	*kwi* 'tree'	*ko-dati* 'grove' ('tree-stand')
e ~ o	*se* 'back'	*so-muku* 'turn' ('back-face')
e ~ a	*me* 'eye'	*ma-pye* 'front' ('eye-side, direction')

There are various proposals about the origin of noun apophony (Yoshitake 1928, Murayama 1962, Whitman 1985); all hold that the compound form directly reflects the root vowel, while freestanding *wi* and *e* originate from contractions like (3a), e.g. *mwi* 'body' < _*mui_; *me* 'eye' < _*mai._

Perhaps the strongest argument for the 4VH is the relative infrequency of *Cwi, Ce, Cye,* and *Cwo*, especially outside of morpheme-final position. However we take the position (2.2) that this distribution has two sources: *Cwi* and *Ce* truly are secondary, but final *ye* and *wo* reflect primary vowels.

2.1 Two sources for o: PJ *ə, *ɨ > OJ o

The 7VH (2a) holds that OJ *o* is the reflex of two PJ vowels, which we reconstruct as _*ɨ_ and _*ə_, a high and a mid central vowel respectively. The basic observation underlying this proposal is evident in (3-4) above: OJ *o* takes part in two alternations, *o ~ wi* and *o ~ e*, reflecting two outcomes of contraction with _*i._ Of these *o ~ e* has previously been thought to be an irregular and/or nonstandard variation of *o ~ wi*, but we argue instead that the alternation *o ~ e* in simply reflects a different source for OJ *o*, as shown in (5); pre-OJ _*ɨ_ and _*ə_ merged after these contractions took place, eventually resulting in OJ *o*.

(5) a. **ɨ* > *o ~ wi* < **ɨi*
b. **ə* > *o ~ e* < **əi*

Below we review relevant cases of the two alternations *o ~ e* and *o ~ wi*.

2.1.1 Lexical Contraction

The examples in (6) seem to be the only solid cases of lexical contraction of an ancestor of OJ *o* with **i*. They do not show **əi > wi* to be regular and **əi > e* irregular: there is but one case of the former versus two of the latter, supporting the distinct PJ sources in (7).

(6) a. *opwisi* (cf. (4.a))
b. *toneri* (cf. (4.a)), *wenu* 'puppy' (cf. *wo* 'small', *inu* 'dog')

(7) a. **ipɨ-isi > opwisi*
b. **tənə-iri > toneri*, **wə-inu > wenu*

2.1.2 Nominal Apophony

Among the monosyllabic apophonic nominal stems, OJ *o* takes part in two alternations, *o- ~ wi* and *o- ~ e*. (8) lists these alternations for monosyllabic stems.[2] Again, the distribution is not persuasive for *o ~ wi < *əi* being regular; instead, two distinct sources should be reconstructed as in (9).

(8) a. *ko- ~ kwi* 'tree'; *no- ~ ni* 'load'; *po- ~ pwi* 'fire';
so demonstrative ~ *si* 3rd sg. personal pronoun.
b. *mo* 'algae; ?seaweed' ~ *me* '(edible) seaweed'; *so- ~ se* 'back';
yo ~ ye 'branch'; *yo- ~ ye-* 'good'.

(9) a. **Cɨ >* *Co- ~ Cwi* < **Cɨi*
b. **Cə- >* *Co- ~ Ce* < **Cəi*

2.1.2 Verb(al) Apophony

The basic stem of the secondary verbs, the Nidan verbs, is thought to derive from contraction of a root or stem final vowel with an **i* (either a derivational morpheme, possibly going back further to **-Ci-*, or the infinitive formant). When the source is reflected independently in OJ, Nidan verbs take part in alternations similar to the apophonic nouns:

[2] Note that *-wi* is neutralized as *-i* after coronals.

(10)

		Nidan verb base
-u- ~ -wi-	_sabu-_ 'lonely'	_sabwi-_ 'get desolate, fade' (< *_sabu-(C)i_)
-o- ~ -wi-	_opo-_ 'big'	_opwi-_ 'get big; grow' (< *_ipi-(C)i_)
-a- ~ -e-	_aka_(-) 'red'	_ake-_ 'redden, lighten' (< *_aka-(C)i_)

Nidan verbs do not regularly take part in the alternation _-o- ~ -e-_, but it is possible to identify a few pairs exhibiting this alternation (11). Of these, only _komor-_, _kome-_ are true lexical verbs. _Se-_ is the basic stem of 'to do'; its root, _so_, is reflected as a fossilized imperative in prohibitive _na-...-so_. _-Koso_ is used as imperative; _to_ is the copula infinitive and _-te_ the derived gerund formant and adverbializer (see Frellesvig 2001:12-16). These roots should be reconstructed as in (12a) and the alternations understood as in (12b).

(11) _komor-_ 'hide' (intr.) ~ _kome-_ 'hide, enclose'; _so ~ se-_ 'do';
-koso ~ -kose- 'do for me'; _to_ copula ~ _te_ adverbializer.

(12) a. *_kəmə_, *_sə_, *_kəsə_, *_tə_
b. *_(-)Cə > (-)Co ~ (-)Ce-_ < *_(-)Cə-(C)i_

2.2 Proto-Japanese *e, *o

Contra the 4VH, the evidence for the OJ nuclei _wo_ and _ye_ being diachronically secondary is far less persuasive than for _wi_ and _e_. While syllables with _wo_ and _ye_ are also relatively infrequent in the OJ lexicon, the vast majority cannot be derived from lexical contractions of the sort in (3b). As noted above, _wo_ and _ye_ do not take part in alternations involved in nominal or verbal apophony. This has led to hypotheses that these nuclei, as opposed to _wi_ and _e_, to a large extent reflect two primary PJ vowels, reconstructed as *_o_ and *_e_. See Hattori (1978-9), Hayata (1998, 2000), Serafim (1999) for proposals based on internal and comparative dialect evidence for reconstruction of PJ *_o_, *_e_. Most recently, the thorough study of Miyake (2003) provides philological evidence for this claim.

Previous reconstructions of front and back mid vowels in PJ have assumed unconditional raising to high vowels (PJ *_o_ > OJ _u_, *_e_ > _i_) or raising conditioned by length; we hypothesize that PJ *_o_ and *_e_ rose to give _wo_ and _ye_ in 'final' position, but _u_, _i_ elsewhere (13). Dialects seem to have differed in the environments and conditions for whether the outcome was 'complete' (> _u_, _i_) or 'incomplete' (> _wo_, _ye_) raising.

(13) *_o_ > _wo_ in final position; _u_ elsewhere
*_e_ > _ye_ in final position; _i_ elsewhere

Internal evidence for raising of **o* may be found in variation between *Cu* and *Cwo* within the OJ lexicon (14), and in dialectal correspondences between Central OJ *Cu* and Eastern OJ *Cwo* (20). See Hayata 1998, Matsumoto 1995:79ff, 132f for *wo~u* forms, also Thorpe 1983.

(14) **yo(-)ri* *ywo(-)ri* 'from' ~ *yuri* 'behind; from'
**mo(-)ko* *mwokwo* 'partner, bridegroom' ~ *mukwo* (> EMJ *muko*)

(15)	Central OJ		Eastern OJ
**yo*	*ywo* 'night'	::	*yu-* (*yutoko* 'night bed')
**no*	*nwo* 'field' (?~ *numa* 'marsh')	::	*nu-* (*nu-no* 'field-Gen.')
*-*o*	-*u* finite primary verb ending	::	-*u* ~ -*wo*

OJ internal evidence for **e* may be found in variation between *ye* and *i* within OJ, see (16), although examples are few, and in dialectal correspondences between Central OJ -*i* and Eastern OJ -*e*, or conversely, Central *ye* and Eastern *i* (17). These examples highlight the fact that different dialects had different criteria for complete and incomplete raising.

(16) **me* *mye* 'woman' ~ -*mi*- (*womina* 'young woman')
**e* *ye* 'placenta' ~ *i*- (*iro* 'of same mother')

(17)	Central OJ		Eastern OJ
**te*	*(mi)ti* 'road'	::	*te* (*miti-no-naga-te*)
**ke*	-*ki* adj.Adn.	::	-*ke*
**ipe*	*ipye* 'house'	::	*ipi*
**kape*	*kapyer-* 'return'	::	*kapir-*

In addition, Ryûkyûan-Japanese comparative evidence gives support for reconstructing PJ **e* (Hattori 1976, 1979-80, Thorpe 1983) where proto-Ryûkyûan **e* corresponds to OJ *i* (23); the PR reconstructions follow Thorpe (1983).

(18) OJ /i/	::	PR **e* < PJ **e*
midu 'water'	::	**medu*
oyobi 'finger'	::	**UyUbe* (*U: PR *u or *o)
piru 'garlic'	::	**peru*
kizu 'wound'	::	**kezu*
idu 'wh-'	::	**edu*
pidi 'elbow'	::	**pedi*

2.2.1 Mid Vowel Raising and Demonstratives

As is well known, the Japanese and Korean systems of demonstrative/interrogative pronouns are structurally identical, with a three way distinction among the demonstratives (19). There is also a good form fit between MK *kɨ*, *tyə*, *ə-* ~ *ənu* and EMJ *ko*, *so*, *i-* ~ *idu-*. However, the semantics do not match in two of the sets: MK mesial *kɨ* corresponds to EMJ proximal *ko*, and MK distal *tyə* to EMJ mesial *so*. Raising of PJ mid vowels offers support for a scenario of changes which has led to this situation.

(19)	proximal	mesial	distal	interrogative
MK	*i*	*kɨ*	*tyə*	*ə-* ~ *ənu*
EMJ	*ko*	*so*	*ka*	*i-* ~ *idu-*

First of all, it is less well known that the EMJ system is an innovation and that OJ in fact, as demonstrated in detail by Hashimoto (1966, 1982), only has a two term plus interrogative system : *ko* (speaker), *so* (non-speaker), *i-* ~ *idu-* (interrogative) (20). The OJ system is entirely speaker based (speaker versus nonspeaker), with no direct reference to hearer, so the semantics are also quite different from the later system. The *ka* usually posited for OJ is a product of projecting the EMJ system unto logographically written portions of the OJ text corpus. In OJ, *ka* was not a productive member of the demonstrative system. Early precursors of the innovative EMJ system are attested three times in OJ: *ka* (as distinct from the adverb *ka* 'this way'), is attested at most twice, both in dialect poems (M 14.3565, 20.4384) and the long form, *kare*, is found once (M 18.4045). Other *ka-* based demonstratives are not attested until EMJ.

(20) OJ demonstratives	speaker	nonspeaker	interrogative
	ko	*so*	*i-* ~ *idu-*

In addition to the productive OJ system, there is some evidence for an earlier proximal demonstrative *i-*, lost by OJ times but vestigially retained in *ima* 'now' < *i* 'this' + *ma* 'interval', and perhaps also as the OJ term of address *i* 'you'. We propose that the OJ system evolved from a PJ system with proximal **i* and interrogative **e*, in addition to mesial and distal, see (21) below. What upset the PJ system, we suggest, was raising of pre-OJ /*e/, resulting in homonymy between pre-OJ proximal **i* (< PJ **i*) and interrogative **i* (< PJ **e*), a stage we represent as pre-OJ(a). We suggest that this 'pernicious homonymy' was resolved by proximal **i* being discarded as a productive member of the system and mesial **ki* and distal **si* being reanalyzed as speech event participant and nonparticipant respectively: pre-OJ(b).

This was subsequently reanalyzed as speaker and nonspeaker, respectively, the system exhibited by OJ. The OJ system was later augmented to include a distal (*ka*), giving the EMJ and later system.[3]

(21)				
PJ	proximal **i*	mesial **kɨ*	distal **sɨ*	interrogative **e*
pre-OJ(a)	proximal **i*	mesial **kɨ*	distal **sɨ*	interrogative **i*
pre-OJ(b)	participant **kɨ*	nonparticipant **sɨ*		interrogative **i*
OJ	speaker *ko*	nonspeaker *so*		interrogative *i- ~ idu-*
EMJ	proximal *ko*	mesial *so*	distal *ka*	interrogative *i- ~ idu-*

The PJ demonstrative system we reconstruct is a good fit, phonologically and semantically, with the MK system (22):

(22)	proximal	mesial	distal	interrogative
MK	*i*	*kɨ*	*tyə*	*ə*
PJ	**i*	**kɨ*	**sɨ*	**e*

2.3 Summary

Recapitulating, we propose the following seven vowel system for PJ. It is worth noting that (23) is a typologically well-attested system. Crothers (1978) reports that vowel system type 7:2 (seven vowels with two of the central vowels /ɨ/, /ə/, or /ü/) is the fifth most common in his sample of vowel systems, and the most common type among seven vowel systems, with 14 exemplars.

(23)			
	***i**	***ɨ**	***u**
	***e**	***ə**	***o**
		***a**	

[3] A change such as the one we propose for pre-OJ of the mesial in a three way demonstrative system to replace the original proximal is attested in the transition from classical to vulgar Latin, with mesial *iste* replacing proximal *hic* of the original three way system of proximal *hic*, mesial *iste*, and distal *ille* (see Väänänen 1963: 128-9).

3. The Japanese-Korean Vowel Correspondences

The system in (23) is not dissimilar to Late Middle Korean (24):

(24) LMK Vowels (15th century; transcription follows Lee 1972a)

i	ɨ	u
	ə	o
	ʌ	
	a	

The main difference between the two systems reflects a peculiarity of the LMK inventory noted by many previous researchers: a four-way height distinction, with no non-high front vowel. 3.1 shows how certain vowel correspondences between Japanese and Korean fall out under the 7VH for OJ. 3.2 examines the structural disparities between the two systems.

3.1 The Basic Correspondences

We propose the basic vowel correspondences in (25):

(25)	MK		OJ		PJ
a.	i	::	i	<	*i
b.	ɨ	::	o	<	*ɨ
c.	u	::	u	<	*u
d.	y*ə* < *e	::	i, ye	<	*e
e.	*ə*	::	o, a	<	**ə*, *a
f.	o	::	u, wo	<	*o
g.	ʌ	::	o, a	<	**ə*, *a
h.	a	::	a	<	a

3.1.1 Correspondences for OJ /o/

In addition to the well known correspondences involving Middle Korean *ɨ* :: OJ *o* (25b), a number of convincing lexical pairs support the correspondence MK ʌ :: OJ *o* (Kôno 1967/1979: 561, Martin 1966: 220) in (25g):

(26)	MK *ɨ*		OJ *o*		PJ **ɨ*
a.	*kɨ* 'that' (mesial)	::	*ko*	<	**kɨ* (demonstrative; cf. 2.2.1))
b.	*mɨsɨ-* 'wh(at)'	::	*mosi*	<	**mɨsi* (conjectural adverb)
c.	*timɨr-* 'rare'	::	*tomo-si*	<	**tɨ mɨ* - 'scarce'
d.	*tɨr-* < **tɨrɨ-* 'hold,lift'	::	*tor-*	<	**tɨr-* 'take'
e.	*mɨrɨ-t* 'all'	::	*moro-*	<	**mɨrɨ* 'all'

(27) MK *ʌ* :: OJ *o* PJ *ə*

a. *tʌrk* 'chicken' :: *tori* < **tər(-i)* 'bird'

b. *kʌth-* 'alike' :: *koto-si* < **kətə-* 'resemble'

c. *mʌt* 'eldest, chief (of kin)' :: *moto* < **mətə* 'base, origin'

d. *nʌr-* 'fly' :: *nor-* < **nər* 'ride'

e. *kʌβʌr* 'county' :: *kopori* < **kəpər(-i)* 'county' (loan)

These two correspondence sets show us that two PJ vowels were involved: OJ *o* < PJ **ɨ* :: MK *ɨ*, and OJ *o* < PJ **ə* :: MK ʌ. The same two sets of correspondences emerge in OJ correspondences for MK words in final /r/ or /y/:

(28) MK *ɨr* OJ *o-, wi* PJ **ɨ y*

a. *pɨr* 'fire' :: *po-, pwi* < **pɨy* 'fire'

b. *mɨri-* < **mɨrɨr-* 'withdraw' :: *mo, mwi-* < **mɨ* -'turn about'

c. *kɨrih* 'stump, counter for trees' :: *ko-, kwi* < **kɨy* 'tree'

(29) MK *ʌr* OJ *e* PJ * *əy*

a. *mʌr* 'seaweed' :: *mo, me* < *mə(y)* 'seaweed'

b. *pʌyam* 'snake' :: *pemi* < *pəym(-i)* 'snake'

c. *pʌy* 'boat' :: *pe* < *pəy* 'boat (prow)'

The seven vowel hypothesis accounts directly for the existence of two sets of Korean correspondences for OJ *o*. Note that the OJ apophonic nouns 'fire' and 'tree' in (28) behave exactly as predicted on internal grounds by the hypothesis that their nuclear vowel results from PJ **ɨ*. Likewise, the vowel in (29a) alternates between *e* and *o*, suggesting on internal grounds the PJ shape * *mə(y)* confirmed by the MK comparison.

3.1.2 Correspondences for PJ *e and *o

Under the mid vowel raising hypothesis, MK *o* is expected to correspond to OJ u, except in final position. This is borne out:

(30) MK *o* :: OJ *u* PJ **o*

a. *kokori* 'stem' :: *kuku-, kukwi,* 'stem' ?< **kokor*

b. *oy* 'melon' :: *uri* 'melon' ?< **ori*

c. *tok* 'jug' :: *tuki* 'jug' ?< **toki*

d. *kom* < *koma* 'bear' :: *kuma* 'bear' ?< **koma*

e. *mom* 'body' :: *mu- mwi* 'body'' ?< **mo(C)(i)*

f. *moyh* 'mountain' :: *mure* 'mountain' ?< **more*

g. *kop-/koB-* < *kopʌ-* 'beautiful' :: *kupasi-* 'beautiful' < **kopa-*

h. *moh* 'corner, side' :: *mwo* 'direction' < **mo*

i. *-to* 'also, too' :: *two* 'outside, other' < **to*

In (30a-f) there is no Japanese-internal evidence that non-final /u/ results from PJ *o, although the vowel shape is consistent with this source. In (g), there is evidence for OJ u < *o: the original vowel survives in the Kami Nidan verb *kwopwi-* 'love, long for'; it is raised in stem-nonfinal position in the adjective *kupasi-* 'fine, beautiful'.

The MK correspondence for OJ *i/ye* < PJ **e* is less clear; as noted above, the MK inventory lacks a non-high front vowel. Following a suggestion from Leon Serafim, brought to our attention by Marc Miyake, we hypothesize a front mid vowel **e* for pre-MK that was centralized to merge with *ə*. In absolute initial position, this vowel appears as MK *ə*, but in non-initial position it palatalized the preceding consonant before being centralized, resulting in syllables of shape *Cyə* in MK. The predicted OJ correspondence for this vowel is *i* in nonfinal (31a-e), *ye* in final position (f-g):

(31)	MK yə	::	OJ *i*		PJ **e*
a.	*syəm* 'island'	::	*sima* 'island'	?<	**syema*
b.	*syəy-* 'whiten' cf. *hʌy-/hɨy-* 'white'	::	*sirwo* 'white'	?<	**sero*
c.	*nyəy-* 'go'	::	*nige-* 'flee'	?<	**nenk(V)-*
d.	*pyərok* 'flea'	::	*piru* 'leech'	<	**peru*
e.	*ə-* 'wh'	::	*i-* 'wh'	<	**e-*
f.	*myəniri* 'wife'	::	*mye, mi-* 'woman'	<	**me*
g.	*cyəs* 'breasts'	::	*ti, titi* 'breasts'	?<	**te*

Previous treatments of correspondences like those in (31) have posited primary **i* for both languages (Lee 1959, Whitman 1985). But (d-e) give Ryûkyûan evidence for PJ **e*, while (f) gives Japanese-internal evidence for *e, as it shows *ye*, not *i*, in the position predicted by the mid vowel raising hypothesis. Our proposal provides a more balanced vowel system for pre-MK and makes sense of this correspondence set.

3.2 Pre-OJ Mid Vowel Raising in Japanese Loans from Korean

The mid vowel raising hypothesis enables us to distinguish loans which entered Japanese after raising from material present in the language at the preraising stage:

(32)	**MK**		**J Preraising**	**Postraising**
a.	*syəm* 'island''	::	*sima* 'island'	*sema* (*Nihon shoki*)
b.	*kyən* 'silk' (Sino-Korean)	::	*kinu* 'silk'	*ken* (Sino-Japanese)
c.	*tyər* 'Buddhist temple'	::		*tera* 'Buddhist temple'
d.	*puthə* 'Buddha' < **putihyə*	::		*potoke* 'Buddha'
e.	*Kokuryə* 'Koguryŏ' (SK)	::	*Kokuri*	*Kure* 'Koguryŏ'
f.	*kom* < *koma* 'bear'	::	*kuma* 'bear'	*koma* Koguryŏ ethnonym
g.	*mosi* 'ramie'	::	*karamusi* '(Korean) ramie'	

Some of the J preraising forms in (32) are certain (b, e) or probable (g) loans, but the raising diagnostic shows them to be older than their counterparts in the right column.

3.3 A Vowel Shift in EMK?

The unbalanced character of the LMK vowel system in (24) has attracted the attention of Korean linguists for over 40 years. One influential proposal is the 'vowel shift' hypothesis of Lee Ki-moon (1972a, b), which posits a series of chain-type shifts from the hypothesized Early Middle Korean system in (33):

(33) The post-EMK Vowel Shift (Lee 1968, 1972a,b)

```
*i    (LMK ɨ) *ü      →   *u
           ↑                ↓
                       (LMK o)
*e   →    *ə (LMK ʌ)  ←    *ɔ
          *a
```

The vowel shift hypothesis has been criticized by a number of linguists (Kang 1980, Kim 1993, Martin 2000, Vovin 2000). Despite the superficial structural similarity between (33) and the reconstructed PJ system in (23), the vowel correspondences we have discussed give no support for (33). (33) predicts correspondences of the type EMK _*e_ > LMK _ə_ :: OJ _i_ < PJ _*e_, but all correspondences of this type in (31) involve LMK _Cyə_, not _Cə_, supporting our hypothesis that only the former descends from a front vowel. Similarly, (33) predicts EMK _*u_ > LMK _o_ :: OJ _u_ < PJ _*u_, but (30) shows that LMK _o_ corresponds to OJ _u_ only in raising environments; elsewhere, it corresponds to OJ _wo_.

4. Conclusion

We have argued for a Proto-Japanese system of seven vowels, three of which (*ɨ, *e, and *o) were completely or largely eliminated by mergers by the period of the central dialect of OJ. We have shown how this system makes sense of similarities between the demonstrative systems of Korean and Japanese and a number of JK vowel correspondences.

Abbreviations

PJ	Proto-Japanese (including Ryûkyûan)
OJ	Old Japanese (700-800)
EMJ	Early Middle Japanese (800-1200)
EMK	Early Middle Korean (900-1400)
LMK	Late Middle Korean (1400-1600)
PR	Proto-Ryûkyûan

References

Crothers, John. 1978. Typology and universals of vowel systems. In Green berg, J. (ed.) *Universals of Human Language, Volume 2: Phonology*, 93-153. Stanford: Stanford University Press.

Frellesvig, Bjarke. 2001. A common Korean and Japanese copula. *Journal of East Asian Linguistics* 10: 1-35.

Frellesvig, Bjarke and John Whitman. Forthcoming.a. The vowels of proto-Japanese. Japanese Language and Literature (spring 2004).

Frellesvig, Bjarke and John Whitman. Forthcoming.b. Evidence for seven vowels in proto-Japanese. Proto-Japanese, Proceedings from ICHL 2003 (2005).

Hashimoto, Shirô. 1966. Kodaigo no shiji-taikei: Jôdai o chûshin ni. *Kokugo Kokubun* 35: 329-41.

Hashimoto, Shirô. 1982. Shijigo no shiteki tenkai. *Kôza nihongogaku*, vol. 2: Bunpôshi, ed. by Kenji Morioka et al., 217-40. Meiji Shoin.

Hattori, Shirô. 1978-9. Nihonsogo ni tsuite 1 - 22. *Gekkan Gengo* vols. 7/1 - 7/3, 7/6 - 8/12.

Hayata, Teruhiro. 1998. Jôdai nihongo no onsetsu kôzô to o-retsu kô-otsu no betsu (The Syllable and the Distinction between o_1 and o_2 in Old Japanese). *Onsei Kenkyû/Journal of the Phonetic Society of Japan* 2: 25-33.

Hayata, Teruhiro. 2000. The Liquid and stem-final vowel alternations of verbs in Ancient Japanese. *Gengo Kenkyû* 118: 5-27.

Kang, Shinhang. 1980. *Kyerim yusa 'Koryŏ pang'ŏn' yŏngu*. Seoul: Sŏng-gyun'gwan University Press.

Kim, Chuwŏn. 1993. *Moŭm chohwa ŭi yŏngu*. Kyŏngsan: Yŏngnam University Press.

Kôno, Rokurô. 1967/1979. *Kôno Rokurô Chosakushû* 1: 555-562. Tokyo: Heibonsha.

Lange, Roland A. 1973. *The Phonology of Eighth-Century Japanese*. Tokyo: Sophia University.

Lee, Ki-Moon. 1959. On the breaking of *i in Korean. *Asia Yengwu* II.2.

Lee, Ki-Moon. 1972a. *Kwugŏ-sa kaesŏl*. Seoul: Minjung Sŏgwan.

Lee, Ki-Moon. 1972b. *Kwugŏ ŭmun-sa yŏn'gu*. Seoul: Han'guk Munhwa Yŏn'gu-so.

Martin, Samuel E. 1966. Lexical evidence relating Korean to Japanese. *Language* 42.2: 185-251.

Martin, Samuel E. 1987. *The Japanese Language Through Time*. Yale University Press.

Martin, Samuel E. 2000. How have Korean vowels changed through time.

Korean Linguistics 10: 1-60
Matsumoto, Katsumi. 1974. Kodai Nihongo boin soshiki kô: naiteki saiken no kokoromi. *Kanazawa Daigaku hô-bungakubu ronshû*: bungaku hen 22: 83-152.

Matsumoto, Katsumi. 1984. Gengoshi no saiken to gengofuhen. *Gengo Kenkyû* 86: 5-32.

Matsumoto, Katsumi. 1995. *Kodai Nihongo boinron : Jôdai tokushu kanazukai no saikaishaku*. Tokyo: Hitsuji Shobô.

Miller, Roy A. 1967. *The Japanese Language*. Chicago: Chicago University Press.

Miyake, Marc. 2003. Philological evidence for *e and *o in Pre-Old Japanese. *Diachronica* 20: 81-136.

Murayama, Shichirô. 1962. Nihongo to kôkurigo no sûshi - Nihongo no keitô mondai ni tuite. *Kokugogaku* 48.

Ohno, Susumu. 1977. On'in no hensen. *Iwanami kôza Nihongo 5, On'in*: 147-220. Tôkyô: Iwanami Shoten.

Serafim, Leon. 1999. Reflexes of Proto-Korea-Japonic Mid Vowels in Japonic and Korean. Paper presented at the Workshop on Korean-Japanese Comparative Linguistics, XIVth International Conference on Historical Linguistics, Vancouver, British Columbia.

Thorpe, Maner L. 1983. *Ryûkyûan Language History*. University of Southern California Ph.D. dissertation.

Unger, J. Marshall. 1977/1993. *Studies in early Japanese morphophonemics*. Yale University dissertation, reproduced by IULC.

Vovin, Alexander. 2000. On the great vowel shift in Middle Korean and position of stress in proto-Korean. *Korean Linguistics* 10, 61-79

Wenck, Günther. *Japanische Phonetik*, Band IV: Erscheinungen und Probleme des japanischen Lautwandels. Wiesbaden: Otto Harrassowitz.

Whitman, John. 1985. *The Phonological Basis for the Comparison of Japanese and Korean*, Harvard University dissertation.

Yoshitake, Saburô. 1928. The history of the Japanese particle *i*. *Bulletin of the School of Oriental Studies* 5: 889-896.

Acoustic Properties of Japanese and English Vowels: Effects of Phonetic and Prosodic Context

MIWAKO HISAGI, KANAE NISHI, AND WINIFRED STRANGE
The City University of New York-Graduate Center

1. Introduction

Adult learners of foreign languages have considerable difficulty learning to perceive and produce some, but not all, non-native vowels (e.g., Nishi et al., 1998). According to Flege's Speech Learning Model (Flege, 1995) non-native vowels that are "phonetically similar" to native vowels will be perceptually assimilated to native categories, resulting in interlanguage (IL) representations which subsume both L1 and L2 vowels. This will lead to accented production of the L2 vowels, and to perceptual confusions if two L2 vowels are assimilated to the same L1 category. In contrast, non-native vowels which are highly dissimilar phonetically from L1 vowels will (with L2 experience) come to be represented separately from all L1 categories in IL, and may be produced as more native-like. In predicting these patterns of perceptual assimilation, many previous studies have inferred phonetic similarity/dissimilarity from cross-language comparisons of the acoustic structure of vowels produced in only one or a few phonetic and prosodic contexts (often in CV or CVC syllables produced in lists). Previous research has documented large differences in the phonetic realization of American English (AE) vowels as a function of phonetic context (Hillenbrand et al., 2001) and prosodic context (Fourakis, 1991; Strange et al., submitted). Less research has been published on the allophonic and prosodic variation of Japanese (J) vowels. Thus, the goal of the present study was to compare the allophonic and prosodic variation in spectral and temporal structure of J and AE vowels, using acoustical analysis of corpora in which the phonetic and prosodic context was varied systematically. To the extent that the type and amount of phonetic variation *differs* across the two languages, we would expect that cross-language perceptual similarity might also vary with contextual variables.

The J vowel inventory includes five spectrally distinctive pairs of vowels that are temporally differentiated (e.g., 1-mora /i/ *vs* 2-mora /ii/), whereas AE has eleven spectrally distinctive (non-rhotic) vowels: seven phonetically long and four phonetically short vowels (Peterson & Lehiste, 1960). In the present study, vowels were produced in utterances which varied in (a) utterance duration (citation-form lists of disyllables *vs* multisyllabic nonsense words imbedded in a carrier sentence), (b) segmental context (labial *vs* alveolar preceding/following consonants), (c) prominence location (narrow Focus *vs* Postfocus sentence position) and (d) speaking rate (normal *vs* rapid sentences). Cross-language comparisons were then conducted to determine how each of these variables influenced the spectral structure (formant frequencies at syllable midpoint) and the temporal structure (syllable duration) of the target syllables. The following comparisons will be presented in this paper:

1) Consonantal Context: vowels in b-p *vs* d-t context produced in multisyllabic nonsense words medially in a sentence produced at normal speaking rate with instructions not to emphasis the target word (no focus).

2) Sentence Prominence: vowels in d-t context produced in multisyllabic nonsense words imbedded in sentences in which the target word was in narrow focus position *vs* following the word with narrow focus (postfocus).

3) Speaking Rate: vowels in d-t context produced in multisyllabic words imbedded in sentences produced with the speakers' self-selected normal conversational rate *vs* at a rapid rate.

Because of limitations of space, the data for the citation-form disyllables will not be presented.

2. Methods

2.1 Subjects

Four Japanese and four Americans participated as speakers in this study. The Japanese participants (2 males, 2 females) were native speakers of Kansai dialect, and ranged in age from 18 to 24 years old (mean=21 years). American participants (2 males, 2 females) were native speakers of New

York dialect and ranged in age from 34 to 41 years old (mean=37 years). All Japanese had never lived outside of the Kansai area in Japan and had not had extensive exposure to spoken English outside of Japan. American participants were not fluent in any other language. All subjects were paid for their participation.

2.2 Stimulus materials

The target vowels for Japanese were the five long vowels, /aa, ee, ii, oo, ɯɯ/ and the five short vowels, /a, e, i, o, ɯ/; for American English the vowels included seven long vowels, /i, e, æ, ɑ, ɔ, o, u/ and four short vowels, /ɪ, ɛ, ʌ, ʊ/. For AE, the carrier sentence was 'I said five gaCVCa this time.' For J, the carrier sentence was 'Kono hon-ga CVCa desu ne ('This book is CVCa.')'.

2.3 Procedure

Instructions given for each condition were as follows: (1) Normal: "Please speak as if you are talking to a native speaker; don't speak slowly and don't emphasize the nonsense word," (2) Focus: "Please speak as if you are answering a question, 'Did you say five <u>gaduta</u>?' when your answer is 'gadita'," (3) Postfocus: "Please speak as if you are answering a question, 'Did you say <u>three</u> gaduta?' when your answer is 'five'," and (4) Rapid: "Please speak as rapidly as possible without leaving any sounds out." Speakers were provided a reading list in which each of the utterances was preceded by a number indicating the target vowel identity. Speakers were instructed to pause briefly between the number and the sentence. Utterances were blocked by segmental/prosodic condition (normal b-p, normal d-t, Focus d-t, Postfocus d-t, rapid d-t) to establish a consistent rhythm and prosody across utterances containing all vowels within each condition. All vowels were produced four times in each condition with conditions randomized across the four speakers of each language. Within blocks, vowels were randomly ordered in four different sequences. Any clearly mispronounced or disfluent utterances were either self-corrected by the speaker or the experimenter asked for a repetition at the end of each block.

Three J speakers were recorded in an anechoic chamber at ATR Human Information Science Laboratories, using a condenser microphone (SONY ECM-77) connected to a DAT recorder (SONY PCM-2500A, B). One J speaker and all AE speakers were recorded in an IAC chamber in the Speech Acoustic and Perception Laboratory at the City University of New York-Graduate Center, using a dynamic microphone (SHURE SM-48) fed to a Preamplifier (Earthworks Lab 101) and then into a PC computer through a soundcard. Stimuli were directly transferred to computer files

(22.05 kHz sampling rate, 16 bit quantization) using "SoundForge 4.5 (Sonic Foundry, inc)" software.

Acoustic analysis was performed on a PC computer, using customized programs written in MATLab. First, time-synchronized waveforms and wideband spectrograms (1024 points, 6 dB pre-emphasis) of an utterance were displayed. The experimenter located the onset and offset of the target syllable by hand. Onset was defined as the initial consonant release burst (the beginning of opening of the vocal tract) and offset was defined as the beginning of silence associated with the beginning of following stop consonant closure. The program then displayed three spectral sections located at 25%, 50%, and 75% durational points in each syllable in which formant center frequencies (derived from LPC analysis – 24 coefficients autocorrelation) were superimposed as lines on the narrow band FFT spectrum (512 pts). In most cases, the LPC analysis selected formant frequencies corresponded closely with spectral peaks in the FFT spectrum. In those cases where the LPC analysis generated spurious peaks or indicated missing or merged formants, values were estimated from the FFT spectra by manual placement of a cursor at the spectral peak. Data from the 50% point are presented in this paper. Average fundamental frequency (voice pitch) was also calculated (autocorrelation method) for the middle half of each syllable (between 25% and 75% points).

3. Results

Results of acoustic comparisons across the three contextual variables are presented below. Changes in vowel quality (formant frequencies at syllable midpoint) are shown in figures which plot the mean Formant 1/Formant 2 (F1/F2) values (in Barks) averaged over tokens and speakers (16 tokens/vowel); coordinates are arranged to display vowel locations in the traditional vowel quadrilateral with high vowels above, low vowels below and front vowels to the left. Long and short vowels for each language are shown separately. Changes in vowel quantity (syllable duration) are also reported in tables for long and short vowels separately for each language, averaged over tokens and speakers. Finally, changes in fundamental frequency (f0) are reported as a function of the prosodic variables of sentence prominence (focus) and speaking rate.

3.1 Effects of Segmental Context: bVp *vs* dVt

3.1.1 Vowel Quality: Figure 1 shows the combined data of males and females. As Figure 1 shows, differences in the average F1/F2 values as a function of consonantal context differed across languages and across long and short vowels in each language. J 2-mora vowels reflected the smallest average change overall; F2 values (corresponding to vowel backness) changed only slightly for the back vowels /aa, oo, ɯɯ/ (mean F2 change =

109 Hz, 124 Hz, 126 Hz, respectively), while front vowels remained stable. In contrast, J 1-mora back vowels showed large increases in average F2 frequencies (i.e. greater fronting) in alveolar contexts relative to labial contexts (a =344 Hz, o =355 Hz, ɯ =377 Hz), and F1 values also decreased for /a/ (raised). Thus, 1-mora and 2-mora back J vowels differed more in spectral structure in alveolar contexts than in labial context and the 1-mora vowels were less differentiated in vowel space in alveolar contexts. The AE vowels showed a somewhat different pattern. For the long vowels, only /u, o/ showed significant fronting (F2 increases of 586 Hz and 210 Hz, respectively), while F2 values for the remaining back vowels /ɑ, ɔ/ and the three front vowels /i, e, æ/ were quite stable across segmental contexts. All four short AE vowels showed increased F2 values in alveolar context relative to labial context, although the average change was greater for back vowels (ʊ=489 Hz; ʌ =242 Hz) than for front vowels (ɪ=155 Hz; ɛ=170 Hz). These changes resulted in differences in the *relative* locations of AE vowels in the vowel space, with so-called back rounded vowels /u, ʊ, o/ much closer to front vowels in alveolar context than in labial context. That is, back rounded high and mid vowels were allophonically produced as front rounded vowels in alveolar context.

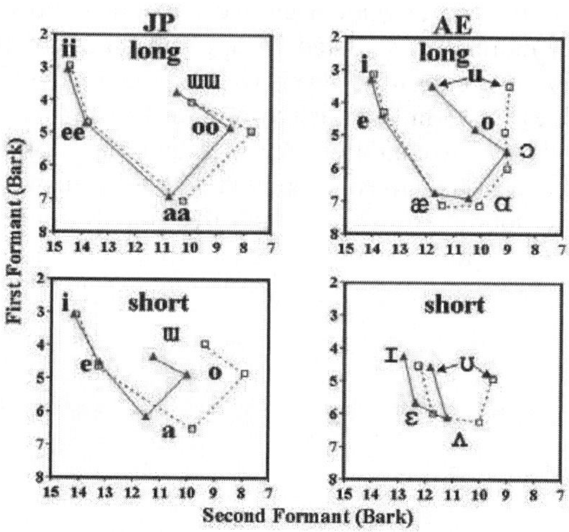

Figure 1. Vowel space for J vowels (left) and AE vowels (right) in /bVp/ (open squares) *vs* /dVt/ (closed triangles) contexts

3.1.2 Vowel Quantity: Table 1 displays the average syllable durations for J and AE vowels in labial and alveolar contexts. Both long and short vowels in both languages were longer in /dVt/ context than in /bVp/ context. Larger differences in AE may be due to the final /t/ being produced as a (voiced) flap in intervocalic context. Note that the ratio of 2-mora to 1-mora vowels in Japanese remained quite constant across contexts, whereas the long/short vowel ratio for AE vowels was reduced in alveolar context.

Table 1. Average durations (in ms) for long and short Japanese and American English vowels in labial and alveolar consonantal context.

JAPANESE	Labial (LB)	Alveolar (AV)	Ratio (LB/AV)
long vowels (L)	142	159	0.89
short vowels (S)	75	86	0.87
Ratio (L/S)	1.89	1.85	

AMERICAN ENGLISH	Labial (LB)	Alveolar (AV)	Ratio (LB/AV)
long vowels (L)	125	158	0.79
short vowels (S)	88	124	0.71
Ratio (L/S)	1.42	1.27	

3.2 Effects of Sentence Prominence: Focus *vs* Postfocus

3.2.1 Vowel Quality: Figure 2 displays the F1/F2 vowel spaces for J and AE vowels, again averaged across tokens and speakers. When the nonsense words containing the target vowels were in Focus position, vowels were, on average, more differentiated in spectral structure in both languages. That is, F1 values for low vowels tended to be higher (vowels were lower) and F2 values for front and back vowels differed more. Note, however, that even in the Focus condition, AE high and mid back vowels were allophonically fronted in this alveolar context. Thus, sentence prominence did not, in general, appear to have a large effect on spectral structure for either J or AE vowels, at least in this one consonantal context.

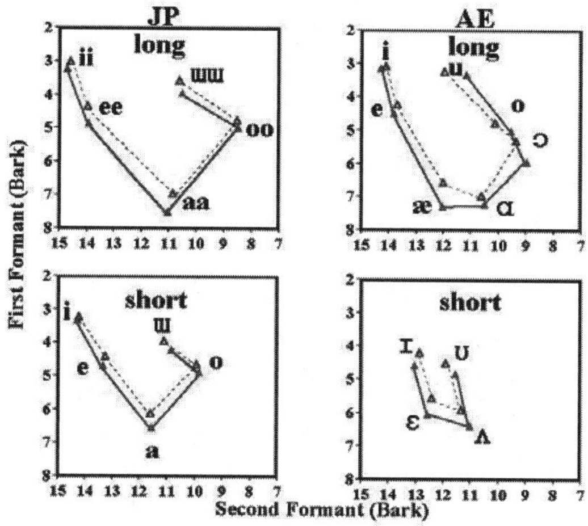

Figure 2. Vowel space for J vowels (left) and AE vowels (right): Focus (solid lines) *vs* Postfocus (dashed lines) in /dVt/ contexts

3.2.2 Vowel Quantity: Table 2 presents the average durations of long and short J and AE vowels and the ratio of long to short vowels. In the righthand column, the duration ratios for the Focus relative to the Postfocus condition are also given. As these data show, J short vowels did not show a change with sentence prominence, while J long vowels were 12% longer in the Focus condition. Thus, the ratio of 2-mora to 1-mora vowels was reduced in the Postfocus prosodic condition, relative to the Focus position, and to the Neutral Focus position reported in Table 1 above (1.85 for alveolar context). Syllable durations for nonsense words in Focus position in AE showed more similar lengthening of long and short vowels relative to Postfocus position (17% and 12% respectively) and to Neutral Focus position shown in Table 1 (12% and 6%, respectively). This resulted in the long/short vowel ratio remaining quite stable over all three conditions in which vowels were preceded and followed by alveolar consonants. Note, however, that even in Postfocus contexts, J 2-mora and 1-mora vowels differed significantly more in relative duration than did AE long and short vowels.

Table 2. Average durations (in ms) for long and short Japanese and American English vowels in Focus and Postfocus context.

JAPANESE		Focus (F)	Postfocus (PF)	Ratio (F/PF)
	long vowels (L)	164	147	1.12
	short vowels (S)	87	86	1.01
	Ratio (L/S)	1.89	1.71	

AMERICAN ENGLISH		Focus (F)	Postfocus (PF)	Ratio (F/PF)
	long vowels (L)	177	151	1.17
	short vowels (S)	132	118	1.12
	Ratio (L/S)	1.34	1.28	

3.2.3 Voice Pitch (f0): For comparison of voice pitch (f0), the male and female data were separated because of gender differences in average voice pitch. Table 3 presents the average data for J and AE males and females. The f0 values represent the pitch of the target vowels, averaged over all ten vowels for J utterances and all eleven vowels for AE utterances. For all groups, the average f0 was greater for syllables in Focus position than in the Postfocus position. However, Japanese males showed somewhat smaller changes in voice pitch than AE males and J and AE females.

Table 3. Average f0 (in Hz) for Japanese and American English vowels in Focus and Postfocus context.

JAPANESE		Focus (F)	Postfocus (PF)	Ratio (F/PF)
	Male	176	150	1.17
	Female	265	213	1.24

AMERICAN ENGLISH		Focus (F)	Postfocus (PF)	Ratio (F/PF)
	Male	159	105	1.51
	Female	237	174	1.36

3.3 Effects of Speaking Rate: Normal *vs* Rapid

3.3.1 Vowel Quality: Figure 3 presents the vowel spaces for J and AE vowels produced in sentences at the speakers' self-selected normal rate of speech *vs* at a rapid rate. As the figure shows, the spectral structure of both long and short vowels in both languages remained very similar, on average, in the two rate conditions. There was some centralization of AE /ɔ, ʌ/ and J /a, o, oo/ in the rapid condition, while J /aa/ showed the opposite effect (higher F1 in rapid condition). Thus, in alveolar context at least, most J and

AE vowels spoken rapidly in sentence length utterances had very similar spectral structure to those produced at slower rates (and more prominent sentence positions) in the same multisyllabic nonsense word context.

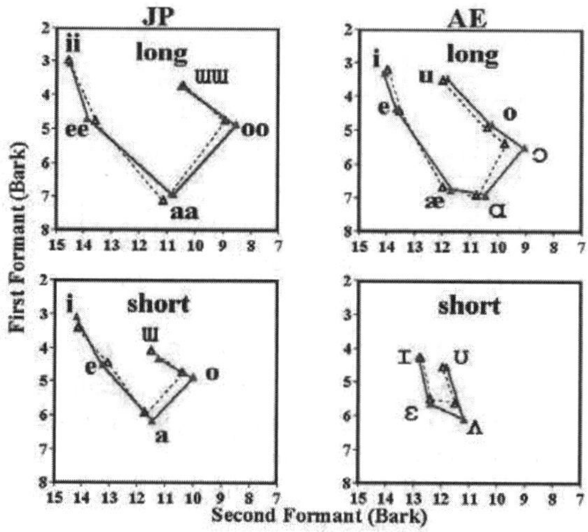

Figure 3. Vowel space for J vowels (left) and AE vowels (right): normal (solid lines) *vs* rapid (dashed lines) in /dVt/ contexts

3.3.2 Vowel Quantity: Table 4 presents the average duration data for the normal rate sentences (also shown in Table 1) and the rapid rate sentences, separately for long and short vowels in J and AE languages. As before, durations of syllables containing J 1-mora vowels did not decrease in the rapid condition, relative to those in the normal rate (Neutral Focus) condition, nor indeed relative to those produced in the Focus condition. In contrast, the 2-mora J vowels were, on average, 28% shorter in the rapid condition. Thus, the 2-mora/1-mora duration ratio decreased considerably in the rapid utterances (1.51). In contrast, both long and short AE vowels decreased in duration proportionally (21% and 22%, respectively) such that the long/short duration ratio remained stable across speaking rates. Note that the vowel length differences in rapidly produced J utterances were still greater than they were in AE utterances.

Table 4. Average durations (in ms) for long and short Japanese and American English vowels in normal and rapid context.

JAPANESE		Normal (N)	Rapid (R)	Ratio(N/R)
	long vowels (L)	159	124	1.28
	short vowels (S)	86	82	1.05
	Ratio (L/S)	1.85	1.51	

AMERICAN ENGLISH		Normal (N)	Rapid (R)	Ratio(N/R)
	long vowels (L)	158	131	1.21
	short vowels (S)	124	102	1.22
	Ratio (L/S)	1.27	1.28	

3.3.3 Voice Pitch (f0): Table 5 gives the average f0 values in normal and rapid conditions, summed over all ten J vowels and all eleven AE vowels, respectively. There were no consistent differences in f0 as a function of speaking rate for the Japanese utterances. For AE speakers' utterances, f0 increased in the rapid condition for both males and females. One J female speaker had a very low f0 which did not increase for rapid utterances. Future studies with more speakers are needed to explore if there are cross-language differences in f0 as a function of speaking rate.

Table 5. Average f0 (in Hz) for Japanese and American English vowels in normal and rapid context.

JAPANESE		Normal (N)	Rapid (R)	Ratio (N/R)
	Male	143	146	0.98
	Female	253	226	1.12

AMERICAN ENGLISH		Normal (N)	Rapid (R)	Ratio (N/R)
	Male	119	138	0.86
	Female	180	187	0.96

4. Discussion

4.1 Summary of Effects of Consonantal Context

Both languages showed acoustic fronting of back vowels in /dVt/ context (higher second formants) and vowels were longer in /dVt/ context. The overall shape of the vowel space (i.e. relative locations of vowels) remained similar across contexts for J vowels; however, the space tended to shrink for 1-mora vowels in alveolar context, due to coarticulatory fronting of back vowels and raising of the low vowel. In contrast, the shape of the vowel space changed across contexts for AE vowels, such that high and mid back vowels were fronted in alveolar context. This resulted in considerable acoustic overlap of instances of front and back short vowels in that context. Finally, syllable durations showed greater change for AE than for J vowels. For the latter, the ratio of 2-mora to 1-mora vowels remained relatively constant.

4.2 Summary of Effects of Sentence Focus

The spectral variation of vowels in sentence Focus *vs* Postfocus context was similar (and relatively small) across languages. In both languages, sentence prominence was also indicated by increases in syllable duration and fundamental frequency. However, in order to maintain the length contrast between 2-mora and 1-mora vowels in Japanese, sentence focus for nonsense words containing J short vowels was achieved by increased pitch instead of increased vocalic duration. For AE vowels, duration differences between long and short vowels were enhanced in Focus context, relative to Neutral and Postfocus context. However, long/short vowel ratios remained considerably smaller for AE vowel contrasts than for J vowel contrasts in both prosodic contexts.

4.3 Summary of Effects of Speaking Rate

Spectral variation as a function of speaking rate was similar across languages, with a few vowels showing a small amount of centralization, while others were either the same or actually more differentiated in rapid condition. As expected, syllable durations decreased for both J and AE rapid utterances. However, in Japanese, only long vowels were shorter, on average, while short vowels did not change. Thus, the ratio of 2-mora to 1-mora vowels decreased in the rapid condition for J vowels, while in AE utterances, the long-short vowel ratio remained stable. However, even in the context of very rapid speech, vowel length was more distinctive for J vowels than for AE vowels, as would be expected given the phonological status of vowel length in Japanese. Finally, results of changes in voice pitch were not conclusive, given individual differences in patterns of change across speakers.

4.4 Implications

These within- and cross-language similarities and differences in the effects of prosodic and segmental context on vowel acoustics reflect both language-universal constraints and language-specific "rules" for changes in vowel quality and quantity. Raising awareness of these cross-linguistic differences may help second language learners of Japanese and English to improve their perception and production.

References

Flege, J.E. (1995). Second language speech learning: Theory, findings, and problems. In *Speech Perception and Linguistic Experience: Issues in Cross-language Research* (W. Strange, editor), pp.233-277. Timonium, MD: York Press.

Fourakis, M. (1991). Tempo, stress, and vowel reduction in American English. *Journal of the Acoustical Society of America, 90,* 1816-1827.

Hillenbrand, J.M., Clark, M.J., & Nearey, T.M. (2001). Effects of consonant environment on vowel formant patterns, *Journal of the Acoustical Society of America, 109,* 748-763.

Nishi, K., Strange, W., Akahane-Yamada, R., Trent, S.A., and Thornton, D.H. (1998). Perceptual assimilation of Japanese vowels by American English listeners: effects of speaking style. Paper presented at the 136th Meeting of the Acoustic Society of America, Norfolk, VA.

Peterson, G. E.,& Lehiste, I. (1960). Duration of syllable nuclei in English, *Journal of the Acoustical Society of America, 97,* 1286-1296.

Strange, W., Bohn, O., Trent, S. and Nishi, K. (submitted). Acoustic and perceptual similarity of North German and American English vowels. *Journal of the Acoustical Society of America.*

Default Prosody and Relative Clause Attachment in Japanese

SUN-AH JUN & CHISATO KOIKE
UCLA

1. Introduction

Sentences with a complex noun phrase modified by a relative clause (e.g., 'Someone shot the servant of the actress who was on the balcony') can be ambiguous regarding the attachment of the relative clause (RC). The RC can modify the whole NP ('the servant of the actress', i.e. the servant), known as *high* attachment, or the NP immediately adjacent to the RC ('the actress'), known as *low* attachment. In English, speakers in general prefer low attachment (Carreiras & Clifton 1993, 1999; Fernández 2000, 2003), but this attachment preference has turned out to be language-specific. High attachment is preferred by speakers of Dutch (Brysbaert & Mitchell 1996), French (Zagar, Pynte, & Rativeau 1997), German (Hemforth, Konieczny, Scheepers, & Strube 1998), Japanese (Kamide & Mitchell 1997), and Spanish (Cuetos & Mitchell 1988), while low attachment is preferred by speakers of Arabic (Quinn, Abdelghany, & Fodor 2000), English (Frazier & Clifton 1996), and Norwegian, Romanian, and Swedish (Ehrlich, Fernández, Fodor, Stenshoel, & Vinereanu 1999). (See Fernández 2000, 2003, for more detail). This apparent cross-linguistic difference in ambiguity resolution preference has raised some dilemmas for the universalist view of sentence processing (Kimball 1973; Frazier & Fodor 1978; Frazier 1979; Frazier & Rayner 1988), which hypothesizes that the human sentence processing mechanism is innate and universal. There have been several attempts to explain the cross-linguistic differences (e.g. Tuning, Two Factor Model, Construal, Attachment-Binding, and Implicit Prosody), and this paper focuses on the Implicit Prosody Hypothesis (IPH) proposed by Fodor (1998, 2002).

The IPH states that a default prosodic contour projected in silent reading favors the syntactic analysis associated with the default prosody for the construction. Since languages differ in their prosody, attachment preferences would differ across languages. This hypothesis is supported by the effect of prosody on attachment resolution. Short RCs tend to attach low and long RCs tend to attach high. Maynell (1999) and Lovri´c et al. (2000, 2001) found that speakers interpret a prosodic break before an RC (in a sequence of NP1 NP2 RC) as a marker of a stronger syntactic boundary, which prompts high attachment (i.e. RC modifying NP1). This suggests that speakers of a language with high attachment preference would tend to produce a prosodic boundary between the RC and the adjacent noun in the default phrasing of a sentence, but not between the two nouns (i.e. NP1 and NP2).

The current study investigates the validity of the IPH in production and perception experiments on Japanese data. In the production experiment, we examine how Japanese speakers, known to prefer high attachment (Kamide & Mitchell 1997), produce the prosodic phrasing of a sentence, especially the default prosodic pattern of a complex noun phrase preceded by an RC. (In Japanese, the word order is the opposite of that in English. In this paper, following the word order in Japanese, we will label the target structure as 'RC NP1 NP2' where NP1 is the noun corresponding to 'the actress' and NP2 is the head noun corresponding to 'the servant' in the English example above. In Japanese, NP1 is followed by the genitive particle *-no*, corresponding to the 'NP1's NP2' structure in English.) The IPH would predict that Japanese speakers produce a larger prosodic break between RC and NP1 than between NP1 and NP2. In the perception experiment, which is preformed about three weeks later, we examine the interpretation (i.e. RC attachment) of the same sentences used in the production experiment by the same subjects who participated in the production experiment. For the target sentences used in both experiments, we changed the length and the accentedness of each RC, NP1, and NP2 as well as the location of the target phrase in a sentence to see if the default phrasing of the target phrase changes depending on these factors, and if so, whether the changed default phrasing is reflected in the speakers' interpretation of RC attachment.

2. Method

2.1. Subjects

Thirty speakers of Tokyo Japanese participated in both the production and the perception experiment. Subjects were randomly divided into two groups (15 speakers each): Group 1 (skimming) and Group 2 (non-skimming).

2.2. Material

Twenty-four sentences were created with six different combinations of accent types for RC, NP1, and NP2, and within each accent type, there were four combinations of length types for RC, NP1, and NP2. Table 1 shows these six types of accents and four types of length combinations. Two combinations of accent, UAU and UUU, were not included since these did not seem to differ from UAA and UUA, respectively, in terms of their influence in phrasing between RC and NP1. It is expected that the accentedness of RC and NP1 would affect the phrasing of the target phrase because it has been found in previous studies that an unaccented word is likely to form one prosodic group with the following word (e.g. Kubozono 1993; Venditti and van Santen 2000).

Factors	Type	RC	NP1	NP2
Accent	AAA	Accented	Accented	Accented
	AAU	Accented	Accented	Unaccented
	AUA	Accented	Unaccented	Accented
	AUU	Accented	Unaccented	Unaccented
	UAA	Unaccented	Accented	Accented
	UUA	Unaccented	Unaccented	Accented
Length	ddd	Default	Default	Default
	ldd	Long	Default	Default
	sls	Short	Long	Short
	ssd	Short	Short	Default

Table 1. Types of Accent and Length of each phrase (RC, NP1, and NP2)

Length combinations were chosen focusing on the length of RC and NP1 so that each length combination may or may not trigger a prosodic break after an RC. For example, 'ldd' would more likely trigger a break after the RC than the default length, 'ddd', while 'ssd' or 'sls' would less likely trigger a break after the RC than 'ddd'. The 'default' length was defined as a 3-4 mora NP and a 7-8 mora RC; the 'short' length was defined as a 1-2 mora NP and a shorter than 6 mora RC, and the 'long' length was defined as a longer than 6 mora NP and a longer than 10 mora RC. The 24 sentences varying in terms of accent types and length types were then located either at the beginning of a sentence (i.e. Sentence initial) or the middle of a sentence (i.e. Sentence medial), resulting in a total 48 target sentences. Example sentences of three types of the Accent-Length combinations are shown in (1). The target structure is italicized, and the location of Accent is shown with an apostrophe.

(1) a. AUA-ddd type; sentence medial
Senshuu Ta'roo wa *joyuu ni na'tta* *koohai no*
Last week Taro-TOP actress into to become-past *junior student-GEN*
one'esan ni guuzen a'tta.
older sister with accidently to meet-past
=> 'Last week Taro happened to meet *the older sister of the junior student who became an actress.*'

b. UAA-ldd; Sentence initial
Kookoo de oshiete-iru one'esan no fi'anse/fia'nse wa
high school at to teach-prog older sister-GEN fiancé-TOP
ryo'ori to karaoke ga shu'mi rashi'i.
cooking and karaoke-NOM hobby seem
=> '*The fiance of my older sister who is teaching at high school* seems to like cooking and karaoke as hobbies.'

c. AAU-ssd type; sentence medial
Yamamoto-kachoo wa *ji'ko de shinda* *bu'ka no*
Yamamoto-section chief-TOP *accident by to die-past subordinate-GEN*
musume-san to ichido denwa de hana'shita koto' ga a'ru.
daughter with once telephone on to have talked
=> 'The section chief Yamamoto had talked once on the phone with *the daughter of his subordinate who died in an accident.*'

2.3. Procedure

2.3.1. Production

The 48 target sentences were randomized together with 36 filler sentences, resulting in a total of 84 sentences. Subjects in Group 1 were instructed to read each sentence after briefly skimming the sentence, and subjects in Group 2 were instructed to read each sentence without skimming first. Each sentence was written on an index card in Japanese orthography, and speakers read each sentence two times in the sound booth at the UCLA Phonetics Lab. We varied the option of skimming vs. non-skimming in order to match closely the default prosody employed by native speakers in their silent reading during the off-line and on-line sentence processing experiment, respectively. Allowing time to skim the sentence before reading and asking subjects to repeat each sentence two times allowed us to investigate how stable the default prosody was -- if there is any default prosody at all for each sentence or structure -- given the different amount of semantic information available to them before reading. All utterances were digitized using PitchWorks (*Scicon*), and the prosodic phrasing was determined by the intonation pattern of the utterance and the degree of juncture between words following the conventions described in Japanese ToBI (Pierrehumbert and Beckman 1988; Venditti 1995, in press; Maegawa et al. 2002)

2.3.2. Perception

The subjects who participated in the production experiment also participated in the perception experiment. Each subject was arranged to come back to the lab about 3 weeks after his/her production experiment. The perception experiment was an off-line questionnaire experiment. The questionnaire consisted of the 48 target sentences used in the production experiment randomized with 57 filler sentences. A comprehension question was added below each sentence (e.g., who was on the balcony?) and two choices were given as a possible answer (e.g. the actress, the servant). The questionnaire was displayed on a computer screen as an html file with each page listing 10 questions and only a forward button shown at the bottom of the page. Subjects were asked to mark an answer on a paper. The experiment took about 30 minutes.

3. Results

3.1. Production

The sequence of RC, NP1, and NP2 was phrased in many ways but grouped into three categories depending on the sub-grouping among the three phrases. The first category was RC//NP1-NP2 (a prosodic break between RC and NP1 and a grouping of NP1 and NP2), which we call 'early' boundary. This includes when the prosodic boundary is either an Intonation Phrase (IP) (i.e. $\{RC\}_{IP}\{NP1\text{-}NP2\}$) or an Accentual Phrase (AP), a phrase smaller than an IP and is defined by an initial rising tone (H-) and the lexical pitch accent (H*+L), if there is one (i.e. $\{RC\}_{AP}\{NP1\text{-}NP2\}$) (See Pierrehumbert and Beckman 1986 and Venditti 1995, in press, for more detail). An example pitch track of the latter is shown in Figure 1. The second category was RC-NP1//NP2 (a prosodic break between NP1 and NP2 and a grouping of RC and NP1), which we call 'late' boundary. Again, the prosodic boundary can be an IP or an AP, and a pitch track example of the AP boundary is shown in Figure 2. Finally, the third category was RC/NP1/NP2 (no sub-grouping among the three), which we call 'neutral' boundary. The third case included three types of phrasing: (1) when the prosodic boundary was an IP, $\{RC\}_{IP}\{NP1\}_{IP}\{NP2\}$, (2) when it was an AP, $\{RC\}_{AP}\{NP1\}_{AP}$ $\{NP2\}$, and (3) when all three phrases together formed one AP, $\{RC\text{-}NP1\text{-}NP2\}_{AP}$. A pitch track example of (2) is shown in Figure 3.

Table 2 shows the percentage of each category of default phrasing in the production of the structure RC NP1 NP2, both in sentence-initial (Initial) and sentence-medial (Medial) position of a sentence, separated by the Groups. Speakers in Group 1 and Group 2 produced different phrasing between the two repetitions, 17.8% and 20.8% of the time, respectively, suggesting that the default phrasing can, but not substantially, change across repetitions. Since the difference between each repetition within each Group does not differ significantly and since the first repetition of Group 2 (no skimming) includes more speech errors in general, the phrasing data from the second repetition of Group 2 were compared with those of the first repetition of Group 1.

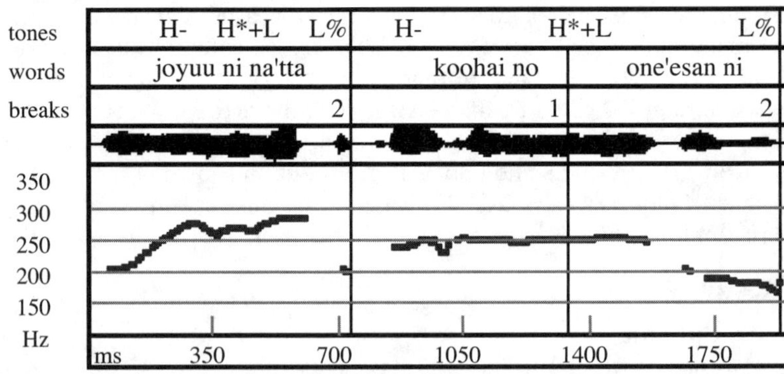

Figure 1. Pitch track of the RC-NP1-NP2 phrase of the sentence in (1a), produced in $\{RC\}_{AP}\{NP1\text{-}NP2\}$ phrasing.

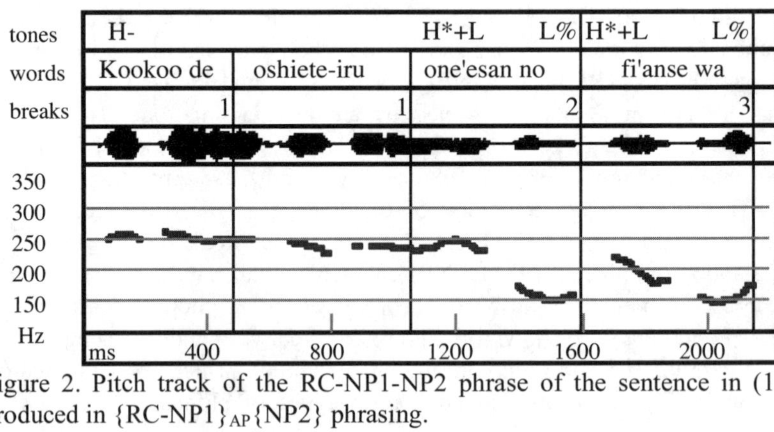

Figure 2. Pitch track of the RC-NP1-NP2 phrase of the sentence in (1b), produced in $\{RC\text{-}NP1\}_{AP}\{NP2\}$ phrasing.

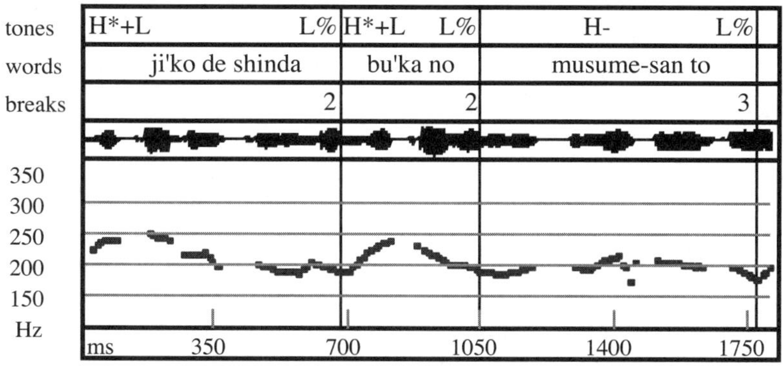

Figure 3. Pitch track of the RC-NP1-NP2 phrase of the sentence in (1c), produced in $\{RC\}_{AP}\{NP1\}_{AP}\{NP2\}$ phrasing.

Results show that, in both Groups, Japanese speakers produced 'early' boundary (RC//NP1-NP2) two thirds of the time (66~67%) and the 'late' boundary (RC-NP1//NP2) only 7~10%. For the rest (22~26%), no grouping was made. This result in itself would support Fodor's IPH because it predicts that the default phrasing of a high attachment language would place a prosodic break between the RC and the adjacent NP, i.e. RC//NP1-NP2.

	Location in S	RC//NP1-NP2	RC-NP1//NP2	RC/NP1/NP2
GR1	Medial	63.88%	10.0%	26.11%
	Initial	69.16%	4.44%	26.38%
	GR 1 Total	66.52%	7.22%	26.25%
GR2	Medial	65.55%	11.94%	22.5%
	Initial	70.0%	8.61%	21.38%
	GR 2 Total	67.77%	10.27%	21.94%
All	Total	67.15%	8.75%	24.09%

Table 2. Percentage of each boundary type of the target structure in each Group (Data for Total for each Group are based on 720 tokens and data for all are based on 1440 tokens).

Logistic Regression analyses show that there is a significant difference between Groups in production data (Chi-square=6.718, p=.0348). Group 1 (skimming) produced more cases of 'neutral' boundary and fewer 'late' boundary cases than Group 2 (non-skimming). Furthermore, there is a significant difference in the Location in Sentence for Group 1 (Chi-square= 8.653, p=.0132). Speakers produced more 'late' boundaries in sentence-medial than sentence–initial position. Speakers in both groups showed the effect of Length (Gr1: Chi-square=35.434, p<.0001; Gr2: Chi-square= 16.629. p=.0107). Compared to the default length (=ddd), speakers produced more 'early' boundaries when the RC was long (=ldd) and fewer 'late' boundaries when RC was short (=ssd or sls). Finally, speakers in both groups showed the effect of Accent (Gr1: Chi-square=114.089, p<.0001; Gr2: Chi-square=149.575. p<.0001). Compared to the AAA type accent, they produced more 'early' boundaries when NP1 was unaccented (=AUU or AUA) and more 'late' boundaries when RC was unaccented (=UAA). The number of 'early' boundary tokens is, from the highest to the lowest: AUU (22.1%), AUA (20.8%), AAU (16.5%), UUA (16.4%), AAA (15.49%), and UAA (8.5%); data based on 967 tokens. This confirms the previous finding that an unaccented word tends to form one prosodic unit together with the following word (e.g. Kubozono 1993; Kondo & Mazuka 1996; Venditti & van Santen 2000; Hirose 2003).

The phrasing of the UAA pattern was very different from other Accent patterns. For all the phrasing data of UAA (240 tokens), 34.58% was 'early' boundary, 27.5% was 'late' boundary, and 37.9% was 'neutral' boundary. The number of 'early' boundaries for this accent pattern was lower than those of other Accent patterns, but the number of 'late' and 'neutral' boundaries was higher than those of others. This suggests that there is an interaction between the accent effect and the syntactic constraint on phrasing. Though a UA sequence often forms one prosodic group, in the UAA pattern where the RC is Unaccented and NP1 is Accented, a clause boundary between RC and NP1 seemed to prevent RC and NP1 from forming one prosodic grouping. The conflict between the accent factor and the syntactic constraint seemed to yield the highest percentage of the 'neutral' boundary for this Accent pattern.

3.2. Perception

Results show that Japanese speakers interpreted the RC as modifying NP2 66% of the time (when combining Group 1 and Group 2); that is, they prefer high attachment, confirming previous findings by Kamide and Mitchell (1997). Table 3 shows the percentage of low and high attachment within each Group and across Groups when the structure was located at the beginning of a sentence (Initial) and in the middle of a sentence (Med).

Logistic Regression analyses show that there is no significant difference between Groups (Chi-square=1.639, p=.2005). The effect of Location on perception was not significant in each Group, but the effect of Length was significant in Group 1 (Chi-square=8.645, p=.0344). The RC in ldd (long RC) was interpreted as high attachment more often than that in the default length (ddd). Finally, the effect of Accent was significant only in Group 2. The RC was interpreted as high attachment more often for AUA and AUU compared to that for AAA. In sum, longer RCs in general generated more high attachment than shorter RCs, and a sequence of Accented RC and Unaccented NP1 generated more high attachment than other Accent types.

Location in S	Group1		Group2		Total	
	Low	High	Low	High	Low	High
Med	32.8%	67.2%	35.0%	65.0%	33.9%	66.1%
Initial	31.9%	68.1%	36.1%	63.8%	34.0%	66%
Total	32.4%	67.6%	35.5%	64.4%	33.9%	66%

Table 3. Percentage of Low and High attachment in each Group and Total (there were 720 tokens in each Group (= 24 sentences x 15 speakers x 2 Locations).

4. Discussion: Default Prosody and the Comparison between Perception and Production

As shown in Jun (2003), speakers in Japanese do not put a phrase break between a relative clause and a head noun when the head noun is a single noun. For example, the prosodic grouping of a sentence *John-ga neko-ni kamitsuita inu-o oikaketa* ('John-NOM cat-at bit dog-ACC chased'=> 'John chased the dog that bit the cat.') is {John-ga} {neko-ni kamitsita inu-o} {oikaketa}. The head noun *inu-o* 'the dog-ACC' forms one prosodic group with the preceding word, the verb of the relative clause. This may be due to a morpho-syntactic fact of Japanese that there is no complementizer marking the boundary of a relative clause. If there is a prosodic break after the verb *kamitsuita*, the verb could be interpreted as a sentence final verb, i.e., 'John bit the cat'. However, when the head noun is complex having the structure of NP1's NP2 as shown in the current experiment, speakers preferred to put a prosodic break after the relative clause, producing RC//NP1-NP2 phrasing. This suggests that the default phrasing changes depending on the internal structure of a sentence. It would be interesting to see if the prosodic phrasing and the interpretation change when the predicate of a relative clause is an adjective, not a verb.

The results from the production and perception experiment show that, though default phasing and interpretation of RC attachment change depending on factors such as Accent and Length, a majority of Japanese speakers produced a prosodic boundary after an RC and preferred high attachment of the RC. This seems to indicate that there is a good match between production and perception as predicted by the IPH.

If the IPH predicts a correlation between production (i.e. prosodic phrasing) and perception, the strongest claim of the IPH would be a perfect match between production and perception. That is, a token produced as RC//NP1-NP2 would be perceived as high attachment, and a token produced as RC-NP1//NP2 would be perceived as low attachment. When individual tokens were examined, however, the match was not very good. Among the 75.9% where speakers produced a grouping (67.15% for RC//NP1-NP2 and 8.75% for RC-NP1//NP2; see Table 2), 63.1% showed matching (i.e. RC//NP1-NP2 with high attachment and RC-NP1//NP2 with low attachment) and 36.8% showed the opposite. When the structure did not show any sub-grouping (24%), subjects preferred high attachment 16.3% and low attachment 7.8%. That is, when there was no prosodic cue for either grouping, subjects preferred to attach the RC to NP2, i.e. the head of the noun phrase, the non-adjacent noun, which is not predicted by the Late Closure Hypothesis (Frazier & Fodor 1978, Frazier 1979). Instead, this may support Frazier's Relativized Relevance Principle (Frazier 1990) because the RC modifies the topic of the complex noun phrase, i.e. the head noun. Mismatch was also observed when we compared the effect of Accent on the production and the perception. The AUU type showed the highest frequency of the RC//NP1-NP2 pattern and the highest percentage of high attachment, thus showing the highest degree of matching (22.8%, 158 out of 691). However, the UAA type showed the lowest frequency of RC//NP1-NP2 while showing the second highest percentage of high attachment, thus showing the lowest degree of matching (11.7%, 81 out of 691).

Given that RC-NP1//NP2 was produced in only 8.75% of the data, a majority of the mismatch cases must have come from the tokens produced with the RC//NP1-NP2 phrasing interpreted as low attachment. At the same time, the higher matching cases could also be a by-product of the common default phrasing and high attachment preference in Japanese. In other words, there may not be a direct connection between the production and the perception of the same sentence token. Rather, the results seem to imply a group behavior as a whole. This view can be supported by the default phrasing patterns of individual speakers. We found that the pattern of default phrasing of the group as a whole was very similar to that of individual speakers, suggesting that there is default phrasing produced for a majority of the time by every speaker, and that this default phrasing is correlated with the attachment preference of the group. A given sentence was not always phrased the same way across all 30 speakers, but when we look at the 48 sentences as a whole, about 70% of them were produced with RC//NP1-NP2 phrasing by every speaker, about 20% of them with RC/NP1/NP2 phrasing, and about 10% of them with RC-NP1//NP2 phrasing. Out of 30 speakers, four did not show the similar ratio (i.e., the RC//NP1-NP2 pattern was 45-60% and the RC/NP1/NP2 pattern was 35-41%), but they still demonstrated a similar perception pattern as the rest of the subjects. It seems that a direct mapping between production and perception of an individual subject is not a way to test the IPH. Instead, the data seem to suggest that there is a gross correlation or mapping between production and perception in a speech community.

In sum, current findings support Fodor's IPH in that there is a correlation between the prosodic pattern of a structure and the interpretation of the structure. But, the data do not show whether the default phrasing is the cause of the perception as claimed by the IPH. In order to generalize the current findings, the prosody of low attachment languages should be examined in a similar way.

References

Brysbaert, M. and D. C. Mitchell. 1996. Modifier Attachment in Sentence Parsing: Evidence from Dutch. *Quarterly Journal of Experimental Psychology* 49A(3): 664-95.

Carreiras, M. and C. Clifton. 1993. Relative Clause Interpretation Preferences in Spanish and English. *Language and Speech* 36: 353-372.

Carreiras, M. and C. Clifton. 1999. Another Word on Parsing Relative Clauses: Eyetracking Evidence from Spanish and English. *Memory and Cognition* 27(5): 826-33.

Cuetos, F. and D. Mitchell. 1988. Cross-linguistic Differences in Parsing: Restrictions on the Use of the Late Closure Strategy in Spanish. *Cognition* 30: 73-105

Ehrlich, K., E. Fernández, J. D. Fodor, E. Stenshoel, and M. Vinereanu. 1999. Low Attachment of Relative Clauses: New Data from Swedish, Norwegian and Romanian. Poster presented at the 12th Annual CUNY Conference, New York.

Fernández, E. 2000. Bilingual Sentence Processing: Relative Clause Attachment in English and Spanish. Doctoral dissertation, CUNY Graduate Center.

Fernández, E. 2003. *Bilingual Sentence Processing: Relative Clause Attachment in English and Spanish.* Amsterdam: John Benjamins.

Fodor, J. D. 1998. Learning to Parse. *Journal of Psycholinguistic Research* 27(2): 285-319.

Fodor, J. D. 2002. Prosodic Disambiguation in Silent Reading. *NELS* 32: 113-32.

Frazier, L. 1979. On Comprehending Sentences: Syntactic Parsing Strategies. Doctoral dissertation, University of Connecticut.

Frazier, L. 1990. Parsing Modifiers: Special Purpose Routines in the Human Sentence Processing Mechanism? *Comprehension Processes in Reading*, ed. D.A. Balota, G. B. Flores d'Arcais, and K. Rayner, 303-30. Hillsdale, NJ: Lawrence Erlbaum.

Frazier, L. and C. Clifton. 1996. *Construal.* Cambridge, MA: MIT Press.

Frazier, L. and J. D. Fodor. 1978. The Sausage Machine: A New Two-stage Parsing Model. *Cognition* 6: 1-34.

Frazier, L. and K. Rayner. 1988. Parameterizing the Language System: Left- vs. right- branching within and across Languages. *Explaining Language Universals*, ed. J. A. Hawkins, Oxford, UK: Basil Blackwell.

Hemforth, B., L. Konieczny, C. Scheepers, and G. Strube. 1998. Syntactic Ambiguity Resolution in German. *Sentence Processing: A Crosslinguistic Perspective. Syntax and Semantics, vol. 31:*, ed. D. Hillert, 293-312. San Diego, CA: Academic Press.

Hirose, Y. 2003. Recycling Prosodic Bounaries. *Journal of Psycholinguistic Research* 32(2): 167-95.

Jun, S.-A. 2003. Prosodic Phrasing and Attachment Preferences. *Journal of Psycholinguistic Research* 32(2): 219-49.

Kamide, Y. and D. C. Mitchell. 1997. Relative Clause Attachment: Non-determinism in Japanese Parsing. *Journal of Psycholinguistic Research* 26: 247-54.

Kimball, J. 1973. Seven Principles of Surface Structure Parsing. *Cognition* 2: 15-47.

Kondo, T. and R. Mazuka. 1996. Prosodic Planning While Reading Aloud: On-line Examination of Japanese Sentences. *Journal of Psycholinguistic Research* 25: 357-81.

Kubozono, H. 1993. *The Organization of Japanese Prosody*. Tokyo: Kurosio Publishers.

Lovric, N., D. Bradley, and J. D. Fodor. 2000. RC Attachment in Croatian with and without Preposition. Poster presented at the AMLaP Conference, Leiden.

Lovric, N., D. Bradley, and J. D. Fodor. 2001. Silent Prosody Resolves Syntactic Ambiguities: Evidence from Croatian. Paper presented at the SUNY/CUNY/NYU Conference, Stonybrook, NY.

Maegawa, K., H. Kikuchi, Y. Igarashi, and J. Venditti. 2002. X-J_ToBI: An Extended J_ToBI for Spontaneous Speech. Proceedings of the ICSLP, Denver, Colorado.

Maynell, L. A. 1999. Effect of Pitch Accent Placement on Resolving Relative Clause Ambiguity in English. Poster presented at the 12th Annual CUNY Conference on Human Sentence Processing, New York.

Pierrehumbert, J. and M. Beckman. 1988. *Japanese Tone Structure*. Cambridge, MA: MIT Press.

Quinn, D., H. Abdelghany, and J. D. Fodor. 2000. More Evidence of Implicit Prosody in Reading: French and Arabic Relative Clauses. Poster presented at the 13th Annual CUNY Conference, La Jolla, CA

Venditti, J. 1995. Japanese ToBI Labeling Guidelines. Ms, Ohio St. Univ. [Ohio State University Working Papers in Linguistics 50: 127-62]

Venditti, J. in press. The J_ToBI Model of Japanese Intonation. *Prosodic Typology: The Phonology of Intonation and Phrasing,* ed. S.-A. Jun, Oxford, UK: Oxford University Press.

Venditti, J. and J. P. H. van Santen. 2000. Japanese Intonation Synthesis Using Superposition and Linear Alignment Models. Proceedings of the International Conference on Spoken Language Processing (ICSLP), Beijing, China.

Zagar, D., J. Pynte, and S. Rativeau. 1997. Evidence for Early-closure Attachment on First-pass Reading Times in French. *Quarterly Journal of Experimental Psychology* 50A(2): 421-38.

On the Proper Treatment of NonCrispEdges[1]

SHIGETO KAWAHARA
University of Massachusetts, Amherst

'While many-to-one and many-to-many associations are not uncommon, there is nonetheless something unusual about them.'
(Goldsmith 1984: 256)

1. Introduction

It is commonly observed that spreading is blocked by an edge of a particular category (e.g. Nespor and Vogel 1986). For example, Indonesian resolves hiatus by spreading the first vowel to the second syllable node, but such spreading is blocked by a prosodic word edge (Cohn and McCarthy 1994), e.g. $_{\text{Wd}}$[dija] 'two' but di-ʔ$_{\text{Wd}}$[ambil] 'taken'. The primary aim of this paper is to develop a general theory that accounts for such blockage of spreading. I propose that such blockage takes place due to the markedness of the structures that result from spreading, which inevitably involve multiply-linked features or segments. To formalize this idea, a general schema of constraints

[1] I wish to thank Michael Becker, Stuart Davis, Kathryn Flack, Maria Gouskova, Shinsook Lee, Hajime Ono, Kazu Kurisu, Taka Shinya, the members of the UMass Phonology Group and the audiences at Japanese/Korean Linguistics Conference 13 who offered many constructive suggestions. I am especially grateful to Jaye Padgett, Joe Pater and John McCarthy for their thoughtful comments, which led to much improvement of this paper. All errors are mine.

is proposed within the framework of Optimality Theory (henceforth OT; Prince and Smolensky 1993). The proposed schema is called UNIQUE AFFILIATION (UA), as it requires an element to be uniquely affiliated with a higher element. The proposed constraint family captures a general pattern of spreading blockage, and further, it provides a new instance of a constraint schema, contributing to the investigation of the internal structure of CON.

The remainder of this paper is structured as follows. §2 presents the formal proposal regarding the markedness of multiple linking. §3 is devoted to justifying the details of the proposal. §4 considers some consequences of the proposed theory. In §5 I consider alternative approaches, mainly focusing on the CRISPEDGE constraints proposed by Ito and Mester, which are functionally quite similar to my proposal. Though the current proposal is much inspired by CRISPEDGE constraints, I will show that CRISPEDGE constraints *per se* are insufficient. Most of the evidence in this paper is drawn from Japanese, although cross-linguistic data are used from time to time.

2. Formalization

The core of my proposal is that structures like (1) are marked because α is not uniquely dominated by β, i.e. α is multiply-linked with respect to β.

(1)

This idea is formally articulated in the following constraint schema:

(2) UNIQUE AFFILIATION (α, β):

Let α, β, γ be variables ranging over linguistic categories and let $x\delta y$ mean that x is dominated by y, then

(i) $\forall\alpha\ [(\alpha\delta\beta) \rightarrow \neg\exists\gamma\ [(\alpha\delta\gamma) \wedge (\neg(\beta\delta\gamma) \wedge \neg(\gamma\delta\beta))]]$
(ii) Assign one violation mark for each instance of α that falsifies (i)

The constraint schema takes two variable arguments, α and β. UA(α, β) requires that, if α is dominated by β, α be not dominated by any γ unless γ dominates β or vice versa. Informally, α must "uniquely affiliate" with β.

Some illustrative examples are given below in (3) to show how violations of UA are computed. (3i) is a structure of a geminate, which is a typical structure violating UA constraints. The C-Place node is dominated by μ_1, and is also dominated by σ_2 which does not dominate μ_1; therefore, the C-Place is not uniquely dominated by either μ_1 or σ_2. Hence, the structure violates UA(C-Place, μ) and UA(C-Place, σ). The second structure (3ii) is part of the traditional prosodic hierarchy (Selkirk 1980 *et seq*). In this case, UA constraints are satisfied, since even though the mora is dominated by both the syllable and the foot, the syllable is also dominated by the foot.

(3)

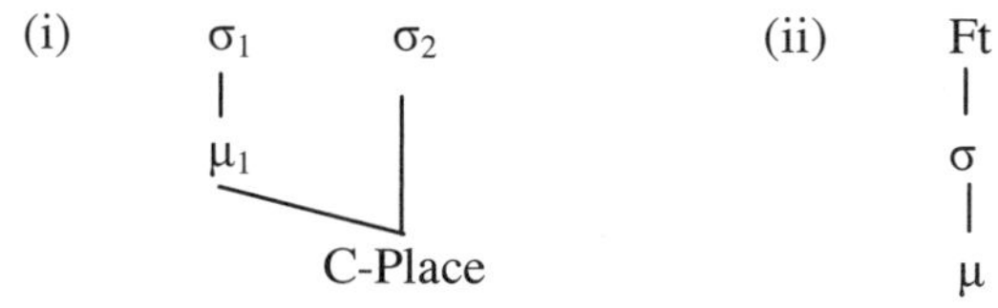

3. Justifying the Proposal

In this section, I justify the details of my proposal. In UA(α, β), α is a subordinate category and β is a superordinate category. It will be shown that a pair of UA constraints where β is held the same and α is varied are different constraints (§3.1). Similarly, constraints where α is held the same while β is varied are shown to be different constraints (§3.2). Finally, following the earlier observation made by Walker (2001), §3.3 briefly discusses how a violation mark for UA constraints is assessed.

3.1. α as a Variable Argument

The use of α as a variable argument is motivated by the observation that, given a superordinate category to which there is a multiply-linked subordinate category, its markedness value differs depending on what kind of subordinate element is linked across that superordinate category. Here I illustrate this point using the distribution of geminates and long vowels in Standard noncolloquial Japanese.

Morpheme-internally, geminates and long vowels are amply attested in Japanese, as in *su<u>pp</u>ai* 'sour' and *ok<u>aa</u>san* 'mother'. However, across a morpheme boundary, only geminates are allowed in noncolloquial Standard Japanese. Cross-morphemic geminates are found in so-called reduced compounds, illustrated below (Poser 1984: 89-91; Ito and Mester 1996: 24):

(4) /but-u/ 'strike'

bu**t**-**t**oosu	'permeate'	bu**p**-**p**anasu	'fire a bullet'
bu**k**-**k**orosu	'kill violently'	bu**n**-**n**aguru	'beat up'

Evidence that cross-morphemic long vowels are illicit comes from the blockage of fusion. Japanese fuses /ei/ and /ou/ into [ee] and [oo] (Vance 1987), as most clearly observed in recent loanwords from English in (5a). However, this fusion is blocked across a morpheme boundary, as in (5bc):

(5) a. /ei/ → [ee]; /ou/ → [oo]

k**ee**ki	'cake'	p**ee**suto	'paste'
k**oo**to	'coat'	h**oo**pu	'hope'

b. (a) is blocked by a morphological boundary

anim**e** **i**rasuto	*anim**ee**rasuto	'anime illustration'
suiit**o** **u**edingu	*suiit**oo**edingu	'sweet wedding'

c.

/tow + u/	→	tou	*too	'inquire (non-past)'
/kow+ u/	→	kou	*koo	'beg (non-past)'

The ungrammaticality of the forms in (5bc) suggests that cross-morphemic long vowels are prohibited in noncolloquial Standard Japanese[2].

Cross-morphemic geminates and long vowels thus have different markedness values in Japanese. It follows that UA(C-Place, Morph), which prohibits cross-morphemic geminates, and UA(V-Place, Morph), which prohibits cross-morphemic long vowels, must be separate constraints, as only the former is violable in Japanese. This supports the hypothesis that α is a variable argument in the proposed constraint schema.

3.2. β as a Variable Argument

In §3.1 I showed that given one superordinate category, the markedness of multiple-linking structures varies depending on what links across that superordinate category. This observation requires the use of α as a variable argument. In this subsection, I will show that β must also be a variable argument, pointing out that for one subordinate element, the markedness value differs depending on to which superordinate category it is multiply linked.

Evidence for this comes from the phonology of Sino-Japanese compounding, analyzed by Ito and Mester (1996). This section recasts their analysis in terms of UA constraints. Root-final vowels delete in Sino-Japanese whenever possible,[3] and the root-final consonant fuses with the root-initial consonant of the following morpheme because a coda cannot license an independent place specification (Ito 1986). This deletion is illustrated in (6):

(6)	Root-final vowel deletion in Sino-Japanese: /hatu/		
	$[\text{hat-tatu}]_{\text{Wd}}$	*hat**u**-tatu	'development'
	$[\text{hak-kaku}]_{\text{Wd}}$	*hat**u**-kaku	'detection'
	$[\text{hap-pjoo}]_{\text{Wd}}$	*hat**u**-pjoo	'presentation'

There is an environment in which the deletion systematically fails in contrast with the words in (6). Sino-Japanese roots are combined into a word, and a vowel adjacent to an edge of a word fails to delete. This is shown in (7) where the bold-faced root-final vowels do not delete:

---

[2] As John Whitman reminds me, in casual speech, the inflectional suffix of [i] can be fused with root-final vowels, as in /taka-i/ → [take:] 'expensive'; even in this style of speech, fusion across stems in (5b) seems impossible (it might not be clear whether fusion in (5c) is possible in casual speech, but according to my intuition, it is possible). This might suggest that there is an independent constraint that actively coerces elimination of an independent syllable for an affix ranked above UA(Morph, V-Place), i.e., *SYLLFORAFFIX. DEP-OO(V) also does the job because it disfavors a vowel that is not found in the uninflected stem (see Gouskova 2003a).

[3] In fact, it might be possible to regard the root-final vowels as epenthetic, as the quality of such a vowel is almost predictable (Tateishi 1990; Ito and Mester 1996; Kurisu 2000): it generally agrees in backness with the first vowel and is always [+high]. However, in some forms, the quality of the second vowel is unpredictable, suggesting that it is underlyingly specified. Further, given Richness of the Base (Prince and Smolensky 1993), the lack of root-final vowels cannot be imposed on inputs (see Kurisu 2000 for discussion).

(7)	[[toku[4]-bets**u**]$_{Wd}$-seki]$_{Wd}$ 'special seat'	*[[tokubes]$_{Wd}$ -seki]$_{Wd}$
	$_{Wd}$[bets**u** $_{Wd}$[hjoo-ki]] 'separate transcription'	*$_{Wd}$[bep $_{Wd}$[pjoo-ki]]

Ito and Mester (1996) assume that a Sino-Japanese morpheme corresponds to a prosodic foot; based on this assumption, the generalization that explains the difference between (6) and (7) is straightforward: multiple linking of a C-Place across a foot boundary is allowed, but a C-Place cannot be multiply linked across a prosodic word boundary. This is why deletion fails in (7).

(8) (i) (ii) *

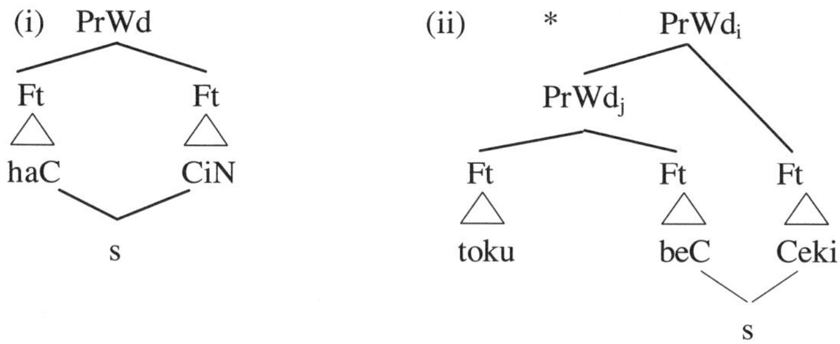

To recast this insight within OT, I employ ALIGN-L(σ, Stem) as a constraint triggering vowel deletion (Spaelti 1997; Kurisu 2000; see also McCarthy and Prince 1993). This constraint requires every syllable to be aligned with the left edge of a stem, and this thus prefers monosyllabic stems. Since vowel deletion takes place at the cost of UA(C-Place, Ft), ALIGN-L(σ, Stem) outranks UA(C-Place, Ft). On the other hand, since the structure (8ii) is not allowed as a result of vowel deletion, UA(C-Place, PrWd) is ranked above ALIGN-L(σ, Stem):

(9) ALIGN-L(σ, Stem) » UA(C-Place, Ft), MAX

/hatu-tatu/	UA(C-Pl, PrWd)	ALIGN-L (σ, Stem)	UA(C-Pl, Ft)	MAX
a. $_{Wd}$[hatu-tatu]		*/*!		
b. ☞ $_{Wd}$[hat-tatu]		*	*	*

(10) UA(C-Place, PrWd) » ALIGN-L(σ, Stem)

/toku-betsu-seki/	UA(C-Pl, PrWd)	ALIGN-L (σ, Stem)	UA(C-Pl, Ft)	MAX
a. ☞$_{Wd}$[toku-betu]-$_{Wd}$[seki]		*/*/*		
b. $_{Wd}$[toku-bes]- $_{Wd}$[seki]	*!	*/*	*	*

[4] Despite that this vowel is word-internal, it fails to delete because the resulting structure [tobbetsu] would have a voiced obstruent geminate, which is prohibited (see e.g. Kurisu 2000).

Some remarks about UA(C-Place, PrWd) in (10) are in order. The candidate (b) violates this constraint because, as seen in (8ii), the lower $PrWd_j$ does not uniquely dominate the C-Place: the C-Place is simultaneously linked to the $PrWd_j$ and the third foot, which is outside of the $PrWd_j$.

In sum, (9) and (10) show that UA(C-Place, Ft) and UA(C-Place, PrWd) are separate constraints, proving that β must be a variable argument.

3.3. How Violation Marks are Accrued

To conclude this section, some remarks on the second clause of the UA definition - that violation marks are assessed for each instance of α - are in order. This clause is based on Walker's claim (2001) about vowel harmony in Classical Manchu, where she argues that being multiply linked to three instances of a superordinate category is no more marked than being multiply linked to two instances of the same category (see Pater 2003 for a parallel example in Balantak). Without evidence to the contrary, I formulate UA in such a way that violations are assessed for each instance of α, rather than for each offending association line[5]. However, if the facts were shown to go the other way, it would be a simple matter to appropriately change or parameterize the definition of UA in (2) (see also §5.1 for related discussion).

4. Some Consequences of the Proposed Theory

I have formulated a hypothesis about the markedness of multiple-linking (§2) and presented justification for the details of the proposal (§3). In this section, I present some further consequences of the proposed theory.

4.1. Expressing the Markedness of Complex Structures

The first favorable consequence of the UA constraints is that they successfully account for the markedness of some autosegmentally complex structures. For example, a H tone associated with more than one tone bearing unit is marked, and this structure is prohibited in some languages (e.g. Sukuma, Bantu: Goldsmith 1990: 18). The markedness of such spread tones can be expressed via UA(H, TBU). Other instances of autosegmentally complex structures include harmonized features (see Beckman's UNIQUE (1998)), long vowels and geminates. The markedness of harmonized features manifests itself through the fact that some languages flop a feature (and avoid spreading) in order to associate a feature to some position (e.g. Esimbi; Hyman 1988), and such a pattern requires a markedness constraint that militates against a harmonized feature (Walker 1999). The markedness of geminates and long vowels is uncontroversial as some languages completely lack such structures (see §3.1). For more on the markedness of long vowels and geminates, see §5.1.

---

[5] This predicts that if α crosses an edge of β, it can cross any number of edges of the same type (as in fact observed in Classical Manchu). This, however, seems incompatible with a so-called non-iterative process, where, for example, spreading penetrates just one syllable into the following domain, but not any further. McCarthy (2003: §5) provides an analysis of such cases, which is compatible with the proposed view.

4.2. Solving an Old Problem of Heteromorphemic Geminates

The second consequence of the proposed UA theory is that it solves an old problem concerning the creation of true geminates across morphemes. It has been noted that creating a true geminate across a morpheme boundary is often prohibited, as in Tigrinya (Schein 1981), but this prohibition does not always hold, as Tiberian Hebrew allows such a structure (McCarthy 1980).

UA(C-Place, Morph) militates against true geminates across two morphemes, but given the violability of constraints in OT, this situation is exactly what is expected. Assuming that the OCP is satisfied by fusion of adjacent identical elements, permutation of the OCP and UA(C-Place, Morph) accounts for the contrast between Tiberian Hebrew and Tigrinya[6].

4.3. Eliminating Domain Specifications in Spreading Constraints

UA(α, β) prevents the spreading of α from a higher superordinate category β. Thus, the interaction of UA constraints with a general spreading constraint yields domain-specific spreading. More concretely,

(11) Let D_n be an n-level prosodic category and if the domain of harmony of the feature F is D_n, then,

$$\text{UA}(F, D_n) \gg \text{S}\textsc{pread}(F) \gg \text{UA}(F, D_{n-1}), \text{UA}(F, D_{n-2}) \ldots$$

As a result, domain specifications can be eliminated from spreading constraints, contra claims by, e.g. Walker (1998: 37) and Padgett (2002a). One prediction of the proposal is that spreading is equally blocked by the left or right edge of a particular category, as UA is not relativized for edges. Whether this prediction is on the right track is left for future investigation.

Another remark about blocking spreading by a set of UA constraints is in order. It is commonly observed that multiple linking across a higher category results in higher markedness value. This derives from the fact that multiple linking across a higher category (e.g. PrWd) usually entails multiple linking across lower categories (e.g. Ft, σ, μ). Thus, spreading across a higher category incurs a superset of violation marks compared to spreading across a lower category, and hence it is universally more marked even without ranking stipulation. In other words, UA for lower categories is more stringent.[7] See de Lacy (2002) for discussion on stringency.

5. Alternatives

Before concluding the paper, in this section, I compare UA constraints with

---

[6] In general, there is an intrinsic tension between UA constraints and the OCP: given two adjacent identical autosegments α, the OCP(α) militates for fusion of them while the UA(α, β) militates against the fusion.

[7] This stringency relationship does not hold for structures that violate exhaustivity. For instance, in a trisyllabic structure with the first two syllables footed and the final syllable being directly attached to a PrWd, spreading from the second syllable to the third violates UA(α, Ft) but it does not violate UA(α, PrWd). Spreading from the third syllable to outside of the PrWd on the other hand violates UA(α, PrWd), but not UA(α, Ft). Whether the latter is universally more marked than the former is yet to be determined in future investigation.

alternatives, first with CRISPEDGE constraints proposed by Ito and Mester (1994, 1999)[8] and second with a faithfulness constraint *SPREAD.

5.1. CRISPEDGE(PCAT)

First, the definition of CRISPEDGE is given below (Ito and Mester 1994: 38).

(12) CRISPEDGE(PCat): PCat is crisp

> Crisp dfn = Let A be a terminal (sub)string in a phonological representation, C a category of type PCat, and A *be-the-content* of C. Then C is *crisp* (or: *has crisp edges*) if and only if A *is-a* PCat.

Informally, if a PCat C dominates an element A, CRISPEDGE(PCat) requires that no other category dominates A. So UA and CRISPEDGE are similar in their function; however, crucially, the locus of violation is the PCat C for CRISPEDGE constraints. I argue that CRISPEDGE constraints have the following problems because of this characteristic.

First, CRISPEDGE does not look at the source of noncrispness (cf. Walker 2001). Thus, it predicts that the markedness of noncrisp edges is consistent regardless of what is linked across that category. However, this prediction is inconsistent with what we saw in §3.1: in Japanese, a C-Place can link across morphemes while a V-Place cannot. By incorporating a variable argument α, the proposed UA theory overcomes this problem.

Second, if we attempt to express the markedness of geminates and long vowels by CRISPEDGE constraints (Baker 1998), it predicts that geminates are always more marked than long vowels. This is because long vowels violate only CRISPEDGE(μ), while geminates violate both CRISPEDGE(μ) and CRISPEDGE(σ) (as well as NOCODA), as observed in (13). As a result geminates incur a superset of the violations incurred by long vowels.

(13) (i) geminates (ii) long vowels

However, this prediction is inconsistent with the actual data. For instance, to create a heavy syllable, some languages resort to gemination rather than vowel lengthening. The Shizuoka dialect of Japanese is one example, as seen in the formation of emphatic forms; /takai/ → [takkai] *taakai 'expensive' (Davis and Ueda 2003). A word formation process found in Japanese motherese also exhibits the same tendency, as in /oki/ → [okki] *[ooki] 'to

[8] CRISPEDGE constraints are further developed and utilized in Baker (1998); Kawahara (2003); Kawasaki (2000); Keer (1999); Noske (1997); Pater (2001); Pineros (2002); Walker (2001) among others.

wake up' (Kawahara 2001). Further, there are languages that only have geminates but no long vowels; Ainu is such an example (Chiri 1951). CRISPEDGE cannot explain these patterns.

On the other hand, in the UA theory, long vowels and geminates are penalized by different constraints: UA(V-Place, μ) for the former and UA(C-place, μ), UA(C-Place, σ) for the latter. If UA(V-Place, μ) » UA(C-place, μ), UA(C-Place, σ), geminates are less marked than long vowels.

Third, according to the formulation of UA given in (2), UA cares about the number of offending subordinate categories (i.e. the number of α), but CRISPEDGE constraints do not. Supporting evidence for this aspect of UA is found in Gã (Padgett 1995, 2002b):

(14) a. **ŋ͡mk͡p**okua 'nipple' **ŋ͡mk͡p**ai 'libation'
b. **ŋ-g͡b**ekɛ 'my child' **ŋ-k͡p**ai 'my cheeks'

As in (14a), morpheme-internally, nasal place assimilation to a complex segment is total. On the other hand, in (14b), across a morpheme boundary assimilation is partial: only the dorsal node spreads. This partial assimilation can be captured as the effort to minimize the number of elements linked across morphemes, i.e. the effect of UA(C-Place, Morph) ranked above the trigger constraint for assimilation. Let this trigger constraint be SPREAD(Place), which requires adjacent consonants to share every place node (Padgett 2002ab). The ranking UA(C-Place, Morph) » SPREAD(Place) alone predicts that no assimilation takes place cross-morphemically, but given that placeless nasals are marked, HAVEPLACE(NAS) can be ranked above UA(C-Place, Morph), requiring that at least one place feature spread.[9] Finally, I follow Padgett's feature class theory (1995, 2002b) and assume that UA(C-Place, Morph) is violated for each C-Place linked across morphemes; hence spreading two C-Places is worse than spreading only one C-Place. The following tableau summarizes the story[10]:

(15) Assimilation only partial across a morpheme boundary

/N#kpai/	HAVEPLACE	UA(C-Pl, Morph)	SPREAD(Place)
a. N kpai (kpai linked to L/D)	*!		**
b. ☞ ŋ kpai (D/L shared by ŋ and kpai)		*	*
c. ŋm kpai (D and L each linked to ŋm and kpai)		*/*!	

[9] See Padgett (2002b) for a hypothesis about why the dorsal node, rather than the labial node, spreads. See also Ohala and Lorentz (1977).

[10] If SPREAD(Pl) » IDENT(Pl), then the underlying specification of the affix does not matter.

Crucially, CRISPEDGE would treat (b) and (c) both as noncrisp and, therefore, cannot distinguish them in terms of markedness. In other words, since the locus of violation for CRISPEDGE is a noncrisp edge *per se*, it does not care about the number of offending subordinate elements. In summary, the data from Gã supports UA's claim that the markedness of multiply-linked structures varies as a function of the number of offending subordinate categories.

5.2. Faithfulness Constraints: *SPREAD

The second alternative is the faithfulness constraint *SPREAD. UA constraints prohibit spreading from a particular domain, so one might wonder whether they could be replaced by a set of faithfulness constraints that prohibit spreading from a particular domain, e.g. *SPREAD(α, β): "don't spread α from the domain β" (see McCarthy 2000). However, there is evidence that markedness constraints are needed to rule out multiply-linked structures. For example, UA(V-Place, μ) expresses the markedness of a long vowel and so, when undominated, it produces a language that has no long vowels. Its counterpart *SPREAD(V-Place, μ), which prohibits spreading of a V-Place which is already linked to a mora, might prohibit the creation of a long vowel, but it does not say anything about underlying long vowels; this then fails to characterize a language without long vowels. More generally, given Richness of the Base, the lack of some structures must be accounted for by markedness constraints rather than by faithfulness constraints. Thus, although *SPREAD and UA partially overlap in their functions, UA constraints are independently required.

6. Concluding Remarks

At a descriptive level, this paper has shown that when an element is multiply linked across a higher category, its markedness is determined on the basis of (i) what is multiply linked (§3.1) (ii) what the superordinate category is (§3.2) and (iii) the number of multiply-linked elements (§5.1). I proposed the UNIQUE AFFILIATION constraint schema to account for this observation. This theory captures the general pattern of spreading blockage, and hence contributes to the investigation of internal structure of CON, which, in this view, is not merely a list of random constraints (see de Lacy 2002; Eisner 2002; Gouskova 2003ab; Ito and Mester 1994, 1999; Keer 1999; McCarthy 2002: 17-22, in press; McCarthy and Prince 1993; Potts and Pullum 2002; Smith 2002; Smolensky 1995 among others for such a view and relevant discussion).

As a final remark, it may have been noticed that for all the UA constraints proposed in this paper, α is smaller than a syllable. In fact, whether a syllable can belong to more than one higher unit is a controversial matter (see Hyde 2002 for recent discussion), and for prosodic categories higher than syllables, it is doubtful that they can ever multiply link to higher categories. This restriction presumably derives from a substantive condition independent of the UA schema: the larger an element is, the more difficult it is to repeat it. It remains to be seen whether some other substantive restrictions interact with UA constraint schema, limiting the range of actual instantiation of UA constraints.

References

Baker, B. 1998. Edge-Crispness: Segment to Mora Isomorphism. *Proceedings of WCCFL* 16: 33-47.

Beckman, J. 1998. Positional Faithfulness. Doctoral dissertation, UMass, Amherst.

Chiri, M. 1952. *Ainu Gohoo Gaisetsu*. Heibonsha.

Cohn, A. and J. McCarthy. 1994. Alignment and Parallelism in Indonesian Phonology. Ms., Cornell University and UMass, Amherst.

Davis, S. and I. Ueda. 2003. Mora Augmentation Processes in Japanese. *Journal of Japanese Linguistics* 18: 1-23.

de Lacy, P. 2002. Formal Expression of Markedness. Doctoral dissertation, UMass, Amherst.

Eisner, J. 2002. Doing OT in a Straightjacket. Ms., Johns Hopkins University.

Goldsmith, J. 1984. Meeussen's Rule. *Language Sound Structure*, eds. M. Aronoff and R. Oehrle, 245-259. Cambridge: MIT Press.

Goldsmith, J. 1990. *Autosegmental and Metrical Phonology*. Oxford: Blackwell.

Gouskova, M. 2003a. Deriving Economy: Syncope in Optimality Theory. Doctoral dissertation, University of Massachusetts, Amherst.

Gouskova, M. 2003b. Relational Hierarchies in OT. Ms., Rutgers University.

Hyde, B. 2002. A Restrictive Theory of Metrical Stress. *Phonology* 19: 313-359.

Hyman, L. 1988. Underspecification and Vowel Height Transfer in Esimbi. *Phonology* 5: 255-273.

Ito, J. 1986. Syllable Theory in Prosodic Phonology. Doctoral dissertation, UMass, Amherst.

Ito, J. and A. Mester. 1994. Reflection on CodaCond and Alignment. *Phonology at Santa Cruz* 3: 22-46.

Ito, J. and A. Mester. 1996. Stem and Word in Sino-Japanese. *Phonological Structure and Language Processing: Cross-linguistic Studies*, eds. T. Otake and A. Cutler, 13-44. New York: Mouton de Gruyter.

Ito, J. and A. Mester. 1999. Realignment. *Prosody-Morphology Interface*, eds. R. Kager, H van der Hulst and W. Zonnenveld, 188-217. Cambridge: Cambridge University Press.

Kawahara, S. 2001. Reduplication not Driven by a RED Morpheme. Talk given at Phonological Association in Kansai (PAIK) at Kobe University. December 14th.

Kawahara, S. 2003. On a Certain Type of Hiatus Resolution in Japanese. *Phonological Studies* 6: 11-20.

Kawasaki, T. 2000. Spreading and Final Exceptionality. *Phonological Studies* 3:3-10.

Keer, E. 1999. Geminates, the OCP and the Nature of CON. Doctoral dissertation, Rutgers University.

Kurisu, K. 2000. Richness of the Base and Root Fusion in Sino-Japanese. *Journal of East Asian Linguistics* 9: 147-185.

McCarthy, J. 1980. The Representation of Consonant Length in Hebrew. *Linguistic Inquiry* 12: 321-327.

McCarthy, J. 2000. Faithfulness and Prosodic Circumscription. *Optimality Theory: Phonology, Syntax and Acquisition*, eds. J. Dekkers, F. van der Leeuw, and J. van de Weijer, 151–189. Oxford: Oxford University Press.

McCarthy, J. 2002. *A Thematic Guide to Optimality Theory*. Cambridge: Cambridge

University Press.
McCarthy, J. 2003. Comparative Markedness. *Theoretical Linguistics* 29: 1-52.
McCarthy, J. in press. OT Constraints are Categorical. To appear in *Phonology* 20.
McCarthy, J. and A. Prince. 1993. Generalized Alignment. *Yearbook of Morphology*. 79-153.
Noske, M. 1997. Feature Spreading as Dealignment: The Distribution of [ç] and [x] in German. *Phonology* 14: 221-234.
Nespor, M and I. Vogel. 1986. *Prosodic Phonology*. Dordrecht: Foris Publications.
Ohala, J and J. Lorentz. 1977. The Story of [w]: An Exercise in the Phonetic Explanation for Sound Patterns. *Proceedings of BLS* 3: 577-599.
Padgett, J. 1995. Partial Class Behavior and Nasal Place Assimilation. *Proceedings of the Arizona Phonology Conference*.
Padgett, J. 2002a. Russian Voicing Assimilation, Final Devoicing, and the Problem of [v]. Ms., University of California, Santa Cruz.
Padgett, J. 2002b. Feature Classes in Phonology. *Language* 78: 81-110.
Pater, J. 2001. Austronesian Nasal Substitution Revisited: What's Wrong with *NC (and What's Not). *Segmental Phonology in Optimality Theory*, ed. L. Lombardi, 159-182. Cambridge: Cambridge University Press.
Pater, J. 2003. Balantak Metathesis and Theories of Possible Repair in Optimality Theory. Ms., UMass, Amherst.
Pineros, C. 2002. On the Interplay between Consonant Alignment and Feature Faithfulness in a Caribbean Spanish Dialects. Ms., University of Iowa.
Poser, W. 1984. The Phonetics and Phonology of Tone and Intonation in Japanese. Doctoral dissertation, MIT.
Potts, C and G. Pullum. 2002. Model Theory and the Content of OT Constraints. *Phonology* 19: 361-393.
Schein, B. 1981. Spirantization in Tigrinya. *Theoretical Issues in the Grammar of Semitic Languages*: *MIT Working Papers in Linguistics* 3: 32-43.
Selkirk, E. 1980. The Role of Prosodic Categories in English Word Stress. *Linguistic Inquiry* 11: 563-605.
Smith, J. 2002. Toward a Compositional Treatment of Positional Constraints: The Case of Positional Augmentation. *Papers in Optimality Theory II: University of Massachusetts Occasional Papers in Linguistics* 26: 337-370.
Smolensky, P. 1995. On the Internal Structure of the Constraint Component CON of UG. Talk given at UCLA. April 7th, 1995.
Spaelti, P. 1997. Dimensions of Variation in Multiple-Pattern Reduplication. Doctoral dissertation, University of California, Santa Cruz.
Tateishi, K. 1990. Phonology of Sino-Japanese Morphemes. *University of Massachusetts Occasional Papers in Linguistics* 13: 209-235.
Vance, T. 1987. *An Introduction to Japanese Phonology*. New York: State University of New York Press.

Walker, R. 1998. Nasalization, Neutral Segments and Opacity Effects. Doctoral dissertation, University of California, Santa Cruz.

Walker, R. 1999. Esimbi Vowel Height Shift: Implications for Faith and Markedness. Ms., University of Southern California.

Walker, R. 2001. Round Licensing, Harmony, and Bisyllabic Triggers in Altaic. *Natural Language and Linguistic Theory* 19: 827-878.

Where Have All the Lax Stops Gone? On the Possible Restructuring of the Korean Stop System*

SEUNG-HOON SHIN AND STUART DAVIS
Dongseo University and Indiana University

1. Introduction

The Korean stop system is well known for its three-way contrast between aspirated, tense, and lax consonants as exemplified in (1).

(1) The three way stop contrast of Korean

a. p^hul - grass	p'ul - horn	pul - fire
b. t^hal - mask	t'al - daughter	tal - moon
c. c^hata - kick	c'ata - is salty	cata - sleep
d. ip^{h}al - 2 X 8	ip'al - teeth	ipal- haircut
e. k^hulk^{h}ul - snoring sound	k'ul - honey	kul - oyster

* The research done by the first author was supported in part through the Research Grant of Dongseo University. We would like to thank Mihui Cho, Ken de Jong, Hyunsook Kang, Hyunsoon Kim, Ock Hwan Kim, Minkyung Lee, Yongsung Lee, Han-Yong Park, Jae-Ick Park, Minsu Shim, Jin-young Tak, John Whitman, Young-mee Yu Cho, and the participants at J/K 13. All errors are our responsibility.

The system contains two laryngeally marked consonants: the aspirated stops with the feature [spread glottis] exemplified in the first column in (1) and the tense (or fortis) stops with the feature [constricted glottis] exemplified in the second column in (1). The laryngeally unmarked lax (or plain) stops lacking any laryngeal features are shown in the third column of (1). In this paper we consider a particular change witnessed in the Korean stop system. Specifically, in Section 2 of this paper we document the expansion of the tense stops in modern spoken Korean mainly at the expense of the lax ones[1]. The tensification phenomena that we focus on has been little discussed in the Korean phonological literature. They include optional tensification of lax stops in spoken Korean, the relexicalization of some lax stops as tense stops in the Kyungsang dialect, tensification and lax stop avoidance in loanword adaptation, and the first language acquisition of tense stops. When taken together these phenomena show that tense stops are expanding to the detriment of lax stops. In the final part of the paper, which is of a speculative nature, we consider some possible reasons for the apparent demise of the lax stop at the expense of the tense ones. While we address the possibility that modern Korean is at an initial stage in a restructuring from a three-way stop system into a two-way system that contrasts tense stops with aspirated ones, we discuss the importance of the observation that tensification largely affects word-initial consonants.

2. Tensification Phenomena

In this section we document the expansion of tense stops in modern spoken Korean at the expense of lax ones. In particular, we focus on stops in onset position in order to abstract away from the effects of coda neutralization which requires all obstruents in coda position to be unreleased without any laryngeal features; see Tak (1997) for one analysis. While the tensification phenomena that we will document in this Section has been little discussed in the Korean phonology literature, there are other tensification processes in Korean that are more well-known which we briefly mention here. Probably the most well-known and discussed tensification phenomena in Korean phonology is the process of post-obstruent tensification (Kim-Renaud 1986, Cho and Inkelas 1994). The post-obstruent tensification rule from Kim-Renaud (1986) is given in (2a) with exemplification in (2b) and (2c).

---

1 The expansion of tense consonants at the expense of lax ones is something that has been noted anecdotedly. Various Korean speakers have mentioned to us that younger speakers seem to have more tensification than older speaker.

(2) Post-obstruent tensification (Kim-Renaud 1986)

a. C ----> [+constricted glottis] / C ____
[-sonorant] [-sonorant]

b. /cap-ta/ --- [capt'a] 'to catch'

c. /nop^h-ta/ --- [nopt'a] 'high (declarative)'

Post-obstruent tensification takes a plain obstruent and tensifies it when it occurs after another obstruent. As the examples in (2b) and (2c) show, the triggering obstruent can either be a plain one or a laryngeally marked one. Less frequently discussed is the issue of whether an aspirated stop undergoes post-obstruent tensification. The possibility for an aspirated stop to undergo post obstruent tensification typically does not arise in native Korean words. There are no native Korean words in which an aspirated stop follows an obstruent. And, as indicated by (2b) and (2c), the environment where post-obstruent tensification is observed occurs over a suffixal boundary within a phonological word; Korean lacks suffixes that begin with an aspirated stop. However, the fact that some borrowed words in Korean display aspirated stops after obstruents (e.g. takt^{h}ə 'doctor') makes clear that post-obstruent tensification only impacts lax obstruents. In this way, one can see a consequence of post-obstruent tensification as the expansion of surface tense consonants at the expense of lax ones.

Another tensification phenomenon that has engendered some discussion in the Korean linguistics literature that we briefly mention here is tensification of ideophones. The phonosemantics of ideophone tensification has been discussed by Martin (1962) and Lee (1992) and is exemplified with the form in (3).

(3) Tensification in ideophones (Martin 1962, Lee 1992)

a. pəltək b. p'əlt'ək c. p^{h}əlt'ək
'sudden gesture of standing, sitting, or lying up/down'

According to Martin (1962) and Lee (1992) the ideophone in (3) whether pronounced with an initial plain, tense, or aspirated bilabial stop has the same basic meaning, with the laryngeal feature of the initial stop modifying the basic meaning in some way. According to Martin (1962) the modification of the meaning has to do with the intensity of the action, with the tense consonants indicating an intensive action and the aspirated consonant indicating an even more intensive action. On the other hand, Lee (1992) views the tense consonant of (3b) as indicating a heavier, slower gesture while the aspirated consonant of (3c) implies a swifter lighter gesture. While the exact characterization of the semantics of tensification of ideophones is beyond the scope of the present paper, we want to distinguish the tensification phenomena that we will present in this section from that illustrated by (2) and (3) in that they are neither purely phonological as in (2) (i.e. predictable from the phonological environment) nor semantic in the sense that tensification is used to modify the meaning of a corresponding form with a lax stop as in (3b)[2].

We now consider four types of tensification phenomena in spoken Korean, distinct from (2) and (3) above, that have received little attention in the Korean phonological literature. These are optional tensification of lax stops, the relexicalization of some lax stops as tense stops in the Kyungsang dialect, tensification in loan word adaptation, and the first language acquisition of tense stops. When taken together these phenomena show that tense stops are expanding to the detriment of lax stops. Let us first consider optional tensification of lax stops. In spoken Korean, there are certain words that have underlying lax stops that can optionally be pronounced as tense without any change in meaning. The data in (4) are representative examples.

(4) Optional tensification of lax stops in spoken Korean

Form with lax stop	*Optional tensification*	*Gloss*
a. kwa	k'wa	department
b. kampaŋ	k'ampaŋ	prison cell
c. tuk	t'uk	dam
d. pon	p'on	model
e. takt'a	t'akt'a	to polish
f. kukita	k'ukita	to crumple
g. pokt'a	p'okt'a	to fry
h. pek'ita	p'ek'ita	to copy
i. cakt'a	c'akt'a	to be small
j. kək'uro	k'ək'uro	bottom up

The optional tensification in (4) occurs with stops in word-initial position. As seen by the variety of data in (4), the place of articulation does not matter. While it is true that only certain words like those in (4) can undergo optional tensification, there are at least two reasons to believe that (4) indeed represents the expansion of tense stops at the expense of lax ones. First, the opposite phenomena does not seem to occur; that is, forms with

2 A third tensification phenomenon that we will not discuss is the tensification that marks an initial obstruent of a second member of a compound. While this type of tensification has typically been analyzed as a result of t-insertion (Ahn 1985), Shin (2002) presents a strong case for it to be analyzed as tensification of the second member without t-insertion.

underlying tense stops do not undergo optional detensification when in word-initial (or onset) position. (We ignore here the regular process of coda neutralization whereby consonants lose laryngeal features in coda position,) And, second, there are no examples that we are aware of in which Korean native words with an initial aspirated consonant can optionally be pronounced as tense.

A second phenomenon that demonstrates the expansion of the tense stops to the detriment of the lax ones is that in certain dialects of the southern part of South Korea there has been a relexicalization of lax stops in some words as tense ones. This is exemplified by the data in (5) from the Kyungsang dialect of Korean and reflects the native speech of the first author.

(5) Relexicalization of lax stops as tense stops in the Kyungsang dialect

Standard Korean	*Kyungsang Dialect*	*Gloss*
a. ke	k'e (k'i)	crab
b. tuk'əpi	t'uk'əpi	toad
c. kotɨŋə	k'otɨŋə	mackerel
d. cok'i	c'ok'i	vest
e. kacuk	k'acuk	leather
f. pətk'ita	p'ətk'ita	unclothe
g. talt'a /talhta/	t'alt'a	to wear down, be rubbed off
h. pulta	p'ult'a	to become soft (noodle)

Again, the opposite does not seem to exist. We are not aware of forms that have a tense stop (or an aspirated stop) in Standard Korean but with a lax stop in Kyungsang dialect. Given that the pronunciation with the lax stop is historically older in (4) and (5) (as reflected by the Korean orthography), the data in (4) and (5) bear witness to the expansion of tense stops at the expense of lax ones.

A third phenomenon that demonstrates the expansion of the tense stops to the detriment of the lax ones come from loanwords. For example, it is interesting that the voiceless unaspirated stops of French typically surface as tense stops rather than lax stops when borrowed into Korean as the examples in (6) illustrate. (Hyunsoon Kim, personal communication)

(6) Borrowing of French voiceless unaspirated stops as tense stops

French	*Korean*	
a. Paris	p'ari	
b. cafe	k'ap^{h}e	
c. Tous Les Jours	t'urecurɨ	(bakery franchise)
d. TGV	t'ecebe	(Train à Grande Vitesse)

e. comme toi k'ommɨt'ɨwa (brand of children's clothes)
f. Qu'est-ce que c'est? k'es'ɨk'ɨs'e

With respect to English loanwords, there are two types of stop consonants in English that might be expected to borrowed as lax stops in Korean. These would be the unaspirated allophones of voiceless stops as well as the voiced stops. Both these have acoustic characteristics that make them seem more similar to the Korean lax stops than to either the aspirated or tense stops. If we first consider English voiceless unaspirated stops as exemplified in the English columns in (7), we note that these unexpectedly do not get borrowed as lax stops but as aspirated ones.

(7) English voiceless unaspirated stops after /s/ are borrowed as aspirated in Korean

English	*Korean*	*English*	*Korean*
a. sketch	$\text{sɨk}^{h}\text{ec}^{h}\text{i}$	b. sprite	$\text{sɨp}^{h}\text{ɨrait}^{h}\text{ɨ}$
c. stop	$\text{sɨt}^{h}\text{op}$	d. piston	$\text{p}^{h}\text{isɨt}^{h}\text{on}$

The data in (7) illustrate a consistent pattern in the borrowing of English words into Korean. The English voiceless unaspirated stop after an /s/ is consistently borrowed as an aspirated stop in Korean. This is somewhat surprising especially given that the Korean aspirated stops are heavily aspirated (with a voice onset time of over 100 milliseconds, Choi 2001, Kang 2001) while the English voiceless stop after /s/ has very little if any aspiration. The effect of the mismatch is that a lax stop is avoided in the borrowing of English voiceless unaspirated stops into Korean. We leave open the question as to why the English stops after /s/ are borrowed as aspirated stops rather than as tense stops, especially given that the Korean tense stops have very little VOT.

In considering the borrowing of English voiced stops into Korean, one would expect that they should be borrowed as the voiceless unaspirated lax stops in Korean. This is because English voiced stops have acoustic characteristics similar to Korean lax stops. In both languages these stops have a short voice onset time in word-initial position. This means that in neither language are these stops fully voiced word-initially. On the other hand, both the English voiced stops and the Korean lax stops are fully voiced intervocalically (Kingston and Diehl 1994). With respect to borrowings, while it is certainly the case that English words with voiced stops are often borrowed with Korean lax stops as would be expected, there does seem to be a rather large number of borrowings where in word-initial position, the English voiced stop is borrowed as a tense stop, thus avoiding a lax stop while expanding the tense ones. Relevant data are provided in (8) where the words in parentheses indicate other examples of English words with initial voiced stops that are borrowed as tense stops.

(8) English word-initial voiced stops are often borrowed with tense stops in Korean

English *Korean*
a. bar p'a
b. bat p'æt (bag, ball, badge, banana, bonus, boxing)
c. dance t'æns'ɨ
d. dollar t'alla (dam, double, down, dubbing, duet)
e. gas k'as'ɨ
f. gum k'əm (game, gang, golf, goal, gown)
g. joke c'ok^{h}ɨ
h. jamc'æm (jab, jazz, jeep, joint, jump)

Much less common is for a word-initial voiceless (aspirated) stop in English to be borrowed as a tense consonant in Korean. Typically, English words with initial voiceless (aspirated) stops are borrowed as aspirated stops in Korean. In (9), though, we show a few cases where they are borrowed as a tense consonant instead.

(9) English word-initial aspirated stops borrowed as tense stops in Korean

English *Korean*
a. tank t'aŋk^{h}ɨ
b. pin p'in
c. pocket p'oket^{h}ɨ

Taken together, the data in (8) and (9) point to the expansion of Korean tense consonants mainly, though not exclusively, at the expense of lax ones.

With respect to the realization of English words borrowed with word-final stops, which are typically not aspirated but can be either released or unreleased in English, in Korean they exhibit variable behavior. They can be borrowed with the word-final stop interpreted as aspirated as in (10), as a lax stop as in (11), and even as a fricative as evidenced by the English words ending in word-final coronal stops shown in (12). The additional vowel-initial case ending shown in (12) makes clear that English word-final [t] or [d] can be lexicalized as the fricative /s/ when borrowed into Korean. One phenomenon that should be noticed in the data in (10)-(12) is that it is quite variable as to whether an English word-final stop is interpreted as having a release. If they are interpreted as having a release they are lexicalized with a word-final *ɨ*, as illustrated by the data in (10) and some of the forms in (11). If they are not interpreted as having a release then no vowel is inserted as illustrated by the data in (12) and (11c).

(10) Word-final voiceless stops are often borrowed as aspirated though they are typically not aspirated in spoken English

English	*Korean*	*English*	*Korean*
a. tank	t’æŋk^{h}ɨ	b. pocket	p’oket^{h}ɨ
c. pipe	p’aip^{h}ɨ	d. joke	c’ok^{h}ɨ
e. rope	rop^{h}ɨ	f. coke	k^{h}ok^{h}ɨ

(11) Word-final voiced stops in English are often borrowed as lax stops in Korean

English	*Korean*	*English*	*Korean*
a. league	likɨ	b. code	k^{h}otɨ
c cab	k^{h}æp	d. mug	məkɨ
e. tube	t^{h}yupɨ		

(12) English words with word-final [t] and [d] lexicalized in Korean with /s/.

English	*Korean*	
a. net	net --- ne*s*+*i* (nom.)	(*nec-i)
b. cabinet	k^{h}epinet --- k^{h}epine*s* - *i*	
c. pyramid	p^{h}iramit --- p^{h}irami*s* - *i*	

The realization of word-final stops of English borrowings into Korean as seen in (10)-(12) is quite complex. A specific analysis of this is beyond the scope of the present paper. The relevant point for our paper is to note that since English word-final stops are unaspirated (whether voiced or voiceless) one would expect that they should be typically borrowed as a Korean lax stop. While this is sometimes the case, especially for voiced stops as shown in (11), there seem to be many examples where a borrowing with a lax stop is avoided. This, thus, presents another situation where the appearance of expected lax stops seems to be avoided in the borrowing of English words into Korean. Consequently, the data in (6)-(12) taken altogether point to an avoidance of lax stops in the realization of borrowed words into Korean in places where they would be expected, given the similar nature of the stops in the source language to that of lax stops in Korean. In some of these cases we see the expansion of tense stops at the expense of the lax ones, but in other cases, we see an expansion of aspirated stops as in (7) and (10) and even fricatives as in (12).

Finally, we would like to note evidence from Korean child language acquisition bearing on tense stops. Both anecdotally and observationally, the early words of children acquiring Korean as their native language do not have lax stops but have tense stops (and nasals). Some commonly assumed early words of Korean children include those in (13).

(13) Some early words in Korean child language acquisition

Words	*Gloss*	*Words*	*Gloss*
a. ap'a	father	b. p'ap'a	milk, food, meal
c. k'ak'a	cookie	d. c'ic'i	breast, milk
e. p'aŋp'aŋ	car		

While the data in (13) is somewhat anecdotal, the data from the Korean child language acquisition study of Cho (2002) show that tense stops (along with nasals) are acquired before both the lax stops and the aspirated stops. It is interesting as to why tense stops would be the first stops acquired given that the lax stops would be unmarked for any laryngeal feature. That the unmarked laryngeal consonants, the lax consonants, are not acquired first may not mean much on its own, but, taken together with the tensification evidence and the loanword evidence presented in this section, it is consistent with the expansion of the tense stops at the expense of the lax ones.

3. Discussion

In the preceding section we have presented evidence showing the expansion of the Korean tense stops mainly at the expense of the lax ones. Evidence comes from optional tensification like in (4), dialectal tensification as in (5), loanword data such as (6)-(12), and observations about early acquisition where the first stops acquired seem to be the tense ones. Moreover, and importantly, we are not aware of an opposite phenomenon, namely, optional detensification of underlying tense stops (in word-initial position, setting aside laryngeal neutralization in coda position which is obligatory). Here we briefly speculate on why there is this expansion of tense stops at the expense of lax ones. One possibility is that we are witnessing the beginning stages of the restructuring of the Korean stop system from one having a three way contrast of plain, tense, and aspirated stops to one having a two way contrast of tense versus aspirated stops. A system with a two way stop contrast would be less marked than the present one with a three way contrast; also a two way contrast in the Korean stop system would make it more symmetrical with the fricative system which witnesses a two way contrast between tense /s'/ and plain /s/ which apparently is made with some degree of aspiration (Cho et al. 2002). However, speculation on the restructuring of the Korean stop system is probably premature. As John Whitman reminds us, historically, in Korean, the tense stops had a low functional load mainly developing historically out of syllable-initial consonant clusters. The current expansion of tense stops as documented in this paper can be viewed as a means by which the language evens out the functional load of the different stops. One can see this over time where certain words of Middle Korean with lax stops currently are pronounced with tense stops (e.g. p'alli "fast").

An important observation about much of the tensification data in Section 2, especially the optional tensification data in (4), the dialectal tensification in (5), and the loanword data in (6) and (8) is that such tensification mainly occurs in word-initial position. This suggests that Korean is promoting a prosodic constraint requiring the alignment of the beginning of the word with a laryngeal feature, so that if a word does not already begin with an aspirated sound, it will begin with a tense one. From an optimality-theoretic perspective, a constraint like that in (14) is becoming high-ranked.

(14) Laryngeal alignment constraint
Align-L(Wd, Laryngeal feature): Align the beginning of the word with a laryngeal feature.

The laryngeal feature would either be [spread glottis] (i.e. aspiration) or [constricted glottis] (i.e. tense). From a functional perspective, one can understand the promoting of such a constraint as a way to demarcate the beginning of the word; this can be seen then as a case of domain-initial strengthening along the lines of Cho and Jun (2000). However, it should be understood that the constraint in (14) would not be undominated since feature cooccurrence constraints such as *[Sonorant, constricted glottis] and *[Sonorant, spread glottis] would prevent a word-initial sonorant from being aspirated or tense. In this light, it is interesting to note that there are virtually no nouns in modern Korean that end in a lexical tense stop and there are very few that end in a lexical aspirated stop (Kang 2003).

Closely related to the issue of word-initial position, and not discussed so far, is the correlation that exists between tense consonants and high pitch on the following vowel. In Korean, the pitch is higher on a vowel immediately following a tense consonant in comparison with a lax consonant. It has been observed (Hyunsook Kang, personal communication) that the tense stops that occur in English loanwords in Korean are most often immediately before a stressed vowel, indicating that the high pitch of a stress vowel is what induces tensification of an immediately preceding stop, as exemplified in (8). This suggests that if the tensification phenomenon mainly occurs in word-initial position, it might be due to intonational factors such as a high pitch being associated with the first syllable or mora. In this regard, it is worth noting that Jun (1993) gives the accentual phrase of Seoul Korean as LHLH unless the initial segment of the phrase is laryngeally marked in which case it is HHLH. Studies such as Choi (2001) have shown that both tense and aspirated consonants are associated with a higher tone on the following vowel. The word-initial tensification phenomenon illustrated in data like (4), (5), (6), and (8) may be tied to the prosodic system of Korean. That is, we can speculate that tense consonants may be used to enhance a word boundary because they are linked to the word initial high pitch and a high tone is more salient than a low tone (assuming the word is phrase-initial; see Jun 1993).

In sum, in this paper we have tried to document the expansion of tense consonants at the expense of lax ones in current spoken Korean. While the expansion is probably unlikely to lead to the restructuring of the Korean stop system, it seems to affect word-initial stops in particular. Formally, this may be evidence for the promotion of a prosodic alignment constraint that aligns the beginning of the word with a laryngeal feature and acoustically this is associated with a high pitch.

References

Ahn, S-C. 1985. The Interplay of Phonology and Morphology in Korean. Doctoral Dissertation, University of Illinois.

Cho, M-H. 2002. Consonant Harmony in Child Korean: A Comparison with Child English. *Japanese/Korean Linguistics* 11:219-231.

Cho, T-H. and S-A Jun. 2000. Domain-Initial Strengthening as Enhancement of Laryngeal Features: Aerodynamic Evidence from Korean. *Chicago Linguistics Society* 36:31-44.

Cho, T-H, S-A Jun and P. Ladefoged. 2002. Acoustic and aerodynamic correlates of Korean stops and fricatives. *Journal of Phonetics* 30/2:193-228.

Cho, Y-M Yu and S. Inkelas. 1994. Post-obstruent Tensification in Korean and Geminate Inalterability. In Young-Key Kim-Renaud (ed.), *Theoretical Issues in Korean Linguistics*. 45-60. Stanford: CSLI Publications.

Choi, H-S. 2001. Acoustic Cues for the Korean Stop Contrast - Dialect Variation. *ZAS Papers in Linguistics* 28:1-12.

Jun, S-A. 1993. The Phonetics and Phonology of Korean Prosody, Doctoral Dissertation, Ohio State University.

Kang, Y-J. 2003. Sound Changes Affecting Non-final Coronal Obstruents in Korean. *Japanese/Korean Linguistics* 12:128-139.

Kim-Renaud, Y-K. 1986. *Studies in Korean Linguistics*. Seoul:Hanshin Publishing Co.

Kingston, J. and R. Diehl. 1994. Phonetic Knowledge, *Language* 70:419-454.

Lee, J-S. 1992. Phonology and Sound Symbolism of Korean Ideophones, Doctoral Dissertation, Indiana University.

Martin, S. 1962. *A Reference Grammar of Korean*. Tokyo:Charles E. Tuttle Co.

Shin, S-H. 2002. Constraint Conjunction in Korean Compounds. *Korean Journal of Linguistics* 27:65-86.

Tak, J-Y. 1997. Issues in Korean Consonantal Phonology. Doctoral Dissertation, Indiana University.

Romanization and Phonemicization of Japanese

TIMOTHY J. VANCE
University of Arizona

1. Introduction

There are two widely used systems of romanization for Japanese. **Hepburn** romanization (*Hebon-shiki rômaji*) is named after James Curtis Hepburn (1815–1911), the American missionary who adopted it in later editions of his Japanese-English dictionary.[1] **Kunrei** romanization (*kunrei-shiki rômaji*) was promulgated by the Japanese government in an official directive (*kunrei*) issued by the cabinet in 1937.[2] Comparisons of the two systems often say that Hepburn romanization is based

[1] Hepburn's original system differs in several respects from what is now called Hepburn romanization. For examples, see the 1867 first edition of his dictionary (reprinted as Hepburn 1983). Seeley (1991:140) explains that modern Hepburn romanization is essentially the system adopted by the *Rômaji kai* 'Romanization Club' in 1885. Hepburn began using this system in his 1886 third edition.

[2] Seeley (1991:140) notes that Kunrei romanization is a slightly modified version of *Nippon-shiki rômaji* 'Japan-style romanization', which was proposed in 1881 by the physicist Tanakadate Aikitsu. The modifications involved eliminating a small number of spelling distinctions that mirrored conservative *kana* spellings but no longer corresponded to different pronunciations.

on English spelling and that Kunrei romanization reflects the Japanese phonemic system.[3] Needless to say, however, there is no phonemic analysis of modern Tokyo Japanese that all linguists agree on. Any claim that one or the other romanization is a better reflection of the phonemic system depends on the preferred solutions to a set of problems that have vexed linguists working on Japanese for many decades.

The table in (1) shows the differences between the two systems, along with a *katakana* spelling for each syllable. The Kunrei system does not provide for syllables that occur only in recent loans, and such syllables will figure prominently in the discussion below.

(1)

Katakana	フィ	フェ	ファ	フォ	フ	フュ	
Hepburn	<fi>	<fe>	<fa>	<fo>	<fu>	<fyu>	
Kunrei	—	—	—	—	<hu>	—	
Katakana	シ	シェ	シャ	ショ	シュ		
Hepburn	<shi>	<she>	<sha>	<sho>	<shu>		
Kunrei	<si>	—	<sya>	<syo>	<syu>		
Katakana	チ	チェ	チャ	チョ	チュ	ティ	テュ
Hepburn	<chi>	<che>	<cha>	<cho>	<chu>	<ti>	<tyu>
Kunrei	<ti>	—	<tya>	<tyo>	<tyu>	—	—
Katakana	ジ	ジェ	ジャ	ジョ	ジュ		
Hepburn	<ji>	<je>	<ja>	<jo>	<ju>		
Kunrei	<zi>	—	<zya>	<zyo>	<zyu>		

2. The Voiceless Bilabial Fricative

Hepburn <fu> and Kunrei <hu> both represent a consonant pronounced [ɸ] followed by /u/ (realized as [ɯ]).[4] Except in recent borrowings, [ɸ] is in complementary distribution both with [ç] (which occurs immediately before /i/) and with [h] (which occurs immediately before /e/, /a/, or /o/).[5] While [ɸ] only occurs immediately before /u/ in native and Sino-Japanese vocabulary items, it can appear immediately before any vowel in recent loans, as in [ɸiɾɯmɯ] 'film', [ɸeɾiː] 'ferry', [ɸaiɾɯ] 'file', and [ɸoːkɯ] 'fork'. One possibility is to say that a garden-variety phonemic split has left modern Tokyo Japanese with a contrast between a phoneme /h/ (realized as [ç] or as [h]) and a phoneme /f/ (realized as

[3] Seeley's (1991:140) statement is typical, though more careful than most: "The Hepburn romanisation, which was based loosely on the conventions of English spelling . . . stood in opposition to what was in effect a phonemically-orientated romanisaton system . . ."

[4] For details on the realization of Japanese /u/, see Vance 1987:10–11.

[5] Depending on other analytical decisions that will come up later, it may be necessary to say that [ç] also occurs immediately before /y/, but I ignore this complication here.

[ɸ]).[6] As (2) shows, this analysis leaves /h/ with a defective distribution, since neither [ç] nor [h] occurs immediately before /u/.[7]

(2) /fi/ [ɸi] /fe/ [ɸe] /fa/ [ɸɑ] /fo/ [ɸo] /fu/ [ɸɯ]

/hi/ [çi] /he/ [he] /ha/ [hɑ] /ho/ [ho] */hu/

An analysis that countenances archiphonemes could treat [ɸ] immediately before /u/ as neither /f/ nor /h/, but an American Descriptivist version of phonemics would require [ɸ] to be a realization of /f/ wherever it occurs.[8] Given this analysis of [ɸ] followed by /u/ as /fu/, Hepburn <fu> is a better reflection of Japanese phonemics than Kunrei <hu>.

Hepburn <f> antedates the borrowed vocabulary items that motivate treating /f/ as a separate phoneme from /h/, but the serendipitous result is that Hepburn romanization easily accommodates the innovative sequences involving /f/ (<firumu>, <ferî>, <fairu>, <fôku>), whereas Kunrei romanization does not. Of course, [ɸ] followed by anything other than /u/ could be treated as a **foreignism** (like the [x] that some English-speaking classical music fans use in *Bach*) and therefore beyond the boundaries of a phonemic analysis of Japanese. Yet another alternative is to stratify the vocabulary and treat the "recent loan" stratum as having a different phonemic system than older strata.[9]

3. Alveopalatal Obstruents

A phonemic analysis of Japanese alveopalatal obstruents requires dealing with an even more challenging set of interrelated questions. The traditional syllabary display suggests that alveopalatal [ɕ] and alveolar [s] are allophones of a single phoneme, and that alveopalatal [cɕ] and alveolar [t] are allophones of a single phoneme as well. Part of this tra-

---

[6] Bloch (1950:116) distinguished an "innovating dialect" from a "conservative dialect" of Tokyo Japanese. One feature of the former was that it allowed [ɸi ɸe ɸɑ ɸo], whereas the latter did not. Assuming the phonemic split interpretation, Bloch's account suggests that the split was still in progress half a century ago, but it is very nearly complete today. My experience is that Tokyo speakers born after World War II react with embarrassment or derision to conservative pronunciations like [hoːkɯ] for the word meaning 'fork'.

[7] Bloch (1950:131–132) actually says that [ɸɯ] and [hɯ] were in free variation. I am not aware of any evidence for such variability in present-day Tokyo Japanese. Perhaps the development of a contrast between [ɸ] and [h] has led to a reduction in variability. On the other hand, it may still be true that non-contrastive [ɸ] (before [ɯ]) varies more than contrastive [ɸ] (before other vowels).

[8] This "once a phoneme always a phoneme" doctrine follows from Hockett's (1942) "non-intersection" requirement, which Chomsky (1964:93–94) calls the "absolute version" of the "invariance condition" in his critique of American Descriptivist phonemic analysis.

[9] For proposals on treating the Japanese vocabulary as stratified, see McCawley 1968: 62–75 and Itô and Mester 1995. For a critique, see Vance 2002.

ditional arrangement appears in (3). For the syllable represented by each *katakana* letter in (3), a phonetic transcription and the two romanizations (H=Hepburn, K=Kunrei) are provided.

(3) ナ [nɑ] H<na> K<na> タ [tɑ] H<ta> K<ta> サ [sɑ] H<sa> K<sa>
ニ [ɲi] H<ni> K<ni> チ [cɕi] H<chi> K<ti> シ [ɕi] H<shi> K<si>
ヌ [nɯ] H<nu> K<nu> ツ [tsɯ] H<tsu> K<tu> ス [sɯ] H<su> K<su>
ネ [ne] H<ne> K<ne> テ [te] H<te> K<te> セ [se] H<se> K<se>
ノ [no] H<no> K<no> ト [to] H<to> K<to> ソ [so] H<so> K<so>

When the *kana* syllabaries (i.e., *hiragana* and *katakana*) first came into use about 1,100 years ago, the syllables in each column in (3) presumably shared a phonemically identical initial consonant, but there is certainly no guarantee that the same must be true of the modern Tokyo descendants of those syllables. The Kunrei romanizations in (3) maintain the parallelism of the traditional display by rendering all the syllables in each column with the same consonant letter. In particular, Kunrei romanization uses <si> for [ɕi] (cf. H<shi>) and <ti> for [cɕi] (cf. H<chi>). "Kunrei-style" will refer here to a phonemic analysis that treats both [ɕ] and [s] as allophones of /s/ and treats both [cɕ] and [t] as allophones of /t/. "Hepburn-style" will refer to a phonemic analysis that treats [ɕ], [s], [cɕ], and [t] as four different phonemes, e.g., an analysis that uses /s/ for [s] (cf. H<sa> for [sɑ]), /š/ for [ɕ] (cf. H<shi> for [ɕi]), /t/ for [t] (cf. H<ta> for [tɑ]), and /č/ for [cɕ] (cf. H<chi> for [cɕi]).

This distinction between Kunrei-style and Hepburn-style phonemic analyses extends naturally to the voiced alveopalatal obstruent [ɟʑ], although historical changes have made this case slightly more complicated than the two considered just above.[10] Adding the *dakuten* voicing diacritic to each of the *katakana* letters in the rightmost column of (3) yields the letters in (4).

(4) ザ [dzɑ]~[zɑ] H<za> K<za> ゼ [dze]~[ze] H<ze> K<ze>
ジ [ɟʑi] H<ji> K<zi> ゾ [dzo]~[zo] H<zo> K<zo>
ズ [dzɯ]~[zɯ] H<zu> K<zu>

For the consonant realized as [dz] or [z], both romanization systems use <z>, but for the syllable realized as [ɟʑi], Kunrei <zi> corresponds to

---

[10] Earlier contrasts between [dz] and [z] and between [ɟʑ] and [ʑ] were lost about 400 years ago in Tokyo Japanese but still reflected in pre-modern *kana* spelling. For discussion, see Toyama 1972:198–202 and Vance 1987:24–25.

Hepburn <ji>.[11] A Kunrei-style phonemic analysis treats [dz], [z], and [ɟʑ] as allophones of /z/. A Hepburn-style analysis treats [dz]~[z] and [ɟʑ] as two different phonemes, e.g., an analysis that uses /z/ for [dz]~[z] (cf. H<za> for [dzɑ]~[zɑ]) and /ǰ/ for [ɟʑ] (cf. H<ji> for [ɟʑi]).

The great majority of modern linguists working on Japanese seem to believe that a Kunrei-style phonemic analysis of alveopalatal obstruents is appropriate for modern Tokyo. The most obvious problem with treating [ɕi cɕi ɟʑi] as /si ti zi/ (cf. K<si ti zi>) is that [ɕ], [cɕ], and [ɟʑ] all appear before vowels other than /i/. These combinations are not recent innovations; they were already well entrenched when the precursors of the two romanization systems were first devised in the 19th century. The examples in (5) are etymologically Sino-Japanese, and all are listed in the 1867 first edition of Hepburn's dictionary.

(5)	[ɕɑɾei] 'token of thanks'	[cɕɑkɯjoː] 'wearing'	[ɟʑɑmɑ] 'obstacle'
	[ɕokɯbɑ] 'workplace'	[cɕosɑkɯ] 'authoring'	[ɟʑosei] 'aid'
	[ɕɯɾɯi] 'type'	[cɕɯːoː] 'center'	[ɟʑɯnoː] 'accepting'

As these examples show, [ɕ] is not in complementary distribution with [s], [cɕ] is not in complementary distribution with [t], and [ɟʑ] is not in complementary distribution with [dz]~[z], despite what the traditional syllabary columns in (3) and (4) suggest.

The two romanization systems represent the combinations of interest as in (6). Notice how Hepburn romanization consistently uses <sh> for [ɕ], <ch> for [cɕ], and <j> for [ɟʑ].

(6)	シ[ɕi] H<shi>K<si>	チ[cɕi] H<chi>K<ti>	ジ[ɟʑi] H<ji>K<zi>
	シャ[ɕɑ] H<sha>K<sya>	チャ[cɕɑ] H<cha>K<tya>	ジャ[ɟʑɑ] H<ja>K<zya>
	ショ[ɕo] H<sho>K<syo>	チョ[cɕo] H<cho>K<tyo>	ジョ[ɟʑo] H<jo>K<zyo>
	シュ[ɕɯ] H<shu>K<syu>	チュ[cɕɯ] H<chu>K<tyu>	ジュ[ɟʑɯ] H<ju>K<zyu>

Since a Hepburn-style phonemic analysis treats [ɕ] as /š/ (not as an allophone of /s/), [cɕ] as /č/ (not as an allophone of /t/), and [ɟʑi] as /ǰ/ (not as an allophone of /z/), the combinations in (6) fit right in: <sh> corresponds to /š/, <ch> corresponds to /č/, and <j> corresponds to /ǰ/. Kunrei romanization, on the other hand, uses <sy> for [ɕ], <ty> for [cɕ], and <zy> for [ɟʑ] when the immediately following vowel is not /i/.

---

[11] According to Kawakami (1977:52–52), [dz] and [z] are in nearly complementary distribution: [dz] word-initially or immediately following a consonant and [z] usually but not always intervocalically. Arecent instrumental study (Matsugu and Vance 2003) indicates that the actual distribution is not so neat, although the word-initial and post-consonantal environments clearly favor the [dz] realization, and the intervocalic environment clearly favors the [z] realization. The syllable realized as [ɟʑi] is also sometimes realized as [ʑi], but the tendency toward fricative realization intervocalically is not as clear.

These Kunrei conventions mirror modern *kana* spellings, which render the syllables [ɕɑ ɕo ɕɯ], [cɕɑ cɕo cɕɯ], and [ɟʑɑ ɟʑo ɟʑɯ] with digraphs. For example, [ɕɑ] (K<sya>) is written with a full-size letter for [ɕi] (K<si>) followed by a reduced-size letter for [jɑ] (K<ya>). In other words, big <si> plus little <ya> equals <sya>, big <ti> plus little <yo> equals <tyo>, and so on, as in (7).

(7)
	K<sya>		K<tyo>	
full-size	— シャ —	reduced-size	full-size — チョ —	reduced-size
K<si>		K<ya>	K<ti>	K<yo>

Although these Kunrei <CyV> combinations correspond consistently to modern *kana* spellings, they could not originally have been based on *kana* in any straightforward way, since modern *kana* spellings were not adopted until 1946.[12] In any case, one possible Kunrei-style phonemic analysis of the combinations in (6) would be to treat an alveopalatal consonant before a vowel other than /i/ as a realization of an underlying cluster: [ɕɑ] realizes /sya/, [cɕo] realizes /tyo/, [ɟʑɯ] realizes /zyu/, etc.

In CV syllables, the Japanese phoneme /y/, realized as the semivowel [j], occurs only before a back vowel, as in (8).

(8) */yi/ */ye/ /ya/ /yo/ /yu/

Both romanization systems represent this /y/ as <y>: <ya yu yo>. Both also suggest that words such as [kjodai] 'gigantic' and [pjokopjoko] 'bounce-bounce' begin with /Cy/ clusters: <kyodai>, <pyokopyoko>. This cluster treatment can be incorporated into either style of phonemic analysis, but the resulting Kunrei-style analysis shows greater "economy" (i.e., fewer phonemes) and much greater "symmetry" (i.e., many fewer gaps) than the resulting Hepburn-style analysis. The comparison in (9) assumes a Kunrei-style analysis in which, before a vowel other than /i/, [ɕ], [cɕ], and [ɟʑ] are phonemically /sy/, /ty/, and /zy/. All the syllables in (9) contain the vowel /a/, but exactly the same pattern holds for /o/ and (leaving recent borrowings aside) for /u/.[13]

(9)
BOTH SYSTEMS:	/pa/	/ba/	/ma/	/na/	/ra/	/ka/	/ga/	/ha/
	/pya/	/bya/	/mya/	/nya/	/rya/	/kya/	/gya/	/hya/
KUNREI-STYLE:	/ta/	/da/	/za/	/sa/				
	/tya/	*/dya/	/zya/	/sya/				
HEPBURN-STYLE:	/ta/	/da/	/za/	/sa/	/ča/	/ǰa/	/ša/	
	*/tya/	*/dya/	*/zya/	*/sya/	*/čya/	*/ǰya/	*/šya/	

[12] See Seeley 1991:104–125,153–154 for the history of *kana* spelling.

[13] The sequence /hy/ in (9) is realized as [çj]. See note 5.

In the Kunrei-style analysis the only phonotactically inadmissible /Cy/ cluster is /dy/, but in the Hepburn-style analysis no /Cy/ cluster begins with a coronal obstruent.

If recent loans are excluded from consideration, before /i/ there is no contrast between [ɕ] and [s], between [cɕ] and [t], or between [ɟʑ] and [dz]~[z]. This lack of contrast makes it possible for a basically Kunrei-style analysis to treat [ɕi] as either /si/ or /syi/, [cɕi] as either /ti/ or /tyi/, and [ɟʑi] as either /zi/ or /zyi/, as shown in (10).

(10)	*/syi/	*/tyi/	*/zyi/	*/si/	*/ti/	*/zi/
	/si/	/ti/	/zi/	/syi/	/tyi/	/zyi/
	[ɕi]	[cɕi]	[ɟʑi]	[ɕi]	[cɕi]	[ɟʑi]

Given the prohibition on /yi/ noted above in (8), it seems more natural to rule out /Cyi/ combinations and adopt the alternative on the left in (10).

4. Accommodating Recent Borrowings

Recent borrowings pose some serious challenges for the Kunrei-style analysis developed in §3. For one thing, there are loanwords containing the phonetic sequence [ti], such as [bɯtikːɯ] 'boutique'. The alternative on the right in (10) provides a way of accommodating such loans, since [cɕi] is /tyi/ rather than /ti/. This choice leaves /ti/ available for innovative [ti]. Notice, however, that analyzing [cɕi] as /tyi/ produces a mismatch between the phonemic analysis and Kunrei <ti>. Parallelism would make [ɟʑi] and [ɕi] phonemically /zyi/ and /syi/, although neither [dzi]~[zi] nor [si] has been integrated into modern Tokyo Japanese.[14]

Recent loans have also produced [ɕ]/[s], [cɕ]/[t], and [ɟʑ]/[dz]~[z] contrasts before /e/. The obvious Kunrei-style solution is to treat [ɕe] (as in [ɕeɸɯ] 'chef'), [cɕe] (as in [cɕeɾo] 'cello'), and [ɟʑe] (as in [ɟʑetːo] 'jet') as /sye/, /tye/, and /zye/. As noted above in (8), however, the syllable /ye/ is typically taken to be phonotactically inadmissible (although it is marginally possible for some speakers; see Vance 1987:26–27). Furthermore, as (11) shows, most syllables that would call for a /Cye/ analysis in a Kunrei-style system do not occur even in recent loans.

(11)	/pe/	/be/	/me/	/ne/	/re/	/ke/	/ge/	/he/
	*/pye/	*/bye/	*/mye/	*/nye/	*/rye/	*/kye/	*/gye/	*/hye/

Treating the innovative combinations [ɕe], [cɕe], and [ɟʑe] as /sye/, /tye/, and /zye/ entails giving up the appealing generalization that a syllable

---

14 The *katakana* spellings スィ and ズィ, which imply [si] and [dzi]~[zi], are sometimes used, but I would argue that [si] and [dzi]~[zi] are still foreignisms. At the same time, I admit that there is no infallible way of deciding what should be considered a foreignism.

cannot begin with a consonant followed by the otherwise disallowed sequence /ye/.[15]

In contrast to a Kunrei-style analysis, a Hepburn-style analysis has distributional gaps that are filled by the innovative sequences that occur in recent borrowings, as (12) shows.

(12)	/pi/	/pu/	*/pyi/	/pyu/	>/ti/	*/tu/	*/tyi/	?/tyu/	/či/	/ču/	*/čyi/	*/čyu/
	/pe/	/po/	*/pye/	/pyo/	/te/	/to/	*/tye/	*/tyo/	>/če/	/čo/	*/čye/	*/čyo/
		/pa/		/pya/		/ta/		*/tya/		/ča/		*/čya/

Notice that innovative /ti/ and /če/ give the phonemes /t/ and /č/ distributions that are more like the distributions of non-coronal obstruents such as /p/. Also, since the Hepburn-style analysis can treat [ɕe cɕe ɟʑe] as /še če ǰe/, there is no need to resort to the otherwise disallowed sequence /ye/. A Kunrei-style analysis treats these three innovative sequences as /sye tye zye/, as noted above, but why the restriction against /ye/ should be lifted only following /s/, /t/, or /z/ remains a mystery. A proponent of Kunrei-style analysis might try to argue that the restriction against /Cye/ has actually been lifted across the board and that the phonotactic prohibitions in (11) do not hold in recent borrowings. There is little doubt that phonetic sequences of the form [Cje] or [Cʲe] are cross-linguistically dispreferred, which limits the potential sources for the starred /Cye/ sequences (11). Nonetheless, the few relevant borrowings from Russian have been assimilated into Japanese with [Ce] rather than [Cye]. An example is Russian печка [pʲeʧkə] 'stove', borrowed into Japanese with initial [pe], not [pje].

On the other hand, there are innovative sequences that force a Hepburn-style analysis to give up a generalization noted above in connection with (9) in §3, namely, that a syllable-initial /Cy/ cluster is phonotactically inadmissible if C is a coronal obstruent. The sequence [djɯ] is well established in loanwords such as [djɯetːo] 'duet', and a Hepburn-style analysis presumably has to treat [djɯ] phonemically as /dyu/.[16] The sequence [tjɯ] is probably still a foreignism for most speakers, so Hepburn-style /tyu/ is marked as questionable in (12). Authoritative Japanese dictionaries list spellings that imply [tjɯ] but cross-reference them to preferred spellings that imply [cɕɯ] instead, e.g., テューバ (implying [tjɯːbɑ]) cross-referenced to チューバ (implying [cɕɯːbɑ]) for 'tuba'. Since a Kunrei-style analysis uses /tyu/ for [cɕɯ], it is not clear how it could accommodate [tjɯ], but the unavailability of a

---

[15] Mester and Itô (1989:283) state a constraint that prohibits /ye/ (preceded by a tautosyllabic C or not) and then mention that the constraint is violated in recent foreign loans.

[16] /dy/ is available for [djɯ] because the contrast [ɟʑ] vs. [ʑ] was lost. See note 10.

phonemicization for [tjɯ] could easily be construed as a virtue. As noted in connection with (9), /dy/ is the only syllable-initial /Cy/ cluster that does not occur in the Kunrei-style analysis developed in §3. Thus, /dyu/ is available for innovative [djɯ] in a Kunrei-style analysis, just as it is in a Hepburn-style analysis. In other words, /dy/ fills a distributional gap in a Kunrei-style analysis. In contrast, Kunrei-style /ty/ is already in use for [cç], which explains why [djɯ] has been integrated so easily into modern Tokyo Japanese while the very similar [tjɯ] has not.

5. Distinctively Palatalized Consonants

As noted both in §3 and in §4, a Hepburn-style phonemic analysis ends up treating almost all /Cy/ sequences as distributional gaps when C is a coronal obstruent, the only exceptions being /dy/ (in innovative /dyu/) and, possibly, /ty/.[17] A Kunrei-style analysis does not involve so many gaps, since it treats [ç cç ɟʑ] as realizations of /sy ty zy/, but it accommodates innovative sequences in recent borrowings much less readily.

A different way to eliminate the distributional gaps that occur in a Hepburn-style analysis is to say that Japanese has distinctively palatalized consonants instead of syllable-initial /Cy/ clusters. On this analysis, *kyôdo* 'intensity' is /kʲoodo/ and *kôdo* 'luminosity' is /koodo/, with /kʲ/ distinct from /k/. To make these words a minimal pair, the apparent [j] between the [kʲ] and [oː] in *kyôdo* can be interpreted as a side-effect of the transition from the palatalized consonant to the vowel rather than as a separate segment: [kʲoːdo] 'intensity' vs. [koːdo] 'luminosity'.[18] This palatalized-consonant analysis adds several phonemes to the inventory, but it also simplifies the phonotactics by eliminating all syllable-initial consonant clusters. The problematic [ç cç ɟʑ] can be transcribed phonemically either as /š č ǰ/, mirroring Hepburn romanization, or as /sʲ tʲ zʲ/, to hint at the morphophonemic alternations between [ç] and /s/, between [cç] and /t/, and between [ɟʑ] and /z/.[19]

---

[17] Since [dj] always precedes [ɯ] in existing words, it is not obvious whether the sequences [djɑ] and [djo] are phonotactically prohibited or just accidental gaps.

[18] Duanmu (2000:28–36) offers a similar analysis of syllable-initial alveopalatal obstruents in Beijing Mandarin. The appeal of the /Cy/ analysis for Mandarin is strengthened by the fact that there is variation among speakers between palatalized "dentals" and alveopalatals. For example, for /sy/ some speakers have [sʲ] and others have [ç].

[19] The morphophonemic alternations of interest occur, for example, in the inflectional forms of verbs, as in *hanasu* [hɑnɑsu] 'speak' with [s] versus *hanashi* [hɑnɑçi] 'speaking' with [ç]. Zoll (1997:264–270) proposes an account of Japanese "mimetic palatalization" that depends crucially on treating [pʲ], [kʲ], etc., as having a secondary articulation (i.e., palaltalization) that [ç], [cç], and [ɟʑ] lack. However, it is the realizations that are relevant in this account, not the "underlying" or phonemic forms, so it is compatible with either /š č ǰ/ or /sʲ tʲ zʲ/.

Except in recent borrowings, the palatalized-consonant analysis has no contrasts between /Cʲe/ and /Ce/ or between /Cʲi/ and /Ci/. Assuming that [te] is /te/ and [cçi] is /tʲi/, this analysis accommodates innovative [cçe] as /tʲe/ and innovative [ti] as /ti/. As noted in §4, if [cçi] is treated in straightforward Kunrei-style fashion as /ti/, accommodating innovative [ti] requires a significant reorganization of the system. Even if recent borrowings are treated as a separate stratum with a distinct phonological system, it seems almost perverse to analyze [cçi] as /tyi/ when it occurs in a recent borrowing but as /ti/ when it occurs in a native or Sino-Japanese word. One way to avoid this undesirable consequence is to take the position that, before [cçe] and [ti] were assimilated into Japanese, [te] and [cçi] involved neither /t/ nor /tʲ/ but a traditional archiphoneme unspecified for palatalization.

The same kind of archiphoneme analysis has at least some appeal in other cases as well. For example, since the stop in [kʲi] 'spirit' is strongly palatalized, phonetic similarity dictates treating it as /kʲ/ rather than as /k/, but this choice has a highly counterintuitive consequence. It leaves /k/ occurring only before /e a o u/ and /kʲ/ only before /i a o u/, which means that [kʲi] 'spirit' and [ke] 'hair' begin with different consonants: /kʲi/ vs. /ke/. The archiphoneme analysis avoids this consequence. On the other hand, it does not capture the intuition that both [kʲi] 'spirit' and [ke] 'hair' begin with the same consonant as [kɑ] 'mosquito', as (13) shows using /K/ for the archiphoneme.[20]

(13) /Ki/ /Ke/ /ka/ /kʲa/ /ko/ /kʲo/ /ku/ /kʲu/

As noted in §4, the obvious way to accommodate innovative [çe], [cçe], and [ɟʑe] in a Kunrei-style analysis is to treat them as /sye/, /tye/, and /zye/, but the syllable /ye/ does not occur. Notice that a palatalized-consonant analysis involves no /Cye/ sequences, which means that a simple phonotactic prohibition on /ye/ can be maintained. A palatalized-consonant analysis can treat the innovative sequence [dʲɯ] (transcribed [djɯ] in §4) as /dʲu/, and it can also accommodate the more dubious sequence [tʲɯ] (transcribed [tjɯ] in §4), provided that [cç] is treated not as a palatalized alveolar (as suggested by the transcription /tʲ/) but simply as an alveopalatal (as suggested by the transcription /č/). Using /ču/ for [cçɯ] leaves /tʲu/ available for [tʲɯ].

---

[20] Depending on exactly how the underspecified consonants are interepreted, this archiphoneme analysis may interfere with the use of distinctive palatalization to predict the fleeting vowel at the end of some Sino-Japanese morphemes. Itô (1988:149–150), for example, represents *iku* 'breeding' as underlyingly /ik/ and *iki* 'region' as underlyingly /ikʲ/, although she assumes palatalization is on a separate autosegmental tier.

6. Conclusion

This paper has examined the dubious notion that Kunrei romanization is a better reflection than Hepburn of the Japanese phonemic system. The approach has been to think through the consequences of some of the analytical choices that a linguist must make in working out a phonemicization. No attempt has been made to go beyond very traditional assumptions about the segmental nature of phonological representations. Kunrei romanization clearly matches present-day *kana* spelling conventions much better, whereas Hepburn romanization sticks much closer to the phonetic ground. But their relative merits as quasi-phonemic transcriptions of modern Tokyo Japanese are in the eye of the beholder.

References

Bloch, B. 1950. Studies in Colloquial Japanese IV: Phonemics. *Language* 26:86–125. [References are to the version in *Bernard Bloch on Japanese*, ed. by R. A. Miller, 113–165. New Haven: Yale University Press, 1970]

Chomsky, N. 1964. Current Issues in Linguistics Theory. *The Structure of Language: Readings in the Philosophy of Language*, ed. by J. A. Fodor and J. J. Katz, 50–118. Englewood Cliffs: Prentice-Hall.

Duanmu, S. 2000. *The Phonology of Standard Chinese*. Oxford: Oxford University Press.

Hepburn, J. C. 1983. *A Japanese and English Dictionary with an English and Japanese Index*. Rutland & Tokyo: Tuttle. [Originally published in 1867.]

Hockett, C. F. 1942. A System of Descriptive Phonology. *Language* 16:3–21.

Itô, J. 1988. *Syllable Theory in Prosodic Phonology*. New York & London: Garland Publishing.

Itô, J., and A. Mester. 1995. Japanese Phonology. *The Handbook of Phonological Theory*, ed. by J. Goldsmith, 817–838. Oxford: Blackwell.

Kawakami, S. 1977. *Nihongo onsei gaisetsu*. Tokyo: Ôfûsha.

Matsugu, Y., and T. J. Vance. 2003. Allophonic Variation of Japanese /z/. Poster presented at the 146th Meeting of the Acoustical Society of America, 11 November, Austin, Texas.

Mester, R. A., and J. Itô. 1989. Feature Predictability and Underspecification: Palatal Prosody in Japanese Mimetics. Language 65:258–293.

Seeley, C. 1991. *A History of Writing in Japan*. Leiden: E. J. Brill.

Toyama, E. 1972. Kindai no On'in. *Kôza Nihongoshi 2: On'inshi, Mojishi*, ed. by N. Nakata, 173–268. Tokyo: Taishûkan.

Vance, T. J. 1987. *An Introduction to Japanese Phonology*. Albany: SUNY Press.

———. 2002. Another Look at Vocabulary Stratification in Japanese. *The Linguist's Linguist: A Collection of Papers in Honour of Alexis Manaster Ramer*, ed. by F. Cavoto, 433–436. Munich & Newcastle: Lincom Europa.

Zoll, C. 1997. Conflicting Directionality. *Phonology* 14:263–286.

Part II

Morphology, Morphosyntax and Syntax

Gerund Phrases as NPs with N Heads: No Empty or Mixed Categories

HEE-RAHK CHAE

Hankuk University. of Foreign Studies

1. Introduction

The gerund phrase construction is one of the most recalcitrant constructions to deal with because it has both nominal and verbal properties. The construction is usually handled by recourse to special categories and/or mechanisms, which are not always well-motivated. In this paper, we will provide an "Indexed Phrase Structure Grammar" analysis of it (Chae 1992), where gerund phrases are analyzed as NPs with N heads.

There are different types of gerund phrases (GPs) in English, Korean and other languages. In this paper, we will focus on two types of GP constructions, which are represented by the examples in (1a/2a) and (1b/2b) below, respectively. The terms used to refer to these constructions are not uniform. For example, in Pullum (1991) the GPs in (1a) and (2a) are called "nominal gerund phrases." Malouf (1998/2000) uses the term "verbal gerunds" to refer to those in both (1a/2a) and (1b/2b). We will simply call these two types GPs. When it is necessary to refer to the two types separately, the former will be called "Poss-GPs" and the latter "Non-Poss-GPs." English has one nominalizer (NML), i.e. *-ing*, which attaches to verb stems and become gerunds. On the other hand, Korean has two different NMLs: *-um* and *-ki*.

2. Properties of Gerund Phrases

English GPs, which appear in the square brackets in (1a-b), are not easy to analyze because we have to deal with their mixed categorial properties.

(1) a. [The girl's (deftly/not) painting her father] alarmed him.
b. [The girl (deftly/not) painting her father] alarmed him.

Some of their nominal properties are as follows. Firstly, they appear in NP positions (as verbal and prepositional complements). Secondly, the "subject" of GPs, e.g. *the girl's* in (1a) or *the girl* in (1b), is optional. This can be regarded as a nominal property because verbs in general require a subject while nouns do not. Lastly, the subject is in the genitive form in (1a), just like the "subject" of nouns.

On the other hand, GPs show verbal properties as well. First of all, the head of the GP, i.e. the gerund, takes the same complements as the verb from which it is derived. For example, in (1) the GP head *painting* takes *her father* as its object just like the verb *paint*. If it is a nominal element, it would take a PP complement, i.e. *of her father*. Besides, GPs can take adverbial modifiers and they can be negated with *not*, as shown in the parentheses in (1). These are usually regarded as verbal properties.[1]

Korean GPs have very similar properties to those of the English GPs which we have observed above (Yoon 1996):

(2) a. [cyon-uy (ppalli) chayk-ul (an) ilk-um-i] nollawu-n sasil-i-ta.
-Gen fast book-Acc not read-NML-Nom surprising fact-be[Pres]-Decl
'John's (fast/not) reading the book is a surprising thing.'
b. [cyon-i (ppalli) chayk-ul (an) ilk-um-i] nollawu-n sasil-i-ta. (*-i*: Nom)

As for the nominal properties, they appear in NP positions and the subject of the GP is in the genitive form in such examples as (2a). As for the verbal properties, gerunds take accusative complements, combine with adverbial modifiers and can be negated with *an*.

There are also some differences between English GP constructions and Korean GP constructions. For example, the subject of the GP in (2b) has the nominative marker *-i* rather than the accusative maker *-ul*. A more significant difference between the two languages is the morphological status of the nominalizers (NMLs). It is very clear that the English NML *-ing* is an affix, a word-internal element. However, the morphological status of the Korean NMLs *-um* and *-ki* is not clear at all. In view of such data as in (3), *-um* seems to be an entity which combines with a phrase, because the coordinate structure as a whole is nominalized.

(3) cyon-i [[chayk-ul ilk-ko] [yenhwa-lul po-ass]]-um-ul al-n-ta.
-Nom book-Acc read-Conj movie-Acc see-Past-NML-Acc know-Pres-Decl
'(I) know (the fact) that John read a book and saw a movie.'

---

[1] Malouf (1988: 35-37), however, argues that those "verbal properties" are not actually unique to verbs (cf. section 4 of this paper).

If we assume that the NML is attached to the second embedded clause, the phrase would become an illegitimate coordinate structure of [VP-and-NP]. On the other hand, the NML seems to combine only with its preceding verb rather than a preceding phrase, in such "gapping" and/or "right node raising" constructions as (4) (Chung, et al. 2001: 773):

(4) [cyon-i sakwa-lul *e*] kuliko [meyli-ka banana-lul mek-ess-um]
-Nom apple-Acc and Mary-Nom banana-Acc eat-Past-NML
'John having eaten apples and Mary (having eaten) bananas.'

If we assume that the NML here is attached to the whole coordinate structure, the gapped part in the first clause would be construed as *mek-ess-*, which leads to an ungrammatical expression of *[[*cyon-i sakwa-lul mek-ess-*] *kuliko* [*meyli-ka banana-lul mek-ess-um*]]. In addition, the "common factor" *mek-ess-um* in (4) would not make a constituent at all if we assume that the NML combines with the whole preceding phrase.

3. Previous Analyses

Among the literature dealing with GP constructions, Pullum (1991: 775-76) proposes three "theoretical desiderata" for a desirable analysis of GPs. These desiderata are established as a set of conditions that any reasonable analysis of GPs should satisfy:

(5) Pullum's (1991) theoretical desiderata:
a. strong lexicalism: syntax operates at the superword level and does not affect the internal structure of words.
b. endocentricity: every constituent has (at least) one distinguished daughter identified as its head.
c. null licensing: no phonologically zero constituent should be posited that is neither semantically contentful nor syntactically bound.

According to him, "all the generative analyses I am aware of violate one or more of the conditions" above in their treatments of the GPs (p. 776). Actually, almost all the previous analyses violate one or more of these principles (Baker 1985, Abney 1987, Yoon 1996, Bresnan 1997, Kaiser 1998) and/or posit unmotivated categories or mechanisms (Lapointe 1993; Malouf 1998; Chung, et al. 2001). Even Pullum's own analysis violates the endocentricity principle, at least conceptually.

Pullum (1991) argues that his analysis satisfies the endocentricity condition even though there is a category mismatch between the mother category and its head daughter category. However, as was pointed out by Malouf (1998: 70-71), his analysis cannot analyze GPs like the one in (1b). He further argues that there is no natural way of extending the analysis to handle these examples. He points out that all the possible extensions would violate the endocentricity condition.

Baker (1985) and Abney (1987) treat the NML *-ing* as an independent syntactic element. It is analyzed as the head of the gerund. Hence, among other problems (cf. Malouf 1998: 58-), their analyses violate the strong lexicalism condition in (5a). In Yoon's (1996) analysis, the NML does not have any function of determining the categorial status of GPs. Instead, he posits an empty category which converts a verbal host category into a nominal category. This analysis violates the null licensing condition in (5c). Lapointe (1993) introduces "dual lexical categories" like <N|V>. In <N|V>, N determines the external syntactic properties and V determines the internal syntactic properties of gerunds. These categories are not very well-motivated and necessarily complicate the whole system a lot. Kaiser (1998) posits a rule which converts a VP into a NP for the Poss-GPs and another rule which converts a VP into a NP dominating a VP for the Non-Poss-GPs. Putting aside the plausibility of these rules, they violate the endocentricity condition.[2]

Malouf (1998/2000) provides a Head-driven Phrase Structure Grammar analysis of GPs. Taking gerunds as a separate category, he analyzes *gerund* as a subtype of both *noun* and "*relational*" in the type hierarchy. Then, he posits a lexical rule to produce gerunds from the corresponding *-ing* forms of the verbs. His system accounts for the major properties of GPs in English. However, it also has some undesirable aspects. For example, the system works only under the assumption that gerunds constitute an independent category of *gerund*. Next, the category *relational*, as is pointed out by Chung, et al. (2001: fn. 10), "has no direct reflex in syntax at all." This is another instance of unmotivated categories/types.

Chung, et al. (2001) provide an "enriched" type hierarchy system for the analysis of GPs. They distinguish two groups of GPs: such English GPs as in (1a), i.e. the English Poss-GP, and such Korean gerunds as in (6a), the "*-ki*-GP," are analyzed as a subtype of *noun* and *verbal*, and others such as the one in (1b), i.e. the English Non-Poss-GP, and the one in (6b), the "*-um*-GP," are analyzed as a subtype of *nominal* and *verb*.

(6) a. cyon-i cip-ul ttena-ki-lul yaksok ha-yess-ta.
-Nom house-Acc leave-NML promise do-Past-Decl
'John promised to leave home.'
b. cyon-i cip-ul ttena-ass-um-i myengpayk-ha-ta.
-Nom house-Acc leave-Past-NML-Nom evident-be-Decl
'It is evident that John left home.'

They seem to provide a comprehensive analysis of English and Korean GPs. However, their analysis has generated more problems than it has solved. It has serious technical and/or conceptual problems. Firstly, one of their basic assumptions is that the English NML *-ing* and the Korean NMLs *-um/ki* are

[2] As for the difficulties with the analyses of Bresnan (1997), refer to Malouf (1988: 79-87).

verbal endings. Then, it becomes mysterious how the Poss-G and the *-ki*-G, which contain these verbal endings, become an element whose HEAD value is *noun*. Secondly, their analysis has contradictory nodes. For example, the HEAD value of a VP is *noun* in their (59), and the HEAD value of a *noun-poss-ph* category is *verb* in their (63).

4. Some Background Issues

Before we provide an Indexed Phrase Structure Grammar analysis of English and Korean GPs, we need to elucidate some issues to better understand their characteristics. We saw before that the morphological status of the Korean NMLs is not clear: they seem to be an entity which combines with a phrase in (3), while they seem to be attached to a word in (4). The NML *-um* cannot stand alone phonologically regardless of whether it is attached to a phrase or a word. Hence, it cannot be a normal word even when it is attached to a phrase. In the case when it is attached to a phrase as in (3), it has to be analyzed as a clitic: a unit which is a word syntactically but cannot stand alone phonologically.

Then, we need to clarify the morphological status of the NML when it is combined with a word. There are two possibilities: it can be an inflectional affix or a clitic. It cannot be a derivational affix because it comes after the inflectional affix *-ess*, as we can see from *mek-ess-um* in (4). In general, derivational suffixes come before inflectional suffixes. Hence, it can only be an inflectional affix if it is a word-internal element. However, it does not seem to be an inflectional affix, either. It occurs as the last element among the verbal elements. Notice that only delimiters and nominal particles can be attached to the right-hand side of it. One might assume that it comes on the same slot as such mood markers as declarative and imperative endings, which occupy the last position among verbal particles. However, we do not have evidence for this assumption (contra Chung, et al. 2001). As we will see shortly, we have even positive evidence which shows that the Korean NMLs, at least the NML *-ki*, occur after these mood markers. It would be very difficult to account for these distributional properties if we assume that they are inflectional affixes. In addition, the NMLs have the function of changing a verbal category into a nominal category. Only derivational affixes and words, including clitics, have this category-changing function. As they cannot be derivational affixes and independent words, we come to the conclusion that they are clitics.

The data in (7) show that the NML *-ki* can be attached to those elements with mood markers, which can stand alone as independent verbal units.

(7) a. pap-ul mek-nun/ess/keyss-ta-ki-ey (cf. mek-nun/ess/keyss-ta)
cooked rice-Acc eat-Pres/Past/Fut-Decl-NML-at
'As (he) tells/told me that (he) eats/ate/will eat meal, ...'

b. pap-ul mek-ø/ess/keyss-(nu)nya-ki-ey (cf. mek-ø/ess/keyss-(nu)nya)
-Pres/Past/Fut-Inter-NML-at
'As (he) asks/asked me if I eat/ate/will eat meal, ...'

c. pap-ul mek-ø-ela-ki-ey (cf. mek-ø-ela)
-Pres-Imp-NML-at 'As (he) orders/ordered me to eat meal, ...'
d. pap-ul mek-ø-ca-ki-ey (cf. mek-ø-ca)
-Pres-Prop-NML-at 'As (he) proposes/proposed to eat meal, ...'

We can see from these examples that the host of the NML *-ki* is not necessarily a dependent element. Hence, we can say at least that its host can be either a dependent element or an independent element. There is even a better way of generalizing its distribution. That is, we can assume that it combines only with independent verbal units. Apparent exceptions to this generalization are those GPs which do not contain the mood marker. However, if we assume that these GPs have a null-form (ø) mood marker, no *-ki*-GPs are exceptions to the generalization. As the mood marker in Korean is an inflectional ending, the empty element posited here is different from those syntactic empty categories which Pullum (1991) opposes to employ (cf. the null licensing condition). It is very common that one or more of the inflectional affixes in the template does not actually appear.

Although the two NMLs *-um* and *-ki* have largely the same properties, they have some differences as well. These differences are just what can be expected from our analysis and the reason for the differences is obvious and simple. The NMLs are different just because they are two different words with different phonological, syntactic and semantic characteristics. Remember that clitics are words syntactically. They are similar in some respects and different in other respects, just like any two words can be.

We concluded that the Korean NML is a clitic. We still need to account for the fact that it can be attached either to a full phrase or to a lower level phrase. We are going to provide a solution to this problem by assuming that GPs like those in (2) are structurally ambiguous (cf. Chae (1996) for light verb constructions). Under this assumption, the GPs can be analyzed as combining with different categories and/or bar-level expressions: [*John-i/uy* [*chay-ul* [[*ilk-ø*]$_{V'}$ [*-um*]$_{N}$]$_{N'}$]$_{NP}$ and [*John-i/uy* [[*chayk-ul ilk-ø*]$_{VP}$ [*-um*]$_{N}$]$_{NP}$]$_{NP}$. Here the NML is attached to a V' and VP, respectively. We assume that it can also be attached to a clausal unit. As for the case-marking, we assume that the nominative and accusative cases are assigned by the verb but the genitive case is assigned by the complex NP structure.

Now we can provide an account of the data in (3-4). In (3), the NML can be attached to the verb *po-ass*, the phrase [*yenhwa-lul po-ass*] or the phrase [*chayk-ul ilk-ko yenhwa-lul po-ass*]. However, the first two possibilities are ruled out because they lead to an ungrammatical coordinate structure of [VP-NP]. In (4), the NML can be attached to the verb *mek-* or higher units. These latter options will be ruled out because they would result in a non-constituent factor. Notice that a common factor in a conjoined structure should always be a constituent.

As for the last issue to be considered, we have to reexamine the "verbal properties" of GPs. In section 2, we saw that GPs can be modified by adverbials and can be negated with *not*. These are usually regarded as verbal properties. However, they are not unique to verbs (Malouf 1998: 35-37):

(8) a. Sandy rarely *gets* enough sleep.
  b. Sandy lives directly *beneath* a dance studio.
  c. Sandy's apartment has an insufficiently *thick* ceiling.
  d. Sandy grumbles about the dancers' nocturnally *rehearsing* Swan Lake.
  e. Sandy's repeated(*-ly) *complaint* brought no satisfaction.

(9) a. Not *surprisingly*, the defendant took the Fifth.
  b. The conference will be held in Saarbruecken, not *far* from the French border.
  c. Not *many* people who has gone over Niagra Falls live to tell about it.
  d. Pat's not *having* bathed for a week disturbed the other diners.
  e. *The not *processing* of the election results created a scandal.

As we can see in (8), adverbials can modify prepositions (b) and adjectives (c), as well as verbs (a) and gerunds (d). Based on such data as in (e), he says that only common nouns cannot be modified by adverbials. The data in (9) show that *not* can be used to negate adverbials (a-b) and determiners (c), as well as gerunds (d). We can see from the example in (e) that only nouns cannot be negated with *not*. These sets of data only show that gerunds behave differently from (common) nouns. They do not prove at all that gerunds have to be analyzed as verbal elements.

One other "verbal properties" of gerunds is that they take verbally case-marked complements like accusative objects. However, these complementation facts do not necessarily prove that gerunds are verbs, either (Malouf 1998: 36). Not only verbs but also postpositions and some other categories can take verbally case-marked complements. Especially, verbal nouns in Korean can have a variety of different complementation patterns. Although we cannot judge the categorial status of gerunds on the basis of the complementation phenomena, it is clear that a gerund takes the same type and number of complements as the verb constituting the gerund:

(10) a. John put a diamond ring into his pocket.
  b. [John's/John putting a diamond ring into his pocket] appalled his girlfriend.

The gerund *putting* in (b) and the verb *put* in (a) have the same set of complements (except some differences in the subjects). We need to account for this relationship whatever theoretical framework we may work in.

5. An IPSG Analysis

In this section, we will show that the special properties of the GPs in English and Korean can be accounted for effectively under an Indexed Phrase Structure Grammar (IPSG) approach. Chae (1992) develops an IPSG framework to provide a unified account of "lexically triggered unbounded discontinuities" in English (in *tough*- and similar constructions, comparative constructions, and result clause constructions). These constructions contain particular lexical items which characterize them and trigger the existence of other parts (i.e. targets) in them. The trigger in these constructions has a LICENSOR feature in a stack (hence, an Indexed Grammar), whose value is its target. The feature propagates through the tree as a FOOT feature and, popping out of the stack, licenses the target.

The main point of the present framework is that each lexical item which induces a particular construction has a stacked [LICENSOR XP] as a part of its syntactic information in the lexicon. LICENSOR is a kind of a FOOT feature and its value (i.e. XP) is the same as the target. The feature in the stack is discharged according to the following principle:

(11) The Principle of LICENSOR Discharge:
[LICENSOR XP] in the stack of a node (pops out of the stack and) licenses one of this node's daughters when the specification of the LICENSOR's value (i.e. XP) is the same as that of this daughter node.

(12) a. John is easy to please.

b.

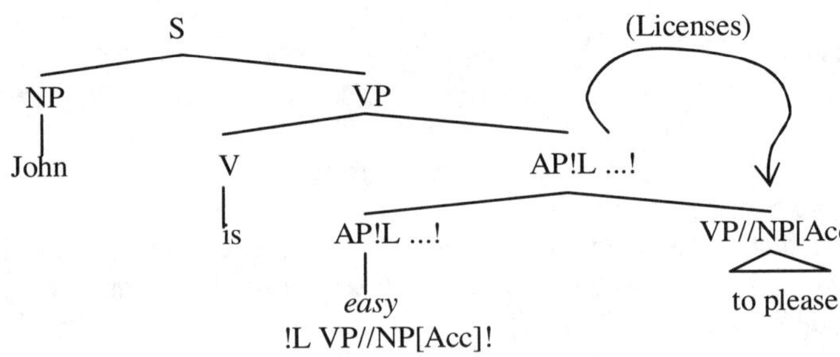

The lexical item *easy* has a stacked LICENSOR feature whose value is a VP with an accusative gap, i.e. !LICENSOR VP//NP[Acc]! (the stack is represented as a set of exclamation marks, !...!). This feature propagates through the tree. When it is instantiated on the upper AP node, it pops out of the stack to license the VP//NP[Acc] daughter, according to the principle (11). Notice that the specification of the licensed node is the same as that of the feature's value. Here we can effectively account for the fact that a particular lexical item is responsible for the existence of the construction concerned.

Under the present framework, we assume that the NMLs, whether they are affixes (as in English) or syntactic entities (as in Korean), have an empty-valued LICENSOR feature in the stack. When it combines with a verbal stem (in the lexicon) or a V'/VP (in syntax), the resulting unit becomes a N or N/'NP. Then, this unit takes the subcategorized elements of its host as the value of its LICENSOR feature. In (1), for example, when the English NML *-ing* combines with *paint*, which has the feature [SUBCAT <NP_1[Nom], NP_2[Acc]>], in the lexicon, the word *painting* becomes a N with [LICENSOR NP_2[Acc]-(NP_1[Acc])] in the stack. A few changes occur due to the lexical rule concerned. First, the subject of the GP, i.e. NP_1, takes the accusative case. This change is due to the fact that the gerund is tenseless while the input verb is potentially tensed. Second, the subject becomes optional, which is also related to the tense status change. Third, we assume that the object complement comes before the subject complement as the value of LICENSOR because the former is licensed first in default cases.

In (2), when the Korean NML *-um* combines with *ilk-*, which has the feature [SUBCAT <NP[Nom], NP[Acc]>], in syntax, the resulting phrase *ilk-um* becomes a N' with [LICENSOR NP[Acc]-NP[Nom]] in the stack. Here we do not have all the changes in the English lexical rule. The difference between English and Korean is that the NML and its host combine in the lexicon in English while they combine in syntax in Korean. The fact can be attributed to a property of lexical rules that the subject of a verb becomes optional when it combines with the NML *-ing* in English. On the other hand, this kind of change does not occur in Korean because the combination is a syntactic process. The subject of the GP is optional in Korean as well, but the deletion here is due to the general pro-drop phenomenon of the language. In Korean, the object can also be deleted naturally in appropriate context.

The present mechanism accounts for the most important "verbal property" of GPs, i.e. the property that they take the same set of complements as the source verb. They show nominal properties just because they are NPs with nominal heads. Now we can provide an IPSG analysis of the English GP sentences in (1) and the Korean GP sentences in (2), as follows:

(13)

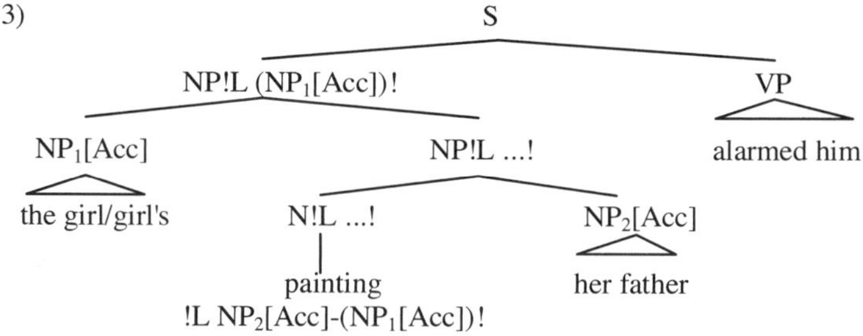

(14)

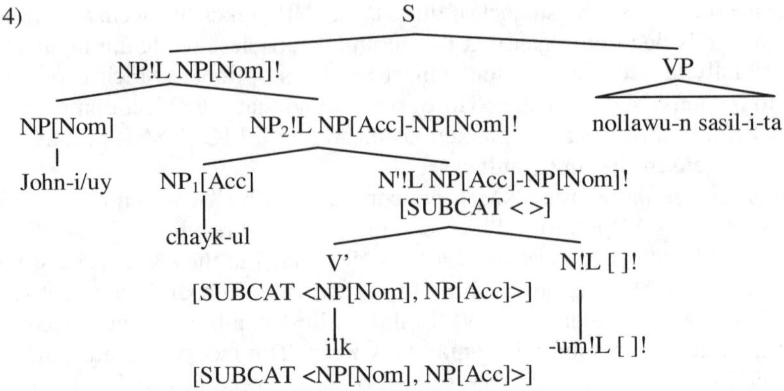

In (13), the lexical item *painting* is specified as having [LICENSOR NP[Acc] -(NP[Acc])] in the stack. In (14), the NML *-um* is specified as having an empty-valued LICENSOR in the lexicon, i.e. !LICENSOR [ ]!. This feature, which is introduced by *-um*, propagates through the tree. When a category with this feature combines with the projection of a verb, the subcategorized elements of the verb become the value of the feature. Notice that the verb *ilk-*, which has NP[Nom] and NP[Acc] as its complements, combines with *-um* as daughters of the N' node.

When a category has a daughter with the same specification as the value of its LICENSOR feature, the daughter will be licensed by the discharge principle in (11). Here we assume that when there is more than one entity as the value of the feature, only the left-most one will be considered. In English, the LICENSOR feature of the gerund has its value "from the beginning" in syntax, but in Korean the feature gets its value when the NML combines with its host verb. The feature will discharge its value when it combines with the verb's complements. For example, in (14), its NP[Acc] value will be discharged on the NP$_2$ node because this node has a node NP[Acc], i.e. NP$_1$, as its daughter.

The case difference between (1a)/(2a) and (1b)/(2b) in the subject can be accounted for with reference to the difference between the structural and inherent case assignment. The subject is in the genitive case in the former, while it is in the accusative/nominative case in the latter. The genitive case in the former is assigned structurally because the subject is in the specifier position of the NP. Here we have to assume that the inherent case is overridden by the structural case. The accusative/nominative case in the latter is assigned by the verb concerned. The accusative and nominative case difference between (1b) and (2b) is due to a parameter difference between English and Korean.

In our approach, gerunds are analyzed as verbal noun constructions in Korean (Chae 1997): they carry their own subcategorized elements and can be modified by adverbs (and adjectives), even though they are nouns. We assume that NML in Korean is a kind of nominal clitic, a noun in syntax but a dependent element in phonology. Then, we have a natural account of the fact that a category-changing element (the NML) can follow an inflectional affix in *mek-ess-um* (cf. (4)). We further assume that its host can be either a V' or VP, which means that the GPs in (2) are structurally ambiguous (as are verbal noun constructions in Korean) between [*chayk-ul* [*ilk-um*]] and [[*chayk-ul ilk*]-*um*]. This ambiguity accounts for the paradox in (3) and (4): only the second type of structure is legitimate in (3) and only the first type in (4).

6. Conclusion

The GP construction is one of the most difficult constructions to analyze effectively. The present research, however, has provided a reasonable analysis of it without adopting any costly mechanisms or special categories like empty or mixed/dual categories. We do not have to assume an arbitrary type hierarchy, either. We analyzed GPs as NPs with nominal heads. GPs are just NPs in observance of the basic principles of category determination[3] even though they have some verbal properties. In English, the word containing the NML affix *-ing* is analyzed as a noun and this noun is treated as the head of the GP. In Korean, the NML *-um* itself is analyzed as the head noun of GPs. In addition, the present analysis does not violate any of the theoretical desiderata Pullum (1991) posited, not only from a technical point of view but also from a conceptual point of view. We have an independent motivation for our analysis: verbal noun constructions in Korean. The result of this research turns out to be a strong evidence for the effectiveness of the theoretical framework employed in this research, i.e. Indexed Phrase Structure Grammar (IPSG).

References

Abney, Steven P. 1987. *The English noun phrase in its sentential aspect*. Ph.D. dissertation, MIT.

Baker, Mark C. 1985. Syntactic affixation and English gerunds. *Proceedings of the 4th West Coast Conference on Formal Linguistics*, 1-11. Stanford, CSLI Publications.

Bresnan, Joan. 1997. Mixed categories as head sharing constructions. *Proceedings of the LFG '97 conference*, 1-17. Stanford, CSLI Online Publications.

Chae, Hee-Rahk. 1992. *Lexically triggered unbounded discontinuities in English: An Indexed Phrase Structure Grammar approach*. Ph.D. dissertation, Ohio State University.

Chae, Hee-Rahk. 1996. Light verb constructions and structural ambiguity. *Language, information and computation* 11, 99-107. Kyunghee University.

Chae, Hee-Rahk. 1997. Verbal nouns and light verbs in Korean. *Language Research* 33.4, 581-600.

Chung, Chan, Jong-Bok Kim, Byung-Soo Park, and Peter Sells. 2001. Mixed categories and multiple inheritance hierarchies in English and Korean gerundive phrases. *Language Research* 37.4, 763-797.

Culicover, Peter. 1999. *Syntactic nuts*. Oxford Univ. Press.

---

[3] One of the most basic principles of category determination is that the category of an element should be determined on the basis of its (morphotactic and) distributional properties.

Kaiser, Lizanne. 1998. *The morphosyntax of clausal nominalization constructions.* Ph.D. dissertation, Yale University.

Lapointe, Steven G. 1993. Dual lexical categories and the syntax of mixed category phrases. *Proceedings of the 10th Eastern States Conference of Linguistics*, 199-210. Cornell Linguistics Circle.

Malouf, Robert P. 1998. *Mixed categories in the hierarchical lexicon*. Ph.D. dissertation, Stanford Univ. Published by CSLI Publications, Stanford, in 2000.

Pullum, Geoffrey K. 1991. English nominal gerund phrases as noun phrases with verb-phrase heads. *Linguistics* 29, 763-799.

Yoon, James H.S. 1996. Nominal gerund phrases in English as phrasal zero derivations. *Linguistics* 34, 329-356.

Extended Parallel Morphology for Korean *V-e V* Compounds

YOUNGJU CHOI
University of Illinois at Urbana-Champaign

0. Introduction

There has been a lot of debate on the locus of complex predicate formation. All complex predicates exhibit argument sharing and act as a single 'word'. However, debates arise when some of complex predicates sometimes show syntactic atomicity while others are transparent to syntactic processes.

Alsina (1997) compared the causatives of Chichewa and those of Catalan. He showed that two causative constructions are identical at the level of argument structure and they are subject to the same constraints. However it was shown that they are different in the phrasal level due to the fact that the former has one verbal form and the latter has two verbal forms. His conclusion is that synthetic morphological objects are formed in the lexicon and analytic or phrasal objects are formed in the syntax.

In response to Alsina (1997)'s Two Source Approach, Ackerman and Lesourd (1997) claimed the Single Source Approach for the causatives of Chichewa and Catalan, and phrasal predicates of Hungarian. They raised a question on the binary typology of Alsina (1997) since Hungarian complex predicates show both synthetic and analytic properties. They claimed that if Lexicalism abandons the lexical integrity hypothesis while keeping the belief that only lexical representations are responsible for information about argument structure, valence, and case government, all the complex predicates including the causatives of both languages and complex predicates of Hungarian fall in the lexicon.

However, this paper argues that the Two Source Approach and the Single Source Approach cannot be maintained for Korean verbal compounds. Empirical data from verbal compounds show that both approaches are not adequate and call for an extension of Parallel Morphology (Borer 1988, Shibatani and Kageyama 1988).

Korean verbal compounds are divided into two types according to types of the second verb in *V-e V* form. When two verbs are main predicates, they form a main verbal compound (MVC) and when the first verb is a main verb and the second verb is an auxiliary verb, two verbs form an auxiliary verbal compound (AVC). Several tests show that MVCs are lexically formed while AVCs are syntactically formed. Since both of the verbal compounds have analytic forms, *V-e V,* the Two Source Approach where the one-to-one correspondence between a synthetic form and lexical formation, and between an analytic form and syntactic formation is kept, cannot cover the data of Korean. The Single Source Approach where only synthetic complex predicates are allowed to have lexical integrity cannot cover the Korean data, either, since one type of analytic verbal compounds, namely AVCs, shows syntactic atomicity.

This calls for an extension of Parallel Morphology where the same morphological phenomena can occur in the lexicon and in the syntax, according to their behavior. Since we are dealing with analytic complex predicates, if Parallel Morphology is extended to cover analytic forms, it fits the Korean data. The same *V-e V* compounds can be formed in the lexicon and in the syntax according as whether they show lexical integrity or not. Moreover, the extension of Parallel Morphology has very positive results in that it explains other Korean affixation phenomenon neatly.

The paper is structured as follows. Section 1 briefly introduces the two approaches to complex predicates. Section 2 demonstrates that Korean verbal compounds behave differently depending on the type they belong to and argues that both of the two approaches introduced in section 1 are not appropriate for the Korean data. Section 3 shows how extended Parallel Morphology can explain the Korean verbal compounds and how it explain other Korean affixation phenomena. Section 4 shows that even though the two types of verbal compound have different behavior in many tests, they still share the same character both in predicate cleft formation and in delimiter insertion. However, it is argued that the same behavior cannot provide counter-evidence for the division in the loci of formation. Section 5 is a conclusion.

1. Two Approaches to Complex Predicates

1.1 The Two Source Approach

Alsina (1997) argues that morphological causatives are formed in the lexicon and syntactic causatives are formed in the syntax using the data from Chichewa and Catalan, respectively. While a single causative affix cannot scope over two conjoined verbal stems in Chichewa, a causative predicate can scope over two conjoined embedded predicates in Catalan. While the causative affix and stem of the former do not show separability, in Catalan, adverbs and parentheticals can be inserted between the causative predicate and the embedded predicate. The causatives of Chichewa can undergo category-changing morphology and those of Catalan cannot. Thus, he claimed that two causatives are formed in two different components of grammar, namely in the lexicon in Chichewa and in the syntax in Catalan.

He argued that argument structures of both causatives are formed by the same mechanism, namely, composition, in each locus of grammar. Example in (1) has a verbal root *-meny*, reciprocal affix *-an-* and causative affix *-its*. Each of them has a PRED value as shown in (2) by downward arrows. Each nonterminal node has a PRED value resulted from the composition of PRED values of two morphemes. First, the PRED value of the verbal root *meny* and that of the reciprocal morpheme *-an-* is composed and has a result of binding two arguments [P-A] and [P-P] since *-an-* is a argument structure binding morpheme. The causative morpheme *-its* is added and the PRED values of *meny-an-* and *-its* are composed again and has a result of binding of two argument structures. The derived complex predicate has a meaning of 'X made them hit each other' roughly.

(1) meny-an-its-a (Chichewa)
hit-RCP-CST-FV

(2)

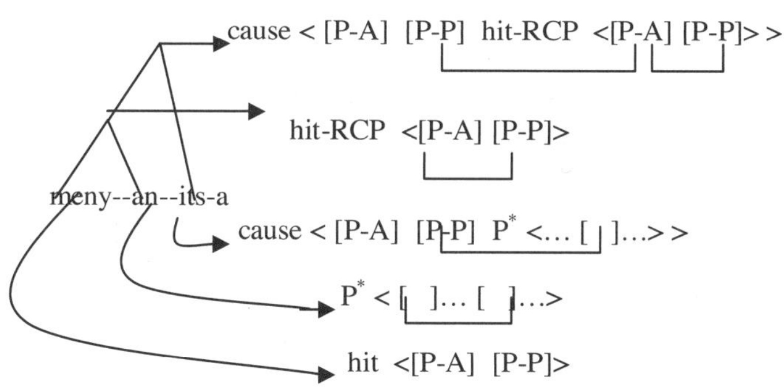

The same composition is applied to the case of Catalan where three separate verbs *faig, acabar,* and *llegir* form a complex predicate. They form a complex predicate in syntax since they show syntactic transparency in that they behave differently in coordination, in separability, and in nominalization from a causative morpheme and a verbal root in Chichewa. In syntax, as well as morphology, predicate composition is allowed, as shown in (4).

(3) Li faig acabar de llegir la carta (Catalan)
him (dat.) I. make finish of read the letter
'I make him finish reading the letter.'

(4)

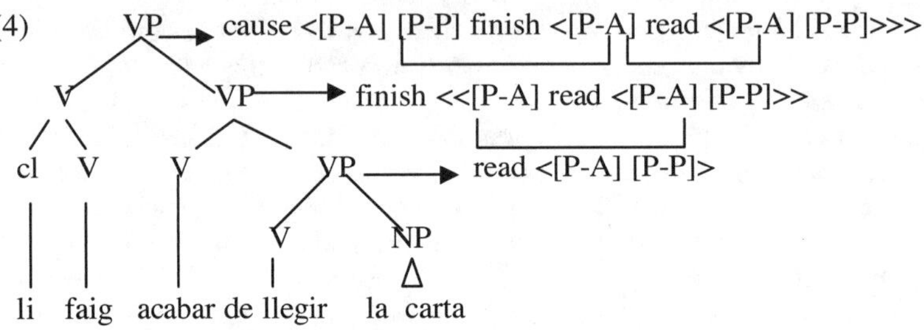

1.2 The Single Source Approach

Ackerman and Lesourd (1997) tried to cover three types of complex predicates; synthetic morphological ones (causatives of Chichew⇓a), analytic morphological ones (phrasal predicates of Hungarian), and non-morphological, syntactic ones (causatives of Catalan). They claimed that all the complex predicates (synthetic or analytic morphological predicates, or syntactic predicates) are formed in the lexicon. The information on argument structures, valency, and case of them is manipulated in the morphological component. Since only synthetic morphological objects show lexical integrity, the syntactic separation of analytic morphological predicates and syntactic predicates is explained by abandoning the lexical integrity hypothesis of lexicalism. Their claim is summarized as in (5).

(5) a. Chichewa : lexical information in the lexicon
synthetic morphological object : $[X\ \ Y]_V$
single syntactic atom : $[X\ \ Y]_V$
b. Hungarian: lexical information in the lexicon
analytic morphological object : $[X]_{Prt'}\ [Y]_V$
two syntactic atoms : $[X]_{Prt'}\ [Y]_V$
c. Catalan : lexical information in the lexicon
non-morphological object : $[X]_{V'}\ [Y]_V$
two syntactic atoms : $[X]_{V'}\ [Y]_V$

2. Different Behaviors of the Two Types of Korean Verbal Compounds

There are two types of verbal compounds in Korean. One is a MVC where both verbs are all main verbs, as in (6) and the other is an AVC where only the first verb is a main verb and the second verb is an auxiliary verb, as in (7).

(6) Haksayng-tul-i kel-e ka-ss-ta
student-Plu-Nom walk-E go-Pst-Dcl
'Students went (to somewhere), walking.'

(7) Haksayng-tul-i kel-e po-ass-ta
student-Plu-Nom walk-E try-Pst-Dcl
'Students tried to walk.'

The existence of two types of verbal compounds challenges the Single Source Approach and the Two Source Approach. The same analytic (*V-e V*) form of Korean verbal compounds seems to be formed in two different components of grammar since they show different behavior in terms of lexical integrity.

2.1 Gapping Test

As discussed in B-K Kim (1993), gapping is allowed in AVCs while it is not allowed in MVCs. Example (8a) is grammatical in the sense 'John dragged the carriage and Mary caught and pulled the string'. However, it is ungrammatical when the gapping is assumed. On the contrary, example (8b) is understood as if it has gapping.

(8) a.*John-i swuley-lul kkul~~-e tangki~~-ko,
J-Nom carriage drag(-E pull)-and
Mary-ka cwul-ul cap-**a tangki**-ess-ta
M-Nom string-Acc catch-E pull-Pst-Dcl
'John dragged and pulled the carriage and
Mary caught and pulled the string.'
b. John-i cheumulo sayngsen-ul yoliha~~-e po~~-ko,
J-Nom first fish-Acc cook-(E try)-and
Mary-ka cheumulo mek-**e po**-ass-ta
M-Nom first eat-E try-Pst-Dcl
'John first tried to cook a fish and Mary first tried to eat it.'

2.2 Verbal Proform Test

The verbal proform *kulehkey ha-* or *kula-* 'so do' can replace the first verb in AVCs but it cannot replace that in MVCs, as shown in the grammatical contrast between (9a) and (9b). In (9a), the proform *kelehkey ha-* or *kela-* cannot replace the first verb *cap-* while, in (9b), it can replace the first verb *tangki-*.

(9) a. *John-i cwul-ul cap-a tangki-ko,
J-Nom string-Acc catch-E pull-and
Mary-to cwul-ul **kulehkey ha/kula**-e tangki-ess-ta
M-also string-Acc so do / so do-E pull-Pst-Dcl
'John caught and pulled the string and Mary also did so and pulled it.'
b. John-i cwul-ul tangki-e po-ko,
J-Nom string-Acc pull-E try-and
Mary-to cwul-ul **kulehkey ha/kula**-e po-ass-ta
M-also string-Acc so do / so do-E try-Pst-Dcl
'John tried to pull the string and Mary also tried to do so.'

2.3 Extractibility Test

An object and the first verb of AVCs can undergo topicalization while those of MVCs cannot. As shown in (10b), when *ha-* is supported, extraction of the object and the first verb is allowed. However, regardless of the *ha*-support, extraction of the object and the first verb is not allowed, as in (10a).

(10) a. *Swuley-lul cap-ki-nun John-i (ha-e-) tangki-ko,
carriage-Acc catch-Nml-Top J-Nom (do-E) pull-and,
cwul-ul cap-ki-nun Mary-ka (ha-e-) tangki-ess-ta
string-Acc catch-Nml-Top M-Nom (do-E) pull-Pst-Dcl
'As for catching the carriage, John did and pulled,
and as for catching the string, Mary did and pulled.'
b. Swuley-ul cap-ki-nun John-i *(ha-e-) po-ko,
carriage-Acc catch-Nml-Top J-Nom (do-E) try-and,
cwul-ul cap-ki-nun Mary-ka *(ha-e-) po-ass-ta
string-Acc catch-Nml-Top M-Nom (do-E) try-Pst-Dcl
'As for catching the carriage, John tried to do so,
and as for catching the string, Mary tried to do so.'

2.4 Combinatorial Restriction

When there is more than one compound in a clause, the main compounds and the auxiliary compounds are never mixed. Both the main compounds and the auxiliary compounds undergo other auxiliary compound formation, as in (11).

(11) a. Cwul-(ul) [[[cap-a tangki $_{\text{MVC}}$]-e cwu $_{\text{AVC}}$]-e po $_{\text{AVC}}$]-a.
string-(Acc) catch-E pull-E give a favor for-E try-Imp
'Try to catch and pull the string for me, please.'

b. Cwul-(ul) [[[cap-a tangki $_{MVC}$]-e po $_{AVC}$]-a cwu $_{AVC}$]-e.
string-(Acc) catch-E pull-E try-E give a favor for-Imp
'Try to catch and pull the string for me, please.'

However, neither of them can undergo main compound formation, as in (12).

(12) a. *Cwul-(ul) [[[cap-a cwu $_{AVC}$]-e tangki $_{MVC}$]-e po $_{AVC}$]-a.
string-(Acc) catch-E give a favor for-E pull-E try-Imp
'Try to catch and pull the string for me, please.'

b. *Cwul-(ul) [[[cap-a po $_{AVC}$]-a tangki $_{MVC}$]-e cwu $_{AVC}$]-e.
string-(Acc) catch-E try-E pull-E give a favor for-Imp
'Try to catch and pull the string for me, please.'

If AVCs and MVCs are formed in the same component of the grammar, then it is predicted that two kinds of complex predicates can be mixed together because both of them use the same strategy, using *–e* between each verb. However, it turns out that the mixed predicates are all ungrammatical, as in (12).

2.5 Prefixation Test

Prefixation, known as a lexical process, is possible for MVCs while it is not possible for AVCs. As shown in (13), the verbal root *tol* 'turn' does not combine with the prefix *toy-* 're'. However, the MVC *tol-a o-* 'come back' combines with the prefix *toy-,* forming *toy-tol-a o-* 'come back again', as in (14).

(13) *Ku ai-tul-i toy-tol-ass-ta
the child-plu-Nom re-turn-Pst-Dcl
'The children returned.'

(14) Ku ai-tul-i toy-tol-a o-ass-ta (cf. tol-a o-ta 'come back')
the child-plu-Nom re-turn-E come-Pst-Dcl
'The children came back again.'

However, the AVCs do not allow prefixation.[1]

(15) a. Ku ai-tul-i tol-a po-ass-ta
the child-plu-Nom turn-E try-Pst-Dcl
'The children tried to turn around.'

b. *Ku ai-tul-i toy-tol-a po-ass-ta
the child-plu-Nom re-turn-E try-Pst-Dcl
'The children tried to return.'

[1] When *toy-tol-a po-ass-ta* has an idiomatic meaning, 'thought of the past', the sentence is grammatical.

In summary, since the MVCs show lexical integrity and the AVCs show syntactic separability, they seem to be formed in different loci of the grammar.

3. A Proposal: Extended Parallel Morphology

The position of Alsina (1997) is inappropriate for Korean verbal compounds. The one-to-one correspondence between morphological complex predicates and lexical formation, and between analytic complex predicates and syntactic formation cannot be maintained since all the analytic verbal compounds in Korean show either opacity or transparency, depending on the type.

The position of Ackerman and Lesourd (1997) is also inappropriate. Since they abandon the lexical integrity hypothesis for analytic objects, they cannot cover the case where some of analytic complex predicates do show lexical integrity. Korean MVCs, though they are analytic objects, show integrity for many tests.

3.1 Parallel Morphology and Extended Parallel Morphology

According to Shibatani and Kageyama (1988), and Borer (1988, 1993), the same morphological processes are allowed both in the lexicon and in the syntax. Some complex predicates are formed in the lexicon and they show the lexical integrity. Others are formed in syntax and they show the syntactic separability.

(16)
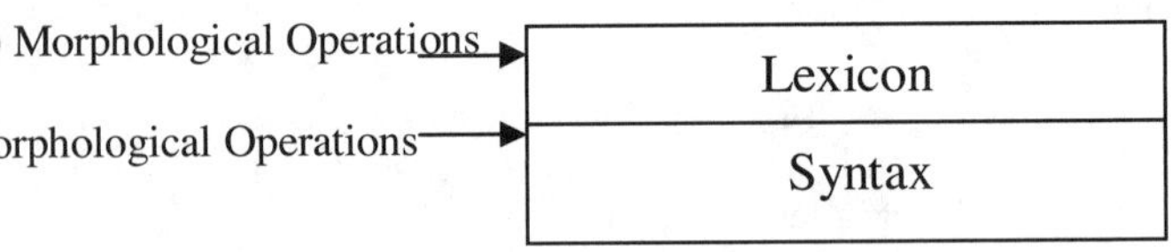

If not only morphological operations but also analytic combinations are carried out in different loci, the different behavior of Korean verbal compounds can be explained. Phrasal composition is allowed in the lexicon or in syntax and shows different properties depending on the locus of formation.

(17)
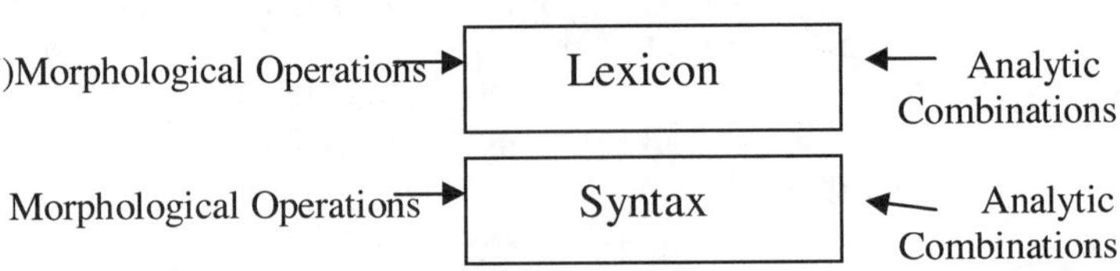

3.2 Further Implication

The result of the extension of Parallel Morphology is very positive when we think of affixation phenomena in Korean. Korean phrasal affixes generally show lexical integrity with the words they are attached (See J. H-S Yoon (1989, 1996), C. Park (2002)).

In (18), even though the affixes *–ass* and *–ta,* attached respectively to the root *nol-* and to the affixed root *nol-ass-,* are not separable from the entire word *nol-ass-ta*, they are attached to the entire phrases *pap-ul mek-ko nol-* and *pap-ul mek-ko nol-ass-*, respectively. Thus, phrasal affixes show lexical integrity.

(18) Chelswu-nun pap-ul mek-ko nol-ass-ta
C-Top meal-Acc eat-and play-Pst-Dcl
'Chelswu ate the meal and played.'

(19)

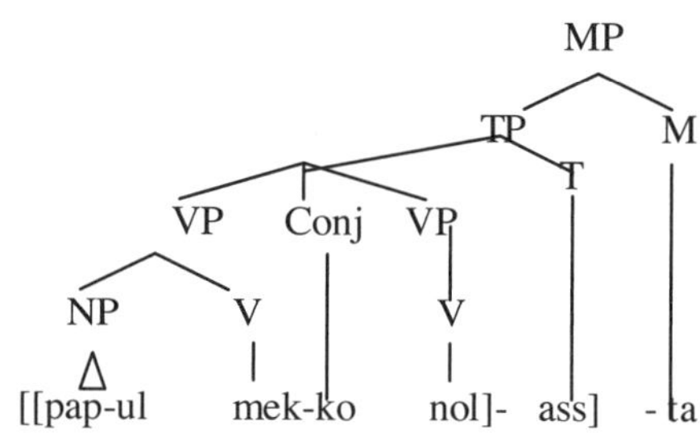

4. The Same Properties of the Two Types of the Verbal Compounds

Even though the two types of verbal compound show differences in many tests, they share the same properties in that both of them allow the insertion of delimiters and they, both, allow partial predicate cleft constructions. However, these two properties do not shake the conclusion of the section 2 and section 3.

The first property MVCs and AVCs share is that both of them allow the insertion of delimiters between two verbs, as in (20).

(20) a. Ku ai-tul-i cwul-ul cap-a-**man** tangki-ess-ta
the child-Plu-Nom string-Acc catch-E-delim pull-Pst-Dcl
'The children only caught and pulled the string.'

b. Ku ai-tul-i cwul-ul cap-a-**man** po-ass-ta
the child-Plu-Nom string-Acc catch-E-delim try-Pst-Dcl
'The children only tried to catch the string.'

The insertion of the delimiters seems to have two requirements. The free form requirement (J H-S Yoon (1995)) is the one and the other is that it needs two X° forms. The *-a* makes a verbal root a free form so that it can host delimiters.

(21)

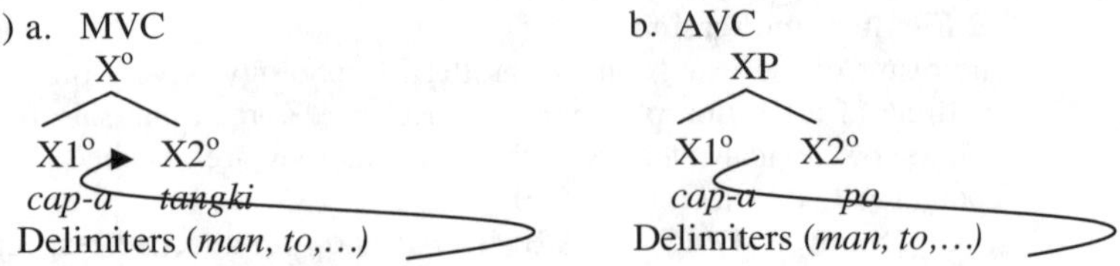

The second property MVCs and AVCs share is that both of them allow partial repetition of predicates in the predicate cleft construction formation. As shown in (22), in both MVCs and AVCs, only the second verb is repeated.

(22) a. Ku ai-tul-i cwul-ul cap-a tangki-ki-nun tangki-ess-ta
the child-Plu-Nom string-Acc catch-E pull-Nml-Top pull-Pst-Dcl
'As for catching and pulling the string, the children pulled it.'
b. Ku ai-tul-i cwul-ul cap-a po-ki-nun po-ass-ta
the child-Plu-Nom string-Acc catch-E try-Nml-Top try-Pst-Dcl
'As for trying to catch the string, the children tried it.'

Some argue that partial repetition is the result of the syntactic separation of two verbs (Yi E-Y 1996). However, the analysis of J-M Jo (2001, 2003) shows that partial repetition is not a syntactic phenomenon but it is the result of partial deletion in PF.[2] As shown in (23a), *ku ai-tul-i cwul-ul cap-a tangki* is moved out and, among the remaining copy, *ku ai-tul-i cwul-ul cap-a* is deleted, resulting in the sentence, *ku ai-tul-i cwul-ul cap-a tangki-ki-nun tangki-ess-ta*. Example (23b) has the same result since it follows the same steps of movement and deletion.

---

[2] According to J-M Jo (2001, 2003), predicate cleft constructions are formed by movement in syntax and optional deletion of the copy of the moved elements in PF. For example, from (ia), *Chelswu-ka ku chayk-ul ilk-* is topicalized and its copy remains in its original position as in (ib). The dummy nominalizer *ki* is inserted for the topical marker *–nun* to be attached, and the copy is optionally deleted in PF, as in (ic). Finally, we get the result (id).

(i) a. Chelswu-ka ku chayk-ul ilk-ess-ta
C-nom the book-acc read-pst-decl
'Chelswu read the book.'
b. Chelswu-ka ku chayk-ul ilk Chelsw-ka ku chayk-ul ilk-ess-ta
C-nom the book-acc read C-nom the book-acc read-pst-decl
(Topicalization and its copy)
c. Chelswu-ka ku chayk-ul ilk-ki-nun (insertion of KI)
C-nom the book-acc read-KI-top
~~Chelsw-ka ku chayk-ul~~ ilk-ess-ta (optional deletion of the copy)
C-nom the book-acc read-pst-decl
d. Chelswu-ka ku chayk-ul ilk-ki-nun ilk-ess-ta (the result)

(23) a. Ku ai-tul-i cwul-ul cap-a tangki-ki-nun
the child-Plu-Nom string-Acc catch-E pull-Nml-Top
[~~Ku ai-tul-i cwul-ul cap-a~~] tangki-ess-ta
the child-Plu-Nom string-Acc catch-E pull-Pst-Dcl
'As for catching and pulling the string, the children pulled it.'

b. Ku ai-tul-i cwul-ul cap-a po-ki-nun
the child-Plu-Nom string-Acc catch-E try-Nml-Top
[~~Ku ai-tul-i cwul-ul cap-a~~] po-ass-ta
the child-Plu-Nom string-Acc catch-E try-Pst-Dcl
'As for trying to catch the string, the children tried it.'

5. Conclusion

The same form of *V-e V* compound is divided into two kinds according to the type of the second verb. The two types of compound behave differently in terms of lexical integrity in many tests. This separation of the same analytic form requires an extension of the Parallel Morphology model. The extension is able to cover not only the verbal compounds but also other affixation phenomena of Korean.

References

Ackerman, F., and P. Lesourd 1997. Toward a lexical representation of phrasal predicates. In Alex Alsina, Joan Bresnan and Peter Sells (eds.) *Complex Predicates*, 67-106. Stanford, CSLI Publications.

Alsina, A. 1997. A theory of complex predicates: Evidence from causatives in Bantu and Romance. In Alex Alsina, Joan Bresnan and Peter Sells (eds.) *Complex Predicates*, 203-246 Stanford, CSLI Publications.

Borer, H. 1988. On the morphological parallelism between compounds and constructs. *Yearbook of Morphology* 1:45-66.

Bresnan, J., and S. Mchombo. 1995. The lexical integrity principle: evidence from Bantu. *Natural Language and Linguistic Theory* 13.2:181-254.

Choi, Y. 2003. Handout for presentation of the 10th Harvard International Symposium on Korean Linguistics. University of Illinois at Urbana-Champaign.

Jo, J-M. 2001. Handout for Syntax Reading Group. Korean (predicate) cleft constructions. University of Illinois at Urbana-Champaign.

Jo, J-M. 2003. Handout for presentation of the 10th Harvard International Symposium on Korean Linguistics. University of Illinois at Urbana-Champaign.

Kageyama, T. 1989. The place of morphology in the grammar: verb-verb compounds in Japanese. *Yearbook of Morphology* 2:73-94.

Kim, B-K. 1993. The structure and the argument-linking convention of V-V compounds in Korean. In Susumu Kuno et al (eds.) *Harvard Studies in Korean Linguistics* V:180-192. Hanshin Publishing Company.

Park, C. 2002. Some evidence for Korean nominalizers as phrasal affixes. *Proceedings of the international summer conference of the LSK*, 475-487. Seoul: Thaehaksa.

Shibatani, M., and T. Kageyama 1988. Word formation in a modular theory of grammar: Postsyntactic compounds in Japanese. *Language* 64: 451-484.

Yi, E-Y. 1996. Verb compound and the serial verb constructions in Korean. In Hee-Don Ahn et.al (eds.) *Morphosyntax in Generative Grammar*. Proceedings of 1996 Seoul International Conference on Generative Grammar, 445-463. Seoul: Hankuk Publishing Co.

Yoon, J. H-S. 1989. *A Restricted Theory of Morphosyntactic Interaction and Its Consequences*. Ph.D. Dissertation, University of Illinois at Urbana-Champaign.

Yoon, J. H-S. 1995. Nominal, verbal and crosscategorial affixation in Korean. *Journal of East Asian Linguistics* 4: 325-356.

Yoon, J. H-S. 1996. A syntactic accounts of category-changing phrasal morphology: nominalizations in English and Korean. In Hee-Don Ahn et.al (eds.) *Morphosyntax in Generative Grammar*. Proceedings of 1996 Seoul International Conference on Generative Grammar, 63-86. Seoul: Hankuk Publishing Co.

Dummy Plural Marker *-Tul* in Gapping and the Theory of Gapping *

DAEHO CHUNG
Hanyang University

1. Introduction

In this paper I observe that gapping in Korean feeds an environment which licenses otherwise unlicensed dummy plural marker (DPM) *-tul* and discuss some implications the observation induces as to the theory of gapping.[1]

Before going into the main discussion, it is in order to have some background knowledge on the behaviors of DPM. As discussed in the

* I would like to thank all the audience at the 13th Japanese/Korean Linguistics Conference. Special thanks to the following people for valuable comments and suggestions: Hee-Rahk Chae, Chung-hye Han, J.R. Hayashishita, Hajime Hoji, Jong-Bok Kim, Hyosang Lee, Mamoru Saito, James Yoon, Ayumi Ueyama, among others.

[1] As will be clear, the term 'gapping' in this paper is to be theory neutrally understood since the so-called gapping construction has been analyzed in various ways. See Sections 3 and 4.

literature (Song 1975, Choe 1988, Kuh 1987, Lee 1991, Park and Sohn 1993, Sohn 1994, Moon 1995, Ym 2002, Hong 2003, among others), DPM in Korean looks like a plural morpheme in its form but does not denote plurality of the element it is attached to. Consider the difference between the underlined plural marker <u>tul</u> and the boldfaced DPM **tul** in (1).

(1) a. yay-<u>tul</u>$_i$-a, e$_i$ ppalli-**tul** mwul-**tul** masi-ela.
guy-PL-VOC fast-DPM water-DPM drink-IMP
'Guys, drink water quickly.'

b. Sue-wa Kim-i ecey chayk-<u>tul</u>-ul-**tul** sa-ess-ta.
S.-and K-NOM yesterday book-PL -ACC-DPM buy-PST-DE
'Sue and Kim bought some books yesterday.'

As in (1a), DPM can be attached not only to count nouns but also to adverbs and mass nouns, which inherently resist plurality.[2]

According to Choe (1988), DPM licensing is licensed by a local plural subject. Thus DPM involves three factors, i.e., subjecthood, plurality, and locality, as exemplified in (2) through (4):

(2) Subjecthood Condition

a. <u>Sue-wa Kim-i</u> swukcey-lul ilccik-**tul** ceychwulha-ess-ta.
S.-and K. -NOM assignment-ACC early-DPM submit-PST-DE
'Sue and Kim submitted their assignment early.'

b. *Tom-i <u>Sue-wa Kim</u>-ul seykey-**tul** ttayli-ess-ta.
T.-NOM S.-and K.-ACC hard-DPM hit-PST-DE
'Tom hit Sue and Kim hard.'

c. *Tom-i <u>Sue-wa Kim</u>-eykey ton-ul manhi-**tul** cwu-ess-ta.
T.-NOM S.-and K.-Dat money much-DPM give-PST-DE
'Tom gave a lot of money to Sue and Kim.'

d. *Tom-i <u>Sue-wa Kim</u>-uloputhe ton-ul manhi-**tul** pat-ess-ta.
T.-NOM S.-and K.-from money-ACC much-DPM receive-PST-DE
'Tom received money from Sue and Kim.'

(3) Plurality Condition
{<u>haksayng-tul</u>-i/Sue<u>-wa Kim</u>-i/*<u>Kim</u>-i} ilccik-**tul** ttena-ess-ta.
Student-PL-NOM/S.-and K.-NOM/K.-NOM early-DPM leave-PST-DE
'{Students/Sue and Kim/Kim} left early.'

---

[2]Plural morpheme *tul* and DPM *tul* take different morphological slots, as shown in (1b), where both appear at the same time. See Lee (1991).

(4) Locality Condition

a. Sue-wa Kim-i ilccik-**tul** ttena-ess-ta.
S.-and K. -NOM early-DPM leave-PST-DE
'Sue and Kim left early.'

b. *Sue-wa Kim-un [Tom-i ilccik-**tul** ttena-ess-ta]-ko malha-n-ta.
S.-and K.-TOP T. -NOM early-DPM leave-PST-DE-C say-PRES-DE
'Sue and Kim say that Tom left early.'

As shown in the contrast between (2a) vs. (2b-d), DPM is licensed by a subject[3] but hardly by other functions such as an object, an indirect object or an oblique adjunct element. The trigger should be plural, as shown in (3). The examples in (4) show that DPM and its trigger should be located in the same clause.[4]

Taking examples like (5) and (6) below,[5] Ym (2002) challenges the subjecthood condition and proposes an event semantics based theory, where DPM is licensed as long as an event plurality is guaranteed.

(5) han sonyen-i phungsen han kay ssik-ul sinnakey-**tul** thettuli-ess-ta.
one boy-NOM balloon one CL each-ACC amusedly-DPM break-PST-DE
'A boy broke each balloon in amusement.'

(6) ku kyengchal-i ai-tul-ul cip-eyse-**tul** ttayli-ess-ta.
that police;officer-NOM child-PL-ACC house-at-DPM beat-PST-DE
'The police officer beat the children at their houses.'

The judgment on the data is controversial. Besides, there is crucial evidence that DPM is constrained by syntactic factors, whether or not it is

---

[3]The triggering subject need not be overtly realized.

(i) a. e eti-tul ka-ni?
where-DPM go-QE
'Where are (you guys) going?

b. [Tom-kwa Mary]$_i$-nun e$_i$ ilccik-tul ka-ess-ni?
T.-and M.-TOP early-DPM go-PST-QE
'Did Tom and Mary leave early?'

[4]According to Moon (1995), the locality condition is loosened in a logophoric environment:

(i) (=Moon 1995:356, his (2))
Salam-tul-i [$_S$ nalssi-ka manhi-**tul** chwuweciessta]-ko malhapnita.
People-PL-NOM weather-NOM a lot-DPM became;cold-Comp say
'People say that the weather became cold a lot.'

He argues that DPM behaves like an anaphor and is subject to Binding Principle A. Logophoricity extends the binding domain for DPM, just as for other regular anaphors.

[5]See Park and Sohn (1993) for similar examples.

constrained by semantics as well. (See Chung 2003 for further discussion.) Notice that DPM licensing is subject to the c-command condition:

(7) *han sonyen-i-**tul** phungsen han kay ssik-ul thettuli-ess-ta.
one boy-NOM-DPM balloon one CL each-ACC break-PST-DE
'A boy broke each balloon.'

(8) *ku kyengchal-i-**tul** ai-tul-ul cip-eyse ttayli-ess-ta.
that police officer-NOM-DPM child-PL-ACC house-at beat-PST-DE
'The police officer beat the children at their houses.'

If the event semantics were solely responsible for DMP licensing, there would be no reason to rule out the sentences in (7) and (8), since they contain elements inducing an event plurality, just as the sentences in (5) and (6) are claimed to do so.

Furthermore, the main discussion in later sections does not crucially hinge on the subjecthood condition. Thus, I will assume that DPM licensing is dependent on syntactic factors such as c-command and locality, whether or not semantics is additionally relevant.

This paper is organized as follows. In Section 2, I observe that gapping feeds DPM licensing. In Section 3 and Section 4, which are the main part of this paper, I discuss what theoretical implications this observation brings forth with regard to the theory of gapping. Section 3 shows that previous analyses put forth in the literature do not adequately account for the DPM licensing in gapping contexts. In Section 4, I compare two alternative analyses and then adopt one. Section 5 summarizes the paper.

2. DPM Licensing Fed by Gapping

In this section I observe that gapping feeds an environment in which otherwise unlicensed DPMs are licensed, as exemplified below:

(9) a. Tom-i nonmwun-ul yelsimhi(*-**tul**) ilk-ko (kuliko)
T.-NOM paper-ACC hard-DPM read-and (and)
Sam-i chayk-ul yelsimhi(*-**tul**) ilk-ess-ta.
M.-NOM book-ACC hard-DPM read-PST-DE
'Tom read papers hard and Sam read books hard.'

b. Tom-i nonmwun-ul (kuliko) Sam-i chayk-ul yelsimhi-**tul**
T.-NOM paper-ACC (and) S.-NOM book-ACC hard-DPM
ilk-ess-ta.
read-PST-DE
'Tom read papers hard and Sam books.'

(10) a. John-i [Mary-eykey nonmwun-ul yelsimhi(*-**tul**) ilk-key] ha-ko
J.-NOM M.-Dat paper-ACC hard-DPM read-cause-and
[Tom-eykey chayk-ul yelsimhi(*-**tul**) ilk-key] ha-ess-ta.
T.-Dat book-ACC hard-DPM read-cause-PST-DE
'John made Mary read papers hard and Tom read books hard.'

b. John-i [Mary-eykey nonmwun-ul] kuliko
J.-NOM M.-Dat paper-ACC and
[Tom-eykey chayk-ul yelsimhi-**tul** ilk-key] ha-ess-ta.
T.-Dat book-ACC hard-DPM read-cause-PST-DE
'John made Mary read papers hard and Tom read books hard.'

In a non-reduced coordinate structure with a singular subject, as in (9a) and (10a), DPMs are not licensed in either conjunct, just as in simple sentences. See (3). If, however, gapping takes place, DPMs become acceptable, as in (9b) and (10b).

The contrast between (9a)/(10a) vs. (9b)/(10b) are of some theoretical significance in the following senses. First, it provides additional evidence that semantics is not solely responsible for DPM licensing: there is little semantic difference between the two (gapped vs. gapless) structures with respect to the event plurality in the sense of Ym (2002). Despite the lack of difference in semantics, the two structures differ in DPM licensing: DPM is licensed only when gapping takes place. Second, the contrast points to a particular theory of gapping, as will be discussed in Sections 3 and 4.

3. DPM Licensing in Gapping and Previous Gapping Analyses

The contrast between (9a)/(10a) vs. (9b)/(10b) cannot be accounted for by previous theories put forth in the literature as to the so-called gapping structure in Korean or Japanese. This section shows that the gapping facts go against three analyses: Abe and Hoshi's (1993, 1997) LF-Copying Analysis, Kim's (1997) PF-Deletion Analysis, and Saito's (1987) Right Node Raising (RNR) Analysis.

Let us first consider Abe and Hoshi's (1993, 1997) analysis, which is illustrated schematically in (11):

(11) a. LF-Raising
XP ... α_i ··· ~~[$_{VP}$ ··· e_i ···]~~ & KP ... β_j ··· [$_{VP}$ ··· e_j V...]

b. LF-copying
XP ... α_i ··· [$_{VP}$ ··· e_i V...] & KP ... β_j ··· [$_{VP}$ ··· e_j V...]

Remnants in gapping move out of the ellipsis site at LF and the phrase in the ellipsis site is copied from the second conjunct.[6]

Kim (1997) proposes a PF-Deletion Analysis, in which remnants move out of the ellipsis site in overt syntax for the purpose of focus feature checking and the phrase in the ellipsis site loses its phonetic content via PF-Deletion, as illustrated in (12).

(12) a. Focus Raising

$\alpha_i \ldots \beta_j \ldots [_{TP}\ e_i \ldots e_j \ldots V]\ \ \&\ \gamma_k \ldots \delta_l \ldots [_{TP}\ e_k \ldots e_l \ldots V]$

b. PF-Deletion

$\alpha_i \ldots \beta_j \ldots$ ~~$[_{TP}\ e_i \ldots e_j \ldots V]$~~ $\&\ \gamma_k \ldots \delta_l \ldots [_{TP}\ e_k \ldots e_l \ldots V]$

What is common in both Abe and Hoshi's analysis and Kim's is that elements in the second conjunct do not have any direct syntactic relation with elements in the first conjunct except that they provide some content identification for the ellipsis site in the first conjunct.

Both Abe & Hoshi's and Kim's analyses incorrectly predict to rule out (9b) and (10b) as well as (9a) and (10a). Notice that the sentences in (b) start out from those in (a), according to them. The subject-predicate relation remains intact in the second conjunct, where there is no appropriate plural element to license the DPM.

Saito's (1987) analysis fails as it stands, too. According to him, gapping is an instance of a stylistic right node raising at PF as illustrated in (13b), where α is RNRed across the board.

(13) a. [[XP…YP…[$_\alpha$ … -DPM …V] AND [KP…LP…[$_\alpha$ … -DPM…V]]

b. [[[XP…YP…e_i] AND [KP…LP…e_i]] [$_\alpha$ … -DPM …V …]$_i$]

ATB RNR

RNR taking place at PF in his system, the syntactic structure will remain intact. Then gapping should display no variation in DPM licensing. This is not borne out as was seen in the previous section. Even if RNR in gapping takes place in syntax, Saito's theory does not properly account for DPM licensing in gapping contexts. Notice that before gapping takes place, DPM is not licensed in either conjunct when there is no appropriate plural subject, as in (9a) and (10a). Even after RNR takes place, there is no appropriate trigger if RNR is upward as an instance of movement and the c-command

[6]I wonder how it is ever possible in (11a) to extract an element from an ellipsis site, which is null before copying takes place.

condition is not satisfied. Notice XP and KP in (13b) do not c-command the DPM contained in α, that is, the RNRed phrase.

What if gapping involves a large-scale RNR, for example, a clausal level RNR. This would be possible, as shown in (14), where the clausal level RNR is preceded by leftward movement of subjects and objects. This seems to be able to remedy the problem, depending on the number interpretation of the subject in the RNRed part, i.e., t_i in (14b).

(14) a. Scrambling or Focus Raising
[[$_{S1}$ Tom$_i$ [$_{S2}$ paper$_j$ [$_{S3}$ t_i t_j hard-DPM read]]] AND
[[$_{S1}$ Sam$_i$ [$_{S2}$ book$_j$ [$_{S3}$ t_i t_j hard-DPM read]]]

b. Right Node Raising
[[$_{S1}$ Tom$_i$ [$_{S2}$ paper$_j$ [$_{S3}$ t_k]]] AND
[[$_{S1}$ Sam$_i$ [$_{S2}$ book$_j$ [$_{S3}$ t_k]]] [$_{S3}$ t_i t_j hard-DPM read]$_k$]

If t_i in S3 in (14b) were interpreted as a plural subject, the DPM would be licensed. However, the problem that remains unexplained is that DPMs in (14a) are unlicensed before the RNR takes place. Notice that both conjuncts have a singular subject at the outset. (14a) with a DPM realized in either conjunct is ungrammatical. One last option left is to assume that DPM is merged after RNR takes place. This would, however, lead to a cyclicity problem in derivation or a violation of Chomky's (1995) so-called extension condition. Notice that the DPM in (14b) is properly contained in the RNRed part.

Furthermore, any theory that resorts to leftward movement faces a serious problem since gapping is immune from various island constraints like the Left Branch Condition, the Complex Noun Phrase Constraint, and the Adjunct Condition, as shown in (15) through (17).[7]

(15) The Left Branch Condition
John-i Mary kuliko Tom-i Sue-uy nonmwun-ul towacwu-ess-ta.
J.-NOM M. and T.-NOM S.-GEN paper-ACC help-PST-DE
(Lit) 'John helped Mary's paper and Tom helped Sue's paper.'

(16) The Complex NP Constraint
John-i Mary kuliko Tom-i Sue-ka ssu-un nonmwun-ul simsaha-ess-ta.
J.-NOM M. and T.-NOM S.-NOM write-ADN paper-ACC review-PST-DE
'John reviewed the paper that Mary wrote and Tom reviewed the paper that Sue wrote.'

---

[7]Kim (1997: 201-202) admits that gapping in Korean may violate the Left Branch Condition, although he claims that it is generally subject to island constraints.

(17) The Adjunct Condition
Tom-un Sam kuliko Jim-un Sue-ka o-ki ttaymwuney ttena-ess-ta.
J.-Con S. and J.-Con S.-NOM come-PST-because leave-PST-DE
'Tom (left because) Sam (is coming) and Jim left early because Sue is coming.'

Being insensitive to such island constraints, gapping in Korean doesn't seem to involve syntactic movement. Once the leftward raising is not guaranteed, the large-scale RNR analysis that crucially hinges on the leftward movement fails to account for the feeding relation of gapping in DPM licensing. Abe & Hoshi's analysis and Kim's, face the same problem since they also assume leftward movement.

4. Toward an Explanation

To satisfy the licensing conditions mentioned in Section 1, especially the plurality condition, DPMs in (9) and (10) should be somehow directly linked to the subjects scattered in both conjuncts. How is this possible? One possible solution is to allow some sort of a (three-dimensional) parallel (or tandem) structure along the similar lines of Goodall (1987), Muadz (1991), and Moltmann (1992), as schematically represented below:

(18) Tom-NOM paper-ACC —— hard-DPM read.
Sam-NOM book-ACC

(19) John-NOM — Mary-DAT [PRO paper-ACC —— hard-DPM read] caused
Tom-DAT [PRO book-ACC

Given the parallel structure, it naturally follows that gapping feeds DPM licensing. As shown below in (20), DPM is linked to a local plural subject, although the subject is scattered across the conjuncts.

(20)

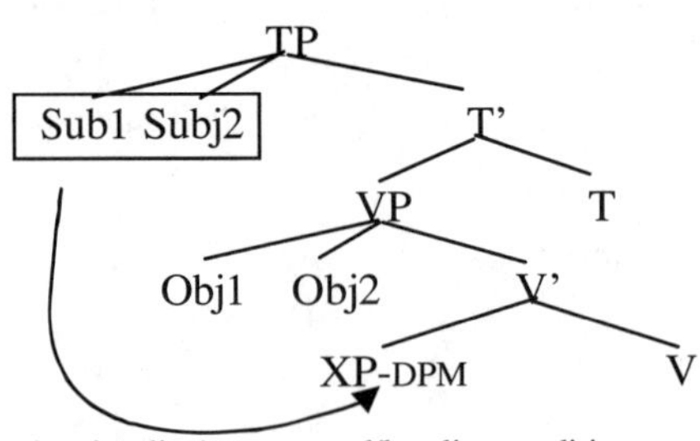

Satisfies the plurality/c-command/locality conditions

The ungrammaticality of (9a) and (10a) with the DPMs realized also follows since DPMs in such sentences have no appropriate plural trigger in the local context, i.e., in each conjunct, as shown in (21).

As far as DPM licensing in gapping contexts is concerned, the three-dimensional parallel structure seems to be better than previously mentioned approaches. However, the three-dimensional structure has some theoretical burden in linearization. So I would like to introduce another solution to DPM licensing in gapping contexts, which does not resort to the three-dimensional structure. It is to adopt Wilder's (1999) multiple dominance analysis that was proposed to account for English RNR phenomena. According to him, the apparently RNRed part or the shared part is dominated both by the first and the second conjunct. Thus, the relevant part of (9b) and (10) will have the following structure:

(21)

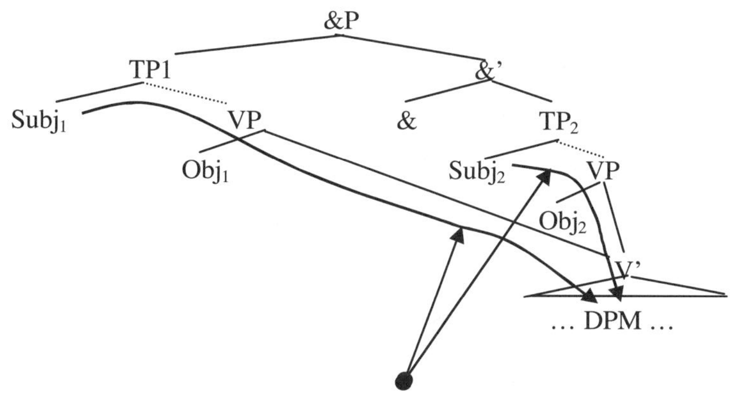

Satisfy the plurality/c-command/locality conditions

The shared part in (9b) or (10b), say V', is simultaneously dominated by both conjuncts. Then the DPM in V' will be co-c-commanded by the subjects scattered across conjuncts, satisfying the plurality condition, the c-command condition, etc.[8]

5. Summary

This paper observed that gapping feeds an environment in which otherwise unlicensed dummy plural marker (DPM) is licensed. This phenomenon cannot be properly accounted for by previous gapping analyses put forth in the literature (Abe and Hoshi 1993, 1997, Kim 1997, Saito 1987, among

[8]With some plausible modification of LCA, Wilder also derives the correct linear order.

others). These analyses fail for the following two reasons. First, no direct link between DPM and its trigger is guaranteed, despite the fact that the licensing triggers can be scattered across conjuncts. Second, these analyses crucially hinge upon leftward movement, despite the lack of island constraints in gapping. This paper compared two solutions that do not suffer from the above-mentioned two problems: a three-dimensional parallel structure (Goodall 1987, Muadz 1991, Moltmann 1992, etc.) and a multiple dominance structure (Wilder 1999). The latter structure is adopted since it is free of linearization problems.

References

Abe, J. and H. Hoshi. 1993. Gapping and P-stranding. In M. Saito (ed.), *Japanese Grammar (II): Second Annual Report for the Research Project, Development of a Formal Grammar of Japanese*. 16-28, University of Connecticut, Connecticut.

Abe, J. and H. Hoshi. 1997. Gapping and P-stranding. *Journal of East Asian Linguistics* 6, 101-136.

Choe, H.-S. 1988. Restructuring Parameters and Complex Predicates: Transformational approach, Ph. D. dissertation, MIT.

Chung, D. 2003. Dummy *–tul* in Gapping Construction. *Proceedings of the 2003 Spring Conference of the Korea Generative Grammar Circle*, 75-83.

Chomsky, N. 1995. *The Minimalist Program*. Cambridge, Mass.: MIT Press.

Goodall, G. 1987. *Parallel Structures in Syntax*. Cambridge University Press, Cambridge.

Hong, Y.-T. 2003. pihaysekseng pokswu phyosi *tul* (Uninterpretable Plural Marker *tul*). Ms. Sungshin Women's University. [written in Korean]

Kim, J.-S. 1997. Syntactic Focus Movement and Ellipsis: a Minimalist Approach. Ph. D. dissertation, University of Connecticut.

Kuh, H. 1987. Plural Copying in Korean. In S. Kuno et al (eds.), *Harvard Studies in Korean Linguistics* II, 239-250.

Lee, H.-G. 1991. Plural Marker Copying in Korean. In S. Kuno et al (eds.), *Harvard Studies in Korean Linguistics* III, 513-528.

Moltmann, F. 1992. Coordination and Comparatives. Ph.D. dissertation, MIT.

Moon, S. 1995. Plural Marker *tul* is Subject to Principle A. In S. Kuno et al (eds.), *Harvard Studies in Korean Linguistics* VI, 355-369.

Muadz, H. 1991. Coordinate Structures: A Planar Representation. Ph.D. dissertation, University of Arizona, Tucson.

Park, M.-K. & K.-W. Sohn. 1993. A Minimalist Approach to Plural Marker Licensing in Korean. *MIT Working Papers in Linguistics* 20, 193-207.

Saito, M. 1987. Three Notes on Syntactic Movement in Japanese. In T. Imai and M. Saito (eds.), *Issues in Japanese Linguistics*, Dordrecht: Foris.

Sohn, K.-W. 1994.On Gapping and Right Node Raising. In Y.-S. Kim et al (eds.), *Explorations in Generative Grammar*, 589-611, Seoul: Hankuk Publishing Co.

Song, S.-C. 1975. Rare Plural Marker and Ubiquitous Plural Marker in Korean. *Papers from the eleventh regional meeting of CLS* 11-32.

Wilder, C. 1999. Right Node Raising and the LCA. S. Bird, A. Carnie, J. Haugen, and P. Norquest (eds.) *WCCFL 18 Proceedings*, 586-598.

Ym, C. 2002. The Semantics of Non-nominal *tul* in Korean. *Journal of the International Circle of Korean Linguistics* 11, 183-202.

A morphological constraint on negation in imperatives in Korean*

CHUNG-HYE HAN
Simon Fraser University

CHUNGMIN LEE
Seoul National University

1 Introduction

Korean has two types of negation: long and short negation. Long negation occurs after the main verb followed by the light verb *ha*, as in (1a). Short negation occurs before the verb, as in (1b).

(1) a. Inho-nun hakkyo-ey ka-ci **ani** ha-yess-ta.
Inho-TOP school-to go-CI NEG ha-PAST-DECL
'Inho did not go to school.'

b. Inho-nun hakkyo-ey **an** ka-ss-ta.
Inho-TOP school-to NEG go-PAST-DECL
'Inho did not go to school.'

Negative imperatives however cannot be formed with short negation. They are instead formed with long negation, but its lexical form *mal* is different from the usual form *ani*.

*We thank Jong-Bok Kim, Hee-Jeong Ko, and the audience at JK 13 for helpful questions and comments. All errors are ours.

(2) a. * hakkyo-ey **an** ka-la.
school-to NEG go-IMP
'Don't go to school.'

b. * hakkyo-ey ka-ci **ani** ha-yela.
school-to go-CI NEG ha-IMP
'Don't go to school.'

c. hakkyo-ey ka-ci **mal**-ala.
school-to go-CI NEG-IMP
'Don't go to school.'

In this paper, we address two questions concerning negative imperatives in Korean: (i) what is the morphosyntactic nature of *mal* in negative imperatives and why is it impossible to form negative imperatives with long negation *ani*?; and (ii) why is it impossible to form negative imperatives with short negation *an*?[1]

In section 2, our discussion on *mal* will lead us to the conclusion that the clause structure of imperatives includes a projection of deontic modality and a projection of imperative operator encoding illocutionary force, and that *mal* is a lexicalization of *ani ha* in the context of deontic modality. We then address the question why short negation is impossible in negative imperatives. In section 3, we will consider a few syntax and semantics based approaches as possible analyses and point out their limitations. In section 4, assuming the clause structure of imperatives with two separate projections for modality and force, we propose that the constraint responsible for ruling out a negative imperative with short negation is morphological in nature, and not syntactic or semantic. We will argue that the constraint follows from Subset Principle and Vocabulary Insertion in Distributed Morphology (Halle and Marantz 1993, 1994).

2 Morphosyntactic nature of *mal*

For an account of the morphosyntactic nature of *mal*, we will extend and refine the approach given in C. Lee (1978): i.e., 'long negation + *ha*' lexicalizes as *mal* in the context of imperatives and propositives.

Tellingly, *mal* can occur in non-imperatives as well, as long as they form deontic modality contexts. For example, it can occur in matrix clauses in

[1]By imperatives, we refer to sentences with distinctive imperative morphology on the verb and/or distinctive imperative syntax. They canonically express the directive illocutionary force associated with commands and requests. Consequently, the term IMPERATIVE has often been used to refer to a sentence's function rather than its form. However, we use the term IMPERATIVE to refer exclusively to a sentence's form. For referring to a sentence's function, we use terms such as COMMAND and REQUEST.

which the verbs are affixed with deontic modal inflections as in (3), and in embedded clauses under directive/volitional verbs as in (4).[2] Given that the imperative also forms a deontic modality context, the proper generalization is that *ani ha* lexicalizes as *mal* in the context of deontic modality, and not just in the context of the imperative. We will formalize this in Distributed Morphology framework in section 4.

(3) Matrix clauses that constitute deontic modality context

a. Cey-ka hakkyo-ey ka-ci **mal**-kkayo?
I-NOM school-to go-CI NEG-Q
'Should I not go to school?'

b. Na-nun hakkyo-ey ka-ci **mal**-ayakeyss-ta.
I-TOP school-to go-CI NEG-should-DECL
'I should not go to school.'

c. Inho-nun hakkyo-ey ka-ci **mal**-aya ha-n-ta.
you-TOP school-to go-CI NEG-should do-PRES-DECL
'Inho should not go to school.'

d. * Inho-nun hakkyo-ey ka-ci **mal**-n-ta.
Inho-TOP school-to go-CI NEG-PRES-DECL
'Inho does not go to school.'

(4) Embedded clauses under directive/volitional verbs

a. Inho-ka Yumi-eykey hakkyo-ey ka-ci **mal**-la-ko
Inho-NOM Yumi-to school-to go-CI NEG-should-COMP
tangpwuha-yess-ta.
tell-PAST-DECL
'Inho told Yumi that she should not go to school.'

b. Inho-nun Yumi-ka hakkyo-ey ka-ci **mal**-ki-lul
Inho-TOP Yumi-NOM school-to go-CI NEG-NMZ-ACC
pala-n-ta.
want-PRES-DECL
'Inho wants Yumi to not go to school.'

c. * Inho-nun Yumi-ka hakkyo-ey ka-ci **mal**-ass-tako
Inho-TOP Yumi-NOM school-to go-CI NEG-PAST-COMP
mit-nun-ta.
believe-PRES-DECL
'Inho believes that Yumi did not go to school.'

---

[2]It is possible to use short negation *an* as well as long form *ani* in the embedded clause of (4b). We take this to mean that the matrix verb *pala* ('want') has two selectional possibilities: it can select a deontic modal clause or a non-deontic modal clause. A similar situation is attested in Romance where some predicates can select a subjunctive or an indicative clause (Quer 1998).

What this implies for the clause structure is that the category for deontic modality and the category for the imperative need to be distinguished somehow. Although there may be different ways of implementing this idea, we will choose to do so by postulating two separate projections for each category: a projection for modality and a projection for illocutionary operator (cf. Sells 2003).

(5)

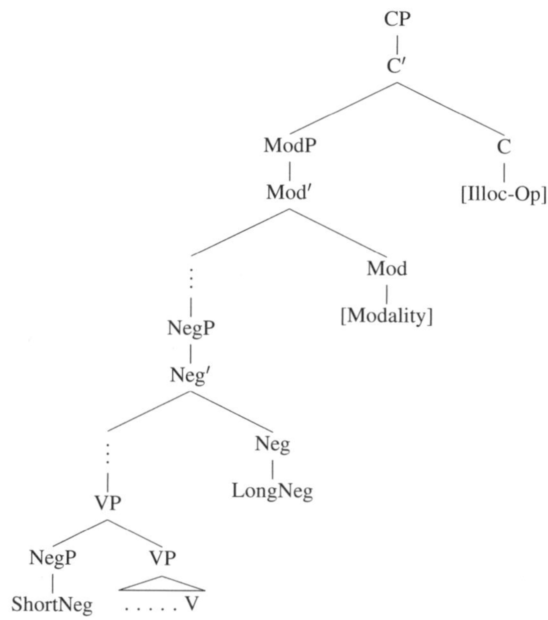

We will further assume that long negation projects NegP, and short negation starts out as a left adjunct of VP but cliticizes to the verb, as in Neg-cliticization in Romance (Cinque 1999). The fact that a sentence can contain both short and long negation as in (6) supports two different positions for the two types of negation (see also A.-R. Kim 2002).

(6) Inho-nun amwu kes-to **an** masi-ci **ani** ha-yess-ta.
Inho-TOP any thing-even NEG drink-CI NEG do-PAST-DECL
'Inho didn't not drink anything. / Inho drank something.'

The fact that *ha*, which is similar to English *do*, is required with long negation supports that long negation is a head that projects a phrase of its own (NegP), and blocks the verb from coming together with inflections (see D.-I. Cho 1994; E.-Y. Yi 1994). Further, while in adult grammar, short negation must occur immediately before the verb, and nothing can intervene between them (see H.-S. Han 1987; Y.-K. No 1988; J.-B. Kim 1999), 2-3 year-old children often produce sentences in which short negation and the verb are separated by an object or an adverb, as in (7) (K.-J. Hahn 1981; Y.-M. Cho & K.-S. Hong 1988; Y.-J. Kim 1997; Y.-K. Baek 1998; Hagstrom 2002). This difference between adult and child grammar can be explained as follows: short negation, which heads its own projection, left-adjoined to VP, cliticizes onto the verb in the adult grammar, but fails to do so in the child grammar (H. Han & M.-K. Park 1994).

(7) a. na **an** pap mek-e.
I NEG rice eat-DECL
'I do not eat rice.' (Y.-M. Cho & K.-S. Hong 1988:34 [2;2-6])

b. **an** mak wul-e.
NEG much cry-DECL
'(I) do not cry much.' (Y.-M. Cho & K.-S. Hong 1988:35 [2;2-6])

Note that while identifying the correlation between *mal* and deontic modal context sheds light on why long form *ani* cannot be used in negative imperatives, it does not explain why short negation cannot be. Assuming the clause structure in (5), we propose an analysis that addresses this issue in section 4.

3 Possible analyses of the incompatibility of imperatives and short negation

Before we present our proposal, we will first rule out a few possible syntax and semantics based approaches, as a way of motivating our own analysis.

A series of works have been proposed to account for the (in)compatibility of negation and the imperative based on various Romance, Balkan, and Germanic languages (Zanuttini 1991, 1994, 1997; Rivero 1994; Rivero and Terzi 1994; Han 2000, 2001). Although the details are different, an idea shared by all these approaches is that in some languages (such as Italian, Spanish, Modern Greek), the syntax of the imperative and the syntax of negation are incompatible, ruling out negative imperative formation, and so negative commands are instead formed with another sentence type, such as subjunctives. Examples from Modern Greek are given in (8).

(8) Modern Greek (C.-H. Han 2001:1)

a. * Mi grapse to!
Neg write-2sg.Imp it
'Don't write it!'

b. (Na) mi to grapsis!
NA Neg it write-2sg.Subj
'Don't write it!'

This approach however cannot be extended to Korean because it would miss the generalization that short negation cannot occur in a wider range of sentences which can be characterized as deontic modal sentences.

Another possible approach is to exploit the assumption that there is scope difference between long and short negation, and formulate an analysis based on this assumption. C.-H. Han & C. Lee (2002) pursue this approach and propose that semantics of short negation restricted by the scope possibility is incompatible with the semantics of negative imperatives. But the problem is that there is no consensus in the literature or among speakers as to what the scope facts are (see C.-H. Cho 1975; J.-H. Suh 1989; H.-H. Park 1998; K. Lee 1989; J.-B. Kim 2000; S.-C. Song 1982; Y.-K. Baek 1998; Hagstrom 2002; Han, Lidz and Musolino 2003). Crucially, the speakers that report that there is no scope difference reject negative imperatives with short negation. Given this, it is doubtful that scope of short negation can tell us anything about why short negation is impossible in imperatives (or deontic modal sentences).[3]

A related approach is to formulate an analysis based on the assumption that there is a semantic difference between short and long negation. But it is doubtful that this will work because as far as semantics is concerned, they are the same type of objects, a function from propositions to propositions ($\lambda p.\neg p$).

4 Our proposal: a morphological constraint

We propose that what is at work is a morphological constraint that applies post-syntactically to the verbal complex, which is formed either through V-raising (D.-I. Cho 1994; Y.-S. Choi 1999) or INFL-lowering (J. Yoon 1994; H. Han and M.-K. Park 1994). The verbal complex will include negation as well as tense, modality and illocutionary (sentence type) morphology because negation behaves like a clitic on the verb in Korean. Within the framework of Distributed Morphology (DM), this verbal complex will have been formed once the structure (e.g., (5)) is shipped off to the morphological component. In what follows, we will argue that the fact that negative imperatives (as well as other types of deontic modal sentences) cannot be formed with short negation follows from Subset Principle and Vocabulary Insertion in DM.

In DM, the output of syntax is a structure with a bundle of morphosyntactic (and semantic) features on each node, as in (9), and that vocabulary insertion takes place post-syntactically, in the morphological component. So, assuming (5), the node dominating the verbal complex in sentences with long negation will include [+Neg, +Modality, +Illoc], and in sentences with short

[3]See C. Lee (1978) for a discussion on scope interaction between *mal* and other quantificational elements in negative imperatives.

negation will include [+V] as well as [+Neg, +Modality, +Illoc] because the negation node cliticizes to V^0 which further incorporates with Mod^0 and C^0.

(9) Feature bundles

Verbal complex in long negation sentence	Verbal complex in short negation sentence
[+Neg, +Modality, +Illoc]	[+Neg, +V, +Modality, +Illoc]

(10)

Vocabulary item	Features
an	+Neg
mal	+Neg, +Deontic

Vocabulary items are also specified with features. For example, as in (10), *an* is specified with [+Neg], and *mal* is specified with [+Neg, +Deontic] (given that it is the negation form in deontic contexts). Vocabulary insertion obeys Subset Principle: for a feature bundle of a given node, the vocabulary item that has the most number of matching features is inserted.

We propose that in the imperative with long negation, the feature bundle of the verbal complex node includes [+Neg, +Deontic, +Imp], where [+Deontic] is a feature value for [+Modality], and [+Imp] is a feature value for [+Illoc]. Through Subset Principle, *mal* is inserted for [+Neg, +Deontic]. This rules out negative imperatives with long negation *ani*. Further, because *mal* is a verbal element, the morpheme for [+Imp] can be inflected on it, generating imperative prohibitive verb *mal-ala*. On the other hand, the verbal complex node in the imperative with short negation would include [+V, +Neg, +Deontic, +Imp]. Since the feature bundle includes [+Neg, +Deontic], *mal* should be inserted, instead of *an* which is simply associated with [+Neg]. Further, a lexical verb will be inserted for [+V]. But then, the verbal complex will end up with two verbal elements, *mal* and the lexical verb, resulting in an ill-formed morphological object. This thus rules out negative imperatives as well as other types of deontic modal sentences with short negation.

Our main supporting argument for the proposed analysis comes from acquisition data. C. Lee (1988, 1993) points out that young children (2-3 years of age) sometimes produce negative imperatives with short negation (11). There are two possible accounts consistent with the proposed morphological analysis. First, notably, children in the same age range sometimes fail to cliticize short negation onto the verb, as was illustrated in (7) (K.-J. Hahn 1981; Y.-M. Cho & K.-S. Hong 1988; Y.-J. Kim 1997; Y.-K. Baek 1998; Hagstrom 2002). What this means is that for the children who have not yet acquired the clitic status of short negation, [+Neg] will not be included in the feature bundle for the verbal complex of an imperative with short negation. That is, the feature bundle for the verbal complex would be [+V, +Deontic, +Imp], and separately, the node for short negation will have [+Neg]. Thus, the condition for inserting *mal* will not be met. Instead *an* will be inserted under Neg^0, and the lexical verb and the corresponding inflections will be inserted for the verbal complex, without any morphological violation.

(11) a. To the father leaving for school

appa, hakkyo **an** ka!
Daddy, school NEG go
'Daddy, don't go to school!' (C. Lee 1993:8 [2;5])

b. **an** pwul kkeyo.
NEG light turn-off
'Don't turn off the light.' (C. Lee 1993:8 [2;1])

Another possible account has to do with the fact that Korean children acquire short negation before long negation. H.-H. Park (1998a) shows that 3 year-olds in general can only produce short negation, whereas 5 year-olds can produce both short and long negation. Given that *mal* has the syntax of long form negation, children who have not yet acquired long form *ani* would not have acquired *mal* either. At this stage, if the child has not yet learned the clitic-status of short negation, then *an* will be inserted for [+Neg] without any violation, as explained above. And if the child has learned the clitic-staus of short negation, then the feature bundle for the verbal complex would include [+Neg, +V, +Deontic, +Imp]. But since *mal* specified with [+Deontic, +Neg] is not in the Vocabulary, the next best choice is *an* with [+Neg] (Subset Principle). This then allows the insertion of lexical verb as well as corresponding inflections.

A prediction that emerges from our proposal is that an imperative should be able to contain short negation if it also contains long form *mal*.

(12) amwu kes-to **an** masi-ci **mal**-ala.
any thing-even NEG drink-CI NEG-IMP
'Don't not drink anything.'

This is because in a sentence with both long and short negations, the lexical verb with cliticized short negation, and the verbal complex with long negation are in separate nodes. Hence, *an* specified with [+Neg], and *mal* specified with [+Neg, +Deontic] can be inserted in separate nodes without any violation. The prediction is borne out in (12).

5 Conclusion

To conclude, we have argued that imperatives project a projection of deontic modality and a projection of the imperative operator contributing the illocutionary force. Assuming this clause structure, we proposed that *mal* in negative imperatives is a lexicalization of long form negation and deontic modality. Assuming further that long and short negations occur in two different positions in a clause structure, we proposed that the reason why short negation is incompatible with imperatives (and other deontic modal sentences) is morphological, not syntactic or semantic. We argued that this incompatibility follows from Subset Principle and Vocabulary Insertion in Distributed Morphology. It remains to be seen whether it is feasible to extend a similar morphology-based analysis to other languages that do not allow negative imperatives, such as Italian, Spanish and Modern Greek.

References

Baek, Judy Yoo-Kyung. 1998. Negation and object shift in early child Korean. In *The Interpretive Tract*, volume 25 of *MIT Working Papers in Linguistics*. MITWPL, Cambridge, 73–86.

Cho, Choon-Hak. 1975. The scope of negation in Korean. In H.-M. Sohn (ed.), *The Korean Language: Its Structure and Social Projection*. The Center for Korean Studies, University of Hawaii, 121–132.

Cho, Dong-In. 1994. Functional projections and verb movement. In Young-key Kim-Renaud (ed.), *Theoretical Issues in Korean Linguistics*. CSLI Publications, 233–254.

Cho, Young-mee Yu and Ki-Sun Hong. 1988. Evidence for the VP constituent from child Korean. In *Papers and Reports on Child Language Development*, volume 27. Department of Linguistics, Stanford University, Stanford, CA.

Choi, Young-Sik. 1999. Negation, its scope and NPI licensing in Korean. In Rebecca Daly and Anastasia Riehl (eds.), *Proceedings of ESCOL'99*, 25–36. CLC, Cornell University.

Cinque, Guglielmo. 1999. *Adverbs and Functional Heads: A Cross-Linguistic Perspective*. Oxford Studies in Comparative Syntax. Oxford University Press, New York, Oxford.

Hagstrom, Paul. 2001. Phrasal movement in Korean negation. In *Proceedings of SCIL*, volume 9 (MITWPL #36). MITWPL, Cambridge.

Hagstrom, Paul. 2002. Implications of child error for the syntax of negation in Korean. *Journal of East Asian Linguistics* 11, 211–242.

Hahn, Kyung-Ja Park. 1981. *The Development of Negation in One Korean Child*. Ph.D. thesis, University of Hawaii.

Halle, Morris and Alec Marantz. 1993. Distributed morphology and the pieces of inflection. In Kenneth Hale and S. Jay Keyser (eds.), *The View from Building 20*. MIT Press, Cambridge, 111–176.

Halle, Morris and Alec Marantz. 1994. Some key features of distributed morphology. In Andrew Carnie and Heidi Harley (eds.), *MIT Working Papers: Papers on Phonology and Morphology*, volume 21. MITWPL, Cambridge, 275–288.

Han, Chung-hye. 2000. *The Structure and Interpretation of Imperatives: Mood and Force in Universal Grammar*. Outstanding Dissertations in Linguistics. Garland Publishing, New York.

Han, Chung-hye. 2001. Force, negation and imperatives. *The Linguistic Review* 18, 289–325.

Han, Chung-hye and Chungmin Lee. 2002. On negative imperatives in Korean. In *Proceedings of the 16th Pacific Asia Conference on Language, Information and Computation*. The Korean Society for Language and Information.

Han, Chung-hye, Jeffrey Lidz, and Julien Musolino. 2003. Verb-movement and grammar competition in Korean: Evidence from negation and quantifier scope. A talk presented at *Workshop on UG Principles and Input Data: How do we get Plato's Heaven into Skinner's Box?*, University of Michigan in East Lansing, Aug. 1-2, 2003.

Han, Haksung. 1987. *The Configurational Structure of the Korean Language*. Ph.D. thesis, University of Texas, Austin.

Han, Ho and Myung-Kwan Park. 1994. The syntax of negation in Korean and its development in child language. In *Proceedings of ESCOL'94*. CLC, Cornell University, 152–162.

Kim, Ae-Ryung. 2002. Two positions for Korean negation. In N. Akatsuka and S. Strauss (eds)., *Japanese/Korean Linguistics*, volume 10. CSLI, Stanford, 587–600.

Kim, Jong-Bok. 1999. On the prefixhood and scope of short form negation. In *Harvard Studies in Korean Linguistics*, volume VIII. Dept. of Linguistics, Harvard University, 403–418.

Kim, Jong-Bok. 2000. *The Grammar of Negation: A Constraint-Based Approach*. CSLI, Stanford.

Kim, Young-Joo. 1997. The acquisition of Korean. In D. Slobin (ed.), *The Crosslinguistic Study of Language Acquisition*, volume 4. Lawrence Erlbaum, Hilsdale, NJ, 335–444.

Lee, Chungmin. 1978. Negative imperatives in Korean. In Chin-Woo Kim (ed.), *Papers in Korean Linguistics*. Hornbeam Press, Columbia, South Carolina, 149–156.

Lee, Chungmin. 1988. Speech act terms and mood indicators (in Korean). *Acta Linguistica Hungarica* 38, 127–141.

Lee, Chungmin. 1993. The acquisition of mood indicators in Korean. In *Harvard Studies in Korean Linguistics*, volume V. Dept. of Linguistics, Harvard University, 41–61.

No, Yongkyoon. 1988. Negative morphemes in Korean: Evidence for a derivational treatment. In Eung-Jin Baek (ed.), *Papers from the Sixth International Conference on Korean Linguistics*. International Circle of Korean Linguistics, 556–567

Park, Heeheon. 1998a. Acquisition of negation in Korean. *Korean Linguistics: Journal of the International Circle of Korean Linguistics* 9, 111–131.

Park, Myung-Kwan. 1998b. Negation and placement of verb in Korean. *Language Research* 34, 709–736.

Quer, Josep. 1998. *Mood at the Interface*. Ph.D. thesis, Utrecht Institute of Linguistics OTS.

Rivero, Maria-Luisa. 1994. Finiteness and second position in long head movement languages: Breton and Slavic. ms. University of Ottawa.

Rivero, Maria-Luisa and Arhonto Terzi. 1995. Imperatives, V-movement and logical mood. *Journal of Linguistics* 31, 301–332.

Sells, Peter. To appear. Negative imperatives in Korean. In *Proceedings of the 10th Harvard International Symposium on Korean Linguistics*. Dept. of Linguistics, Harvard University.

Song, Seok Choong. 1982. On interpreting the scope of negation in Korean. *Language Research* 18, 197–215.

Suh, Jinhee. 1989. Scope interaction in negation. In *Harvard Studies in Korena Linguistics*, volume III. Department of Linguistics, Harvard University, 527–536.

Yi, Eun-Young. 1994. NegP in Korean. In H. Grabois, D. Parkinson, and D. Yeager (eds.), *Cornell Working Papers in Linguistics*, volume 12. Cornell University, Ithaca, 193–208.

Yoon, James Hye-Suk. 1994. Korean verbal inflection and checking theory. In *The Morphology-Syntax Connection*, volume 22 of *MIT Working Papers in Linguistics*. MITWPL, Cambridge, 251–270.

Zanuttini, Raffaella. 1991. *Syntactic properties of sentential negation: A comparative study of Romance languages*. Ph.D. thesis, University of Pennsylvania.

Zanuttini, Raffaella. 1994. Speculations on negative imperatives. *Rivista di Linguistica* 6, 67–89.

Zanuttini, Raffaella. 1997. *Negation and Clausal Structure: a Comparative Study of Romance Languages*. Oxford Studies in Comparative Syntax. Oxford University Press, New York, Oxford.

On Adnominal 'Focus-Sensitive' Particles in Japanese[*]

J.-R. HAYASHISHITA
Kyoto University
University of Southern California

1. Introduction

In the generative tradition, words like *only* and *even* in their adnominal uses (and adverbial uses) are assumed to have the property of a scope-bearing element (henceforth scope properties). The meaning of (1a) is, for example, assumed to be (1b).

(1) a. John greeted only Mary.

b. There is no one other than Mary such that John greeted him or her.

---

[*]I am much indebted to Hajime Hoji and Emi Mukai for the conception and development of the line of thinking presented in this paper. The comments and suggestions by Teruhiko Fukaya, Maki Irie, Kiyoko Kataoka, Utpal Lahiri, Bill McClure, Yasuhiko Miura, Barry Schein, Yukinori Takubo, Yukiko Tsuboi, Ayumi Ueyama, and John Whitman also helped me understand various issues relevant for the content of the paper. This research is supported by Grant-in-Aid for JSPS Fellow, No. 2196, Japan Society of the Promotion of Science, The Ministry of Education, Culture, Sports, Science and Technology.

To account for the scope properties, a number of analyses have been put forth; cf. Kuroda 1965, Peters & Karttunen 1979, Rooth 1985, 1992, and Büring & Hartmann 2001, among others.

Japanese words corresponding to *only* and *even*, are *dake* and *sae*, and they can precede or follow a *case-marker* or *postposition* (henceforth simply *CM*), as illustrated in (2)-(3).[1]

(2) a. John-wa Kimura sensei-ni-dake/sae aisatusita.
John-TOP Kimura teacher-DAT-only/even greeted
'John greeted only/even Prof. Kimura.'
b. John-wa Kimura sensei-dake/sae-ni aisatusita.

(3) a. John-wa Kyoto daigaku-de-dake/sae enzetusita.
John-TOP Kyoto university-at-only/even spoke
'John spoke only/even at Kyoto University.'
b. John-wa Kyoto daigaku-dake/sae-de enzetusita.

Although works in generative grammar such as Kuroda 1969/70 and Hoji 1985 uniformly treat FPs in both cases as having scope properties, functional grammarians such as Morita (1974) and Kuno & Monane (1979) observe that there are some semantic differences, depending on their locations with respect to a CM. As pointed out in Morita 1974, for example, (4a) necessarily mean that this disease can be cured by injection, but not by any other method, while (4b) does not. (4b) can additionally mean that this disease can be cured by injection alone (but something other than injection may also cure it).

(4) a. Kono byooki-wa tyuusya-de-dake naoru.
this disease-TOP injection-with-only cure
'This disease is cured only with injection.'
b. Kono byooki-wa tyuusya-dake-de naoru.

In the following discussion, I refer to words like *dake* and *sae* as *'focus-sensitive' particles* (henceforth *FPs*), and the FP in an NP-CM-FP (e.g., (2a) and (3a)) is called *NP-external FP* and the FP in an NP-FP-CM (e.g., (2b) and (3b)) *NP-internal FP*.

The aim of this paper is to provide a theoretical characterization of the semantic difference between NP-external FPs and NP-internal FPs observed in the works of functional grammar. The rest of the paper is organized as follows. In Section 2, I argue for (5).

---

[1]The nominative-marker *ga*, the accusative-marker *o*, and the dative-marker *ni* can all follow words like *dake* and *sae*, but only the dative-marker can precede them. Postpositions, on the other hand, can all follow or precede them.

(5) NP-external FPs can be considered to have scope properties while NP-internal FPs cannot.

Sections 3 and 4 provide analyses for NP-external FPs and NP-internal FPs. Analyses proposed in generative grammar are all designed to capture the scope properties of FPs. Once (5) is established, therefore, it is reasonable to consider which of the analyses should be adopted for NP-external FPs. However, we must seek a new analysis for NP-internal FPs. Regarding NP-external FPs, I review two major analyses: the analysis that assumes an NP plus an FP to undergo QR (cf. Kuroda 1965, Peters & Karttunen 1979, and Hoji 1985), and the one that is based on the theory of the association of focus in Rooth 1985 and need not assume QR (cf. Rooth 1985, 1992, and Büring & Hartmann 2001). I argue that the former should be adopted over the latter. Section 5 concludes the paper.

In the interests of space, the generalizations to be maintained below are illustrated only with *dake* 'only'; however, they should hold for other FPs, e.g, *sae* 'even', *sura* 'even', *nomi* 'only', *bakari* 'nothing but', etc.

2. NP-external FPs Can Be Considered to Have Scope Properties while NP-internal FPs Cannot

When simple cases are considered, NP-internal FPs and NP-external FPs appear to have scope properties on a par with each other. For example, both (6a) and (6b) can be truthfully uttered in (7a), but not in (7b).

(6) a. John-wa Kimura sensei-ni-dake soodansita.
John-TOP Kimura teacher-DAT-only consulted
'John consulted only with Prof. Kimura.'
b. John-wa Kimura sensei-dake-ni soodansita.

(7) There are only two professors, Profs. Kimura and Yamada.
a. Situation 1
John consulted with Prof. Kimura, but not with Prof. Yamada.
b. Situation 2
John consulted both with Prof. Kimura and with Prof. Yamada.

One may thus conclude that they both can be taken to mean (8), the interpretation that is expected under the assumption that *dake* 'only' has scope properties.

(8) There is no one other than Prof. Kimura such that John consulted with him or her.

Once we consider more complicated examples, however, some difference emerges between NP-external FPs and NP-internal FPs. It seems that the former can be understood as having scope properties while the latter cannot. For example, consider the examples in (9) together with the situations in (10).

(9) a. John-wa Kimura sensei-ni-dake email-de soodansita.
John-TOP Kimura teacher-DAT-only email-with consulted
'John consulted only with Prof. Kimura by email.'
b. John-wa Kimura sensei-dake-ni email-de soodansita.

(10) There are only two professors, Profs. Kimura and Yamada.
a. Situation 1
John consulted with Prof. Kimura by email and with Prof. Yamada by phone.
b. Situation 2
John consulted with Prof. Kimura by email, but with no other person.

(10a) is a situation where John consulted someone other than Prof. Kimura but Prof. Kimura is the only person that he consulted by email. (10b) is a situation where John consulted no one except Prof. Kimura. (9a) can be truthfully uttered in both situations. By contrast, (9b) is true in (10b), but false in (10a). It thus seems that (9a), but not (9b), can be taken to mean (11).

(11) There is no one other than Prof. Kimura such that John consulted with him or her by email.

Given that if an element α has scope properties, then α can be understood as having scope over a clause, I take the contrast just observed (i.e., (9a), but not (9b), can be taken to mean (11)) as evidence that NP-external FPs can be considered as having scope properties while NP-internal FPs cannot.

3. Theoretical Characterization

In this section, I put forth analyses for NP-external FPs and NP-internal FPs. I start with NP-external FPs.

3.1. NP-external FPs

Given the conclusion that NP-external FPs can be understood as having scope properties, it is reasonable to consider which proposal in generative grammar should be adopted for NP-external FPs. The existing proposals are roughly classified into two types. One type adopts the assumptions in (12) or their notational variants (henceforth the QR analysis); cf. Kuroda 1965, Peters & Karttunen 1979, and Hoji 1985.

(12) a. An NP plus an FP (e.g., *only Mary*) is an instance of a generalized quantifier, i.e., of type <et, t>.
b. An NP plus an FP (e.g., *only Mary*) undergoes QR for interpretive purposes, i.e., to avoid a type mismatch problem.

Under this analysis, (13a), for example, is represented as (13b) at LF. The meaning of *only Mary* is roughly (14a), and by compositionally combining *only Mary* and *John kissed t*, the scope properties of *only* is derived as in (14b).

(13) a. PF: John kissed only Mary
b. LF: [$_{IP}$ only Mary$_1$ [$_{IP}$ John kissed t_1]]

(14) a. ← [$_{DP}$ only Mary] → = the set of all properties p which no one other than Mary has
b. ← [$_{IP}$ only Mary$_1$ [$_{IP}$ John kissed t_1]] → = the set of worlds in which the property of John's kissing is one which no one other than Mary has.

The other is based on the theory of the association of focus in Rooth 1985 (henceforth the Roothian analysis); cf. Rooth 1985, 1992, and Büring & Hartmann 2001. The assumptions adopted by the Roothian analysis are summarized in (15).

(15) a. *Focus* is a grammatical concept: Focused elements are marked at LF with 'F', which is realized as a pitch accent on the main stress-bearing syllable.
b. Each node is interpreted with its *ordinary semantic value* and its *focus semantic value*.
i. The focus semantic value of any node X, ←X→^{f}, consists of a set of alternatives to its ordinary semantic value ←X→.
ii. The set of alternatives is derived by substitution of the meaning of the focused constituent by alternatives.
iii. if X contains no 'F' at all, ←X→^{f} is the singleton set containing X's ordinary semantic value, e.g., ←*kissed*→^{f} = {←*kissed*→}

To illustrate how this analysis derives the scope properties associated with FPs, let us consider (16), where the capitalization of *Mary* indicates that it receives a pitch accent on the main stress-bearing syllable.

(16) a. PF: John kissed only MARY.
b. LF: [$_{IP}$ John kissed only Mary$_F$]

First of all, the phonetic form in (16a) corresponds to the LF in (16b), where ‘F’-marking is placed on *Mary*. As mentioned above, each node is interpreted with its ordinary and focus semantic values. The two semantic values of *Mary* are as in (17a) and (17b).

(17) a. ← $[_{DP}$ Mary$_F]$ → = the set of all properties p which Mary has.
b. ← $[_{DP}$ Mary$_F]$ →^{f} = the set of all sets P of properties p such that there is an alternative to Mary who has the properties p in P.

Assuming the interpretive rule for *only* in (18), which manipulates ordinary and focus semantic values, we can derive the ordinary and focus semantic values of *only Mary* as in (19a) and (19b), respectively.

(18) The interpretive rule for *only* (= Büring & Hartmann 2001 (31))
If *A* is of type <α, t>, *only A* is of type <α, t>, too, and ←*only A*→ is the set of all *B* of type α such that *B* has the property ←*A*→ (i.e., *B* ∈ ←*A*→), and no other property that is an alternative to that (i.e., in ←*A*→^{f}); ←*only A*→^{f} = {←*only A*→}.

(19) a. ← $[_{DP}$ only Mary$_F]$ → = the set of all properties p that Mary has and that no alternative to Mary has.
b. ← $[_{DP}$ only Mary$_F]$ →^{f} = ← $[_{DP}$ only Mary$_F]$ →

And, compositionally combining the semantic values of *only Mary* and those of the rest of the sentence, the scope properties of *only* can be derived as in (20).

(20) ← $[_{IP}$ John kissed only Mary$_F]$ → = the set of worlds in which the property of John’s kissing is one that Mary has and that no alternative to Mary has.

In summary, the QR analysis must assume (21a) while the Roothian analysis need not (since it manipulates type-shifting operations), and conversely, the Roothian analysis must assume (21b) while the QR analysis need not.

(21) a. An NP plus an FP undergoes QR.
b. Focus, ‘F’-marking at LF, is a grammatical notion.

I adopt the QR analysis over the Roothian analysis for NP-external FPs, because (i) the generalizations to be presented in Section 4 cannot be accounted for without assuming (21a), and (ii) (21b) cannot be maintained for Japanese. In the interests of space, however, the evidence in support of (ii) will not be given in this paper.

3.2. NP-internal FPs

For NP-internal FPs, we must seek a new analysis. Furthermore, the new analysis must capture their apparent scope properties. I suggest that the phonetic string in (22a), for example, is represented as (22b) at LF (with *Mary-dake-ni* in situ), and interpreted as in (23).

(22) a. PF: John-ga Mary-dake-ni soodansita (koto).
'(Lit.) (That) John consulted with only Mary.'
b. LF: [$_{IP}$ John-ga Mary-dake-ni soodansita]

(23) a. ←Mary-dake-ni→ = Mary, who is the unique individual that satisfies the contextually most salient proposition under consideration.
b. ←John-ga Mary-dake-ni soodansita→ = the set of worlds in which John consulted with Mary, who is the unique individual that satisfies the contextually most salient proposition under consideration.

Notice that the analysis suggested above can account for the apparent scope properties of NP-internal FPs. In the case of (22a), assuming the contextually most salient proposition to be *John consulted with x*, the derived meaning is indistinguishable from the meaning of the NP-external FP counterpart.[2]

4. Confirmation

In this section, I present two sets of generalizations, which further distinguish NP-external FPs from NP-internal FPs and, at the same time, lend support to their analyses I have just adopted.

4.1. Generalization 1

First, (24a) is infelicitous while (24b) is not, despite the fact that they differ from each other only in the location of the FP.

(24) a. #Boku-wa kimi-ni-dake meguriau tameni umaretekita.
I-TOP you-DAT-only meet in:order:to was:born
'I was born in order to meet only you.'
b. Boku-wa kimi-dake-ni meguriau tameni umaretekita.

---

[2]One may wonder how we can account for the observations that (9b) can be truthfully uttered in (10b), but not in (10a), based on which I have argued that NP-internal FPs do not have scope properties. I wish to maintain that due to the pragmatic principle in (i), the contextually most salient proposition under discussion can be *John consulted with x*, but not *John consulted with x through email*.

(i) Pragmatic Principle (Cf. Kuno's 1978 discourse principles.)
Do not repeat old information in the matrix clause, except a verb and a WA-marked NP.

Since the embedded scope reading is infelicitous while the matrix scope reading is not, as indicated in (25), I interpret the contrast as indicating (26).

(25) a. The embedded scope reading
#I was born so that I meet no one other than you.
b. The matrix scope reading
There is no one other than you that I was born to meet (i.e., my birth is for you!).

(26) a. The scope of NP-external FPs is clause-bounded.
b. NP-internal FPs appear to take scope beyond the clause they originate in.

Given the assumption that QR is clause-bounded, (26a) follows directly from the QR analysis, which assumes that an NP-CM-FP undergoes QR. The Roothian analysis, on the other hand, fails to account for such locality effects.[3] (25b) is compatible with the analysis of NP-internal FPs suggested above, provided that the contextually most salient proposition under discussion for (24b) can be *I was born in order to meet x*.

4.2. Generalization 2

The scope order between a QP and an NP-external FP seems to be determined by their c-command relation prior to QR. An NP-internal FP, on the other hand, appears to take scope above or below a QP, irrespective of their c-command relation.

First, consider the sentences in (27), where a QP c-commands an NP plus an FP prior to QR (cf. Kuroda 1969/70 and Hoji 1985).

(27) a. Sanninizyoo-no sensei-ga Toyota-ni-dake John-o suisensita.
three:more-GEN teacher-NOM Toyota-DAT-only John-ACC recommended
'Three or more professors recommended John only to Toyota'
b. Sanninizyoo-no sensei-ga Toyota-dake-ni John-o suisensita.

(27a), which contains an NP-external FP, gives rise to the QP>FP reading in (28a), but not the FP>QP reading in (28b). (27b), the NP-internal FP counterpart of (27a), on the other hand, appears to allow both readings in (28)

(28) a. The QP>FP reading
There are three or more *x*'s, *x* is a professor such that there is no company other than Toyota to which *x* recommended John.

---

[3] I thank John Whitman (p.c. August 2003) for pointing out that this generalization speaks against the Roothian analysis.

b. The FP>QP reading
There is no company other than Toyota such that there are three or more *x*'s, *x* is a professor such that *x* recommended John to it.

Now consider the sentences in (29), where an NP plus an FP c-commands a QP prior to QR (cf. Hoji 1985 and Hayashishita 2000).

(29) a. John-wa Toyota-ni-dake sanninizyoo-no gakusei-o suisensita.
John-TOP Toyota-DAT-only three:more-GEN student-ACC recommended
'(Lit.) John recommended only to Toyota three or more students.'
b. John-wa Toyota-dake-ni sanninizyoo-no gakusei-o suisensita.

(29a) allows the FP>QP reading in (30b), but not the QP>FP reading in (30a). By contrast, (29b) appears to give rise to both readings in (30).

(30) a. The QP>FP reading
There are three or more *x*'s, *x* is student such that there is no company other than Toyota to which John recommended *x*.
b. The FP>QP reading
There is no company other than Toyota such that there are three or more *x*'s, *x* is a student such that John recommended *x* to it.

The generalization regarding the scope interaction between a QP and an NP-external FP thus seems to be (31).

(31) Let a QP be α, and an NP plus an NP-external FP β.
a. α can take wide scope with respect to β only if α c-commands β, prior to QR.
b. α can take narrow scope with respect to β only if α is c-commanded by β, prior to QR.

Note also that (32), a 'scrambling' counterpart of (27a), contrasts with (27a), and gives rise to the FP>QP reading (as well as the QP>FP reading).

(32) Toyota-ni-dake sanninizyoo-no sensei-ga John-o suisensita
'(Lit.) Only to Toyota, three or more professors recommended John'

This contrast can be taken as further evidence in support of (31b), for the NP_2 can c-command, or be c-commanded by, the NP_1 in NP_2-*ni/o* NP_1-*ga* Verb, prior to QR (cf. Hoji 1985, Saito 1992 Ueyama 2002).

Similarly, (33), a 'scrambling' counterpart of (29a), gives rise to the QP>FP reading (in addition to the FP>QP reading) in contrast to (29a).

(33) John-wa sanninizyoo-no gakusei-o Toyota-ni-dake suisensita
'John recommended three or more students only to Toyota.'

Given the assumption that the NP_3 can c-command, or be c-commanded by, the NP_2 in NP_1-*ga* NP_3-*o* NP_2-*ni* Verb, prior to QR (cf. Hoji 1985 and Kitagawa 1994), this contrast renders further support to (31a).

The generalizations in (31) are naturally explained by the QR analysis, together with the isomorphism principle in Huang 1982 that when two noun phrases undergo covert movement, their c-command relation prior to the movement cannot be altered. The Roothian analysis, on the other hand, cannot account for them.

I wish to maintain that the observations about (27b) and (29b) are compatible with the analysis of NP-internal FPs suggested above. (27b), for example, is analyzed to be *there are three or more x*'s, *x is a professor such that x recommended John to Toyota, who is the unique individual that satisfies the contextually most salient proposition under consideration*. Assuming that the contextually most salient proposition in this situation is *there are three or more x*'s, *x is a professor such that x recommended John to y*, we can derive a reading analogous to the FP>QP reading. When the salient proposition is *they (= the same set of three or more professors) recommended John to y*, on the other hand, a reading analogous to the QP>FP reading can emerge.

5. Concluding Remarks

In summary, I have argued that NP-external FPs can be understood as having scope properties while NP-internal FPs cannot, and the apparent scope properties associated with the latter should be treated by pragmatics. One of the implications is, therefore, that our linguistic intuitions labeled as 'scope interpretations' may not always reveal LF properties of the grammar (see also Hayashishita forthcoming). Finally, this paper suggests that we should reevaluate works on FPs in languages where NP-external FPs and NP-internal FPs are not morphologically differentiated.

References

Büring, D. & K. Hartmann. 2001. The Syntax and Semantics of Focus-Sensitive Particles in German. *Natural Language & Linguistic Theory* 19:229-281.

Hayashishita, J.-R. forthcoming. *Syntactic Scope and Non-Syntactic Scope*. Doctoral dissertation, University of Southern California.

Hayashishita, J.-R. 2000. The Scope Ambiguity and Scrambling. *Proceedings of WCCFL XIX*, 204-17, Somerville: Cascadilla Press.

Hoji, H. 1985. *Logical Form Constraints and Configurational Structures in*

Japanese. Doctoral dissertation, University of Washington.

Huang, J. 1982. *Logical Relations in Chinese and the Theory of Grammar*. Doctoral dissertation, MIT.

Karttunen, L. & S. Peters. 1979. Conventional Implicature. *Syntax and Semantics vol.11: Presupposition*, Academic Press.

Kitagawa, Y. 1994. "Shells, Yolks, and Scrambled E.g.s. *NELS* 24, 221-239.

Kuno, S. 1978. *Danwa-no Bunpoo* 'Discourse Grammar'. Taishuukan publisher.

Kuno, S. & T. Monane. 1979. Postpositioning of Quantifier-like Particles *Journal of the Association of Teachers of Japanese* 14: 115-140.

Kuroda, S.-Y. 1965. *Generative Grammatical Studies in the Japanese Language*. Doctoral dissertation, MIT.

Kuroda, S.-Y. 1969/1970. Remarks on the Notion of subject with Reference to Words like *Also*, *Even* or *Only*. *Annual Bulletin*, vol.3: 111-29, and vol.4: 127-52. Research Institute of Logopedics and Phoniatrics, University of Tokyo

Morita, Y. 1971. The Usage of -dake and -bakari. *Bulletin of the Institute of Language Teaching* 10: 1-27, Tokyo: Waseda Univserity.

Rooth, M. 1985. *Association with Focus*, Doctoral dissertation, University of Massachusetts.

Rooth. M. 1992. A Theory of Focus Interpretation. *Natural Language Semantics* 1: 75-116.

Saito, M. 1992. Long Distance Scrambling in Japanese. *Journal of East Asian Linguistics* 1: 69-118.

Ueyama, A. 2002. Two Types of Scrambling Constructions in Japanese. *Anaphora: A Reference Guide*, ed. A. Barss, 23-71 Cambridge: Blackwell.

Reconstruction Effects in Passive and Scrambling in Japanese*

HAJIME HOJI
University of Southern California

1. Introduction

The typical treatment of the English passive (e.g., (2b)) in the generative tradition is as in (1b).

(1) a. NP1 V NP2.
    b. $NP2_i$ be V-en t_i (by NP1).

(2) a. John broke the vase.
    b. The vase was broken (by John).

Informally speaking, *-en* is understood to have the following two effects, forcing the movement of NP2 as indicated in (1b).[1]

(3) a. The *V* of *V-en* loses its external argument.
    b. The internal argument of the *V* of *V-en* can no longer be 'licensed'

* This paper is based on my handout/presentation at the JK conference, August 1-3, 2003 "Falsifiability and Repeatability in Generative Grammar: A Case Study of Passive and Scrambling in Japanese." Page restrictions have forced me to present only a small portion of the empirical, theoretical, and methodological issues that I initially intended to address in the paper. The readers are referred to http://www.gges.org/hoji/ for further discussion. Acknowledgements are given there.

[1] Among the early standard references are Burzio 1986 and Jaeggli 1986.

as an object; i.e., the Case cannot be assigned/checked in the object position.

In effect, then, *be broken* in (2b) is much like the intransitive *break* as in *the vase broke*. Both in *the vase was broken* and in *the vase broke*, the surface subject is understood to originate in the object position and get raised to its surface position due to the considerations of the sort alluded to in (3b). This type of movement is called *A-movement* and is understood to be involved in sentences of the form in (4) as well (e.g., (5)).

(4) NP_i seems to NP [t_i to VP]

(5) $John_i$ seems to Mary [t_i to be a nice person]

Japanese has a pair that appears to correspond to (1).

(6) a. NP1-ga NP2-o V-ru/ta
-NOM -ACC -TENSE

b. NP2-ga (NP1-{ni/niyotte}) V-(r)are-ru/ta
-NOM -by -PASS-TENSE

(7) a. Mary-ga John-o hihansi-ta
-NOM -ACC criticize-PAST
'Mary criticized John.'

b. John-ga Mary-ni/niyotte hihans-are-ta
-NOM -by criticize-PASS-PAST
'John was criticized by Mary.'

In both (1) and (6), the 'object' in the active sentence corresponds to the 'subject' in the passive, and the 'subject' in the active sentence corresponds to an oblique in the passive.

The functional equivalence, however, does not necessarily mean the sharing of the same formal properties.[2] In other words, it is not clear that (6b) has a structure like (8), involving the same type of movement as in (1b) and (4).

(8) NP2-ga_i (NP1-{ni/niyotte}) t_i V-(r)are-ru/ta

Whether it does or not will have much bearing on the overall characterization of the Japanese language one might pursue. For example, if *-rare* in Japanese had the effects of the sort alluded to in (3b), necessarily resulting in a structure like (8), that would provide support for the view in (9).

(9) There are items in Japanese, as in English and other languages, that bear a feature responsible for agreement/checking (a formal feature that is hypothesized to be responsible for obligatory displacement of elements); and agreement/checking (or its variant) plays a central role in the generation of Japanese sentences.

In contrast to (9), a thesis like (10) has been pursued in Fukui 1986, 1993,

---

[2]See, for example, Chomsky 1976: 181-183 and Hoji 2003: note 80 for some concrete illustration of this point.

and Fukui & Sakai 2003; see also Kuroda 1988.[3]

(10) No items in Japanese bear a feature that is responsible for agreement/checking; and hence agreement/checking plays no role in Japanese, unlike in English and other languages.

If (10) is correct, the Japanese passive morpheme *-rare* should not have the property that results in the effects of the sort alluded to in (3b). Note, however, that the hypothesis in (10) does not necessarily entail the absence of movement in general in Japanese, since it need not be assumed that every movement should be driven by formal feature agreement/checking.

The choice between (9) and (10) in regard to passives in Japanese should thus be contingent upon (i) whether Japanese passives involve movement as indicated in (8), and (ii) whether such movement has properties of A-movement of the sort that is understood to be involved in the derivation of (2b) and (4) in English.

I will argue that examination of the reconstruction effects for variable binding in passive sentences in Japanese leads us to conclude that movement observed in the Japanese passive is not A-movement but rather the same types of movement involved in the derivation of the so-called scrambling construction in Japanese as analyzed in Ueyama 1998. Since some instances of 'scrambled order' have been argued in the literature to be in effect due to A-movement, the thesis to be defended below can also be understood as denying the claim that 'scrambling' in Japanese *can* be an instance of A-movement.

2. Reconstruction Effects in the Japanese 'Scrambling' Constructions

Following Ueyama 1998, let us refer to the sentences of the form *NP1-NOM NP2-DAT/ACC V* and those of the form *NP2-DAT/ACC NP1-NOM* as *SO-type* (Subject-Object word order) and *OS-type* (Object-Subject word order) sentences, respectively. It has been known that *NP2-DAT/ACC* in the OS-type construction in Japanese may show either A- or A'-properties. Thus the OS-type generally allows BVA(*QP*, *so-ko*) in (11a) as well as (11b).[4]

---

[3]It is assumed here that the differences among languages are attributable solely to the differences in (the functional domain of) the lexicons of the languages, as in Borer 1984 and Fukui 1986.

[4]Given in (i)-(iii) is the minimally necessary background to the present discussion concerning the formal basis of the type of BVA that we are concerned with; see Hoji 1998, Ueyama 1998, and Hoji 2003 for more details.

(i) *BVA(A, B)* expresses an intuition that (i) B does not have an inherent value of its own, and (ii) the value of B co-varies with the value of A. (e.g., BVA(*every boy*, *his*) in *every boy loves his mother*)

(ii) *FD(α, β)* is a formal relation established between two linguistic objects, and it has the properties given in (iii) (leaving aside the condition having to do with local

(11) a. 'Absence of the WCO effects':
QP-ACC/DAT ... [... *so-ko* ...]-NOM ... V

b. Reconstruction effects:
[... *so-ko* ...]-ACC/DAT ... *QP*-NOM ... V

In part on the basis of the observation that the effects in (11a) and (11b) never obtain simultaneously, as illustrated in (12), Ueyama (1998) argues that the OS-type construction is structurally two-way ambiguous, and calls the type which shows the effect in (11a) 'Deep OS-type', and the one that shows the effects in (11b) 'Surface OS-type'.

(12) (Ueyama 2002: Section 3.2, (47))

?*[So-ko$_i$-no kaikeisi-o-sae]$_j$ [so-itu$_j$-no kookoo-no
that-place-GEN accountant-ACC-even that-guy-GEN high:school-GEN
sensei]-ga [subete-no zidoosyagaisya]$_i$-ni *ec*$_j$ suisensita.
teacher-NOM every-GEN automobile:company-DAT recommended
'[Even its$_i$ accountant]$_j$, [his$_j$ high school teacher] recommended to [every automobile company]$_i$.'

Intended (but impossible) interpretation:

$\forall x$ (x=automobile company) [it holds of even y, who is x's accountant, that y's high school teacher recommended y to x]

Ueyama's (1998) analysis of the two OS-type constructions, which I adopt here, is as follows.[5]

(13) Surface OS-type:
PF: NP$_1$-DAT/ACC [NP-NOM ... t_1 ...] (← PF movement)
LF: [NP-NOM NP-DAT/ACC ...]

(14) Deep OS-type:
PF: NP$_1$-DAT/ACC [NP-NOM *pro*$_1$ ...]
LF: NP$_1$-DAT/ACC [*pro*$_1$ [NP-NOM t_1 ...]] (← LF movement of *pro*)
(*pro* acting as an empty operator)

According to Ueyama 1998, the OS order in *Surface OS*[6] is derived by the PF movement of the O across the S, and in *Deep OS*, the clause-initial O is 'base-generated' in a position sister to an IP, and is related to 'its theta-position' by means of (i) the 'base-generation' of an empty nominal (represented as *pro* in (14)) in 'the theta position' with which the O is re-

disjointness effects), and a certain type of BVA(A, B) (e.g., BVA(*even Toyota*, *it*)) arises only if FD(t, B) is established at LF, with the t being the trace of A.

(iii) a. (Hoji 2003: (83))
*FD(α, β) if α does not c-command β.

b. (Hoji 2003: (84))
Given FD(α, β), the value of β must be identical to that of α.

[5]A 'pre-QR' structure is given as an LF representation, to avoid unnecessary complications that might result from adding another trace in the representation.

[6]In the ensuing discussion, I will refer to the *Surface OS-type* and the *Deep OS-type* simply as *Surface OS* and *Deep OS*, respectively.

lated, (ii) the LF adjunction of the empty nominal to the IP, and (iii) the formation of the predication relation between the O and the IP (more precisely the λ predicate that the IP gets mapped to), with the O functioning as the subject, much as in the case of the subject of the *tough* construction in English.

Given this analysis, one might suspect that an overt nominal category A can appear in place of the empty nominal in (14), as long as it is possible for A to function in essentially the same way as the empty nominal. Examples like (15) suggest that such is indeed the case; see Hoji 2003: Section 3.1 for discussion on various related issues including judgmental fluctuation on the relevant examples and its theoretical characterization.

(15) [*Toyota-ni-sae*]$_1$ [*so-ko*-o tekitaisisiteiru kaisya]-ga [*so-ko*-ni]$_1$
Toyota-DAT-even that-place-ACC be:hostile company-NOM that-place-DAT
Nissan-o suisensita
Nissan-ACC recommended
'[*To even Toyota*]$_1$, the company which is hostile to *it* recommended Nissan to it$_1$.'

Notice that the presence of such an overt nominal (let us call it *resumption*) is possible in Deep OS but not in Surface OS, as is expected under Ueyama's (1998) account of the OS constructions in Japanese. We are thus led to expect that resumption disambiguates the OS construction, forcing it to be Deep OS and predicting the unavailability of reconstruction effects. The unavailability of the intended BVA in (17) (in contrast to (16)) confirms this prediction.[7]

(16) a. [*So-ko*-o tekitaisisiteiru kaisya]$_1$-o *Toyota-sae*-ga *ec*$_1$ uttaeta
that-place-ACC be:hostile company-ACC Toyota-even-NOM sued
'[The company which is hostile to *it*]$_1$, *even Toyota* sued *ec*$_1$.'

b. [*So-ko*-o tekitaisisiteiru kaisya]$_1$-o Nissan-ga *Toyota-ni-sae*
that-place-ACC be:hostile company-ACC Nissan-NOM Toyota-DAT-even
ec$_1$ suisensita
recommended
'[the company which is hostile to *it*]$_1$, Nissan recommended *to even Toyota ec*$_1$.'

(17) a. *[*So-ko*-o tekitaisisiteiru kaisya]$_1$-o *Toyota-sae*-ga [so-ko-o]$_1$ uttaeta

b. *[*So-ko*-o tekitaisisiteiru kaisya]$_1$-o Nissan-ga *Toyota-ni-sae* [so-ko-o]$_1$ suisensita

Resumption is thus possible only when the 'dislocated' phrase in the OS construction exhibits A-properties, and this constitutes strong supporting

[7]The observations that resumption is possible in Deep OS but not in Surface OS and that reconstruction effects are not observed with resumption are made in unpublished work by J.-R. Hayashishita in 1997; see Ueyama 1998: Appendix A.2, Appendix B.1.1.

evidence in favor of Ueyama's analysis of the OS constructions in Japanese, as opposed to the other analyses offered in the literature.[8]

Summarized in (18) are the consequences of Ueyama's (1998, 2003) analysis of the OS construction in Japanese that are crucial to the present discussion.

(18) a. Reconstruction effects obtain only in Surface OS (i.e., in the OS construction that is derived by PF movement of the O over the S).

b. The O in the OS construction necessarily shows A-properties (hence no reconstruction effects) if the theta-position corresponding to the O is occupied by resumption.

3. Reconstruction Effects in Japanese Passives

Turning to passives, reconstruction effects are observed in examples like (19) but not in examples like (20).[9]

(19) Reconstruction of BVA in Japanese passives:

a. [so-ko$_1$-ni hairitagatteita gakusei]-ga Abe kyoozyu-**niyotte**
that-place-DAT wanted:to:work:for student –NOM Abe Prof.-by
[itutu izyoo-no kaisya]$_1$-ni __ suisensareta
5 more-GEN company-DAT was:recommended
'[a student who wanted to work for it$_1$] was recommended by Prof. Abe to [five or more companies]$_1$'

b. [so-ko$_1$-ni hairitagatteita gakusei]-ga Abe kyoozyu-**niyotte**
that-place-DAT wanted:to:work:for student-NOM Abe Prof.-by
[Toyota-ni-sae]$_1$ __ suisensareta
-DAT-even was:recommended
'[a student who wanted to work for it$_1$] was recommended by Prof. Abe to [even Toyota]$_1$'

(20) a. *[so-ko$_1$-ni hairitagatteita gakusei]-ga Abe kyoozyu-**ni**
that-place-DAT wanted:to:work:for student-NOM Abe Prof.-by
[itutu izyoo-no kaisya]$_1$-ni suisensareta
5 more-GEN company -DAT was:recommended
'[a student who wanted to work for it$_1$] was recommended by Prof. Abe to [five or more companies]$_1$'

b. *[so-ko$_1$-ni hairitagatteita gakusei]-ga Abe kyoozyu-**ni**
that-place-DAT wanted:to:work:for student-NOM Abe Prof.-by
[Toyota-ni-sae]$_1$ suisensareta
-DAT-even was:recommended
'[a student who wanted to work for it$_1$] was recommended by Prof. Abe to [even Toyota]$_1$'

---

[8] I will return to this point briefly in Section 6.

[9] A full paradigm would include acceptable examples corresponding to (20), where the BVA reconstruction is not at stake.

With resumption, the BVA in (19) becomes unavailable; see (21).[10]

(21) a. *[*soko*$_1$-ni hairitagatteita gakusei]-ga Abe kyoozyu-**niyotte**
it-DAT wanted:to:work:for student -NOM Abe Prof.-by
[*itutu izyoo-no kaisya*]$_1$-ni soitu-ga suisensareta
5:or:more-GEN company-DAT was:recommended
'[a student who wanted to work for it$_1$] was recommended by Prof. Abe to [five or more companies]$_1$'

b. *[*soko*$_1$-ni hairitagatteita gakusei]-ga Abe kyoozyu-**niyotte**
it-DAT wanted:to:work:for student-NOM Abe Prof.-by
[*Toyota-ni-sae*]$_1$ soitu-ga suisensareta
-DAT-even was:recommended
'[a student who wanted to work for it$_1$] was recommended by Prof. Abe to [even Toyota]$_1$'

The similarities between OS-type constructions and the passive observed above suggest the possibility that the examples in (19) are instances of Surface OS while those in (20) are not. If such is indeed the case, the 'base order' of (19) should be as in *NP-ni NP-ga V-rare*, among the argument NPs, and *NP-ga NP-ni V-rare* can be derived by the PF movement of *NP-ga* across *NP-ni*, giving rise to the reconstruction effects in (19). Before we turn to the various predictions under such an analysis, I will first try to state the hypothesis about the passives in Japanese I wish to pursue.

4. Hypothesis about Japanese Passives

The case-marking on *NP2* differs between (6a) and (6b). Given the assumption that marking with *-ga* or *-o* reflects the argument structure of the predicate in question, it seems reasonable to assume that the addition of *-rare* affects the argument structure. The observation that there are two sentence patterns with *-rare* that correspond to (22)—the so-called indirect passive (as in (23a)) and direct passive (as in (23b))—suggests that there are two *-rare*'s, as proposed in Kuroda 1979, and that one has an argument-taking property and the other an argument-reducing property.[11]

---

[10]The status of (21) is not due to the use of *so-itu* as resumption. Examples corresponding to the English translations in (i), where *so-ko* is used as the resumption, are also unacceptable (while their status without the resumption is analogous to that of (19)).

(i) [a company that wanted to join it$_1$] was recommended by Mr. Abe to {[five or more organizations]$_1$/[even this organization]$_1$}

[11]The phonetic string corresponding to (23b) can in fact be of the structure in (23a). I.e., nothing seems to prevent (i-b) from being the passive counterpart of (i-a), with the argument-taking *-rare*, where *NP2* is the external argument taken by the argument-taking *-rare*, and *ec2* is an empty nominal that is anaphorically related to *NP2*. The case-markers in the parentheses are provided below just to clarify what is intended.

(i) a. ec1(-ga) ec2(-o) V
b. NP2-ga [$_{VP}$ ec1(-ni) ec2(-o) V]-rare

We will address the issue of how to identify an instance of passive with the argument-reducing *-rare* in the next section.

(22) NP1-ga NP2-o V

(23) (Corresponding to (22))

a. NP3-ga [$_{\text{VP}}$ NP1-ni NP2-o V]-rare

b. NP2-ga (NP1-ni(yotte)) V-rare

Rare in (23a) takes an NP (as its external argument) and a VP as its complement, assigning the NP the experiencer theta-role. *NP-ni* within the VP that expresses the agent remains to be an argument of the V; see footnote 12. The 'base' form of the passive with the argument-taking *-rare* is thus as in (24b) (as proposed in Kuroda 1965: Chapter 5, 1979), with (24a) being its active counterpart.

(24) a. A-ga (B-ni) (C-o) V (e.g., 'A introduced C to B')

b. D-ga [A-ni (B-ni) (C-o) V]-rare

The argument-reducing *-rare* as in (23b) eliminates an argument of the V to which it is attached,[12] and the 'base' form of the passive of this type corresponding to (25a) is as in (25b), and it is possible for an adjunct *NP-niyotte* to appear, for example, at the sentence-initial position in (25b) (e.g., *NP-niyotte (B-ni) C-ga V-rare*).[13]

(25) a. A-ga (B-ni) C-o V (e.g., 'A criticized B', 'A introduced C to B')

b. (B-ni) C-ga V-rare (e.g., 'C was criticized', 'C was introduced to B')

I assume, crucially, that *C* in (25b) can be marked by *-ga* in situ, by a version of the case-marking mechanism of Kuroda 1978, the crucial aspect of which is that it assigns *-ga* to the *first unmarked NP* and *-o* to the rest of the *unmarked NPs* in each cycle.[14] This allows *C* to stay where it is in (25b). Given that (24b) and (25b) are the 'base orders', the other 'word orders' corresponding to them can be understood as instances of 'scram-

---

[12]*V-rare* with the argument-reducing *-rare* is then identical in its formal properties to an unaccusative verb. Although I cannot supply any relevant examples in this paper due to the space limit, reconstruction effects of binding and scope in the examples with an unaccusative verb are observed exactly as expected under the view pursued here. This provides confirmation that the movement in such examples is also what is involved in the OS construction, as in the case of examples with the argument-reducing *-rare*, and is not the A-movement of the sort involved in (1b) and (4) in English. See also Section 6.

[13]The agentive *NP-ni* is an argument but the 'agentive' *NP-niyotte* is an adjunct. *NP-niyotte* means something like 'due to ....', and nothing special is stated in the lexicon or elsewhere in Japanese about *-niyotte* (which is a *renyookei* (adverbial form) of *-niyoru* 'to depend upon'), and its use does not necessarily signal a passive with the argument-reducing *-rare* (e.g., *A-ga B-niyotte C-ni naru* 'A becomes C {by/with/because of} B' (as in some chemical reaction)), the point already noted in Kuroda 1979: note 14.

[14]*NP-ni* is considered a *marked NP*. I assume in this paper that the case-marking in question applies before the PF movement takes place. I also assume that the *-ni* marking on the embedded subject *NP1* in (23a), which has been extremely productive and stable throughout the history of the Japanese language, is achieved by a mechanism independent of the marking of *-ga* and *-o*; cf. Kuroda's (1965, 1978/1992:222) *Subject ni-raising*.

bled' sentences. We could thus make predictions in regard to the possibility of bound variable anaphora once we adopt a specific analysis of the 'scrambled' sentences, and I will discuss several predictions adopting Ueyama's (1998) analysis introduced in Section 3.

5. Predictions

Consider the schematic structures in (26), with *A*, *B*, *C* and *V* being constant.[15]

(26) a. A-ga B-ni C-o V
b. D-ga [$_{VP}$ A-ni B-ni C-o V]-rare (with the argument-taking *-rare*)
c. B-ni C-ga V-rare (with the argument-reducing *-rare*)

If *C* is an empty category and anaphorically related to *D* in (26b), we get *D-ga [$_{VP}$ A-ni B-ni pro V]-rare*. Since *D* is anaphorically related to, and presumably has the same value as, *pro* in such cases, we might represent it as *C-ga [$_{VP}$ A-ni B-ni pro V]-rare*. We can then have (27a) and (27b) as corresponding to (26a).

(27) a. C-ga [$_{VP}$ A-ni B-ni *pro* V]-rare (with the argument-taking *-rare*)
b. B-ni C-ga V-rare (with the argument-reducing *-rare*)

Recall that *A-ni* is the agentive phrase and *B-ni* is the indirect object of the ditransitive construction in question. Given that (27a) and (27b) represent the 'base orders', we see that *C* c-commands *B* in (27a) while *B* c-commands *C* in (27b) in their 'base orders'. The other word orders are then instances of 'scrambled orders', which may be either Surface OS or Deep OS.

Consider (28).

(28) a. C-ga A-ni B-ni V-rare (with the argument-taking *-rare*)
b. C-ga B-ni V-rare (with the argument-reducing *-rare*)

In both (28a) and (28b) *C-ga* precedes *B-ni*. According to the proposed analysis, however, (28b) is an instance of the OS construction while (28a) represents the 'base order'. Given the possibility that (28b) is an instance of the Surface OS type, it should be possible for its LF representation to be identical to its SO counterpart, i.e., (27b), where *B* c-commands *C*. Since (28a) is claimed to be the 'base order', there cannot be an LF representation for (28a) where *B* c-commands *C*. We thus predict that BVA(B, β) is not possible in (29a) but we do not predict it to be impossible in (29b).[16]

---

[15]I assume that *NP-ni NP-o* is the 'base order'; see Hayashishita 2000 for empirical paradigms and arguments in support of this which are significantly more compelling than those given in Hoji 1985.

[16]While the judgments on the availability of the BVA(B, β) in (29b) may not be stable or uniform, we can facilitate its availability by adding the adjunct *NP-niyotte*, as in (29b), since it seems to help the speaker to associate the phonetic string in question with a structural description in which the argument-reducing *-rare* is used instead of the argument-taking *-rare*. Note

(29) a. [... β ...]-ga A-ni B-ni V-rare *BVA(B, β)
b. [... β ...]-ga (A-niyotte) B-ni V-rare BVA(B, β)

Recall from Section 2 that a given OS construction cannot be both Deep OS and Surface OS simultaneously, that reconstruction effects obtain only in Surface OS, and that resumption forces a given OS to be an instance of Deep OS. We thus predict that resumption makes BVA(B, β) unavailable in (29b). The paradigms given in (19)-(21) above confirm these predictions.

Let us now consider (30), where *A-ni(yotte)* is the agentive phrase and *B-ni* is the indirect object.

(30) a. B-ni C-ga A-ni V-rare (with the argument-taking *-rare*)
b. B-ni C-ga A-niyotte V-rare (with the argument-reducing *-rare*)

Given our analysis, (30a) must be an instance of the OS type while (30b) represents the 'base order' of the argument NPs; see the 'base orders' in (27). Hence we predict that the BVA(C, β) is not possible in (31b) insofar as the *-rare* in (31b) is taken to be the argument-reducing *-rare*,[17] but we do not predict BVA(C, β) to be impossible in (31a), which can be an instance of Surface OS.[18]

(31) a. [... β ...]-ni C-ga A-ni V-rare
b. [... β ...]-ni C-ga A-niyotte V-rare

It is further predicted that even those speakers who accept BVA(C, β) in (31a) will find the BVA to be unavailable if the 'base position' of the 'dislocated phrase' is occupied by resumption.

I will briefly illustrate how the predictions regarding (31a) are borne out. (32) is an instance of (31a), and BVA(*55% izyoo-no gakusei*, *so-itu*) seems possible.

(32) [*so-itu*-ga hairitakunakatta kaisya]-ni *55% izyoo-no gakusei*-ga
that-guy-NOM did:not:want:to:join company-DAT 55% more-GEN student-NOM
(a-no) Yamada kyoozyu-ni *ec* syookais-areta (koto)
that-GEN Yamada professor-by was:introduced fact
'to a company *he* did not want to join, *each of the 55% or more of the students* was introduced *ec* by (that notorious) Prof. Yamada'

If the *ec* in (32) is replaced by resumption *so-ko-ni* 'that place-DAT', how-

---

in this connection that the use of the agentive *NP-ni* clearly signals the use of the argument-taking *-rare*, according to the hypothesis pursued here; see footnote 13.

[17]This should be the case at least to the extent that BVA(C, β) is not possible for *[... β ...]-ni C-o V*; see footnote 15 and 18.

[18]It is noted in Hoji 1985: Chapter 4, footnote 37 that the judgments on the WCO and reconstruction paradigms involving the direct and the indirect objects of a ditransitive verb is not as clear as examples involving the subject and the object NPs; see also footnote 15.

ever, the BVA becomes unavailable, much as in (17) and (21).[19, 20]

6. Concluding remarks

In the preceding sections, I have argued that what underlies the word order variations in the Japanese passive is identical to that in non-passive sentences in the language. I have further argued that A-movement is not involved in the derivation of any instance of the OS construction in Japanese, now including the OS versions of passive sentences. The empirical argument for this comes from the fact that those OS constructions in which the 'dislocated phrase' exhibits A-properties are precisely those in which resumption is allowed in the theta-position related to the 'dislocated phrase'. Once we adopt the assumption that A-movement is forced for Case reasons and if the relevant part of the Case theory states that overt categories must have Case, it is not possible to maintain that the movement in question is due to Case reasons since an overt category can indeed appear in what would be the launching site of the A-movement.[21]

It has been argued in Belletti & Rizzi 1988 and Barss 2001, among others, that A-movement exhibits reconstruction effects. The availability of BVA(*every boy*, *his*) in examples like (33) is among the bases for such a claim.

(33) ?[His$_1$ first girl friend]$_2$ seems to every boy$_1$ t_2 to be the most unforgettable. (Kitagawa & Kuroda 1992: (35c))

---

[19]The availability of BVA(*55% izyoo-no gakusei*, *so-itu*) in (i), an instance of Deep OS under the account adopted here, indicates that the unavailability of the BVA in (32) with resumption cannot be attributed to (some processing difficulty associated with) the sequence of *NP-ni NP-ga NP-ni NP-ni*.

(i) [*55% izyoo-no kaisya*]-ni [*so-ko*-ni hairitakunakatta gakusei]-ga
55% more-GEN company-DAT that-place-DAT did:not:want:to:join student-NOM
(ano) Yamada kyoozyu-ni *so-ko*-ni syookaisareta (koto)
that-GEN Yamada professor-by that-place-DAT was:introduced
'to *each of the 55% or more companies*, a student who did not want to join *it* was introduced to *it* by Prof. Yamada'

Furthermore, the unavailability of the BVA with resumption in an example corresponding to (32) cannot be attributed to the use of *so-itu* 'that-guy' as the dependent term; see footnote 10. The choice of the particular example in (32) is to make it only minimally different from (i) above in terms of their 'semantico-functional' aspects.

[20]So far, we have been concerned with the availability of BVA in the Surface OS (see (11b)). Ueyama (1998: Chapter 2, 2002) also discusses empirical generalizations in regard to Deep OS and specifies conditions on when a given 'dislocated phrase' can exhibit A-properties, making reference to 'long-distance scrambling', 'multiple scrambling', and the clause types. Ueyama's generalizations and analysis of Deep OS thus yield a number of predictions beyond what has been discussed above, but the relevant discussion will have to be presented on a different occasion.

[21]The text discussion could be restated in the terms of a more recent (e.g., the EPP-based) technical execution as to what triggers the movement in question, without losing any of its force, as far as I can tell.

The status of such examples seems to be more analogous to that of (34a) than to that of (34b).

(34) a. It seems to every boy_1 that [his_1 first girl friend] is the most unforgettable. (Kitagawa & Kuroda 1992: (35a))

b. *[His_1 (own) $daughter]_2$ promised every $father_1$ [PRO_2 to take good care of her little brother]. (Kitagawa & Kuroda 1992: (38b))

A closer inspection, however, leads us to conclude that A-movement (in English) does not exhibit BVA reconstruction. It is argued in Ueyama 1998, Hayashishita 2004, and Hoji 2003 that the use of certain QPs must be part of a design of a successful syntactic experiment intended to probe into structures at LF. With such QPs (e.g., *at least one NP*), reconstruction effects are not observed in the raising construction in English (while they are in A'-movement such as *wh*-movement). In (35), due to J.-R. Hayashishita, for example, BVA(*at least one professor*, *his*) seems unavailable.

(35) *his_1 *student* seems to [at least one $professor]_1$ t to be worth promoting

If *his student* were indeed in its theta-position (i.e., the embedded subject position) at the point where the grammatical basis for the BVA is checked, the intended binding in (35) would be expected to be as readily available as in (36).

(36) it seems to [at least one $professor]_1$ that his_1 student is quite promising

It is perhaps worth noting that Ueyama's (1998) generalizations discussed in Section 2 have been arrived at by focusing on paradigms *without resumption* that involve a certain type of binder-bindee pairs and by concentrating on the distribution of BVA that is crucially based on a c-command relation at LF. If we considered BVA that can arise independently of LF c-command, we would no longer be able to maintain the generalizations in question, and a different set of generalizations emerges, as discussed in Ueyama 1998 in some depth. In the preceding discussion, I have used such QPs without providing detailed background.[22] As pointed out in Ueyama 1998: Section 3.1 and Hoji 2003: Section 2.2, if we use QPs like *everyone*, *every teacher*, etc., the speaker judgments on BVA paradigms are not as robust as when we use certain other QPs, including *at least one NP*. I thus conclude that A-movement (in English) does not exhibit reconstruction effects, at least in the way the OS constructions in Japanese do.[23]

---

[22]Hoji 2003 provides a summary of the relevant empirical materials.

[23]Recall that the Japanese passive with agentive *NP-ni* does not exhibit reconstruction effects; see (20). One might thus suggest that it is the Japanese passive with agentive *NP-ni* that involves A-movement. Such a position, however, does not seem tenable at least for the following reason: if the so-called *ni*-passive were derived via A-movement, the animacy requirement on the subject of such passive sentences would be mysterious.

The essentials of the analysis outlined above are made in Kuroda 1979, where two types of passives are recognized in Japanese, the *ni* passive and the *niyotte* passive, and the former is explicitly argued in Kuroda 1979 to involve the argument-taking *-rare*. It is also clear that for Kuroda 1979 the agentive *NP-ni* is an argument in the sense relevant here and *NP-niyotte* an adjunct. This work can thus be understood as an attempt to substantiate the essentials of Kuroda's proposal.[24] Unlike Kuroda 1979, however, we maintain that the dichotomy is not between *-ni* and *-niyotte* passives, but it is between the argument-taking *-rare* and the argument-reducing *-rare*. While this new dichotomy makes it less straightforward to test two distinct types of passives in Japanese, the reconstruction effects of BVA have provided an effective testing ground for the proposed hypothesis, and the empirical considerations in Sections 2-5 point to a conclusion that is consistent with (10), repeated here.

(10) No items in Japanese bear a feature that is responsible for agreement/checking, and hence agreement/checking plays no role in Japanese, unlike in English and other languages.

References

Barss, A. 2001. Syntactic Reconstruction Effects. In M. Baltin, and C. Collins, eds., *The Handbook of Contemporary Syntactic Theory*, 670-696, Blackwell Publishers.

Belletti, A. & Luigi R. 1988. Psych-Verbs and Theta-Theory, *Natural Language and Linguistic Theory* 6-3, 291-352.

Borer, H. 1984. *Parametric Syntax*, Foris Publications, Dordrecht.

Burzio, L. 1986. *Italian Syntax: A Government-Binding Approach*. Reidel, Dordrecht.

Chomsky, N. 1976. Conditions on Rules of Grammar, in *Essays on Form and Interpretation*, North-Holland, New York, 163-210.

Fukui, N. 1986. *A Theory of Category Projection and Its Applications*. Doctoral dissertation. Cambridge, MA: MIT.

(i) a. (Inoue 1976: 83, (40b))
Kaikai ga gityoo ni yotte sengen sareta
opening chairman was:announced
'The opening of the meeting was announced by the chairman'
b. (Kuroda 1979: (18))
*Kaikai ga gityoo ni sengen sareta

(ii) (Kuroda 1979: (19) and (20))
a. Siroi booru ga Oo ni yotte takadakato utiage-rareta
white ball high hit-up
'A white ball was hit high in the air by Oo'
b. *Siroi booru ga Oo ni takadakato utiage-rareta

Given the analysis of the passive with the argument-taking *-rare* adopted here, this is not unexpected, as already discussed in Kuroda 1979; see Section 4.

[24]Space limitations prevent me from discussing many important works on Japanese passives in the literature, including Miyagawa 1989, and Hoshi 1994, 1999.

Fukui, N. 1993. Parameters and Optionality. *Linguistic Inquiry* 24-3, 399-420.
Fukui, N. and H. Sakai, 2003. The Visibility Guidelines for Functional Categories: Verb Raising in Japanese and Related Issues. *Lingua* 113/4-6, 321-375.
Hayashishita, J.-R. 2000. Scope Ambiguity and 'Scrambling', *WCCFL* 19, 204-217, Cascadilla Press Somerville, MA.
Hayashishita, J.-R. 2004. *Syntactic and Non-Syntactic Scope*, Doctoral Dissertation, University of Southern California.
Hoji, H. 1985. *Logical Form Constraints and Configurational Structures in Japanese*, Doctoral dissertation, University of Washington.
Hoji, H. 1998. Formal Dependency, Organization of Grammar, and Japanese Demonstratives, *Japanese/Korean Linguistics*, vol.7, 649-677, CSLI Publications.
Hoji, H. 2003. Falsifiability and Repeatability in Generative Grammar: A Case Study of Anaphora and Scope Dependency in Japanese. *Lingua* 113/4-6, 377-446.
Hoshi, H. 1994. *Passive, Causative and Light Verbs: A Study on Theta Role Assignment*, Doctoral dissertation. University of Connecticut.
Hoshi, H. 1999. Passives, in Natsuko Tsujimura, ed., *The Handbook of Japanese Linguistics*, 191-235, Blackwell Publishers.
Inoue, K. 1976. *Henkeibunpoo to nihongo: Joo, toogoron o tyuusin-ni (Transformational Grammar and Japanese: (I) On Syntactic Structures)*, Taishuukan, Tokyo.
Jaeggli, O. 1986. Passive, *Linguistic Inquiry* 17, 587-622.
Kitagawa, Y., and S.-Y. Kuroda, 1992. Passive in Japanese. Ms., University of Rochester and University of California, San Diego.
Kuroda, S.-Y. 1965. *Generative Grammatical Studies in the Japanese Language*, Doctoral dissertation, Massachusetts Institute of Technology, Cambridge.
Kuroda, S.-Y. 1978. Case-marking, Canonical Sentence Patterns, and Counter Equi in Japanese (A Preliminary Survey), in Hinds ed., *Problems in Japanese Syntax and Semantics*. 30-51, Kaitakusha, Tokyo. (Reprinted in Kuroda,1992, 222-239).
Kuroda, S.-Y. 1979. On Japanese Passives, in Bedell et al., eds., *Explorations in Linguistics: Paper in Honor of Kazuko Inoue*, 305-347, Kenkyuusya, Tokyo. (Reproduced as Kuroda, 1992: Chapter 5. (183-221). The page reference is to Kuroda 1992.))
Kuroda, S.-Y. 1988. Whether We Agree or Not: A Comparative Syntax of English and Japanese, *Linguisticae Investigationes* 12, 1-47, also in Kuroda (1992) 315-357.
Kuroda, S.-Y. 1992. *Japanese Syntax and Semantics*, Kluwer Academic Publishers, Dordrecht, Boston and London.
Miyagawa, S. 1989. *Structure and Case Marking in Japanese*, Syntax and Semantics 22, Academic Press, San Diego.
Miyagawa, S. 1997. Against Optional Scrambling, *Linguistic Inquiry* 28-1, 1-25.
Miyagawa, S. and K. Arikawa. 2003. Locality in syntax and floated numeral quantifiers. A talk given at UCLA.
Saito, M. 1992. Long Distance Scrambling in Japanese, *Journal of East Asian Linguistics*, 1-1, 69-118.
Saito, M. 2003. A Derivational Approach to the Interpretation of Scrambling Chains. *Lingua* 113/4-6, 481-518.
Ueyama, A. 1998. *Two Types of Dependency*. Doctoral dissertation. Los Angeles: University of Southern California. (Distributed by GSIL publications. Los Ange-

les: University of Southern California).

Ueyama, A. 2003. Two Types of Scrambling Constructions in Japanese. In: A. Barss (ed.), *Anaphora: A Reference Guide*, 23-71. Blackwell, Cambridge.

Classifiers and Plural Marking*

CHONGHYUCK KIM
University of Delaware

1. Introduction

Numerals directly combine with (count) nouns in English:

(1) five lions

However, the Korean counterpart of the English noun *lion* cannot combine with a numeral without a classifier:[1]

(2) a.*?tases saca	b. saca tases **mari**
five lion	lion five CL_{animal}

One popular way to account for the contrast is to assimilate the Korean facts in (2) to the obligatory use of classifiers with English mass nouns in (3):

(3) a. *five waters b. five bottles of water

Under this view, Korean counterparts of English count nouns are in fact *mass nouns*. Hence, the obligatory use of classifiers follows. I will call this view the *mass view*. Chierchia (1998) is an influential theory of this view.

---

*I would like to thank Satoshi Tomioka and Benjamin Bruening for their encouragements and insightful comments. Thanks are also due to Changyong Sim for his judgments.

[1] Abbreviations used: Acc=accusative, CL=classifier, Cop=copular, Dat=dative, Gen=genitive, Loc=locative, Nom=nominative, PL=plural marker, Pst=past, Pres=present, Top=topic.

In this paper, I argue against the mass view and show that a generalized classifier system in a language does not mean that the language has a mass lexicon. The argument is mainly based on a crucial prediction that the mass view makes: the complementary distribution of a generalized classifier system and plural marking. The mass view predicts the lack of plural marking in a classifier language for the same reason it is not available with English mass nouns. I will show that this predicted correlation between the two does not hold in Korean: Korean is a classifier language, but it *does* have a fairly productive plural marker *-tul*. If we take *-tul* in Korean as the evidence that there exists a count/mass distinction in the language, as the mass view does for English *-s*, it is no longer possible to attribute its obligatory use of classifiers to the lack of the count/mass distinction. It is simply contradictory. Based on the observation from Korean that classifiers are required even in the count domain, I will argue following Krifka (1989, 1995) that classifiers are universally required when a numeral combines with a noun, and reduce the difference between Korean and English to an overt vs. covert use of classifiers.

This paper is organized as follows. Section 2 reviews the relevant part of Chierchia's theory. Section 3 presents Korean as a problematic case for the mass view. Section 4 shows that the problematic case falls out naturally from the hypothesis that classifiers are universal. Section 5 concludes the paper.

2. The Mass View: Chierchia (1998)

In order to understand how pluralization and classifiers are defined to be in complementary distribution in Chierchia's theory, we need to start with the count/mass distinction. The count/mass distinction is considered to be a difference in what a noun denotes in the lexicon. If it denotes a set of singular entities as in (4a), it is a count noun. If it denotes plural entities as well as singular entities, it is a mass noun, as shown in (4b):[2]

(4) a. Count

A= [a, b, c]

lexicon

b. Mass

B= [{a,b,c}
{a,b}{a,c}{b,c}
a, b, c]

lexicon (already pluralized)

---

[2] In contrast to the traditional view (e.g. Bunt 1985), which maintains that mass nouns do not have atomic parts, Chierchia argues that mass nouns have atomic parts just like count nouns, although the size of their minimal parts may be vague.

Pluralization (PL) builds on the count/mass distinction in (4). It applies in the syntax and derives plural individuals from singular individuals, as defined in (5):

(5) PL(A) = A* – A, where A* is a set of singular and plural individuals.

To give an example, under the assumption that there are three cows, *a*, *b*, *c*, in the world, the domain of quantifications for *cow* and *cows* are **←cow→** = {a, b, c}, **←cows→** = {{a,b}, {a,c}, {b,c}, {a,b,c}}. PL can apply to a count noun since it comes out of the lexicon as a set of singularities. However, PL cannot apply to a mass noun. Applying PL to a mass noun A (=PL(A)) is to subtract A from A*. But A* equals A. Thus, subtracting A from A* yields an empty set, thereby making PL undefined for the mass noun. This accounts for why the plural morphology *-s* is only available with count nouns.

The concept of *counting* also relies on the distinction given in (4). According to Chierchia, counting requires a level of individuation. Individuation corresponds to a set of singularities singled out in the syntax. Plural-marked nouns, which are derived from sets of singular individuals in the syntax, presuppose a level of individuation. So, they can combine with numerals without classifiers. Mass nouns come out of the lexicon already pluralized, with no distinction between singulars and plurals. Due to the lack of singled-out singular entities, they cannot combine directly with numerals. They can be counted only with the help of classifiers, whose function is assumed to be that of providing a counting level (singularities) in the syntax.

In sum, pluralization and direct counting are both dependent on the presence of singled-out singularities, whereas the use of a classifier is based on the lack of singled-out singularities. As a result, classifiers and pluralization are mutually exclusive in a language. (6) summarizes our discussion:

(6) a. pluralization → no classifiers (direct counting)
    b. classifiers (no direct counting) → no pluralization

Crucially, (6) predicts a classifier language *not* to have plural marking.

3. Korean

In this section, I will first show that Korean is a classifier language that requires classifiers across the board. Then, I show that Korean has plural marker *-tul*, which is very similar to English *-s*. Combining the two observations together falsifies the mass view.

3.1. Korean is a Classifier Language

As mentioned in the introduction, numerals, generally, cannot attach to nouns in Korean:

(7) a. *sey mwul　　b. *?sey so　　c. *sey chayk
　　three water　　three cow　　three book

Despite the intuitive semantic difference between *water* and *cow/book* with respect to the existence of natural (atomic) units, they both require classifiers in order to be counted:[3]

(8) a. mwul sey **pyeng**　　b. so sey **mari**　　c. chayk sey **kwuen**
　　water three bottle(CL)　　cow three CL_{animal}　　book three CL_{book}

An obvious conclusion we can draw from (7) and (8) is that Korean is a classifier language. However, there is some complication we need to consider before we reach that conclusion. In the literature on Korean nouns (e.g. Kang 1994), it has often been reported that Korean numerals can combine with nouns *with* or *without* classifiers. A typical example is given in (9):

(9) a haksayng twu **myeng**　　b. twu haksayng
　　student two CL_{human}　　two student

Now, the question is whether we can conclude that Korean is a non-classifier language based on examples like (9). The answer, I argue, is *no*. First of all, the possibility of direct combination of numerals and nouns is restricted to certain human nouns.[4] As was shown in (7) and (8), numerals are not allowed to combine with nonhuman nouns directly. Also, the fact that the direct combination is restricted to only certain types within the human nouns suggests that it is some kind of exception (see footnote 4). Second, a non-classifier phrase always has its alternative classifier phrase, as shown in (9). Third, even when the direct combination is possible, it is only possible with small numbers. The higher the number, the worse the direct combination:

---

[3]The classifier phrases in (8) have alternative forms as well. A Numeral+Classifier sequence can precede head nouns with the genitive marker *uy* in between, e.g. [*sey* **pyeng**-*uy*] mwul 'three bottle-Gen water'. Since the form in (8) is generally considered to be more natural and basic (see Kang (1994)), the genitive marked classifier phrase will not be considered.

[4]It is hard to draw a dividing line within human nouns in terms of the possibility of direct combination with numerals. Nouns whose number of members is big such as *salam* 'human' and *haksayng* 'student' are the best candidates for direct combination. Words of respected or specific occupations such as *kyoswunim*, 'professor', and *chengsopwu* 'janitor' cannot easily combine with numerals.

(10) twu haksayng #yetelp haksayng #yel haksayng #sumwu haksayng
two student eight student ten student twenty student

We certainly need to account for why some restricted classes of human nouns can exceptionally combine with small numbers. But, this does not, by any means, jeopardize the conclusion that Korean is a classifier language.

3.2. Korean Plural Marker *-tul*

Korean nouns can appear bare without numerals, classifiers, or determiners:

(11) Chelswu-ka *haksayng-ul* manassta.
Chelwu-Nom student-Acc met
'Chelswu met a student/students.'

The bare noun *haksayng* 'student' can be singular or plural depending on the context. Its singular reading, however, disappears when *-tul* is present:[5]

(12) Chelswu-ka *haksayng-**tul***-ul manassta.
Chelwu-Nom student-tul-Acc met
'Chelswu met students.'

Korean *-tul* and English *-s* both exclude singular interpretations. Another similarity between *-tul* and *-s* is that they are defined only for count nouns:

(13) a. saca-**tul** b. *mwul-**tul**
lion-PL water-PL
'lions' '*waters'

It is tempting to conclude on the basis of (12) and (13) that we would be justified in assigning to *-tul* whatever semantic function we may assign to *-s*. Considering Chinese and Japanese at this point is helpful in making the decision. Chinese and Japanese have *-men* and *-tachi,* respectively. They also share the properties shown in (12) and (13). But, there are still controversies over the status of these morphemes. For instance, Cheng and Sybesma (1999) and Iljic (1994) argue that *-men* is *not* a plural marker like we usually find in languages such as English, but a special category, a *collective marker*. Their major objection against *-men* as a plural marker is that unlike English *-s*, its interpretation is restricted in various ways. Thus, it is important to show how Korean *-tul* behaves in those respects in which Eng-

[5]Korean *-tul* can appear on categories other than nouns, such as PPs, VPs, etc. Traditionally, this type of *-tul* is distinguished from the *-tul* on an NP. Following the tradition, I assume that these two are different and do not discuss the non-nominal use of *-tul* in this paper. See Kim (1994) and Song (1997) for the non-nominal use of *-tul*.

lish *-s* and Chinese *-men*/Japanese *-tachi* do not go together. The following is a comparison of English *-s*, Korean *-tul*, and Japanese *-tachi*.[6]

***Property 1**: Associative Reading*

Japanese *-tachi* can attach to a proper name. *Proper name + tachi* refers to a group represented by the individual with the name:

(14) Taro-**tachi**-wa moo kae-tta.
Taro-TACHI-Top already go-home-Pst
'The group of people represented by Taro went home already.'

This reading is available neither with English *-s* nor with Korean *-tul*:

(15) Wuripan-ey-nun Edison-***tul***-i manhta.
Our.class-Loc-Top Edison-PL-Nom many
'There are many Edisons in our class.'

Edison-tul in (15) refers to either people whose names are Edison or people with the properties of Edison.

***Property 2**: Weak Existential readings*

An English bare plural can only be interpreted existentially when it is used as an argument of a stage level predicate, as in (16). Its Korean counterpart with *-tul,* however, can either be indefinite or definite, as shown in (17):[7]

(16) John met *students* yesterday

(17) Chelswu-ka ecey *haksayng-**tul***-ul mannassta.
Chelswu-Nom yesterday student-PL-Acc met
'Chelswu met (the) students yesterday.'

This difference, however, is not due to a meaning difference between the two plural markers. It can be linked to the fact that Korean is an article-less language. If Chierchia's (1998) claim that covert operators are freely used in article-less languages is correct, definiteness in (17) is achieved by an iota (ι) operator. The use of the iota operator is blocked in (16) by *the* in English (see Chierchia 1998 for details). Unlike *-tul* and *-s*, Japanese *-tachi* can only be interpreted as definite, as shown in (18):[8]

---

[6] I only consider Japanese *-tachi* in this paper, since Japanese is typologically closer to Korean than Chinese. Nevertheless, *-tachi* and *-men* have more or less the same properties.
[7] Carlson (1977) showed the various interpretational possibilities of English bare plurals.
[8] I have somewhat simplified the Japanese data here. In fact, there are controversies over whether Japanese *-tachi* plurals can be interpreted as indefinites. For instance, Nakanishi and Tomioka (to appear) argue that they can be indefinite, while Kurafuji (2002) argues for the

(18) John-wa *gakusee-**tachi**-*ni at-ta.
John-Top student-TACHI-Dat meet-Pst
'John met the students.' (Kurafuji 2002)

***Property 3**: Generic/Kind readings*

An English bare plural receives a generic interpretation when it appears as the subject of a generic sentence (19a). While Korean bare plurals pattern with English bare plurals, as shown in (19b), the intended generic interpretation is hardly available for Japanese bare plurals with *-tachi* as in (19c):

(19) a. *Italians* are cheerful.

b. *Italiasalam-**tul***-un myenglanghata.
Italian-PL-Top cheerful

c. Itaiajin-***tachi***-wa yooki-da. (Nakanishi and Tomioka)
Italian-TACHI-Topic cheerful-Cop
'√Some group of Italians is cheerful. / ???Italians are cheerful.'

The same pattern is observed with respect to the availability of kind readings:

(20) a. Dinosaurs are extinct.

. b *konglyong-**tul***-un myelcong-toyessta.
dinosaur-PL-Top extinct-became

c. zyosei-tantei(?*-***tachi***)-wa mezurasii.
female-detective-TACHI-top rare
'Female private detectives are rare.' (Nakanishi and Tomioka)

***Property 4**: Scopelessness*

When a bare plural appears with a scope bearing element such as an intensional verb, it necessarily takes narrow scope:

(21) John wants to meet politicians.
(want > politicians ,*politicians > want)

The bare plural *politicians* in (21) cannot take wide scope over the intensional verb *want*. Turning to Korean *-tul* in (22),

(22) Chelswu-nun *cengcyin-**tul***-ul manna-ko *shypehanta.*
Chelswu-Top politician-PL-Acc meet-Comp want
√want > politicians √politicians > want

---

opposite. The point I want to make here is that in contexts where Japanese *-tachi* plurals cannot easily be interpreted as indefinite, Korean *-tul* plurals can.

we find that Korean bare plurals can have either a narrow scope or a wide scope reading. This difference is not problematic, however. The wide scope reading is due to the lack of articles in Korean. When an overt article such as *some* appears with a plural noun in English, the noun phrase is also ambiguous between the wide and narrow scope readings:

(23) John wants to meet some politicians. (ambiguous)

Assuming that there is a covert operator corresponding to English *some* and it is freely available only in an article-less language, we can directly assimilate (22) to (23) and block the use of the covert operator in (21) by the fact that English has an overt counterpart of the covert operator, *some*. Under this analysis, Korean *-tul* is transparent with respect to scope relations just like English *-s*. Let us now look at Japanese *-tachi*:

(24) sono byooin-wa kangohu-***tachi***-o sagasi-teiru.
that hospital-Top nurse-TACHI-Acc seek-Prog
*?seek > nurses: 'That hospital is looking for nurses (to hire).'
√nurses > seek: 'There is a group of nurses that hospital is looking for.'

-Tachi gives rise to an unambiguous wide scope reading and excludes the narrow scope reading. This shows that *-tul* and *-s* are both transparent with respect to scope relations, but *-tachi* is not. (25) summarizes our discussion:

(25) Summary of the interpretational possibilities of *-s, -tul, and -tachi*.

	-s	*-tul*	*-tachi*
Associative reading	No	No	Yes
Weak existential reading	Yes	Yes	No (?)
Generic/Kind reading	Yes	Yes	No (?)
Narrow scope reading with intensional transitive verbs	Yes (obligatory)	Yes (optional)	No

Korean *-tul* is strikingly similar to English *-s*, as (25) shows. Unlike Japanese *-tachi,* Korean *-tul* has all the interpretational possibilities that English *-s* may have. I conclude from this that it is unreasonable to treat *-tul* as something different from *-s,* as people often do with Chinese *-men* and Japanese *-tachi,* and we are justified in treating *-tul* in line with English *-s*.

3.3. Implications of Korean -*Tul* and the Count/Mass Distinction

The coexistence of plural marking and a generalized classifier system in Korean entails that one of the following correlations cannot be valid:

(26) a. Plural morphology → count nouns
b. A generalized classifier system → mass nouns

Recall that *-tul* can only attach to count nouns. Besides, as summarized in Kang (1994), the count/mass distinction is reflected in the use of some quantifying expressions. For instance, *yele/myech-myech* 'several', *kak* 'each' are only compatible with count nouns:

(27) kak/yele sakwa   *kak/*yele mwul
     each/several apple   each/several water   (Kang, 1994)

As an opposite case of (27), we have quantity expressions that are only compatible with mass nouns:

(28) yakkan-uy mwul   *?yakkan-uy cayksang
     little-Poss water   little-Poss desk
     'little water'   *'little desk'

Therefore, the second correlation in (26) cannot be correct in Korean. The presence of a generalized classifier system in a language does not mean that the language has only mass nouns. A classifier system can be required even if the language has count nouns.

4. Classifiers Are Universal

The claim that a generalized classifier system can be required even in a count domain brings up a new set of important questions. Among those, I will address the ones that beg an answer most urgently: what is the function of classifiers, why is it required even if there is a count/mass distinction, and how do we account for the difference between Korean and English in terms of the use of classifiers?[9] In order to answer these questions, I propose that we look at English from a Korean perspective. More specifically, I propose that classifiers are universal across languages.[10]

Under the proposed universal classifier view, the difference between Korean and English is reduced to an overt vs. covert use of classifiers. An apparent direct combination of a numeral and a noun, as in (29a), has in fact a null classifier in line with its Korean counterpart, as in (29b):

(29) a. three ϕ lions (ϕ = null classifier)
     b. saca-(tul) sey mary
        lion-(PL) three CL_{animal}

[9] Other important questions arise regarding differences in terms of plural marking between English and Korean. I have to leave these issues open in this paper for space reasons. These issues are part of my dissertation in progress.

[10] This claim is not new. Although Krifka does not make an argument for a classifier as a universal category, he explicitly hypothesizes it in his many works. The contribution of this paper, if any, would be providing an argument for his idea.

As for the question of why classifiers are universal and obligatory, Krifka (1989, 1995) provides a straightforward answer. Hence, I adopt his system. In Krifka's theory, numbers are arguments of type <n> (they are not quantifiers) and thus cannot combine with nouns which are predicates of type <e,t>, because of a type mismatch. Numbers and nouns can only be combined with the help of a classifier, whose function is to provide an open number argument position to a predicate, as illustrated below:[11]

(30) $[CL] = \lambda n\ \lambda P\ \lambda x\ [P(x) \wedge NU(P)(x) = n]$

where a given P denotes a set of singular and plural entities and x ranges over the elements of the set.

(30) simply says that classifiers mediate between numbers and predicates. NU is short for 'Natural Unit'. Its function is to take a predicate as its argument, and pick out an entity within the domain of quantification denoted by the predicate, and then return a number corresponding to the number of natural units making up the entity.

Let me illustrate how the English phrase in (29a) is derived under the proposed analysis:

(31)

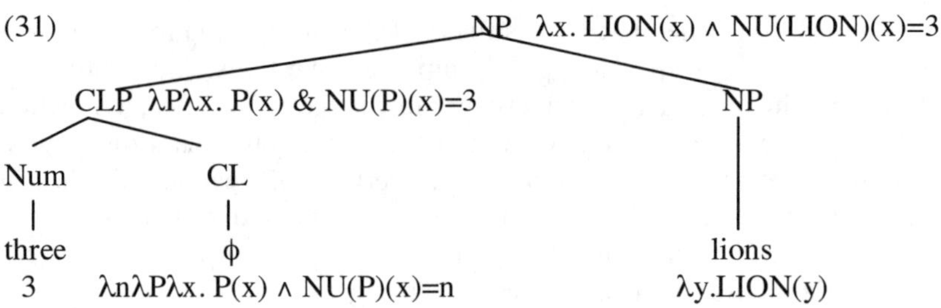

The derivation of its corresponding Korean phrase in (29) is given below:

(32)

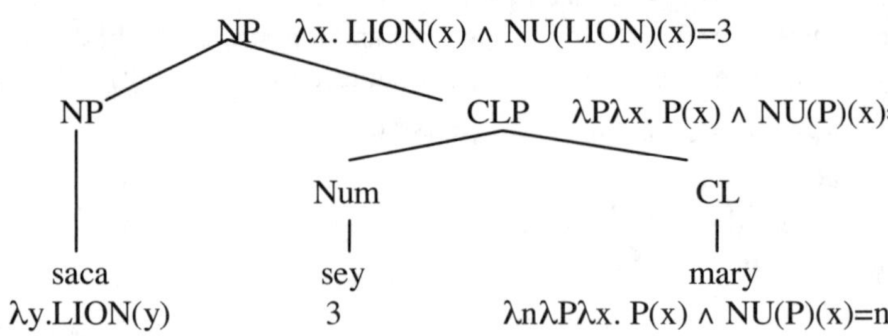

[11] The order of λn and λP can be reversed depending on which element a given classifier combines with first in the syntax.

Note that without CL, Num and NP cannot combine in (32) because of their type mismatch. Their direct combination is blocked since neither of these two categories takes the other as its argument.

In addition to providing answers to the questions raised at the beginning of this section, the universal classifier view has other desirable consequences. First, it predicts that pluralizing a head noun won't make the combination of [Numeral+Noun] any better, since pluralization does not induce a type shifting operation in any of the theories of plurality that I know of. This prediction is borne out:

(33) a. *?sey saca-**tul**
three lion-PL

b. saca-**tul** sey mari
lion-PL three CL_{animal}

Second, we can provide a simple account for why [Noun+Classifier] without a numeral is ungrammatical:

(34) *saca-(tul) mari
lion-(PL) CL_{animal}

The noun phrase in (34) is interpreted as $\lambda n \lambda x[\text{LION}(x) \wedge \text{NU}(\text{LION})(x)=n]$. Without a numeral to bind the open number argument in the phrase, it cannot receive a proper interpretation, leading to the ungrammaticality of the phrase.

To sum up, all the problematic Korean cases for the mass view fall out naturally from the hypothesis of the universal classifier view that a number is a category of type <n> and thus cannot combine with a predicate of type <e,t> without a mediating classifier. It is important to note that under the proposed analysis, both English and Korean count nouns require classifiers. The difference between the two languages is reduced to whether a classifier is visible or not.

5. Conclusion

The attempt to reduce the obligatory use of classifiers in a classifier language to that of English mass nouns was shown to fail in Korean. A generalized classifier system is required in Korean count nouns. Based on this fact, I proposed that classifiers are universal, and reduced the difference between Korean and English to the overt/covert use of classifiers.

References

Bunt, H. 1985. *Mass terms and model-theoretic semantics*. Cambridge: Cambridge University Press.

Carlson, G. N. 1977. Reference to Kinds in English. Doctoral disseration, University of Massachusetts, Amherst.

Chierchia, G. 1998. Reference to kinds across languages. *Natural Language Semantics*, 6(4), 339-405.

Iljic, R. 1994. Quantification in Mandarin Chinese: Two markers of plurality. *Linguistics* 32, 91-116.

Kang, B. 1994. Plurality and other Semantic Aspect of Common Nouns in Korean. *Journal of East Asian Linguistics* 3(1), 1-25.

Kim, Y. 1994. A non-spurious account of 'spurious' Korean plurals. In *Theoretical Issues in Korean Linguistics*, ed. Young-Key Kim-Renaud, 303-323.

Krifka, M. 1989. Nominal Reference, Temporal Constitution and Quantification in Event Semantics. Bartsch, R., van Benthem, J., van Emde Boas, P. eds. *Semantics and Contextual Expressions*, Dordrecht. Foris: 75-115.

Krifka, M. 1995. Common nouns in Chinese and English. In G. Carlson and F.J. Pelletier eds. *The Generic Book*, 398-411. Chicago: University of Chicago Press.

Kurafuji, T. 2002 Plural Morphemes. Definiteness and the notion of Semantic Parameter. Downloadable from http://glow.ling.edu.tw/3-4-2Kurafuji.pdf

Nakanishi, K. and Satoshi, T. to appear. Japanese Plurals are exceptional, *Journal of East Asian Linguistics*.

Song, J. 1997. The so-called Plural Copy in Korean as a marker of distribution and focus. *Journal of Pragmatics* 27, 203-224.

Korean Copular Constructions: A Lexical Sharing Approach

JONG-BOK KIM
Kyung Hee University

PETER SELLS
Stanford University

MICHAEL T. WESCOAT
University of California, Santa Cruz

1 Introduction

While the Korean copula *-i-* forms a phonological word with its preceding N host (see Oh (1991)), it also shows evidence of being an independent syntactic head which takes a phrasal complement, as in (1). The negative copula *ani-* shows a similar structure, but without the phonological cohesion.

(1) a. ku haksayng-un ilpon-eyse o-n salam-i-ta
that student-TOP Japan-from come-PST person-COP-DECL
'That student is a person from Japan.'

b. ku haksayng-un ilpon-eyse o-n salam-i ani-ta
person-NOM NCOP-DECL
'That student is not a person from Japan.'

In canonical predicative uses the copula *-i-* does not allow case-marking on the complement N, nor any other final suffix such as *-(n)un* or *-to* (see (2)a), as it competes with them for the word-final position. The negative copula *ani-ta*, however, allows any suffix, as seen in (2)b.

(2) a. apeci-nun hakca(*-ka/*-nun/*-to)-i-ta
father-TOP scholar(*-NOM/*-FOC/*-FOC)-COP-DECL
'My father is a scholar.'

b. apeci-nun hakca(-ka/-nun/-to) ani-ta
father-TOP scholar(-NOM/-FOC/-FOC) NCOP-DECL
'My father is not a scholar.'

In (1) the modifier *ilpon-eyse o-n* forms a constituent with the N *salam*, which is also the host of the positive copula, and so a favored analysis has been that *-i-* is a clitic (e.g., Yoon (2003)) – a V in syntax forming a phonological word with its adjacent N host, indicated by the '=' in (3). We refer to this as the 'clitic analysis'. The negative copula has the same syntax but is not a clitic.

(3)

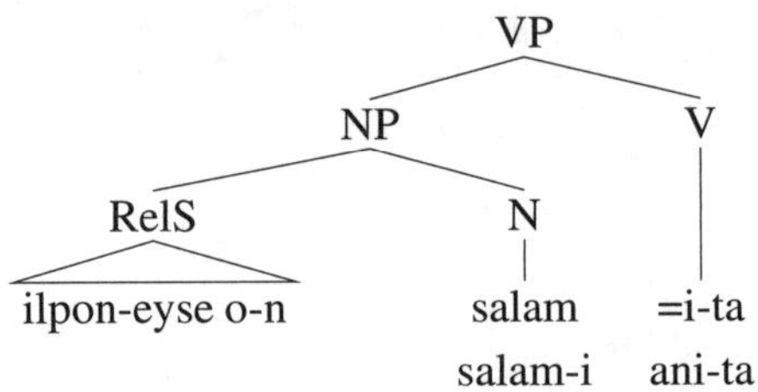

We argue in this paper that while both copula forms do have a syntactic structure which allows for modification of the N *salam* inside NP, the clitic analysis of the copula is not correct. Rather, the copula forms a true lexical word with its N host, shown by three kinds of evidence:

(4) a. the absence of final suffixes on the complement N (as in (2)a);

b. the rules of Palatalization and Coda Neutralization which show that N+Copula is a lexical unit (see Cho and Sells (1995));

c. a novel syntactic argument, coming from the Echo Constrastive Construction (ECC).

The copula-as-clitic analysis makes incorrect predictions for (4)b and (4)c, as it gives the wrong account of what the lexical units are, and leaves the correlation of lexical status with the restriction in (4)a as accidental.

The apparent conflict between these 3 lexical properties and the structure in (3) for *-i-* is predicted by the Lexical Sharing approach of Wescoat (2002), a theory of the relation between words and the syntactic structures they instantiate, motivated for phenomena including English possessives (*'s*), contracted auxiliaries (e.g., *I'll*), and pronominal determiners (e.g., *[These] are good*), Hindi noun incorporation, and Romance and Germanic preposition-determiner compounds, and second-word clitics. In sections 2–4 of this paper we address each of the properties in (4) in turn. Section 5 presents the Lexical Sharing analysis of the copula that resolves the apparent conflict just mentioned, formalized within HPSG (see Ginzburg and Sag (2000)).

2 Lexical Status I: No Final Particles

2.1 Types of Copula

Yoon (2003) identifies two different uses of the Korean copula, the canonical predicational use (in (5)a), and the 'inverse' (in (5)b), which intuitively puts the predicate initial and has the subject as the complement of the copula:

(5) a. ku haysayng-un [ilpon-eyse o-n salam]-i-ta
that student-TOP [Japan-from come-MOD person]-COP-DECL
'That student is actually a person from Japan.'

b. ilpon-eyse o-n salam-un [ku haksayng]-i-ta
Japan-from come-MOD person-TOP [that student]-COP-DECL
'The person from Japan is actually that student.'

We believe that there are 4 types of copula construction in Korean: the *predicational* copula construction (= canonical), the *specificational* copula construction (= inverse), the *cleft* construction, and the *fragment* construction. The first 3 types have similar, though not identical, syntactic structures, while fragments are rather different, as we now explain. The fragment uses provide counterexamples to the claim (see (2) above) that final particles and the copula compete for the same position, and hence cannot cooccur:

(6) a. yeki-eyse-to-i-nya
here-at-also-COP.PRES-Q
'Is it here also?'

b. pwusan-eyse-nun-i-lkka
Pusan-in-FOC-COP-Q
'Even in Pusan?'

These fragments work best in interrogative environments ('Is it X?') and no example corresponds directly to a full clause with a missing argument. Rather, they are fragments which lack full sentential structure and which can only be used in specific contexts, in contrast to other uses of the copula which do not require any special context. In fact, the copula seems to be used in a way that depends pragmatically on the verb in the previous linguistic context, though the best literal translation of an example like (6)b may just be 'Is that the case even in Pusan?', where *that* is anaphoric to something in the context. This context-dependence is illustrated by the following exchange:

(7) A: Mary-nun etten yuklyu-to mek-ci anh-nun-ta
Mary-TOP any meat-kind eat-COMP NEG-PRES-DECL
'Mary doesn't eat any meat.'

B: kyeylan-kkaci-to(-i)-ta
egg-even-also-COP.PRES-DECL
'(Not) even eggs.'

In the typology of lexical rules that we develop below, the fragment use of the copula is a word-to-word rule (see (17)c).

2.2 Korean Nominal Morphology and the Copula

As far as we can determine, the restriction illustrated by (2)a holds for all non-fragment uses of the copula, and it is this restriction that we focus on here. To account for it, Yoon (2003) proposes that the positive copula takes a complement which is marked for Null Case (which has ∅ realization), but which is a case alongside Nominative or Accusative. An NP with Null Case is not the same as an NP which lacks a case marker at all (where case has been 'dropped'). In a similar analysis, Kim and Chung (2002) stipulate that the complement of the copula cannot be specified for structural case, giving the same effect as Yoon's Null Case, by blocking other structural cases.

However, it is an accident on these approaches that it is precisely the form of the copula which cannot stand alone as a syntactic word which is also the form that takes a Null Case complement. The lexicalist analysis attempts to link these two facts. In our view, the negative copula *ani-ta* takes a phrasal complement and as (noun) phrases have case in Korean, this complement has case. That case is the default Nominative, as the special semantic conditions which license Accusative or Dative are not met. In contrast, the lexical attachment of the positive copula *-i-* prevents case from appearing, without appeals to unmotivated values for a case feature.

Based on the classification of Yang (1972), Cho and Sells (1995) adopt the well-known template in (8) for the Korean nominal system:[1]

(8) N-stem - Postposition - Conjunctive - Delim (X-LIM) - Delim (Z-LIM)

The canonical predicative copula does not allow any Z-LIM element on the host N, while all other suffixes are possible, in principle.[2]

Nominative and Accusative case markers appear on NP arguments, but in Korean these case markers may be 'supplanted' by other particles indicating emphasis or focus. The phrasal complement to the negative copula *ani-* is no different in this regard. In (9), the complement to the negative copula bears the particle *-to*, meaning 'also'.

(9) ku i-nun uysa-to ani-ko umak-ka-to
that one-TOP doctor-also NEG.COP-CONJ music-person-also
ani-ta
NEG.COP.PRES-DECL
'He is neither a doctor nor a musician.'

However, it is not possible to attach *-to* directly to the predicate nominal before the positive copula, as in (10):

[1] We present the template here for illustrative purposes, while fully recognizing that its descriptive effects should follow from more principled morphological constraints (see Sells (1997), Yoon (2002), and also section 2.3).

[2] The relevant Z-LIMs are *-(n)un* 'TOPIC/FOCUS', *-i/-ka* (NOM), *-(l)ul* (ACC), and *-to* 'also'. The same morphological restrictions hold for the Japanese copula *-da*, and the corresponding 'Z-LIM' elements in Japanese are: *-wa* ('TOPIC/FOCUS'), *-ga* (NOM), and *-o* (ACC).

(10) *. . . umak-ka-to-i-ta
. . . music-person-also-COP.PRES-DECL
'. . . is also a musician.'

Instead, if a Z-LIM like *-to* is to cooccur with the positive copula, it is necessary use the periphrastic construction in (11).

(11) ku i-nun uysa-i-ki-to ha-ko
that one-TOP doctor-COP-NOMIN-also do-CONJ
umak-ka-i-ki-to ha-ta
music-person-COP-NOMIN-also do.PRES-DECL
'He is both a doctor and a musician.'

Note that the explanation for (10) cannot involve some problem with *-to* taking scope within the complement of the copula, as the same semantic structure obtains in (9), which is acceptable.

The same contrast (anything but a Z-LIM) shows up in (12), in a cleft use:

(12) a. ilen iyaki-ka cekyong toy-nun kes-un
this.kind story-NOM apply PASS-PRES.MOD NOMIN-TOP
swuni-hanthey-man-i-ta
Sooni-DAT-only-COP.PRES-DECL
'It is only to Sooni that this story is applicable.'

b.*. . . swuni-hanthey-man-un-i-ta
. . . Sooni-DAT-only-FOC-COP.PRES-DECL
'It is only to Sooni . . . .'

Other examples of the contrastive difference between the positive and negative copulas can be found in Sells (1997) and Yoon (2003). The clear generalization then about the positive copula is that it effectively attaches in the last (Z-LIM)slot of the templatic structure in (8), and therefore any suffix that falls in that slot cannot cooccur with the copula. However, the negative copula takes a full syntactic complement, and so it shows no restrictions on suffixes.

2.3 Lexical Analysis

Sells (1997) and Yoon (2002) agree that the most important generalizations about nominal suffix ordering are those in (13):

(13) a. The Postposition particles attach right after the N stem.

b. The ZLIM particles are final within the word.

In a hierarchical lexicon, we set up different types corresponding to meaningful classes of (sub-)lexical items. For nominals, we would start with the sorts in (14)a, which participate in suffixal processes as described in b–d:

(14) a. Korean nominal sorts: *stem*, *sub-word*, *word* (see (22) below).

b. Any sort can inherit directly as the next sort 'up', so no suffix is obligatory (for a noun) (see Yoon (1995)).

c. Postposition maps a *stem* to a *sub-word*.

d. ZLIM maps a *sub-word* to a *word*.

These will be expressed as exponent-creating lexical rules (see section 5 below), rather like the realizational approach to morphology of Stump (2001), which also has rules applying sequentially to successively add phonological exponents of morpho-syntactic information. Essentially, these rules realize inflection on a noun, and the sorts give a familiar structure to a Korean word:

(15)

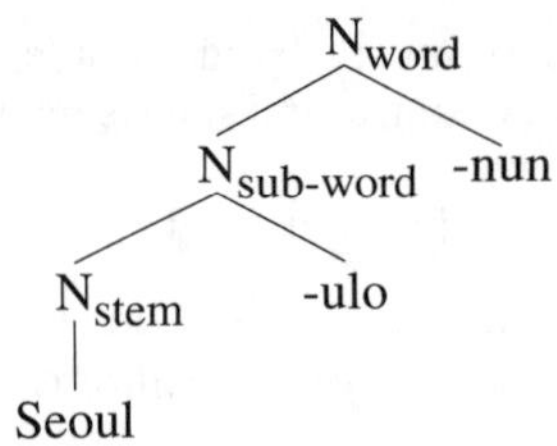

As noted, any sort can directly inherit as the next sort 'up', so that just *Seoul* can also be classified as a *word* (and a *sub-word*) without any suffixation.

Korean grammar also involves some verbalizing rules which create forms like *N-kath-ta* ('look like') and *N-tap-ta* ('be N-ish'), which are effectively derivational processes which take an N *stem* into the verbal part of the lexicon hierarchy (see (17) below). These verbalizing suffixes do not allow any of the nominal suffixes in (8) on the N, hence the restriction to a *stem*, in clear contrast to the copula:

(16) a. salam(*-man)/(*-kkaci)-kath-ta
'looks (only/even) like a person'

b. salam(-man)/(-kkaci)-i-ta
'is (only/even) a person'

We note that the differential sub-lexical selection of *-tap-ta* and *-i-ta* seems impossible to account on an account that takes them both to be syntactic heads which take phrasal complements. The relevant 'derivational' rules (in (17)) will create new verbal roots:

(17) a. For *-kath-ta*, *tap-ta*: map N_{stem} to V_{root}.

b. For copula *-i*: map $N_{sub\text{-}word}$ to V_{root}.

There are only two main classes of lexical rules which change the type of the input element: those which take a *stem* as input, or which take a *sub-word* as input. There are also lexical rules which preserve type. For instance, a semantic delimiter like *-man* can map a *stem* to a *stem* or a *sub-word* to a *sub-word*, though it never applies to a *word*, appearing outside a Z-LIM. Hence words like *Seoul-man-ulo* and *Seoul-ulo-man* are both predicted well-formed.

Korean does have some *word-word* rules, which are completely category-blind, like the spurious/copy marker *-tul* and the discourse-politeness marker *-yo*. These suffixes do not provide or add any information about the internal properties of the word they inflect, but rather about the larger context of use. As noted above, the fragment copula falls in this class, in the sense that it takes a word as input:

(17) c. For fragment copula *-i*: map N_{word} to V_{root}.

So, in summary, the grammar gives the same explanation for the complementary distribution of the Nominative case marker *-i/ka* and the Topic/Focus marker *-(n)un* – both are the result of morphological exponent rules which apply to a *sub-word* to create a different object in the lexicon – and the complementary distribution of the copula *-i* and the Topic/Focus marker *-(n)un*.

3 Lexical Status II: Lexical Phonological Rules

The second argument for lexical status comes from phonology, though we do not illustrate it here due to limitations on space. Cho and Sells (1995) argue that two phonological rules, Palatalization and Coda Neutralization, apply in strictly lexical rather than phonological domains, and hence can distinguish affixes from clitics. They show that the copula is not just part of the same Phonological Word as its N host, but part of the same Lexical Word, which is inconsistent with the clitic analysis.

4 Lexical Status III: The Echo Construction

The Echo Contrastive Construction (ECC) allows the doubling of Vs but none of their phrasal arguments and adjuncts, and sets up a negative implicature in the interpretation of the whole sentence (see Nishiyama and Cho (1998), Choi (2003), Kim (2002), Jo (2003)). The domain of the Korean ECC construction is in fact any syntactic V^0 (see Cho, Kim and Sells (2003)):

(18) chelswu-ka seoul-ul pangmwun ha-ki-nun (pangmwun)
chelswu-NOM Seoul-ACC visit do-NOMIN-FOC (visit)
hay-ss-ta
do-PST-DECL
'Chelswu did visit Seoul (but …).'

Both versions instantiate the ECC: *pangmwun ha-ta* is a syntactically complex V^0 – a V with a preceding VN complement; or just the final V alone can be copied, for it is also a V^0.

Crucially, the positive copula behaves differently, and the only grammatical form of an ECC with the positive copula also involves doubling the preceding N, as in (19) (see Oh (1991), Kim and Chung (2002)). Under the clitic analysis of the copula, the copula and its complement are never a syntactic constituent (see (3) above); however, the ECC treats N+Copula as a syntactic constituent, and so *pangmwun ha-ki-nun hay-ss-ta* above constrasts the impossible **haksayng-i-ki-nun-i-ta* version of (19). This string ought to be fully acceptable under the clitic analysis of the copula, with the first clitic *-i-* hosted at PF by *haksayng* and the second clitic *-i-* hosted at PF by *-nun*.[3]

(19) ku salam-i [mikwuk-eyse kongpwu ha-n]
that person-NOM America-at study do-PST
haksayng-i-ki-nun *(haksayng)-i-ta
student-COP-NMLZ-TOP *(student)-COP-DECL
'That person is a student who studied in America (but he still doesn't speak English well).'

Needless to say, the ECC facts with the negative copula are different: just the *ani-* part can be doubled, as in (20)a. And in fact while the doubling of N + negative copula as in (20)b is grammatical, this example does not have the 'negative implicature' interpretation typical of the ECC, but rather has a VP-topic interpretation:

(20) a. papo-ka ani-ki-nun ani-ta
fool-NOM NCOP-NMLZ-TOP NCOP-DECL
'He's not a fool (but he's not so smart).'

b. papo-ka ani-ki-nun papo-ka ani-ta
fool-NOM NCOP-NMLZ-TOP fool-NOM NCOP-DECL
'It is true that he's not a fool.'

In summary, the ECC treats the negative copula *ani-ta* as a single syntactic V^0 which takes a phrasal complement, while the only V^0 that the ECC has access to with *-i-* is the V^0 formed by it and the N together.

5 Formal Analysis with Lexical Sharing

We believe that the facts above require an analysis of the positive copula grounded in the lexicality of the N+copula complex. Our analysis uses lexical sharing, designed by Wescoat (2002) to handle numerous phenomena across languages in which a word that is demonstrably an output of the lexicon – not a postsyntactic amalgam – exhibits complex syntactic behavior suggesting that it corresponds to two lexical-category constitutents in phrase structure.

[3]Under the clitic analysis of the copula, the copula and its complement are never a syntactic constituent, so it must be that ECC applies only to phonological constituents (as suggested in the analysis of Jo (2003)).

5.1 Lexical Sharing and HPSG

Wescoat (2002) argues that the atomic units of phrase structure are neither words nor morphemes, but rather lexical-category-bearing *atomic constituents*, each of which maps into a *lexical exponent*, i.e. a word which is said to *instantiate* the atomic constituent. The basic idea of lexical sharing is then that two or more atomic constituents may 'share' the same exponent, or equivalently, that a single word may instantiate multiple atomic constituents. This scheme provides a straightforward model of words that appear to straddle a phrase boundary. Diagramatically, we distinguish the exponence relation from the usual dominance relation by employing arrows in place of simple lines, as illustrated in (21), which outlines our analysis of the lexicality of *haksayng-i-* in (19).

(21)

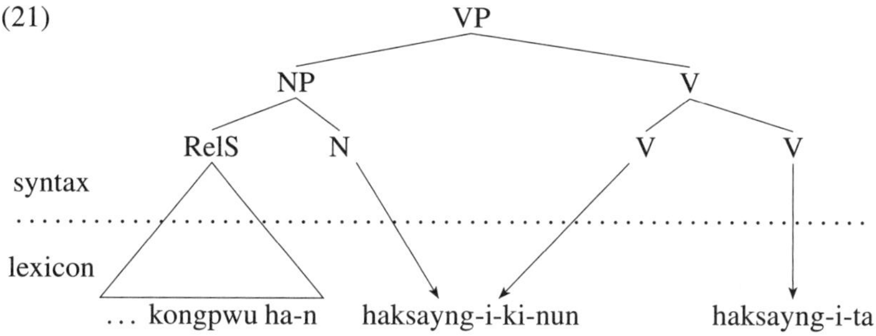

Crucially for our purposes, it is a theorem of Wescoat's axiomatization of lexical sharing that a single word can be the exponent of multiple atom only if those atoms are adjacent.

Lexical sharing may be simply implemented using the basic machinery of HPSG, in which there is a basic sort of *sign*. Two subtypes of *sign*, namely *phrase* and *word*, have been traditionally employed for representing phrase-structure constituents; thus, standard HPSG is among those theories that regard words as the atoms of phrase structure. In the lexical sharing approach we divorce the type *word* from this role, and have a new, properly syntactic type to represent atomic constituents in phrase-structure, namely *atom*. The modified *sign* hierarchy, for our purposes here, is shown in (22).

(22)

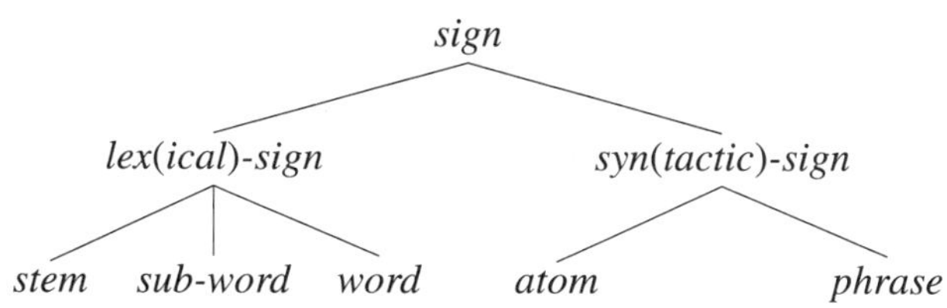

The type (in *italics*) of an AVM determines what attributes (in SMALL CAPS) and what types of values the AVM may contain. The principal new type declarations are given in (23).

(23) a. $\begin{bmatrix} \textit{lex-sign} & \\ \text{PHON(OLOGY)} & \textit{list(form)} \\ \text{INST(ANTIATE)S} & \textit{non-empty-list(atom)} \end{bmatrix}$

b. $\begin{bmatrix} \textit{syn-sign} & \\ \text{SYNSEM} & \textit{synsem} \end{bmatrix}$

c. $\begin{bmatrix} \textit{atom} & \\ \text{EXPON(ENT)} & \textit{word} \\ \text{ARG(UMENT)-ST(RUCTURE)} & \textit{list(synsem)} \end{bmatrix}$

d. $\begin{bmatrix} \textit{phrase} & \\ \text{D(AUGH)T(E)RS} & \textit{non-empty-list(syn-sign)} \end{bmatrix}$

The new attributes EXPON and INSTS in (23) implement lexical sharing: each *atom* is linked via EXPON to a lexical exponent of type *word*; additionally, every *word* contains, as the value of INSTS, an ordered list enumerating each *atom* that the *word* instantiates. We ensure reciprocal linkage between *word* and *atom* with the constraints in (24).

(24) a. $\textit{atom} \Rightarrow \boxed{1}\begin{bmatrix} \text{EXPON} \begin{bmatrix} \textit{word} \\ \text{INSTS } \langle \ldots, \boxed{1}, \ldots \rangle \end{bmatrix} \end{bmatrix}$

b. $\textit{word} \Rightarrow \boxed{1}\begin{bmatrix} \text{INSTS} \left\langle \begin{bmatrix} \textit{atom} \\ \text{EXPON } \boxed{1} \end{bmatrix}, \ldots, \begin{bmatrix} \textit{atom} \\ \text{EXPON } \boxed{1} \end{bmatrix} \right\rangle \end{bmatrix}$

The effect of (24) is illustrated by the schematization in (25) of an instance of lexical sharing (compare with the *haksayng-i-ki-nun* part of (21)).

(25)
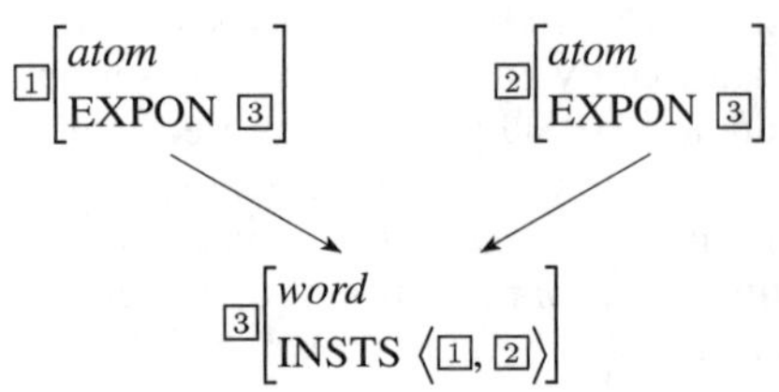

The tags $\boxed{1}$, $\boxed{2}$, and $\boxed{3}$ reveal the interpenetration of the AVMs which they index: both *atom* $\boxed{1}$ and *atom* $\boxed{2}$ have the same *word* $\boxed{3}$ as value of EXPON, giving rise to lexical sharing; moreover, *word* $\boxed{3}$ contains both *atom* $\boxed{1}$ and *atom* $\boxed{2}$ in its INSTS list, thereby enabling the *word* to determine individually the syntactic features of each *atom*. When there is no actual lexical 'sharing', i.e. when a *word* is exponent of a single *atom*, the INSTS list is of length one.

5.2 Copularization

The analysis of *-i-* will be easier to see if we start with the negative copula first. The entry for this form is shown in (26) (we assume a sort *verb-root* for the basic representation of verb roots in Korean):

(26)
$$
\boxed{1}\begin{bmatrix} \textit{verb-root} & \\ \text{PHON} & \text{ani} \\ \text{INSTS} & \left\langle \begin{bmatrix} \textit{atom} & \\ \text{EXPON} & \boxed{1} \\ \text{SYNSEM|LOC} & \begin{bmatrix} \text{CAT|HEAD} & \begin{bmatrix}\textit{verb}\end{bmatrix} \\ \text{CONT} & \begin{bmatrix} \textit{be-rel} & \\ \text{QUANTS} & \langle\ \textit{not-rel}\ \rangle \\ \text{ARG1} & i \\ \text{ARG2} & j \end{bmatrix} \end{bmatrix} \\ \text{ARG-ST} & \left\langle \text{NP}_i, \begin{bmatrix} \text{CAT|HEAD} & \begin{bmatrix} \textit{noun} \\ \text{CASE } \textit{nom} \end{bmatrix} \\ \text{CONT} & \begin{bmatrix}\text{INDEX } j\end{bmatrix} \end{bmatrix} \right\rangle \end{bmatrix} \right\rangle \end{bmatrix}
$$

This is the entry of a two-place predicate which expresses negation of the *be-rel* between those arguments. We adopt the analysis of negation in Ginzburg and Sag (2000), where *neg-rel* appears on the QUANTS list. The first argument is the subject, and the second argument is a nominative-marked complement.

Such an entry would also be appropriate for a positive copula, without the *neg-rel*. The different uses of the non-fragment copula mentioned in section 2 would involve related entries that differ in terms of information-structure properties and also possibly in terms of subtly different sub-types of *be-rel*. The fragment use of the copula inherits the value of the semantic relation from the context.

The positive copula *-i* is treated by a rule (see (27)) which takes a noun *sub-word* as input, and which returns a *verb-root*. That new lexical item can instantiate two syntactic atoms, the first of which is the noun that was input to the rule, and the second is a two-place predicate which expresses the *be-rel*. This lexical rule applies to an N sub-word and creates a form of type *verb-root*. That new form instantiates two atoms in the syntax, an N (which heads NP) and a V (which heads VP), and may be input to further lexical rules. Hence, this is appropriate for the form *haksayng-i-ki-nun* in (21). The lexical rule puts the relevant syntax and semantics of the host N as information about the second argument of the V that the output form instantiates. Nevertheless, this is still a two-place V, an atom which will eventually combine in syntax with a complement NP and then a subject NP.

(27) **Copularization Rule**

$$\boxed{1}\left[\begin{array}{ll} \textit{sub-word} & \\ \text{PHON} & \phi \\ \text{INSTS} & \left\langle \boxed{2}\left[\begin{array}{ll}\textit{atom} & \\ \text{EXPON} & \boxed{1} \\ \text{SYNSEM|LOC} & \left[\begin{array}{ll}\text{CAT|HEAD} & \boxed{3}\left[\textit{noun}\right] \\ \text{CONT} & \boxed{4}\left[\text{INDEX } j\right]\end{array}\right]\end{array}\right]\right\rangle \end{array}\right] \Rightarrow$$

$$\boxed{5}\left[\begin{array}{ll} \textit{verb-root} & \\ \text{PHON} & \phi\text{-}i\text{-} \\ \text{INSTS} & \left\langle \boxed{2}, \left[\begin{array}{ll}\textit{atom} & \\ \text{EXPON} & \boxed{5} \\ \text{SYNSEM|LOC} & \left[\begin{array}{ll}\text{CAT|HEAD} & \left[\textit{verb}\right] \\ \text{CONT} & \left[\begin{array}{ll}\textit{be-rel} & \\ \text{QUANTS} & \langle\ \rangle \\ \text{ARG1} & i \\ \text{ARG2} & j\end{array}\right]\end{array}\right] \\ \text{ARG-ST} & \left\langle \text{NP}_i, \left[\begin{array}{ll}\text{CAT|HEAD} & \boxed{3} \\ \text{CONT} & \boxed{4}\left[\text{INDEX } j\right]\end{array}\right]\right\rangle\end{array}\right]\right\rangle \end{array}\right]$$

For the final word *haksayng-i-ta* in (21), we need an optional modification to the rule in (27) which truly incorporates the N; a model HPSG analysis for this can be found in Malouf (1999). The INSTS list is modified to just have V on it, and the second element on the ARG-ST list is of a *non-canonical* type, namely *incorp(orated)*, which means that although it is present in the lexical entry and in the semantics, it does not correspond to an overt dependent of the verb in the syntax.

6 Conclusion

Under the Lexical Sharing account developed above, *haksayng-i-* is formed in the lexicon and may then be input to any processes of verbal affixation. As it is a lexical unit, it necessarily has the properties enumerated in sections 3–5 above, properties which are either accidental or uncapturable on accounts that do not recognize the lexicality of this form. The Lexical Sharing approach nevertheless allows this single word to instantiate the two atoms N and V in (3) above, showing how a morphologically unitary form can participate in complex syntactic behavior.

References

Cho, Sae-Youn, Jong-Bok Kim, and Peter Sells. 2003. Contrastive verb constructions in Korean. Paper presented at ISOKL-10, Harvard.

Cho, Young-mee Yu, and Peter Sells. 1995. A lexical account of inflectional suffixes in Korean. *Journal of East Asian Linguistics* 4, 119–174.

Choi, Kiyong. 2003. The echoed verb construction in Korean: Evidence for V-raising. In P. M. Clancy (ed.), *Japanese/Korean Linguistics*, Vol. 11. CSLI, Stanford Linguistics Association, 457–470.

Ginzburg, Jonathan, and Ivan Sag. 2000. *Interrogative Investigations*. CSLI Publications.

Jo, Jung-Min. 2003. Variation in predicate cleft constructions in Korean: Epiphenomena at the Syntax-PF interface. Paper presented at ISOKL-10, Harvard.

Kim, Jong-Bok, and Chan Chung. 2002. Korean copula constructions: A construction and linearization perspective. *Ene* 27, 171–193.

Kim, Youngsun. 2002. The syntax of Korean verbal focus constructions. In *Proceedings of the 2002 LSK International Summer Conference*. The Linguistic Society of Korea, 333–344.

Malouf, Robert. 1999. West Greenlandic noun incorporation in a monohierarchical theory of gramar. In G. Webelhuth, J.-P. Koenig, and A. Kathol (eds.), *Lexical and Constructional Aspects of Linguistic Explanation*. Stanford, CSLI Publications, 47–62.

Nishiyama, Kunio, and Eun Cho. 1998. Predicate cleft constructions in Japanese and Korean: The role of dummy verbs in TP/VP-preposing. In N. Akatsuka et al. (eds.), *Japanese/Korean Linguistics*, Vol. 7. CSLI, Stanford Linguistics Association, 463–479.

Oh, Mira. 1991. The Korean copula and palatalization. *Language Research* 27, 701–724.

Sells, Peter. 1997. Positional constraints and faithfulness in morphology. In S. Kuno et al. (eds.), *Harvard Studies in Korean Linguistics*, Vol. 7. Dept. of Linguistics, Harvard University, 488–503.

Stump, Gregory. 2001. *Inflectional Morphology: A Paradigm Structure Approach*. Cambridge, Cambridge University Press.

Wescoat, Michael T. 2002. *On Lexical Sharing*. Doctoral dissertation, Stanford University.

Yang, In-Seok. 1972. *Korean Syntax: Case Marking, Delimiters, Complementation and Relativization*. Seoul, Paek Hap Sa.

Yoon, James Hye-Suk. 1995. Nominal, verbal, and cross-categorial affixation in Korean. *Journal of East Asian Linguistics* 4, 325–356.

Yoon, James Hye-Suk. 2002. Non-morphological determination of nominal affix ordering in Korean. In L. Heggie and F. Ordonez (eds.), *Theoretical Perspectives on Clitic and Affix Combinations*. Amsterdam/Philadelphia, John Benjamins, to appear.

Yoon, James Hye-Suk. 2003. What the Korean copula reveals about the interaction of morphology and syntax. In P. M. Clancy (ed.), *Japanese/Korean Linguistics*, Vol. 11. CSLI, Stanford Linguistics Association, 34–49.

Subject Scrambling*

HEEJEONG KO
Massachusetts Institute of Technology

1. Introduction

The position of the subject in Korean and Japanese has been widely discussed in the literature. In particular, whether a subject undergoes movement in the overt syntax has been quite controversial (Saito 1985; Y-S Lee 1993; Sells 1995; K-W Sohn 1995; Fukui and Sakai 2003, and references therein). Most of the literature, however, has limited the discussion to movement of a subject from [Spec,*v*P] to [Spec,TP] for nominative Case checking purposes (Miyagawa 1997b; Fukui and Sakai 2003, among others; cf. K-W Sohn 1995). In this paper, I provide a new perspective on this issue by extending the empirical domain of the question.

The main goal of the paper is to examine the possibility of clause internal scrambling of a subject to [Spec,CP], which would clearly not be

* I am thankful to the participants of *Japanese/Korean Linguistics 13* at MSU for their helpful questions. I am also grateful to Sylvain Bromberger, Rajesh Bhatt, Noam Chomsky, Sabine Iatridou, Shigeru Miyagawa, Norvin Richards, Luigi Rizzi, Mamoru Saito, William Snyder, Akira Watanabe, Ken Wexler, John Whitman, James Yoon, and others with whom I discussed earlier versions of the paper. Special thanks go to David Pesetsky and Danny Fox for helpful comments and discussions in developing this work. Finally, I thank Philip Monahan for proofreading this paper. Of course, all errors in the paper are mine.

Case-driven. Investigating *why*-questions in adult and child Korean, I argue that a subject must be able to scramble to [Spec,CP].

The paper is organized as follows. Section 2 points out that previous arguments against Subject Scrambling (SS) are inconclusive. Section 3 investigates the position of *way* 'why' in Korean and proposes that *way* is directly merged in [Spec,CP] in the overt syntax. Section 4 demonstrates that subjects can scramble to [Spec,CP], providing evidence from the distribution of floating quantifiers in Korean *why*-questions. Section 5 shows that the proposal is supported by unique word order patterns in child Korean *why*-questions. Section 6 discusses the implications of the paper.

2. Previous Arguments

The controversy regarding the position of the subject is rooted in the fact that subject movement is, in most cases, string vacuous, as shown in (1).

(1) $[_{CP}$ S $[_{TP}$ t_S $[_{vP}$ t_S $[_{VP}$ O V] *v*] T] C]

In the absence of clear word order tests, indirect evidence has led researchers to different conclusions (see Saito 1985; Hoji 1985; Y-S Lee 1993;K-W Sohn 1995; as Yoon (2003) notes, the same issue arises in the discussions of verb movement in Korean and Japanese). This section points out that the key arguments against Subject Scrambling (SS) are, in fact, inconclusive.

Saito (1985) argues that a subject never undergoes scrambling, discussing the contrast between (2) and (3). (The same fact holds in Korean.) While the scrambled object in (2) may license the object-oriented floating quantifier, the scrambled subject in (3) cannot license the subject-oriented floating quantifier.

(2) **Sake-o**$_j$ gakusei-ga$_i$ t_j **san-bon** nondeiru
Beer-Acc student-Nom three-CL$_{bottle}$ drinking
'A student is drinking three bottles of beer.' (J: Japanese)

(3) ***Gakusei- ga**$_i$ sake-o$_j$ t_j **san-nin** t_j nondeiru
Student-Nom beer-Acc three-CL$_{people}$ drinking
'Three students are drinking beer.' (J)

Saito (1985) claims that if *gakusei-ga* may scramble over the scrambled *sake-o* in (3), the numeral *san-nin* could be licensed by the trace of the subject. Since (3) is ungrammatical, Saito (1985) concluded that subjects never scramble (see Saito 1985 for details).

Under close inspection, however, this argument does not constitute evidence against SS. Consider, first, the example in (4), which shows that a subject does sometimes float a numeral quantifier.

(4) **Hakpwumo-tul-i**$_i$ ecey t_i **sey-myeng** Mary-lul mannassta
Parent-Pl-Nom yesterday three-CL_{people} M-Acc met
'Three parents met Mary yesterday.' (K: Korean)

As demonstrated in (4), the subject *hakpwumo* licenses the numeral *sey-myeng* across the temporal adverbial *ecey* (Miyagawa 1989 for Japanese). This indicates that a certain amount of subject movement should be allowed. Since Saito (1985) was built on the theoretical frame that the subject is base-generated at [Spec,IP], we might accommodate (4) by adopting the *v*P-internal subject hypothesis (Kitagawa 1986, among others), as shown in (5).

(5) $[_{IP}$ $Subj_j$ $[_{vP}$ Adv $[_{vP}$ t_j FQ_{subj} $[_{VP}$ Obj V]]]]

Once we adopt the *v*P-internal subject hypothesis, however, Saito's original argument against SS becomes inconclusive. As illustrated in (6), if the subject undergoes Case-driven-movement to [Spec,IP] across the scrambled object at the *v*P-edge, we expect (3) to be grammatical, regardless of SS. However, this is not true. This indicates that the ungrammaticality of (3), in fact, does not crucially rely on the inability of the subject to scramble.

(6) $[_{IP}$ $Subj_j$ $[_{vP}$ Obj_i $[_{vP}$ t_j FQ_{subj} $[_{VP}$ t_i V]]]]

Further, arguments against clause-external SS are also indecisive. Saito (1985) argues that clause-external SS is impossible. Apparently, however, counterexamples like (7) do exist. Saito argues that (7) can be explained by assuming that the matrix subject is 'downgraded as a parenthetical expression'. The grammaticality of (7), however, may simply demonstrate that the clause-external SS is possible (see K-W Sohn 1995 for this position).

(7) John-i$_i$ [na-nun [t_i Mary-lul salangha-n-ta-ko]] sayngkakhanta
J-Nom I-Top M-Acc love-Pres-Dec-C think
'John, I think that _ loves Mary.' (K)

Given the controversy concerning SS, we are in need of a configuration like (8) to test the availability of SS.

(8) $[_{CP}$ $Subj_j$ Adv $[_{IP}$ t_j $[_{vP}$ t_j $[_{VP}$ Obj V]]]]

Since the adverb in (8) is base-generated higher than [Spec,IP], Case-driven subject movement is not an issue. Further, the subject movement in (8) is not string vacuous, we may obtain direct evidence for SS. In the following sections, I show that the adverb 'why' provides such a case.

3. The Position of *Way* 'why' in Korean

In this section, I demonstrate that *way* 'why' in Korean is (externally-) merged into [Spec,CP] of the clause it modifies. The crucial evidence comes from the interaction between the Intervention Effect (Beck and Kim 1997) and the distribution of *way* 'why' in Korean (cf. E Cho 1998).

In Korean (and Japanese), there is a well-known word order restriction between *wh*-words and some Scope-Bearing Elements (SBE) (see Hoji 1985; S W Kim 1991; Beck and Kim 1997, among others).

(9) a. ***Amwuto** **mwues**-ul ilk-ci-**anh**-ass-ni?
Anyone what-Acc read-CI-not-Past-Q
'What did no one read?'
b. **Mwues**-ul$_1$ **amwuto** t$_1$ ilk-ci-**anh**-ass-ni? (K)

As illustrated in (9), *wh*-words cannot be preceded (and c-commanded) by a scope-bearing element, such as *amwuto* 'anyone'. This phenomenon was analyzed as the *LF blocking effect* (Beck and Kim 1997) and reanalyzed as the *LF Intervention Effect* (IE: Hagstrom 1998). A descriptive statement of the effect is given in (10). (The technical details implementing (10) may vary.) On this approach, while LF movement of *mwues* 'what' in (9a) to its checking position is blocked by *amwuto*, overt scrambling of *mwues* in (9b) is allowed.

(10) A *wh*-phrase cannot move across some SBEs at LF to its checking position–such SBEs include 'anyone', 'only', 'even', and 'not'.

What is interesting is the behavior of *way* 'why' with respect to the IE. As noted by Cho (1998), *way* may precede or follow *amwuto*, unlike other *wh*-words. This is illustrated in (11) (see Miyagawa 1997a for Japanese).

(11) a. **Amwuto** **way** ku chayk-ul ilk-ci-**anh**-ass-ni?
Anyone why the book-Acc read-CI-not-Past-Q
'Why did no one read the book?'
b. **Way** **amwuto** ku chayk-ul ilk-ci-**anh**-ass-ni? (K)

Given the contrast between (9) and (11), one might think that *way* is simply exceptional to the IE (see E Cho 1998 for this approach). Under closer investigation, however, this conjecture is not correct.

If *way* is simply exceptional to the IE, we expect that *way* can be preceded by an SBE in any structural configuration. As demonstrated in (12), however, this is not the case. When *way* is merged in the (embedded) declarative clause, the higher negation or 'anyone' makes the sentence ungrammatical. Compare (12) with (13), which shows that *way* may obtain a long-distance reading when there is no SBE in the higher clause.

(12) *__Amwuto__ [John-i __way__ saimha-yess-ta-ko] malha-ci-__anh__-ass-ni?
Anyone J-Nom way resign-Past-Dec-C say-CI-not-Past-Q
'What is the reason x such that (s.t.) no one said John resigned for x?' (K)

(13) Mary-nun [John-i __way__ saimha-yess-ta-ko] malhay-ss-ni?
M-Top [J-Nom why resign-Past-Dec-C] say-Past-Q
'What is the reason x s.t. Mary said that John resigned for x?' (K)

Given (11) and (12), one may think that *way* cannot be preceded by an SBE only when the SBE is in a higher clause (Miyagawa 1997a for Japanese *naze* 'why'). Under closer inspection, however, this hypothesis is also incorrect. As demonstrated in (14), even the clausemate SBE incurs ungrammaticality when *way* is merged in a declarative clause.

(14) *Ne-nun [__amwuto way__ ku chayk-ul ilk-ci-__anh__-ass-ta-__ko__]
You-Top [anyone why the book-Acc read-CI-not-Past-Dec-C]
malhay-ss-ni?
say-Past-Q
'What is the reason x s.t. you said no one read the book for x?'(K)

By contrast, when *way* is merged in an embedded interrogative clause, *way* can be preceded by an SBE. This is illustrated in (15).

(15) I-nun [__amwuto way__ ku chayk-ul ilk-ci-__anh__-ass-__nunci__] anta
I-Top [anyone why the book-Acc read-CI-not-Past-Q] know
'I know why no one read the book.'(K)

The generalization capturing the distribution of *way* is presented in (16).

(16) When *way* is merged in an interrogative clause, SBEs may precede it. On the other hand, when *way* is merged in a declarative clause, SBEs cannot precede it.

On the surface, the generalization in (16) may seem puzzling because there is no obvious reason why the position of the SBE should be correlated with the types of the clause that *way* merges into. However, once we understand the position of *way* in the syntax, (16) is captured in a principled way.

I argue that the peculiar behaviors of *way* with respect to the IE are attributed to its base position in the syntax. Specifically, I propose that *way* is *a clausal modifier*, which is externally-merged (base-generated) in [Spec,CP] of the clause it semantically modifies.[1] I label this proposal the *Clausal Modifier Hypothesis* (CMH). In the following, I demonstrate how the generalization in (16) is explained under the CMH.

Consider first the behavior of *way* merged in interrogative clauses (see (11) and (15)). As illustrated in (17), when *way* is merged in an interrogative clause, the clause has a Q-morpheme that licenses *way* in [Spec,CP]. Through Spec-Head agreement between *way* and *Q*, thus, *way* is licensed in the overt syntax (cf. Chomsky 2000).[2] After *way* is merged in [Spec,CP], an SBE may scramble over *way*, as illustrated in (18) (see Y-S Lee 1993 and K-W Sohn 1995 for independent evidence that SBEs may scramble in Korean). This movement, however, does not trigger the IE because *way* has already been licensed in the overt syntax. Hence, (11a) is grammatical. The tree structure for (11a) is given in (19). The same account extends to (15).

(17) $[_{CP}$ way$_{\text{[uWH]}}$ **Q** ... SBE ...]: External-Merge of *way*

(18) $[_{CP}$ SBE$_1$ $[_{CP}$ way$_{\text{[uWH]}}$ **Q** .... t_1..]]: SBE-Scrambling over *way*

(19)

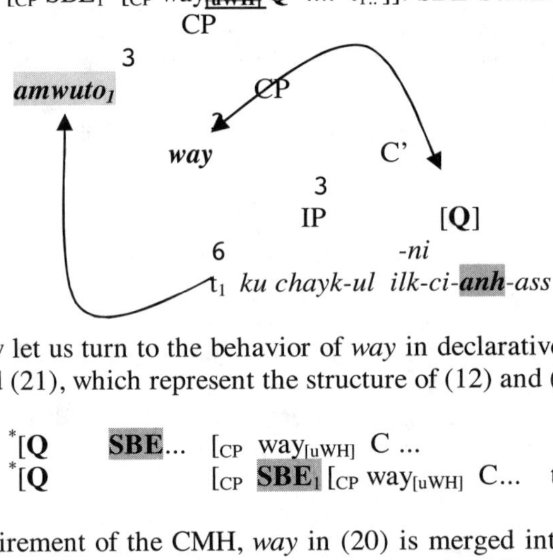

Now let us turn to the behavior of *way* in declarative clauses. Consider (20) and (21), which represent the structure of (12) and (14), respectively.

(20) *[**Q** **SBE**... $[_{CP}$ way$_{\text{[uWH]}}$ C ...]]; see (12)

(21) *[**Q** $[_{CP}$ **SBE**$_1$ $[_{CP}$ way$_{\text{[uWH]}}$ C... t_1]]; see (14)

By requirement of the CMH, *way* in (20) is merged into [Spec,CP] of the declarative clause. Importantly, however, *way* in (20) cannot be licensed in

[1] Similar proposals have been made for *wh*-fronting languages like French and Italian (Rizzi 1990, 1999). See also Lin (1992) for Chinese *weishenme* 'why'.

[2] Chomsky (2000) does not allow Spec-Head relationship as a legitimate configuration for agreement. The CMH can be accommodated into Chomsky (2000) by assuming that *way* is a 'head' that probes the head C (see the similar analysis on expletives and T in Chomsky 2000).

its External-Merge position, in contrast to *way* in (17). Since the declarative clause does not contain the Q-morpheme, *way* in (20) must undergo LF-movement to be licensed. The SBE preceding *way*, however, blocks this LF-movement. Hence, the sentence is ungrammatical. The same account extends to (21). In short, *way* is merged into [Spec,CP] in the overt syntax, and this property leads to the non-uniform behavior of *way* with respect to the Intervention Effect.

4. Subject Scrambling in *Why*-questions

One of the immediate consequences of the CMH is that we have direct evidence for SS. As illustrated in (22), the subject *John* may topicalize or scramble across *way*. Under the CMH, this indicates that a subject may scramble over [Spec,CP] clause-internally. Hence, to the extent that the CMH is successful, we have a strong argument for the existence of SS.

(22) **John$_i$-i/un** **way** t_i ku chayk-ul ilk-ess-ni?
John-Nom/Top why the book-Acc read-Past-Q
'Why did John read the book?' (K)

The floating numeral quantifier test provides further evidence for the existence of SS. If a subject is indeed base-generated below *way*, we predict that the subject licenses a subject-oriented floating quantifier across *way*.[3] As demonstrated in (23), this prediction is borne out. (*Way*-question is embedded in (23) to preserve the naturalness of colloquial speech. However, the same fact holds in root *way*-questions.)

(23) (Na-nun) [**haksayng-tul-i** way **sey-myeng** hakkyo-lul
(I-Top) student-Pl-Nom why three-CL school-Acc
pangmwunha-yess-nunci] an-ta
visit-Past-Q know-Dec
'I know why three students visited the school.'(K)

In sum, interesting facts concerning the Intervention Effect lead us to pinpoint the position of *way* in the overt syntax as [Spec,CP]. This, in turn, provides a direct way of testing non-string vacuous scrambling of a subject. Given that *way* is in [Spec,CP], the fact that a subject may precede *way* constitutes a genuine instance of SS without involving Case-checking.[4]

---

[3] I thank Howard Lasnik (p.c.) for pointing out this prediction.

[4] As for Japanese, there are differences among speakers about whether (11a) is allowed (Miyagawa 1997a; cf. Tanaka 1997; Ayumi Ueyama (p.c.)). The Korean paradigm shown in section 3 and 4, however, holds for those Japanese speakers allowing (11a). Thus, the CMH may extend to those Japanese speakers. For the lack of space, Japanese examples are omitted.

5. Child Korean *Why*-questions

Considering that adult Korean freely allows scrambling, it is not surprising that we find both sentences in (24) grammatical.

(24) a. **Way John-i** ku chayk-ul ilk-ess-ni?
Why John-Nom the book-Acc read-Past-Q
'Why did John read the book?'
b. **John-i way** ku chayk-ul ilk-ess-ni?

Suppose, however, that some Korean speakers do not allow scrambling. Then, under the CMH, we predict that this group of speakers would not utter (24b). Particularly, since these speakers do not allow SS, the CMH predicts that a subject, in general, would not precede *way* for these speakers. Of course, it is difficult to test the prediction with adult Korean speakers due to their ability to scramble. Interestingly, however, child Korean does provide such an opportunity.

It has been noted that Korean children are not good at word order changing operations, such as scrambling, when they are in the early stages of language acquisition (2;00-3;00) (Kim 1997 for details; but see also Otsu 1994 for perception tests with Japanese children).[5] An interesting prediction follows from this observation.

(25) If child Korean does not allow scrambling in contrast to adult Korean, child utterances will show the original word order between *way* and a (non-topic) subject. Under the CMH, we predict that *way* in child Korean will precede the subject, in most cases.

To evaluate this prediction, I examined a corpus containing 53 files of Korean child JK's spontaneous speech, whose age ranged from (2;00) to (2;11).[6] The main concerns of the study were the following: (i) to find the word order pattern in child *way*-questions, (ii) to compare *way* 'why' and *wh*-adjunct *eti* 'where' in their distributions with respect to the subject, (iii) to compare child and adult *way*-questions in terms of word order.[7]

Overall, I found 111 tokens of *way*-questions with more than one word in the JK speech. But most of them did not represent the subject overtly

---

[5]Kim (1997) examined five children's spontaneous production data, showing that non-canonical word order is rare (ranging from 6% to 27%) in early child Korean.

[6] I am deeply grateful to Seung-Bok Lee for allowing me to study the JK data. I am thankful to Tania Ionin and William Snyder for helping me perform the statistical analyses on the data.

[7] The following method was employed for the analysis. A token was counted as one utterance. Each utterance of self-repetition was counted as one token. Total imitation of adult speech was not counted as a token. Partial or transformed imitation of adult speech was counted as one token. If the nominative marker is dropped, it is hard to tell whether the subject has undergone topicalization or scrambling. Thus, I counted only the subjects clearly marked with a nominative marker.

(72.97%, 81/111) or did not mark it with the Case-marker (12.6%, 14/111). Crucially, however, when the subject was overtly marked with the nominative Case marker, a remarkably consistent pattern was observed. The table in (26) summarizes this pattern in JK *way*-questions.

(26) *Way*-questions with a nominative marked subject in JK speech

Word Order	Tokens	%
way S_{NOM} (O) (Verb)	12	75%
S_{NOM} *way* (O) (Verb)	4	25%
Total	16	100%

As illustrated in (26), *way* in the JK data precedes the nominative marked subject at a very high rate: 75% (12/16). Thus, the data in (26) support the prediction of the CMH in (25). (There were extremely rare instances of object scrambling (*object* <*way*) in JK *way*-questions (2/111, 1.8%)).

One might think that the pattern in (26) could be a general pattern occurring with any *wh*-adjunct in child Korean. The data, however, show that this is not the case. In sharp contrast to *way*, *eti* 'where' never preceded the nominative subject. This is illustrated in (27).[8] As described in (28), the difference between *way* and *eti* in their placement is statistically significant.

(27) *Eti*-questions with a nominative marked subject in JK speech

Word Order	Tokens	%
eti S_{NOM} (O) (Verb)	0	0%
S_{NOM} *eti* (O) (Verb)	14	100%
Total	14	100%

(28) The contrast between *way*- and *eti*-questions in JK speech

Child WH	wh S_{NOM}	S_{NOM} wh
way 'why'	12	4
eti 'where'	0	14

(χ^2=17.5, p<.001; Fisher Exact, p<0.0001)

Finally, one might wonder whether the pattern in (26) may result from mere imitation of adult input. The data, however, demonstrate that this is not the case. Refer to the table (29).

[8] Overall, in *eti*-questions, there were a large number of subject omissions (45.2 %, 66/146) and nominative Case-drop (45.2 %, 66/146). The rate of object scrambling in JK *eti*-questions was extremely low (3.42%, 5/146), as in *way*-questions.

(29) Adult *way*-questions in the JK files

Word Order	Tokens	%
way S_{NOM} (O) (Verb)	32	34%
S_{NOM} *way* (O) (Verb)	63	66%
Total	95	100%

In contrast to the child data, the *subject<way* order was the dominant order (66%) for adults communicating with JK. This contrast shows that the result in (26) did not originate from the influence of the adult input. In fact, the child reversed the predominant *subject<way* order in the adult input into the *way<subject* order in his own speech. Statistically, the difference between the adult and child in the placement of *way* reached significance, as illustrated in (30).

(30) Child vs. Adult *way*-questions

	way S_{NOM}	S_{NOM} *way*
Child	12	4
Adult	32	63

(χ^2=9.7694744, p<.01)

6. Summary and Implications

With close examination of the distribution of *way* 'why' in Korean, I proposed that *way* is directly merged in [Spec,CP] and showed that *way* is subject to the Intervention Effect, contrary to the previous suggestions. Further, investigating the behaviors of *way* both in adult and child Korean, this paper demonstrated that a subject may undergo clause-internal scrambling over [Spec,CP]. This paper implies that given that subject scrambling is allowed, previous arguments relying on 'the ban on subject scrambling' should be reconsidered. In particular, the floating quantifier paradigm discussed in Saito (1985) requires a new account.

References

Beck, S. and S.-S. Kim. 1997. On Wh- and Operator Scope in Korean. *Journal of East Asian Linguistics* 6:339–384.

Cho, E. 1998. Why, Contrastive Topic and LF Movement. *Japanese/Korean Linguistics* 8:403-415.

Chomsky, N. 2000. Minimalist Inquiries: The Framework. *Step by Step*, eds. R. Martin, D. Michael, and J. Uriagereka, 89-157. Cambridge: MIT Press.

Fukui, N. and H. Sakai. 2003. The Visibility Guideline for Functional Categories: Verb Raising in Japanese and Related issues. *Lingua* 113:321-375.

Hagstrom, P. 1998. Decomposing Questions. Doctoral dissertation, MIT.

Hoji, H. 1985. Logical Form Constraints and Configurational Structures in Japanese. Doctoral dissertation, University of Washington.

Kim, S. W. 1991. Chain Scope and Quantification Structure. Doctoral dissertation, Brandeis University.

Kim, Y.-J. 1997. The Acquisition of Korean. *The Crosslinguistic Study of Language Acquisition Vol. 4*, ed. D. I. Slobin, 336-443. Mahwah: Lawrence Erlbaum Associates.

Kitagawa, Y. 1986. Subjects in Japanese and English. Doctoral dissertation, University of Massachusetts, Amherst.

Lee, Y.-S. 1993. Scrambling as Case-Driven Obligatory Movement. Doctoral dissertation, University of Pennsylvania.

Lin, J.-W. 1992. The Syntax of Zenmeyang 'how' and Weishenme 'why' in Mandarin Chinese. *Journal of East Asian Linguistics* 1:293-331.

Miyagawa, S. 1989. *Structure and Case Marking in Japanese* (Syntax and Semantics, 22). San Diego: Academic Press.

Miyagawa, S. 1997a. On the Nature of Wh-Scope. Ms, MIT.

Miyagawa, S. 1997b. Against Optional Scrambling. *Linguistic Inquiry* 28:1-26.

Otsu, Y. 1994. Early Acquisition of Scrambling in Japanese. *Language Acquisition Studies in Generative Grammar*, eds. T. Hoekstra and B. D. Schwartz, 253-264. Amsterdam: Benjamins.

Rizzi, L. 1990. *Relativized Minimality*. Cambridge: MIT Press.

Rizzi, L. 1999. On the Position of "Int(errogative)" in the Left Periphery of the Clause. Ms, Universita di Siena.

Saito, M. 1985. Some Asymmetries in Japanese and Their Theoretical Implications. Doctoral dissertation, MIT.

Sells, P. 1995. Korean and Japanese Morphology from a Lexical Perspective. *Linguistic Inquiry* 26:277-335.

Sohn, K.-W. 1995. Negative Polarity Items, Scope and Economy. Doctoral dissertation, University of Connecticut.

Tanaka, H. 1997. Invisible Movement in Sika-Nai and the Linear Crossing Constraint. *Journal of East Asian Linguistics* 6:143–188.

Yoon, J. H.-S. 2003. How are Inflected Verbs Formed? Handout distributed at Korean Syntax Class, LSA Summer Institute, Michigan State University.

Part II

(continued)

A Phonologically Null Copula Functioning as a Light Verb in Japanese*

YUTAKA SATO
International Christian University

1. Introduction

The syntactic category of verbal nouns (VNs, Martin 1975) such as *kensetu* 'construction' and *haisi* 'abolition' in Japanese has been controversial and postulated as noun, verb, or a category in-between noun and verb. The source of controversy is that VNs behave morphologically like nouns and syntactically like verbs. This paper argues that VNs are nouns but they combine with a phonologically null copula functioning as a light verb to derive complex verbs. Postulating such a light verb dispenses with the assumption, contrary to their morphological behavior, that VNs are of a verbal category or a special category in-between nouns and verbs. Nor do we have to assume that nouns with argument structure like VNs can assign verbal cases when concatenated with an element with some aspectual feature (Iida 1987). Moreover, postulation of such a zero light verb accounts for externalization of themes in some constructions with VNs (Ono 1997).

The nominal status of VNs is obvious in terms of what suffixes they can host and what syntactic positions they can appear in. VNs can host such suffixes as case markers (e.g., *kensetu-ga* 'construction-NOMINATIVE'), but never inflectional or derivational suffixes for verbs (e.g., **kensetu-ru* 'construction-NONPAST TENSE). Marked with a case marker, they can occupy subject or object positions as well as other positions that bona fide nouns can appear in. Their syntactic behavior, however, is peculiar in that they appear to license verbal cases (e.g., nominative and accusative cases) in constructions like (1)-(3). (VNs are highlighted in small capitals.)

(1) **Temporal Affix Construction (TAC)**
Biru o KENSETU go ni ziken ga okita.
building ACC construction after at accident NOM happened
After (they) constructed the building, an accident happened.'

(2) ***ni*-Purposive Construction (*ni*-PC)**
John ga Bill o SUISEN ni itta.
John NOM Bill ACC recommendation to/for went
'John went to recommend Bill.'

(3) **Coordinate Construction (CC)**
Kusiro-Sinso wa Abasiri-Sinso no 9-tenpo no uti Monbetu-
Kushiro-CU TOP Abashiri-CU GEN 9-branch GEN among Monbetsu-
siten o HAISI, nokori no 8-tenpo o hikitotta.
branch ACC abolition remaining GEN 8-branch ACC took-over
'Of the nine branches of the Abashiri Credit Union, the Kushiro Credit Union shut down the Monbetsu branch and took over the remaining eight branches.' (Asahi News Paper, 07/08/2002)

The VNs in (1)-(3) are all preceded by their theme arguments in the accusative case despite the fact that no overt verb appears in the same clause. The coordination construction in (3) is an actual datum from the Asahi newsaper. This type of construction is commonly found in news paper and magazine articles.[1] In (3), the first conjunct has a VN preceded by its theme in the accusative, and the second conjunct contains a heavy verb (other than *suru*). Many different approaches to accounting for the facts in (1) and (2) have been made, of which we list five in (4).

---

[1] A search on the *Asahi Sinbun Digital News Archives* (*DNA*) was done to see if twenty VNs (ten activity and ten accomplishment VNs) would occur in constructions like (3). All except for two activity VNs (for which there were either no or very few articles that contained them) were found to occur in this type. These twenty VNs are the first ten of the activity and accomplishment VNs examined in Sato (2002).

(4) Five approaches to accounting for (1) and (2):

a. VNs, argument structure-bearing nouns, can assign verbal cases when concatenated with a [+Asp] element: Iida 1987, Sells 1990, Miyagawa 1991, Matsumoto 1996, Nakajima 1993, Iwasaki 1999.

b. VNs, morphologically nouns, can syntactically project VPs (where they can license verbal cases) when concatenated with a [+Asp] element: Manning 1993, Sells 1996a, Ohara 2000.

c. VNs are verbs: Hasegawa 1991, Takahashi 2000.

d. VNs share some syntactic feature(s) with verbs (as well as nouns): Kageyama 1993, Shibatani & Kageyama 1988, Ohta 1994.

e. VNs are nouns, but a phonologically null verbal element/projection that occurs with them licenses verbal cases: Sato 1993, Hoshi 1994.

Having shown the problem (i.e., how to account for the syntactically verbal behavior of VNs that are morphologically nominal) and different approaches to this problem, data and arguments will be presented in the following sections to argue against approaches a-c in favor of approach e, particularly Sato's (1993, 2000) position. The organization of this paper is as follows: section 2 presents data against approaches a-c (but in keeping with approach e), section 3 presents data that shows a zero light verb behave the same way as an overt copula, and section 4 presents a conclusion.

2. Externalization Data

Ono (1997) has pointed out that accomplishment VNs (which Ono calls the causative type), but not activity VNs, permit externalization of their theme argument (and suppression of their agentive subject at the same time) in the Temporal Affix Construction, as shown in (5). The same applies in the Coordinate Construction in (6). It will be shown in this section how the different approaches fare with these data.

(5) **Temporal Affix Construction (TAC)**

Biru	ga	KENSETU	go	ni	ziken	ga	okita.
building	NOM	construction	after	at	accident	NOM	happened

'After the building was constructed, an accident happened.'

(6) **Coordinate Construction (CC)**

Nisitetu-romen-densya	ga	HAISI,	sinai	kara	densya	kieru.
Nishitetsu-streetcar	NOM	abolition	city	from	train	disappear

'The Nishitetsu streetcar will be shut down, and streetcars will go out of sight from the city.' (Asahi News Paper, 05/24/2002)

Note that the VNs in question are not responsible for such externalization of a theme argument. These VNs never allow their theme to appear as subject when followed by the light verb *suru* 'do', as shown below.

(7) a. Tatemono o/*ga KENSETU-suru.
building ACC/NOM construction-do
'(They) will construct a building/A building will be constructed.'

b. Romen-densya o/*ga HAISI-suru.
streetcar ACC/NOM abolition-do
'(They) will shut down streetcars/Streetcars will be shut down.'

In contrast, VNs that denote events equally interpretable as either the theme spontaneously undergoing change of state or the agent/causer bringing about such change (e.g., *kanryoo* 'completion') permit either argument to be realized as subject when followed by *suru* (Jacobsen 1992), as in (8).

(8) Sigoto o/ga KANRYOO-suru.
work ACC/NOM completion-do
'(They) will finish the work/The work will be done.'

VNs denoting events like 'construction' and 'abolition', which require the involvement of some agent for the denoted events to take place are expected to appear as transitive from their semantics (Jacobsen 1992). For the internal argument of such VNs to appear as subject as in (5)-(6) is unexpected. It is probably not unfair to assume that there is some null morpheme, i.e., null passivizer, in these constructions.[2]

The CC of the type in (6) is not as common as the CC of the type in (3) (see footnote 1). Sato (2002), however, found eight of thirty accomplishment VNs appearing in constructions like (6) and none of thirty activity VNs appearing in this pattern (for details of the survey, see Sato 2002). This supports Ono's (1997) claim that only accomplishment VNs undergo externalization of themes in constructions like (5).

How do, then, the different approaches fare with the above data? Ono (1997), assuming the position held by Iida (1987) (i.e., a VN when concatenated with a [+Asp] element assigns verbal cases), attributed the cause of externalization in (5) to 'aspectualizers' (e.g., *go* 'after' and *tyuu* 'during'). Ono argued that an aspectualizer can alternatively foreground one of the subevents of an accomplishment VN's complex event structure[3]: A transitive construction results when the process subevent is foregrounded, as in (1), or a passivized construction results when the result subevent is foregrounded, as in (5). Ono, however, faces a problem (so do approaches a and b): That is, accomplishment VNs passivize even when there is no as-

---

[2]Kageyama (1993: 238-39) postulates a null passivizer for constructions similar to (5), as will be discussed later.

[3]That is, it foregrounds either the process or the result subevent, or the activity or the change-of-state component of the following LCS [*x* DO-something] CAUSE [*y* BECOME *CONSTRUCTED*].

pectualizer as in the case of the CC in (6). We need to look for something other than an aspectualizer that is responsible for externalization.

Approaches a and b, in fact, have another problem with constructions like (3) and (6): They cannot account for why verbal cases are licensed in those constructions, because the VN is not followed by any element with an aspectual feature there. If they would argue that the functional head Infl/T is extracted across-the-board from both the conjuncts, and that this Infl/T bears some aspectual feature that licenses verbal cases when affixed to the VN, there would be little difference from approach e. This is because Infl/T is an extended projection of V (Grimshaw 2000), and, the argument that VNs, although nominal, can license verbal cases when combined with some verbal head is very similar to what is assumed in approach e.

Approach c also faces a problem with the CC in (6), although it fares fine with the CC in (3). If the VN in the CC in (6), which is taken as a verb, undergoes passivization (due to some null passivizer, for example), other bona fide verbs (maybe of the accomplishment type) should be able to be passivized as well. As the example in (9) indicates, however, bona fide verbs (e.g., *toriyame* 'shut down') never passivize in the CC. The example in (9) with the theme in the nominative is completely ungrammatical.

(9) Romen-densya o/*ga toriyame, huben-ni natta.
streetcar ACC/NOM shut-down inconvenient became
'(They) have shut down the streetcars/The streetcars have been shut down, and it is inconvenient.'

If we postulate, as Sato (2002) did, that there is a zero light verb (ø) in the constructions where VNs alone appear to license verbal cases, as shown in (10) and (11), and that this zero light verb optionally externalizes an affected theme (and suppresses an agent), we can account for the data so far presented.

(10) … M-siten o HAISI ø, … 8-tenpo o hikitotta.
M-branch ACC abolition 8-branch ACC took-over
'(They) shut down the M-branch and took over the eight branches.'

(11) Romen-densya ga HAISI ø, densya ga kieru.
streetcar NOM abolition train NOM disappear
'The streetcars will be shut down, and they will be out of sight.'

In (10), the zero light verb functions as light *suru*, that is, it forms a complex predicate with the preceding VN, and the complex predicate thus formed inherits the argument structure of the VN and assigns theta-roles and verbal cases to its arguments (via its extended projections, Grimshaw 2000). Although VNs are nouns and thus are not capable of assigning verbal cases by themselves, derived complex predicates are verbal because they are compounded with a zero light verb and, thus, have the capacity to assign verbal cases. In (11), the zero light verb functions like the Korean partially light verb *toy* 'become': It forms a complex predicate with the preceding VN and externalizes its theme (and suppresses its agent). Unlike *toy*, which externalizes any theme argument (and suppresses an agent, if any), however, this zero light verb externalizes only affected themes.[4]

There are some apparent problems with this account, however. First, although externalization occurs in the TAC and CC, it does not take place in the *ni*-PC in (2), for which a zero light verb must also be postulated. The example in (12) is ungrammatical for the intended reading without overt *sare* 'be-done'. But if a zero light verb can optionally externalize the theme argument of the VN, the example in (12) should be possible without *sare*.

(12) John ga SUISEN *(sare) ni itta.
John NOM recommendation be-done to went
'John went to get recommended.'

The problem with the *ni*-PC above is accounted for by the parallel phenomenon in the corresponding Korean sentence with *toy*. The partially light verb *toy* can form a passive complex verb *chwuchen-toy* 'be recommended' as shown in (13), but this complex predicate cannot appear in the purpose clause as shown in (14). Replacing the partially light verb by the heavy verb *pat* 'receive' salvages the sentence as shown in (15).

(13) John-i CHWUCHEN-toy-essta.
John-NOM recommendation-become-past
'John was recommended.'

(14) *John-i CHWUCHEN-toy-lo kassta.
John-NOM recommendation-become-to went
'John went to be recommended.'

(15) John-i CHWUCHEN-ul pat-ulo kassta.
John- NOM recommendation-acc receive-to went
'John went to get recommended.'

I assume that the intentional reading of the controlled subject is not possible with a complex passive verb derived with some (partially) light verb. This rules out both the Korean example in (14) and the Japanese example without *sare* in (12).[5]

---

[4]For the exact mechanism of how this is formally done, see Sato 2003.

[5]*Sare* is not subject to this constraint, as can be seen from the fact that the example in (12) with it is grammatical. I just have to state that it is just an exception.

If the preceding argument is on the right track, we can generalize that externalization of affected themes is possible in the constructions where a zero light verb is postulated, unless such externalization is ruled out by an independent rule, such as the ban on intentional subject.

Having presented a solution to the problem with the *ni*-CP, we still have some questions to deal with: How can one and the same morpheme act as a completely light and a partially light verb?, Is there overt form of the zero light verb postulated above? I argue that there is an overt lexical item that corresponds to this zero light verb, and since this overt form optionally causes externalization, it should not be surprising for the non-overt equivalent to behave in the same way. The overt lexical item in question, I argue, is the copular verb *da* in Japanese. The phonologically null form of *da* is widely accepted in the literature, as in (16). It will be shown in the next section how the overt copula behaves with VNs.

(16) Kore wa hon ø.
this TOP book COP
'This is a book.'

3. An overt copula functioning as a light verb

Constructions with VNs followed by an overt copula that functions as a light verb have been sporadically mentioned in the literature. Iwasaki (1999) and Matsumoto (1996) argue that *no*, the adnominal form of the copula *da*, follows a VN and plays the role of *suru* in the VN-*no* Construction. Iwasaki (1999), Matsumoto (1996), and Sells (1996b) present sentences with VNs followed by *da*, which, however, vary in grammaticality depending on the type of arguments that the VNs take. Let us first look at the data with *da* and next at the data with *no*.

Matsumoto (1996) and Sells (1996b) give grammatical sentences with VNs followed by *da*, where the VNs occur with the locative postposition *e* 'to', as in (17).

(17) Kyoo kara Jon wa Tookyoo e SYUTTYOO da.
today from Jon TOP Tokyo to business-trip COP
'John will be on a business trip to Tokyo from today on.' (Matsumoto's example, 1996: 81, footnote 10)

Iwasaki (1999), however, presents an 'ungrammatical' sentence with a VN followed by *da*, where the VN occurs with the theme in the accusative case, as shown in (18). The grammaticality judgment in (18) is Iwasaki's.

(18) *John ga ainugo o KENKYUU da/dat-ta.
John NOM Ainu ACC research COP-PRES/COP-PAST

'John does/did research on Ainu.' (Iwasaki's (16) 1999: 121)

He states that 'the finite conclusive form of the copula does not usually co-occur with VN...' (ibid., p. 121). It is true that some sentences of the type in (18), i.e., some VNs with accusatively marked arguments followed by *da*, sound marginal. But there are many instances of this type that are well-formed. The examples in (19) and (20) are the actual data I found through online search on the Google site (http://www.google.co.jp).

(19) kenpoo 9-zyoo o HAISI da na
constitution article-9 ACC abolition COP PARTICLE
'(Now, we) are abolishing article 9 of the constitution.'

(20) *ongaku riron o BENKYOO da* ('music theory ACC study COP'); *saa kyoo mo gyookai o KENKYUU da!* ('now, today too industry ACC study COP'); *mittu no kihon o RENSYUU da* ('three basic ACC practice COP'); *sintin-taisya o SOKUSIN da!* ('metablism ACC activation COP'); *saibu o SYUUSEI da* ('detail ACC revision COP'); *FF o TYUUSI da* ('FF ACC cancellation COP'); *OT34 o HAITI da* ('OT34 ACC arrangement COP'); *dekki o TYOOSEI da* ('deck ACC adjustment COP'); *sosite densyoku o KYOOKA da* ('and electric ornament ACC enrichment COP'); *fyueru-firutaa o KOOKAN da* ('fuel filter ACC change COP'); *hoosoohoo o KAISEI da* ('broadcasting law ACC revision COP')[6]

Iwasaki (1999, note 11, p. 175) notes that examples like (17) are 'a kind of exclamatory' sentence. This exclamatory nuance, however, seems to come from the nonpast copula *da*. Even in sentences where ordinary nouns precede, they often sound exclamatory with *da*, as shown in (21).

(21) Ame da.
rain COP
'It's raining!'

Crucially, accomplishment VNs followed by a copula permit externalization of their themes, as shown in (22). It is also an actual datum found on the Google web site.

(22) Haiguusya-tokubetu-koozyo ga HAISI da nante.
spouse-special-deduction NOM abolition COP PARTICLE
'(Oh well), the special deduction for spouses will be abolished.'

---

[6]The form of the copula that follows NP-*o* VN (a VN preceded by its theme argument in the accusative) is not limited to *no* and *da*. I found on the Google site NP-*o HAISI* na *no* ('it's that ...'), *HAISI* de *wa naku* ('it is not ...'), *HAISI* de *wa gozaimasen* ('it is not ...'—in the polite style), *HAISI* de ('being ...'), and *HAISI* desita *kke* ('was it ...?').

In (22), the theme argument of *haisi* appears in the nominative, when followed by the copula, although it is not possible when it is followed by *suru*, as shown in (7b). The agentive phrase can appear as an adjunct, *seihu ni-yotte* 'by the government', in (22).

Now let us turn to the data with the adnominal copula *no*. The construction in (23) is similar to the TAC in (1) but differs from it in having *no* in-between a VN and a temporal affix.

(23) Keisatu ga otoko o TAIHO no sai, ziko ga okita.
police NOM man ACC arrest COP time accident NOM happened
'When the police arrested the man, an accident happened.'

Shibatani and Kageyama (1988), Kageyama (1993), and Sato (1993) assumed that *no* is a genitive marker. Iwasaki (1999) and Matsumoto (1996) argued that it is a copula in the adnominal form. The evidence Iwasaki (1999: 113) presented was that it '...permits of both present-tense and past-tense interpretations.' That is, adverbial clauses like *keisatu ga otoko o taiho no sai* ('at the time of the police arresting the man') in (23) permits of either a present-tense or a past-tense interpretation. It is true that this adverbial clause can be interpreted either way depending on the tense of the main clause, but it is not readily clear, to me at least, how one can conclude from this fact that *no* in such a construction is a copula.

Interestingly, however, as noted by Kageyama (1993:238-39), this construction also allows the theme of an accomplishment VN to be externalized. The VN *taiho* 'arrest' in (24) only turns transitive when followed by *suru* (*taiho-suru* 'to arrest'), but it can appear passivized when *no* follows.

(24) Otoko ga keisatu ni-yotte TAIHO no sai, ziko ga okita.
man NOM police by arrest COP time accident NOM happened
'When the man was arrested by the police, an accident happened.'

The syntactic behavior of *no* in (24) parallel to that of *da* in (22) seems to indicate that this *no* indeed is the adnominal form of copula.

To sum up, (i) a copular verb can occur after a VN and license verbal case marking on its arguments ((19)-(24)), and (ii) when a copular verb follows a VN, it permits externalization of the internal argument of the VN (which only occurs as transitive when followed by *suru*) ((22), (24)). If we postulate that there is a zero copula in the TAC and CC (and the *ni*-PC as well), as shown in (10) and (11), we can account for verbal case marking in those constructions. Verbal cases such as accusative and nominative can be licensed (via extended projections) by a covert copular verb (or by a complex predicate that it forms with a VN), just as in the case of an overt copula. Externalization of the theme of accomplishment VNs in the TAC and CC can be also accounted for, assuming that a covert copula can cause externalization on a par with an overt one.

4. Conclusion

I have presented data in which the theme of accomplishment VNs externalizes (despite the fact that those VNs only permit their agentive argument to occur as subject when followed by *suru*) in TAC and CC. I have also demonstrated that the overt copula in Japanese can form a complex predicate with a VN, and that it can trigger externalization of accomplishment VNs' internal argument. Based on these facts, I argued that there is a phonologically null copula in the constructions where VNs alone appear to license verbal cases (i.e., the TAC, CC, and *ni*-PC). Postulation of such a phonologically null copula should not be remarkable because it is needed any way to account for many of Japanese sentences with nominal predicates. Postulating some verbal element that forms a complex predicate with VNs in those constructions allows us to account for verbal case marking on the arguments in the constructions where there is no overt verbal element. If such a verbal element is responsible for verbal case marking, we do not have to assume that VNs are verbs or behave as verbs when concatenated with an element with [+Asp]. Moreover, we can also account for why those constructions where VNs appear to license verbal cases are where externalization of accomplishment can take place.

***Acknowledgments:** This paper was presented at the 13th Japanese/Korean Linguistics Conference, 2003, and some parts of it have been presented at the 19th National Conference of the English Society of Japan, 2001, and the 124th Conference of the Linguistics Society of Japan, 2002. I thank all those who made comments on earlier versions of this paper there and the organizers of those conferences.

References

Grimshaw, J. 2000. Locality and extended projection. *Lexical Specification and Insertion*, eds. P. Coopmans, M. Everaert, & J. Grimshaw, 115-33. Amsterdam: John Benjamins Publishing Company.

Hasegawa, N. 1991. On head movement in Japanese: The case of verbal nouns. *Proceedings of Sophia Linguistic Society* 6: 8-32.

Hoshi, H. 1994. Passive, Causative, and Light Verbs: A Study on Theta Role Assignment. Doctoral dissertation, University of Connecticut, Storrs, Connecticut.

Iida, M. 1987. Case assignment by Nominals in Japanese. *Working Papers in Grammatical Theory and Discourse Structure: Interactions of Morphology, Syntax, and Discourse,* eds. M. Iida, S. Wechsler, & D. Zec, 93-138. Stanford: CSLI.

Iwasaki, Y. 1999. Three Subcategories of Nouns in Japanese. Doctoral dissertation,

University of Illinois at Urbana-Champaign.

Jacobsen, W. M. 1991. *The transitive Strucutre of Events in Japanese*. Tokyo: Kurosio Shuppan.

Kageyama, T. 1993. *Bunpoo to Gokeisei* [Grammar and Word Formation]. Kasukabe: Hituzi Syobo.

Manning, C. 1993. Analyzing the verbal noun: Internal and external constraints. *Japanese/Korean Linguistics*, vol. 3, ed. S. Choi, 236-253. Stanford: CSLI.

Martin, S. E. 1975. *A Reference Grammar of Japanese*. New Haven: Yale University Press.

Matsumoto, Y. 1996. *Complex Predicates in Japanese: A Syntactic and Semantic Study of the Notion 'Word.'* Stanford: CSLI.

Miyagawa, S. 1991. Case realization and scrambling. Ms., Ohio State University.

Nakajima, T. 1993. Syntactic analysis of the light verb construction. *Cornell Working Papers in Linguistics* 11, eds. E. J. Rubin & M. Bernstein, 125-148. Department of Linguistics, Cornell University, Ithaca, N.Y.

Ohara, M. 2000. An analysis of verbal nouns in Japanese. Doctoral dissertation, University of Essex.

Ohta, K. 1994. Verbal Nouns in Japanese. Doctoral dissertation, UCLA.

Ono, N. 1997. Externalization and Event Structure. *Verb Semantics and Syntactic Structure*, ed. T. Kageyama, 149-176. Tokyo: Kurosio Shuppan.

Sato, Y. 1993. Complex predicate formation with verbal nouns in Japanese and Korean: Argument transfer at LF. Doctoral dissertation, University of Hawaii at Manoa.

Sato, Y. 2000. Some evidence for a zero light verb in Japanese. *Japanese/Korean Linguistics*, Volume 9, eds. M. Nakayama and C. Quinn, 365-378. Stanford: CSLI.

Sato, Y. 2002. Doomeishi to ketsugoo suru zero no judookaji [A null passivizer that combines with verbal nouns]. Paper presented at the 124th Conference of the Linguistics Society of Japan.

Sato, Y. 2003. Externalization in the Temporal Affix Construction. *Asian Cultural Studies* 29, 105-121. International Christian University.

Sells, P. 1990. More on light verbs and θ-marking. Ms., Stanford University.

Sells, P. 1996a. Case, categories and projection. *Proceedings of 1996 Seoul International Conference on Generative Grammar*, eds. H.-D. Ahn, M.-Y. Kang, Y.-S. Kim, and S. Lee, 47-62. Seoul: Hankwuk Publishing Co.

Sells, P. 1996b. Morphological expression and ordering in Korean and Japanese. *Language Research* 32: 601-620.

Shibatani, M. & Kageyama, T. 1988. Word formation in a modular theory of grammar: postsyntactic compounds in Japanese. *Language* 63: 451-484.

Takahashi, M. 2000. The Syntax and Morphology of Japanese Verbal Nouns. Doctoral dissertation, University of Massachusetts at Amherst.

A Unified Syntactic Account of Morphological Causatives in Korean

MINJEONG SON[1]
University of Delaware

1. Introduction

This paper is primarily concerned with morphological causatives (henceforth, MCs) in Korean with a causative morpheme *-i-*.[2] It is often suggested that morphological causatives are divided into at least two different groups, a decomposable type and a nondecomposable type. Most theories of Korean causatives have argued that MCs that are not decomposable must be treated differently from those that are. Kim (1998), for instance, has argued the decomposable type is formed in the syntax, whereas the nondecomposable type is formed in the lexicon.

---

[1]This paper was presented at the Annual Graduate Student Conference at the University of Delaware, the 13th Japanese/Korean Linguistics Conference at Michigan State University, and the 4th Asian GLOW conference at Seoul National University. I would like to thank the audience of each conference for their comments and criticisms. I am especially grateful to James Yoon and Mamoru Saito for their comments and enjoyable discussions on this topic. I am also greatly benefited from insightful comments, suggestions, and discussions with Satoshi Tomioka and Benjamin Bruening. All the shortcomings are of course my own.

[2]The causative suffix in Korean is realized in various forms, such as ***i, -hi, -li, -ki,*** and ***-khi.***

In this paper, I challenge these analyses and propose that all MC formation in Korean takes place in the syntax. By demonstrating the scope ambiguity of the adverb *tasi* 'again', as used by von Stechow (1998) for German, I show that those MCs, which have been believed to be unanalysable, in fact, involve complex event structure with a separable result state denoted by VP. Following recent proponents of event decomposition in the syntax (e.g., Hale and Keyser 1993; Harley 1995; Travis 2000), I argue that the decomposition of the complex causative verb is reflected in the syntax by a separate verbal projection headed by CAUSE, similar to *v*P in Hale and Keyser (1993) and v_{CAUSE} in Folli and Harley (2004).

2. Two Types of Morphological Causatives

Let us first consider two different types of MCs in Korean which differ syntactically and semantically based on the scope of adverbial modification and the semantics of the causee.

In the first type, the causee acts as an agent of the caused event, and manner adverbs often create scope ambiguities, as illustrated in (1).[3]

(1)	Mary-ka	tongsayng-eykey	chayk-ul	*ppalli*	ilk-hi-ess-ta.
	Mary-NOM	sister-DAT	book-ACC	*quickly*	read-CAU-PST-DEC

a. 'Mary made her sister quickly read the book.'
b. 'Mary quickly made her sister read the book.'

The causee 'sister' is interpreted as an agent of reading a book, and the subject 'Mary' is interpreted as a causer that brings about the event 'Sister reads the book'. In addition, the property of 'quickly' can be attributed both to the caused event and the causing event, as shown in (1a) and (1b). For this reason, it has often been claimed that the morphological causative with an agentive causee (Agentive MCs) is decomposable and involves two events (e.g., Um 1995; Kim 1998).

In the second type, the causee does not participate in the caused event as an agent. Rather, it behaves as a goal, as illustrated in (2).

(2)	Emma-ka	ai-eykey	sinpal-ul	*ppalli*	sin-ki-ess-ta.
	mother-NOM	child-DAT	shoes-ACC	*quickly*	put.on-CAU-PST-DEC

a. 'Mother quickly put the shoes on the child.'
b. *'Mother caused the shoes to be quickly put on the child.'

Ai-eykey 'the child' in (2) is not an agent of the caused eventuality, but a goal who is the target of the action carried out by the causer 'Mother'; the

---

[3]The following abbreviations are used in this paper.
NOM: Nominative ACC: Accusative DAT: Dative CAU: Causative Morpheme
PST: Past Tense DEC: Declarative Marker

child is not the participant in control of the event of putting the shoes on, but the Mother is. The state of the shoes being put on the child is a result state of Mother's action performed on the child. Furthermore, no ambiguity is observed with respect to adverbial modification; the adverb 'quickly' only describes how the action of Mother was carried out which results in the state of the shoes being put on the child. Hence, it has been argued that MCs with a non-agentive causee (Non-agentive MCs) involve only a single event and cannot be decomposed (e.g., Um, 1995).

The tables in (3-4) illustrate examples of these two types of MCs in Korean.

(3) Agentive MCs

	a. Non-Causatives		b. Causatives	
In-tran.	i. wus-ta	'laugh'	wus-***ki***-ta	'cause x to laugh'
	ii. wul-ta	'cry'	wul-***li***-ta	'cause x to cry'
	iii. ket-ta	'walk'	ket-***li***-ta	'cause x to walk'
Trans.	iv. ilk-ta	'read'	ilk-***hi***-ta	'cause x to read'
	v. kal-ta	'plow'	kal-***li***-ta	'cause x to plow'
	vi. palp-ta	'tread'	palp-***hi***-ta	'cause x to tread'

(4) Non-Agentive MCs

	a. Non-Causatives		b. Causatives	
In-tran.	i. cwuk-ta	'die'	cwuk-***i***-ta	'kill x'
	ii. nok-ta	'melt'	nok-***i***-ta	'melt x'
	iii. el-ta	'freeze'	el-***i***-ta	'freeze x'
Trans	iv. mek-ta	'eat'	mek-***i***-ta	'feed x'
	v. ip-ta	'put on clothes'	ip-***i***-ta	'dress x'
	vi. sin-ta	'put on shoes'	sin-***ki***-ta	'put shoes on x'

As seen in (3) and (4), the intransitive verb bases appearing in each type of MCs are unambiguously unergatives and unaccusatives, respectively. In particular, the relation between the pairs of transitive versus unaccusative verbs in non-agentive MCs is comparable to the inchoative-transitive alternation in English like 'The ice melted' and 'John melted the ice.'[4]

As mentioned earlier, on the bases of examples like (1), the addition of the causative morpheme *-i-* to the type of unergative (or some transitive) verbs, shown in (3), is often considered to be compositional and decom-

[4]For the transitive verb bases in (3-4), native speakers of Korean have an intuition that specific members of predicates in each type are difficult to predict, and hence no systematic classification has been attempted so far. See Son (2003) for an argument that systematically distinguishes transitive verb bases of agentive MCs from those of non-agentive MCs.

posable into the verb stem and the causative morpheme. In contrast, for non-agentive MCs in (4), including both intransitive and transitive bases, it is claimed (e.g., Kim 1998) that speakers of Korean have a strong intuition that the verb plus the causative morpheme *–i-* combination forms a unitary 'word'; the type of morphological causatives in (4) is idiosyncratic and nondecomposable.

However, consideration of further data associated with an event adverb like 'again' suggests that the non-agentive MCs in (4) are also decomposable into two separable events, a causing event and a caused eventuality (i.e., a result state). In what follows, I will show that the adverb *tasi* 'again' in Korean creates two different readings in non-agentive MCs, in which *tasi* modifies both a causing event and a result state. This phenomenon, which has not drawn much attention in connection with Korean causatives, will provide new evidence that non-agentive MCs are decomposable into two events, and that the component expressing a result state is not only conceptually available in the logical meaning of the non-agentive MC verbs but also receives a grammatical realization in the syntax.

3. Scope Ambiguity of *tasi* 'again' in Non-agentive MCs

Sentence (5) is ambiguous between two readings: A restitutive reading in (5a) and a repetitive reading in (5b).

(5) Emma-ka ai-eykey sinpal-ul ***tasi*** sin-ki-ess-ta
Mother-NOM child-DAT shoes-ACC again put.on-CAU-PST-DEC
a. 'Mother made [the child put on his shoes again].'
b. 'Mother again made the child put on his shoes.'

The restitutive reading presupposes that there had been an event in which the child was wearing the shoes sometime before, but it is not required that Mother herself caused that event before. In fact, it is not necessary that anyone had caused that event. In contrast, the repetitive reading presupposes that Mother herself had made the child put on the shoes before. That is, *tasi* can modify either the caused event or the result state.

Adopting a structural theory of 'again' proposed by von Stechow (1998), I suggest that this ambiguity with respect to the scope of *tasi*, which is also observed in the corresponding syntactic causatives (as well as agentive MCs), is sufficient evidence that the non-agentive MC involves two events, and thus has a complex underlying structure. I argue that the scope ambiguity of *tasi* in (5) can be easily accounted for if we decompose the verb *sinkita* into 'put on + CAUSE' and this decomposition is reflected in the syntax. For instance, the ambiguity of (5) can be explained by assuming that *tasi* has narrow scope with respect to CAUSE, if it is generated in the lower position, as in (6a), hence the restitutive reading. If *tasi* is generated in the higher position, it has wide scope with respect to CAUSE, as shown in (6b), and we get the repetitive reading.[5]

(6) a. [[$_{VP}$ ***again*** [$_{VP}$ put-on]] CAUSE] **Restitutive reading**
 b. [***again*** [$_{VP}$ [$_{VP}$ put-on] CAUSE]] **Repetitive reading**

The syntactic and semantic patterns of the two MCs we have seen thus far are summarized in (7).

(7)	**Morphological Causatives**	
	Non-Agentive MCs	**Agentive MCs**
a. Event Modification of Caused Events with 'again'	✓	✓
b. Some Manner Adverbial Modification of Caused Event	✕	✓
c. Thematic Role of the Causee	Goal	Agent

In the following section, I will discuss two important issues that arise from MC formation in Korean based on the facts outlined above: First, what determines different realizations of the argument structure (e.g., a thematic role of the causee as an agent versus a goal) in agentive and non-agentive MCs? Secondly, how is the argument composition in causatives inherited from their non-causative counterparts, and where do the alternations of argument structure in causatives and non-causatives come from?

Following recent proponents of predicate decomposition in the syntax (e.g., Hale & Keyser 1993; Harley 1995; von Stechow 1998; Travis 2000), I would like to derive the patterns in (7) from independent lexical-semantic and structural considerations of the verb root. The basic idea is that non-agentive MCs are always formed on verbal roots lacking an external argument, in particular, an agent (e.g., VP). Agentive MCs are formed on stems that already contain an agent-introducing projection, i.e., VoiceP, in their lexical conceptual representations. By allowing different sizes of complements for which CAUSE selects, an explanation for the contrast (e.g., 7b) and the similarity (e.g., 7a) in adverbial modification between agentive and non-agentive MCs will follow naturally.

---

[5]The same scope ambiguity of *tasi* is also observed in non-agentive MCs whose base form is unaccusative, as exemplified in (1).

(1) a. Chelswu-ka sakwacup-ul ***tasi*** nok-***i***-ess-ta.
 Chelswu-NOM apple.juice-ACC again melt-CAU-PST-DEC
 (i) 'Chelswu caused [the apple juice to melt again]'.
 (ii) 'Chelswu again caused the apple juice to melt.'

4. Analysis[6]

Building upon the notion of eventiveness (Harley 1995) and following Kratzer (1996), I assume that the agent is introduced by the functional head Voice, and that VP and VoiceP are the minimal domains for event semantics and agentive semantics, respectively. In Harley's theory of eventiveness, EventP's (equivalent to VoiceP's) semantic contribution to the meaning of a verb is essentially 'change of state', regardless of whether the Event head has an argument in its specifier. If the event denoted by the head has an external argument (e.g., an agent or a causer), the Event head is interpreted as *CAUSE*; if, on the other hand, there is no argument in the specifier of EventP, the Event head is interpreted as *BECOME/HAPPEN*. Harley (1995) further argues that the complement for which the Event head selects (e.g., BaseP such as AdjP or VP) is devoid of information related to the eventiveness of the verb and denotes a non-dynamic eventuality, i.e., a state. Hence, simple stative predicates like *dead* are represented without a projection of EventP, whereas eventive predicates like *die* are merged with EventP without an external argument. I also adopt the idea of Folli and Harley (2004) that there are different flavors of a single Voice head, one which introduces an external argument with CAUSE meaning (CAUSE-Voice), and one which does not project an external argument (BECOME-Voice), and one which necessarily introduces an agent argument (DO-Voice).

Based on these assumptions, I argue that an explanation for the MC split in Korean follows from a difference in the size of the complement for which the CAUSE head selects, namely VoiceP versus VP. I assume that in the agentive MC, CAUSE merges with VoiceP, which denotes an agentive eventiveness. In the non-agentive MC, in contrast, CAUSE merges with VP, which lacks an external argument and denotes a result state. The syntactic structure of each type under the present proposal is represented in (8).

(8) a. Agentive MCs (e.g., (1)) b. Non-agentive MCs (e.g., (2))

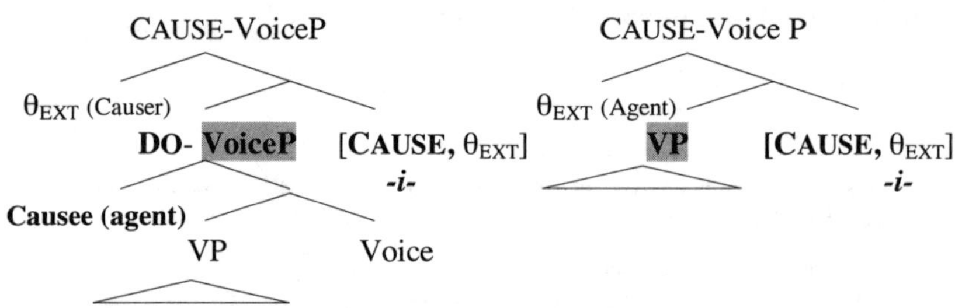

[6] The analysis presented in this paper relies on the notion of 'Late-Insertion', as proposed by Halle and Marantz (1993), according to which lexical realization occurs en route to Phonological Form.

As shown in (8a), the CAUSE head in agentive MCs takes an event, i.e., an agent-introducing VoiceP, as its complement, which explains the thematic role of the causee as an agent. Since the agent is explicitly expressed in the underlying structure of the base predicate with which the CAUSE head merges, the external argument introduced by the θ_{EXT} feature of the causative head cannot be interpreted as an agent, but a causer. This structure is true for both unergative and transitive verb bases. In (8b), non-agentive MCs take a smaller verbal projection than the VoiceP, i.e., a VP, which lacks an external-argument-introducing Voice and hence denotes a state. The structure proposed in (8b) with the VP as a complement straightforwardly accounts for the non-agentive MCs whose base predicates are unaccusative. Assuming that the subject in unaccusative sentences is underlyingly an internal argument of the verb root (and is moved to the subject position, e.g., [Spec,VoiceP], to satisfy an EPP feature of some sort), their causative counterparts are formed by merging the CAUSE head with the VP, as illustrated in (9a).

(9)[7] a. *cwuk-i-ta* 'kill (dead-CAUSE)' b. *cwuk-ta* 'die (dead-BECOME)'

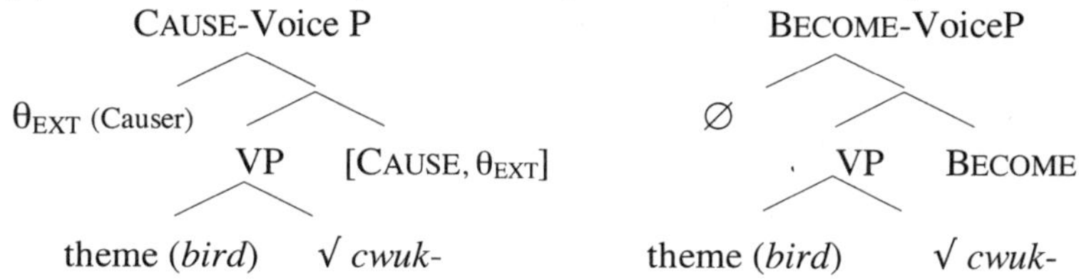

Following Harley (1995), I assume that the eventiveness of predicates is determined by the presence of a Voice projection which contributes the meaning 'change of state', 'change of location', etc. The interpretation of the Voice head for the inchoative-causative pair, therefore, is determined by whether or not it has an argument in its specifier position; if the Voice head has an argument in its Spec, the Voice head is interpreted as CAUSE, hence CAUSE-Voice as in (9a); if the Voice head is devoid of an argument in its Spec, the Voice head is interpreted as BECOME, hence BECOME-Voice, as in (9b). Therefore, I assume that the inchoative-causative alternation is attributable to whether or not the Voice head contains an external argument, i.e., whether the verb root merges with BECOME-Voice or CAUSE-Voice.

Based on the structure in (8b=9a), which straightforwardly accounts for the MCs with unaccusative bases, it is still unclear how the argument composition is inherited from the base verb in the non-agentive MC whose base

---

[7] I use Pesetsky's notation of √ to express the root morpheme.

is a transitive verb; it is not evident how and from where *ai-eykey* 'child-DAT' in (2), repeated as (10), receives a thematic role as a goal.

(10) Emma-ka ai-eykey sinpal-ul (ppali) sin-ki-ess-ta.
mother-NOM child-DAT shoes-ACC (quickly) put.on-CAU-PST-DEC
'Mother (quickly) put the shoes on the child.'

To differentiate the semantics of the causee in the two types of MCs in (1) and (2), I further propose that a VP whose base form is transitive in non-agentive MCs has a more complex internal structure than that of unaccusative verb bases; the VP of transitive verb bases contains an abstract applicative head above the verb root, as shown in (11) with the fully specified semantic interpretation.[8]

(11)[9,10]

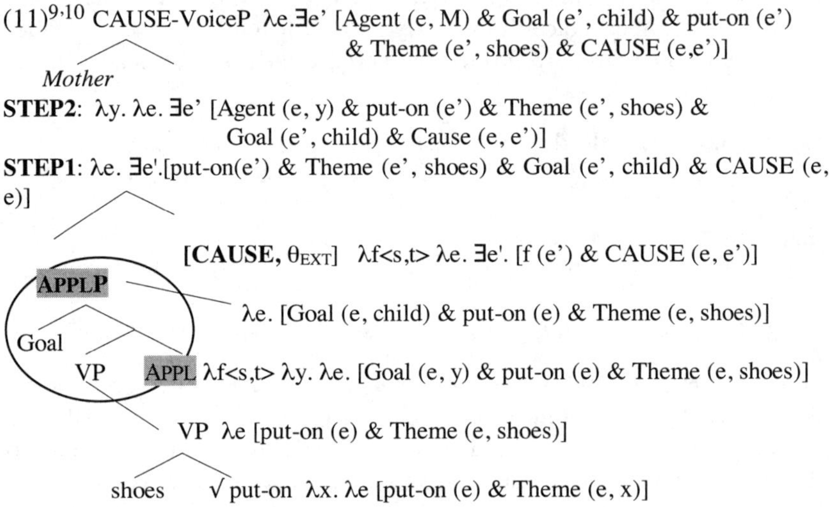

The APPL head denotes a relation between an individual (e.g., a goal) and an eventuality denoted by the verb; the argument introduced by the APPL head is a positional endpoint of the theme that undergoes a change of location. I further assume that the APPLP resides in the lexical conceptual level of the verb meaning, and a goal argument introduced by APPL is part of the lexical entry of the verb. The interpretation based on the semantic computation in (11) can be roughly paraphrased as: 'There exists *e'* such

[8]The postulation of APPLP is assumed for all transitive verb bases, not just for causatives. See Son (2003) for the syntactic and semantic representation of the transitive verb base of (11).

[9]The syntactic and semantic configuration proposed for non-agentive MCs with transitive bases is similar to that of high applicatives proposed by Pylkkänen (2000a).

[10]I follow Pylkkänen (2000b) for the representation and interpretation of the CAUSE head.

that the shoes are put on the child in *e'* and *e'* is a result state of *e* such that the Mother is an agent in *e*.' The underlying structure with the abstract APPL in (11), therefore, determines the thematic role of the causee as a goal, rather than an agent.

5. Syntax and Semantics of the Scope Ambiguity of *tasi* 'again'

The MC split observed in Korean thus far has been attributed to two different complements for which CAUSE selects, VoiceP versus VP/APPLP, which denotes an event versus a state, respectively. Under the current analysis of non-agentive MCs, the explanation for two different readings of *tasi* in (2) falls out naturally. By having an APPLP for transitive bases and a VP for unaccusative bases as a complement of CAUSE, *tasi* can be adjoined either to the APPLP/VP, where it takes scope over the caused event, or to the VoiceP, where it takes scope over CAUSE (i.e., a causing event). Different syntactic positions of *tasi*, therefore, trigger two different interpretations, the restitutive reading, as in (12b), and the repetitive reading, as in (12a).

(12) a. **CAUSE-VoiceP** ➔ ***again*** ([λe. ∃e' [Agent (e, M) & Goal (e', child) & put-on (e') & Theme (e', shoes) & CAUSE (e,e')])(e")

tasi **CAUSE-Voice P** λe. ∃e' [Agent (e, M) & Goal (e', child) & put-on (e') & Theme (e', shoes) & CAUSE (e,e')]

Repetitive

Mother STEP2: λy. λe. ∃e' [Agent (e, y) & Goal (e', child) & put-on (e') & Theme (e', shoes) & CAUSE (e,e')]

STEP1: λe. ∃e'.[Goal (e', child) & put-on(e') & Theme (e', shoes) & CAUSE (e,e')]

[CAUSE, θ_{EXT}] λf<s,t> λe. ∃e'. [f (e') & CAUSE (e, e')]

b. **APPLP** ➔ ***again*** ([λe'. [Goal (e', child) & put-on (e') & Theme (e', shoes)]])(e")

tasi **APPLP** λe'. [Goal (e', child) & put-on (e') & Theme (e', shoes)]

Restitutive

child λf<s,t> λy. λe'. [Goal (e', y) & f (e')]

VP APPL

λe. [put-on (e) & Theme (e, shoes)]

For the meaning of 'again', I adopt the semantics proposed by von Stechow (1998); 'again' is of type <<s,t><s,t>>, a function taking two event arguments. Its meaning is defined as (13) and (14).[11]

(13) Let P be a property of eventualities and let *e* be an eventuality.

[11]The definition is read as: P is a property of eventualities, and '<' is the relation of temporal precedence. It is true of any two eventualities if the first is temporally located entirely before the second. MAX(P)(e') means that e' is a maximal P-event, where MAX is defined as (14).

again(P)(e) is defined only if $\exists e'$ [$[\![MAX]\!]$ (P)(e')=1 & e' < e]
Where defined, $[\![again]\!]$ (P)(e)=1 iff P(e)=1

(14) MAX is a symbol of type <<s,t>,<s,t>>. $[\![MAX]\!]$ (P)(e)=1 iff P(e) and there is no e' such that e is a proper part of e' and P(e')=1

The semantics of *again* presupposes that there had been a same kind of the event that had occurred previously. Therefore, the denotation of the higher APPLP in (12b), the restitutive reading, can be read as '*e'* is an event such that the shoes are being put on the child in *e'* and there has been a maximal event of the same kind before.' The repetitive reading is derived by adjoining *tasi* to the CAUSE-VoiceP. The denotation of the higher CAUSE-VoiceP in (12a), therefore, can be read as 'there exists *e'* such that the shoes are put on the child in *e'* and *e'* is a caused event of *e* in which the Mother is an agent in *e*, and there has been a maximal event of the same kind as *e* before'.

6. Manner Adverbial Modification (e.g., *quickly*)

The contrast between agentive MCs and non-agentive MCs in adverbial modification with adverbs like 'quickly' also follows from the current proposal. In line with Cinque (1999), among others, I assume that adverbs can be base-adjoined to various maximal projections in the sentence depending on their semantics. I suggest that manner adverbs like 'quickly' are base-adjoined to an event-denoting VoiceP (e.g., CAUSE-VoiceP) and describe how an action or event took place.[12] Based on this assumption, an explanation for the contrast between agentive MCs and non-agentive MCs shown in (7b) falls out naturally; the contrast can be accounted for by the number of VoicePs, as shown in (15).

(15) a. Agentive MCs b. Non-agentive MCs

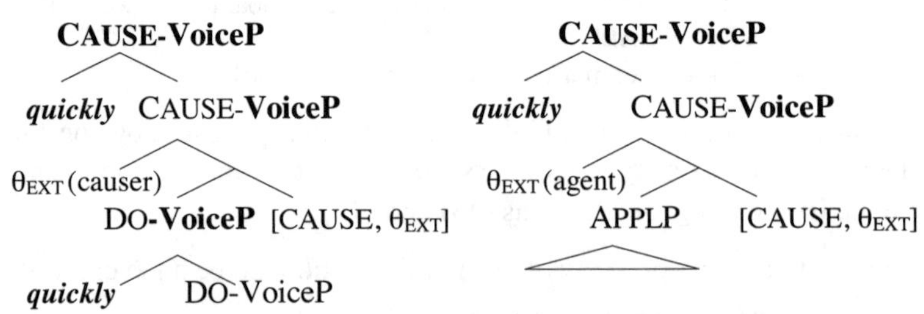

[12] See Son (2003) for justification of this approach.

In the agentive MCs, there exist two VoiceP projections, CAUSE-VoiceP and DO-VoiceP, and 'quickly' can be adjoined to either one of them, hence the scope ambiguity. In the non-agentive MCs, however, only one VoiceP is projected and thus there is only one position available for the adverb to be adjoined to. Therefore, as we would expect, no scope ambiguity is observed.

7. Conclusion

By demonstrating the scope ambiguity of *tasi* 'again' in non-agentive MCs, I argued that all MC formation in Korean takes place in the syntax. The MC split in Korean then was argued to be attributable to the different sizes of complements for which the CAUSE head selects, an event-denoting VoiceP versus a result-state-denoting APPL/VP. The postulation of subevents has been argued to be syntactically substantial since certain internal aspectual articulations of lexical verbs have been shown to be motivated by a number of syntactic and semantic facts with respect to adverbial modification (e.g., the ambiguity of *wieder* 'again' in German, von Stechow 1998; the ambiguity of 'almost' in English, Folli & Harley 2004). The scope ambiguity of *tasi* 'again' in Korean not only provides more evidence for the grammatical realization of complex event structure but also leads to a unified syntactic treatment of morphological causatives.

References

Cinque, G. 1999. *Adverbs and Functional Heads. A Cross-linguistic Perspective.* New York, OUP.

Folli, Raffaella. and Heidi Harley. 2004. Consuming results: Flavors of v. Forthcoming in Roumyana Slabakova and Paula Kempchinsky, (eds.), *Aspectual Inquiries*. Dordrecht: Kluwer

Hale, Ken and Keyser, Jay. 1993. On Argument Structure and The Lexical Expression of Syntactic Relations. In Ken Hale and Jay Keyster (eds.) *The View from Building 20: A Festschrift for Sylvain Bromberger*. pp. 53-108. Cambridge, MIT Press.

Halle, Morris and Marantz, Alec. 1993. Distributed Morphology. In Ken Hale and Jay Keyster (eds.) *The View from Building 20: A Festschrift for Sylvain Bromberger*. pp. 111-176. Cambridge, MIT Press.

Harley, Heidi. 1995. *Subjects, Events, and Licensing*. Ph.D. Thesis, MIT.

Kim, A. R. 1998. VP complement of HI-Causative. In David James Silva (eds.), *Japanese/Korean Linguistics 8*. pp. 445-458. Stanford: CSLI Publications.

Kratzer, Angelika. 1996. Severing the External Argument from Its Verb. In Johan Rooryck and Laurie Zaring, (eds). *Phrase Structure and The Lexicon*, pp. 109-137. Dordrecht: Kluwer.

Pylkkänen, Liina. 2000a. What Applicative Heads Apply To. In M.A. Minnick, A. Williams and E. Kaiser (eds.), *Proceedings of the 24th Annual Penn Linguistics Colloquium*, pp, 197-210. UPenn Working Papers in Linguistics, Volume 7.1.

Pylkkänen, Liina. 2000b. Representing Causatives. In B. Jackson and T. Matthews (eds.), *SALT X Proceedings*. CLC Publications. Cornell University, Ithaca, NY.

Son, M.J. 2003. Two Types of Morphological Causatives and the Scope Ambiguity of *tasi* 'again'. Ms. University of Delaware.

Travis, Lisa. 2000. Event Structure in Syntax. In C. Tenny and J. Pustejovsky (eds.), *Events as Grammatical Objects*. pp. 145-185. Stanford: CSLI Publications.

Um, H. 1995. Argument Structure of Korean Causatives. In S. Kuno et al (eds.). *Harvard Studies in Korean Linguistics 6*. pp.413-428. Harvard University: Dept. of Linguistics.

Von Stechow, Armin. 1996. The Different Readings of *wieder* 'again': A structural Account. *Journal of Semantics* 13, pp. 87-138.

Process Nominals and Morphological Complexity

James Hye Suk Yoon and Chongwon Park
University of Illinois, Urbana-Champaign

1. Introduction

Argument-bearing nominals – known as process nominals or complex event nominals – have played a central role in the development of generative grammar (Lees 1960; Chomsky 1970; Grimshaw 1990, etc.). An interesting fact about such nominals is that they seem to be deverbal, as shown by (1) from English:

(1) a. John examined the evidence
    b. John's examination of the evidence

In one way or another, existing analyses of process nominals are designed to allow nominals to bear argument structure only when they are deverbal. The inquiry that motivates this paper is whether this is true in languages that seem to contain morphologically simple process nouns. In this paper we argue that such process nominals – exemplified *par excellence* by Verbal Nouns (VN) in languages like Korean and Japanese – can in fact be associated with 'verbal' properties such as argument structure, even in the absence of a verbal base.

The principal argument for our conclusion comes from the fact that while VNs within DPs show properties derivative of the presence of argument structure, other 'verbal' properties are systematically lacking from such structures. The question then arises as to why 'verbal' properties such as argument structure can be associated with nouns in one (Korean and Japanese) but not another (English) type of language. We seek to find our answer in the fact that a high percentage of verbs in languages like Japanese and Korean are denominal (Iwasaki 1999; Jun 2002; Nam 1996). Since verbs are built around a nominal base combined with a semantically bleached grammatical verb, it is only natural that the indispensable ingredient for verb meanings - argument structure - should be supplied by the nominal base. In contrast, the majority of verbs in English cannot be morphologically decomposed into a nominal base and verbalizing affixes. Thus, argument structure inheres in the verb root and nouns that possess argument structure do so only in virtue of a derivational relationship with a base verb.

The organization of the paper is as follows. In section 2, we will show verb-like properties of process nominals in English. After showing the properties of Korean and Japanese process nouns (or verbal nouns) in section 3, we will argue that VNs projecting as DPs do not embed a verbal sub-structure in Japanese and Korean. Then, in section 5, differences between process nominals in English and Japanese/Korean will be discussed. Section 6 concludes the paper with exploration of some consequences and implications of putting forth the view on verbal nouns with nominal base.

2. Verb-like properties of process nominals in English

Recently, Borer (1999, 2003) and FBR (2001) have argued for a return to the transformational analysis of deverbal nominals in English based on the possibility of VP-adverbs and VP pro-forms in DPs projected from process nominals, shown below:

(4) a. Sam's destruction of his documents this morning was preceded by Bill's *doing so*. (FBR 2001: 571)
b. His explanation of the accident *thoroughly*. (FBR 2001: 555)

This move is a significant about-face from the established tradition of analyzing such DPs as thoroughly nominal in the syntax. (Chomsky 1970; Grimshaw 1990, *inter alia*). Though interesting, we are not interested in entering the debate about whether process nominals should be derived in the lexicon or in the syntax. What we wish to focus on is the following:

while Grimshaw (1990) and FBR (2001) disagree about the locus of the formation of process nominals, they are in agreement that the verbal properties of such nominals derive from the verbal base.

3. Process Nominals in Korean (and Japanese)

Korean possesses two types of deverbal nominalizations: phrasal (syntactic) nominalizations and lexical nominalizations. Phrasal nominalizations are constructed by affixing *-um* or *-ki* to verbal projections headed by native stock predicate roots, whereas lexical nominalizations are formed by attaching affixes such as *-kay*, *-i*, etc., to such roots. The former are clearly syntactic (Yoon 1989; C-W Park 2002), while the latter clearly result nominals lacking argument structure. In (5), a syntactic nominalization, the subject and object argument appear in canonical verbal case marking, suggesting that nominalization targets TP, rather than the verb. Lexical nominalization in (6) show a sharp contrast with (5) in that it does not allow arguments of the base verb to be inherited.

(5) Chelswu-ka chayk-ul ppali ilk-ess-**um**-i pwunmyengha-ta
Chelswu-Nom book-Acc quickly read-Pst-Nml evident-Dcl
'It is evident that Chelswu read the book quickly.'

(6) ma(k)-kay (cf.) * John-uy kwumeng-uy ma(k)-kay
stop-Nml J-gen hole-gen stop-nml
'stopper/cork' Intended: 'John's plugging/stopping of the hole.'

However, this is not to say that there are no argument-bearing nominals in Korean (and Japanese) that have properties similar to process nominals in English. There are such nominals, in abundance. Most argument-bearing nominals in Korean are Sino-Korean Verbal Nouns (VN):

(7) Roma-ceykwuk-uy Masada-yosay-uy kongkyek
R-empire-gen Masada-fort-gen attack (VN)
'Roman Empire's attack of Masada fort"

There is extensive research on VNs, especially when they form complex predicates that exhibit verbal properties, in the Light Verb Construction and the Aspectual Noun Construction (H-D Ahn 199; H-R Chae 1996, 1997; J-S Jun 2002, inter alia):

(8) LVC:
John-i Yenghi-lul simha-key kongkyek-(ul) hay-ss-ta
J-nom Y-acc severe-adv attack-(acc) do-pst-decl
'John attacked/criticized Mary severely'

(9) ANC:

[Kim-paksa-ka wencahayk-ul yenkwu-cwung]-ey cencayng-i
K-doctor-nom atom.nucleus-acc research-midst-loc war-nom
ilena-ss-ta
break.out-pst-decl
'The war broke out while Dr. Kim was doing research on atom nucleus'

Among the many debated issues in the analysis of these constructions is the debate on the category of the VN. Given that it displays verbal properties in these constructions, is VN a verb, a noun, a special category that is a mixture of noun and verb?

Up to now, resolution of this issue of the category of the VN and the source of verbal properties in constructions containing VNs has not been sought through investigation of properties of structures where VNs project as DPs – as in (7) above. The reason for excluding structures like (7) from the debate was in turn based on the assumption that (i) everything in such DPs is nominal; and (ii) argument/event structure is possible in nominals, so that the verbal properties in such DPs is derivative of argument structure.

However, given recent developments in the investigation of English process nominals, these assumptions need not necessarily be valid. First, nominal marking of dependents need not imply the lack of syntactic VP, since 'VP' is deconstructed (to v+VP, to AspP+VP, etc) and arguments are case-licensed in positions outside VP. Therefore, verbal elements licensed 'low' in VP may still surface in such structures. Second, it is possible that properties attributed to the presence of argument/event structure (Ev role) in fact are due to the presence of VP (cf. FBR).

4. VNs projecting as DPs do not embed a verbal sub-structure

The analysis of process nominals in Borer (1999, 2003) and FBR allow us to pinpoint the loci of various verb-like properties in process nominals. Specifically, their analyses imply the following:

(10) a. VP pro-forms, VP-adverbs, etc. are the **lowest** verbal property
b. Argument/event structure licensing is an **intermediate** verbal properties
c. Case licensing is the **highest** verbal property

English process nominals are verbal from (a) to (b), but not (c), while English gerunds are verbal up to (c) (in the case of Acc-Ing gerunds).

(11) Kim's explanation of the problem to the tenants (did not prevent a riot).
(12) * John's removal the garbage.

With this as background, we now turn to the question of what verbal properties are found in Korean VNs which project as DPs. Korean VNs projecting as DP show (b) properties but not (a) or (c). (13) shows that Korean VNs can be used with an agent-oriented modifier. In (14), the verbal noun *kongkyek* 'attack' is modified by the aspectual modifier *samil-tongan-uy* 'for three days'. (15) shows adverbial modification is infelicitous. (16) is an acceptable example of implicit argument/event control. However, as shown in (17), VP-pro-forms are not allowed for Korean process nominals.

(13) Cheli-uy uytocek-in Yenghi-eytayhan pinan
C-gen intentional-and Y-about criticism
'Cheli-uy intentional criticism of Yenghi'
(14) Mikwun-uy samil-tongan-uy/*?samil-man-uy
American.army-gen three.days-during-gen/three.days-only-gen
Baghdad-uy kongkyek
Baghdad-gen attack
'American troops attack of Baghdad for three days (* in three days)'
(15) Mikwun-uy Baghdad-lo-uy sinsok-*hi/han cinkyek
American.soldier-gen B-to-gen quick-*advz/adn incursion
'American troops' quick (*quickly) incursion into Baghdad'
(16) [PRO haksayngtul-ul top-ki wihan] canghakkum-uy coseng
student-pl help-nml in.order.to scholarship-gen formation
'The formation of fellowship fund to help students'
(17) 2003-nyen Mikwun-uy Baghdad-uy kongkyek-un
2003-year American.troops-gen B-gen attack-top
1917-nyen Yengkwukkwun-uy *kulehkey hay-ss-te-n
1917-year British.soldier-gen so do-past-ret-adn
kes/?kukes-pota te hyokwa-cek-i-ess-ta
fact/?that-than more effective-and-cop-past-decl

As the above examples show, roughly, only (b) properties are found, not (a) or (c) properties. That is, the intermediate verbal property is found but not high or low verbal properties.

This is unexpected if VNs embed a V, that is, if they are deverbal, since deverbal nominalizations – whether they are syntactic or lexical ---

are characterized by the fact that verbal properties split from nominal properties around a single point of articulation in the projection path below which everything is verbal and above which everything is nominal (i.e., what Malouf 1998 calls *Phrasal Coherence* holds). Different kinds of gerunds (syntactic nominalizations) as well as process nominals projecting as DPs in English abide by this generalization as we just saw.

Now, if DPs projected from VNs contain a verbal component, albeit an invisible one, we do not expect Phrasal Coherence to be violated. We are thus led to conclude that there is no verbal source from which VNs are derived.

Assuming that VNs cannot be deconstructed to a structure that contains a verbal projection but that VNs are nevertheless capable of bearing a-structure, we would like to know why process nominals in E and J/K differ the way they do. We seek an answer to this question in the next section.

5. Differences between process nominals in English and Korean

We believe that an interesting perspective on the differences emerges when we focus on the morphological composition of verbs/predicates in the languages in question. In languages such as English, verbs tend not to be denominal in that while they may be morphologically complex, the percentage of denominal verbs in the lexicon is rather low. Thus, nominals with verb-like properties are derived from verbs (so that we have 'Remarks on nominalization'). In contrast, in Korean and Japanese, a large percentage of verbs are denominal in that they contain a nominal base plus a verbalizing element (so that we should have 'Remarks on verbalization'). That is, the 'radical' (Sapir 1921) around which verbs/predicates is constructed are nominal in character.

According to Iwasaki (1999), both simple and complex verbs (as well as adjectives – based on the light verbs *su-ru* and the copula) in Japanese can be analyzed as having a morphological structure in which the radical of the predicate is nominal, followed by a denominalizing suffix which is in turn followed by predicate inflections. And while not all predicate roots of native stock in Korean can be traced to a nominal source, there are some predicates of native stock that are clearly denominal (John Whitman, p.c.).

(18) Nolang ~ nolah-ta 'yellow'/ Ppalkang ~ ppalkah-ta 'red'

The percentage of denominal verbs in the Korean lexicon is rather high. According to J-S Nam (1996), around 60 percent of verbs in Korean are denominal. Many denominal verbs are based on the verb *ha-ta*, which is found in the LVC construction. However, *ha-ta* isn't the only denominal (light) verb in Korean. As C-S Hong et al. (1997) shows, close to 30 odd verbs in Korean function as denominal light verbs.

This then leads to the question as to why there are so many denominal verbs in Korean (and Japanese) compared to languages like English. Iwasaki (1999) suggests the following as a possible explanation of the 'systemic forces' that endow the K/J lexicon with such a high proportion of denominal verbs.

<u>The rise of denominal verbs in the K/J lexicon</u> (Iwasaki 1999):

a. Native predicate roots are bound forms.
b. Predicate (V, A) inflection attaches to bound forms.
c. There aren't that many basic roots of native stock (bound roots).
d. The language relies on borrowing to supply new predicates.
e. Borrowed predicates are treated as free forms.
f. Noun roots in K/J are free forms. Thus borrowed roots are conducive to categorization as nouns rather than verbs/adjectives.
g. As nouns, they can project DPs without the need for special morphology.
h. But when used as verbs, they need to be verbalized, in order for predicate inflection to be able to attach to them.

The scenario sketched above is intuitively plausible and explains, *inter alia*, why no special morphosyntax is needed to license VNs when they project as DPs, but special elements are needed to license VNs when they function as (denominal) complex verbs.[1]

6. Consequences and Implications

The crosslinguistic comparison of process nominals that this paper has engaged itself in has numerous consequences and implications.

[1] Category of VN and the licensing of 'verbal' properties:

The most immediate implication of the investigation has to do with the debate on the category of VN and the presumed source of verbal properties in complex predicate constructions containing VNs. For one, our results imply that the attempt to account for the verbal properties of complex predicate constructions by **taking the VN to be a verb** (Ahn 1991, for example) is misguided, both empirically and conceptually.

---

1 Why is English different? For one, English is a 'word inflection' language where inflections, including verbal inflections, attach to free-form 'words'. Thus, when borrowing takes place, there is no need for language-internal adjustment of the borrowed form as a verbal root.

On the empirical side, as pointed out by Yoon (1991) and H-R Chae (1996) among many others, VN simply fails to behave morphologically as a verb (Yoon 1991). On the conceptual side, this analysis must posit a zero derivation of V → N when VNs project as DPs. However, while this may work technically, the analysis fails to capture the fact that no special licensing is needed for VNs in the nominal context but special licensing is required in verbal contexts. Finally, if the recent work of FBR is on the right track, we expect to find evidence of VP sub-structure, which we don't.

Similar considerations extend to analyses that take **VN to be an underspecified category** that is categorized as N or V depending on the context (Sells 1995; Manning 1993; Pak 2001, etc.). Again, on the conceptual side, such analyses fail to capture the asymmetry between the nominal and verbal uses of VNs; only the latter require special licensing. They also make some factually wrong predictions. Under the underspecification-categorization approach, the VN in ANC is categorized as a verb (Sells 1995, 1996). However, no evidence other than case-marking indicates that VN is a V. *VN+cwung* is a noun compound (may be 'postsyntactic'). V-roots/stem cannot compound with '*cwung' (*mek-cwung, *mek-ess-cwung, *mek-e-cwung*, etc.).[2]

[2] Predicates in Korean/Japanese need not be verbal:

The realization that the majority of predicates in Korean/Japanese are denominal sheds new light on the fact that unlike languages like English, nominal predicates abound in these languages. A cursory examination of the headlines of a Korean-language newspaper reveals that a high percentage of headlines have nominal predicates headed by verbal nouns, whereas headlines in English-language newspapers contain verbs:

(19) a. Samsung-cenca-to sayngsancik-un **kwuin-nan**
S-electronics-even production.jobs-top manpower-difficulty
'Even Samsung Electronics is experiencing manpower difficulties in the production branch'

---

2 What does this suggest about the source of 'verbal' cases in Korean (and Japanese)? The perspective defended here which takes VN to be an N and ANC to contain an aspectual nominal compound necessitates that the so-called 'verbal cases' do not require a morphological verb. Instead, functional heads with aspectual properties – whether they are nominal or verbal in character – in construction with an argument licensing head must be capable of assigning 'verbal' cases.

b. Mwun-kyuhyen-sinpwu Ro-taythonglyeng-ey **toksel**
M-priest R-present-dat harsh.words
'Father Mwun hurled invectives against President Ro'
(*Chosun Ilbo*, internet edition, 7/30/03)

(20) a. Bush **acknowledges** 'real threat' of terrorism
b. President **urges** compromise on medicare prescription plan
(*The New York Times*, internet edition, 7/30/03)

Why are predicates in telegraphic registers predominantly verbal in English while they are predominantly nominal in Korean (and Japanese)? The difference has to do with the fact that in the former, argument structure is licensed only in the presence of verbs, while in the latter, a nominal predicate root is capable of assigning arguments on its own.

[3] Productive deverbal nominalizations are syntactic in Korean:

This may appear at first to be related to the fact that Korean has a large number of denominal verbs. However, on a moment's reflection, it is not. Consider the following paradigm (H-S Han 1987):

(21) a. John-uy swuhak-uy yenkwu
J-gen math-gen research (VN)
'John's research of mathematics'
b. John-i swuhak-ul yenkwu-hay-ss-ta
J-nom math-acc research-do-past-decl
'John researched mathematics'
c. John-i swuhak-ul yenkwu-hay-ss-um
J-nom math-acc research-do-past-nml
'John researching mathematics'
d. *John-uy swuhak-uy yenkwu-hay-ss-um
J-gen math-gen research-do-past-decl
'John's researching of mathematics'

While the nominalizing suffixes *-um* (and *-ki*) can form both syntactic and lexical nominalizations, what is notably missing are lexical nominalizations formed with these nominalizers that inherit the arguments from the base verb, in sharp contrast to English where argument-bearing nominals are deverbal, as we have seen.

We propose to explain the ungrammaticality of (21d) above by taking it to be a form of Blocking. Specifically, (21d) is blocked by (21a). Since there is an underived process nominal, there is no reason to denominalize the nominal, and then nominalize it again. In contrast, in English, there are no underived process nominals, thus for a nominal to have arguments, it must have a verbal base.

Why then are syntactic nominalizations not blocked by the presence of (21a)? One answer is that while (21a) (and 21d which it blocks) are formed in the lexicon, syntactic nominalizations are formed in the syntax, and usually blocking does not traverse the lexicon-syntax boundary. Another answer is that the marking of dependents in (21a,d) and (21c) are different, which means that the features of the underived process nominal and the nominalized denominal verb are not equivalent, and there is no blocking.

[4] Morphological make-up is a significant clue to syntactico-semantic composition:

A lesson drawn from the comparison of process nominals in English and Korean-Japanese is that there must be a rather transparent relationship between morphological form and syntactic composition. If it weren't so, there is no reason why a morphologically underived VN could not be derived from an abstract verbal source.

There is confirmation of this point from English. In English, complex event nominals and simple event nominals differ in that while the derivation of the former (deverbal) nominal shows evidence of an underlying VP, the latter (not deverbal) do not, even when their meanings are similar.

(22) a. The destruction of the city so thoroughly (to impress the general)
b. *?The journey so desperately (to reach India)

This is a sobering lesson for recent approaches where morphological complexity (or lack thereof) has no bearing on syntactic structural complexity. Morphological complexity is not always a direct determinant of syntactic complexity, since not all complex words are derived by syntactic mechanisms, but in cases such as process nominals, it is a measure that syntax can ill afford to ignore.

References

Ahn, Hee-Don 1991. *Light Verbs, VP-movement, Negation, and Clausal Architecture in Korean and English.* Doctoral dissertation, University of Wisconsin-Madison.

Borer, Hagit 1999. "The Form, the Forming, and the Formation of Nominals". Ms., University of Southern California.

Borer, Hagit 2003. "Exo-skeletal vs. Endo-skeletal Explanations: Syntactic Projections and the Lexicon", in M. Polinsky and J. Moore (eds.), Explanation in Linguistic Theory, 31-67. Stanford: CSLI Publications.

Chae, Hee-Rahk 1996. "Properties of ha- and Light Predicate Constructions". *Language Research* 32.3: 409-476.

Chae, Hee-Rahk 1997. "Verbal Nouns and Light Verbs in Korean". *Language Research* 33.4: 581-600.

Chomsky, Noam 1970. "Remarks on Nominalizations". *Readings in English Transformational Grammar*, ed. R Jacobs and P Rosenbaum, 184-221. New York: Plenum Press.

Fu, Jingqui, Thomas Roeper, and Hagit Borer [=FBR] 2001. "The VP within Process Nominals: Evidence from Adverbs and the VP Anaphora *Do-So*", *NLLT* 19: 549-582.

Grimshaw, Jane 1990. *Argument Structure*. MIT Press, Cambridge: MA.

Han, Hak-Sung 1987. *The Configurational Structure of the Korean Language*. Doctoral dissertation, University of Texas at Austin.

Hong, Chai-song et al. 1997. *The dictionary of modern Korean verbal constructions*. Twusan Tonga Press, Seoul.

Iwasaki, Yasufumi 1999. *Three Categories of Nouns in Japanese*. Doctoral dissertation, University of Illinois at Urbana-Champaign.

Jun, Jong Sup 2003. *Syntactic and Semantic Bases of Case Assignment*. Doctoral dissertation, Brandeis University.

Lees, Robert 1960. *The Grammar of English Nominalizations*. TheHague: Mouton.

Malouf, Robert 1998. *Mixed Categories in the Hierachical Lexicon*. Doctoral dissertation, Stanford University.

Manning, Christopher 1993. "Analyzing the Verbal Noun: Internal and External Constraints". *Japanese/Korean Linguistics* 3, ed. Soonja Choi, 236-253. CSLI, Stanford Linguistics Association.

Nam, Jee-Sun 1996. "Lexicon of Korean Predicative Terms Classified by Morphological Ending Forms". *IGM 97-8/96-9* Vol. I/II, Universite de Marne-la-Vallee, France.

No, Yongkyoon 1997. "Parellels between Korean Verbs and Nouns in Subcategorization". *Language and Information* 1, The Korean Society for Language and Information, 27-65.

Pak, Miok 2001. "Verbal Nouns in Korean: Categorically Unspecified Lexical Roots". *Harvard Studies in Korean Linguistics* IX: 517-531.

Park, Chongwon 2002. "Some Evidence for Korean Nominalizers as Phrasal Affixes". *Proceedings of the 2002 LSK Summer Conference*.

Sapir, Edward 1921. *Language: An Introduction to the Study of Speech*. New York: Harcourt, Brace and Company.

Sells, Peter 1995. "The Category and Case Marking Properties of Verbal Nouns in Korean". *Harvard Studies in Korean Linguistics* VI: 370-386.

Sells, Peter 1996. "Case, Categories, and Projection in Korean and Japanese". *Morphosyntax in Generative Grammar*, eds Hee-Don Ahn et al., 47-62, The Korean Generative Grammar Circle, Hankwuk Publishing Co., Seoul.

Yoon, James H. S. 1991. Theta Operations and the Syntax of Multiple Complement Constructions in Korean. *Harvard Studies in Korean Linguistics* IV: 433-446.

Part III

Semantics, Acquisition and Psycholinguistics

Scope Inversion in Japanese: Contrastive Topics Require Scalar Implicatures

YURIE HARA
University of Delaware

1. Introduction

Japanese has a scope inversion phenomenon by a Contrastive Topic (CTopic) marking that is similar to the Korean Contrastive Topic marking (see Lee, 2000) and the Topic-Focus contour observed in German (see Büring, 1997, among others). For instance, the example (1a) which contains two logical operators, quantifier and negation, is ambiguous. If we change the nominative marker *ga* into *wa* as in (1b), we only have the negation wide scope reading. (Note: the availability of the $\neg\forall$ reading of (1a) varies among individuals).

(1) a. Mary-ga zen'in-ni choko-o age-nakat-ta
Mary-Nom everyone-Dat chocolate-Acc give-Neg-Past
' as for everyone Mary did not give a chocolate to them.'
'it is not the case that Mary gave a chocolate to everyone.'

b. Mary-ga zen'in-ni-wa choko-o age-nakat-ta
Mary-Nom everyone-Dat-Top chocolate-Acc give-Neg-Past
* 'as for everyone Mary did not give a chocolate to them.'
'it is not the case that Mary gave a chocolate to everyone.'

Another observation on the CTopic marker *wa* is that it induces implicatures. In this paper, first I will show what kind of implicatures Contrastive

Topics generate. Second, I will summarize Büring's (1997) account on German. Büring (1997) claims that a sentence which contains a topic must 'have reasonable implicatures' and thus when a topic-marked sentence is ambiguous, only the reading which has implicatures can survive. I adopt the same idea to explain the Japanese data. In other words, only the $\neg\forall$ reading in (1b)has implicatures, therefore it is the only available reading. Based on the prosodic pattern of German, Büring (1997) further provides a mechanism of Focus and Topic value to elicit implicatures. Since Japanese has a different pattern of prosody, however, it is not clear whether his system can be applied to Japanese case presented above. Third, I will present an alternative account of Japanese based on Sauerland's (2001) mechanism of computing implicatures. I claim that a Contrastive Topic presupposes a particular set of scalar alternatives, i.e. stronger propositions than the asserted one. Thus, if one of the possible propositions of the ambiguous sentence fails to have this set of scalar alternatives, it causes a presupposition failure. This is the source of disambiguation.

2. Implicatures

It is observed that Contrastive Topics always induce implicatures. In (2), for instance, compared to the utterance without CTopic-marking, *John-ga kita*. 'John-nom came', (2b) includes the speaker's indication that the asserted proposition is the most informative answer that he or she can give. Similarly, CTopic-marking of numerals as in (3b) seems to have an effect similar to 'at least N', namely it specifies the number the speaker is certain of and indicates the uncertainty of bigger numbers (Teramura, 1991).

(2) a. Who came to the party?

b. JOHN-wa ki-ta
John-CTop come-Past
As for John, he came (Implicature: I don't know about others)

(3) a. How many people came to the party?

b. 3-nin-wa kita
3-Class-CTop came
3 people came (Implicature: I don't know whether more than three came)

I claim that the scope inversion is due to this property of CTopic: CTopic always induces implicatures. If a sentence contains a CTopic, only the reading that has implicatures can survive. In (4), the $\neg\forall$ reading implies "Some people came", while the $\forall\neg$ reading exhaustively entails or contradicts all the variants of the asserted proposition, "Some people didn't come", "Most people came", etc. and therefore no propositions are left to be implied. Consequently, $\neg\forall$ is the only available reading for (4). The same reasoning can be made to explain why CTopic-marked quantifiers, like *minna* 'everyone', cannot appear in an affirmative context. Since (5) has only one logical operator, *minna*, there is only one possible proposition "Everyone came". This proposition is the strongest proposition among the possible alternatives, therefore no implicature can be derived. Therefore, (5) is infelicitous, since the asserted proposition is not compatible with the property of CTopic-marking.

(4) MINNA-wa ko-nakat-ta
Everyone-CTop come-Neg-Past

a. It is not the case that all the people came.
(Implicature: Probably some people came. (available reading))

b. All the people are such that they didn't come. (no implicatures (unavailable reading))

(5) # Minna-wa kita.
Everyone-CTop came (no implicatures)

The next question pertains to how we compute the implicatures. In the next section, I summarize the system developed by Büring (1997) for a scope inversion in German.

3. Büring 1997

German has a scope inversion effect similar to the Japanese case. For instance, sentence (6a) can be disambiguated by a specific prosody as in (6b) (Féry, 1993, Büring, 1997, Krifka, 1998, among others). Büring (1997) calls the rising accent on *alle* a Topic accent and the falling accent on *nicht* a Focus accent.

(6) a. Alle Politiker sind nicht korrupt
all politicians are not currupt
i. No politician is corrupt. ($\forall\neg$)
ii. It is not the case that all politicians are corrupt.($\neg\forall$)

b. /ALLE Politiker sind NICHT\ korrupt
all politicians are not currupt
It is not the case that all politicians are corrupt.($\neg\forall$ only)

Büring (1997) provides the following analysis in the framework of Rooth's (1985, 1992) *Alternative Semantics for Focus*. By having the Topic-Focus prosody, (6b) elicits three different types of semantic values: first it has the ordinary semantic value $[\![(6b)]\!]^o$. Second, the Focus accent generates the Focus semantic value $[\![(6b)]\!]^f$, which is a set of propositions obtained by replacing the focused element with some type-identical alteratives to it (*not* and the identity function). Third, the Topic accent generates the Topic semantic value $[\![(6b)]\!]^t$, which is a set of sets of propositions obtained by replacing the topical element with alternatives (generalized quantifiers).

(7) a. $[\![(6b)]\!]^o$=It is not the case that all politicians are corrupt

b. $[\![(6b)]\!]^f$={All politicians are corrupt, It is not the case that all politicians are corrupt}

c. $[\![(6b)]\!]^t$={{All politicians are corrupt, It is not the case that all politicians are corrupt},
{Most politicians are corrupt, It is not the case that most politicians are corrupt},
{Some politicians are corrupt, It is not the case that some politicians are corrupt},
{No politicians are corrupt, It is not the case that no politicians are corrupt}}

Büring (1997) explains the availability of the $\neg\forall$ reading by means of the notion of Residual Topic ("a set of disputable propositions induced by a Topic"):

(8) If a sentence S with a Topic accent is uttered given some Context CX, and there is no disputable Residual Topic the sentence establishes, the utterance of S in CX is infelicitous.

In the $\neg\forall$ reading of (6b), there are Residual Topics since the proposition asserting that not all politicians are corrupt can cross out only one set of propositions in the Topic value. It neither entails nor excludes other sets of propositions. In other words, we are still able to ask whether there are some corrupt politicians or how many are not corrupt.

(9) $[\![\neg\forall]\!]^t$

a. [[not]$_F$ [[all]$_T$ politician [[corrupt]]]]

b. {~~$\neg$ all(politician)(λx.corrupt(x)), all(politician)(λx.corrupt(x))~~},
{$\neg$ most(politician)(λx.corrupt(x)),
most(politician)(λx.corrupt(x))},
{$\neg$ some(politician)(λx.corrupt(x)),
some(politician)(λx.corrupt(x))},
{$\neg$ one(politician)(λx.corrupt(x)),
one(politician)(λx.corrupt(x))}

On the other hand, the $\forall\neg$ reading is not available for (6b), there is no room for dispute in this reading. If all politicians are such that they are not corrupt, all sets of propositions in the topic value are either entailed or contradicted. All propositions in the Topic value are crossed out since none of them are disputable.

(10) $[\![\forall\neg]\!]^t$

a. $[[\text{all}]_T$ politician [$[\text{not}]_F$ [corrupt]]]

b. {~~all(politician)($\lambda x.\neg$corrupt(x))~~, ~~all(politician)($\lambda x.$corrupt(x))~~},
{~~most(politician)($\lambda x.\neg$corrupt(x))~~,
~~most(politician)($\lambda x.$corrupt(x))~~},
{~~some(politician)($\lambda x.\neg$corrupt(x))~~,
~~some(politician)($\lambda x.$corrupt(x))~~},
{~~one(politician)($\lambda x.\neg$corrupt(x))~~,
~~one(politician)($\lambda x.$corrupt(x))~~}

Accordingly, (10) does not satisfy (8), and thus the quantifier wide scope reading of (6b) is not available. The quantifier narrow scope reading is possible since (9) has disputable propositions.

Büring (1997) notes that the scope inversion is not obligatory for all quantifiers. For instance, (11) remains ambiguous even with Topic Focus contour.

(11) Zwei /DRITTEL Politiker sind NICHT\ korrupt
Two $[\text{thirds}]_T$ of the politicians are $[\text{not}]_F$ corrupt

This follows from the fact that both readings have disputable questions:

(12) a. It is not the case that two thirds of the politicians are corrupt

b. ... and it might or might not be the case that there are in fact no corrupt politicians

(13) a. Two thirds of the politicians are non-corrupt

b. ... and it might or might not be the case that some corrupt

As shown above, in Büring's (1997) system, it is crucial that negation is in Focus to make a set of propositions (Focus value). A sentence with Topic marking necessarily has disputable questions in its Topic value, which are derived from the Focus value. In the next section, it is considered whether Büring's (1997) system can be directly applied to the Japanese case.

4. Japanese

In Section 2., following Büring (1997), I have proposed that the scope inversion phenomenon discussed in this paper is due to the requirement on

Contrastive Topics: Contrastive Topics always induce implicatures. In Section 3., we have seen that Büring (1997) characterized implicatures as disputable propositions in Topic values generated by Focus accent on the negation and Topic accent on the quantifier. In Japanese, it is not clear whether the negation is Focus-marked in the CTopic sentences.

When negation is in Focus, the stress falls onto the verb in Japanese as follows:

(14) a. John-ga ki-ta-no?
John-Nom come-Past-QP
'Did John came?'

b. Iiya, KO-nakat-ta.
No, come-Neg-Past
'No, (he) did NOT.'

In the case of scope inversion, no focus is marked on negation in Japanese. When a sentence (15b) is uttered, *zen'in* 'everyone' receives a stress as indicated by capitals. However, neither the verb stem nor the negation morpheme *nakat* indicates any phonological or morphological difference relative to the non-Topic counterpart (15a).

(15) a. John-wa zen'in-o tasuke-nakat-ta
John-Nom Everyone-Acc help-Neg-Past
'John didn't help anyone'
'it is not the case that John helped everyone'

b. John-wa MINNA-wa tasuke-nakat-ta
John-Nom Everyone-Top help-Neg-Past
*'John didn't help anyone'
'it is not the case that John helped everyone'

Similarly, it is observed that English also has a scope inversion by intonation (Jackendoff, 1972) but the phonological marking is not on the negation but at the end of the sentence .

(16) a. All the men didn't come\. ($\forall\neg$)

b. All the men didn't come/. ($\neg\forall$)

It is possible to assume that the negation does not have a particular prosodic pattern as in German although it is in Focus. Rather than generalizing Büring's (1997) analysis to Japanese data, however, I will offer an alternative analysis that captures the same kind of intuition (uncertainty or disputability of alternatives) without assuming that negation is in Focus.

4.1. Presupposition Failure: Sauerland 2001

I employ the mechanism developed by Sauerland (2001) to compute implicatures and propose that, if a sentence contains a CTopic, it presupposes a particular subset of scalar alternatives (also see Oshima, 2002).

Sauerland (2001) states that a scalar alternative becomes an implicature 'only if the scalar alternative is stronger than the assertion.' In our case, since CTopic-marked sentences always induce implicatures, a CTopic-marked sentence must have a scalar alternative stronger than the assertion in order to be interpreted properly. I formulate this condition as in (17), when a sentence contains a CTopic, it presupposes a set of scalar alternatives ψ such that ψ entails the asserted proposition but the asserted proposition does not entail ψ.

(17) CONTRASTIVE(<B, F>)
$\exists$F$'$[F$'$ $\in$ALT$_C$(F) & B(F$'$) entails B(F) & B(F) doesn't entail B(F$'$)]
(presupposition))

Let us start with the acceptable reading for (4), the negation wide scope reading, $\neg\forall x$[[person(x)][come(x)]] has a scalar alternative $\neg$some(x)[[person(x)][come(x)]]. $\neg$some(x)[[person(x)][come(x)]] entails $\neg\forall x$[[person (x)][come(x)] but not the other way around. Therefore, the existence of the scalar alternative $\neg$some(x)[[person(x)][come(x)]] makes the $\neg\forall$ reading compatible with the presupposition.

(4) MINNA-wa ko-nakat-ta
Everyone-CTop come-Neg-Past

a. It is not the case that all the people came.
(Implicature: Probably some people came. (available reading))

b. All the people are such that they didn't come. (no implicatures (unavailable reading))

(18) B=$\lambda\wp \in D_{<<e,t>,t>}.\neg\wp(\lambda y.\text{come}(y))$

(19) F=λP.$\forall x$[person(x)][P(x)]

(20) F$'$=λP.some(x)[person(x)][P(x)]

(21) a. $\neg\forall x$[[person(x)][come(x)]] (=B(F))

b. scalar alternative: $\neg$some(x)[[person(x)] [come(x)]] (=B(F$'$))

c. B(F$'$) entails B(F)

d. B(F) doesn't entail B(F$'$)

Further, the following operation of the CTopic-marking induces implicatures (see the appendix to the paper for further technical details):

(22) CONTRASTIVE(<B, F>) $\Leftrightarrow$

a. F(B) (assertion)

b. $\forall$F′[F′ $\in$ ALT$_C$(F) & B(F′) entails B(F) & B(F) doesn't entail B(F′)] $\rightarrow$ *Poss*($\neg$B(F′))] (implicature)

Following (22), *Poss*(some(x)[[person(x)][come(x)]]) (the double negations cancel each other), is an implicature of $\neg\forall x$[[person(x)][come(x)]] as we saw in (4a).

On the other hand, a scalar alternative of the quantifier wide scope reading (23) is given in (23a). The negation of (23a) cannot be a scalar implicature since (23a) does not entail the asserted proposition. We get the same result for other scalar alternatives, few(x)[[person(x)][$\neg$come(x)]], most(x)[[person(x)][$\neg$come(x)]], more-than-half(x)[[person(x)][$\neg$come(x)]], etc. Therefore, this reading causes a presupposition failure and thus is unavailable for (4).

(23) $\forall x$ [[person(x)][$\neg$ come(x)]]) (=B(F))

a. scalar alternative: some(x)[[person(x)][$\neg$come(x)]] (=B(F′))

b. B(F′) doesn't entail B(F)

c. B(F) entails B(F′)

4.2. Topic in affirmatives

As mentioned briefly in Section 2., some quantifiers with Topic marking are infelicitous in affirmative context as in (5).

(5) # zen'in-wa kita.
Everyone-Top came

This can be directly explained by my analysis as follows. (5) has only one possible reading, namely (24), because it only contains one logical operator. None of the scalar alternatives of (24), entails (24). Therefore, Proposition (24) with CTopic is not compatible with the presupposition. Since (24) is the only possible reading for (5), the sentence (5) is infelicitous in any context.

(24) $\forall x$ [[person(x)][come(x)]] (=B(F))

a. scalar alternative:
some(x)[[person(x)][come(x)]] (=B(F′))

b. B(F′) doesn't entail B(F)

c. B(F) entails B(F′)

4.3. Proportional and Cardinal *Many*

The interesting contrast between cardinal 'many', *takusan*, and proportional 'many', *ooku*, is explained in this analysis as well. *Takusan* behaves just like *minna* 'everyone'. In other words, if it is CTopic-marked, the sentence is disambiguated into the negation-wide-scope reading in negative context and it is infelicitous in an affirmative context. On the other hand, the sentence which contains the CTopic-marked *ooku* remains ambiguous in a negative context and it is felicitous in an affirmative context.

(25) a. TAKUSAN-no-hito-wa ko-nakat-ta
Many-people-CTop come-Neg-Past
It is not the case that many people came. ($\neg$many only)

b. OOKU-no-hito-wa ko-nakat-ta
Many of the people are such that they didn't come. (many$\neg$)
It is not the case that many of the people came. ($\neg$many)

(26) a. # Takusan-no-hito-wa ki-ta.
Many-people-CTop come-Past
'Many people came'

b. Ooku-no-hito-wa ki-ta.
Many-people-CTop come-Past
'Many of the people came'

Some scalar alternatives such as no(x)[[person(x)][$\neg$come(x)]], some(x) [[person(x)][$\neg$come(x)]], etc. do not entail many(x)[[person(x)][$\neg$come(x)]] regardless of *many* being cardinal or proportional. The contrast here is due to the fact that $\forall x$[[person(x)][$\neg$come(x)]] does not entail many$_{card}$(x)[[person(x)][$\neg$come(x)]] but $\forall x$[[person(x)][$\neg$come(x)]] does entail many$_{prop}$(x)[[person(x)][$\neg$come(x)]].

The asserted proposition of the quantifier-wide-scope reading of (25a) can be written as (27). $\forall x$[[person(x)][$\neg$come(x)]] does not entail many$_{card}$ [[person(x)][$\neg$come(x)]]. Suppose that there are 80 people in the domain and we say "many people" only when there are more than 100 people; then $\forall x$[[person(x)][$\neg$come(x)]] is true but many$_{card}$[[person(x)][$\neg$come(x)] is false.

(27) many$_{card}$[[person(x)][$\neg$come(x)]] (=B(F))

a. scalar alternative: $\forall x$[[person(x)][$\neg$come(x)]] (=B(F$'$))

b. B(F$'$) doesn't entail B(F)

c. B(F) entails B(F$'$)

As a result, $\text{many}_{card}\neg$ reading of (25a) causes a presupposition failure and thus it cannot be an available reading for (25a). On the other hand, $\forall x$[[person(x)][$\neg$come(x)]] entails many_{prop}[[person (x)][$\neg$come(x)]] since, by definition, the number of being proportionally many cannot overwhelm the number of all the individuals. Therefore, the $\text{many}_{prop}\ \neg$ reading of (25b) induces an implicature, namely $Poss(\neg\forall x$ [[person(x)][$\neg$ come(x)]]).

5. Conclusion

Scope inversion in both Japanese and German can be attributed to the same property of Contrastive Topics: a sentence containing Contrastive Topics induces implicatures. The mechanism for the computation of implicatures, however, is still controversial. Büring's (1997) system generates implicatures by forming a Focus value which is assigned to the negation. In Japanese, on the other hand, there is no overt assignment of Focus to the negation. Rather than generalizing Büring's (1997) system, this paper characterizes the property of Contrastive Topic as a presuppositional requirement of stronger scalar alternatives, using Sauerland's (2001) mechanism. Finally, this analysis of Contrastive Topics allows us to attribute the scope inversion to presupposition failure.

Appendix

In Sauerland (2001), the negation of the scalar alternative that is stronger than the asserted proposition becomes an implicature.

(28) $\neg\alpha'$ is an implicature of α if the following three hold: Sauerland (2001)

a. α' is a scalar alternative of α

b. α' entails α

c. α doesn't entail α'

For instance, some(x)[[person(x)] [come(x)]] is an implicature of $\neg\forall x$[[person(x)][come(x)]]. This computation of implicature, however, becomes inappropriate for Japanese CTopic-marking when other types of scalar is considered.

As mentioned in Section 2., the impressions we get from the following examples are "the speaker is not sure whether people other than John came" or "the speaker is not sure whether more than 3 people came"

(29) John-wa kita
John-top came

(30) 3-nin-wa kita
3-class-top came
$\approx$ At least 3 people came

If we adopt Sauerland's (2001) mechanism directly, the computed implicature would be too strong compared with the actual intuition. For example, (29) would imply "Mary didn't come" and (30) would imply "it is not the case that 4 people came" rather than "the speaker is not sure."

(31) $[_{\text{CT}}$ John$]$ came

a. John $\ll$ John and Mary $\ll$ John, Mary and Bill

b. λP.P(John)(come(x)) (=α)

   i. scalar alternative: λP.P(John & Mary)(come(x)) $(= \alpha')$

   ii. α' is a scalar alternative of α

   iii. α' entails α

   iv. α doesn't entail α'

   v. Implicature:
   $\neg\lambda$P.P(John & Mary)(come(x)) $(= \neg\alpha')$

(32) $[_{\text{CT}}$ Three$]$ people came

a. $1 \ll 2 \ll 3 \ll 4$

b. $|\{x : \text{person}(x) \cap \text{come}(x)\}| = 3$ (=α)

   i. scalar alternative: $|\{x : \text{person}(x) \cap \text{come}(x)\}| = 4$ $(= \alpha')$

   ii. α' is a scalar alternative of α

   iii. α' entails α

   iv. α doesn't entail α'

   v. Implicature:
   $|\{x : = \text{person}(x) \cap \text{come}(x)\}| \neq 4$ $(= \neg\alpha')$

Therefore, we need to add an epistemic logic operator (or consider Indeterminate value of Kleene's strong three-valued logic as Oshima (2002) did) to avoid computing implicatures that are too strong.

References

Büring, D. 1997. The great scope inversion conspiracy. *Linguistics and Philosophy* 20:175–194.

Féry, C. 1993. *German Intonational Patterns*. Tübingen: Niemeyer.

Jackendoff, R. 1972. *Semantic Interpretation in Generative Grammar*. Cambridge, MA: MIT Press.

Krifka, M. 1998. Scope inversion under rise-fall contour in German. *Linguistic Inquiry* 29:1:75–112.

Lee, C. 2000. Contrastive predicates and conventional scales. In A. Okrent and J. Boyle, eds., *CLS*, vol. 36-1, pages 243–257.

Oshima, D. Y. 2002. Contrastive topic as a paradigmatic operator. paper presented at Workshop on Information Structure in Context, Stuttgart University.

Rooth, M. 1985. *Association with Focus*. Ph.D. thesis, University of Massachusetts at Amherst.

Rooth, M. 1992. A theory of focus interpretation. *Natural Language Semantics* 1:75–116.

Sauerland, U. 2001. On the computation of conversational implicatures. In *Proceedings of SALT 11*. Cornell University, Ithaca: CLC Publications.

Teramura, H. 1991. *Nihongo no sintakusu to imi (Japanese Syntax and Semantics) III*. Kurosio Publishers.

Korean Children's Syntactic and Semantic Development of Dative Constructions in L1

HEE-SOOK KIM AND EUN-JOO MOON
Korea National University of Education

1. Introduction

This paper, based on an observational study of first language (L1) acquisition by Korean children, focuses on the nature of dative constructions. Specifically, the issue of whether the prepositional dative (PD) or the double object dative (DOD) is the unmarked structure is examined.[1] This is one of major issues related to Universal Grammar (UG) which needs to be determined empirically through various types of acquisition data.

(1) a. Jack gave a book to Ann. (PD)
b. Jack gave Ann a book. (DOD)

[1] The prepositional dative (PD) is often referred to as the indirect object dative (IOD) or *to*-dative. Prepositions are used to mark the case of the indirect object in English, but in many other languages such as Korean and Japanese the case is marked by an affix or postpositions. Although the term IOD is more widely used in the literature because it is crosslinguistically more neutral, the term PD will be used in this study to rule out any confusion. For instance, some Koreans confuse IOD with DOD because the first NP in DOD is an indirect object (IO).

2. Theoretical Background

2.1. Derivational Approach to Dative Constructions

Kim (2003) criticizes the positing of the existence of two different subcategorizations of the issue. On the basis of Fillmore (1965), Larson (1988), and Emonds (1993), Kim (2003) proposes a derivational approach showing that the PD (1a) is a more unmarked structure than the DOD (1b) with the following major key assumptions: the binarity principle, vp-shell analysis of complex predicates, the uniform theta assignment hypothesis, localism with a tier model, and the concept of inherent case.[2]

It is claimed that the PD construction is formed by head-to-head movement from the third underlying form of a three-term argument structure and the DOD by the optional V'-reanalysis adapted from Larson (1988). This study assumes that the PD is a more basic structure than the DOD.

2.2. Head Parameter and Korean Equivalents to English Dative Constructions

It is generally agreed that a sentence like (3) is the unmarked dative construction in Korean. Though controversial, it is assumed in this paper that the generally agreed upon unmarked dative construction in Korean corresponds to the unmarked PD construction in English.[3]

---

[2] The key assumptions are as follows:

a. Binarity principle in combining (merging) elements
b. VP-shell analysis of complex predicates
c. Uniform Theta Assignment Hypothesis (UTAH): Identical thematic relationships are represented by identical structural relations between the items at the level of D-Structure.
d. Localism (Anderson, 1971) and two thematic tiers (Jackendoff, 2002)
   i) Thematic tier (spatial tier): source (FROM), goal (TO), theme/moving object (Ø)
   ii) Action tier: agent–patient

[3] The rationale for selecting the English equivalents for Korean sentences is accounted for in the following. If the word orders of the two given languages are compared focusing on the relationship between the verb and the thematic roles of internal arguments, the unmarked dative construction in Korean is analyzed as an equivalent of the unmarked PD construction in English as shown in Figure (1a). When the thematic hierarchy is looked at this way, the default word order in Korean follows this hierarchy: Agent precedes Recipient, and Recipient precedes Theme (Wechsler, 1995). In both Korean and English sentences, the Theme is closer to the verb than the Recipient is. Surprisingly, the relations regarding the semantic roles and syntactic cases in both languages remain consistent. The direction is the only difference. Within this

(3) 'Minswu-ka[NOM] Ceyni-eykey[DAT] kkem-ul[ACC] cwu-ess-ta.'
'Minsu gave a stick of gum to Jenny.'

Based on the head parameter theory and thematic hierarchy theory, dative structures in Korean and English are symmetrical with the arguments branching in opposite directions centering around the verb/head, as if in a mirror image, illustrated in Figure 1 below. For convenience, the subjects are not specified. Kiparsky (1987) presents the thematic hierarchy in terms of semantic constituency where lower roles are closer to the verb: <Agent<Recipient/Goal<Theme verb>>>.[4] The rationale for selecting the English equivalents for Korean sentences is illustrated in Figure 1.

Goal/PP	**Theme**/NP	**Verb**		
Ceyni-eykey	kkem-ul	cwu-ta		
		Verb	**Theme**/NP	Goal/PP
		Give	a stick of gum	to Jenny

(a)The correspondence of the Korean dative structure with the English PD

Theme/NP	**Goal**/NP	**Verb**		
Kkem-ul	Ceyni(?:Ø/lul/-hanthey)	cwu-ta		
		Verb	**Goal**/NP	Theme/NP
		Give	Jenny	a stick of gum

(b) The correspondence of the Korean dative structure with the English DOD

Figure 1. Symmetry of dative constructions in Korean and English

---

analysis, prepositional features are assumed to be incorporated into the verbs in DOD sentences. Thus, the Korean equivalent corresponding to the English DOD construction would be one close to the figure (1b).

Considering that word order is an important mechanism children use to help communicate semantic relations, Korean children consistently followed pattern 'a' (PD type) rather than pattern 'b' (DOD type) when both Theme and Recipient were present in a sentence.

[4] In this paper, the terms Goal and Recipient are used interchangeably. Grimshaw (1990) uses the term GOAL (the entity towards which the activity expressed by the predicate is directed) in a broad sense to include both animate and inanimate entities. On the other hand, Kiparsky (1987) uses the term Recipient to refer to only animate indirect objects.

3. An Observational Study: Acquisition of Dative Constructions in L1 by Korean Children

3.1. Subjects

The data collected for the L1 study comes from longitudinal observations of ten Korean children aged between one and four years; see (4). They are ranked in order of age in months at the beginning of their first recordings.

(4)

SW	**12-30 months**	**TS**	**19-37 months**
BJ	**14-32 months**	**DY**	**20-38 months**
MS	**18-36 months**	**DH**	**20-38 months**
SH	**18-36 months**	**HW**	**23-41 months**
TY	**18-36 months**	**HI**	**30-48 months**

3.2. Materials and Procedure

To observe when and how Korean children acquire the argument structure of dative constructions in L1, a diary (Appendix) was distributed to the mothers of the subjects and collected 18 months later. The mothers were asked to write down actual dative sentences containing verbs specified in the diaries and the age at which their child produced them. Then the transcriptions were analyzed sentence by sentence with special reference to the missing arguments. The verbs used in this study are dative verbs in Korean that correspond to those in English, selected from the word list in the Curriculum for Foreign Language Education edited by the Ministry of Education of Korea.

4. Results and Discussion

4.1. General Developmental Sequence

Although the age at which each child produced his or her first example of a dative construction varied significantly, the subjects seemed to follow a general pattern regarding the sequence of production as detailed in (5).

(5) General sequence in L1 acquisition of dative constructions in Korean

① At the prelinguistic stage, children use pointing/gestures or call their mom/caretakers to express the dative meaning.

② Children use the word 'ike' (this thing) or specific nouns which are to be realized as the direct objects in the dative constructions later on (e.g., 'ike 'this thing'; wuyu 'milk'; mwul 'water'; mal 'horse') (20 months±5).

③ They start to use dative verbs with or without the objects (e.g., (ike) cwe 'Give this to me'; (mal) sacwe 'Buy a horse for me') (24 months±5).

④ They add indirect objects without overt case markers (28 months±5).

a. Appa-ka Minswu-Ø chong-Ø sajwesse.
   Daddy-Nom Minsu-DAT gun-ACC bought
   'Daddy bought a gun for Minsu (me).'

b. Swuhyeni-Ø chak-Ø ilkecwe.
   Suhyeon-DAT book-ACC read
   'Read a book to Suhyeon (me).'

⑤ They use indirect objects with the dative markers 'eykey/hanthey' (32 months±5).

a. Halapeci-ka Minswu-hanthey ton-Ø cwess-ta.
   Grandpa-NOM Minsu-DAT money-ACC gave
   'Grandpa gave some money to Minsu (me)'

b. Emma-ka na-hanthey tencyepwa.
   Mommy-NOM I-DAT throw
   'Mommy, throw (the ball) to me.'

Surprisingly, although the dative markers *eykey* and *hanthey* can be used interchangeably in Korean, only 'hanthey' was found in the speech of children. It has been observed that the dative marker 'hanthey' emerged at a later stage of development, usually after thirty months. It is also interesting to note that when the Goal expressed was the children themselves, they usually omitted the indirect object (i.e., goal), but some of them consistently used their own name in that place for a certain period of time.

4.2. Sentence Types and Dative Constructions in L1 data

Table 1 shows that more than 65 percent of the sample sentences were imperatives (i.e., directives such as commands or requests) in Korean children's speech. This is probably closely related with the fact that about 70 percent of the sentences had missing subjects.

Sentence type	Total number of sentences (180)	In percentage (%)
Imperative	118	65.5
Interrogative	20	11.1
Declarative	42	23.3

Table 1. Types of sentences produced by children using dative constructions

4.3. Development of Nouns and Verbs in Dative Constructions

The findings also seem to confirm the claim made by Gentner (1982), that children universally acquire nouns earlier than verbs. Their earliest words spoken were nouns closely related to their surroundings such as *emma* 'mommy', *wuyu* 'milk', and *kkakka* 'cookie'. In mother-child interaction where new referents are usually present objects, the use of deictic pronouns such as *ike* 'this thing' is a very common referential strategy for first mentions (Clancy, 1996). Many of the children in our corpus also began producing dative construction with the word *ike*.

The development of verbs in dative constructions in Korean also appears to follow particular patterns. First of all, the analysis of the data shows that Korean children produced the most typical dative verb *cwu-ta* 'give' first. Then verbs that combine with the verb *cwu-ta*, such as *sa+cwuta* 'buy', *ilke+cwuta* 'read', *poye+cwuta* 'show', were produced by children based on their needs. In general, the verbs corresponding to 'teach', 'send', and 'write' in English did not appear until quite later on (e.g., around 35 months). As mentioned above, children tend to omit indirect objects very frequently, but they usually specified the indirect objects for the Korean verbs equivalent to 'throw' and 'send'.

4.4. Word Order and Development of Dative Case Markers

Word order in Korean is relatively loose compared to that in English. However, the general word order of dative constructions shown in this acquisition data was fairly consistent with the unmarked dative construction in Korean which was assumed to be equivalent to the English PD: Agent precedes Goal, and Goal precedes Theme. This point is further illustrated below.

i. When one internal argument is present:
The development of the pattern [DO + Action] precedes [IO + Action] and the former is used much more frequently.

ii. When two internal arguments are present:

The productive word order was as follows: Agent precedes Goal, and Goal precedes Theme.

An interesting finding was that, in general, children rarely produced the Accusative case marker (-ul/lul) overtly in comparison with the Dative case marker. Therefore only the dative markers will be examined. In examples in (6), there is no overt dative marker present. On the other hand, in (7), it is shown that children produced the dative markers overtly.

(6) Without dative markers

a. Enni-ka Minswu-Ø aiskhulim-Ø cwesse. (MS, 23)
girl-NOM Minsu-DAT ice-cream-ACC
'The girl gave some ice-cream to Minsu.'

b. Swuhyeni-Ø wuyu-Ø cwe. (SH, 26)
Suhyeon-DAT milk-ACC give
'Give some milk to me.'

c. Emma, Na-Ø phinikhio-Ø poyecwe. (MS, 36)
Mommy I-DAT Pinnochio-ACC show
'Mommy, show Pinnochio to me.'

(7) With dative markers

a. Hikwani-hanthey wuyu-Ø cwela. (HW, 32)
Heekwan-DAT milk-ACC give
'Give some milk to Heekwan.'

b. Emma, Ceyhyeni-hanthey aiskhulim-Ø sacwulkkeci? (DH, 38)
mommy, Jehyeon-DAT ice-cream-ACC will buy
'Mommy, will you buy some ice-cream for Jehyeon?'

c. Appa-ka cincca na-hanthey os-Ø sacwuntako-haysse. (HI, 48)
daddy-NOM really I-DAT clothes-ACC will buy said
'Daddy said he will really buy some clothes for me.'

In either case, the basic word order remained the same: Agent precedes Goal, and Goal precedes Theme. There were only a few exceptions to this productive word order.[5]

---

[5] There were only a few exceptions to the general word order as shown below.

a. Kuke-Ø nahanthey phaseyyo. (while playing house) (HY, 45)
that-ACC I-DAT sell
'Sell that one to me.'

b. Ike-Ø Cwunseki-Ø poyecwu-myen coahakeyssta. (HI, 45)
This-ACC Junseok-DAT show-if pleased-will be
'If we show this to Junseok, he will be pleased.'

These results on word order seem to suggest that the PD (=IOD) is the unmarked structure.

4.5. Missing Arguments (DO vs. IO)

The most striking feature found in this acquisition data is that indirect objects are very often omitted, especially when the IO is in the first or second person. There were many more indirect objects missing (54 percent) than direct objects missing (9 percent) in the L1 data as shown in Table 2.

Missing arguments	Total (180)	In percentage (%)
DO (Theme)	16	8.9
IO (Goal)	98	54.4
Both IO and DO	36	20.0
Overt IO and DO	30	16.6
Subject	130	73

Table 2. Missing arguments in dative constructions in Korean (L1)

From the observed phenomena described in this section, it is interesting to note that there exists a relationship between the prominence theory of Grimshaw (1990) and the missing argument phenomenon in the L1 acquisition of dative constructions by Korean children. According to Grimshaw, the external argument is the most prominent in the argument structure, and the internal arguments also have prominence relative to each other: (Agent (Goal[4] (Theme))). The more prominent an argument, the more likely it is that that argument can be omitted as shown below in (8).

(8) Prominence relations: Agent /Experiencer/Source > Goal > Theme
Relative frequency of the missing arguments: Subject > IO > DO

4.6. Datives from Locatives

Martin (1992), cited in Aristar (1996), claims that, diachronically, both *ey* and *eykey* originate in locatives, a locative marker *-ey*. When this marker took an animate nominal as its argument, it was marked as indicating the place at which the animate was found. *-key* (my/your/his place) appeared after the case particle, and this produced the animate locative *eykey*. The string *eykey*, which had begun as an animate locative, is now interpreted as a dative marker.

As has been mentioned earlier, although *-eykey* and *-hanthey* can be used inter-changeably, children only used *-hanthey*. If we posit that -

hanthey is equivalent to *-eykey*, it may be inferred that the data seems to provide support for Kuryowicz's (1964) claim that dative cases are diachronically derived from locatives. Korean children seem to acquire the locative 'to' *(-ey)* relatively earlier than they acquire the dative 'to' (*-eykey*) as shown in the examples (9) and (10). Notice in (9a) that *-hanthey* can also be used as a [+animate] locative marker.

(9) a. Appa-hanthey kalkkeya. (MS, 25)
daddy-LOCATIVE will go
'I will go to daddy.'
b. Mal-Ø kaciko ceki-ey kalkkeya. (MS, 24)
horse-ACC take there-LOCATIVE will go
'I will go there with the horse.'

(10) a. Emma-ka na-hanthey tencye. (MS, 28; SH, 34)
mommy-NOM I-DAT throw
'Mommy, throw (the ball) to me.
b. Emma-hanthey phyenci-Ø ponaylkkeya.(MS, 33; DY, 32; HI, 38)
mommy-DAT a letter-ACC will send
'I will send a letter to mommy.'

Also, in Korean, there is a pattern with dative and locative marking which is in some ways reminiscent of Indo-European itself. The language shows a complex blending of animacy with dative and locative marking: *-ey* is used only with inanimates and *-eykey* is used only with animates. An interesting finding was that children were fairly sensitive to the animacy feature and correctly used *-ey* with inanimates and *-eykey* (*-hanthey*) with animates without making overgeneralizations.

5. Conclusion and Implications

The results of this study are generally consistent with Kim's (2003) predictions that the PD structure is the more basic unmarked structure and therefore acquired before the DOD. Thus, this study provides support for the position that the PD is the unmarked structure, and consequently, this theoretical implication supports the UG-based markedness theory.

Further implications are as follows: 1) The rarity of the ACCUSATIVE case marker could be interpreted to support Kim's proposal that Objective is an inherent case and hence the structural Objective case could be redundant. 2) Children are sensitive to animacy features.

References

Anderson, J. 1971. *The Grammar of Case: Towards a Localistic Theory*. Cambridge University Press.

Aoun, J. & Y. Li. 1989. Scope and Constituency. *Linguistic Inquiry* 20: 141-172.

Aristar, A. 1996. The Relationship Between Dative and Locative: Kurylowicz's Argument from a Typological Perspective. *Diachronica* □□: 207-224.

Clancy, P. 1996. Referential Strategies and the Co-construction of Argument Structure in Korean Acquisition. *Studies in Anaphora*, ed. B. Fox, 33-68. Amsterdam and Philadelphia: Benjamins.

Emonds, J. 1993. Projecting Indirect Objects. *The Linguistic Review* 10: 211-263.

Fillmore, C. 1965. *Indirect Object Constructions in English and the Ordering of Transformations*. The Hague: Mouton and Co.

Gentner, D. 1982. Why Nouns Are Learned Before Verbs: Linguistic Relativity Versus Natural Partitioning. *Language Development 2: Language Thought, and Culture*, ed. S. A. Kuczaj, 301-334. Hillsdale, NJ: Erlbaum.

Grimshaw, J. 1990. *Argument Structure*. MIT Press.

Jackendoff, R. 2002. *Foundations of Language: Brain, Meaning, Grammar, Evolution*. Oxford University Press.

Kim, H. S. 2003. Double Objects' Puzzles for Syntactic Analysis. *Proceedings of the Spring Meeting of the Korean Generative Grammar Circle.*

Kiparsky, P. 1987. *Morphology and Grammatical relations*. Manuscript, Stanford University.

Kurylowicz, J. 1964. *The Inflectional Categories of Indo-European*. Heidelberg: Carl Winter.

Larson, R. 1988. On the Double Object Construction. *Linguistic Inquiry* 19: 335-391.

Martin, S. 1992. *A Reference Grammar of Korean*. Rutland, Vermont: Charles E. Tuttle.

Moon, E. J. 2003. *Acquisition of Argument Structures in L1 and L2 by Korean Learners of English: With Special Reference to Dative Constructions*. Doctoral dissertation, Korea National University of Education.

Pinker, S. 1989. *Learnability and Cognition: The Acquisition of Argument Structure*. Cambridge, Mass.: MIT Press.

Wechsler, S. 1995. *The Semantic Basis of Argument structure*. Stanford, California: CSLI Publications.

Appendix

This diary is devised to examine when and how Korean children acquire the dative constructions in L1. Please write down the actually produced sentences containing the given dative verbs and the time each utterance occurred.

Name: Birth date:

1. cwuta (give---to)
_______(12 months) --->________ (18 months) ---> _______ (24 months) --->________________ (36months) --->_________________ (48months)
2. sacwuta (buy---for)
3. ilkecwuta (read---to)
4. mantulecwuta (make---for)
5. poyecwuta (show---to)
6. tencita (throw---to)
7. kacyeota/kacyekata (bring/take---to)
8. iyakihaycwuta (tell---to)
9. kaluchyecwuta (teach---to)
10. ponayta (send---to)
11. phalta (sell---to)
12. phyencilul ssuta (write---to)
13. others

Korean Children's Interpretation of Sentences Containing 'Every' and 'Not'

MEESOOK KIM, CHUNG-HYE HAN, JEFFREY LIDZ, AND JULIEN MUSOLINO
Sangji University, Simon Fraser University, University of Maryland, and Indiana University

1. Introduction

Recently, a number of acquisition studies have paid considerable attention to children's difficulty with quantified expressions (Donaldson & Lloyd, 1974; Inhelder & Piaget, 1964; Philip, 1995, among others). This phenomenon has been found in a variety of languages including English (Donaldson & Lloyd, 1974), French (Inhelder & Piaget, 1964), Chinese (Lee, 1986), Japanese (Philip, 1995), and Korean (Kang, 2001). Interestingly, whereas most of the previous studies have focused on children's interpretation of sentences containing a universally quantified NP and an existentially quantified one, few researchers have examined interactions involving quantifiers and negation (but see Drozd and Philip, 1993; Musolino, Crain, and Thornton, 2000; O'Leary and Crain, 1994). In particular, by testing English-speaking children's knowledge on the scope interaction of the universal quantifier and negation, Musolino et al. (2000) found that children, unlike adults, show a strong preference for the scopal interpretation of the quantified elements which corresponds to their surface syntactic position (i.e. isomorphic readings).

In this paper we present data from an experiment designed to investigate how child and adult speakers of Korean interpret sentences containing universally quantified noun phrases and negation, in particular focusing on the scope interaction of object quantifiers and negation, with the use of Truth Value Judgment Task methodology (Crain and Thornton, 1998; Musolino et al., 2000). The discussion is organized as follows: Section 2 introduces the phenomenon and considers previous studies on the acquisition of the phenomenon in English. Section 3 discusses previous studies on the scope interaction of universal quantifiers and negation in Korean. Section 4 is the main experimental section of the paper. Section 5 shows the results of the present experiment. Finally, section 6 discusses some important implications.

II. Negation and Quantifiers in English

A number of researchers in linguistics have noticed that sentences like (1), where a universally quantified NP occurs in the subject position of a negated clause, show scope ambiguity (Horn, 1989; Jackendoff, 1972; Lasnik, 1972, among others). In one interpretation, (1) can be paraphrased as meaning that no horse jumped over the fence. Here the universally quantified subject is interpreted outside the scope of negation (abbreviated every>not), as shown in (1a). Musolino et al. (2000) call this an *isomorphic* interpretation because in this case the scope relation between the universally quantified noun phrase (NP) and negation matches their surface positions. Another possible interpretation of (1) is that not all of the horses jumped over the fence. In this case, the universally quantified subject is interpreted within the scope of negation (not>every), as shown in (1b). That is, the fact that negation takes scope over the universal quantifier involves a mismatch between their surface positions and the semantic interpretation. This phenomenon is referred to as a *non-isomorphic* interpretation (a 'not all' reading) because the interpretation of *every horse* with respect to negation is based on a reversal of their surface positions.

(1) **Every** horse did**n't** jump over the fence.
a. No horse jumped over the fence (every > not)
$\forall(x)\neg$ [horse (x) $\rightarrow$ $\neg$ jump over the fence (x)]
b. Not every horse jumped over the fence (not > every)
$\neg\forall(x)$ [horse (x) $\rightarrow$ jump over the fence (x)]

Interestingly, not all sentences with a universally quantified NP and negation demonstrate scope ambiguity. As shown in (2), object quantifiers in a negated sentence allow a 'not all' (narrow scope) reading because negation takes scope over the object quantifier. That is, (2) can only be paraphrased as meaning that not every orange was bought by the Smurf (not>every). Notice that unlike the example in (1), in this case the 'not all' reading corresponds to an isomorphic interpretation because the scope relation between negation and the universally quantified NP coincides with their surface position.

(2) The Smurf did**n't** buy **every** orange.
$\neg\forall(x)$ [orange (x) $\rightarrow$ the Smurf bought (x)] (not > every)

Based on the fact that there is a scope difference between subject quantifier and object quantifier with respect to negation in English, Musolino et al. (2000) tested English-speaking children's knowledge of the scope interaction of the universal quantifier and negation, using the Truth Value Judgment Task methodology (Crain and Thornton, 1998). The main finding from Musolino et al.'s study was that while adults can easily access the non-isomorphic interpretation of sentences like (1b), 4-to-7-year-old children systematically assign sentences an isomorphic interpretation only. For example, one of the stories used to test children's comprehension of (1) involved three horses trying to jump over a fence. Two of the horses successfully jumped over the fence but the third one didn't. At the end of the story, a puppet described the situation as follows: Every horse didn't jump over the fence. Note that this statement is true in the non-isomorphic (i.e. not all) reading of the sentence since it is true that not all of the horses jumped over the fence. However, the puppet's statement is false in the isomorphic reading since two horses did jump over the fence. They found that in this case adults accepted the puppet's statement 100% of the time, indicating that they could easily access the non-isomorphic interpretation (i.e. not>every). In contrast, children systematically rejected the puppet's statements, 92.5% of the time, thereby showing that children seem to only be able to access the isomorphic reading of the sentence (i.e. every>not).

Musolino et al. (2000) also tested sentences like (2), where the universal quantifier *every* occurs in the object position of a negated sentence. The example in (2) was used in the context of a story where a Smurf had bought only one of three oranges, and therefore not all of them. They found that in this case children had no difficulty accepting the puppet's statements that the Smurf didn't buy every orange (i.e. not>every). Notice that in this case the not all reading corresponds to an isomorphic interpretation, unlike the example in (1).

So far we have seen a phenomenon involving the scope interaction of the universal quantifier and negation in English. An important finding was that there are systematic differences in the way that children and adults interpret sentences containing the universal quantifier and negation. That is, English-speaking children are initially restricted to isomorphic interpretations in sentences where both isomorphic and non-isomorphic interpretations are available in adult grammar. In the following section, we examine the scope interpretation of the universal quantifier *every* in negated sentences in adult Koreans.

III. Negation and Quantifiers in Korean

It is a well-known fact that Korean has two types of negation, short negation (S-Neg) in (3) and long negation (L-Neg) in (4). In S-Neg, the negative morpheme *an* appears immediately before the verb. In contrast, in L-Neg, the negative morpheme *ani* appears between the verb stem containing a suffix *ci* and the dummy verb *ha* 'do' which bears the tense morphology.

(3)	John-i	sakwa-lul	**an**	mek-ess-ta.	
	J-nom	apple-acc	neg	eat-past-decl	
	'John did not eat the apple.'			(Short Negation)	
(4)	John-i	sakwa-lul	mek-**ci**	**ani**	**ha**-yess-ta.
	J-nom	apple-acc	eat-CI	neg	do-past-decl
	'John did not eat the apple.'			(Long Negation)	

The structure of negation in Korean has received considerable attention from many researchers in theoretical syntax (Ahn, 1991; Cho, 1993; Lee, 1993; Park, 1994; Sohn, 1995; Hagstrom, 1998, among others), even though there is still considerable debate. While recent researchers have proposed the same underlying structure for two types of negation (Hagstrom, 1998), most studies on negation assume that there are two different structures for negation in Korean in order to explain scope-related phenomena (Ahn, 1991; Choe, 1997; Kim, 1997).[1]

More interestingly, it has been reported in the literature that the interaction of quantifier and negation in Korean shows a scope difference between S-Neg and L-Neg in both subject quantifiers and object quantifiers, as shown in (5) and (6), although there is considerable debate about this. In particular, the facts about the scope of object quantifiers in S-Neg are controversial. For example, the literature generally agrees with the judgment

[1] Since the syntactic structure of the two types of negation in Korean is still controversial, I will not discuss the issue in detail here.

that examples like (6) are ambiguous. In contrast, the majority find (5) to be unambiguous (Cho, 1975; Park, 1994; Suh, 1989, etc.), although some do find (5) to be ambiguous (Choe, 1997; Lee, 1993; Sohn, 1995).

(5)	John-i	**motun**	chayk-ul	**an**	ilk-ess-ta	
	J-nom	every	book-acc	neg	read-past-decl	
	'John didn't read every book.'					
(6)	John-i	**motun**	chayk-ul	ilk-**ci**	**ani**	hay-ss-ta
	J-nom	every	book-acc	read-CI	neg	do-past-decl
	'John didn't read every book.'					

In spite of the existence of some disagreement about judgments of the above sentences, it can be generally assumed that object quantifiers allow only wide scope with respect to short negation (every>not), while object quantifiers allow either wide (every>not) or narrow scope (not>every) with respect to long negation. Accordingly, the example in (5) can be paraphrased as meaning that none of the books were read by John (every>not). In this case, the quantified NP *every book* is interpreted in the scope of negation, leading to an isomorphic interpretation (a wide scope reading).

On the other hand, the example in (6), containing the object quantifier and long negation, shows scope ambiguity. In one interpretation, (6) can be paraphrased as meaning that none of the books were read by John (every>not), as in (5). In this case, the quantified NP *every book* takes scope over negation, causing an isomorphic interpretation (a wide scope reading). Another possible interpretation of (6) is that not all of the books were read by John (not>every). In this case, negation takes scope over the quantified NP *every book*, lead to a non-isomorphic interpretation (a narrow scope reading).

Therefore, it would be interesting to find out experimentally whether the unambiguity of sentences in (5) and the scope ambiguity of sentences in (6) can be verified by the judgments of adult speakers of Korean. Furthermore, it would be interesting to investigate how Korean children interpret the interaction of object quantifiers and long negation, where both isomorphic and non-isomorphic readings are available in the adult grammar.

IV. Experiment on Korean

Sixty Korean-speaking children aged 4;0-4;11 (mean 4;5) and sixty Korean-speaking adults (all undergraduate students) participated in our experiment. As in the experiment by Musolino et al. (2000), speakers of Korean were tested using the Truth Value Judgment Task (TVJT) methodology (Crain and Thornton, 1998; Musolino et al., 2000). The TVJT involved two experimenters. Using small toys and props, the first experimenter acted out short stories in front of the participants. The second experimenter played the role of a puppet (in this case Mickey) who watched the stories with the participants. At the end of the story, the puppet made a statement about what happened in the story. The participants had to determine whether the puppet's statement was correct or not. Finally, the participants were asked to explain why they thought that the puppet was right or wrong, in order to confirm that the participants' responses were based on their correct understanding of the story.

The children were tested individually. Two pretest stories were given to each child. In the first story, the statement made by the puppet was true. In the second story, the puppet's statement was false. The statements made by the puppet about two pretest stories included the scope interaction of negation and object quantifiers. If the child could answer those correctly, they would then hear eight more stories: four test stories involving sentences of types (5) and (6) and four control stories.

Adult participants were shown a videotaped version of the stories. They were given a score sheet and were instructed to indicate, for each story, whether the puppet was right or wrong. They were also asked to provide a brief justification for their answers. Adult participants were tested in groups.

In this experiment, the stories were made in such a way that one of the readings was true and the other reading was false. Therefore, YES or NO answers to the puppet's statements were taken as a measure of the subjects' abilities to access one reading or the other. Notice that children were tested using the same method and similar materials as those used by Musolino et al. (2000).

Each of four test stories with short negation and long negation was given to each subject. Furthermore, two versions of the stories were constructed; that is, a “none” condition and a “not-all” condition. Take for example the "none" condition in the interaction of the object quantifier and the two types of negation.

Object Quantifiers with S-Neg

(7) ku yeoja ai-ka **motun** panci-lul **an** sa-ss-ta
the girl-nom every ring-acc neg buy-past-Decl
'The girl didn't buy every ring.'

Object Quantifiers with L-Neg

(8) ku yeoja ai-ka **motun** panci-lul **sa-ci** **ani** hay-ss-ta
the girl-nom every ring-acc buy-CI neg do-past-Decl
'The girl didn't buy every ring.'

In one story, for example, a girl decided to go to the stationery store to buy some toys. There were three balloons and three rings in the store. She first decided to buy three balloons. Next, the girl examined the three rings in the store to see if she would buy them. The first two were too small, and the third one was too expensive. The girl then decided not to buy the rings. At the end of the story, the puppet makes a statement using either the sentence in (7) or the sentence in (8). Notice that in the context of the story just described, (7) and (8) are true in an isomorphic (i.e. 'none') reading since it is true that none of the rings were bought by the girl. If subjects access the isomorphic interpretation of (7) and (8), we expect them to accept the puppet's statement. In contrast, (7) and (8) are false in a non-isomorphic interpretation (i.e. not all).

Let us now consider the "not-all" condition. In one story, for example, a girl decided to go to the stationery store to buy some toys. There were three balloons and three rings in the store. She first decided to buy three balloons. Next, the girls examined the three rings in the store to see if she would buy them. The first one was red and pretty, and she decided to buy it. The second one was blue and cheap, and she decided to buy it. But the third one was too expensive and the girl ended up only buying two of the three rings. At the end of the story, the puppet makes a statement using either the sentence in (7) or the sentence in (8). Notice that in the context of the story just described, (7) and (8) are false in an isomorphic (i.e. 'none') reading since it is not the case that none of the rings were bought by the girl. If subjects access the isomorphic interpretation of (7) and (8), we expect them to reject the puppet's statement. By contrast, (7) and (8) are true in a non-isomorphic interpretation (i.e. not all). Accordingly, if subjects access the non-isomorphic interpretation, we expect them to accept the puppet's statement.

V. Results

First of all, we found that in the "none" condition with short negation, children accepted the puppet's statements about 82% of the time and adults almost always (98% of the time) accepted the puppet's statements. In contrast, in the "not-all" condition with short negation, children gave YES answers to the short negation 36.7% of the time and adults gave YES answers to the short negation 33.3% of the time. That is, in the "none" condition, children and adults showed no significant difference in the interaction of object quantifiers and short negation (p=1.06). In the "not-all" condition as well, no reliable difference between children and adults was found in the interaction of object quantifiers and short negation (p=.189).

Notice that in the "none" condition, the test items with short negation were true in an isomorphic (i.e. 'none') reading and were false in a non-isomorphic (i.e. 'not all') reading. In contrast, in the "not-all" condition, the test items with short negation were true in a non-isomorphic (not>every) reading and were false in an isomorphic (every>not) reading. Accordingly, we predicted that if subjects could access the isomorphic reading for the test items in the "none"-condition, they would accept the puppet's statement. By contrast, if subjects could access the isomorphic interpretation in the "not-all" condition, they would reject the puppet's statement. As we predicted, both children and adults accepted the puppet's statements in the "none" condition, whereas they rejected the puppet's statements in the "not-all" condition. Therefore, the results indicate that both 4-year-olds and adults accept only the isomorphic reading (every>not) with respect to the scope interaction between object quantifiers and short negation.

Second, we found that in the "none"-condition with long negation, children accepted the puppet's statements 87% of the time, and adults almost always (93% of the time) accepted the puppet's statements. In the "none" condition, we found no significant difference between children and adults in the understanding of object quantifiers and long negation (p=.582). By contrast, in the "not-all" condition with long negation, children gave YES answers to long negation 40% of the time, whereas adults gave YES answers to long negation 76.7% of the time. That is, in the "not-all" condition, we found a significant difference between children and adults in the interpretation of object quantifiers and long negation (p=.037).

Recall that in the "none" condition, the test items with long negation were true in an isomorphic (i.e. every>not or 'none') reading and were false in a non-isomorphic (i.e. not>every or 'not all') reading. By contrast, in the "not-all" condition, the test items with long negation were true in a non-isomorphic (not>every) reading and were false in an isomorphic (every>not) reading. Accordingly, we predicted that if subjects could access the isomorphic reading for the test items in the "none" condition, they would accept the puppet's statement. In addition, if subjects could access the isomorphic reading in the "not-all" condition, they would reject the puppet's statement. By contrast, if subjects could access the non-isomorphic interpretation in the "not-all" condition, they would accept the puppet's statement.

As we predicted, both children and adults accepted the puppet's statements in the "none" condition with long negation. In contrast, in the "not-all" condition with long negation, children rejected the puppet's statements but adults accepted the puppet's statements. That is, the results imply that adults accept both isomorphic (every>not) and non-isomorphic (not>every) readings, whereas children are restricted to the isomorphic reading (every>not) with respect to the scope interaction of object quantifiers and long negation.

In addition, both children and adults showed no significant difference between short negation and long negation in the "none"-condition (p=.59 for children; p=.48 for adults). Second, we found no reliable difference between adults and children in short negation (p=.106) as well as in long negation (p=.58). Third, children showed no significant difference between short negation and long negation in the "not-all" condition (p=.86), whereas adults showed a significant difference between the two types of negation (p=.008). Finally, no reliable difference between adults and children was found in short negation (p=.18), whereas a significant difference between adults and children was found in long negation (p=.03).

VI. Summary and Discussion

Let us summarize the findings. In the experiments presented here, we asked whether the scope ambiguities in sentences with object quantifiers and long negation and the lack of scope ambiguities in sentences with object quantifiers and short negation in Korean could be experimentally confirmed by native speakers of Korean. In addition, we asked whether children's preference for isomorphic readings could be confirmed cross-linguistically, based on the same experimental methodology (i.e. Crain and Thornton's TVJT).

First, the results presented above experimentally confirm previous assumptions about the scope interaction between object quantifiers and the two types of negation in Korean. More specifically, while adult speakers of Korean can easily assign either scope interpretation in the interaction of object quantifiers and long negation, they assign only wide scope interpretation in the interaction of object quantifiers and short negation. This shows that there is a scope difference between short negation and long negation with respect to the scope interaction of object quantifiers and negation in Korean. Therefore, the results confirm experimentally the existence of scope ambiguities in sentences containing object quantifiers and long negation and a lack of scope ambiguities in sentences containing object quantifiers and short negation.

Second, the results from the experiment show that 4-year-old children did not show a scope difference between short negation and long negation in each condition, unlike adults. For both types of negation, Korean children showed a strong preference for the wide scope interpretation, that is, for the isomorphic interpretation. Accordingly, the results strengthen the findings of Musolino et al. (2000) by showing that 4-year-old children have a reliable preference for the isomorphic reading of quantified objects, where both readings are available in adult grammar. Therefore, these experiments based on the TVJT methodology show that regardless of language, children are restricted to the isomorphic reading, in terms of the scope interaction of the universal quantifier and negation.

Now we may ask why children differ from adults in the way that we have observed. In other words, why are children initially restricted to the isomorphic reading of such sentences cross-linguistically? Following Musolino et al. (2000), we assume that children's failure to assign non-isomorphic readings may be due to their processing or parsing limitations. According to this view, differences in processing ability between children and adults may be responsible for children's inability to access the non-isomorphic reading of sentences containing quantifiers and negation. Since the isomorphic reading is a direct result of a left to right parse, the scope relation between quantified objects and negation is initially interpreted based on the isomorphic reading (i.e. every>not). In contrast, a non-isomorphic reading requires an additional step to reverse the scope relation between quantified objects and negation, and then to assign an interpretation in which negation has scope over the universal quantifier (i.e. not>every). Therefore, children's preference for isomorphic readings may reflect processing effects. Nevertheless, because the data presented here do not allow us to determine whether the preference for isomorphic interpretations is due to performance factors, as the processing account claims, further investigation is needed.

References

Ahn, H. 1991. Light Verbs, VP-movement, Negation and Clausal Architecture in Korean and English. Doctoral dissertation, University of Wisconsin, Madison.

Cho, C. 1975. The Sscope of Nnegation in Korean. *The Korean Language*. Ed. H.-M. Sohn, page numbers. Center for Korean Studies: University of Hawaii Press.

Cho, D. 1993. Emphasis, Negation, and Verb Movement. *Papers from the Fifth Student Conference in Linguistics*, eds. V. Lindblad & M. Gamon, 50-69. MIT Working Papers in Linguistics 20: Cambridge, MA.

Choe, H. 1997. *TwoFfunctions of Negation: Negating and Licensing*. Manuscript, MIT/Yeungnam University.

Crain, S., & Thornton, R. 1998. *Investigations in Universal Grammar: A Guide to Research on the Acquisition of Syntax and Semantics*. Cambridge, MA: MIT Press.

Donaldson, M., & Lloyd, P. 1974. Sentences and Situations: Children's Judgments of Match and Mismatch. *Current Problems in Psycholinguistics,* ed. F. Bresson, page numbers. Paris: Centre National de la Rechernche Scientifique.

Drozd, K., & Philip, W. 1993. Event Quantification in Preschoolers' Comprehension of Negation. *Proceedings of the 24th Annual Child Language Research Forum*, ed. E. V. Clark , 72-86. Stanford, CA: CSLI.

Hagstrom, P. 1998. Phrasal Movement in Korean Negation. *Proceedings of the 9th Student Conference in Linguistics,* eds. L. Veselinova, S. Robinson, and L. Antieau, 180-215. MIT Working Papers in Linguistics 31: Cambridge, MA.

Horn, L. 1989. *A Natural History of Negation.* Chicago: University of Chicago Press.

Inhelder, B., & Piaget, J. 1964. *The Early Growth of Logic in the Child.* London: Routledge and Kegan Paul.

Jackendoff, R. 1972. *Semantic Interpretation in Generative Grammar.* Cambridge, MA: MIT Press.

Kang, H. 2001. Quantifier Spreading: Linguistic and Pragmatic Considerations. *Lingua* 111: 591-627.

Kim, Y. 1997. The Acquisition of Korean. *The Crosslinguistic Study of Language Acquisition,* Vol, 4, ed. D. Slobin, 335-444. Hillsdale, NJ: Erlbaum.

Lasnik, H. 1972. *Analyses of Negation in English.* Doctoral dissertation, MIT.

Lee, J. 1993. Postverbal Adverbs and Verb Movement in Korean *Japanese/Korean Linguistics* 2, ed. P. Clancy, 420-443. Stanford, CA: SLA/CSLI.

Lee, T. 1986. *Studies in Quantification in Chinese.* Doctoral dissertation, University of California, specify which campus.

Musolino, J., Crain, S., & Thornton, R. 2000. Navigating Negative Quantificational Space. *Linguistic,* 38(1): 1-32.

O'Leary, C., & Crain, S. 1994. *Negative Polarity Items (A Positive Result), Positive Polarity Items (A Negative Result).* Paper presented at the 1994 Boston University Conference on Language Development, Boston, MA.

Park, M. 1994. *A Morpho-syntactic Study of Korean Verbal Inflection.* Doctoral dissertation, University of Connecticut.

Philip, W. 1995. *Event Quantification in the Acquisition of Universal Quantification.* Doctoral dissertation, University of Massachusetts, Amherst.

Sohn, K. 1995. *Negative Polarity Items, Scope, and Economy.* Doctoral dissertation, University of Connecticut.

Suh 1989. Please supply this reference, cited in the first paragraph of p. 5.

Internally Headed Relatives Parallel Direct Perception Complements*

MIN-JOO KIM
Texas Tech University

1. Introduction

It has been noted in the literature that in Korean, the Internally Headed Relative Clause Construction (henceforth IHRC) and the Direct Perception Construction (henceforth DPC) take an identical syntactic form (e.g. N.-K. Kim 1984, B. Park 1994, Jhang 1994, Chung 1999, Chung and Kim 2003, M.-J. Kim to appear):[1] In both constructions, the complement of the embedding predicate consists of a gapless relative clause and a grammatical element *kes*, as illustrated in (1) and (2), respectively.[2]

---

*I am deeply grateful to Makoto Kadowaki, Chris Potts, Peggy Speas, and Ellen Woolford for the helpful comments and suggestions on an earlier version of the paper. I also benefited greatly from discussions with Kyle Johnson and Chisato Kitagawa. In addition, I would like to thank the audience at the 13th J/K Conference for questions and comments, in particular Professors Daeho Chung, Chungmin Lee, John Whitman, and James Hyesuk Yoon.

[1]As far as I am aware, this parallel is also found in Japanese (Makoto Kadowaki and Chisato Kitagawa personal communication) and the dialects of Quechua (Lefebvre and Muyskin 1988).

[2]In Korean, the relative marker *–nun* inflects for the tense/aspect of the embedded clause: *–nun* denotes imperfective aspect, *–(u)n* perfect/perfective, and *–(u)l* prospective.

(1) Internally Headed Relative Clause Construction (IHRC)

John-un	[[totwuk-i	tomangka]-**nun**	**kes**]-ul
J.-top	[[thief-nom	run.away]-**rel.imprf**	**kes**]-acc

cap-ess-ta
catch-pst-decl
'John caught a/the thief running away.'

(2) Direct Perception Construction (DPC)

John-un	[[totwuk-i	tomangka]-**nun**	**kes**]-ul
J.-top	[[thief-nom	run.away]-**rel.imprf**	**kes**]-acc

po-ess-ta
see-pst-decl
'John saw the event of a/the thief running away.'

Despite their identical surface form, however, the two constructions have been classified separately and, to my knowledge, the relationship between them has not been much studied in a systematic way (but see M.-J. Kim to appear). In fact, the DPC has been often treated as a kind of factive propositional attitude construction, as illustrated in (5) (e.g. Kim 1984, Jhang 1994, Chung and Kim 2003). In my understanding, this separate classification is due to the fact that the complements of the two constructions receive different interpretations: The IHRC complement receives an entity interpretation such as the thief, as shown in (1), whereas the DPC complement receives an eventuality interpretation such as the event of a/the thief running away, as shown in (2).

In this paper, I show that this interpretive difference between IHRC and DPC complements is only apparent; it merely reflects the embedding predicate's selectional properties, that is, entity-selecting vs. eventuality-selecting. By drawing on more substantive parallels between the two constructions than their surface form, and by bringing together the insights of previous research on each construction (e.g., Shimoyama 1999, Basilico 2003), I argue that they have an identical syntax and semantics. The gist of the proposal is that (i) their complements have a DP structure which consists of an event-denoting small clause and a pronominal definite description *kes* and (ii) the small clause provides the descriptive content for *kes*, whereby getting indirectly linked to the embedding clause (compare Hoshi 1996, Shimoyama 1999, Chung and Kim 2003). I show that by treating *kes* as a pronominal definite description, we can derive the apparently different interpretations of IHRC and DPC complements in a unified way.

In Section 2, I discuss the parallel between the IHRC and the DPC. In this section, I also show that the DPC differs from the factive propositional attitude construction, challenging the prevailing view in the literature. In Section 3, I propose a syntactic and semantic analysis of the IHRC and the DPC, which essentially unifies the two constructions. In Section 4, I return to the common properties of the two constructions outlined in Section 2 and show how they follow from the proposed analysis. Finally, Section 5 summarizes and concludes the paper.

2. The Parallel between the IHRC and the DPC

As far as I am aware, the similarity between the IHRC and the DPC has not been much discussed in the literature beyond noting their surface parallel. In this section, I show that they are alike in at least three aspects. In addition, I show that these parallels are not shared by other constructions that have the same form such as factive propositional complements and psych-predicate complements.

First, as noted by several authors, the embedded clause of the IHRC cannot contain an I(ndividual)-level predicate in the sense of Carlson (1977), i.e., a predicate that denotes a (semi) permanent property of an individual (see Matsuda 2002, Y.-B. Kim 2002, Chung and Kim 2003, C.-M. Lee 2001, M. Lee 2003). This property is illustrated in (3).

(3) *John-un [ku yeca-ka **yeppu**]-n kes-ul
J.-top [that woman-nom **pretty**]-rel kes-acc
tallay-ess-ta
comfort-pst-decl
Intended: 'John comforted the woman who was pretty.'

Note that this restriction also holds for the DPC complement, as illustrated in (4), but not for the complements of factive propositional attitude verbs or psych-predicates, even though they take the exactly identical syntactic form, as shown in (5) and (6). This suggests that the incompatibility with I-level predicates is not intrinsic to the gapless clause and *kes* string itself.

(4) *John-un [ku yeca-ka **yeppu**]-n kes-ul
J.-top [that woman-nom **pretty**]-rel kes-acc
po-ess-ta
see-pst-decl
Intended: 'John saw the woman who was pretty.'

(5) John-un [ku yeca-ka **yeppu**]-n kes-ul
J.-top [that woman-nom **pretty**]-rel kes-acc
al-ess-ta
know-pst-decl
'John knew that the woman was pretty.'

(6) Na-nun [John-i **chakha**-n kes]-i
I-top [J.-nom **good.hearted**-rel kes]-nom
maum-ey tun-ta
heart-loc come.in-decl
'I like John's being good-hearted.'

Second, as noted by M.-J. Kim (to appear), neither the IHRC nor the DPC allows the indicative mood marker *–ta* to occur in the embedded relative clause, as illustrated in (7) and (8).

(7) *John-un [totwuk-i tomangka-n-**ta**-nun
J.-top [thief-nom run.away-imprf-**ind**-rel.imprf
kes]-ul **cap-ess-ta**
kes]-acc **catch-pst-decl**
Intended: 'John caught the thief running away.'

(8) *John-un [totwuk-i tomangka-n-**ta**-nun
J.-top [thief-nom run.away-imprf-**ind**-rel.imprf
kes]-ul **po-ess-ta**
kes]-acc **see-pst-decl**
Intended: 'John saw the thief running away.'

Again, this property does not hold for the complements of factive propositional attitude verbs, as illustrated in (9), suggesting that this is a unique property of the IHRC and the DPC.

(9) John-un [totwuk-i tomangka-(n-**ta**-)nun
J.-top [thief-nom run.away-(imprf-**ind**-)rel.imprf
kes]-ul **al-ess-ta**
kes]-acc know**-pst-decl**
'John knew that the thief was running away.'

Third, as noted by Kuroda (1992), in the IHRC, the embedded event time cannot be posterior to the embedding event time, as shown in (10).

(10) *John-un [Mary-ka ttena-**l** kes]-ul
J.-top [M.-nom leave-**rel.fut** kes]-acc
cap-ess-ta
catch-pst-decl
Intended: 'John caught Mary, who will/would be leaving.'

This temporal restriction also holds for DPC complements, as shown in (11), but not for factive complements, as shown in (12), again suggesting that it is a defining property of the IHRC and the DPC, rather than the same string of words.

(11) *John-un [Mary-ka ttena-**l** kes]-ul
J.-top [M.-nom leave-**rel.fut** kes]-acc
po-ess-ta
see-pst-decl
Intended: 'John saw the event, where Mary will/would be leaving.'

(12) John-un [Mary-ka ttena-**l** kes]-ul
J.-top [M.-nom leave-**rel.fut** kes]-acc
al-ess-ta
know-pst-decl
'John knew that Mary will/would be leaving.'

3. Analysis

In this section, I offer an analysis that unifies the IHRC and the DPC. The upshot of the proposal is that in both constructions, the complement consists of event-denoting clausal material and a pronominal definite description, and that this pronoun links the embedded clause to the embedding clause.

3.1. The Syntax and Semantics of the Embedded Clause

I propose that the embedded clause in the IHRC and the DPC, i.e. the relative clause that occurs preceding *kes*, consists of a functional projection that is smaller than a full clause. The exact label of this clause is immaterial to our purpose. Hence, to keep matters simple, I will label it as XP. This proposal is schematically represented in (13).

(13)

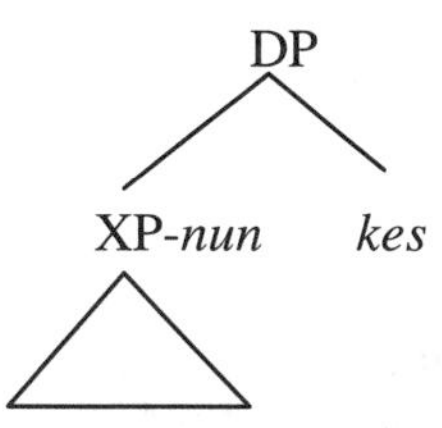

Support for this small clause analysis of the embedded clause comes from at least three sources. First, several authors have argued that the embedded clause of the IHRC carries only new information or informational focus (e.g. Chung and Kim 2003, M. Lee 2003), which is projected VP-internally (Kiss 1998) or at the left edge of VP (Valluví 1995). This is evidenced by the fact that IHRC complements do not tolerate topics, as shown in (14).

(14) ??/*John-i [**Mary-nun** ppang-ul kaci-e
J.-nom [**M.-nun** bread-acc bring-comp
o]-n kes]-ul mek-ess-ta
aux-rel.prf kes]-acc eat-pst-decl
Intended: 'As for Mary, she brought bread and John ate it.'

If we assume that the information structure of a sentence is reflected in its syntactic structure, then we can infer from (14) that IHRC complements lack the functional projection that hosts topics or old information.

It has also been independently claimed that the IHRC and DPC complements instantiate a thetic judgment as opposed to a categorical judgment (Kuroda 1992, Matsuda 2002, H. Park 1998, Basilico 1998). Thetic judgments only contain the nuclear scope in the tripartite logical structure of Heim (1982), whereas categorial judgments contain a quantifier and its restrictive clause as well (von Fintel 1989). If we follow Diesing (1992) and assume that there is a direct syntax and semantics mapping, we are then led to conclude that a thetic judgment must have a smaller syntactic structure than a categorical judgment and hence a smaller logical structure as well.[3]

Further support for the present proposal comes from the event-sensitivity of the IHRC and the DPC. It has been suggested by several authors that the semantics of the IHRC involves describing a whole/scene relation (e.g. Ohara 1992) or a relation between two sets of eventualities (e.g. Kuroda 1992, Y.-B. Kim 2002, Matsuda 2002, Chung and Kim 2003). It has also been argued that the DPC in various languages describes a part-whole relation between two eventualities (e.g. Higginbotham 1983, Felser 1999, Basilico 2003). If these analyses are correct, then it follows that IHRC and DPC complements contain a truncated syntactic structure which receives an event-level, but not a world-level, interpretation.

3.2. The Syntax and Semantics of *kes*

Hoshi (1996) and Shimoyama (1999) propose that the Japanese counterpart of *kes*, i.e. *no*, instantiates a so-called E-type pronoun. The basis for this proposal is that *no* is interpreted in a way analogous to a typical E-type interpretation: The preceding relative clause sets up a context which provides a predicate-level restrictor for it.

My analysis of *kes* builds upon these E-type pronoun analyses of *no*, but it diverges from them in its details. First, I propose that *kes* is a pronominal definite description, rather than an E-type pronoun. The motivation for this departure is that pronouns are inherently ambiguous and hence can behave like bound variables or E-type pronouns depending on the syntactic environment in which they occur (see Elbourne 2002 for similar arguments for

---

[3]For discussion of thetic vs. categorical distinction and their cross-linguistic manifestations, see, among others, Ladusaw 2000 and references therein.

English pronouns). With this pronoun analysis of *kes*, we can now capture the semantic variability of *kes* in various syntactic environments without any stipulation, thereby overcoming the shortcomings of the previous E-type pronoun analyses (see Kitagawa 2002 for a critique of these analyses).

Second, unlike the previous analyses which analyze *no* or *kes* as a nominalizer, I propose that it is a pronoun that spells out a definite article and its elided NP sister (modulo the licensing conditions for NP ellipsis) (compare Chung and Kim 2003). This idea is represented in (15), where ∅ stands for a phonologically null element.[4]

(15)

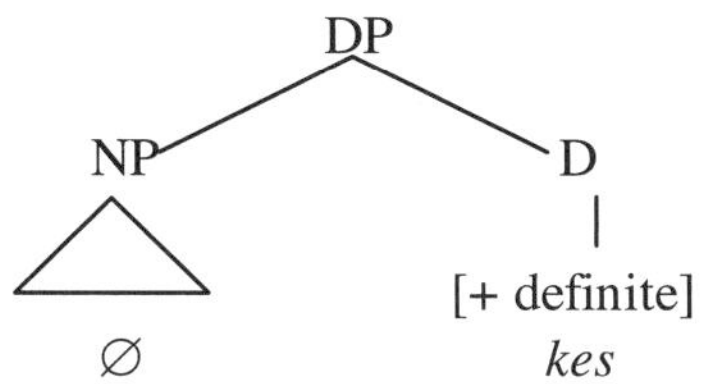

Support for the definiteness of *kes* in the IHRC and the DPC comes from the fact that *kes* is always interpreted as referring to a unique, maximal entity that has a salient property recovered from the context which is provided by the embedded relative clause (see Hoshi 1996, Shimoyama 1999 for Japanese IHRC).

To illustrate this, consider (16) and (17). In (16), *kes* is interpreted to refer to all the cookies that Mary put in the box, not just some of them. Hence the sentence will be judged false if it is uttered in a context where John ate only three cookies.[5] Similarly, in (17), *kes* refers to the unique sound of the event where the thief was running away.

(16) John-un [[Mary-ka sangca-ey kwaca-lul **tases-kay**
J.-top [[M.-nom box-loc cookie-acc **five-CL**
noh-a twu]-n **kes**]-ul mek-ess-ta
put-comp aux]-rel.pst **kes**]-acc eat-pst-decl
'Mary put <u>five</u> cookies in the box and John ate <u>them</u>.'

(17) John-un [[totwuk-i tomangka]-nun **kes**]-ul
J.-top [[thief-nom run.away]-rel.imprf **kes**]-acc
tul-ess-ta
hear-pst-decl
'The thief was running away and John heard <u>it</u>.'

---

[4]See Elbourne 2002 for a similar treatment of English pronouns.
[5]Hoshi (1996) and Shimoyama (1999) offer similar observations about the Japanese IHRC.

Turning now to the semantics of *kes*, I adopt Chierchia's (1995:221) treatment of definite descriptions; the previous E-type pronoun analyses adopt versions of Cooper's (1979) analysis. This is to capture the fact that the denotation of *kes* stands in a relation to the content of the embedded clause.

Under the present proposal, *kes* is a spell out of a definite article with an elided NP sister. According to Chierchia, the denotation of *the NP* in English can contain a relational free variable and its arguments, as given in (18).

(18) $\iota x[R_w(y_{1..n}, x) \& N_w(x)]$, where *R, y* are free variables.

Under this view, the denotation of the NP is something like 'the unique (maximal) individual x such that x stands in an R relation with a contextually salient individual y and x has the property N'.

Extending this approach to the definite descriptions in Korean, I propose (19) as the denotation of *kes* (ignoring the world variable and the indices in Chierchia's original proposal).

(19) $\iota x[R(x, y) \& P(x)]$, where *R, P, y* are free variables, and R is a relation that holds between individuals, i.e. entities and eventualities, and P corresponds to the denotation of the elided NP sister of the definite article.

I assume that these free variables' values are determined by the context which is set up by the embedded clause, in conjunction with the embedding predicate's selectional properties.[6] What this means is that if the embedding predicate selects for an entity-denoting element, then *kes* will denote an entity; if the embedding predicate selects for an eventuality, then *kes* will denote an eventuality. The first case instantiates the IHRC and the second case instantiates the DPC.

3.3. Application of the Present Proposal

We are now ready to apply the present proposal to actual sentences and derive their truth-conditions. Consider first (20) and (21).

[6]This bears on the problem of 'formal link,' which refers to the phenomenon where the antecedent of the predicate-level restrictor for the definite article inside an E-type pronoun must be linguistically present in the preceding sentence (for details, see Kadmon 1987, Elbourne 2002 and references therein). For a possible solution to the formal linking problem of the Korean IHRC, see M.-J. Kim 2003.

(20) John-un [[totwuk-i tomangka]-nun kes]-ul
J.-top [[thief-nom run.away]-rel.imprf kes]-acc
cap-ess-ta
catch-pst-decl
'John caught a/the thief running away.'

(21) John-un [[totwuk-i tomangka]-nun kes]-ul
J.-top [[thief-nom run.away]-rel.imprf kes]-acc
po-ess-ta
see-pst-decl
'John saw the event of a/the thief running away.'

Given the selectional properties of the embedding predicate and the context provided by the embedded clause, our intuitions tell us that the *kes* in (20) should be interpreted as something like (22) and that in (21) as something like (23).

(22) ι_ex[Agent(x, e) & thief(x)] (this reads as 'the unique x such that x is the Agent of the event e and x has the property of being a thief')

(23) ι_ex[visual aspect(x, e) & scene(x)] (this reads as 'the unique x such that x is the visual aspect of the event e and x has the property of being a scene')

Applying these interpretations of *kes* to the semantics of the entire sentences, we arrive at (24) and (25) as the truth-conditions for (20) and (21), respectively.[7]

(24) $\exists e_1 \exists x$[running away(e_1) & Agent(x)(e_1) & thief(x) & $\exists e_2$[**catch**(e_2) & Agent(John)(e_2) & **Theme(**$\boldsymbol{\iota_e}$**uAgent(u, e**$_\mathbf{1}$**) & thief(u))(e**$_\mathbf{2}$**)**)].

(This reads as 'there is an event e_1 and an entity x such that e_1 is a running away event and the agent of e_1 is x and x is a thief and there is another event e_2 such that e_2 is a <u>catching</u> event and its agent is John and its theme is the unique u such that u is the <u>Agent </u>of the event e_1 and u has the property of being <u>a thief</u>'.)

(25) $\exists e_1 \exists x$[running away(e_1) & Agent(x)(e_1) & thief(x) & & $\exists e_2$[**see**(e_2) & Agent(John)(e_2) & **Theme(**$\boldsymbol{\iota_e}$**uVisual aspect(u, e**$_\mathbf{1}$**) & scene(u))(e**$_\mathbf{2}$**)**)].

---

[7]Here I ignore the semantic contribution of tense/aspect. In addition, I abstract away from the relation between the embedded event and the embedding event.

(This reads as 'there is an event e_1 and an entity x such that e_1 is a running away event and the agent of e_1 is x and x is a thief and there is another event e_2 such that e_2 is a seeing event and its agent is John and its theme is the unique u such that u is the visual aspect of the event e_1 and u has the property of being a scene'.)

These truth-conditions are compatible with native speakers' intuitions about the meanings of (20) and (21), suggesting that the present analysis of *kes* is on the right track. They also show that the semantics of the IHRC and the DPC can be derived via the same mechanism. Although the truth-conditions given in (24) and (25) may seem to differ from each other, they are essentially identical. In one case, *kes* refers to an entity and in the other case, it refers to an eventuality or the perceptual aspect thereof. Under the proposed analysis, this semantic variability of *kes* is in fact expected; being a pronoun, it can refer to an entity or an eventuality, depending on the semantics of the predicate that selects for it. Given this, we can conclude that the IHRC and the DPC have an identical semantics; that is, they both connect two sets of eventualities via a pronominal definite description.

4. Explaining the Common Properties of the Two Constructions

Let us now return to the parallels between the IHRC and the DPC which were outlined in Section 2 and see how they follow from the proposed analysis.

The first and the second common properties of the two constructions follow from the truncated syntactic structure of the embedded clause. The embedded clause cannot contain an I-level predicate, because I-level predicates ascribe permanent properties to individuals and hence can only occur in a categorical statement, for it has a tripartite logical structure in the sense of Heim (1982), as argued by von Fintel (1989) and Deising (1992), among others. Similarly, the embedded clause cannot tolerate indicative mood, because mood is concerned with the illocutionary force of the sentence and hence can only occur in a full-blown clausal structure.

On the other hand, the temporal restriction on the embedded clause follows from the way in which *kes* is interpreted. If the embedded event time is posterior to the embedding event time, then *kes* will refer to a unique individual which stands in a relation to an event which has not occurred at the time of the embedding event. But when *kes* receives such an interpretation, the sentence cannot be interpreted, as shown in (10) and (11). This is illustrated by (26) and (27), which paraphrase (10) and (11).

(26) #There will be an event of Mary leaving and John caught her in that event.

(27) #There will be an event of Mary leaving and John saw the scene of that event.

These interpretations are anomalous, since due to our physical limitations, we cannot catch or perceive an individual which is part of a future event.

5. Summary and Conclusion

In this paper, I compared the IHRC and the DPC, which have been treated as separate constructions. I claimed that they have an identical syntax and semantics and hence need to be subsumed under the same category. I proposed that the complements of these constructions are DPs which consist of an event-denoting small clause and a pronominal definite description *kes*. I argued that the small clause sets up a context which provides a predicate level restrictor for *kes* and this way it gets indirectly linked to an event-level denotation of the embedded clause. If correct, these findings suggest a strong connection between the IHRC/DPC and small clauses.

References

Basilico, D. 1998. Object Position and Predication Forms. *Natural Language and Linguistic Theory* 16:541-595.

Basilico, D. 2003. The Topic of Small Clauses. *Linguistic Inquiry* 34:1-35.

Carlson, G. N. 1977. *Reference to Kinds in English*. PhD thesis. UMass-Amherst.

Chierchia, G. 1995. *Dynamics of Meaning*. The University of Chicago Press.

Chung, D.-H. 1999. A Ccomplement Analysis of the Head Internal Relative Clauses. *Language and Information* 3:1-12.

Chung, C. and J.-B. Kim. 2003. Differences between Externally and Internally Headed Relative Clause Constructions, *On-line Proceedings of HPSG 2002*, ed. J.-B. Kim, 3-25. Stanford: CSLI.

Cooper, R. 1979. The Interpretation of Pronouns, *Syntax and Semantics 10: Selections from the Third Groningen Round Table*, eds. F. Heny and H. S. Schnelle, 61-92. New York: Academic Press.

Diesing, M. 1992. *Indefinites*. Cambridge, MA: MIT Press.

Elbourne, P. 2002. E-type Anaphora as NP-deletion. *Natural Language Semantics* 9: 241-288.

Felser, C. 1999. *Verbal Complement Clauses: A Minimalist Study of Direct Perception Constructions*. Amsterdam: John Benjamins.

von Fintel, K. 1989. Theticity in Generative Grammar. Ms. UMass-Amherst. Heim, I. 1982. *The Semantics of Definite and Indefinite Noun Phrases*. PhD thesis. UMass-Amherst.

Higginbotham, J. 1983. The Logic of Perceptual Reports: An Extensional Alternative to Situation Semantics. *The Journal of Philosophy* 80:100-127.

Hoshi, K. 1996. *Structural and Interpretive Aspects of Head-internal and Head-external Relative Clauses*, PhD thesis. University of Rochester.

Jhang, S.-E. 1994. *Headed Nominalizations in Korean: Relative Clauses, Clefts, and Comparatives*, PhD thesis. Simon Fraser University.

Kadmon, N. 1987. *On Unique and Non-unique Reference and Asymmetric Quantification*, PhD thesis. UMass-Amherst.

Kim, M.-J. 2003. Internally-headed Relatives Instantiate Situation Subordination. Paper Presented at NELS 34. Stony Brook University. November 7-9.

Kim, M.-J. To appear. Three Types of *Kes*-nominalization in Korean. *Harvard Studies in Korean Linguistics* 10, eds. I. Lee et al. Seoul: Hanshin.

Kim, N.-K. 1984. *The Grammar of Korean Complementation*. University of Hawaii at Manoa: Center for Korean Studies.

Kim, Y.-B. 2002. Relevancy in Internally Headed Relative Clauses in Korean. *Lingua* 112:541-559.

Kiss, K. E. 1998. Identificational Focus and Information Focus. *Language* 74:245-273.

Kitagawa, C. 2002. Internally Headed Relative Clauses in Japanese and Their Typological Implications. Ms. UMass-Amherst.

Kuroda, S.-Y. 1992. *Japanese Syntax and Semantics*. Dordrecht: Kluwer.

Ladusaw, W. 2000. Thetic and Categorical, Stage and Individual, and Weak and Strong, *Negation and Polarity: Syntactic and Semantic Perspectives*, eds. L. Horn and Y. Kato, 232-242, Oxford University Press.

Lee, C. 2001. Acquisition of Topic and Subject Markers in Korean. *Issues in East Asian Language Acquisition*, ed. M. Nakayama. Tokyo: Kurosio.

Lee, M. 2003. Focus-induced Constraints on Head-internal Relatives. Paper Presented at the 10th Harvard International Conference on Korean Linguistics.

Lefebvre, C. and P. Muyskin. 1988. *Mixed Categories, Nominalizations in Quechua*. Boston: Kluwer Academic Publishers.

Matsuda, Y. 2002. Event Sensitivity of Head-internal Relatives in Japanese. *Japanese/Korean Linguistics* 10:629-643.

Ohara, H. K. 1993. On Japanese Internally Headed Relative Clauses. *Proceedings of BLS* 18, eds. Buszard-Wechsler et al., 100-109.

Park, B.-S. 1994. Modification vs. Complementation: The so-called Internally Headed Relative Clauses Reconsidered. *Proceedings of the 1994 Kyoto Conference: A Festschrift for Professor Akira Ikeya*.

Park, H. 1998. Thetic/Categorical Judgment and Relative Clauses in Korean. *Proceedings of WECOL '98*.

Shimoyama, J. 1999. Internally Headed Relative Clauses in Japanese and E-type Pronoun Anaphora. *Journal of East Asian Linguistics* 8:147-182.

Vallduví, E. 1995. Structural Properties of Information Packaging in Catalan. *Discourse Configurational Languages*, 122-152, Oxford University Press.

Motion and State: Verbs *tul-/na-* (K) and *hairu/deru* (J) 'enter'/'exit'

CHUNGMIN LEE
Seoul National University

1. Introduction

This paper examines how change of location is related to change of state or transition, particularly in the case of *tul-/na-* (K) and *hairu/deru* (J) 'enter'/ 'exit.[1] With these verbs the process subevent is not explicit.

Change always involves a shift in state from $\neg P$ to P as well as a shift in location in the flow of time. The verbs 'enter'/'exit' involve subevents having the result states **inside (of)** and **outside (of)**, with point-monotone increasing and decreasing, respectively (Zwarts and Winter 2000). When we consider the motion involved, 'exit' is not monotonic; the Source space counts. A shift in state is more abstract. When the transition is psychological, it becomes even more abstract. To convey motion, deictic verbs are added in K/J.

[1] I would like to express my gratitude to Mustsuko Endo Hudson, the J/K 13 organizer, for orchestrating J/K 13, inviting me as a keynote speaker, and to the audience for questions and comments. I am deeply indebted to Pat Clancy for her thorough editing in style and everything. My thanks also go to consultants Eri Tanaka, Hiroshi Aoyagi, Naoko Sugita, Kuniko Nielsen for Japanese, as well as Harold Torrence and Nathan Klinedinst for English. An earlier, longer version was given at LP 2002 (Mekai University, Japan; Lee 2006). Contact: clee@snu.ac.kr.

2. Enter/exit Verbs and Unaccusativization

In verb-framed languages (Talmy 2000) such as K/J, Hindi, Romance languages, as opposed to satellite-framed (co-event) languages such as English, Finno-Ugric and Chinese, a stative location adposition, e.g. *–ey* (K), *-ni* (J), *à* (French), *-meN* (Hindi), is used only for deictic directed motion verbs but not for intransitive manner verbs. Path-oriented Goal adpositions in verb-framed languages, e.g. *kkaci* (K), *mada* (J), *hasta* (Sp), and *jusqu'à* (Fr) can co-occur with manner motion verbs, denoting a Path all the way to the telic point, forming an accomplishment.

Transitive manner motion verbs such as *pus-* 'pour' (K) have the Figure as the object and the Goal as a PP (with *–ey*), and do not show any alternation between object and Goal PP cross-linguistically. With verbs that do alternate, the Goal PP is promoted to a 'globally affected' **derived Theme** (Lee 1997). Verbs corresponding to 'load', 'pile', and 'spray', which alternate in English, do not alternate in K/J. The verbs 'paint', 'stuff', and 'wrap' do show alternation cross-linguistically (Kim 1999, Lee et al 1999), between a derived Theme and a Goal PP. These two patterns correspond to Jackendoff's (1996) distinction between 'final-distributive' as opposed to 'Path-distributive' *spray*. The latter, non-alternating pattern, , which is the one found in K/J, places more weight on Path.

All four types of transitive motion verbs in K show an Agent-NOM Figure-ACC Goal-PP pattern. The second type of verb, e.g. *tam-* 'put (into)' and *sit-* 'load', show this pattern as well as Goal-NOM Figure-ACC in K/J. The latter pattern gives prominence to the container, rather than to its affected state. Thus Thematization does not occur for this type in K/J. In English **The truck loaded the hay* (cf. *Store-rooms store things*) is unacceptable; *truck* is affected but not prominent.

The third type of verb, e.g. *chaywu* 'fill' and *teph-* 'cover' in K/J, show both the Goal PP and the Goal Thematization patterns. The latter is impossible in English (**Mary filled water into the bottle* (reported to occur in child English, Gropen et al. 1992). Figure-NOM Goal-ACC is also possible for Type 3. When the Instrumental case is attached to the Figure in Thematization, the derived Theme is affected together with Agent, and the Figure is prominent. This is why the Figure can be a subject in Type 3 but not in Type 4 (*puthi-* 'attach') verbs.

To deal with Type 3 verbs, we can consider using **underspecification of headedness** between process and state. If a process is headd, a Goal PP appears, while if a state is headed, Thematization of the Goal occurs. This must be distinguished from achievement verbs, for which I propose an implicit process (**I-process**) for the pre-telic stage.

The Path verbs 'enter'/'exit' in K/J, i.e. *tul-/na-* (K) and *hairu/deru* (J), show an interesting development. As pure Path verbs they hardly show any meaning of explicit motion in modern K, but in J they are freely used, as in (1). In modern K their use in the Path reading is mostly blocked, as in (2a), although in Middle K they were used freely in this reading just as in modern J.

(1) Taro-ga heya-ni hait-ta /heya -kara/-o de -ta
-NOM room-at enter-PAST /room-from/-ACC exit-PAST
'Taro entered/exited from the room.'
(2) a. *Yumi-ka pang-ey tul-ess-ta / *pang-eyse na-ss-ta
-NOM room-at enter–PAST-DEC room-from exited
b. Yumi-ka pang-ey tul-e ka -ess-ta /pang-eyse na-o-ass-ta
-NOM room-at enter go-PAST-DEC exit-come-PAST-DEC
(a, b) 'Yumi entered/exited from the room.'
c. Yumi-ka pang-ey tul-e ka –ko iss-ta /pang-eyse na-o-ko iss-ta
-NOM room-at enter go-PROGR-DEC exit-come-PROGR-DEC
'Yumi is entering/exiting from the room.'

In K, as in (2b), a directed motion verb *ka-* 'go' or *o-* 'come' must be attached to these Path verbs, forming complex verb forms such as *tul–e ka-* 'go into' and *tul–e o-* 'come into,' for grammaticality and a process progressive reading (2c). The complex verb just conveys physical motion and freely takes the progressive form, denoting motion explicitly. The simple verb *tul-* 'enter' in (3a,b) below is different from the complex form in that its use is limited to contexts of entering a sleeping place (hotel/bed/nest). It cannot be used in the progressive in K, as illustrated in (3a);it takes an event for the telic quale of the Goal enclosure nominal, i.e. 'to stay' for a hotel and 'to sleep' for a bed. The Path verb *na-* 'exit' is not used in the Path reading at all in K (3c).

(3) a. Insu-ka cumak/camcari-ey tul-ess-ta /*tul-ko iss-ta
-NOM hotel/bed -at enter-PAST-DEC / enter-PROG-DEC
'Insu entered/*is entering/put up at a hotel/bed.'
b. say-tul-i tungci-ey tul-ess-ta
-PL-NOM nest-at enter-PAST-DEC
'Birds entered their nest.'
c. *Insu-ka cumak/camcari-eyse na –ass-ta
-NOM hotel/bed -from exit-PAST-DEC
'Insu exited from a hotel/bed.'

In (3a), a durative modification such as *sahul tongan* 'for three days' is possible because the result state is salient in connection with the TELIC quale involved in the Goal nominal, i.e., 'to sleep.' The verb *arrive* or its correspondent *tochak-ha-* in K lacks this kind of post hoc state saliency. Its culmination or transition (from a journey to a standstill) point is clear.

The complex verb with the deictic verb *ka-*, i.e. *tul-e ka-* 'go into', may be represented as a composition consisting of E1, a process of change in location (because of *ka-* 'go') and E2, the result state via Path (because of *tul-* ('enter'). The E1 process is headed, which is why the progressive is possible with the complex verb. Even in English, *enter* as opposed to *go into* seems weighted toward the result state.[2] The complex verb, unlike *tul-* 'enter', does not require a strict selection restriction on the object, except a general one: enclosure.

Other possible contexts for the Path verb *tul-* are the following:

(4) a. uri cip-ey totwuk-i tul-ess-ta
our house-at thief-NOM entered
'A thief invaded my house.'
b. tongcen-i cikap-ey tul –e iss-ta
coin-NOM wallet-in enter-RESULTATIVE
'Coins are contained in the wallet.'
c. ?Yumi-ka pang-ey tul –e iss-ta
-NOM room-in enter-RESULTATIVE
'Yumi is (confined) in the room.'
d. Yumi-ka kamok-ey tul –e iss-ta
-NOM prison-in enter-RESULTATIVE
'Yumi is (confined) in the prison.'

In (4a), our house experienced invasion by a thief. With the resultative construction, an inanimate object can be in a container , as in (4b). If the subject happens to be a human, however, as in (4c), the same construction with a loose enclosure is odd; Yumi can go into the room on her own free will.Accordingly, --- *tul-e ka iss-*, with the directed motion verb, is perfect. If the location is a prison cell, she is put into it against her will by external causation (as with causative verbs), with *tul-* 'enter' in its unaccusative sense.

Those sentences in which *tul-* is felicitous do not allow replacing the locative *–ey* by the Path-oriented postposition *–kkaci* 'up to' or the atelic

---

[2] (a) is more natural than (b) for some people; for *enter*, the head slightly leans toward the result state and the process tends to be slightly implicit and instantaneous. That is why (c) is more natural than (b).

a. Mary was going into the room.
b. Mary was entering the room.
c. Mary was entering the room when the lights went out. (H. Torrence, p.c.)

directional postposition *–uro* 'toward,' as with other achievement verbs. This again implies absence of explicit process. Observe:

(5) a. *Inho-nun cumak –kkaci/-uro tul-ess-ta
Lit: 'Inho entered up to/toward a hotel.'
b. ?* Inho-nun cip –kkaci/-uro tochakha-yess-ta
Lit: 'Inho arrived up to/toward his house.'

The verb *tul-* is felicitous with the **resultative form *–e iss-***.How, then, does this differ from the **progressive form *–ko iss-*** in distribution and meaning? In J, one form, *–te iru,* is used for both functions. This has much to do with aspectual classes of verbs. If the verb is an instantaneous achievement, the progressive is not allowed, but the resultative is, e.g. **cuk-ko iss-ta* 'is dying'; *cuk-e iss-ta* 'died and remains in that state'. The adverbial *kutayro* 'in that state' can be inserted before *iss-* 'exist,' with the original meaning of *iss-* still largelypreserved, it cannot be inserted with the progressive form. Therefore, if we say, *kui-nun yeki sal-ko iss-ta* 'He is living here,' it is progressive and has the implication of temporariness (Lee 1999), whereas *kui-nun acik sal-a iss-ta* 'He is still alive' is resultative, implying he was once on the verge of death or was assumed or expected to be dead.

With transitive verbs, the resultative form *-e iss-* is not used. Instead, with verbs of wearing, the progressive form *–ko iss-* is used and is ambiguous between the process-progressive reading and the resultative reading. For example, if we say, usingthe Type 4 verb *puthi-* 'attach, paste,' *kui-nun kasum*[body-part]*-ey irumphyo-rul puthi-ko iss-ta* 'He is attaching/wearing a name tag on his chest', the sentence can be ambiguous.There is a coherent connection between the result of attaching a name tag on the agent's body part and his remaining in the state of having it on. The adverbial *kutayro* 'in that state', inserted before *iss-,* this relationship explicit. Here again, we can represent the lexical meaning of the verb by underspecifying the headedness of subevents **e1: process** and **e2: state** for verbs of wearing. If, however, *kui-nun pyek-ey kwanggo-rul puthi-ko iss-ta* 'He is pasting ads on the wall', it only has the process-progressive reading. There is no coherent connection between the result of 'pasting ads on the wall' and the agent remaining in the result state of having pasted ads on the wall. Therefore, no resultative reading is involved.Why, then, do we not use the separate resultative form *-e iss-* for this reading with transitive verbs? With transitive verbs, the process event can be headed and progressive-marked and the same form *–ko*, with its original function of conjunction, can easily license temporal sequence between e1 and e2 by implicature, with the perfective aspect reading of e1. Therefore, there is no need to mark the resultative aspect by a separate form.

That is why the same form is used for the two readings in the case of process-bearing transitive verbs of wearing. In the progressive form *-ko iss-*, the conjunctive *–ko*, like *–myense* 'while –ing,' had the meaning of simultaneity, producing the overall meaning of *–myense iss-* 'be -ing'. For achievement verbs, e2 is headed from the beginning and only the resultative form can be used. For example, in Japanese *toochaku-shi-**te iru*** '---arrived and remains' has only a resultative reading (*-te iru* but not the past form *toochaku-shit-ta* can be modified by *go hun* 'for 5 minutes'). In Korean, *tochakha-**ye iss**-* in the resultative form is natural, whereas the progressive form in the process-progressive reading *tochakha-**ko iss**-* is unacceptable for the older generation but becoming acceptable for younger speakers. The progressive in K, however, does not denote the preparatory stage or futurate as in English, hence, *He is leaving* vs. **kui-ka ttena-ko iss-ta* 'He is leaving.'[3]

Let us consider the following progressive accomplishment sentence:

(6) noin-i kil-ul kenne-ko iss-ta /??kenne-e issta
old man-NOM road-ACC cross-PROG-DEC exist [RESULT]
'An old man is crossing the street.'

Unlike the Source-based achievement verb *ttena-* 'leave' or the Goal oriented *tochak-ha-* 'arrive,' the verb in (6) is Path-oriented and is a process-headed accomplishment. The second subevent **e2: state** denotes the Agent=Figure's being at/on the other edge of the street, which is the Path. The Source edge of the street is implicit. Naturally, (6) does not entail the perfective *noin-i kil-ul kenne-ess-ta* 'An old man has crossed the street,' i.e. it exhibits the imperfective paradox. It also passes the test (?)*noin-un kil-ul kenne-ki-rul machi-ess-ta* 'The old man finished crossing the street,' whereas the achievement verb *ttena-* 'leave' does not. Progressive *kil-ul kenne-ko iss-ta* 'crossing the street' denotes part of a complete street-crossing, which may be interrupted and unrealized. In inertia worlds, without any interruption the old man would have crossed the street. Because of the nature of temporal part, the progressive shows the implicature of

[3] Another interesting kind of non-process progressive occurs with the so-called 'criterion predicates', such as *break the law/promise* (Kearns 2003). The sentence *In reading the document Jones was breaking the law* shows a non-process progressive; *break the law* has the representation **D–E1=e2: process-headed**; **RESTR=e2≤e1** and **FORMAL** = illegal (e1, [1]); the progressive is to apply to the default event e2 (*reading the document* or a similar implicit event) with the declaration of the criterion (of being *illegal* from the **FORMAL** quale).

temporariness of the event involved.[4] In English, an active sentence with 'cross' can be passivized but this is not the case with 'enter' (*The street has been crossed by people* vs. **The auditorium was entered by the crowd*). For the J *hairu* 'enter' and *deru* 'exit' pair, Kita (1999) argues that they lack semantic encoding of motion and therefore a discrete change of state must be posited in the set of spatial semantic primitives in addition to motion and location. But Tsujimura (1999) argues against Kita's claim that this pair of verbs lacks 'motion,' claiming that they pattern with motion verbs in J. This controversy is natural since the motion exists physically but not cognitively or perceptually so as to be encoded. Also in J, when this pair of verbs appears in the *-te iru* form, they do not take the progressive, as in (7), according to Kita; according to Tsujimura, however, they can have a progressive reading if they have a Source role and a time adverbial reinforcing the action-in-progress, as in (8).

(7) uma-ga saku –no naka-ni hait -te iru
horse-NOM fence-GEN inside-into enter
'A horse has been in/*is entering the fence-enclosure.'

(8) uma-ga ima umagoya-kara de -te iru (-no o mitegoaran)
horse-NOM now barn-from exit COMP ACC look
'(Look at) the horse that is exiting from the barn right now.'

(9) ima mise-ni hait-te iru tokoro da yo.
now shop-in enter- PROG right.now COP PRT
Intended: "I am entering the shop right now."

However, (8) seems to have the predominant reading of result state, even in the given context of the focused time adverbial *ima*, according to most native J speakers I have consulted. To denote a process-progressive, a directed motion verb *ku-ru* 'come' or *ik-u* 'go' must be used (instead of *i-ru* 'be, exist'), as in (10). Although one consultant felt that (9) can be used in the progressive reading in a cell phone conversation, others believe that it

---

[4] a. For Dowty (1979), the progressive is: [PROG φ] is true at $<I, w>$ iff for some interval *I'* such that $I \subset I'$ and *I* is not a final subinterval for *I'*, and for all *w'* such that *w' Inertia*($<I, w>$), φ is true at $<I', w'>$.

b. *The cloud crossed the sky in/for a minute* is also possible but, contrary to Jackendoff's (1996) claim that it is ambiguous, 'for a minute' seems to be allowed due to the vagueness of the edges of the sky (N. Klinedinst agrees with this, p.c., although some do not like this sentence).

still conveys a result state, with the progressive reading perhaps reflecting the influence of Western dialects in Japan.[5]

The lack of an explicit durative process is responsible for the prohibition against co-occurrence of 'enter' and 'exit' with an aspectual verb. A durative adverbial can modify the result state, not the process; the time span adverbial 'in' can be used to modify the preparatory/preliminary stage before the onset of the event of entering or exiting.[6]

(10) uma-ga ima umagoya-kara de-te kuru/iku (-no o mitegoran)
horse-NOM now barn-from exit come/go (look.at)
'(Look at) the horse that is coming/going out of the barn right now.'

In K, neither (7) nor (8) is possible in the progressive. It is interesting to see that the J counterparts are still widely used in contexts of physical motion, though their process-progressive is largely impossible. In both languages, in combination (composition) with the deictic verbs 'go' and 'come', they are freely associated with the progressive form. Otherwise, they are felt to denote the transition or change from the state of 'outside' to 'inside' or vice versa. The two opposite states may be felt to be discrete. Change of location develops into change of state, while maintaining the flavor of location change. I see this as unaccusativization. Canonical achievements lack agentivity and get unaccusativized. Pinon's (1997) claim that their non-agentivity is due to their lack of duration does not seem to be entirely tenable; degree achievements are not instantaneous and have duration but lack agentivity (e.g., *The snow is gradually melting*). When they are completely unaccusative, they become devoid of agency and can denote an abstract change of state productively. Thus, they can take a causative morpheme, producing causative transitive verbs, both in K and J. Tsujimura (1999) nicely observed intransitive-causative pairs in J but did not capture the tendency for the intransitive member of the pair to be unaccusative. Observe:

---

[5] There are two forms that correspond to the two interpretations of *te-iru:* (a) *mise-ni hairi-yoru* [progressive] and (b) *mise-ni hait-toru* [result state]. Both *yoru* and *toru* are from 'oru' 'be' for animate themes; *-yoru*: attaches to infinitival form, *-toru* is a reduction of V-*te-oru*)(E. Tanaka).

[6] (with 'finish') *Yumi-wa sono heya-ni/kara hairi-oe-ta/de-oe-ta
Lit: 'Yumi finished entering/exiting that room.'
(with durative) Yumi-wa 5 hun (kan) sono heya-ni/kara hait(-te i)-ta /de-te i-ta
'Yumi entered and was/stayed in that room for five minutes.'
(with time span) Yumi-wa 5 hun-de sono heya-ni/kara hait-ta/de-ta (*-de* 'in')
'Yumi went into that room in five minutes.'

(11) Unaccusative-causative
(unacc) causative (unacc) causative
hairu ireru 'put in' (J) *deru desu* 'take out' (J)
tul- tul-i- (K) *na- na-y-* (K)
(12) sonnim/kaku-rul tul-i-ess-ta
guest/furniture-ACC enter-CAUS-PAST-DEC
'(We) admitted/put in guests/furniture.'

With the causative transitive form, we can have the progressive. We can notice a similar [sweeping (or often unaccusativity) sense tendency] with other Path verbs in K, such as *ttu-* 'float', *oru-* 'rise', *nayri-* 'fall, get down', *huru-* 'flow', (and *sos-* 'soar', *ci-* 'set', 'fall') and they have causative counterparts with causative morphemes (*nayri-* having the same form). This is Talmy's (2000) [conformation] (geometric complex) subcomponent of Path verbs. The other two components are vector (arrival, traversal, and departure) and deixis(hither, hence). In the case of *ttu-* 'float', there seems to be an implicit or presupposed preceding upward motion due to buoyancy, which may or may not be linguistically encoded in different languages; we can represent its event structure simply as E1 = **e1: state,** as Pustejovsky (1995) did for *float* in English), or as follows for *ttu-* 'float' in K:

(13) E1 = **e1: state**; D-E1=**e2: I-process**; **Restr = e2 < e1**; **Head=e1**

Therefore, the stage-level of *ttu-* 'float' is expressed by the resultative form *ttu-e iss-* 'is floating' or the perfective form *ttu-ess,* which means 'be up (in the air, on the surface of water, etc.) as an immediate result of the past default upward motion. Otherwise, we cannot explain why we necessarily have the perfective (past) form for this situation (the progressive *ttu-ko iss-* being rarely used, except in the case where a pop singer's name is rising or becoming more popular). If we use the present form of the verb, it conveys an individual level predicate, e.g., *kirum-un mul wi-ey ttu-n-ta* 'Oil floats on water', a generic statement (or a stage level on-going situation). We feel a weaker sense of Path motion with the manner verb *ttu-* 'float,' which involves no exertion of force (or being out of control), compared to the verbs *oru-* 'rise' and *nayri-* 'fall, get down'. Subtly different degrees of motion are perceived with these verbs but the latter two express motion more explicitly in composition with the directed motion verbs 'go' and 'come.' Therefore, I propose that we distinguish between two different types of processes or initial events:

(14) E1 = **e1:I**(mplicit)-**Process** and E1 = **e1:E**(xplicit)-**process**

In this formulation **e1:I-process** applies to achievement/unaccusative verbs such as *tul-* (K), *hairu* (J) 'enter' and *na-* (K), *deru* (J) 'exit', and to other verbs that behave similarly. The verb *kwuru-* 'roll' is an unaccusative verb but not, by itself, an achievement verb . Pustejovsky's (1995) differentiation in terms of headedness is not sufficient in light of the transitive motion verbs that we have dealt with.

The event of 'entering a hotel' with the verb *tul-* in K is understood to be instantaneously achieved at a telic point.Accordingly, the **lexical semantic representation** of the verbs ***tul-*** and ***hairu*** 'enter' must have:

(15) **e1: I-process** and
e2: state but **e2** is headed and **e1** is not headed and is implicit.
FORMAL = **be inside of** (**e2, x, y**)
(**inside'** $=_{def} \lambda A.\ \lambda \mathbf{v}.internal(\mathbf{v}, A)$, mapping a set of points to the set of internally closest vectors, Zwarts and Winter 2000)

The result states **be inside of** for 'enter' and **be outside of** for 'exit' are point monotone increasing and decreasing, respectively (Zwarts and Winter 2000), but when a dynamic process of motion with Path is included, 'exit' is not monotonic; the Source space counts, e.g., *France-eyse na-ka-ass-ta* '- exited France' =/=> *Paris-eyse na-ka-ass-ta* '- exited Paris.' The verb *ture ka-* 'enter' is Goal-oriented and is still monotone increasing. *Paris-ey ture-ka-ass-ta* '- entered Paris' ==> *France-ey ture-ka-ass-ta* '- entered France.'

The Kita-Tsujimura controversy has a precedent in K in the disagreement over whether the verb *tul-* encodes just Path or motion+Path in the verb complex *tul-e o-/ka-*. Choi & Bowerman (1991) argue that the deictic verb in the complex encodes motion+deixis, whereas Kim (1997) argues that it encodes only deixis. Kim, cites the impossibility of *–se* insertion as evidence (*ku-nun san-ey olla-*(**-se*) *kass-ta* 'He went up the mountain.' But other conformation verbs with *–se* are grammatical, e.g., *ku-nun san-ul neme-se ka-ss-ta* 'He went over the mountain.' Here the motion of 'going' can extend beyond '(moving) over the mountain,' whereas there is one identical Goal telic point for 'rising' and 'going' in *olla ka-* (see Im 2001). Because the verb *tul-* lost its explicit motion reading in modern K, the attached deictic verb can be sai to have taken over the motion component. This is why the progressive is possible with the complex *tul-e o-/ka-*, but not with *tul-* alone.

Additional contexts for the use of *tule-/na-* (K) and *hairu/deru* (J) are purely unaccusative; they must co-occur with deictic motion verbs to be used freely in the physical motional Path reading. Due to their lack of an explicit process sense, the Path verbs themselves came to be extended and used for involuntary, natural or abstract changes of state rather easily and productively in K.[7] Observe:

(16) Yumi-nun cam –i tul-ess-ta
-TOP sleep-NOM enter-PAST-DEC
'Yumi fell asleep.'

(17) a. Yumi-nun chel-i tul-ess-ta (cf. chel-i na-ss-ta)
–TOP sense-NOM enter-PAST-DEC
'Yumi became sensible.'

b. icey sayngkak-i na-ass-ta
now idea-NOM exit-PAST-DEC
'Now it occurred to me.'

c. Yumi-ka cengshin-i na-ss-ta vs. na-ka-ss-ta
-NOM spirit-NOM exit-PAST-DEC exit-go-PAST-DEC
'Yumi became sober' vs. 'got crazy'

d. na-nun Yumi-ka maum-ey tu-n-ta
I-NOM -NOM mind-LOC enter-PRES-DEC
'I am satisfied with Yumi.'

An abstract change of state, as in (16), is expressed by *tul-* with the perfective form of the verb. The motion involved may be merely fictive; otherwise, the verb is stative, expressing the result state. Changes in mental state are expressed as in (17a,b) and in psychological state as in (17c). These new meanings are generated by combining the verb with mental or psychological nominals, constituting an **I-process.state-lcp**. The formal quale of the second argument of (17) must be **mental/psychological** or **abastract**. In (17a), the Experiencer Topic (the original Goal) undergoes a process or change in mental state from being not sensible to being sensible. The complex predicate *chel-i tul-* 'become sensible' is result-salient as an

---

[7] See: (1) a. nwun-ey meng-i tul -ess-ta 'got a black eye'
b. suyem-i na -ass -ta '(his) beard started to grow'
c. elkul-ey hok-i na-ass-ta 'has a growth on his face'
(2) a. yuhok-ey ppaci-e-tul-ess-ta 'fell into the temptation'
b. mul-i mwun thum-uro sumi-e-tul-ess-ta
'Water soaked into the room through a crack in the door'
(3) a. i kos-ey-nun pyeth-i tul-ci anh-nun-ta
'The sun does not shine into this place'.
b. ppang-ey komphangi-ka na-ass-ta 'The bread got moldy'
c. sako-ka na-ass-ta 'An accident happened'
(4) Yumi-nun pan-esyse 10 tung –an-ey tul-ess-ta
'Yumi was placed within the top ten positions in class'.
'Enter' can also be combined with 'attack' verbs, adding Path into a personal domain:
a. koyangi-ka kay-hanthey tempi-e tul-ess-ta
'The cat set on the dog/entered the dog's territory'.
b. talli-e-tu-l 'go at, rush at,' ttwui-e-tul- 'jump onto'

individual-level predicate; the past form in this case entails present relevance. In contrast, *cengshin-i na-* 'become sober' in (17b) is a stage-level predicate. Here, *na-* means 'come out, come into being' but *na-ka-* with the motion verb *ka-*'go' means 'go out of'. Therefore, when the former combines with *cengshin* 'spirit, mind' it means 'become sober instantly' but when the latter combines with the mental nominal it means 'go crazy.' In (17d), the composed predicate with the psychological nominal *maum* 'heart' is purely psychological, and subject to the subjectivity constraint (i.e. permitting only a first person Experiencer in the present). Here, *maum* belongs to the Experiencer and retains the original Loc/Goal marker *ey-* 'in,' 'at'; the composed predicate is stage-level. The causative verb *n-ay-* 'let out,' derived from *na-* 'exit,' is also extended to a psychological use in combination with the psychological noun *hwa* 'anger.' The combined expression *hwa-rul n-ay-* comes to mean 'get angry, have one's blood up.'[8]

Unergative verbs such as *run* and *talli-*(K) have internal causation (Levin and Hovav 1995) and agentive exertion of force, forming a pseudo-reflexive in English (though limited) and a hyperbolic resultative in K, unlike unaccusative verbs. Compare (18) – (19a) with (19b,c):

(18) I ran myself ragged/(breathless).
(19) a. na-nun cwuk-torok talli-ess-ta
I –TOP die-to run-PAST-DEC
Lit. 'I ran so as to die'. 'I ran myself to death.'[9]
b. * na-nun cwuk-torok cip-ey tochak-hay-ss-ta (Lee and Lee 2000)
'I arrived home so as to die.'
c. * na-nun cwuk-torok yekwan-ey tul-ess-ta
'I entered a hotel so as to die.'

Therefore, in order to block progressive and hyperbolic resultative forms, we can posit an implicit or void initial event (e1) and a result state event (e2), with the second event being the head, for the pair of verbs *tul-* and *na-* (K)/*hairu* and *deru* (J) and other similar unaccusative verbs. Various psychologically extended uses of motion verbs are witnessed in K. In derived psychological verbs, the Theme/Stimulus argument in the psychological verb template shows ambivalent behavior in case realization between the original (Goal) Dative case (20a) and the NOM case (20b),

8 The process-involving verb *na-ka-* 'go out' is used in an abstract sense for attending a public institution (with some sense of pride/prestige) such as a conference, class or company in connection with one's purpose/work. It is typically used for engagement (with courage), e.g. going into a bullring, sports arena, or war. On the other hand, *ture ka-* 'go into' is used for being admitted (to study or work in connection with the organization's purpose: Appearing on TV is *TV-ey na o-ass-ta* 'She came out on TV' (Kim and Lee 1997).

9 This hyperbolic resultative use is also possible in English (Pat Clancy, p.c.).

which co-occurs with psychological verbs, although they are basically psychological verbs. Observe:

(20) a. na –nun Yumi –eke maum-i kkul-i-n-ta/ka-n-ta
I-TOP -to mind -NOM draw-PASS-PRES-DEC
b. . na –nun Yumi –ka maum-i kkul-i-n-ta/ka-n-ta
I-TOP -NOM mind -NOM draw-PASS-PRES-DEC
'I am attracted by Yumi.' (Psychological Verb)

(21) Yumi-uy chwulhyen-i *maywu* kincangkam-ul coseng-ha-yess-ta
-of appearance NOM very tension sense-ACC built
Lit. 'Yumi's appearance (presence) *very* built tension.'

Motion verbs and spatial directive prepositions become psychological when combined with psychological nominals, losing their original sense of physical motion. As seen in (21), indirect constitutive causation in the verb *coseng-ha-* 'build, construct' (with the qualia [CONST = **PART_OF(z,y)**; FORMAL = **α_result(e2,y)**; AGENTIVE = **α_act(e1,x,z)**]) changes to experienced (direct) causation (with QUALIA = [FORMAL = **α_result(e2,x)**; AGENTIVE = **α_act(e1,x, ---)**]) and does not need any part of the object such as 'material' (from a default argument). This is 'derived unaccusativity' (Pustejovsky 1995), which, I argue, allows for modification by the degree adverbial *maywu* 'very' in K, as in (21). The same can apply to (20). Furthermore, the progressive form of (21) entails (21). The imperfective paradox disappears because no telicity is involved anymore. When the transition is mental/psychological, it becomes even more abstract and its structure is reduced; its default argument 'material' and its quale CONST = **PART_OF(z,y)** disappear, unlike *build a house*. The progressive in K/J, V-*ko -iss-*/V-*te iru*, can co-occur with psychological/cognitive verbs like 'know' (because of their original coincidence or result state meaning), unlike in English. However, the progressive largely denotes continuation of a psychological state and implicates the temporariness of the given event (Lee 1999).

As numeral classifier languages, K and J exhibit quantization in terms of numeral classifiers. Otherwise their nominals remain underspecified, unlike in English (Lee 2000; see Kennedy 2002).[10]

---

[10] Consider how telicity is defined:

A predicate *P* is *quantized* iff no entity that is *P* can be a subset of another entity that is *P* (see Krifka 1998). An event description *R* is *telic* iff it applies to events *e* such that all parts of *e* that fall under *R* are initial and final parts of *e* (see Krifka 1998, Kennedy 2002).

5. Conclusion

We have seen various phases and degrees of abstraction with verbs of entering and exiting in K and J, from change of location (spatial motion) to other changes, such as changes of state and telic (transitional) events of accomplishment. Even within changes of location, we have seen case alternation with more abstract changes of state in which Path-involving 'enter'/'exit' verbs in K/J become unaccusativized, moreso in K than in J. My proposed implicit **I-Process** is involved here. The relation between progressive and resultative has been explored. In use, the verbs 'enter'/'exit' in K/J tend to restore process by adding deitic verbs. Abstraction involves argument reduction and changes in syntactic behavior.

We have also seen that point monotonicity works for the result states of the verbs, **inside** and **outside,** but does not work for 'exit' verbs of motion. Finally, we have noted that modification of psychological events produces expressions with degree modifiers in K/J.

References

Choi, S. and M. Bowerman. 1991. Learning to Express Motion Events in English and Koran: The Influence of Language-specific Lexicalization Patterns. *Cognition* 41: 83-121.

Dowty, D. 1991. Thematic Proto-roles and Argument Selection. *Language* 67: 547-619.

Im, S.-C. 2001. Typological Patterns of Motion Verbs in Korean. Doctoral dissertation, SUNY Buffalo.

Joe, J. and C. Lee 2002. A 'Removal' Type of Negative Predicates. In N. Akatsuka & S. Strauss (eds.) *Japanese/Korean Linguistics* 10, 559-572. Stanford: CSLI.

Kennedy, C. 2002. UCLA mini-lecture titled 'Telicity Corresponds to Degree of Change.'

Kim, A. and C. Lee 1997. The Antonymic Dichotomy 'EXIT' VS. 'ENTER' in a Single Lexeme: Space Categorization in Korean. In X. Li, L. Lopez, and T. Stroika (eds.), *Papers from 1997 Mid-America Linguistics Conference,* 195-205. University of Missouri-Columbia..

Kim, Y. 1997.Verb Lexicalization Patterns in Korean – with Focus on Motion Conflation in Complex Verb Constructions. In H. Sohn & J. Haig (eds.), *Japanese/Korean Linguistics* 6, 495-511. Stanford: CSLI.

Kita, S. 1999. Japanese Enter/Exit Verbs without Motion Semantics. *Studies in Language* 23: 307-330.

Krifka, M. 1998. The Origins of Telicity. In S. Rothstein (ed.), *Events and Grammar*. Kluwer.

Lee, C. 1997. Argument Structure and the Role of Theme. In M. Shafto & P. Langley (eds.), *Proceedings of the Cognitive Science Society Conference*, 983. Mahwah, NJ: Lawrence Erlbaum.

Lee, C. 1999. Aspects of Aspect in Korean Psych-predicates: Implications for Psych-predicates in General. In W. Abraham and L. Kulikov (eds.) *Transitivity and TAM: Papers Presented to Vladimir Nedjalkov on the Occasion of His 70th Birthday*. Amsterdam: John Benjamins.

Lee, C. 2000. Numeral Classifiers, (In-)Definites and Incremental Theme in Korean. In C. Lee and J. Whitman (eds.), *Korean Syntax and Semantics: LSA Institute Workshop, Santa Cruz, '91*, 109-131. Seoul: Thaehaksa.

Lee, C. 2006. Change of Location: With Reference to Change of State, Creation/ Removal, Degree and Telicity. In S. Haraguchi, O. Fujimura, and B. Palek (eds.), *LP 2002: Studies in Language, Speech and Communication*, vols. I, II, 487-521. Prague: The Karolinum Press.

Lee, C., B. Kang, S. Nam and Y. Kim 1999. Underspecification in Transitive Motion Verbs in Korean. The Texas Linguistic Society Workshop on Argument Structure.

Lee, C., and H. Kim. 2000. Telicity and Scale-Boundedness of Change-of-state/Creation Verbs in Korean. *Web Journal of Cognitive Approach to Verb Semantics*, Kazan State University, Russia.

Levin, B. and M.R. Hovav. 1995. *Unaccusativity at the Syntax-Lexical Semantics Interface*. Cambridge, MA: MIT Press.

Levin, B. & S. Pinker (eds.). 1991. *Lexical and Conceptual Semantics*. Blackwell.

Talmy, Leonard 2000 *Toward a Cognitive Semantics*, Vols I and II. Cambridge, MA: MIT Press.

Tenny, C. 1987. *Grammaticalizing Aspect and Affectedness*. MIT Dissertation.

Pinon, C. 1993. Paths and their Names. In K. Beals et al. (eds), *CLS II. The Correspondence of Conceptual, Semantic and Grammatical Representations*, 287-303.

Pustejovsky J. 1995. *The Generative Lexicon*. Cambridge, MA: MIT Press.

Tsujimura, N. 2002. Japanese Enter/Exit Verbs Revisited. *Studies in Language* 23: 165.

Yoon, Y. 1996. Total and Partial Predicates and the Weak and Strong Interpretations. *Natural Language Semantics* 4/3: 217-36.

Zwarts, J. and Y. Winter. 2000. Vector Space Semantics: a Modeltheoretic Analysis of Locative Prepositions. *Journal of Logic, Language and Information* 9: 169-211.

Semantic Divergence of *-(R)are*: from a different perspective

DAVID Y. OSHIMA
Stanford University

1 Introduction

The Japanese passive morpheme *-(r)are* (*-(r)ar* in classical Japanese) has four distinct uses that are historically related: passive, spontaneous, potential (ability), and honorific. Although the path and driving force of this divergence have been widely discussed and to some extent clarified by traditional Japanese grammarians (Karashima 1993; Kuginuki 1991; Onoe 1998/9 among others), on several points consensus and satisfactory accounts have not been reached yet.

This paper addresses the paths through which the meaning of *-(r)are* diverged, under the new light posed by the analysis of the Japanese passive by Oshima (2002), who proposes that the core meaning of the Japanese passive is the triadic relation of "lack of control". Namely, I argue (i) that the relation between the spontaneous and the passive can be captured in terms of the relation between "general" and "particular", (ii) that the proposed analysis of the spontaneous construction gives a straightforward account of its development into the potential use, and (iii) that the proposed analysis of the spontaneous construction gives support to the hypothesis that the honorific emerged from the spontaneous.

2 The Four Uses of *-(R)are*

In this section I provide an overview of the four uses of *-(r)are* in modern and classical Japanese. I also illustrate the analysis of the Japanese passive, which is adopted here and which plays an important role in the following discussion.

2.1 Passive

It is well known that the Japanese passive is "non-canonical", in that it allows so-called possessive and indirect passives. In the literature, it has been commonly assumed (i) that two or more types of passives (direct/possessive/indirect etc.) must be postulated to explain various facts related to the construction, and (ii) that the "indirect" passive lexically implies an adversative effect caused by the described event on the referent of the subject (Kuno 1973; Gunji 1987; Uda 1994 among others). Alleged varieties of the Japanese passive are exemplified below, with corresponding active sentences (if any):

(1) direct passive

a. Max-ga Pat-ni nagur-are-ta.
Max-Nom Pat-Dat hit-RARE-Past
'Max was hit by Pat.'

b. Pat-ga Max-o nagut-ta.
Pat-Nom Max-o hit-Past

(2) possessive passive

a. Max$_i$-ga Pat-ni (zibun$_i$-no) musuko-o nagur-are-ta.
Max-Nom Pat-Dat self-Gen son-Acc hit-RARE-Past
'Max had his son hit by Pat.'

b. Pat-ga Max-no musuko-o nagut-ta.
Pat-Nom Max-Gen son-Acc hit-Past

(3) indirect passive

Max-ga Pat-ni John-o nagu-rare-ta.
Max-Nom Pat-Dat John-Acc hit-RARE-Past
'Pat hit John on Max.'

Among the three types illustrated above, only the direct passive has the basic characteristics of a cross-linguistically canonical passive, involving "promotion" of an object of the stem to subject and "demotion" of the subject of the stem into a peripheral function marked by an oblique case, *-ni*.

In Oshima (2002), I argued that a uniform account of Japanese passives is possible and plausible. I proposed that the core semantics of the Japanese passive is the triadic relation of "lack of control" among an agent, undergoer and event; a simplified lexical representation of a passive verb, formalized in the framework of HPSG (Head-driven Phrase Structure Grammar; Pollard and Sag 1994), is given as follows:

(4) Lexical representation of *nagur-are-* 'be hit':

$$\begin{bmatrix} \textit{nagur-are-} & \\ \text{HEAD} & \textit{verb} \\ \text{ARG-ST} & <\text{NP[NOM]}_i, \text{NP[DAT]}_j, < \text{PRO}_j, \text{NP[ACC]}_k >> \\ \text{CONTENT} & \begin{bmatrix} \textit{lack-control-rel} & \\ \text{ACTOR} & i \\ \text{UNDERGOER} & j \\ \text{EVENT} & \begin{bmatrix} \textit{hit-rel} & \\ \text{ACTOR} & j \\ \text{UNDERGOER} & k \end{bmatrix} \end{bmatrix} \end{bmatrix}$$

This analysis provides a straightforward account of the adversative effect implicature induced by the indirect passive. The account goes as follows: For a statement of the form: "an event P is out of x's control" to be felicitous, there must be some pragmatically significant relation between P and x; i.e. it must be the case either (i) that x is directly or indirectly involved in P, or (ii) that P causes some effect on x. In case (ii), the effect is usually construed as an adversative one by the inference that: "when an uncontrolled event has some effect on an individual, that effect tends to be a bad one".[1]

According to this analysis, the semantics of the Japanese passive morpheme *-(r)are* is antonymous to the causative morpheme *-(s)ase*, whose core semantics is (the triadic relation of) "exert (positive) control", and whose

---

[1] The following data illustrate this point:

(i) a. That Patricia nominated him$_i$ as her heir was out of Max's$_i$ control.
+/> "Max was adversely affected."
b. That Patricia nominated his$_i$ son as her heir was out of Max's$_i$ control.
+/> "Max was adversely affected."
c. That Patricia nominated John as her heir was out of Max's control.
+> "Max was adversely affected."

These three sentences semantically correspond to the three types of passives given in (ii). Importantly, the adversative effect on the individual to whom the absence of control force is attributed, in this example, Max, arises only when he is not directly or indirectly participating in the subordinate event.

(ii) a. Max-wa Patricia-ni soozokunin-to-site simei-s-are-ta.
Max-Top Patricia-Dat heir-as nominate-Pass-Past
b. Max-wa Patricia-ni musuko-o soozokunin-to-site simei-s-are-ta.
Max-Top Patricia-Dat son-Acc heir-as nominate-Pass-Past
c. Max-wa Patricia-ni John-o soozokunin-to-site simei-s-are-ta.
Max-Top Patricia-Dat John-Acc heir-as nominate-Pass-Past

morphological properties are symmetrical to those of *-(r)are* (cf. Kuginuki 1991:15).[2] The semilattice diagram below illustrates the relation between the causative and the passive in a lucid way; the meaning of the passive, *lack-control-relation*, is a sister type of the supertype of the meaning of the causative (*positive-exert-control-relation*).

(5)

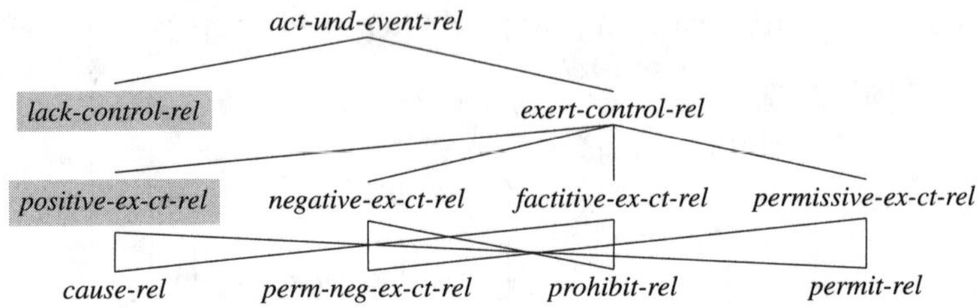

2.2 Spontaneous

The spontaneous construction in modern Japanese is used to depict situations where certain thoughts, attitudes, mental states etc. are brought about to some agent's (typically the speaker's) mind by virtue of environments/situations.

(6) Mukasi-ga sinob-are-ru.
old.time-Nom think.about-RARE-Pres
'Old times come to mind.'

(7) Kokyoo-no haha-no koto-ga omoidas-are-ru.
hometown-Gen mother-Gen fact-Nom recall-RARE-Pres
'I can't help remembering my mother in my hometown.'

The case-marking pattern of the spontaneous in modern Japanese is similar to that of the passive; also, only those verbs that denote psychological or perceptional activities/states have spontaneous forms.

At earlier stages of Japanese, namely up to the Chuuko stage (approx. A.D. 794–1192), in contrast, spontaneous forms (with *-(ra)y* and *-(ra)r*; see below) can be formed with a wider variety of stem verbs, and do not affect the argument pattern of the base verb.

For example, in (8), where the base verb is *mau* 'dance', the actor is not demoted to a peripheral function and marked by the particle *-ni*, as in the case of the passive. In (9), the perceived theme of the event of surprising, which is the sound of wind, is not promoted to subject (see Onoe 2003, 1998/9;

[2]The Japanese causative can mean either causation (factitive causation) or permission (permissive causation), and thus can be understood as their semantic supertype.

Shibatani 2000).

(8) Kikoribito-domo-mo kokoronarazu maw-are-keri.
wood.cutter-Pl-also involuntarily dance-RAR-Past
'Wood cutters too danced willy-nilly.'
(*Konjaku Monogatari*, vol.28; 11c)

(9) Kaze-no oto-ni-zo odorok-are-nuru.
wind-Gen sound-at-Emph be.surprised-RAR-Perf
'(I) got surprised at the sound of the wind.'
(*Kokin Wakashu*, 169; 10c)

2.3 Potential (Ability)

In modern Japanese, only vowel-final verbs (so-called *ichidan doosi*) and *kuru* 'come' can form a potential form with *-(r)are*.

(10) Taro-wa doko-demo sugu-ni ne-rare-ru.
Taro-Top wherever soon sleep-RARE-Pres
'Taro is able to fall asleep at once, wherever he is.'

(11) Tenki-ga waruku-te ko-rare-nakat-ta.
weather-Nom bad-Gerund come-RARE-Neg-Past
'(I/You/He) could not come because of the bad weather.'

Consonant-final verbs (*godan doosi*), on the other hand, gradually lost their potential forms with *-(r)are* from the Muromachi to Meiji periods (during 14–20c), and instead obtained new potential forms (*kanoo doosi* 'potential verbs', e.g. *hanaseru, kakeru*).

Recently, potential verbs derived from vowel-final verbs (*ichidan dooshi*) and *kuru*, which are called *ra-nuki* ('*ra* dropping')-forms, began to be used, in various areas, dialects, and registers; e.g. *nereru, koreru*). This change can be explained as the process in which (i) potential verbs derived from vowel-ending verbs arose in favor of explicitness (mitigation of ambiguity), (ii) *ra-nuki* forms are arising in favor of explicitness and the symmetry of the paradigm (see Inoue 1998; Kinsui 2003). Whereas potential verbs derived from consonant-final verbs are now considered a part of the normative usage, *ra-nuki* forms have not been accepted in formal registers.

2.4 Honorific

Japanese has a rich system of honorific verb morphology (cf. Kikuchi 1994; Nishida 1987). The V-*(r)are* form can be used to manifest the speaker's high esteem of the referent of the subject.

(12) a. Sensei-ga hon-o kat-ta.
teacher-Nom book-Acc buy-Past
'The teacher bought a book.'
b. Sensei-ga hon-o kaw-are-ta.
teacher-Nom book-Acc buy-RARE-Past
'The teacher bought a book. (hon.)'

This use of the V-*(r)are* form is synonymous to *o*-V-*ninaru* (e.g. *Sensei-ga hon-o o-kai-ninat-ta*), except that the former is considered to be more formal.

3 Diachronic Relations among the Four Uses

This section explores how the meaning of *-(r)are* and its predecessors diverged.

3.1 Overview

The morpheme *-(ra)r* (the direct predecessor of *-(r)are*) arose at the beginning of the Chuuko stage (around A.D. 800), taking over *-(ra)y*, which already exhibited three distinct uses: passive, spontaneous and potential. The emergence of the causative ending *-(sa)s* took place at the same period, which took over the old form *-sim* (Kuginuki 1991; Minegishi 1968).

(13)

passive etc.	**causative**	
-(ra)y	*-sim*	
↓	↓	**early Chuuko** (around A.D. 800)
-(ra)r	*-(sa)s*	
↓	↓	**late Kinsei** (Edo period)
-(r)are	*-(s)ase*	

The passive and spontaneous uses of *-(r)are* are said to be oldest among the four uses; the ambiguity is present in the oldest records available (Kuginuki 1991; Hashimoto 1969). The potential use of *-(ra)y*/*-(ra)r* was limited in negative contexts until the end of Heian period (A.D. 794-1192); the tendency that the potential construction occurs with negation continued from the Chusei period (A.D. 1192-1573) onward. The honorific use arose in the Heian period, but it was then subject to certain stylistic constraints (Karashima 1993).

3.2 Passive to Spontaneous, or Spontaneous to Passive?

In the literature, there is no consensus as to which of the passive and spontaneous uses is prior. Shibatani (2000) proposes that the passive arose from the spontaneous; the reasoning is as follows:

(i) The basic function of the spontaneous construction is to defocus the volitionality/intention of the thematic agent.

(ii) This leads to the rearrangement of the case marking pattern: the thematic agent in the spontaneous came not to be realized as the subject, whereas the theme argument was "promoted" and came to be *ga*- (nominative-) marked.

(iii) As a result, the spontaneous form developed into an (inchoative-like) intransitive form, which in turn developed into a passive form that could accompany an agent realized as a peripheral function.

Shibatani's hypothesis assumes that the Japanese passive is "de-transitivized" or argument-decrementing. As mentioned in Section 2.1, however, the Japanese passive is argument-incrementing rather than argument-decrementing. For this reason, I believe it is unlikely that the passive arose from an intransitive, inchoative form (on a par with the passives in Spanish, Russian etc.; see Haspelmath 1990).

An alternative analysis I propose here is that the relation between the spontaneous and the passive can be interpreted as the one between "general" and "particular". In a passive construction, the absence of control force is attributed to a particular individual, namely the referent of the (matrix) subject; on the other hand, in a spontaneous the control force is just absent in the relevant environment.

(14) a. Format of the passive construction:

$$\begin{bmatrix} \textit{passive-stem} & \\ \text{HEAD} & \textit{verb} \\ \text{ARG-ST} & \langle \text{NP[NOM]}_i, \text{NP[DAT]}_j, \langle \text{PRO}_j, \ldots \rangle\rangle \\ \text{CONTENT} & \begin{bmatrix} \textit{lack-control-rel} & \\ \text{ACTOR} & i \\ \text{UNDERGOER} & j \\ \text{EVENT} & \begin{bmatrix} \textit{relation} & \\ \ldots & j \\ \ldots & \ldots \end{bmatrix} \end{bmatrix} \end{bmatrix}$$

b. Format of the spontaneous construction:

$$\begin{bmatrix} \textit{spontaneous-stem} & \\ \text{HEAD} & \textit{verb} \\ \text{ARG-ST} & \langle \text{NP[NOM]}_i, \ldots \rangle \\ \text{CONTENT} & \begin{bmatrix} \textit{general-lack-control-rel} & \\ \text{EVENT} & \begin{bmatrix} \textit{relation} & \\ \ldots & i \\ \ldots & \ldots \end{bmatrix} \end{bmatrix} \end{bmatrix}$$

According to this analysis, the relation between the spontaneous and the passive is to some extent reminiscent of the one between the existential and the possessive, which are often encoded by the same form, as in the Japanese *aru* construction and the French *avoir* construction:

(15) a. (Tukue-no ue-ni) hon-ga aru. (existence)
desk-Gen top-Loc book-Nom be.Pres
'There is a book (on the desk).'

b. Taro-ni [musuko-ga aru]. (possession)
Taro-Dat son-Nom be.Pres
'Taro has a son.'

(16) a. Il y a un livre. (existence)
it(expl.) there have a book
'There is a book.'

b. Il a un livre. (possession)
he have a book
'He has a book.'

That is, possession can be metaphorically construed as existence particularized to a certain agent, and vice versa (Kageyama 1996, Freeze 1992; cf. Tham 2003).

What bearings does this analysis have on the directionality between the passive and spontaneous? To my knowledge, the semantic extension from particular to general and that from general to particular are both commonly attested (e.g. possession→existence, existence→possession), and thus the analysis above does not provide a decisive hint on the directionality in either way.

3.3 Spontaneous to Potential

It has been widely acknowledged that the potential use arose from the spontaneous use. Shibatani (1985) remarks: 'It is only one small step from the spontaneous to the potential. An event that occurs spontaneously has a strong propensity to happen. If this automatic happening is negated, then a reading of impotentiality is implied. [. . .] A generalization of the spontaneous/potential correlation leads to the positive potential reading of an agent-defocusing form, as in Japanese.' (see also Shibatani 2000:171).

The analysis of the spontaneous proposed above provides a straightforward account of the process through which it led to the meaning of "(im)potentiality". The negation of an event of the form "there is no external control on the occurrence of P" is logically equivalent to "there is some external control on the occurrence of P". The external control can be either positive (i.e. "some external force made/let it happen that P") or negative (i.e. "some external force blocks it from happening that P"):

(17) ¬ (GENERAL-LACK-CONTROL (P)) =
GENERAL-POSITIVE-CONTROL (P) ∨
GENERAL-NEGATIVE-CONTROL (P)

However, the negation of a spontaneous implicates the negation of the core (subordinate) event. For instance, the contrast in a pair of (18a) and (18b) mostly concerns the speaker's construal of the event, rather than the truth conditional difference about the way the event was caused (Shibatani 2000:168); the negation of (18b) implicates that one did not remember the past time (hence the marginal status of (18c)).

(18) a. Mukasi-o omoidas-ita.
old.time-Acc recall-Past
'(I) recalled old times.'
b. Mukasi-ga omoidas-are-ta.
old.time-Nom recall-RARE-Past
'Old times came to (my) mind.'
c. ?Mukasi-ga omoidas-are-ru koto-wa-nakat-ta-ga,
old.time-Nom recall-RARE it.was.not.the.case-though
mukasi-o omoidasi-ta.
old.time-Acc recall-Past

In sum, negating the spontaneous implicates a blocking force which prohibits an event from happening. As the final step, the presence of an external blocking force leads to the meaning of impossibility, which generalizes to the potential/ability meaning that can be used in both positive and negative contexts.

3.4 Spontaneous to Honorific, or Passive to Honorific?

The honorific use arose in a relatively late stage (during the Heian period). Traditionally, the view that the honorific arose from the spontaneous has been predominant (Tokieda 1941; Minegishi 1968; Hashimoto 1969 among others). The fact that *-(ra)r*/*-(r)are* in their honorific use do not affect the argument pattern of the stem seems to support this hypothesis.

Shibatani (2000) too takes this view and claims that the honorific use of *-(ra)r* is motivated by a cross-linguistically common strategy to encode honorific meaning, i.e. the avoidance of direct mention of the agent; the spontaneous construction, he claims, brings about this effect by defocusing the direct link between the honorified agent and the action. In a similar vein, Onoe (1998/9) proposes that the honorific *-(r)are* indicates the nobility of the agent by depicting an event as an emergence of a certain situation, rather than as his/her volitional action. The analysis of the spontaneous as "(general) lack of control" provides an additional motivation for the emergence of the honorific; to say that there is nothing that forces or prohibits some person's actions readily leads to acknowledge the absolute might of that person, and thus is an appropriate way to manifest one's respects towards him or her.

Another possibility, that the honorific is derived from the passive, is advocated by authors like Matsushita (1930), Kinoshita (1972), Karashima (1993) and Otsubo (1993), based on different motivations. The settlement of the issue, I believe, waits for further studies.

4 Summary

This paper examined the process through which the meaning of *-(r)are* and its predecessors diverged. I proposed that the spontaneous and the passive shares the core meaning of "lack of control", and that the relation between them can be understood as the one between "general" and "particular". I also argued that the proposed analysis of the spontaneous gives a straightforward account of its development into the potential use, and that it also gives support to the hypothesis that the honorific developed from the spontaneous.

Acknowledgements

I would like to express my gratitude to Paul Kiparsky, Satoshi Kinsui, John Beavers, Peter Sells, Ivan A. Sag, and Shiao Wei Tham for valuable comments and helpful discussions. Thanks also to the participants of the 13th Japanese/Korean Linguistics Conference. Any remaining errors are my own.

References

Freeze, R. 1992. Existentials and other Locatives. *Language* 68(3):553–595.

Hashimoto, S. 1969. *Zyosi, zyodoosi no kenkyuu.* Tokyo: Iwanami Shoten.

Haspelmath, M. 1990. The Grammaticization of Passive Morphology. *Studies in Linguistics* 14(1):25–72.

Inoue, H. 1998. *Nihongo uocchingu.* Tokyo: Iwanami Shoten.

Kageyama, T. 1996. *Doosi imiron.* Tokyo: Kuroshio Shuppan.

Karashima, M. 1993. *Ru/raru* no sonkeiyoohoo no hassei to tenkai: komonzyo hoka no yoorei kara. *Kokugogaku* 172:1–14.

Kikuchi, Y. 1994. *Keigo.* Tokyo: Kadokawa Shoten.

Kinoshita, M. 1972. *Manyoosyuu gohoo no kenkyuu* . Tokyo: Hanawa Shobo.

Kinsui, S. 2003. *Ra*-nuki kotoba no rekisiteki kenkyuu. *Gengo* 32(4):56–62.

Kuginuki, T. 1991. Zyodoosi *ru/raru, su/sasu* no seiritu no rekisitekizyooken ni tuite. *Kokugogaku* 164:15–28.

Kuno, S. 1973. *The Structure of Japanese Language.* Cambridge, Mass.: MIT Press.

Matsushita, D. 1930. *Kaisen hyoozyun nihon bunpoo* . Tokyo: Chubunkan.

Minegishi, A. 1968. Zihatu, kanoo, ukemi, sonkei, sieki. *Kokugokokubun* S43(10):16–34.

Nishida, N. 1984. *Keigo.* Tokyo: Tokyodo Shuppan.

Onoe, K. 1998/9. Bunpoo o kangaeru: syuttaibun. *Nihongogaku* 17-7:76–83/17-10:90–97/18-1:86–93.

Onoe, K. 2003. *Rareru*-bun no tagisei to syugo. *Gengo* 32(4):34–42.

Oshima, D. Y. 2002. Out of Control: A Unified Analysis of Japanese Passive Constructions. In *The Proceedings of the 9th International Conference on Head-Driven Phrase Structure Grammar*, 245-265.

Otsubo, H. 1993. Kanbunkundokubun de '見' o ru/raru to yomu baai no ichikoosatu. *Kokugokokubun* 62(4):1–17/62(5):36–48.

Pollard, C. and I. A. Sag. 1994. *Head-Driven Phrase Structure Grammar.* Stanford: CSLI.

Shibatani, M. 1985. Passives and Related Constructions: A Prototype Analysis. *Language* 61(4):821–848.

Shibatani, M. 2000. Boisu. In Y. Nitta and T. Masuoka, eds., *Bun no kokkaku*, vol. 1 of *Nihongo no bunpoo*, 117–186. Tokyo: Iwanami Shoten.

Tham, S. W. 2003. *Representing Possession: Semantic Dimensions and Pragmatic Bases*. Ph.D. thesis, Stanford University.

Tokieda, M. 1941. *Kokugogakugenron*. Tokyo: Iwanami Shoten.

Uda, C. 1994. *Complex Predicates in Japanese*. New York: Garland Publishing.

Motion Verbs, Telicity, and Argument Projection*

NATSUKO TSUJIMURA
Indiana University

1. Introduction

Issues revolving around the question of to what extent syntactic projection of argument (or argument linking) is influenced by specific properties of individual lexical items have recently renewed the controversy that focuses on the relationship between argument projection and aspectual roles. The opposing views that arise from this question are referred to by Borer (1998), for instance, as 'lexical-entry-driven approaches' and 'syntactic predicate-based approaches'. The lexical-entry-driven approaches have had their impetus based on the assumption that lexical items are the bearer of the information leading to argument projection, as is reflected, among many others, in Chomsky (1981), the Uniformity of Theta Alignment Hypothesis by Baker (1988), and the projectionist view advanced in a series of lexical semantic works by Beth Levin and Malka Rappaport Hovav (e.g. Rappaport Hovav and Levin 1998, 2002; Levin and Rappaport Hovav, to appear). A motivation for considering the syntactic predicate-based approaches, on the

* I would like to thank Stuart Davis for his comments on earlier versions of this paper. The presentation of the paper was made possible through a faculty travel grant awarded by the East Asian Studies Center at Indiana University.

other hand, is found in Geuder and Butt's (1998: 2) introductory comment on the issue:

> ...we believe that a closer inspection of the wider array of crosslinguistic data now available points to the conclusion that the projection of arguments into the syntax depends on factors which go beyond the kind of information that can plausibly be projected from lexical entries alone.

One of the factors motivating the syntactic predicate-based approaches in recent research concerns aspectual roles, as expressed by Tenny's (1994) Aspectual Interface Hypothesis in (1).

(1) Aspectual Interface Hypothesis (Tenny 1994: 2)
The universal principles of mapping between thematic structure and syntactic argument structure are governed by aspectual properties. Constraints on the aspectual properties associated with direct internal arguments, indirect internal arguments, and external arguments in syntactic structure constrains the kinds of event participants that can occupy these positions. Only the aspectual part of thematic structure is visible to the universal linking principle.

The aspectual properties that are considered to play a major role in argument projection have been characterized by invoking notions with a wide range of names: They include, but are not limited to, delimitedness and measuring-out (Tenny 1994, Ritter and Rosen 1998); telicity and boundedness (van Hout 1998); subject of result (Borer 1998); and incremental theme (Dowty 1991, McClure 2002). Continuing recognition of the relevance of aspectual properties to argument projection has provided grounds to cast doubt on the central tenet of the long-held view of the lexical-entry-driven approaches. Rappaport Hovav and Levin (2002) outline the two hypotheses in (2) that conjunctively or disjunctively underlie many, if not all, of the syntactic predicate-based approaches.

(2) a. Hypothesis I: Argument projection is aspectually driven.
b. Hypothesis II: Argument expression is not lexically determined.

Rappaport Hovav and Levin (2002) discuss variable behavior verbs like those in (3-4) for a concrete illustration.

(3) a. Dana read the book.
b. Dana read from the book.

(4) a. Kerry wiped the table clean.
b. Kerry wiped the crumbs off the table.

According to approaches that adopt the hypotheses in (2), telicity is syntactically encoded: The direct object leads to the telic interpretation, as in (3a), while the oblique argument to the atelic reading, as in (3b). The direct objects in (4) serve as measuring arguments in the sense of Tenny (1994), giving rise to the telic interpretation in both. Rappaport Hovav and Levin (2002), however, argue that semantic properties pertinent to argument projection cannot be reduced to aspectual roles and that semantic determinants should not be overlooked. Importantly, they demonstrate that change of state verbs that exhibit a uniform argument projection pattern do not necessarily show a homogeneous aspectual pattern. Compare the two sets of change of state verbs, *break* and *dim*, in (5-9).

(5) *Pat broke/dimmed.
(6) a. *My kids broke me into the poorhouse.
    b. *The stagehand dimmed the scene dark.
(7) a. *The two-year old outbroke the three-year old.
    b. *The stagehand outdimmed the director.
(8) a. Alex broke the vase/*Alex broke at the vase.
    b. Sam dimmed the lights/*Sam dimmed at/from the lights.
(Rappaport Hovav and Levin 2002)
(9) a. Alex broke the vase in/*for a minute.
    b. Sam dimmed the lights in/for a minute.

Both *break* and *dim* show the same range of syntactic argument projection patterns: unspecified object deletion in (5), nonsubcategorized NP resultatives in (6), *out*-prefixation in (7), and conative alternation in (8). And yet, in (9) *break* is telic while *dim* is either telic or atelic. Rappaport Hovav and Levin, moreover, go on to say that *break* is punctual but *dim* is durative, again displaying lack of uniformity in aspecual properties.

In this paper I will demonstrate that an examination of the lexicalization pattern, telicity, and argument expressions of motion verbs in Japanese lends support to the lexical-entry-driven approaches: That is, argument projection cannot be explained on solely aspectual grounds but is to a great extent motivated by lexical considerations. Investigation of lexicalization or conflation patterns, discussed in detail by Talmy (1985) and also by Muehleisen and Imai (1996) for Japanese, coupled with telicity and argument expressions observed with motion verbs reveal that motion verbs do not show a uniform aspectual pattern. More specifically, I will show that traversal objects that often accompany motion verbs exhibit a uniform syntactic pattern while telicity interpretations vary. This discrepancy is not what would be predicted by the hypothesis in (2a). Building on Muehleisen and Imai's work, I will then demonstrate that traversal objects are associated with motion verbs for different reasons, constrained by specific semantic information that is available in the architecture of verb meaning. This suggests that lexically-determined argument expression cannot be eliminated, weakening the hypothesis in (2b). In this paper I will primarily discuss these two issues separately.

2. Traversal Objects and Telicity

It is well known that the majority of motion verbs in Japanese can cooccur with what Martin (1975) calls traversal objects, which are marked by the Accusative Case particle. Examples of motion verbs with traversal objects are given in (10-16).

(10) Sumie-ga haikingukoosu-o/saka-o aruita/subetta.
Sumie-Nom hiking course-Acc/hill-Acc walked/slid
'Sumie walked on the hiking course/slid (down) the hill.'

(11) Kodomo-ga kaidan-o/kono miti-o orita/itta.
child-Nom stairs-Acc/this street-Acc went down/went
'The child went down the stairs/went on this street.'

(12) Kisya-ga tonneru-o kugutta.
train-Nom tunnel-Acc passed through
'The train passed through the tunnel.'

(13) Doroboo-ga uramiti-o nuketa.
thief-Nom alley-Acc passed through
'The thief passed through an alley.'

(14) Ikkoo-wa yama-o koeta.
party-Top mountain-Acc went over
'The party went over the mountain.'

Kuno (1973: 97) explains the semantic role of traversal objects as follows: 'NP-*o* indicates that the motion designated by the verb takes place covering the entire dimension (or the major portion thereof) of the NP continuously and unidirectionally.' This description has in fact led many researchers to the assumption that traversal objects serve to 'measure out' or delimit motion events, and hence give rise to the telic interpretation (cf. Sugamoto 1982). In fact, a correlation between traversal objects and telicity, if it exists at all, would be consistent with Tenny's Aspectual Interface Hypothesis in (1), which further extends to the claim that direct object is the position (or the syntactic position which direct [internation?] arguments are mapped onto) for a delimiter.

Contrary to this prediction, the telicity interpretations of motion verbs in (10-14) vary. Some motion verbs with traversal objects are either telic or atelic, as in (15-16), while others with traversal objects must be telic, as in (17-19).

(15) Sumie-ga haikingukoosu-o itizikan/itizikande aruita.
Sumie-Nom hiking course-Acc for/in an hour walked
'Sumie walked on the hiking course for/in an hour.'

(16) Kodomo-ga (nagai) kaidan-o sanpun/sanpunde orita.
child-Nom (long) stairs-Acc for/in three minutes went down
'The child went down the long stairs for/in three minutes.'

(17) Kisya-ga tonneru-o *zyuppun/zyuppunde kugutta.
train-Nom tunnel-Acc *for/in ten minutes passed through
'The train passed through the tunnel *for/in ten minutes.'

(18) Doroboo-ga uramiti-o *gohun/gohunde nuketa.
thief-Nom alley-Acc *for/in five minutes passed through
'The thief passed through an alley *for/in five minutes.'

(19) Ikkoo-wa yama-o *nizikan/nizikande koeta.
party-Top mountain-acc *for/in two hours went over
'The party went over the mountain *for/in two hours.'

The selection of time adverbials with the motion verbs in (15-16) indicates that traversal objects do not always guarantee the telic interpretation. These sentences are interpreted either as telic or atelic, and contextual information often comes into play for telicity judgments. The motion verbs in (17-19) with traversal objects, by contrast, invariably impose the telic interpretation, and adverbial selection in these sentences cannot fluctuate with contextual information, unlike the case with (15-16). That is, motion verbs with traversal objects in (17-19) are unequivocally telic.

Recall that under the hypothesis in (2a), argument projection is motivated by aspectual considerations. Many syntactic approaches under this hypothesis adopt the view that aspectual distinctions are derived from syntactic differences, and that the interaction of constituents serving as delimiters and functional projections, for instance, is supposed to accommodate such syntactic encoding (Borer 1998, McClure 1994, 2002, Ritter and Rosen 1998). Thus, in syntactic predicate-based approaches, it is expected that traversal objects in (15-16) and those in (17-19) should display contrasting syntactic behavior. This is the question which we now examine.

The question of to what degree traversal objects should be assimilated into more conventional transitive objects has not found a straightforward answer primarily because they share syntactic and semantic properties in some environments but not in others. The same question has also led to the debate as to whether traversal objects are arguments or adjuncts. This is part of the reason why the NP-*o* under discussion has received labels, such as 'traversal objects' and 'quasi-objects' (Miyagawa 1989), separate from traditional direct objects. The question of objecthood that traversal objects raise will not be discussed in this paper since it does not directly concern the issue examined here. I would, instead, like to examine whether the telicity difference observed between (15-16) and (17-19) results in a non-uniform pattern in syntactic phenomena that are considered to involve direct objects, as would be predicted by approaches that adopt the hypotheses in (2). We will discuss just a few of these phenomena.

First, when suffixed to a transitive verb, the desiderative morpheme *–tai* and the potential morpheme *–(rar)eru* can change the Accusative Case marking on the direct object to the Nominative Case although it is also acceptable to maintain the Accusative marking, as is shown in (20).

(20) a. Noriko-ga suppai ringo-o tabeta.
Noriko-Nom sour apple-Acc ate
'Noriko ate a sour apple.'
b. desiderative *–tai*
Suppai ringo-ga/o tabe-tai.
sour apple-Nom/Acc eat-Des
'(I) want to eat sour apples.'
c. potential *–(rar)eru*
Suppai ringo-ga/o tabe-rareru?
sour apple-Nom/Acc eat-Pot
'Can you eat sour apples?'

The formation of desiderative and potential sentences does not distinguish between the two groups that have exhibited a difference in telicity. Consider (21-22), where verbs in the (a) and (b) sentences show ambiguous telicity, corresponding to (15-16), while those in the (c) sentences require the telic interpretation, corresponding to (17-19).

(21) desiderative
a. Donna haikingukoosu-ga/o aruki-tai?
what kind of hiking course-Nom/Acc walk-Des
'What kind of hiking course do you want to walk on?'
b. Yooroppa-no yama-ga/o nobori-tai.
Europe-Gen mountains-Nom/Acc climb-Des
'I want to climb mountains in Europe.'
c. Ookii kawa-ga/o watari-tai.
big river-Nom/Acc cross-Des
'I want to cross a big river.'

(22) potential
a. Konna dekoboko-no miti-ga/o aruk-eru?
this kind of bumpy-Gen road-Nom/Acc walk-Pot
'Can you walk on this kind of bumpy road?'

b. Kyuuna kaidai-ga/o ori-rareru?
steep stairs-Nom/Acc go down-Pot
'Can you go down steep stairs?'

c. Kono te-no torakku-wa semai tonneru-ga/o
this kind-Gen truck-Top narrow tunnel-Nom/Acc
kugur-e-nai.
pass through-Pot-Neg
'This kind of truck cannot pass through narrow tunnels.'

Second, the causative construction can potentially have two patterns, one marking the causee with the Accusative Case and the other with the Dative Case, but when the base sentence is transitive with a direct object marked with the Accusative Case, only the causative sentence with the causee marked with the Dative Case is allowed. This is to avoid the Double-*o* Constraint. An example is given in (23).

(23) a. Kodomo-ga ringo-o tabeta.
child-Nom apple-Acc ate
'A child ate an apple.'

b. Ziroo-ga kodomo-ni/*o ringo-o tabe-sase-ta.
Ziro-Nom child-Dat/Acc apple-Acc eat-Cause-Past
'Ziro made the child eat an apple.'

It has been pointed out by Matsumoto (1990) that violations of the Double-*o* Constraint are relaxed with motion verbs. In particular, when traversal objects are scrambled to the beginning of sentences, the violation is not as completely ruled out as is the case with conventional transitive causative sentences. As the examples in (24) illustrate, traversal objects pattern in a parallel fashion regardless of the observed aspectual difference among the verbs.

(24) a. (?)Ano nagai haikingukoosu-o Tanaka-ga musume-o
that long hiking course-Acc Tanaka-Nom daughter-Acc
aruk-ase-ta(-sooda).
walk-Cause-Past(-I hear)
'(I hear that) Tanaka made his daughter walk on that long hiking course.'

b. (?)Konna kyuuna saka-o sensei-ga
this kind of steep hill-Acc teacher-Nom
syoogakusei-o nobor-ase-ta(-sooda).
elementary students-Acc climb-Cause-Past(-I hear)
'(I hear that) the teacher made the elementary school students go up this steep hill.'

c. (?)Nagare-no hayai kawa-o daikan-ga
flowing-Gen rapid river-Acc local magistrate-Nom
hyakusyoo-o watar-ase-ta(-sooda).
farmer-Acc cross-Cause-Past(-I hear)
'(I hear that) the local magistrate made the farmer cross the fast-flowing river.'

Finally, the distribution of floating numeral quantifiers, discussed extensively in Miyagawa (1989), shows that the mutual c-command condition is satisfied between traversal objects and numeral quantifiers, leading to the argument status of the traversal objects. Again, traversal objects of all motion verbs behave uniformly in the numeral quantifier test.

(25) a. Kinoo haikingukoosu-o mittu(mo) aruita-kara,
yesterday hiking course-Acc three(as many as) walked-since
kyoo-wa asi-ga itai.
today-Top legs-Nom hurt
'Since I walked on as many as three hiking courses yesterday, my legs hurt today.'

b. Mitiko-wa yooroppa-no yama-o itutu nobotta(-sooda).
Michiko-Top Europe-Gen mountain-Acc five climbed(-I hear)
'(I hear that) Michiko climbed five mountains in Europe.'

c. Ikkoo-wa hasi-o yottu watatte, yado-ni tuita.
party-Top bridge-Acc four cross hotel-at arrived
'The party arrived at the hotel after crossing four bridges.'

Under the hypotheses in (2), we would expect syntactic encoding of the aspectual differences in (15-19), but as far as the range of data shown in (20-25) is concerned, traversal objects exhibit uniform patterns despite the aspectual differences in (15-19). There seems to be very little basis for the position that the aspectual distinctions observed in (15-19) should be accounted for in syntactic terms. The projection of traversal objects is, thus, not aspectually driven, nor is the aspectual difference among motion verbs syntactically derived.

3. Conflation Patterns and Traversal Objects

Let us now turn to the question underlying the hypothesis in (2b). I will contend that the projection of traversal objects is not homogeneous among motion verbs, and that their projection in a subclass of motion verbs is triggered by the critical role that a semantic component plays in constructing the verb meaning. To this end, I will begin with a discussion of conflation patterns extensively investigated by Talmy (1985).

Talmy (1985) argues that motion events are dissected into various components, and that languages differ in the way in which these components are incorporated to constitute a meaning of a verb. The motion components that Talmy names are Motion, Figure, Ground, Path, and Manner. Talmy describes Figure and Ground as follows: 'The basic motion event consists of one object (the "Figure") moving or located with respect to another object (the reference-object or "Ground")'; whereas Path is defined as 'the course followed or site occupied by the Figure object with respect to the Ground object.' (p.61) Japanese motion verbs have customarily been divided into two, Manner verbs and Path verbs, where Manner verbs express manner of motion such as walking and running while Path verbs contrast in directions of motion such as upward and downward movements. Typical members of each group of verbs are given in (26-27), where for our purposes only verbs that can occur with traversal objects are included.

(26) Manner verbs: *aruku* 'walk', *hasiru* 'run', *tobu* 'fly', *oyogu* 'swim', *korogaru* 'roll', *suberu* 'slide', *hau* 'crawl', ...

(27) Path verbs: *iku* 'go', *kuru* 'come', *agaru* 'go up', *oriru* 'go down', *otiru* 'fall', *susumu* 'proceed', *noboru* 'climb', *modoru* 'return', *kudaru* 'descend', ...

Interestingly, Talmy notes that the conflation of Motion and Ground does not even form a minor system in any language, although he gives *emplane* and *deplane* as sporadic examples of the Ground conflation pattern.

Contrary to Talmy's crosslinguistic conclusion about Ground conflation, Muehleisen and Imai (1996) claim that what have been classified as Path verbs in Japanese should be divided into subclasses: Ground-Path verbs, which conflate Motion and Ground, and Direction-Path verbs, which conflate Motion and Direction. The members of Ground-Path verbs include those in (28) while verbs in (29) are now called Direction-Path verbs.

(28) *koeru* 'cross', *kuguru* 'pass through [under]', *wataru* 'go over', *nukeru* 'pass [cut] through', *magaru* 'turn', ?*tooru* 'go along', ?*yokogiru* 'cross', ?*tukkiru* 'cross', ...

The motion event described by *koeru* 'cross, go over', for example, involves a barrier-like entity or space as a reference object, namely, the Ground. Barrier-like entities may be vertically extended, normally with the impression of being higher than one's height, such as a fence and a mountain, and the motion event is achieved by changing location from one side of the Ground to the other by going over the Ground object. The Ground, however, may be a line or a space, such as a border, an ocean, or a desert. Examples with *koeru* are given in (29).

(29) a. hei/yama/oka-o koeru 'go over a fence/mountain/hill'
b. kokkyoo/umi/kawa/sabaku-o koeru 'cross over a border/ocean/river/desert'

Another example of Ground-Path verbs, *kuguru* 'pass through [under]', describes a motion in which the Figure moves from one side of the Ground to the other by going under the Ground. The Ground object generally stands over the Figure, as exemplified by an arch-shaped gate, the *noren*-curtain of a shop (a traditional shop curtain hung at the entrance), a tunnel, and even a ring through which animals in a circus jump. This is shown in (30).

(30) a. mon/torii/tonneru/noren-o kuguru 'go through/under a gate/gateway at the entrance to a Shinto shrine/*noren*-curtain'
b. hi-no wa-o kuguru '(a lion) passing through a fire ring'

The semantic component of Ground specified in the Ground-Path verb's meaning is uniformly projected in syntax as a traversal object, perhaps as an obligatory constituent (see Muehleisen and Imai 1996). The projection of a traversal object is lexically motivated for Ground-Path verbs because the Ground component, which is mapped onto a traversal object, is an integral ingredient that comprises the verb meaning. The projection of the Ground component as traversal objects in syntax is, thus, not random, but instead is strictly imposed by the lexical specification of Ground-Path verbs.

Unlike the English verbs *emplane* and *deplane*, which are considered by Talmy (1985) to be sporadic instances of Ground conflation verbs, the Ground objects of Ground-Path verbs in Japanese do not appear in the actual morphological makeup of the verbs as a sort of denominal verb, so specific instantiation of the Ground needs to appear in a separate lexical item. That is, the Ground component in the verb's meaning provides some guidelines as to the range of general appearances, and its syntactically projected traversal object needs to be within the guidelines. As Muehleisen and Imai (1996) point out, if a traversal object refers to something outside the range, the result is anomalous, as is shown in (31-32), which are modified from Muehleisen and Imai's examples (pp. 334-335).

(31) *Ikkoo-wa torii-o koeta.
party-Top shrine-gate-Acc went over
'(lit.) The group went over the shrine gate.'

(32) *Watasi-wa hirobirotosita heigen-o nuketa.
I-Top wide open plain-Acc went out of
'(lit.) I went out of the plain.'

No lexical specification as to the nature of the Ground component constitutes the meaning of Manner verbs and Direction-Path verbs. With these subclasses of motion verbs, then, information concerning the Ground object will be additional, supplementing the more critical motion component of Manner or Direction, respectively. In other words, the intrinsic meanings of Manner and Direction-Path verbs are defined without reference to the Ground; whereas, as mentioned above, the Ground is integral to constructing the meaning of Ground-Path verbs. This distinction leads to my conjecture that the projection of traversal objects is lexically forced by Ground-Path verbs while it is optional with Manner and Direction-Path verbs. In this regard, we may consider the telic interpretation in (17-19) as a consequence of the obligatory projection of the Ground component of Ground-Path verbs. But, importantly, such a connection is relevant in so far as the aspectual property pertinent to Ground-Path verbs comes from a semantically defined notion of event.

4. Conclusion

In this paper I have taken up the issues of whether argument projection is aspectually determined and whether argument projection is not lexically determined, as summarized in the form of the two hypotheses in (2). The focus of the examination has been on motion verbs in Japanese and the range of telicity interpretations that these verbs demonstrate. Despite the fact that traversal objects with these verbs exhibit a uniform pattern in various syntactic phenomena, they are aspectually non-uniform. The range of data indicates that the projection of traversal objects is not aspectually motivated. The discussion of conflation patterns available in motion verbs in Japanese has shown that traversal objects associated with motion verbs are not necessarily projected for the same reason. Classification of motion verbs based on their conflation patterns has led us to two situations. Traversal objects of Ground-Path verbs are obligatorily projected from the Ground component because this event component constitutes a critical element in defining the verb meaning. Traversal objects of Manner and Direction-Path verbs are projected optionally. These two situations are constrained by the lexical specification of classes of motion verbs in Japanese. Thus, the information provided by the lexical entry plays a vital role in the determination of argument expression.

References

Baker, M. 1988. *Incorporation*. Chicago: University of Chicago Press.

Borer, H. 1998. Deriving Passive Without Theta Roles. *Morphology and its Relation to Phonology and Syntax*, eds. S. Lapointe, D. Brentari, and P. Farrell, 60-99. Stanford: CSLI.

Chomsky, N. 1981. *Lectures on Government and Binding*, Dordrecht: Foris.

Dowty, D. 1991. Thematic Proto-Roles and Argument Selection. *Language* 67: 547-619.

Geuder, W. and Butt, M. 1998. Introduction. *The Projection of Arguments: Lexical and Compositional Factors*, ed. M. Butt and W. Geuder, 1-20. Stanford: CSLI.

Kuno, S. 1973. *The Structure of the Japanese Language*. Cambridge, MA: MIT Press.

Levin, B. and Rappaport Hovav, M. to appear. The Semantic Determinants of Argument Expression: A View from the English Resultative Construction. *The Syntax of Time,* ed. J. Gueron and J. Lecarme. Cambridge, MA: MIT Press.

McClure, W. 1994. *Syntactic Projections of the Semantics of Aspect*. Ph.D dissertation. Ithaca: Cornell University.

McClure, W. 2002. Change of State Syntax. Unpublished ms. New York: CUNY.

Martin, S. 1975. *Reference Grammar of Japanese*. New Haven: Yale University Press.

Matsumoto, Y. 1990. Still More on Light Verbs. Unpublished ms. Stanford: Stanford University.

Miyagawa, S. 1989. *Structure and Case Marking in Japanese*. San Diego: Academic Press.

Muehleisen, V. and Imai, M. 1996. Transitivity and the Incorporation of Ground Information in Japanese Path Verbs. *Lexical and Syntactical Constructions and the Construction of Meaning*, ed. M. Verspoor, K.D. Lee, and E. Sweetser, 329-346. Amsterdam: John Benjamins.

Rappaport Hovav, M. and Levin, B. 1998. Building Verb Meanings. *The Projection of Arguments: Lexical and Compositional Factors,* ed. M. Butt and W. Geuder, 97-134. Stanford: CSLI.

Rappaport Hovav, M. and Levin, B. 2002. Change of State Verbs: Implications for Theories of Argument Projection. *BLS* 28: page numbers.

Ritter, E. and Rosen, S. 1998. Delimiting Events in Syntax. *The Projection of Arguments: Lexical and Compositional Factors,* eds. M. Butt and W. Geuder, 60-99. Stanford: CSLI.

Sugamoto, N. 1982. Transitivity and Objecthood in Japanese. *Studies in Transitivity,* eds. P. Hopper and S. Thomson, 423-447. New York: Academic Press.

Talmy, L. 1985. Lexicalization Patterns: Semantic Structure in Lexical Forms. *Grammatical Categories and the Lexicon*, ed. T. Shopen, 57-149. Cambridge: Cambridge University Press.

Tenny, C. 1994. *Aspectual Roles and the Syntax-Semantics Interface*. Dordrecht: Kluwer.

van Hout, Angeliek. 1998. *Event Semantics of Verb Frame Alternations: A case Study of Dutch and its Acquisition*. New York: Garland.

Part IV

Grammaticalization and Functional Grammar

A Corpus-based Study of the Grammaticalization of the Korean Connectives *mye* and *myense* to Sentence Final Particles*

MINJU KIM
Claremont McKenna College

1. Introduction

The functional extension of a clausal connective to a sentence final particle (hereafter SFP), functioning to mark stance in discourse has been commonly observed in Korean and Japanese. Table 1 on the next page summarizes some of the most prototypical cases of this phenomenon. This study will investigate an additional development of this kind, that is, how the Korean simultaneous connectives *mye* and *myense* grammaticalized into SFPs.

* I sincerely thank Sung-Ock Sohn, Shoichi Iwasaki, Hongyin Tao, and Russell Schuh at UCLA for their helpful comments and suggestions on an earlier version of this paper. The abbreviations used in this paper are Acc (Accusative), Conn (Connective), Cop (Copular), Dec (Declarative), Gen (Genitive), Imp (Imperative), Nom (Nominative), Prog (Progressive), Q (Question), Qt (Quotative), Retro (Retrospective), Rl (Relativizer), and Top (Topic).

	Form	Connective	SFP	Studies
Korean	*ko*	juxtaposition	reinforcement	Sohn 1997
	nuntey	circumstantial	mitigation	Park 1997
	nikka	causal, temporal	reassertion	Sohn to appear
Japanese	*to*	quotative	hedging, etc	Hayashi 1997

Table 1. From connectives to sentence final particles (SFPs)

Examples (2) and (3) below compare these two distinctive functions of *mye* and *myense* - as connectives and as SFPs. In (2), *mye* and *myense* are located before the declarative sentence ender *ta* and function as simultaneous connectives denoting 'while'. On the other hand, in (3), *mye* and *myense* are located after the sentence ender *ta* and function as SFPs. As such, their role is to seek the hearer's validation of what the speaker has heard previously and can be translated as 'is it true?'

(2) *John-i umak-ul tulu-mye/myense kongpwuha-yss-ta.*
John-Nom music-Acc hear-*mye/myense* study-Pst-Dec:End
'While listening to music, John studied.'

(3) *John-i Jane hako kyelhonha-yss-ta-mye/myense?*
John Nom Jane with marry-Pst-Dec:End-*mye/myense*
'I heard that John and Jane got married, is it true?'

Besides marking simultaneity, both connectives have additional functions: *Mye* can mark juxtaposition and *myense* can mark concessivity. Yet despite these distinct additional functions, they followed the same path in their development into SFPs. Moreover, Kim (2003) showed that *myense* was coined by the combination of *mye* and *isye* 'to exist'. Because of this, the present study will discuss them together unless a separate treatment is deemed necessary.

This study analyzed both diachronic corpus and natural conversation data and the size of data corpus for each century is shown in Table 2.

	No. of words		No. of words
15th C	653,108	19th C	405,701
16th C	202,276	PDK (WR: written)	439,365
17th C	360,515	PDK (SP: spoken)*	61,639
18th C	415,462	**Total**	**2,538,066**

Table 2. Size of data corpus for each century

* The Present Day Korean (hereafter, PDK) spoken data consists of transcriptions of about 470 minutes of natural conversation data.

Based on the analysis of these data corpora, this study first proposes that the functional extension of *mye* and *myense* to SFPs was made possible through two stages of development: first, from simultaneous to quotative, and second, from quotative to hearsay evidential.

Next, this study will reveal that the grammaticalization of the quotative function in *mye* and *myense* shows striking parallelism with the previous grammaticalization of the quotative markers *hAya* and *hako* in that they all follow the same developmental path – from a 'say' verb construction to a quotative marker.

Finally, drawing on the cases of *hAya*, *hako*, *mye*, and *myense*, this study will also demonstrate that the grammaticalization from the 'say' verb construction to the quotative marker took place in the discourse contexts where the 'say' verb construction was used with another speech act verb of a specific denotation.

In the next section, I will examine the grammaticalization from the 'say' verb construction to the quotative marker, and in Section 3, I will discuss the functional extension from the quotative to the hearsay evidential marker.

2. From 'Say' Verb Constructions to Quotative Markers

Cross-linguistically, it is common for a construction with a 'say' verb to grammaticalize into a quotative marker. This has been shown to be the case in Nama (Hagman 1977), Twi (Lord 1989), Kusasi (Lord 1993), Pe (Lord 1989), Thai (Matisoff 1991), and Buru (Klamer 2000).

In the history of Korean, the grammaticalization from a 'say' verb construction to a quotative has occurred three times: first, before the 15th C with *hAya* (*ha* 'say', 'do' plus *ya* 'and'), second, in the 16th C with *hAko* (*ha* 'say', 'do' plus *ko* 'and'), and third, currently taking place with *mye* and *myense*. I will examine these three cases in this order.

2.1. First Quotative Marker with Connective *e*

The construction *hAya* consists of *hA* 'say' (old form of *ha*) and the connective *e* 'and'. *Ya* is the old form of *ye*, which is an allomorph of the connective *e*. The Korean alphabet started in the 15th C and as King (1994) pointed out, by the 15th C *hAya* was already functioning both as a 'say' verb construction, as in (5), and as a quotative marker, as in (6).

(5) [*Sekpo sangcel* 1447, 24:6a]
kasep-conca-i kyeycoksan-ay ka-lila hA-ya atoseywang-ksontAy ka
Kasep-teacher-Nom Mt. Kyeycok-Loc go-Fut: Dec say-and King Atosey-Dat go
'Saying that he will go to Mountain Kyeycok, Teacher Kasep went to King Atosey.'

(6) [*Sekpo Sangcel* 1447, 24:28a]
cwuk-un hwu-ey-za nwuyuch-untAl mit-uli-ye hAya nilu-ko
die-Rl after-at-only regret-although reach-Fut-Q Quot say-and
'He said, "after you die, even if you have regret, you will not be able to reach enlightenment."'

In (5), *hAya* retains its literal meaning of 'saying'. However, in (6), *hAya* functions as a quotative marker meaning 'that' and is followed by another 'say' verb *nilu*. In (6), *hAya* is a quotative marker and not a 'say' verb construction. If it were not functioning as such, the sentence would have two 'say' verbs, *ha* and *nilu*, resulting in the awkward phrase 'he said-said "after you die"'. Based on this, I propose that in the grammaticalization from the 'say' verb construction to the quotative, the addition of a new semantically general 'say' verb verifies that the old 'say' verb construction has transformed into the quotative marker.

2.2. Second Quotative Marker with Connective *ko*

hAko (> *hako*) is composed of *hA* 'say' (the old form of *ha*) and the connective *ko* 'and'. It is well known that historically the connective *ko* replaced the connective *e* (Lee 1981). In accordance with this trend, *hAko* replaced the quotative *hAya*. Today *hako* and its reduced form *ko* function as the prototypical quotative markers in Korean. Although the quotative *hAko* first emerged in the 16th C, I found examples similar to (7) in the 15th C corpus, where the interpretation of *hAko* can be ambiguous.

(7) [*Samkang yel* 1481, 30]
nayil-ey-n ne-lul tul-ye kwungin sam-oli-la hAko elwu-lyehA-ntay
tomorrow-at-Top you-Acc take-Conn concubine entitle-Int-Dec *hAko* coax-Int-Conn
'(The King) coaxed (her) saying "tomorrow I will take you in (to the palace) and entitle you my concubine."'

The action of coaxing *elwu* usually iherently implies the action of speaking *hA*. Due to this semantic overlap, the meaning of 'saying' becomes demoted in the verb *hA*. Moreover, the propositional content of 'saying' can be subcategorized under the verb *elwu*, rendering the interpretation 'the king coaxed *that* tomorrow he would take her into the palace'. With this inference, *hako* can be analyzed as a quotative marker meaning 'that' rather than as a 'say' verb. Ambiguity in examples like (7) proposes that the 'say' verb construction grammaticalized into the quotative marker in the context where it is used with another speech act verb of a specific denotation, such as 'coax'. This proposition will be discussed further when I examine the grammaticalization of *mye* and *myense* below.

2.3. Third Quotative Markers, *mye* and *myense*

2.3.1. Similarities among the Connectives *e*, *ko*, and *mye*

The quotative marker *hAya* consists of *ha* and the connective *e* (its allomorph *ya*), whereas *hAko* consists of *ha* and the connective *ko*. The next connective we will discuss is *mye*. Kim (2003) illustrates that in the past, the connectives *e*, *ko*, and *mye* shared significant similarities. For instance, in Middle Korean, they all expressed the rather general conjunction meaning 'and'. Due to their functional similarities, when the use of *ko* started to increase in the 15th C, it encroached on and replaced *e* and *mye*.[1] In the history of Korean, their similarities are also manifested in that of all the connectives, only these three grammaticalized with the verb *isye* 'to exist' to engender another set of connectives with *se* - *ese*, *kose*, and *myense*. The emergence of the quotative function with *mye* can be better understood through such historical connections with *e* and *ko*.

2.3.2. Statistical Evidence

	Total*	In quot.**	Quot %		Total*	In quot.**	Quot %
15th C	22,079	294	**1%**	18th C	13,277	299	**2%**
16th C	25,065	361	**1%**	19th C	9,369	343	**4%**
17th C	13,594	103	**1%**	PDK(WR)	5,560	262	**5%**

Table 3. Diachronic distribution of *mye*

*Raw frequency counts are normalized for diachronic comparison and the numbers represent occurrences per million words. ** In quot: used in quotation sentences with 'say' verbs.

	Total*	In quot	Quotative	SFP
Myense	218	58 (27%)	52 (24%)	4 (2%)

Table 4. Distribution of *myense* in Present Day Korean (PDK) spoken data

* Numbers represent raw frequency counts. Size of the PDK spoken data is smaller than that of the written data and thus, its total number of tokens is fewer.

Table 3 shows the diachronic distribution of the connective *mye*. Since the 16th C, the frequencies of *mye* have been in steady decline. Interestingly, however, in spite of its overall decrease, the percentage of the use of *mye* in the quotation sentences with 'say' verbs (as in (8) below) has increased over time.

Compared to *mye*, the frequency of *myense* in the historical data is marginal, averaging only 21 tokens per century. Yet in PDK, the frequency of *myense* is surging. Currently it is in the process of replacing its cognate *mye*, especially in the spoken register. In the PDK spoken data, 218 tokens of *myense* were found, compared to only 19 tokens of *mye*. Table 4 exhibits the functional distribution of *myense*. In the PDK spoken data, the use of

---

[1]The following examples (Kim 2003) demonstrate the historical replacement of *mye* by *ko*. The two examples are Korean translations of the same Chinese text, *nokeltay,* made at different times. Hence, the English translation of (a) and (b) is the same.

(a) [*penyek nokeltay* 1517, 2:42a]

tyohi ket-te-n mAl-to talAni thA-mye tyohAn os-to talAni nip-umye

well walk-Retro-Rel horse-also other ride-*mye* good clothes-also other wear-*mye*

(b) [*monge nokeltay* 1790, 7:9b]

tyohAn cayn mAl-ila-to talAn salam-i thA-ko tyohAn os-ila-to talAn salAm-i nip-ko

good fast horse-COP-also other-NOM ride-*ko* good clothes-COP-also other-NOM wear-*ko*

"Once you die, others will ride your strong horses, they will wear your good clothes, and..."

myense in quotation sentences is as high as 27 percent. In the same data, *myense* is used not only in the quotation sentences, but also as a quotative marker.

Through frequent use in quotation sentences with a 'say' verb (as in (8) and (9)), *mye* and *myense* emerged as part of the 'say' verb construction. This, in turn, provided them the potential to take up the new quotative function.

2.3.3. Semantic Extension

Using examples (8) and (9), I will now illustrate the semantic extension from a 'say' verb construction to quotative with *mye* and *myense*. Please note that although *mye* is used in these examples, *myense* can also be used in its place.

(8) Simultaneous Stage (use of *mye* in a quotation sentence)
ku-nun nayil o-kess-ta-(ko ha)-mye ttena-ss-ta
he-Top tomorrow come-Fut-Ded-(Qt say)-while leave-Pst-Dec
'He left saying he will come tomorrow.'

(9) Ambiguous Stage (from simultaneous to quotative)
ku-nun nayil sa-cwu-kess-ta-(ko ha)-mye yaksokhay-ss-ta
he-TOP tomorrow buy-Benef-Fut-Dec-(Qt say)-while promise-Pst-Dec
'He promised saying he will buy it tomorrow.' -> He promised that he will buy it tomorrow.

In (8), *mye* is used as part of the 'say' verb construction in combination with the 'say' verb *ha* before it. I noted earlier that despite the overall decrease in the frequency of *mye*, its use in quotation sentences with a 'say' verb has been increasing. It should be noted that, as shown in (8), the quotative marker *ko* and the 'say' verb can be omitted before *mye* and, when they are omitted, *mye* is attached directly to the quoted message. This syntactic condition made the incumbent quotative marker *ko* invisible and must have further facilitated the reanalysis of *mye* as a quotative marker.

I propose that the grammaticalization of *mye* into the quotative marker is initiated in the contexts such as the one in (9), where *mye* combines a 'say' verb before it with another speech act verb of some specific denotation. In (9), since the action of promising is normally conducted through speech, the propositional content of speaking (the 'say' verb *ha*) becomes subcategorized under the verb 'promise'. In turn, the inference invited from (9) is that 'he promised that he will buy it tomorrow.' In this reading, the connective *mye* is analyzed as the quotative marker 'that'.

On the basis of the discussion thus far, I propose the grammaticalization from a 'say' verb construction to a quotative marker as follows. First, it is well known that the source constructions for grammaticalization are lexical items with general denotations. This holds true for the grammaticalization under discussion as well, as it has been shown that the source item is a semantically general 'say' verb (Klamer 2000). Second, a construction with this general 'say' verb grammaticalizes into the quotative marker in contexts similar to that of (9), where it is used with another speech act verb of a specific denotation, such as 'answer' and 'promise'. Finally, the transformation of the 'say' verb construction into the quotative marker can be verified by the addition of a new general 'say' verb (in the case of Korean, positioned after the new quotative marker), as shown in (6).

3. Examples of the Quotative *myense* from Conversation Data

In the natural conversation data, I found 52 tokens of *myense* functioning as a quotative marker. I will examine some of them here. Please note that when *myense* functions as part of a 'say' verb construction, a 'say' verb precedes *myense* whereas when *myense* functions as a quotative marker, a new 'say' verb follows it.

In (11), two married women are talking about their mutual friend.

(11) [From *Two Ladies*]

1 W: *=kuliko caki-ka ku- kule-te-la*
and self-Nom th- say:Med-Ret-Dec
'And she herself said…'

2 *imsin-cwung-ey nemwuna manhun nappun sayngkak-ul hay-ss-ess-tay*
pregnant-middle-at too much bad thought-Acc do-Pst-Plup-Qt:Hearsay
'during the pregnancy she had a lot of bad thoughts.'

3 H: *u ung* 'I see'

4 W: *hoksi kulen (0.2) ki-kihyengcekin-kel-lo*
maybe that de-deformed-Dn-Dir

5=> *sayngkak-ul nemwu manhi hay-ss-ta-myense kule-te-la-ko*
thought-Acc too many do-Pst-Dec-*myense* say:Med-Ret-Det-SFP
'She said that she had many bad thoughts about the possibility of de- deformation.'

6 H: *um, tatul naitul-ese imsinha-myen*
right all old-when pregnant-Cond
"Right, we all do when pregnant at an old age."

In line 5, the quotative *myense* is 'followed' by a 'say' verb *kule*. Kim (2003) showed that in conversations, the most frequent 'say' verb is *kule* ('say', 'do') rather than *ha*. In this example, *myense* functions as a quotative and not as a simultaneous marker. In order for *myense* to mark simultaneity, it has to combine a verb preceding *myense* with the following verb *kule*. The existence of the sentence ender *ta* before *myense* indicates that the only possible verb that can be restored before *myense* is the say verb *ha*, as in (8) and (9). On the other hand, if we restore *ha* and force the simultaneous reading, the sentence becomes ungrammatical since it contains two 'say' verbs for one quoted message (see (6) for a discussion on this). Hence, *myense* in (11) has already transformed into a quotative marker and thus cannot mark simultaneity.

In (12) also, *myense* functions as the quotative marker and is followed by the 'say' verb *kule*. Here, two teenage girls are talking about another girl who was recently elected as captain of their church group.

(12) [From *Teenage Girls*]

1 P: *ani sasil mwe ce-pen-ey nay ka mwe-la kule-n-cwul-a-ni?*
Well in fact last-time-at I what-Cop say:Med-Rel-DN know-Q
'Do you know what I said (to her) last time?'

2=> *pwucang caki mos-ha-kess-ta-<u>myense</u> kule-teni-man cal-man hako tani-tey*
captain self Neg-do-Int-Dec-<u>*myense*</u> say:Med-Ret-although well do-around
'Although you said you cannot be the captain, you go around acting like the captain so well (i.e. being bossy).'

3 S: *e kulay na-nun kukey nemwu silh-ta-nikkan*
yeah right I-Top that too dislike-Dec-SFP:assert
'Yeah, right. That is what I really dislike (about her).'

A minor functional difference between the prototypical quotative marker *ko* and the quotative *myense* is that *myense* can deliver the feeling of an outpour of multiple utterances, probably due to its original simultaneous meaning. In (13), Y recounts a fight with her husband over their teenager son. With the use of the quotative *myense*, she vividly expresses how she poured out complaints to her husband.

(13) [From *Family Problems*]

1 Y: *ecey po-nikka sok-ey chenpwul-i na-te-lay.*
yesterday watch-Caus inside-Loc anger-Nom arise-Ret-HSay
'He said watching him (son) one day brought about so much anger.'

2=> *Tangsin-un ecey halwu po-nikka chenpwul na-ci na-nun maynnal po-ko iss-ta-<u>myense</u>*
you-Top yesterday one -day watch-Caus anger arise-Tag I-Top everyday watch-Prog-Dec-<u>myense</u>
'(I said) "you feel that much anger after watching him for one day? I watch him everyday."'

3=> *na-poko solicilu-nta-ko kule-ci mala-<u>myense</u>*
I-Dat yell-Dec-Qt say:Med-Comp Neg:Imp-<u>*myense*</u>
'(and I said) "don't tell me not to yell (at him)."'

(0.2)

4 *nonun tongan-man-ila-to ai ay-lul kakkawun tey-lato*
vacation during-only-Cop-even kids-Acc near place-even
'Even only during the vacation'

5=> *eti tongney twyssan-ila-to teyli-ko-tani-ko ha-la-ko*
where neighbor mountain-Cop-even take-Conn-go-Conn do-Ipm-Qt
'(I said) "you should take the kids to the mountain even near our neighborhood."'

The quotative *ko* in line 5 is used in alternation with the quotative *myense* in 2 and 3. This alternation also supports the argument of this paper - that *myense* has started to function as a quotative marker in the spoken register.

In addition, what should be noted from this excerpt is that the quotative markers *ko* and *myense* in lines 2, 3, and 5 are not followed by reporting 'say' verbs. At the end of her long turn, Y eventually omits the 'say' verb, and in my translation 'I said' is put inside parenthesis. Without a 'say' verb, adding the quotative marker at the end of the sentence can manifest that what has been mentioned is in fact a quoted message. Such uses of the quotative *ko* and *myense* without main 'say' verbs, as shown here, are closely related to the next functional extension of these constructions to hearsay evidential markers.

4. From Quotative to Hearsay Evidential

Drawing on the discussions thus far, I will now account for the functional extension of *mye* and *myense* to SFPs. First of all, I suggest that the sentence final function of *mye* and *myense* is derived from their quotative function rather than the simultaneous function, based on the following evidence. As mentioned earlier, when *mye* and *myense* function as simultaneous markers, the 'say' verb can be inserted before them. In contrast, when they function as quotative markers and SFPs, such insertion is not permitted. Second, it is well known that the quotative marker *ko* also developed into a SFP with a confirmatory function similar to that of *mye* and *myense*. Hence, in (14), the SFP *ko* can be used instead of *mye* and *myense*.

(14) John i Jane hako kyelhonha-ss-ta-*ko/mye/myense* ?
John Nom Jane with marry-Pst-Dec-*ko/mye/myense*
'I heard that John and Jane got married, is it true?'

This connection between the quotative function and the confirmatory sentence final function demonstrates that the sentence final function of *mye* and *myense* has been derived from their quotative function rather than directly from their simultaneous function.

Next, I suggest that the SFPs *mye* and *myense* are in essence hearsay evidential markers, derived from the quotative function. In different languages, such functional shift from quotative to hearsay evidential marking has been observed (Haspelmath 1993, Givon 1991). I argue that in the case of *mye* and *myense* as well, after acquiring the quotative function, they further developed to mark hearsay evidentiality.

The functional extension from the quotative to the hearsay evidential marking can be described as a change in focus. In the quotative marking, the focus lies in the original speech action, that is, the original speaker (who) stated some information (what). On the other hand, in the hearsay evidential marking, the focus changes to the information itself and its status as second-hand, while the original speech action becomes eclipsed. With Korean *ko*, *mye*, and *myense*, this change in focus is manifested as a syntactic rule. When they are used as SFPs, as in (14), neither the original speaker of the quotation nor the verb of saying can occur with *ko*, *mye*, and *myense*. This syntactic reduction attests that, in the sentence final position, they are operating as hearsay evidential markers rather than quotative markers.

By marking a question as hearsay, the speaker can signify his limited access and commitment to, as well as responsibility for, the inquiring content. Such discourse strategy seems to have motivated the utilization of *ko*, *mye*, and *myense* as SFPs in questions.

5. Conclusion

Drawing on the findings from diachronic and synchronic corpus data, in this paper I have proposed that the sentence final use of *mye* and *myense* should not be treated as a syntactically reduced variation of the simultaneous use. Rather, it should be understood under the more theoretically feasible functional extension from simultaneity to quotative to hearsay evidentiality.

Although I proposed that the path of these functional extensions takes the aforementioned order, it is true that their use as SFPs is more prominent than as quotatives, suggesting the reverse order in their development. Yet an explanation for this can be found in that for a long time they have been used as pseudo-quotatives, albeit limited to specific contexts.

The functional extension of *mye* and *myense* to the quotative has long been emerging in local contexts like (9) (i.e. with speech act verbs of specific denotations). In these contexts, their function is very similar to the quotative and they can even collocate with verbs like 'shout' (which is not possible with English 'while'). Through their frequent use as a quotative in these specific contexts, they could develop to the SFPs, where they are not followed by any verbs.

In general, a form starts its grammaticalization in a specific local context and, over time, generalizes by expanding its collocational contexts. What we have observed in Section 3 of this paper is the incipient expansion of the quotative *myense* to collocational contexts where it is used with more general 'say' verbs. This is why, unlike its use with specific speech act verbs, its use with general 'say' verbs is still confined to natural conversation data.

References

Givon, T. 1991. Serial Verbs and the Mental Reality of 'event': Grammatical vs. Cognitive Packing. *Approaches to Grammaticalization*, eds. E. Traugott & B. Heine, 81-127. Amsterdam: John Benjamins.

Hagman, R.S. 1977. *Nama Hottentot grammar*. Bloomington: Indiana Unviersity Publications.

Haspelmath, M. 1993. *A Grammar of Lezgina*. Berlin/New York: Mouton de Gruyter.

Kim, M. J. 2003. *Discourse, Frequency, and the Emergence of Grammar: A Corpus-based Study of the Grammaticalization of the Korean Existential Verb is(i)-ta*. Doctoral Dissertation, UCLA.

King, R. 1994. History of Reported Speech in Korean. *Korean Linguistics: Journal of the International Circle of Korean Linguistics* 8:1-38.

Klamer, M. 2000. How report verbs become quote markers and complementisers. *Lingua* 110: 69-98.

Lee, K. K. 1981. Ssikuth {-a} wa {-ko} uy ukesacek kyochey. *Kwekeuy thongsa uymilon*, eds. Y. K. Ko & Y. Y. Park, 317-329. Seoul: Tower.

Lord, C. 1989 *Syntactic reanalysis in the historical development of serial verb constructions in languages of West Africa*. Doctoral Dissertation, UCLA.

Lord, C. 1993. *Historical change in serial verb constructions*. Amsterdam: John Benjamins.

Matisoff, J. 1991. Areal and universal dimensions of grammaticalization in Lahu. *Approaches to Grammaticalization*, eds. E. Traugott & B. Heine, 383-454. Amsterdam: John Benjamins.

Park, Y. Y. 1997. *A Cross-linguistic Study of the Use of Contrastive Connectives in English, Korean, and Japanese Conversation*. Doctoral Dissertation, UCLA.

Sohn, S. O. 1997. From quotation to sentence-final particle: The analysis of *–ko* in modern Korean. *9th International Conference on Korean Linguistics* ed. R. King, New York: SUNY.

Sohn, S. O. to appear. On the Emergence of Intersubjectivity: An Analysis of the Sentence-final *nikka* in Korean. presented at *12th Japanese/Korean Linguistics*.

Morpheme Insertions in Japanese Causative and Potential Expressions*

JUDY OKADA
University of California, Los Angeles

1. Introduction

This study focuses on the insertion of partially and fully reduplicated morphemes of voice in present-day Japanese. Previous studies have traced the historical development of the modern potential suffix *–(r)are-* and causative suffix *–(s)as(e)-* (Komatsu 1999, Inoue 1998 and others). However, they do not account for the more recent developments in the use of morpheme insertions, which are: 1) the morpheme *sa* for causative structures; 2) the partially reduplicated morpheme *re* for potential structures; and 3) the fully reduplicated morpheme *rare* for potential structures. This author previously focused on the insertion of the morpheme *sa* in causative constructions (Okada 2003). Here, the causative *sa*-insertion and the more

*I would like to thank Shoichi Iwasaki, Satoshi Kinsui, and Hongyin Tao for their guidance and suggestions on this and earlier versions of this paper. Much gratitude also go to Chigusa Saito and Megumi Yoda for bringing to my attention valuable examples used in this paper, and to John Kuratani for many hours of help and support in the presentation of this paper.

familiar potential *re*-insertion will be reviewed. Also, a new fully reduplicated potential *rare*-insertion will be introduced.

The Japanese language rarely accounts for morpheme reduplications even in cases of double causative constructions such as 'A had B make C do ~' (Shibatani 1976a: 244). However, two years of accumulated internet data show that not only do partial reduplication of morphemes appear frequently, but complete reduplications appear as well.

This author proposes that a systematic change in the Japanese causatives and potentials is taking place. Following a process of reduction and reanalysis, what began as an attempt to intensify the meaning of the relevant morpheme appears to be developing into a means to substantiate the relevant morpheme. Moreover, this change contributes to the gradual move of the language over the centuries to simplify the conjugation paradigm. The mechanism involved here is reanalysis.

2. Reanalysis

These inserted morphemes *sa* and *re* emerged from a process of reanalysis in a competitive environment between what Langacker calls 'signal simplicity' and 'transparency'. Langacker (1977: 58) describes reanalysis as '...change in the structure of an expression or class of expressions that does not involve any immediate or intrinsic modification of its surface manifestation'.

One type of reanalysis, resegmentation, has three types: boundary loss, boundary creation, and boundary shift. Such boundary changes are involved in the reanalysis that has brought about the inserted morphemes, and each may also contribute to the formation of a clearer and more distinct form of the morphemes.

2.1. Signal Simplicity vs. Transparency

One characteristic of language change described by Langacker (1977: 102) as 'signal simplicity' is 'economy in regard to production of the physical speech signal ... making its articulation less exacting.' This is in direct competition with 'transparency' where 'every semantic element in a sentence will be associated with a distinct and recognizable surface form.'

Transparency seeks a clear and recognizable surface form for every semantic element, whereas simplicity is associated with shortening or loss of semantic or syntactic elements. Thus, there is an on-going competition among different elements of optimality, clarity of surface form, ease of speech production, and ease of speech perception. This continuous discord between simplicity and clarity is one reason language continues to change.

2.2. Reanalysis in *Sa*-Insertion

Below are some examples of sentences with causative *sa*-insertion, taken from a TV variety show.[1] The capitalized portion is the inserted, redundant morpheme. Taking this out would produce a traditionally acceptable sentence.

(1) *Honjitsu shikai-o yar-**aS-Ase**-te-itadakimasu*
today host-ACC do-**CAUS-CAUS**-TE-AUX:POL:NONP
'Allow me to be your host today.'

(2) *Otayori yom-**aS-Ase**-te-itadakimasu*
letter read-**CAUS-CAUS**-TE-AUX:POL:NONP
'Allow me to read this letter.'

(3) *Tsugi-ni ik-**aS-Ase**-te-itadakimasu*
next-DAT go-**CAUS-CAUS**-TE-AUX:POL:NONP
'Allow me to go on (to the next explanation).'

The various existing causative forms demonstrate resegmentation and competition between 'signal simplicity' and 'transparency'. With the vowel verbs, there exists a reduced, often more colloquial *–as-* form of the *–sase-*, which is the most frequently encountered morpheme insertion form observed (Okada 2003: 31). This form resembles many existing transitive and lexical causative verbs.[2] The reduplication of the causative morpheme or *sa*-insertion helps to clarify the causative meaning when so intended. Subsequently, a reanalysis occurs, whereby the *sa* morpheme emerges, as shown in (4) below.

---

[1]The speaker for examples (1)~(3) is a young entertainer (Nakai) of the popular singing group SMAP.

[2]Examples where the intransitive vowel verbs have reduced causative forms that are similar to the transitive verb and to the causative form of the relevant transitive verb include the following:

Intransitive	Causative (short)	Transitive	Causative (or ***sa***-ins.)
hiye- 'cool'	*hiye-**sas**-*	*hiyas-*	*hiy**asas**-*
kare- 'wilt'	*kare-**sas**-*	*karas-*	*kar**asas**-*
okure- 'be late'	*okure-**sas**-*	*okuras-*	*okur**asas**-*

(4) Causative (vowel verb *mi-ru* 'to see'):

mi-ru	basic form
mi-sase-ru	causative form
or: *mi-**sas**-u*	optional, reduced (more colloquial) form
*mi-**saS**-**Ase**-ru*	*sa*-insertion onto reduced form
*mi-**[sa]-[SA]-se**-ru*	reanalysis of causative morpheme (renewal of a causative reinforcer *SA*)

In the case of consonant verbs, there exists the traditional causative form, as well as a reduced (or simplified) version. However, this reduced, colloquial form of the causative morpheme resembles existing transitive and lexical causative verbs (see (11a) below for examples). A doubling at this point to intensify the causative meaning (and for more transparency) leads to a reanalysis, producing a *SA*-morpheme that can even be used again, as in (5) below, which is from actual data.

(5) Causative (consonant verb *yom-u* 'to read'):

yom-u	basic form
yom-ase-ru	causative form
or: *yom-**as**-u*	optional, reduced (colloquial) form
*yom-**aS-Ase**-ru*	*sa*-insertion onto reduced form
*yom-a-**[SA]-se**-ru*	reanalysis of causative morpheme (renewal of a causative reinforcer *SA*)
*yom-**a-SA-SA-s**[**e**-r]u*	tripled causative morpheme (from actual data)

2.3. Reanalysis in *Re*-Insertion

Below are internet examples of sentences with potential *re*-insertion. In these also, the capitalized portion is the redundant morpheme.

(6) *...firutaringu-tte...okona-**e**-**RE**-ru n deshoo ka?*[3]
filtering-QUOT perform-**POT**-**POT**-NONP NMLZ CONJ Q
'...can filtering...be performed...?'

(7) *Sake-ga are-ba sawag-**e**-**RE**-ru hitobito...*[4]
sake-NOM exist-COND make.noise-**POT**-**POT**-NONP people
'People who can become noisy with *sake*...'

[3]Data taken from: http://www.users.gr.jp/ml/archive/win2k/8454.asp

[4]Data taken from: http://www.trpg.net/talk/IRC/kataribe/2002/03/20020330.kataribe.txt

(8) *Terebi-ga mi-**re-RE**-ru kedo kekkoo hima-na no ne* [5]
TV-NOM see-**POT-POT**-NONP but quite boring-COP NMLZ P
'I can watch TV, but it's quite boring...'

One observes even more resegmentation and competition between 'signal simplicity' and 'transparency' in the development and changes in the potential expressions. With vowel verbs a reduced version results from the *ra*-deletion[6] effect. The reduction contributes to 'signal simplicity' and brings the conjugation paradigm closer to that of the consonant verbs, not to mention structural separation from passive, spontaneous, and honorific forms. However, this deletion seems to leave a lacking of a potential 'feel' in the verb (Mizuno 1995: 94). Thus, to intensify the 'potential' feel, a reanalysis occurs, whereby the potential meaning is associated with the morpheme *re* (instead of *–are*), leading to a doubling of the *re*-morpheme, or *re*-insertion.

(9) Potential (vowel verb *mi-ru* 'to see'):

mi-ru	basic form
mi-rare-ru	potential form
mi-r [ar] e-ru	reduction (separates from honorific, passive & spontaneous)
*mi**r-e**-ru*	reduced *RA* (or *-ar-)*-deleted potential form (similar in form to the consonant verb)
mi-[re]-ru	reanalysis of the potential morpheme
*mi-**re-RE**-ru*	doubled *RE*-inserted potential form

The consonant verbs follow what has emerged from the vowel verbs. However, the *re*-insertion among consonant verbs produces a distinct potential morpheme that does not exist for traditional potential verbs, namely *–ere*. This allows for consonant verbs to have a potential 'form' *(kanô-kei)* of the verb, rather than being referred to as a potential 'verb' *(kanô-dôshi)*. *Re*-insertion also helps to distinguish potential forms from structurally similar transitive verbs (see (11b) below for examples).

[5] Data taken from: http://homepage1.nifty.com/SHIGE/second/2002_11.htm

[6] *Ra*-deletion is believed to have begun around the end of the Taisho Period (1912~1926) (Kinsui 2003, Inoue 1998).

(10) Potential (consonant verb *sum-u* 'to live/reside'):

sum-u	basic form
sum-e-ru	potential verb *(kanô-dôshi)*
*sum-e-**re**-ru*	doubled *RE*-inserted potential form *(kanô-kei)*

2.4. Effects of Morpheme Insertions

The effects of the *sa* and *re*-insertions may be summarized as follows:

1. Insertion provides a more distinct morpheme: for causatives, a clear *sa* morpheme (*-a-SAs-* vs. *–as-*), and for potentials, a clear *re* morpheme (*-e-RE-* vs. *–e-*).
2. Insertion provides a common morpheme for all regular verbs; that is, both causative *sa*-insertion and potential *re*-insertion produce verb endings that are identical to those of vowel verbs *(yoma-SAse-ru / mi-sase-ru; yome-RE-ru / mi-re-ru).*
3. Insertions distinguish causative and potential forms of the verb from transitive verbs that are similar in form. The following are examples of transitive verbs that are similar in form to causative forms (11a), and potential forms (11b):

(11) Similarities of Transitive Verbs to Causative and Potential Forms

a. Intransitive	Causative (short)	Transitive	Causative (or ***sa***-ins.)
tob- 'fly'	*tob-**as**-*	*tobas-*	*tob**asas**-*
ugok- 'move'	*ugok-**as**-*	*ugokas-*	*ugok**asas**-*
nak- 'cry'	*nak-**as**-*	*nakas-*	*nak**asas**-*
b. Intransitive	**Potential**	**Transitive**	**Potential (or *re*-ins.)**
tat- 'stand'	*tat-**e**-*	*tate-*	*tat**ere-***
susum- 'proceed'	*susum-**e**-*	*susume-*	*susum**ere-***
tok- 'solve'	*tok-**e**-*	*toke-*	*tok**ere-***

4. Insertions unify the conjugation paradigm for all regular verbs. For instance, for potentials, both consonant and vowel verbs can have the same conjugation system *(yom-e-RE-ru / mir-e-RE-ru).* For causatives, provided that dialectal influence prevails for the vowel verbs,[7] here too

[7]Inoue (1998: 28) states that in various regions of Eastern and Western Japan, vowel verbs such as *ki-ru* 'to wear' and *mi-ru* 'to see' are changing their causative forms from the traditional *ki-sase-ru* and *mi-sase-ru* to a newer *kir-ase-ru* and *mir-ase-ru*, respectively. The newer forms

the same conjugation system will result for both consonant and vowel verbs *(yom-a-SAse-ru* / *mir-a-SAse-ru).*

2.5 Further Effects of *Re*-Insertion

With respect to *re*-insertion, one can also add the following effects:

1. *Re*-insertion provides a potential 'form' *(kanô-kei)* instead of a potential 'verb' *(kanô-dôshi)* for consonant verbs; i.e., a clear morpheme exists that is separable from the verb to have potential meaning.
2. *Re*-insertion retains the structural separation from the honorific, passive, and spontaneous forms that results from the *ra*-deletion effect.
3. *Re*-insertion provides a solution to the feeling of 'deficiency' after the *ra*-deletion effect.

However, *re*-insertions are not without problems. One is that *re*-inserted potential forms can be difficult to articulate, especially in the conditional form using *–ba* where there is a series of three instances of *re* in a row, as in the following examples:

(12) Examples of *re-re-re*

Vowel verb	*re*-inserted potential		*re*-inserted conditional
mi-ru 'see'	*mi-re-RE-ru*	>	*mi-re-RE-re-ba*
tabe-ru 'eat'	*tabe-re-RE-ru*	>	*tabe-re-RE-re-ba*

3. Increase in Use of *Sa*-Insertion

In 2002 this author examined the top eight verbs that most frequently appeared with causative *sa*-insertion (data taken from the internet). These same verbs analyzed one year later demonstrated a significant increase in the occurrence of *sa*-inserted causatives. The data compare those collected in summer 2002 with those from summer 2003:

(13) Comparison of *Sa*-Insertion Occurrence: 2002 vs. 2003

			May 2002	July 2003
Consonant verbs:	*owar-u*	'end'	123	524
	ik-u	'go'	119	791
	yom-u	'read'	1	718
	kak-u	'write'	1	802
	tsuka-u	'use'	0	832

follow the same rule as those of consonant verbs, where the *r* of *–ru* is retained as part of the root of the verb, and final *–u* is replaced with the causative *–ase-*.

Vowel verbs:	*mi-ru*	'see'	18	13
	tabe-ru	'eat'	10	8
	kangae-ru	'think'	7	9
		total:	282	3,697

Over a period of one year, the numbers have increased considerably for each of the consonant verbs mentioned above, while the vowel verbs remain pretty much unchanged. One explanation is the advantageous formation of a clear and transparent causative morpheme for the consonant verbs. However, consonant verbs such as *hanas-u* 'to speak,' *sagas-u* 'to search,' and *naos-u* 'to fix' (with *–s-u* endings) are low or zero in occurrence of *sa*-insertion. This may be due to the fact that these already form the *–asas*-ending, and by avoiding *sa*-insertion it can prevent the occurrence of a series of *sa (-asasas-)* that would be more difficult to articulate.

4. *Rare*-Insertion

In addition to *re*-insertion, insertion of a full potential morpheme *rare* is also observed in the internet data. Examples of sentences with insertion of the fully-reduplicated potential *rare* are as follows:

(14) *...katsuyoo.sure-ba, kiroku-o motto nobas-**e-RARE**-ru* [8]
use-COND record-ACC more improve-**POT**-**POT**-NONP
'…if you use it, you can improve your (speed) record even more.'

(15) *...anshin.shi-te waiwai sawag-**e-RARE**-ru ryokan* [9]
be.worriless-TE noisily make.noise-**POT**-**POT**-NONP inn
'an inn where one can be noisy without worry'

(16) *Ookii gamen-ga mi-**re-RARE**-ru yoo-ni nat-te-imasu* [10]
big screen-NOM see-**POT**-**POT**-NONP like-ADV be-TE-AUX:NONP
'It's set up so that one can watch on a big screen.'

4.1. Comparison of *Re-* versus *Rare*-Insertions

When comparing the partially reduplicated *re* with the fully reduplicated *rare*, the shorter *re*-insertion is preferred among the consonant verbs, while the longer *rare*-insertion is more popular among the vowel verbs.

[8]Data taken from a magazine advertisement of the Seiko brand Super Athlete watch (February 2003)

[9]Data taken from: http://www.rankei.com/mail-Monthly/0010/answer/a3.htm

[10]Data taken from: http://homepage2.nifty.com/n-cinema/cinemas/niigata-ken/t-joy-niigata/t-joy-niigata.html

(17) Vowel Verbs: *re*-insertion vs. *rare*-insertion

	re-insertion	*rare*-insertion
mi-ru 'see'	124	162
tabe-ru 'eat'	115	305

(18) Consonant Verbs: *re*-insertion vs. *rare*-insertion

	re-insertion	*rare*-insertion
tuka-u 'use'	173	54
erab-u 'choose'	422	283

The *rare*-insertion is more popular with the vowel verbs. While the advantages of *re*-insertion are retained, the longer *rare*-insertion prevents the overly redundant sequence of *re,* especially for the conditional *ba* constructions *(-re-re-re-ba).*

4.2. Effects of *Rare*-Insertion in Potentials

The effects of the potential *rare*-insertion may be summarized as follows:

1. *Rare*-insertion provides a distinct morpheme for potentials: a clear *rare* morpheme *(-e-RARE-* vs. *–e-).*
2. *Rare*-insertion provides a common morpheme for all regular verbs; that is, potential *rare*-insertion produces verb endings that are identical to those of vowel verbs *(yome-RARE-ru / mi-reRARE-ru).*
3. *Rare*-insertion distinguishes potential forms of the verb from transitive verbs that are similar in form.
4. *Rare*-insertion provides a potential 'form' *(kanô-kei)* instead of a potential 'verb' *(kanô-dôshi)* for consonant verbs.
5. *Rare*-insertion retains the separation from the honorifics, passives, and spontaneous forms.
6. *Rare*-insertion provides a solution to the feeling of 'deficiency' after the *ra*-deletion effect.
7. *Rare*-insertion eliminates the *re-re-re* series for conditional *ba*-expressions.

5. Conclusion

Morpheme insertions appear to have begun as a way of intensifying the meaning of the morpheme by means of reananlysis, especially in cases where the option of reduction (signal simplicity) exists.[11] However, from a broader perspective, causative *sa*-insertion, potential *re*-insertion, and potential *rare*-insertion all contribute to making their respective morphemes

[11] A more detailed analysis of the *sa*-insertion appears in Okada (2003).

more transparent with clearly distinguishable morphemes. At the same time, they unite the conjugation paradigms of all regular (i.e., consonant and vowel) verbs. Furthermore, these morpheme insertions help to avoid confusion with other verbs, especially transitive verbs that are structurally similar.

Although morpheme insertions in the case of verbs still remain outside mainstream Japanese grammar, they are indisputably on the rise, and appear to be fast becoming an accepted part of the language.

List of abbreviations

ACC	accusative	NMLZ	nominalizer
AUX	auxiliary	NOM	nominative
CAUS	causative	NONP	nonpast
COND	conditional	PASS	passive
CONJ	conjecture	PAST	past
COP	copula	POL	polite
DAT	dative	POT	potential
GEN	genitive	Q	question
HON	honorific	QUOT	quotative
INST	instrumental	TE	*te*-form of the verb
NEG	negative	TOP	topic

References

Hopper, P. J. and E. C. Traugott. 1993. *Grammaticalization*. Cambridge: Cambridge University Press.

Inoue, F. 1998. *Nihongo Wotchingu* (Watching the Japanese Language). Iwanami Shinsho #540. Tokyo: Iwanami Shoten.

Iwasaki, S. 2002. *Japanese*. London Oriental African Linguistics Library, No. 5. Amsterdam & Philadelphia: John Benjamins.

Kinsui, S. 2003. *Ra-nuki Kotoba no Rekishi-teki Kenkyû* (The Historical Research of the *Ra*-deletion). Gengo, *Vol. 4*. Tokyo: Taishukan Shoten.

Komatsu, H. 1999. *Nihongo wa Naze Henka Suru ka* (Dynamics of the Japanese Language: From a Universal Point of View). Tokyo: Kasama Shoin.

Langacker, R. W. 1977. Syntactic Reanalysis. *Mechanisms of Syntactic Change*, ed. C. N. Li, 57-139. Austin: University of Texas Press.

Miyagawa, S. 1999. Causatives. *The Handbook of Japanese Linguistics,* ed. N. Tsujimura, 236-68. Oxford: Blackwell Publishers.

Mizuno, M. 1995. *Kanô Dôshi no Hattatsu to Goyô* (The Development and Misuses of the Potential Verbs). Kyushu Ôtani Kenkyû Kiyô (Kyushu Otani Gakkai), 22:89-98.

Okada, J. 2003. Recent Trends in Japanese Causatives: The *Sa*-insertion Phenomenon. *Japanese/Korean Linguistics, Vol. 12,* ed. W. McClure, 28-39. Stanford: CSLI Publications.

Shibatani, M. 1976a. Causativization. *Syntax and Semantics, Vol. 5: Japanese Generative Grammar*, ed. M. Shibatani, 239-94. New York: Academic Press.

Shibatani, M. 1976b. The Grammar of Causative Constructions: A Conspectus. *Syntax and Semantics, Vol. 6: The Grammar of Causative Constructions,* ed. M. Shibatani, 1-40. New York: Academic Press.

Internet search engine used: www.yahoo.co.jp

From Rhetoric to Grammar: Grammaticalization of Rhetorical Strategies in Korean

SEONGHA RHEE
Hankuk University of Foreign Studies / Stanford University

1. Introduction

In grammaticalization studies there is a general agreement that discourse is where grammaticalization is triggered, or that discourse and grammar are in mutual feeding relationship in their formation (Givón 1979a&b, Lichtenberk 1991, Heine et al. 1991, inter alia). There is even a view that there is no *a priori* grammar: The so-called grammar is nothing but a constant movement in discourse toward a structure, hence the notion, 'the emergent grammar'. Referring to the process whereby previously discourse pragmatic elements become syntactic elements, Sankoff (1977) and Givón (1979b) use the term syntacticization, which may be regarded as a subset of grammaticalization.

If we thus acknowledge the prominent role of discourse in grammar formation and the fact that discourse is the locus of active meaning negotiation filled with various kinds of discourse strategies to fulfill intended persuasion, then we would expect rhetorical strategies to surface as one of the most researched subjects of grammaticalization. However, this type of investigation into the dynamics of linguistic manipulations which gradually become elements of grammar has been largely underrepresented.

The term 'rhetoric' has been used in various senses in different disciplines. Following Leech (1983) and Leith and Myerson (1989), among others, we use the term from a broad pragmatic perspective, i.e. a means of persuasion, producing a social discourse with affective meaning, or a perlocutionary effect on the addressee (Wales 2001). Assuming such a perspective, rhetorical strategies such as rhetorical questions and rhetorical negations, which will be addressed in this paper, are defined as strategic uses of questions, negations, and negative questions just for discourse effect, without soliciting answers or negating certain lexical content of a linguistic form.

There has been some insightful research that illustrated that certain grammatical markers have discourse-pragmatic origins, e.g. Givón (1979) for clause subordinators, and Hopper (1982) and Herring (1988) for perfective aspect markers. Of special importance is Herring (1991), who illustrated that Tamil rhetorical questions grammaticalized into markers of clausal subordination.

This paper focuses on various rhetorical structures that have been grammaticalized, or are grammaticalizing, into various markers of grammatical functions. It deals with question expressions, including interrogative sentential endings and interrogative pronouns; and negation expressions, including negation marker *an* 'not',[1] and some words lexically, i.e. inherently and non-derivationally, marked with the semantics of negation,[2] such as *anita* 'not.be', *anihata* 'not.do', *moluta* 'not.know', *malta* 'not.continue', and *epsta* 'not.exist'. [3]

---

[1]This *an* is related to *anita*. Another negation marker *mos* 'cannot', for unknown reasons, does not display comparable roles in forming grammaticalizing constructions as *an* does.

[2]The notion of lexical negation is hard to define as evidenced by the fact that all the marked items in polar antonymy, as e.g. 'die' (vs. unmarked 'live'), 'absent' (vs. unmarked 'present'), etc., may also qualify as lexical negations at a certain conceptual level, making the selection of these items rather arbitrary. However, these are non-derived lexical items intuitively perceived as prominent negation exemplars in Korean.

[3]The verbal ending *–ta* is the lexicographic device used to indicate that the verb is in its dictionary entry form. Therefore, verb forms may appear in inflected forms of *ani-*, *aniha-*, etc. Abbreviations used here are: Adn: adnominal, Caus: causative; Fut: future, Int: interrogative sentential ending, N: noun, Q: interrogative pronoun, and V: verb.

2. Discourse Markers

The most prominent domain of grammatical functions into which rhetorical strategies are grammaticalized is that of discourse markers including its many subcategories, as shown in (1).

(1)

Function	Form	Source Meaning
Discourse Initiators	issci	Exist?
	isscanha	Not exist?
Topic Presenters	kukey Q-nyamyen	If (you) ask what/why...it is
	Proposition-nyamyen	If you ask whether Proposition
	way N-isscanha	Why, does N not exist?
Pause Fillers	mwelalkka	What should (I) say?
	ku Q-nya	What/why...is it?
	ku Q-latela	What/who...did (they) say?
Mitigators	Q-lalkka	Shall I say what/who...?
	eti	Where?
	mwe	What?
	ettehkey	How?
	moluci	(I) don't know
Attention Attractors	ettay	How is it?
	N-inka?	Is it N?
	N-itenka?	Was it N?
	N-ilkka?	Will it be N?
	way	Why?
	ani	No. / Not so.
Emphaticals	way?	Why?
	eti?	Where?
	kulehkomalko	So and not so.
	kuletamata	So. Not so.
	way anikyesse	Why will it not be?

As seen in the above table, many of these discourse markers have complex internal structures, sometimes containing multiple sentences (see e.g. emphatical *kuletamata*). Synchronically, however, many or most Korean speakers write those multiple word-group items without spacing, which deviates from the National Standard Orthographic Regulation, and reflects the Korean speakers' perception of these units as single items.

Most of these discourse makers make use of rhetorical questions for source constructions, presumably because questions, in general, make strong engaging forces on the addressee. Sometimes questions are used to engage the speaker himself or herself in monologue style in the case of pause fillers and some mitigators. Discourse initiators and topic presenters carry similar functions but they are dissimilar in that the former is usually used to begin an interaction while the latter leads into a smaller-scale thematic unit.

It is interesting to note that some of these forms are not fully unitized as a single word unit but are templates containing a slot as indicated by Q (interrogative pronoun) or N (noun) that allows for insertion of a range of items in the same paradigm. For this reason, the items dealt with here are unlike those addressed in traditional grammaticalization research where highly unitized forms like words or morphemes rather than constructions have been the primary focus.

Some of these discourse markers are formally identical with interrogative pronouns or pronoun-only interrogative sentences. However, these forms are entirely deviant in semantics from the pronominal sources; e.g., mitigators 'where', 'what', and 'how' do not make reference to a space, an entity, or a manner, but instead take the entire proposition as their scope and tone down the assertiveness of the proposition. Likewise, emphatical 'why' and 'where' can also mean 'Absolutely!' and 'Absolutely not!', respectively, instead of their pronominal meanings.

3. Auxiliaries

The next category of grammaticalized function is the auxiliaries, as in (2).

(2)

Function	Form	Source Meaning
Attenuative	V-lkkahata	(I'm) doing '[Question]'
	V-nahata	"
	V-kahata	"
Prohibitive	V-ci malta	Not continue V-ing
	A-e malta	Not continue being A
Determinative	V-ko malta	V and then not continue
	V-koya malta	Only after V-ing and then not continue
Completive	V-ko malta	V and then not continue
	V-koya malta	Only after V-ing and then not continue
Cessative	V-ta malta	Approach V and not continue
	V-taka malta	"

Attenuative auxiliaries invariably contain embedded interrogative clauses. The attenuative illocutionary force comes from the strategy that the speaker's opinion is given as if it is not final and still in the examining or questioning process. The verb *malta* is frequently used for auxiliary formation, where the participating particles, *-ci, -e, -ko,* and *–koya*, play a crucial role in determining the ultimate grammatical function (Rhee 2003). For example, with *-ko*, the isolating 'and', the sense of completion arises from a structure of [V-and.then-not.continue] with the highlighted juncture between two events. Completive and Determinative are closely related not only in form but also in meaning: Completive tends to have no selectional restriction on the subject, whereas Determinative tends to appear with the first person subject, thus encoding the speaker's will to complete an event.

4. Derivational Morphemes

Derivational morphemes consist of adjectivizers and adverbializers. They are all built on the verb *malta* 'not continue'. They take verbs and nouns and transform the constructions into adjectives or adverbs, as shown below.

(3)

Function	Form	Source Meaning
Approximative Adjectivizer	V-lkkamalkkahata	say 'shall I V or not?'
	V-ltusmaltushata	be in state of V-ing and not V-ing
	V-llakmalkakhata	be in alternating state of V-ing and not V-ing
	N-manhalkkahata	say 'shall I be the size of N?'
	Measure.Noun-toylkka malkkahata	say 'shall I become MN or not?'
Approximative Adverbializer	V-lkkamalkka	'Shall I V or not?'
	V-ltusmaltus	In the state of being V or not
	V-llakmallak	In alternating state of V-ing and not V-ing
	V-namana	Either V or not V
	V-nuntwung manuntwung	In state of V-ing and not V-ing
	V-tunmaltun	If V or not V
	V-tuncimaltunci	If V or not V

One interesting aspect of these derivational morphemes is that the speakers attribute not only animacy but also volitional capacity to inanimate sentential subjects. Take the following example.

(4) a. po-i-l-kka-ma-l-kka-ha-nun sem
see-Caus-Fut-Q-not.continue-Fut-Q-say-Adn island
'a barely visible island'

b. 30 acre-toy-l-kka-ma-l-kka-ha-nun swuph
30 acre-become-Fut-Q-not.continue-Fut-Q-say-Adn forest
'a forest that is about 30 acres'

The literal meaning of (4a) is 'an island that says, "Shall I be seen or shall I not continue (to be seen)?"', where the island is conceived of as one that is speaking to itself whether it should be seen or not, thus due to this insular 'indecision' the island is barely visible. Likewise, the approximate nature of the figure in (4b) is also described as if the forest is in indeterminacy as to its intention of assuming a certain size. These are paradigm examples of personification and also instances of subjectification in the sense that the speaker construes the objective reality with more subjective attitude toward the physical world (Traugott and Dasher 2002, Traugott 2003).

Another important aspect of these derivational morphemes is that the two subcategories are intimately related as some of their forms suggest.

When some adverbializers are combined with the verb *hata* 'do/say', they become adjectivizers, which is tantamount to saying that adverbializers are adjectivizers minus their predicating capacity.

5. Connectives

The verb *malta* sometimes develops into connectives with some particles in source construction, as shown in (5).

(5)

Function	Form	Source Meaning
Cessative	V-tamalko V-takamalko	Not continue to V, and "
Protinative	V-camaca	At the moment of V-ing and stopping V-ing
Depreciative	V-kenmalken V-kenamalkena	Whether V or not V "
Exclusive	N-malko	Not continue with N, and

As shown above, four major categories of the connectives are Cessative, meaning ceasing an activity; Protinative, resembling English connective 'as soon as'; Depreciative, signaling that the connected item is of no significance; and Exclusive, meaning that the connected item is to be excluded from consideration. In the case of Cessative, the two forms *-tamalko* and *-takamalko* are synonymous, the only difference being that the former is the more phonologically eroded form of the latter, which is also the case with the two forms of Depreciative connectives.

6. Sentential Endings

The next category is a number of sentential endings including Exclamative, Emphatic, and Mitigative endings, as shown below.

(6)

Function	Form	Source Meaning
Exclamative	N-icanha?	Is it not N?
	N-anya?	Is it not N?
Emphatic	Proposition-i anil swu epsta	There is no way of Proposition not being the case.
	Proposition-ilako haci anhul swu epsta	There is no way of not saying Proposition.
	Proposition-ka aniko mwuesikeyssnunka	Proposition is not the case and what will it be?
	Proposition-aninka	Is Proposition not the case?
	Proposition-anikeyssna	Will Proposition not be the case?
Mitigative	Proposition-i aninka sayngkakhata	(I) think 'Is Proposition not the case?'
	Proposition-i aninka siphta	It seems 'Is Proposition not the case?'
	Proposition-i anhulkka siphta	It seems 'Will Proposition be not the case?'

Most of these forms make use of questions and negations at the same time, and they are all sentence-completing constructions, thus fitting the label 'sentential endings'. When *-anya* is used as a regular negative predicate, the preceding noun normally accompanies a nominative case marker. In the case of Exclamative *-anya*, however, the eroded form is so much fossilized that such a case marker is not allowed to be attached.

These endings comprise highly complex source constructions which are still transparent because they are in the early stage of becoming fixed constructions and have undergone less phonological erosion. This trait is also revealed in the fact that these sentential endings are still subject to further inflection for formality and politeness agreements. It is noteworthy that the emphatic illocutionary force is derived from circumlocution, sometimes involving multiple negations. Rhetorical maneuvers allow even more complex source constructions making use of more negations.

7. Pronouns and Adverbs

The last category is a non-homogeneous group of pronouns and adverbs. The first set of pronouns and adverbs are those developed from question pronouns as in (7).

(7)

Function	Form	Source Meaning	New Meaning
Indefinite Pronouns	nwukwu	who	someone
	nwuka	Who is/does?	someone
	nwukwunka	Who is it?	someone
	nwukwunci	who it is	someone
	nwukwulato	whoever it is	anyone
	mwe	what	something
	mwenka	What is it?	something
	mwenci	what it is	something
	mwelato	whatever it is	anything
Indefinite Adverbs	encey	when	some time
	enceynka	When is it?	some time
	eti	where	somewhere
	etinka	Where is it?	somewhere
	etilonka	To where is it?	to somewhere
	ettehkey	how	somehow
	ettekkey ettehkey	how how	somehow
	waynka	Why is it?	for some reason
	waynci	Why is it?	for some reason

Interrogative pronouns denoting 'who' and 'what' develop into indefinite pronouns; whereas 'when', 'where', and 'how' develop into indefinite adverbs. Furthermore, certain constructions containing 'who' and 'what' develop into indefinite pronouns, whereas those with 'when', 'where', 'how', and 'why' develop into indefinite adverbs. The processes involved in the formation of these two categories are nearly identical. The only difference seems to be the different interrogative pronouns being used.

It is precisely for this reason that this is the area where the boundary of lexicalization and grammaticalization becomes unclear. The items in the single grammatical domain, i.e. interrogative pronouns, undergo seemingly identical processes but produce different end-results in terms of the grammatical categories. In the case of indefinite adverbs, since the source items, i.e. interrogative pronouns, are more grammatical than the target items, the development in this direction is clearly a lexicalization process. In the case of indefinite pronouns, however, the relative degrees of grammaticality between the two categories, i.e. interrogative pronouns and indefinite pronouns, cannot be unequivocally determined. Since the final product belongs to the grammatical category, the process may qualify for grammaticalization. However, from a different perspective stressing that the indefinite pronoun is less abstract than the interrogative pronoun, this process may be argued as an instance of lexicalization. From still another perspective, if the relative degrees of grammaticality of the two categories are thought to be undeterminable, this process may have to remain undefined.

There is another group of adverbs that are developed from the rhetorical constructions as shown in (8).

(8)

Form	**Source Meaning**	**New Meaning**
macimoshay	being unable not to continue	unwillingly
aninkey anila	it is not the case that it is not	truly
kuleci anhato	even if you don't do so	in a timely manner
molukin molato	even if I don't know what I don't know	supposedly
molukin hayto	even if I don't know	supposedly
mwenka molukey	not knowing 'What is it?'	somehow
mwenci molukey	not knowing what it is	somehow
etinci molukey	not knowing where	somehow
etinka molukey	not knowing 'where is it?'	somehow
waynci molukey	not knowing why it is	for some reason
waynka molukey	not knowing 'Why is it?'	for some reason
nammolay	so that others wouldn't know	secretly
halswuepsi	there being no way of doing	helplessly
mwenimwenihayto	even though they say what is, what is	after all

Even though these adverbs look complex in terms of internal structure, they are mostly perceived as single units. Many speakers of Korean tend to write them without internal spaces, even though the orthographic regulations require them; and most of these forms are fossilized to such an extent that they are opaque to most morpho-syntactic operations (cf. 'univerbation' Lehmann 1995[1982]). For example, these forms resist lexical substitutions, and, therefore, we cannot replace the lexical negation word in the construction, such as *moluta* 'not know' and *epsta* 'not exist', with affirmative counterparts, *alta* 'know' and *issta* 'exist', in order to derive expressions of opposite meaning.

The adverbs presented in (8) above show how complex the source structures can be for apparently simple units in synchronic grammar. This compacting process is largely due to frequent uses whereby forms become entrenched. A linguistic form needs to contain a certain amount of novelty to create salience and impose forces on the addressee, but these highly entrenched forms no longer produce such effects. In this sense, these forms may be called dead rhetorical forms.

8. Discussions and Conclusions

The grammaticalization phenomena treated here raise some intriguing issues. The first of these involves intersubjectification. Crosslinguistically, there is a strong tendency for words, particularly in grammaticalization, to acquire subjective, and further intersubjective, meanings over time. Intersubjectivity is closely related to 'face' and 'image needs' and may be most prominently displayed by honorification systems (Traugott and Dasher 2002, Traugott 2003). Korean is a language in which honorification is rigidly grammaticalized, and all sentences or fragments of sentences constituting an utterance must be properly marked according to honorification levels. Rhetorical structures are no exceptions. However, some of these, especially rhetorical questions, appear to be directed to the addressee in form, which, however, are in monologue styles that are marked with [-honorific]. In these cases fully grammaticalized intersubjectivity markers are losing their intersubjective force in the course of grammaticalization, a case of development in the direction opposite to that of wide crosslinguistic attestation.

The second issue concerns the grammar-lexicon continuum. The phenomena illustrated here suggest that grammar and lexicon do not have a distinct boundary between them. A linguistic form fully compositional on the surface may function as a single grammatical item. Furthermore, due to variations among individual speakers, some may use certain emerging forms as grammatical markers while others may consider them still combinatory strings of lexical items. Since rhetorical questions and rhetorical negations are fundamentally discursive and involve large chunks of linguistic strings rather than single words, their grammaticalization phenomena are unavoidably unclear in certain aspects. But at the same time, they effectively show that grammar and lexicon form a continuum rather than exist as two separate entities. Similarly, grammaticalization and lexicalization are not always distinct processes but may be identical in certain cases.

Drawing on exemplars in rhetorical strategies, this paper tried to show how large chunks of discourse materials can gradually move toward grammar, and thus blur the grammar-lexicon distinction. In addition, in cases in which an identical process involving items in the same category may produce items that belong to different categories, we tried to show that the two notions that are traditionally conceived of not only as distinct but sometimes opposite processes, i.e. grammaticalization and lexicalization, may be in fact indistinguishable at least in certain cases.

References

Givón, T. 1979a. *On Understanding Grammar*. New York and San Francisco: Academic Press.

Givón, T. 1979b. From Discourse to Syntax: Grammar as a Processing Strategy. In *Discourse and Syntax,* ed. T. Givón, 81-112. New York: Academic Press.

Heine, B., U. Claudi, and F. Hünnemeyer. 1991. *Grammaticalization: A Conceptual Framework*. Chicago: The University of Chicago Press.

Hopper, P. J. 1982. Aspect between Discourse and Grammar. In *Tense-Aspect: Between Semantics and Pragmatics,* ed. P. J. Hopper, 3-18. Amsterdam: Benjamins.

Hopper, P. J. 1987. Emergent Grammar. *BLS* 13:139-57.

Herring, S. 1988. Aspect as a Discourse Strategy in Tamil. *BLS* 14: 280-292.

Herring, S. 1991. The Grammaticalization of Rhetorical Questions in Tamil. In *Approaches to Grammaticalization,* eds. E. C. Traugott and B. Heine. Vol. 1:253-84. Amsterdam & Philadelphia: Benjamins.

Leech, G. N. 1983. *Principles of Pragmatics*. New York: Longman.

Lehmann, C. 1995[1982]. *Thoughts on Grammaticalization*. Müchen & Newcastle: Lincom Europa.

Leith, D. and G. Myerson. 1989. *The Power of Address: Explorations in Rhetoric*. London: Routledge.

Lichtenberk, F. 1991. On the Gradualness of Grammaticalization. In *Approaches to Grammaticalization,* eds. E. C. Traugott and B. Heine. Vol. I:37-80. Amsterdam & Philadelphia: Benjamins.

Rhee, S. 2003. Particle Selection in Auxiliary Formation in Korean. Paper presented at LASSO 32, Oct. 17-19, University of Texas-Pan American, Edinburg, TX.

Sankoff, G. 1977. Variability and Explanation in Language and Culture: Cliticization in New Guinea Tok Pisin. In *GURT 1977*, ed. M. Saville-Troike, 59-73. Washington: Georgetown University Press.

Traugott, E. C. 2003. From Subjectification to Intersubjectification. In *Motives for Language Change*, ed. Raymond Hickey. 124-39. Cambridge: Cambridge University Press.

Traugott, E. C. and R. Dasher. 2002. *Regularity in Semantic Change*. Cambrige: Cambridge University Press.

Wales, K. 2001. *A Dictionary of Stylistics*. New York: Longman.

Nominalized Predicates as Directives in Japanese Discourse

NINA A. YOSHIDA*
University of California, Los Angeles

1. Introduction

Recent studies (e.g. Clancy, Akatsuka, and Strauss 1997, Akatsuka 1998) have noted the relationship in Japanese between deontic modality and conditionality; namely, that Japanese employs the morphosyntax of conditionals as the conventional way of expressing deontic concepts typically expressed by modal verbs in English.

The present study seeks to point out another grammatical form through which directives may be expressed in Japanese; that is, through a predicate nominalized by the formal nouns (*keishiki meishi*) *no, mono,* and *koto*, followed by the copula *da*.[1] The following are a few examples:[2]

---

*I wish to thank Professors Noriko Akatsuka, Shoichi Iwasaki, and Robert S. Kirsner for their invaluable comments and suggestions on earlier versions of this paper.

[1] In colloquial or informal speech, *no* and *mono* are often contracted to *n* and *mon*, respectively, resulting in the semifixed or 'grammaticalized' forms *-nda* and *-monda*.

[2] The following abbreviations are used in this paper:

ACC: Accusative; COP: Copula; COND: Conditional; GEN: Genitive; IMP: Imperative; NOM: Nominative; NPST: Nonpast; TOP: Topic

(1) Mother: *Akai hoo o taberu* ***no***.[3]
red ones ACC eat:NPST **NO**
'(You're) supposed to eat the red ones./Eat the red ones.'
(2) Kitamura: *Koo yuu toki ni wa tasukeau* ***monda***.[4]
like this times in TOP help out:mutual:NPST **MONO** COP
'In times like these, (we) should help each other out.'
(3) Commander: *Kisamatati wa happyakukiro no bakudan ni narikiru* ***kotoda***.[5]
you all NOM 800 kilogram GEN bombs into completely
become:NPST **KOTO** COP
'Turn yourselves completely into 800 kilogram bombs.'

In light of the fact that Japanese already possesses a highly grammaticized system for expressing deontic modality (i.e. conditionals), the occurrence of such utterances in authentic spoken discourse gives rise to two questions: (i) What specific features of nominalized predicates lend themselves to receiving the deontic reading in certain contexts? (ii) What are the (semantic and pragmatic) differences between expressing the same deontic message as a nominal as opposed to a conditional, or simple imperative?

By analyzing the form-function relationship in Japanese between nominalized predicates[6] and their interpretations in various discourse contexts, this study aims to shed some light on the semantics and pragmatics of deontically modalized utterances expressed in this manner.

2. Nominalized Predicates and Modality

Nominalized predicates that occupy the 'comment' position of topic-comment sentences[7] have been the subject of a number of past studies (Teramura 1984, Agetsuma 1991, Tsubone 1994), particularly with respect to their modal functions.

The current study proposes that the structure's striking formal semblance to the commentary predicate—namely the *B (da)* portion of a A *wa*

[3]Data source: an audiotaped mother-child interaction.

[4]Data source: the TV movie *'Kita no Kuni kara: '83 Fuyu'* ('From the Northern Country: Winter '83'), 1983. Tokyo: Fuji T.V.

[5]Data source: the movie *'Aa, Dooki no Sakura'* ('Oh, (We are) Comrades of a Shared Destiny') 1959. Tokyo: Toei Company.

[6]By 'nominalized predicates', I am referring to constructions in which the formal nouns *no, mono*, and *koto* are functioning as complementizers, and correspond to the syntactic pattern of *no, mono*, and *koto* preceded by a clause or phrase in the *rentaikei* 'attributive form' and followed by an optional copula *da*.

[7]Although usually employed in specific reference to an established unit of written data, the term 'sentence' is used generically here to refer synonymously to 'utterance' in spoken data.

B *(da)*[8] type sentence, where the propositional content of this predicate has been made 'nonchallengeable'[9] through its nominalization[10], and where *no, mono,* and *koto* take on a 'nonreferential'[11] reading—that these are the foremost syntactic factors contributing to such pragmatic capabilities. The nominalized predicate takes the propositional contents of what appears, superficially, to be an objectivized event or state, and repackages it as either a *no, mono,* or *koto* in indication of how these contents are to be received. It is this repackaged proposition, made nonchallengeable through its nominalization, and embellished with the speaker's attitudinal stance through his choice of *no, mono,* or *koto*, which is then presented to the hearer when a *no(da), mono(da), koto(da),* or nonreferential type nominal predicate, is uttered.

I further suggest that this attitudinal stance (of the speaker) derives itself from the underlying meanings *no, mono,* and *koto* possess as nominals in this construction. Next, I present what these semantics are, and how the different attitudinal stances arise and are inferenced from them.

3. The Semantics of *No*, *Mono*, and *Koto*

Grammatically speaking, *no* is generally inserted as an associative particle between two noun phrases to mark that a relationship of modifier-modified exists between them. *No* also functions as an indefinite pronoun. In this use, *no* functions as a substitute for a noun whose referent is clear and anaphorically recoverable from the discourse or situational context. *No*, together with *koto*, are also the most commonly recognized nominalizers in Japanese. Although their uses are mutually interchangeable in many cases,

---

[8]The copula *da* is enclosed in parentheses to indicate that it is an optional element in this construction. I will be taking the view that *da* encodes an additional feature here that is compatible with, but not essential to the topic-comment (i.e. A *wa* B) type utterance; namely, that its overt use marks the speaker's explicit assertion of his certainty in his knowledge or his belief in his affirmative judgment about the truth of the sentential content so marked--what Narahara (2002) terms the 'anti-ignorative mode' (Narahara 2002: 163-6).

[9]As initially noted by Givon (1982), the propositional contents of a clause modifying a nominal element have been shown cross-linguistically to be 'nonchallengeable', or shielded from challenge (Givon 1982: 100).

[10]Iwasaki (1985) claims that the discourse-cohesive powers of the nominalized predicate *n(o)da* are a derivational outcome of the clause's structural similarity to a relative clause, and suggests this stems from the 'nonchallengeable' property of the propositional content of its modifying clause (Iwasaki 1985: 128).

[11]Based on Agetsuma (1991), I use the term 'referential' to refer to 'regular' nominalized predicates, where the nominal element serving as the head noun retains its nominal status as the referential object of the *wa*-marked topic, and 'nonreferential' for those which have become formulaic or grammaticalized to the extent that the head noun has lost its nominal status and bears only a modal meaning.

as pointed out in Akatsuka-McCawley (1978), *no* tends to be used when the nominalized clause expresses a directly perceivable event (e.g. *Watasi wa zibun ga furueteiru no/*koto o kanzita*. 'I felt my body trembling.')[12] Thus, based on these three functions, I propose that the morpheme *no* semantically signals the existence of some anaphorically recoverable referent or associative relationship as existing between the element preceding *no* with something that is contextually inferable. It is this inherent 'meaning' of *no* which is being manipulated by the speaker to perform its host of pragmatic functions.

Roughly speaking, the formal nouns *mono* and *koto* express the meaning 'thing' of English. Reference grammars for students of Japanese commonly explain the choice between them as being governed by the opposing semantic notions of 'concrete' versus 'abstract' (e.g. McGloin 1989), or 'tangible' vs. 'intangible' (e.g. Makino and Tsutsui 1989). Teramura (1981) insightfully claims that *mono* most typically signals an object, or a category thereof, possessing some type of physical concreteness which can be perceived by one of the five bodily senses. Moreover, *mono*'s meaning also encompasses those phenomena which one can sense or perceive psychologically (e.g. *tanosimi* 'enjoyment').

Based on such past accounts, I propose the following core meanings for *mono* and *koto*: *Mono* signals an existence that is 'sensorily' perceptible (i.e. through the bodily senses of sight, smell, sound, taste, and touch—as well as one's inner state experiences, such as pain, hunger, emotions, etc.); hence, *mono* is indicative of a physically perceived, and by extension of this notion, a 'nonrationalized' experience, an existence which can essentially be directly sensed without the aid or use of one's mind and its rationalizing powers. In contrast, *koto*, refers to an intellectually or cognitively perceived existence. This is to say, marking an existence as *koto* signals that it will require processing within one's mental faculties and that one's powers of rationalization must be called in to enable this *koto* to become perceptible. Thus, *koto* may be termed an indicator of a 'mental/rationalized experience' to be conceived, or sensed indirectly within the mind. I hypothesize that these opposing semantics of 'physically sensed/unrationalized' existence versus 'cognitively conceived/rationalized' existence are the key, definitive features distinguishing *mono* from *koto* in instances when they are to take on a referential reading.

4. The Deontic Reading of Nominalized Predicates

As pointed out by Lyons (1977), when we impose upon someone the obligation to perform (or to refrain from performing) a particular act, we are

[12] Example adapted from Akatsuka 1978: 181.

describing the desirable results that will obtain if the act in question is performed (Lyons 1977: 823). Deontic necessity, moreover, typically proceeds or derives from some source or cause. If we recognize that we are obliged to perform some act, then we usually acknowledge that someone or something is responsible for our obligation (Lyons 1997: 824).

Likewise, the deontic interpretation of predicates nominalized by *no, mono,* or *koto* typically emerges (i) when the clause modifying *no, mono,* or *koto* contains a verb with nonpast inflection (i.e. future) denoting an agent-controllable action, and (ii) the utterance containing this nominalized predicate is directed toward an overt or implied second-person referent. The fact that the propositional content expressed by the modifying clause has been made nonchallengeable through its nominalization is what syntactically imbues this construction with the illocutionary force of a directive. The speaker's embellishment of this nominalized clause with the choice of either *no, mono,* or *koto* functions not just to indicate to the hearer that he has an obligation to carry out the designated action, but to direct him to the authoritative 'source' or basis behind why he is obligated to perform it. Hence, I claim that the function of *no, mono,* or *koto* in a nonreferential nominalized predicate, when employed in this directive sense, is to denote the existence of this authoritative 'voice' behind utterances so marked.

I further suggest that the differences in the type of authoritative source they each reference derive themselves from the degree of epistemic truth value, and thus deontic necessity, accorded to an existence marked as either a *no, mono,* or *koto*. Moreover, this 'existence = obligation' interpretation arises in part as a result of the metaphorical extension (i.e. SPACE > TIME) of the original, 'core' meanings of *no*, *mono*, and *koto* as nominals. Namely, the semantics signaled by them 'shifts' by way of metaphorical inferencing from denoting an existence with a spatial orientation, to referencing a basis for an obligation with a temporal orientation. It is the synergistic combination of such syntactic and semantic components which results in the strong pragmatic force or illocutionary 'impact' of the nominalized predicate employed as a directive.

In the following, I present a contextualized analysis of directive tokens of *no(da), mono(da)*, and *koto(da)*, as they occur in authentic spoken Japanese discourse.[13] By doing so, I wish to illustrate how the pragmatic effects conveyed by these three nominalized predicate constructions vary by

---

[13]The data tokens for the present analysis were derived from spoken discourse data collected from popular Japanese television dramas and movies that depict the common superior-subordinate type relationships in Japanese society (e.g. police officer-suspect, teacher-student, *sempai* 'senior'-*koohai* 'junior') where directives are most typically found to be issued.

virtue of their formal differences and how they are borne out within the actual context of discourse.

5. Directive uses of *no(da)* in Japanese discourse

As stated previously, referential *no* signals the existence of some anaphorically recoverable referent, or that some associative relationship exists between the element preceding *no* with something that is contextually inferable. In the nonreferential function, *no* marks a propositional content which finds the basis of its validity in a prior context which the hearer can access or identify through the one in which it occurs.

Accordingly, when the speaker marks a clause denoting the performance of a future act with *no*, he is presenting the obligation the hearer has toward carrying out the designated act as finding its grounds in the past (i.e. a prior context). Namely, the existence of this obligation is true and compelling for the hearer because it is linked to and backed by this anaphorically identifiable 'basis'. Frequently, this is a bare imperative conveying the same directive which had been uttered in the discourse context immediately prior to *no(da)*'s occurrence, tokens of which are provided below. In (4), the suspect, Nakao, is holding a man hostage at gunpoint, and threatening the police to move more quickly in meeting his demands if they wish to prevent him from harming the hostage, whereas in (5), the detective, Takami, is attempting to stop the suspect, Nakao, from harming the hostage:

(4) Nakao: *Hayaku siro!* 'Hurry up/Move (it),
quickly do: IMP
→ *Hayaku suru* ***nda***. 'Move (it)!'
quickly do:NPST **NO** COP

(5) Takami: *Nakao-san yamero*, 'Stop (it), Mr. Nakao,'
(name)-Mr. quit:IMP
→ *Yameru* ***nda***[14] 'Stop (it)!'
quit:NPST **NO** COP

As seen above, when two imperatives are uttered in sequence, a common pattern found in actual discourse is for the first to be in the imperative form, immediately followed up by a nominalization of it with *no(da)*. The desirable action to be performed is introduced into the discourse first as a directive taking the imperative inflection, and once the knowledge of its desirability has been 'established' in this way, the speaker then employs

[14] Data source for (4) and (5): The Japanese TV drama series '*Hamidasi Keezi: Joonetu-kee*' ('Maverick Detective: Passionate Series'), Episode 8: 2002. Tokyo: T.V. Asahi

no(da) to ‘remind’ the hearer that the reasons for the action’s obligation are now known to him; hence, by citing the basis of its validity as recoverable from the prior context, the use of *no(da)* serves to reinforce upon the hearer the necessity of his carrying out this action.[15]

The *no(da)* construction, however, can often be found to mark directives which have no prior mention in the discourse by another imperative. In such cases, by employing *no(da)*, the speaker is presenting the obligatory act named in the nominalized clause as having a basis which is known to the hearer by its anaphoric recoverability from the context. In (6) below, the detective, Takami, has received a radio dispatch from police headquarters that the suspect, Yûta, has kidnapped a female office worker. Takami drives over to the apartment of Yûta’s girlfriend, Hitomi, and knocks on her door. When Hitomi answers the door, the following exchange ensues:

(6) 1.	Takami:	*Yuuta ga*	‘(It) appears Yûta
		matui no kaisya no	has kidnapped
		ooeru o	an office worker
		yuukai-sita rasii.	at Matsui’s company.’
2.	Hitomi:	(look of shock)	
3.	Takami:	*Denwa ga attara,*	‘If you get a phone call,
		phone NOM exist:COND	
		zisyu suru yoo-ni	tell (Yûta) without fail
		surrender:NPST so that	
	→	*kanarazu iu* ***nda.***	to turn himself in.’
		without fail say:NPST **NO** COP	
		Ii na.	‘Understand/Alright?’
4.	Hitomi:	(nods reluctantly)	

The propositional content *zisyu suru yooni kanarazu iu* (‘to tell [him] without fail to turn [him]self in’) is presented with *no(da)* by the speaker (Takami) to mark that there exist reasons linked to a prior context which obligate the hearer (Hitomi) to carry out this act, and that these are known to her.[16] Hence, her awareness of it is what obligates her to do so.

When the reasons for the necessity of the act are not anaphorically recoverable from the prior linguistic context, *no(da)* functions in appealing to

---

[15]It should be noted, however, that its utterance in a previous context alone is not what serves to establish its obligatoriness to the hearer. The obligation arises from the context with which it is associated: namely, that the imperative was initially uttered by an authoritative figure (e.g. a police officer), and thus reflects the will of someone whom the hearer recognizes in that context as having the power or authority to impose this will upon him.

[16]Namely, that she has been informed by an authoritative source (i.e. a police detective) in a prior discourse context (i.e. line 1) that Yûta has committed a criminal act (i.e. kidnapping), and as Yûta’s girlfriend, she should have Yûta’s best interests in mind.

the hearer that it is identifiable from the extralinguistic one, as seen in (7) below. As the detective, Takami, turns to leave, Hitomi's cell phone rings. Judging from her nervous looks, Takami figures out the caller is Yûta, takes the phone away from Hitomi, and begins speaking to Yûta.

(7) 1.	Yûta:	*Dare da, omae.*	'You— who are you?'
2.	Takami:	*Keezi no takami da.*	'I'm Takami, a detective.'
		Yuuta,	'Yûta,
		moo baka-na mane wa	stop your foolish actions.'
		already foolish act TOP	
	→	*yameru* ***nda***.[17]	
		quit:NPST **NO** COP	

In line 2 above, the detective Takami employs *no(da)* in an attempt to make Yûta see that the necessity of refraining from his intended actions is something that he must surely be aware of by virtue of his knowledge of what constitutes (or doesn't constitute) acceptable conduct in society.

From this example, it can be seen that the decision of whether to mark an obligatory act and its basis as 'known/identifiable' to the hearer with *no(da)* is a choice based on the speaker's subjective judgement. The actual discourse context may reveal that the knowledge is in fact not shared. However, the speaker's use of *no(da)* shows that, within the context of this particular discourse and among its particular participants, it is he who has the authority to render this judgement and herein lies the authoritative 'force' or impact of directives delivered employing this morphosyntactic format.

6. Directive uses of *mono(da)* in Japanese discourse.

It was proposed that 'physically sensed/unrationalized' existence versus 'cognitively conceived/rationalized' existence are the opposing semantics distinguishing *mono* from *koto* when they are to take on a referential reading. When *mono* receives a nonreferential reading, its semantics 'shifts' by way of metaphorical inferencing (i.e. SPACE > TIME) from denoting an entity with a fixed spatial orientation to that of a temporal one. Accordingly, when employed in the *mono(da)* construction, *mono* is reinterpreted from denoting an existence whose dimensions remain constant in space, to a proposition whose validity remains constant or has endured throughout time; namely, a general, universal, or consensual 'truth'.

Thus, when the speaker marks a clause denoting the performance of a future act with *mono*, he is presenting the obligation the hearer has toward

[17] Data source for (6) and (7): The Japanese TV drama series '*Hamidasi Keezi: Joonetu-kee*' ('Maverick Detective: Passionate Series'), Episode 1: 2002. Tokyo: T.V. Asahi

carrying out the designated act as finding its grounds in a general norm that has persisted throughout time. Hence, the existence of the obligation is true and compelling for the hearer because it corresponds to what has been traditionally and socially regarded as proper, natural, or normal behavior by others. The truth or legitimacy behind a *mono*-marked existence (i.e. obligation) is something to be accepted 'as is', without any attempt to rationalize the logical reasoning behind its necessity; hence, it represents something that appeals to 'common sense'.

The following token of *mono(da)* was taken from the long running television drama and movie series *'Kita no Kuni kara'* ('From the Northern Country').[18] It finds Gorô toiling away in knee-deep winter snow, trying to lay out piping for a waterway system he has designed to direct water from a nearby river to the log cabin where he and his two small children currently live without electricity or running water. An elderly neighbor (Kasamatsu) stops by to see what Gorô is doing. Since his house has access to both tap water and a T.V., he offers to put Gorô in contact with a town official to get water piped to his cabin, but Gorô refuses his offer, saying that he will manage fine on his own resources. This results in the exchange below:

(8) 1. Kasamatsu:	*Kodomo wa*	'(Your) kids
	terebi o mitagatteru.	want to watch T.V.'
	Asu wa oomisoka da.	'Tomorrow is New Years eve.'
	Uti e yokose.	'Send them over to our place.'
2. Gorô:	*Sore wa doomo.*	'Thank you for (the offer).'
	Demo kodomo to	'But I've (already) discussed
	soodan-sitemasu	(it) with the kids.'
3. Kasamatsu:	*Goroo*	'Gorô.'
4. Gorô:	*Hai.*	'Yes?'
5. Kasamatsu:	*Hito no kooi wa,*	'You should graciously accept,
	people GEN goodwill TOP	
→	*arigataku ukeru* ***monda****.*	the goodwill of others.'
	gratefully receive:NPST **MONO** COP	
6. Gorô:	*Hai.*	'I see.'
	(bows head)[19]	

[18] As its name indicates, the series depicts the experiences of a male protagonist (Gorô) who, after a bitter divorce and custody battle, takes his two young children away from the modern city life they knew in Tokyo, to a rustic and austere one in a rural farming town on the outskirts of Furano, Hokkaido. The town's residents are few, but its community is tightknit, and live according to the rules and traditions established by their predecessors.

[19] Data source: The Japanese TV drama series: '*Kita no Kuni kara*' ('From the Northern Country'), Episode 6: 1982. Tokyo: Fuji T.V.

In terms of pragmatics, a directive delivered with *mono(da)* is closer to a strong suggestion than an imperative. It expresses what has been regarded throughout time by others as the proper or normal behavior for a given situation, and by presenting this 'model' before the hearer, strongly urges him to follow suit. The utterer of a *mono(da)* directive must therefore be someone who has the authority to acknowledge or identify what constitutes the norm in the community he is representing. Thus, by implication, this individual must necessarily be someone of greater superiority in age or experience than his hearer.

7. Directive uses of *koto(da)* in Japanese discourse.

It was previously claimed that the semantics of referential *koto* denote a 'cognitively conceived/rationalized' existence. It was further suggested that when *koto* takes on a nonreferential interpretation as in the *koto(da)* construction, metaphorical inferencing[20] causes it to take on the extended meaning of connoting a proposition that only comes into existence at the specific instance of its conception; hence, it indicates a 'particular truth', or one whose validity applies only to a specific time or situation.

Accordingly, when the speaker marks a clause denoting the performance of a future act with *koto*, he is presenting the obligation the hearer has toward carrying out the designated act as finding its basis in something that was conceived within the speaker's mind. Thus, it sends the message that the existence of this obligation is true and valid because its necessity is known solely to the speaker or 'source' of the utterance. In this sense, a directive marked with *koto(da)* stands in contrast to *no(da)* in terms of its implications that the basis for its obligation is known or identifiable only to the speaker (and not the hearer) at the time of its utterance.

The following exchange takes place between a newly hired, middle school teacher (Kinpati-sensee) and his student (Imai). The teacher has just finished passing back the graded tests his students recently took in class:

(9)1. Kinpati:	*Iidesu ka.*	'Listen up.'
	Zyuken wa kimitati no	'The entrance exams are
	mondai-na-n da kara	a concern for all of you,
	itteokimasu kedo,	so I'll say (this) to you (now),
	sikasi	but…
	kono teedo no tesuto de	with scores of less than 60 pts.
	rokuzyutten ika de	on a test of this level,
	hutuu kookoo	those of you aspiring to

[20] Okamoto (2003) claims that the reanalysis of *koto*, from complementizer to sentence-final particle, involved metonymic processes.

	siboo no mono wa=	(get into) regular (academic)
	high schools...'	
2. Imai:	*=Doo naru-n desu ka?*	'What'll happen (to us)?'
3. Kinpati:	*Sore wa,*	'That is (something)
	that TOP	
	zibun de yoku	(you) need to think over well
	self INST well	
→	*kangaetemiru* ***koto***.[21]	yourselves (to find out).'
	try thinking:NPST **KOTO**	

In line 3, Kinpati-sensee's directive to Imai is marked with *koto(da)*[22] to present the basis for the necessity of performing the designated act (i.e. *zibun de yoku kangaetemiru* 'to try thinking [it] over well by yourself') as something known only to the speaker (Kinpati-sensee) at the time of its utterance. *Mono(da)* would be inappropriate here, since the necessity came into existence in its applicability to this particular situation; it does not refer to a persisting norm or 'truth' applicable (to students like Imai) in general.

8. Conclusion

This study has proposed that directives expressed as nominalized predicates present the authoritative 'source' or basis for the hearer's obligation to perform the designated act as extending beyond the simple will of the speaker at speech time. The speaker's choice of employing *no, mono,* or *koto* in such directives functions to further characterize this basis in the following ways:

- *No(da)* marks it as assumed known or accessible to both the speaker and hearer (i.e. established in a past context, but recoverable through the present one).
- *Mono(da)* marks it as having a validity which has endured throughout time (i.e. represents a generally accepted norm or truth-by-consensus).

21Data source: The Japanese TV drama series: 'Sannen Biigumi: Kinpati Sensee' ('Mr. Kinpatchi: Teacher of 9th Grade, Class B'), Series 5, Episode 1: 1980. Tokyo: Tokyo Broadcasing Services

22Kinpati-sensee is a male teacher, and in terms of established hierarchical relationships in Japanese society, is in a position of superiority vis-a-vis his students, particularly in a classroom setting. However, in this particular context, he is also a relative newcomer to the school, and the class he has been assigned to has a reputation for rebelling against authority. Therefore, I suggest that the (optional) da has been omitted here to avoid marking for an explicit assertion by Kinpati-sensee of his certainty in his knowledge, and thus to strategically 'tone-down' the effects of a direct expression of his authority as the source of this knowledge.

- *Ko(da)* marks it as known or identifiable to the speaker (but the not hearer).

The ability to cite this source or basis, in turn, serves to mark its user (i.e. the speaker) as standing in a position of higher authority than the hearer. For this reason, a directive delivered with *no(da), mono(da) or koto*(da) may in certain situations present a 'stronger' or more compelling argument for the hearer's compliance to it than one in the form of a bare imperative or conditional.

References

Agetsuma, Y. 1991. Zissituteki 'mono' to keisikiteki yoohoo to no imiteki tunagari ('The semantic link between "things" of substance and their formal uses'). *Toohoku Daigaku Bungakubu Nihongogakka Ronshuu* 1: 2-11.

Akatsuka, N. and A. Tsukamoto. 1998. *Modaritii to hatsuwa kooi* ('Modality and speech acts'). Tokyo: Kenkyuusha.

Akatsuka-McCawley, N. 1978. Another look at *no*, *koto*, and *to*: Epistemology and complementizer choice in Japanese. *Problems in Japanese Syntax and Semantics,* ed. by J. Hinds and I. Hayward, 178-212. Tokyo: Kaitakusha.

Clancy, P. M., N. Akatsuka and S. Strauss. 1997. Deontic Modality and Conditionality in Discourse: A Cross-linguistic Study of Adult Speech to Young Children. *Directions in Functional Linguistics*, ed. A. Kamio, Amsterdam and Philadelphia: John Benjamins Publishing Company.

Givon, T. 1982. Evidentiality and Epistemic Space. *Studies in Language* 6:23-49.

Iwasaki, S. 1985. Cohesion, nonchallengeablility and the n-desu clause in Japanese spoken discourse. *Journal of Asian Culture* 9:125-140

Lyons, J. 1977. Semantics Vol. II Cambridge/Great Britain: Cambridge University Press.

Makino, S & Tsutsui, M.. 1986. *A Dictionary Of Basic Japanese Grammar*. Tokyo: The Japan Times.

McGloin, N. H. 1989. *A Student's Guide to Japanese Grammar*. Tokyo: Taishuukan Publishing Company.

Narahara, T. 2002. *The Japanese Copula: Forms and Functions*. New York: Palgrave Macmillan.

Okamoto, S. 2003. Metonymy and Pragmatic Inference in the Functional Reanalysis of Grammatical Morphemes in Japanese. *Metonymy and Pragmatic Inferencing*, eds. K. Pather and L. Thornburg, 205-220. Amsterdam and Philadelphia: John Benjamins Publishing Company.

Teramura, H. 1981. Mono to koto. ('*Mono* and *koto*'). *Kokugogaku ronsyuu: Festscrift for Dr. Kazuo Mabuchi*. 743-62.

Teramura, H. 1984. *Nihongo no sintakusu to imi* ('Japanese syntax and semantics')., vol. 2. Tokyo: Kuroshio Publishers.

Tsubone, Y. 1994. 'Monoda' ni kansuru ichi koosatsu. ('A study of *monoda*') *Nihongo Kyoiku* 84: 65-77.

Part V

Pragmatics, Discourse and Sociolinguistics

The Pragmatics of Japanese Sentence-final Forms

HARUKO MINEGISHI COOK
University of Hawaii at Manoa

1. Introduction

In Japanese, sentence-final forms are one of the major resources that mark gender differences. A number of researchers who have studied gendered expressions in Japanese have discussed sentence-final forms (e.g. Ide 1982; Kitagawa 1977; McGloin 1986, 1990; Okamoto 1995; Reynolds 1985; Shibamoto 1985; Uyeno 1971). In these studies, certain sentence-final forms are judged as feminine, certain others, as masculine, and some, as neutral. Such judgments are generally based on native speakers' intuition as well as by observation of usage. However, there have not been any systematic accounts as to why certain collocations of sentence-final forms sound more feminine and others, more masculine. This paper examines collocations of sentence-final forms, and proposes that what is responsible for the gendered speech associated with sentence-final forms is the grammatical categories of nominals and verbals and their intensifiers. This systematically accounts for why certain sentence-final forms in Japanese sound more feminine and certain others more masculine.[1]

[1] The present analysis is based on standard Japanese.

2. Japanese Sentence-final Particles and Gender

Sentence-final particles in Japanese provide metapragmatic instructions as to how the referential message is to be interpreted in speech context. The particles frequently discussed in the literature are *ne*, *yo*, *no*, *wa*, *zo* and *ze*. The particle *ne* is primarily a marker of the speaker's affective stance (see Cook 1992). Other scholars contrast the particles *ne* and *yo*, claiming that while *yo* is a marker of completeness, *ne* is a marker of 'incompleteness' of the speaker's information (Katagiri 1995, Kinsui 1993) or of the speaker's authority in relation to other participants (Morita 2002). Thus, *ne* elicits cooperation from the addressee whereas *yo* asserts the speaker's information or authority. *No* is a nominalizer but it also functions as a sentence-final particle. It indexes a fact (e.g. Aoki 1986) or information accessible to the speaker and the addressee and/or the speaker's group (Cook 1990). The particles *wa*, *no*, *zo*, and *ze* are considered to be directly linked to gendered speech. The particles *wa* and *no* are typically classified as female particles, and the particles *zo* and *ze*, as male particles (Ide 1982; Kitagawa 1977; McGloin 1986, 1990; Okamoto 1995; Shibamoto 1985). The particles *ne* and *yo*, besides the pragmatic functions mentioned above, are often considered to be neutral. However, Shibamoto (1985: 62) makes the following observation:

> Particles used by both men and women are *yo* and *ne*. Whereas men use these forms directly after plain and polite forms of the copula, adjectives and verbs, women are limited to the following combinations of forms:

(1)
$$\text{V} + \begin{Bmatrix} \text{no} \\ \text{wa} \end{Bmatrix} + \text{(yo) (ne)}$$

$$\text{N} + \begin{Bmatrix} \text{(na) no (yo) (ne)} \\ \text{(yo) (ne)} \end{Bmatrix}$$

Shibamoto's observation can be paraphrased as follows: When the plain form of a verb is directly followed by *ne* and/or *yo*, the sequence sounds masculine. In order to soften the strong force of the sequence Verb + *ne* and/or *yo*, the particle *wa* or *no* must be inserted after the verb. When a noun is directly followed by *ne* and/or *yo*, the sequence sounds feminine.[2]

Shibamoto's observation suggests that the categories Noun and Verb have something to do with sentence-final forms sounding either feminine or masculine. Below, I will i) investigate the pragmatic properties of nominals and verbals, ii) propose two types of relations that hold between the nomi-

---

[2] In the sequence, N + (na) no (yo) (ne), *na* is a form of the copula *da*. Since the copula is a type of verb, this sequence is analyzed as $[\text{N} + \text{(na)}]_{\text{V}}$ + no (yo) (ne). Thus it is identical with V + no (yo) (ne).

nal or verbal and the particles, and iii) relate the present analysis to the gendered-speech analysis in Japanese discussed in the literature.

3. Pragmatic Functions of Nominals and Verbals

In this section, I argue that nominals and verbals have their own pragmatic force:the softer effect of Noun + *ne* and/or *yo* comes from the weaker pragmatic force of nominals, and the forceful effect of Verb + *ne* and/or *yo* comes from the stronger pragmatic force of verbals.

Nouns and verbs are universal and fundamental grammatical categories (Langacker 1991). A number of linguists have suggested that verbs prototypically express actions and nouns prototypically express objects (Bates and MacWhinney 1982; Givón 1984; Hopper and Thompson 1984; Langacker 1991; Lyons 1968; Maynard 1997).[3] For example, Bates and MacWhinney suggest that prototypically nouns are visible objects and verbs are concrete, kinetic, visible actions. Givón characterizes nouns as 'time-stable' and verbs as 'non-time-stable'. These characterizations are based on the referential functions of nouns and verbs, i.e. what type of entities nouns typically refer to and what type of entities verbs typically refer to. It has been claimed that in addition to such referential functions, nouns and verbs have pragmatic functions as well. Nouns and verbs index the manner in which something is said. Pragmatic meaning is not just something peripheral added to referential meaning. It is an equally important part of the meaning of nouns and verbs. In English, nominalizations indicate a more formal use of language (Brown and Fraser 1979). For example, to say 'I am surprised at your early arrival' is more formal and impersonal than to say 'I am surprised that you arrived early'. Not only the nominalization of verbs but also expressions with a noun are more formal than expressions involving a verb. For example, 'No smoking' is more often used than 'Don't smoke' in formal situations. In Japanese, nominal expressions are more polite too. Expressions involving a nominalizer, e.g. *tabako o suwanai koto* 'no smoking' and the Chinese compound noun *kinen* 'no smoking' are more polite than expressions involving a verb, *tabako o suuna* or *tabako o sutte wa ikenai* 'Don't smoke'. Brown and Levinson (1987: 208) point out, '... the more nouny an expression, the more removed an actor is from doing or feeling or being something.'[4] Maynard states that nominalized sentences are descriptively distant, for they form an abstract conceptual unit. In other words, nouns are more remote and indirect than verbs in general. Thus, the pragmatic force of nouns is weaker than that of verbs. In Brown and Levinson's terms, nouns are more 'negatively polite' because of their weak pragmatic force.

---

[3] While Langacker (1991:60) accepts these prototypical values for nouns and verbs, he also argues for universally schematic values for these categories.

[4] By 'actor', Brown and Levinson mean a speech act participant and not an agent in an event.

The case of Japanese nominal and verbal forms is consistent with Brown and Levinson's proposal, especially when they are followed by the sentence-final particles *ne* and/or *yo*.[5] Consider examples (2) to (6), in which the sentence-final particles *ne*, *yo,* or *yo ne* follow a nominal or a verbal. Nominals include nouns, adjectival nominals and nominalizers such as *no, wake, koto*, and *mono*. Verbals include verbs and adjectives.

<u>Nominals</u>

(2) Noun
[Hon]$_N$ ne/yo/yo ne
book PART
'It is a book *ne/yo/yo ne*.'

(3) Adjectival nominal
[Genki]$_N$ ne/yo/yo ne
healthy PART
'I/you/he/she/we/they are fine *ne/yo/yo ne*.'

(4) Nominalizer (*no*)
[Iku no]$_N$ ne/yo/yo ne
go NOM PART
'I/you/he/she/we/they will go *ne/yo/yo ne*.'

<u>Verbals</u>

(5) Verbs
[Iku]$_V$ ne/yo/yo ne
go PART
'I/you/he/she/we/they will go *ne/yo/yo ne*.'

(6) Adjective
[Atsui]$_V$ ne/yo/yo ne.
hot PART
'It's hot *ne/yo/yo ne*.'

In line with Shibamoto's observation, the examples involving a nominal ((2), (3), and (4)) consistently sound softer than examples involving a verbal ((5) and (6)). Hence, examples (2), (3) and (4) sound more feminine than examples (5) and (6). In particular, examples (4) and (5) are identical except for the presence or absence of the nominalizer *no*. In the literature, the nominalizer *no* is considered to be a female particle when the copula *da* does not immediately follow it (McGloin 1990). The fact that the sentences in (2), (3), and (4) all sound softer as opposed to sentences in (5) and (6) indicates that the nature of 'nouniness' makes examples (2) (3) and (4) sound softer. The soft effect of the particle *no* derives from the fact that *no* is a type of nominal. Thus, it is clear that the distinction between nominals and verbals is responsible for indexing gender differences. The particles *yo* and *ne* make the contrast in pragmatic force between nominals and verbals more noticeable but do not reverse their pragmatic force.

---

[5] When a particle such as *ne* or *yo* follows a nominal or verbal element, the pragmatic force of the nominal or verbal becomes more noticeable. The particles seem to highlight the pragmatic effect of nominals and verbals.

The pragmatic meanings of each element in examples (2) to (6) are added to one another. For example, the collocation *yo ne* is used to seek a cooperative relation with the addressee or confirmation from the addressee (*ne*) while making an assertion or pointing out some information to the addressee (*yo*). The collocation *no yo ne* points out (*yo*) a fact or accessible information (*no*) to the addressee and *ne* seeks confirmation, agreement, cooperation, etc. from the addressee. In these collocated sequences, the particles do not modify one another. Thus, I call this type of collocation 'additive'. Additive collocations provide an efficient way of achieving two or three different pragmatic functions simultaneously in one utterance.

4. The Modifier Relation

Now we consider the copula *da* and the particles *wa*, *zo* and *ze*, which index gendered speech in Japanese. I will argue that these particles are intensifiers (deintensifiers) of nominals and verbals. The term 'intensifier' includes both intensifiers and deintensifiers. In the literature, the particle *wa* is said to be a female particle (Ide 1982; McGloin 1986, 1990; Okamoto 1995; Uyeno 1971). In contrast, the plain form copula *da* is called *hanteishi* 'judgment' (Teramura 1984). It makes a statement decisive, and hence is often associated with male speech because of its forcefulness. Consider examples (7) and (8). With respect to the structure of the sentences, (7) only differs from (4) in that the plain copula form *da* is added. Now in contrast with (4), which sounds soft and feminine, (7) sounds forceful and masculine. Similarly, (8) only differs from (5) in that the particle *wa* is added. In contrast with (5), which sounds forceful and masculine, (8) sounds soft and feminine. Since the morphological difference between (4) and (7), and (5) and (8), is the absence or presence of *da* and *wa*, respectively, *da* and *wa* must be responsible for the pragmatic conversion of softness to forcefulness and vice versa.

(7) [Iku n(o)]$_N$ da ne/yo/yo ne[6]
go NOM COP PART
'I/you/s/he/we/they will go
ne/yo/yo ne.'

(8) [Iku]$_V$ wa ne/yo/yo ne
go PART PART
'I/you/s/he/we/they will go
ne/yo/yo ne.'

It is a well-known fact that in Japanese the plain form copula *da* occurs only after a nominal and cannot occur after a verbal, as shown in example (9). What has not been clearly pointed out is the fact that the copula *da* and the sentence-final particle *wa* are in complementary distribution in this regard. The particle *wa* only occurs after a verbal, but cannot occur after a nominal, as shown in (10).[7]

---

[6] Before the copula *da*, *o* in *no* is usually omitted in informal speech.
[7] The *wa* that occurs immediately after a noun is the topic marker.

*(9) [Iku]$_V$ da ne
go COP PART
'I/you/s/he/we/they will go *ne*'

*(10) [Iku n(o)]$_N$ wa ne
go NOM PART PART
'I/you/s/he/we/they will go *ne*'

One might argue that the softness of the particle *wa* comes from the rising intonation (e.g. Kitagawa 1977). However, when we compare *iku wa yo* and *iku yo*, the former definitely sounds softer and more feminine. The pitch patterns of *iku wa, iku wa yo* and *iku yo* show that the softness of *wa* is not solely attributable to the rising intonation. Figures 1, 2, and 3 indicate the pitch patterns of the three sentences produced by a speaker of Tokyo dialect.[8]

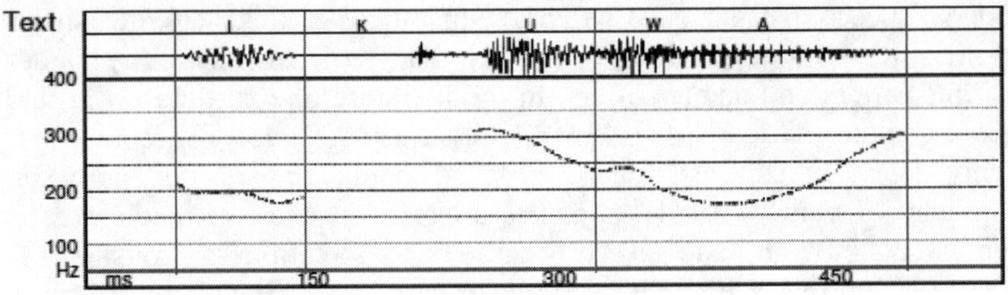

Figure 1: *wa* (rising)

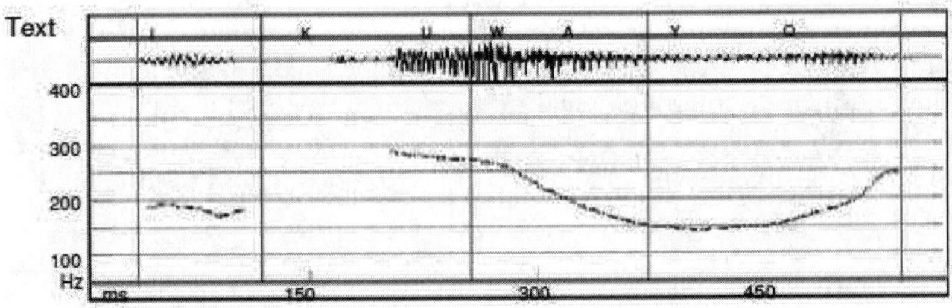

Figure 2: *wa yo*

[8] Hiroyuki Nagahara provided technical assistance. The software program 'PitchWorks' was used to measure pitch patterns. Each drawing indicates, from the top, the text of the utterance in question (with vertical lines aligned with the beginnings of *i-*, *k-*, and *w-*); the sound wave of the utterance; the pitch track of the utterance; and the time line in milliseconds at the bottom. The vertical lines represent mora boundaries.

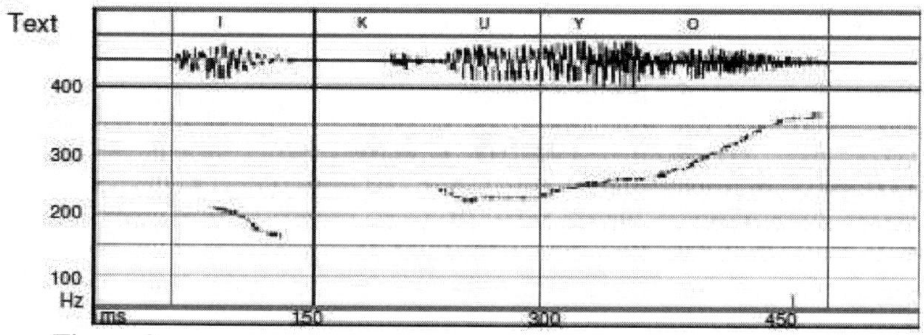

Figure 3: *yo*

In Figure 1, since it is unaccented, the verb *iku* is a low-high sequence. The particle *wa* here is rising in pitch. In Figure 2, *wa yo* is a falling-rising pattern. The shape of the pitch pattern associated with *wa* in *wa yo* is falling. And yet *iku wa yo* sounds as soft as *iku wa*, which indicates that it is not the pitch inflection associated with *wa* alone that conveys softness. One could also argue that the final rising pitch pattern found both in Figures 1 and 2 is responsible for the soft effect of these sentences. However, as shown in Figure 3, the pitch pattern of *iku yo* also shows a final rising pattern. Since both *iku wa yo* and *iku yo* exhibit a final rising pitch pattern, it is not the rising pitch pattern that is solely responsible for the softness of *iku wa yo*. This is evidence that the particle *wa* itself has the pragmatic effect of softening.

From these observations, we can say that the forcefulness of the plain form copula *da* decreases the softness of a nominal and the softness of the particle *wa* deintensifies the forcefulness of a verbal. The structural constraints on intensifiers are that they occur after either a nominal or a verbal, but not after both. Since they modify the pragmatic force of a nominal or verbal, we can characterize *da* and *wa* as modifiers of nominals and verbals, respectively, as shown in (13) and (14).

(13) Nominal

a. [Hon]$_N$ da
book COP
'It is a book.'

b. [Genki]$_N$ da
healthy COP
'I/you/s/he/we/they are fine.'

c. [Iku n(o)]$_N$ da
go NOM COP
'I/you/he/she/we/they will go *ne*/*yo*/*yo ne*.'

(14) Verbal

a. [Iku]$_V$ wa
go PART
'I/you/s/he/we/they will go.'

b. [Atsui]$_V$ wa
hot PART
'It's hot.'

In addition to *da* and *wa*, the particles *zo* and *ze* are also intensifiers. In the literature, the particles *zo* and *ze* are classified as strongly masculine particles (McGloin 1990; Okamoto 1995; Shibamoto 1985; Sturtz Sreetharan 2004). The structural constraint on *zo* and *ze* is similar to that on *wa* in that they only occur after a verbal, as shown in (15) and (16). While *wa* deintensifies the forcefulness of a verbal, *zo* and *ze* further intensify it.

(15) [Iku]$_V$ zo/ze
go PART
'I/you/he/she/we/they will go *zo/ze*.'

*(16) [Hon]$_N$ zo/ze
book PART
'It is a book *zo/ze*.'

Since *zo* and *ze* intensify verbals, which are pragmatically forceful, the collocation of a verbal and *zo* or *ze* is extremely forceful. The present framework can account for the strongly masculine nature of *zo* and *ze*.

In sum, modifiers are particles that intensify or deintensify a nominal or verbal. They either reverse the force of a nominal or verbal (*da* and *wa*) or further intensify the force of a verbal (*zo* and *ze*).

5. Overall Framework for Sentence-final Forms

I now attempt to articulate a framework for analyzing sentence sentence-final forms, based on the analysis presented above. Table 1 presents this framework.

Grammatical category		Intensifier	Additive particle(s)
Nominal	<—	—(da)	(yo) (ne)
	<---	------------------	-----l-----l--
Verbal	<—	—(wa)	(yo) (ne)
	<---	------------------	-----l-----l--
	<—	—(zo)	(yo?)[9]
	<—	—(ze)	

Table 1: A framework for relating sentence-final forms
<— modifying relation, <--- additive relation, ( ) indicates optionality

In this analysis, sentence-final forms in Japanese fall into three categories: (i) the grammatical categories of nominals and verbals, (ii) intensifiers/deintensifiers (*da*, *wa*, *zo* and *ze*) and (iii) additive particles (*yo* and *ne*).[10] An intensifier/deintensifier holds a modifier relation with a nominal or

[9] It is possible for the particle *yo* to occur after *zo*, but this sounds very archaic.

[10] Studies in traditional Japanese grammar classify sentence-final particles into a few categories. For example, Saji (1956) classifies them in terms of the speaker's attitude toward the addressee and the speaker's judgment on the message. He states that *ne* and *yo* belong to the former category and *wa* to the latter.

verbal, while the additive particles stand in an additive relation with one another and with the grammatical category they follow. It is important to point out that the additive and modifier relations are separate and independent of each other. For example, *n(o) da yo ne* and *no yo ne* are different in terms of the modifier relation but they are identical in terms of the additive relation. The intervening presence of *da* does not affect the additive relation of the nominal *no* and the particles *yo* and *ne*. In the additive collocation, the meaning of each particle remains in the collocated sequence. In contrast, in the modifier relation, the modifier can reverse the pragmatic force of the nominal or verbal.

The constraints on order in collocations of particles can be partly explained by the two different relations involved in collocations (i.e. modifier and additive relations). Since the modifier directly intensifies or deintensifies the nominal or verbal, it is ordered immediately following the nominal or verbal. Thus, the intensifiers are ordered before the additive particles. In this sense, the modifier relation is tighter than the additive relation. The particles *wa, zo* and *ze* are verbal modifiers and the copula *da* is a nominal modifier. In addition, only one intensifier modifies the nominal or verbal. Therefore, sequences such as V + *wa zo* and V + *zo wa* are not acceptable. However, the sequence N + *da* + *wa* is possible. In this case, the rule of one modifier to one nominal or verbal applies cyclically to the sequence. First the copula *da* as an intensifier modifies the nominal. Since the copula *da* is also a verbal, *wa* as a deintensifier modifies the verbal sequence ending with *da,* as shown in (17).

(17) $[[\text{Nominal}]_N + \text{da}]_V$ + wa

The constraints on the additive particles are different from those on the intensifiers. The particles *yo* and *ne* can follow either a nominal or a verbal. Since in the additive relation, the meaning of each element is added to that of the others, it is possible for more than one additive particle to occur after a nominal or verbal. The additive particles *yo* and/or *ne*, however, do not occur after the verbal intensifiers *zo* and *ze*.[11] This is perhaps the case because the extreme forcefulness of the collocation verbal + intensifier is in conflict with the pragmatic meanings of *yo* and *ne*. In addition, the additive particles can follow the non-finite gerund, i.e. the *-te* form, whereas the intensifiers cannot.[12]

---

[11]See footnote 10.

[12]The sequence *–te wa* means 'if' but in this case *wa* is a nominal particle.

(18) Matte ne/yo/yo ne.
wait ADD. PART
'Wait *ne/yo/yo ne*.'

*(19) Matte da/wa/zo/ze.
wait INTENSIFIER
'Wait *da/wa/zo/ze*.'

This constraint further supports the present analysis, in which there are at least two different types of sentence-final elements, namely, additive particles and intensifiers.

6. Relationship between Sentence-final Forms and Gendered Speech

Although Japanese sentence-final particles have been classified as female and male particles, recent studies of Japanese women's language have documented that Japanese women are not limited to so-called 'women's particles' but use various sentence-final forms depending upon the social context (Matsumoto 2002; Okamoto 1995; Shibamoto 1985). Furthermore, recent studies of Japanese men's language have found that men also use so-called 'women's particles' in some social contexts (Sturtz Sreetharan 2004). It is clear from these studies that there is no straightforward one-to-one relationship between sentence-final forms and the gender of the speaker. Ochs (1992) claims that most social identities, including gender identity, are not directly indexed by linguistic forms but rather are mediated by the ideology of the society in question. Okamoto (1995) further explains that the pragmatic meanings of softness and forcefulness of the sentence-final forms are related to the gender images of women and men in Japanese society. Thus, certain sentence-final forms reflect the ideal image of a woman in society because of their softness, so they are more often used by women. The proposal that linguistic forms do not directly index gender but that their pragmatic meanings evoke the ideal images of men and women in society is insightful and has contributed to the advancement of research on gender and language. In particular, it can account for the changes that take place in the language of women and men when the ideal gender images change in society. The present analysis relates the nature of nouns and verbs to the pragmatic contributions of sentence-final particles. The conceptual framework proposed in this study systematically explains why certain linguistic forms sound softer and others more forceful. By providing an account of how pragmatic forces derive from linguistic forms, the present study strengthens the claim made by Ochs, Okamoto, and others that the relationship between linguistic forms and gender identity is indirect.

References

Aoki, H. 1986. Evidentials in Japanese. *Evidentiality: The Linguistic Coding of Epistemology*, eds. W. Chafe & J. Nichols, 223-38. Norwood, New Jersey: Ablex.

Bates, E. and MacWhinney, B. 1982. Functional Approaches to Grammar. *Language Acquisition: The State of the Art*, eds. E. Warner and L. Gleitman, 173-218. Cambridge: Cambridge University Press.

Brown, P. and Fraser C. 1979. Speech as a Marker of Situation. *Social Markers in Speech*, eds. K. R. Sherer and H. Giles, 33-63. Cambridge: Cambridge University Press.

Brown, P. and Levinson, S. 1987. *Politeness: Some Universals in Language Usage*. Cambridge: Cambridge University Press.

Cook, H. M. 1990. An Indexical Account of the Japanese Sentence-final Particle *no*. *Discourse Processes* 13: 401-439.

Cook, H. M. 1992. Meanings of Non-referential Indexes: A Case of the Japanese Particle *ne*. *Text* 12: 507-539.

Givón, T. 1984. *Functional-typological Introduction*. Vol. 1. Amsterdam: Benjamins.

Hopper, P. and Thompson, S. 1984. The Discourse Basis for Lexical Categories in Universal Grammar. *Language* 60: 703-752.

Ide, S. 1982. Japanese Sociolinguistics: Politeness and Women's Language. *Lingua* 57: 357-85.

Katagiri, Y. 1995. Shuujoshi ni yoru Taiwa Choosei (Conversational Adjustments by Sentence-final Particles) *Gengo* 24: 38-45.

Kinsui, S. 1993. Shuujoshi yo, ne (The sentence-final particles *yo* and *ne*). *Gengo* 22: 118-121.

Kitagawa, C. 1977. A Source of Femininity in Japanese: In Defense of Robin Lakoff's 'Language and Woman's Place.' *Papers in Linguistics* 10: 275-298.

Langacker, R. 1991. *Concept, Image, and Symbol: The Cognitive Basis of Grammar*. Berlin: Mouton de Gruyter.

Lyons, J. 1968. *Introduction to Theoretical Linguistics*. Cambridge: Cambridge University Press.

Matsumoto, Y. 2002. Gender Identity and the Presentation of Self in Japanese. Paper presented at the Symposium on Japanese Style Shift, Tuscon, Arizona.

Maynard, S. K. 1997. Shifting Contexts: The Sociolinguistic Significance of Nominalization in Japanese Television News. *Language in Society* 26: 381-99.

McGloin, N. H. 1986. Feminine *wa* and *no*: Why Do Women Use Them? *Journal of the Association of Teachers of Japanese* 20: 7-21.

McGloin, N. H. 1990. Sex Difference and Sentence-sentence-final Particles. *Aspects of Japanese Women's Language,* eds. S. Ide and N. McGloin, 23-41. Tokyo: Kuroshio Shuppan.

Morita, E. 2002. Stance Marking in the Collaborative Completion of Sentences: Final Particles as Epistemic Markers in Japanese. *Japanese/Korean Linguistics* 10, eds. N. Akatsuka and S. Strauss, 220-34. Stanford, CA: CSLI Publications.

Ochs, E. 1992. Indexing Gender. *Rethinking Context: Language as an Interactive Phenomenon*, eds. A. Duranti and C. Goodwin, 335-58. Cambridge: Cambridge University Press.

Okamoto, S. 1995. "Tasteless" Japanese: Less "Feminine" Speech among Young Japanese Women. *Gender Articulated: Language and the Socially Constructed Self*, eds. K. Hall and M. Bucholtz, 297-325. New York: Routledge.

Reynolds, K. 1985. Female Speakers of Japanese. *Feminist Issues* 5: 13-46.

Saji, K. 1956. Shuujoshi no Kinoo (Functions of the Final Particles). *Kokugo Kokubun* 26: 696-735.

Shibamoto, J. 1985. *Japanese Women's Language*. New York: Academic Press.

Sturtz Sreetharan, C. 2004. Regions of Masculinity: Japanese Men's Conversational Stereotypes and Realities. *Japanese Language, Gender, and Ideology: Cultural Models and Real People,* eds. S. Okamoto and J. Shibamoto Smith, 275-289. Oxford: Oxford University Press.

Teramura, H. 1984. *Nihongo no Shintakkusu to Imi* (Japanese Syntax and Semantics). Tokyo: Kuroshio Shuppan.

Uyeno, T. 1971. *A Study of Japanese Modality: A Perfo*rmative Analysis of Sentence Particles. Doctoral dissertation, University of Michigan.

Turn Extensions as Turn-Constructional Practice: Word Order Variability in Korean Conversation

HAEYEON KIM
Chung-Ang University

1. Introduction

In discourse analysis, word order variability has often been analyzed from textual and cognitive perspectives (Downing and Noonan 1995). In recent years, a number of researchers in the field of interactional linguistics have explored the interactive nature of conversation, paying serious attention to the intricate processes in which participants are engaged. Some researchers have begun to reexamine word order variability in conversation in sequential and interactional contexts from a conversation-analytic perspective, paying attention to the interactive nature of word order variability in terms of turn increments or extensions (Ford, Fox, and Thompson 2002, Kim 2001, Ono and Suzuki 1992).

The purpose of this paper is to examine turn extensions or increments as instances of word order variability in Korean conversation in terms of turn-constructional practice, mainly from an interactive perspective. As is well known, Korean is widely accepted to be a canonical verb-final language and the verb-final constraint is strictly observed in the overwhelming majority of cases. In conversation, however, many instances of constructions with non-canonical word order *do* occur when one closely examines Korean conversational data. In this regard, this research will explore word order variability in Korean, considering discourse-pragmatic and interactive factors that are responsible for the occurrence of constructions with non-canonical word order.

To characterize word order variability in conversation, this research first classifies turn increments into four types according to prosody and constituency (see Ono and Suzuki 1992). After that, it will examine frequency of turn increments that occur after the predicate in terms of grammatical units such as word, phrase, or clause. Furthermore, this inquiry will examine elements of turn extensions in terms of the grammatical functions they perform as constituents in the constructions where they fit. Based on the frequency and classification of types of turn extensions used in word variability, this research will explore motivations for the occurrence of instances of constructions with non-canonical word order in Korean conversation. After that, it will examine the functions of three types of grammatical forms of turn extensions in their sequential and interactional contexts. Finally, it will suggest that an interaction-based explanation of the use of turn increments in their sequential contexts can provide a better way of understanding word order variability in Korean than do pragmatic or cognitive explanations.

2. Context of the Research

In typological, functional linguistics and discourse analysis, word order has often been discussed in terms of information flow and taxonomy of information states from textual and cognitive perspectives. In such approaches, terms such as given/old-new information, shared or assumed information, newsworthiness, theme, topic, afterthought, emphasis, and contrast have been used to explain word order variability.

Since the research on turn-taking carried out by Sacks et al. (1974), interaction-based research has provided a new way of examining word order variability in conversation in terms of interactional needs and motivations (Ford, Fox and Thompson 2002, Kim 2001, Ono and Suzuki 1992, Schegloff et al. 1977). Among many topics discussed in conversation analysis and interactional linguistics, Ford et al. (2002) and Kim (2001) show that non-canonical word order variability can be explained in terms of turn extensions or increments. They claim that turn increments are closely related with interactional contingencies, including lack of recipient uptake.

As discussed above, interaction-based research has provided a way of exploring how forms and types of turn-constructional units (TCUs) are interactionally determined by the negotiation between participants in talk-in-interaction. In this regard, it is necessary to examine instances of word-order variability in their sequential and interactional contexts as a way of characterizing the nature of TCUs.

3. Database, Types and Frequency of Grammatical Forms of Non-canonical Word Order Variability

In carrying out this research on interactional and structural aspects of word order variability, four audio-taped face-to-face conversations in Korean were used. Based on these four conversations, this research will explore the contexts in which instances of non-canonical word order variability are produced. In the present data, a total of 96 instances of non-canonical word order variability were found. Based on these data, the research will characterize word order variability in terms of turn-constructional practice. This research will explore word order variability in terms of the syntactically-defined notion of clauses and the prosodically-defined notion of intonation units (IUs).

When notions defined in terms of prosody and constituency are applied to the classification of turn increments, there are four theoretically possible combinations.[1] This research is mainly concerned with forms and functions of turn increments of Type I (a constituent turn increment in the same IU) and Type II (a constituent turn increment in the next IU), considering syntactically- and prosodically-defined notions of turn increments.

First, let us examine turn increments in terms of the intonation unit. There has been some research that has dealt with the relationship between IUs and grammatical forms, particularly clausal units (Chafe 1994, Kim 1996, Iwasaki and Tao 1993). In this regard, there is a need to examine whether the added elements occur in the same intonation unit or in the next separate intonation unit. Bearing this in mind, let us consider Excerpt (1).[2]

---

[1] The four possible types of turn increments are: (i) Type I: a constituent turn increment in the same IU, (ii) Type II: a constituent turn increment in the next IU, (iii) Type III: a non-constituent turn increment in the same IU, and (iv) Type IV: a non-constituent turn increment in the next IU. Among these four types, Ford et al. (2002) call Types I and II turn extensions, though they do not make a distinction between intra-IU and inter-IU turn increments.

[2] The Korean conversational data are transcribed basically following the transcription conventions proposed by Du Bois et al. (1993), each line representing an intonation unit. The transcription of Korean examples in this research follows the conventions of the Yale Romanization system. The abbreviations used in glossing Korean examples are as follows:

CIRCUM: Circumstantial connective	COMM: Committal connective
COND: Conditional connective	CONN: Connective
HON: Honorific marker	IE: Informal sentence-ender

(1) [Graduate students are talking about a phonetic analysis of voices.]
1 Y: kunkka Yumi enni-ka cham kulehkey kkaykkusha-tay-yo ikey ←A
that:is Yumi Sister-NM well such clear-QUOT-HON this
'That is, Sister Yumi's is clear, this.'
2 S: uuum.
'uhum.'
3 Y: moksoli cachey-ka ←B
voice itself-NM
'the voice itself.'
(3 intonation units deleted)
4 J: tutki-ey-nun an nangnangha-ntey.
hearing-LOC-TM not clear-CIRCUM
'as for hearing, (it's) not clear?'
5 Y: nangnangh-ay,
clear-IE
'(It's) clear,'
6 tutki-ey-to ←C
hearing-LOC-too
'even for hearing.'
7 nangnangha-cyo Yumi-enni moksoli ←D
clear-COMM:HON Yumi-sister voice
'(It's) clear,sister Yumi's voice.'

In (1), A and D occur at the end of a clausal TCU in the same intonation unit, and B and C occur in separate intonation units. Examination of the present data shows that 69 instances (i.e. 71.9%) of turn increments occur in separate intonation units, and 27 (i.e. 28.1%) in the same intonation unit, out of the total 96 cases.

Next, grammatical forms of turn increments that occur immediately after sentential TCUs are classified in such terms as nominal elements, adjuncts or adverbials, and adverbial clauses. Examination of the present data shows the following distribution of types of grammatical forms:

INTRP: Interruptive connective
NM: Nominative case marker
Q: Question marker
REASON: Reason connective
LOC: Locative marker
PST: Past tense marker
QUOT: Quotative
TM: Topic marker

	Inter-IU	Intra-IU	Total
Noun phrases	37	18	55 (57.3%)
Adv. phrases	17	4	21 (21.9%)
Adv. clauses	15	5	20 (20.8%)
Total	69 (71.9%)	27 (28.1%)	96 (100%)

Table 1. Distribution of types of grammatical forms of turn increments.

Table 1 shows that noun phrases (NPs) are the most frequently used grammatical forms that function as turn increments, and that there is no significant difference in frequency rates of grammatical forms between inter-IU and intra-IU turn increments.

4. Motivations for the Occurrence of Turn Extensions as Non-Canonical Word Order Variability

In this section, let us discuss motivations that are responsible for the occurrence of turn extensions based on the types and frequency of turn increments shown in Section 3.

First of all, the occurrence of intra-IU turn extensions is closely related to a rush-through (Schegloff 1996). Schegloff states that when a speaker is approaching the possible completion point of a TCU, (s)he can speed up the talk, and shape the prosody so as not to come to a completion point, but to proceed immediately into the start of a new TCU. Ford and Thompson (1996) state that a possible transition-relevance place (TRP), which they call a complex transition-relevance place (CTRP), is characterized by syntactic, prosodic, and pragmatic properties. In the production of turn increments, pauses arising in the interaction between speaker and hearer serve as good TRPs, where the next speaker may start his or her turn according to turn-taking rules. However, when there is no such prosodic cue, turn-taking does not take place, which results in an intra-IU turn increment. In this regard, intra-IU turn extensions can be explained in terms of a rush-through.

Second, the occurrence of intra-IU turn increments can be explained in terms of the motivation of presenting an urgently relevant thing first, and a less urgent thing later (see Givón 1983: 20, Hudson 1991), as shown in (2).

(2) (Six IUs of Excerpt (1) are deleted because of space constraints).
Y: nangnangha-cyo Yumi-enni moksoli. ←
clear-COMM:HON Yumi-sister voice
'(It's) clear, sister Yumi's voice.'

As shown in Excerpt (1), the speakers are arguing about whether the voice quality of a fellow student is clear or not. In her claim marked by an arrow in (2), Y presents the predicate first, which is more urgent and relevant than the subject NP because the question of whether the voice quality is clear or not is at issue. In this context, the motivation for presenting an urgently relevant element first produces a turn extension that elaborates the immediately preceding host TCU.

Third, another motivation responsible for the occurrence of turn increments as instances of word order variability is recipient design (Sacks and Schegloff 1979). Recipient design can be understood in the sense that speakers produce turns to be understood in terms of what the speaker knows or assumes about existing mutual knowledge among participants. Examination of the present data shows that speakers produce NP extensions according to the speaker's assumption about mutual knowledge among interactants. In this regard, the use of NP turn extensions can be explained in terms of recipient design.

Fourth, the occurrence of inter-IU turn extensions is directly related to interactional contingencies, i.e. the absence of recipient uptake at a possible completion point (Ford et al. 2002, Kim 2001). When there is lack of recipient uptake, the current speaker adds segments to provide a renewed possible completion point, as shown in Excerpt (3).

(3) 1 HS: (one IU deleted)
    2   i- wenlay nayil-i-cyo
          this originally tomorrow-be-COMM:HON
          'this- originally (it) is tomorrow,'
    3   kuki,
          'that'
    4   uimi:-,
          'semantic-
    5 Y: a:
          'ah'
    6 HS: hwayong--,
          'pragmatics (conference)'
    7 Y: wenlay nayil-i-ess-na?
          originally tomorrow-be-PST-Q
          '(Was it) originally scheduled tomorrow?'

In (3), HS asks fellow students about the exact date for the conference. In his inquiry, first he simply produces a predicate without a subject NP, assuming that the recipient would share the information about the conference. However, at the end of a sentential TCU that would function as a completion point, there is no uptake from the recipient. Then, he produces a pronominal element, which also fails to get recipient uptake. After that, he renews his turn with a partial full NP, which then succeeds in getting recipient uptake in the form of a reactive token. As this excerpt shows, turns are incremented on the basis of interactional needs, such as inviting recipient uptake.

5. Functions of Turn Extensions and Word Order Variability

In this section, let us consider the functions of turn extensions as instances of non-canonical word order variability. These functions will be discussed in terms of the grammatical categories discussed above.

First, let us consider the functions of NP turn extensions. Both argument NPs and non-arguments occur after predicates as NP turn extensions. In addition, NP turn extensions occur either in the same or next, separate intonation units, functioning as intra-IU and inter-IU NP extensions. NP turn extensions perform many functions. They are used to provide specific or additional information, and to reformulate what has been said before, particularly in elliptical constructions in Korean, as shown in Excerpt (4).

(4) a. Y: yenge-nun etten pangpep-ulo hatun ta pisusha-canh-a, ←
English-TM which method-with do all similar-COMM-IE
[keyllon-un].
result-TM
'As for (studying) English, whatever methods you use,
(it is) similar, the result.'
S: [ung].
'Yeah.'
b. J: .. pisushaci anh-a?
similar not-IE
.. twu kay-ka?
two thing-NM ←
'(Aren't they) similar? The two (classes)?'

(4) shows two instances of NP extensions that occur after the host sentential TCUs. In (4a), when Y's turn without a subject reaches a possible completion point, Y produces an NP extension. At the same time, the next speaker produces a reactive token, resulting in the overlapping of two utterances. In (4b), on the other hand, when J produces a sentential TCU without a subject with rising intonation, there is no immediate response from the recipient. Then, J adds an NP extension which serves as subject of the preceding host TCU. When constructions lack arguments, there is a possibility of confusion and ambiguity among participants. If participants

share the information delivered, ellipsis of arguments is allowed in Korean. However, if the information is not shared, the ellipted constructions sound like 'general' statements. In such a case, there occurs a need for more specific information, and there is a negotiation for more specific information among the participants. This fact shows that NP extensions are used to fulfill the need for more specific information when ellipted constructions are used.

NP arguments also occur when the current speaker revises or reformulate what (s)he has said in the immediately preceding host TCU. Speakers sometimes use pronominal elements or full NPs in the host TCU. In such a case, the current speaker either provides a full NP for the pronominal NP or replaces the full NP with another more informative one, as shown in (5).

(5) S: ...ilkwa-ka swipci anhun kyocaytul-i manhi iss-eyo
lesson one-NM easy not materials-NM many be-HON
..kyokwase-ka-yo ←
textbooks-NM-HON
'There are many books whose Lesson One is not easy, textbooks.'

In (5), S is talking about high school English textbooks. He first presents a more general statement about (English) books as teaching materials. But he revises his statement about the English books, providing more specific information in the sense that what he means by books are (English) textbooks. This excerpt shows that full NP turns used as turn increments occur in the next intonation unit as a way of revising or reformulating what has been said, providing more specific information to elaborate the preceding host TCU retroactively.

Second, let us discuss the functions of 17 instances of adverbial phrases used as turn increments that occur after clausal or sentential TCUs that form separate IUs. As has been discussed above, adverbial phrases as turn increments are used to provide additional information, to specify or modify the statement of the preceding host TCUs, among others, as shown in (6).

(6) M: (two intonation units are deleted)
...hye ccalpu-myen,
tongue short-COND
.. hye ccalpun soli-na-cyo,
tongue short sound-produce-COMM:HON
.. yenge hal ttay. ←A
English speak time
'If you have a short tongue, you will produce
short-tongued sounds, when speaking English.'

S: ..hye-ka kileya-ci,
tongue-NM long-COMM
..yakkan, ←B
a:bit
..te cohun kes kath-a.
more good thing seem-IE
'the tongue should be long, a bit, (then) it would be better.'

In (6), two instances of adverbial phrases are used as turn increments, forming separate intonation units. Thus, the ends of the immediately preceding sentential TCUs function as possible completion points. However, there is no uptake from the recipient, which allows for the current speaker to continue her turn. In such situations, the added segments provide additional, more specific information about the 'general' statements made in the preceding host TCUs in both cases.

Third, the use of adverbial clauses as turn increments is mainly concerned with either providing additional circumstantial information or providing an account for the statement/claim expressed in the immediately preceding host TCU (see Ford 1993). In Korean, adverbial clauses usually occur before main clauses, and they are accompanied with clausal connectives to combine with 'main' clauses. The function of providing circumstantial information in the form of an adverbial clause is found in Excerpt (7).

(7) S: (1.5) akka ce=,
before well
Tongswu manna-ss-eyo,
Tongsoo see-PST-HON
tuleo-taka, ←
enter-INTRP
'A while ago, well, I saw Tongsoo,
when I came in (i.e. on my way here).'
P: yey yey.
'Yes, yes.'

In (7), S tells P about seeing a student on his way to the office. In this excerpt, the arrow-marked adverbial clause occurs after a sentential TCU, functioning as a turn increment. If S had kept the canonical [adverbial clause + main clause] word order, the arrow-marked adverbial clause should have preceded the sentential TCU. Here, however, S presents the more relevant information first in the main clause. But realizing that his delivery of information is not sufficient, and that there is no uptake from the recipient, S provides additional circumstantial information in the form of an adverbial clause, elaborating the preceding host TCU retroactively.

Another function of adverbial clauses used as turn increments is providing an account for the statement/claim expressed in the immediately preceding host TCU. Speakers often make a statement or claim based upon the contingencies of the on-going conversation. When such a statement or claim is presented in the main clause, the speaker produces an account or explanation for the statement/claim that (s)he has made, forming a [statement/claim + account/explanation] schema, as shown in Excerpt (8).

(8) A: ...umchengnakey khecy-ess-ci,
    enormously grow-PST-COMM
    emci sonkalak-manhakey khecy-ess-unikka, ←
    thumb finger-like grow-PST-REASON
    '(it (i.e. the swollen flesh)) has grown enormously,
    because (it) has grown as big as a thumb.'
  B: ung,
    'Yeah'

In (8), Speaker A, a flight attendant, talks about her experience of having an accident on the plane. She says the injured part of her arm has become swollen as big as a thumb. In such a situation, she first makes a statement that the swollen flesh has grown unusually big in a sentential TCU. When there is no uptake from the recipient at the completion point, Speaker A produces a turn extension in the form of an adverbial clause as a way of providing an account for the statement retroactively. This excerpt shows that the action of providing an account for a claim or statement retroactively is responsible for the occurrence of the non-canonical word order variability.

6. Summary and Conclusions

This research has explored turn increments used for elaborating the preceding host TCU retroactively as a way of understanding non-canonical word order variability in Korean conversation. Adopting the assumption that turn extensions or increments are closely related to interactional contingencies, this research has discussed types and functions of turn increments, paying attention to word order variability. In characterizing types of turn increments as turn-constructional practice, types of turn increments are classified in terms of the syntactically-defined notion of the clause and the prosodically-defined notion of the intonation unit. Among the four possible types of turn increments, this research has focused on turn extensions, subdividing them into intra-IU and inter-IU turn increments. In addition, the types of grammatical forms are classified into three: (i) argument and non-argument NPs, (ii) adverbial phrases, and (iii) adverbial clauses. Based on the classification of types of turn increments, this research has explored motivations that are responsible for the occurrence of instances of non-canonical word variability.

This research has first shown that the following motivations are mainly responsible for the occurrence of turn increments: (i) a rush-through, (ii) the motivation of presenting an urgently relevant element first, (iii) recipient design, and (iv) pursuing recipient uptake. This research has illustrated how these motivations trigger the occurrence of turn increments. In particular, it has shown that the occurrence of inter-IU turn increments can be explained by the interactional contingency of the absence of recipient uptake at a possible completion point (Ford et al. 2002, and Kim 200E)xamination of three types of grammatical forms of turn shows that they perform the following functions: (i) NP arguments are used to elaborate the preceding host TCUs retroactively by providing additional information, to revise what has been said before, to add new information, particularly in the case when the next speaker does not share the information that the current speaker possesses, (ii) adverbial phrases are used to provide additional information, to specify, or to modify the statement in the preceding host TCUs, among others, and (iii) adverbial clauses are used mainly either to provide additional circumstantial information or to provide an account for the statement/claim expressed in the immediately preceding host TCU.

In sum, the findings of the present research have shown the interactive nature of conversation manifested in the act of retroactive elaboration performed in the manner of revising, specifying, and extending what has been said in the host TCU, particularly when faced with a lack of recipient uptake. In addition, this research suggests that an interaction-based explanation of the use of turn increments in their sequential contexts can provide a better understanding of word order variability in conversation.

References

Chafe, W. 1994. *Discourse, Consciousness, and Time*. Chicago: University of Chicago Press.

Downing, P. and M. Noonan. 1995. *Word Order in Discourse*. Amsterdam/ Philadelphia: Benjamins.

Du Bois, J., S. Schuetze-Coburn, D. Paolino, and S. Cumming. 1993. Outline of Discourse Transcription. *Talking Data: Transcription and Coding Methods for Language Research*, ed. J. Edwards and M. Lampert, 221-260. Hillsdale, NJ: Erlbaum.

Ford, C. 1993. *Grammar in Interaction: Adverbial Clauses in American English*. Cambridge: Cambridge University Press.

Ford, C., B. Fox, and S. A. Thompson. 2002. Constituency and the Grammar of Turn Increments. *The Language of Turn and Sequence*, eds. C. Ford, B. Fox, and S. A. Thompson, 14-38. Oxford: Oxford University Press.

Ford, C., and S. A. Thompson. 1996. Interactional Units in Conversation: Syntactic, Intonational, and Pragmatic Resources for the Management of Turns. *Interaction and Grammar*, eds. E. Ochs, E. Schegloff, and S. A. Thompson, 134-184. Cambridge: Cambridge University Press.

Givón, T. (ed.). 1983. *Topic Continuity in Discourse: A Quantitative Cross-linguistic Study*. Amsterdam/Philadelphia: Benjamins.

Hudson, M. 1991. Discourse Functions of Postposing in Japanese. Paper Presented at the Annual Linguistics Symposium. University of Wisconsin-Milwaukee.

Iwasaki, S. and H. Tao. 1993. A Comparative Study of the Intonation Unit in English, Japanese, and Mandarin Chinese. Paper presented at the 67th annual LSA meeting, Los Angeles.

Kim, H. 1996. The Structure of the Intonation Unit and Verbal Affixes in Korean Conversation. *Discourse and Cognition* 2: 47-74.

Kim, K. 2001. Turn-constructional Practice in Korean Conversation: Organization of Turn Increments. *Language Research* 37.4: 885-922.

Ochs, E., E. Schegloff, and S. A. Thompson. eds. 1996. *Interaction and Grammar*. Cambridge: Cambridge University Press.

Ono, T. and R. Suzuki. 1992. Word Order Variability in Japanese Conversation: Motivations and Grammaticization. *Text* 12: 429-455.

Sacks, H., E. Schegloff & G. Jefferson. 1974. A Simplest Systematics for the Organization of Turn-taking for Conversation. *Language* 50: 696-735.

Sacks, H. and E. Schegloff. 1979. Two Preferences in the Organisation of Reference to Persons in Conversation and their Interaction. *Everyday Language: Studies in Ethnomethodology*, ed. G. Psathas, 15-21. Hillsdale, NJ: Erlbaum.

Schegloff, E. 1996. Turn Organization: One Intersection of Grammar and Interaction. *Interaction and Grammar*, ed. E. Ochs, E. Schegloff, and S. A. Thompson, 52-133. Cambridge: Cambridge University Press.

Schegloff, E., H. Sacks, and G. Jefferson. 1977. The Preference for Self-Correction in the Organization of Repair in Conversation. *Language* 53: 361-382.

Single Full NP Turns with Rising Intonation in Korean Conversation

HAEYEON KIM AND YOUNG-CHEOL YIM
Chung-Ang University

1. Introduction

In the area of interactional linguistics, there has been a significant amount of research that has dealt with sequential structures as a way of characterizing the interactional nature of conversation. In recent years, much research on turn-taking, turn organization, transitional relevance places (TRPs), and turn-constructional units (TCUs) has been carried out as a way of understanding the nature of the turn-constructional component (Sacks et al. 1974, Goodwin 1981, Ford and Thompson 1996, among others). However, little attention has been paid to the properties of single phrasal units, particularly full noun phrases (NPs), which function as unit-types or TCUs in conversation, with only a few exceptions (Matsumoto 1997, Ono and Thompson 1994, and Ono et al. 1998, among others). Their studies, however, do not focus on the full NPs that function as single, independent TCUs, dealing only with limited aspects of interactional and grammatical properties of full NP turns.

The purpose of this research is to explore sequential and interactional contexts of full NPs with a marked rising intonation (NPRIs) that function as single, independent TCUs, as a way of understanding the interactional nature of full NP turns in conversation and the turn-constructional component in the turn-taking system (see Sacks et al. 1974). In this research, we would like to explore the following questions concerning the occurrence of full NPRI turns: (i) when are full NPRIs used as single independent TCUs? and (ii) what social actions are involved in the use of full NPs as independent TCUs?

This research will show that full NPRI turns cannot be described adequately in simple terms such as echo utterances or declarative questions (see Quirk et al. 1985). Rather, we will show that single full NPRI turns should be explored and characterized in sequential and interactional contexts where the full NPRI turns occur (Freed 1994, Weber 1993). This research will show that the forms and functions of TCUs are determined by negotiation between speaker and hearer in talk-in-interaction in the process of performing social actions. Finally, we will suggest that it is necessary to explore the interaction between conversation and grammar, which shapes forms of grammar through negotiation between speaker and hearer. Consequently, this research contributes to a better understanding of the turn-constructional component.

2. Context of the Research

Since the research on turn-taking by Sacks et al. (1974), there has been much research that deals with the nature of TCUs, and the relationship between turn-taking and TCUs in conversation (Schegloff 1996; Ford and Thompson 1996; Ford, Fox, and Thompson 1996; Ono and Thompson 1995; and Tanaka 1999; among others). These studies have dealt with the questions of how turns are organized and how TCUs are related to their sequential and interactional contexts in turn-taking between speaker and hearer. Among recent research findings on turn-taking and TCUs, only a few studies have dealt with the properties of full NP turns (Kim 2002, Matsumoto 1997, and Ono and Thompson 1994). Ono and Thompson (1994) explored 'unattached NPs' in conversation as a way of integrating syntax and interaction. Matsumoto (1997) examined NPs in Japanese conversation in terms of their relation to intonation units as basic units of discourse production and information flow. Although these studies deal with NPs in conversation, they do not pay much attention to the roles and properties of full NPs that constitute single, independent TCUs. Kim (2002) explored the contexts in which full NP turns occur, and functions that full NP turns perform in conversation, as a way of understanding the nature of TCUs.

Ono et al. (1998) is a study of NPs with a marked rising intonation uttered in the form of intonation units. They characterize NPRIs in terms of the following dimensions: interaction, cognition, syntax, and individual differences. They state that the use of NPRIs is heavily interactionally-oriented in the sense that ratification from the involved participants allows the talk to proceed.[1] They show that the speaker continues his/her utterance only after the NP is ratified by other interactants, expressed in the forms of backchannels or head movement. This research, however, does not focus on the full NPs that function as single, independent TCUs. Their research focuses on limited aspects of interactional and grammatical properties of full NP turns.

In spite of some recent research on NPs in conversation, there has not been any serious research on single full NP turns that function as single, independent turns. This research, which is partly inspired by Ono et al.'s research on NPRIs, will attempt to explore the forms and functions of full NPRI turns as a way of understanding the behaviors of NPs as TCUs. It is also related to recent research on questioning that deals with the types and functions of questions in English conversation (Weber 1993, Freed 1994).

3. Database

This research examined four transcripts of spontaneous, informal conversations in Korean, and three telephone conversations. Each conversation is 13 to 30 minutes long, totaling approximately three hours. Among the data, two are multi-party conversations among graduate students, another two are dialogues between two friends, and three are telephone conversations between Koreans studying in the United States. The topics of the conversations are school life, teaching English, and job experiences, among others.

The total number of single full NPRI turns in the database amounts to approximately 53 cases. This number may vary slightly because of the difficulty in making a judgment about single full NPRIs as independent TCUs. Based on the examination of the seven conversations, we will explore in what contexts full NPRI turns are used and what social actions are involved in the production of full NPRI turns.

---

[1]Ono et al. (1998) give Excerpt (i) as evidence for their characterization of full NP intonation units in terms of ratification from the addressee.

(i) (Y talks about what happened at her apartment during the Northridge Earthquake).

1 Y:	de nanka anoo,	Y:	and uh	
2	...takosu no bin=?		a taco bottle?	
3 S:	hai hai hai hai	S:	yes, yes, yes, yes	←
4 Y:	..ga=,	Y:	(Nominative Case Marker)	
5	ochitan da kedo=,		dropped, but	

As shown in (i), when the NPRI is followed by a backchannel, the speaker continues her current talk. Based on this observation, Ono et al. (1998) claim that the speaker continues his/her turn only after the NP is ratified by other interactants.

4. Contexts for the Occurrence of NPRI Turns in Conversation

Full NPRI turns that function as independent TCUs can be found in many different contexts. When we try to account for usage of NPRIs in terms of interaction, we have to examine their contexts in conversation. In conversation, various units are employed for the production of talk in constructing turns. Thus, TCUs are expressed in terms of words, phrases, clauses, or sentences, as pointed out by Sacks et al. (1974:709). In this regard, there is a need to examine the contexts in which NPRIs function as single, independent TCUs. Examination of the present database shows that single NPRIs turns occur in limited contexts, performing certain social actions.

First of all, full NPRI turns occur as instances of repetition of prior turns. In conversation, it is not uncommon that speakers often repeat part or whole of the preceding talk in the process of communicating. Examination of the present data shows that full NPs are used to repeat as a whole or in part of what has been said by another speaker in the immediately preceding turn. It also shows that thirty cases of full NPRIs are examples of partial or whole repetitions from the immediately preceding turn. Repetition is either self-repetition in the same turn, or other-repetition in the next turn, as shown in Excerpt (1).[2]

(1) B: ...(1.7) kulayto ilpon- ilpone ceyil manhci anh-ni aytul-i?
though Japan- Japanese the most not-Q students-NM
..paywunta-nun [aytul-i]? ← A
learn-ATTR students-NM
'But still, don't the Japanese (classes) have the most students?'
students willing to learn?'
A: [hankwukay]tul-to ilpone manhi hay-yo.
Koreans-too Japanese much do-HON
'Many Korean students also study Japanese.'
B: ..hankwukaytul-i? ←B
..Korean:students-NM
'Korean students?'

---

[2]The Korean conversational data are transcribed basically following the transcription conventions proposed by Du Bois et al. (1993), with each line representing an intonation unit (IU). The transcription of Korean examples in this research follows the conventions of Yale Romanization. The abbreviations used in glossing Korean examples are as follows:

ATTR:	Attributive	DECL:	Declarative
HON:	Honorific marker	IE:	Informal sentence-ender
NM:	Nominative case marker	PST:	Past tense marker
Q:	Question marker	RETRO:	Retrospective marker

In (1), we can see two instances of repetition. The repetition marked as A is a partial but expanded self-repetition in the same turn initiated by the speaker herself. The other one, marked as B, is a partial repetition from a critical element of the immediately preceding turn. In particular, the repetition with rising intonation marked as B constitutes a single, independent turn. In traditional grammar, Quirk et al. (1985: 835) call repetitions echo utterances. They state that echo utterances are those which repeat all or part of what has been said by another speaker. According to them, the functions of echo utterances in discourse can be either questions or exclamations. Echo questions are either recapitulatory or explicatory. A recapitulatory echo question is one that repeats part or all of a message, as a way of having its content confirmed. An explicatory echo question, however, is a question that asks for clarification, rather than repetition, of something just said. In this regard, full NPs accompanied with an upward intonation contour as in A and B are treated as echo questions. However, such a term cannot explain properly the functions or social actions that NPRIs perform in their interactional contexts.

Second, full NPRI turns occur as candidate answers or a try markers when there is an ellipsis, or when pronominal elements are used in the immediately preceding turn, as shown in Excerpt (2).

(2) S: cey-ka keki myech pen ka-ass-ess-e-yo.
I-NM there couple times go-PST-PST-IE-HON
'I went there a couple of times.'
P: a, Senam tayhakkyo-yo? ←
ah, Suhnahm University-HON?
'Ah, Suhnahm University?'

In (2), S talks about his experiences of visiting the university where his friend was teaching. In his talk, he uses the pronominal element *keki* 'there' in referring to the university. Then, P produces a full NPRI turn as a way of clarifying what the pronominal element refers to. As this shows, a full NPRI turn occurs as a candidate answer or a try marker when there is an ellipsis or when a pronominal element is used in the immediately preceding turn.

Third, full NPRI turns occur as single independent TCUs when turns form question-answer sequences, particularly with *wh*-questions. The question-answer sequence is one of the most frequently used types that forms an adjacency pair in talk-in-interaction. In question-answer sequences, when the first speaker produces a question, it is normal for the next speaker to provide an answer to it. However, when the next speaker does not have an appropriate answer for the question, (s)he provides a candidate answer, often in the form of a full NPRI turn, as in Excerpt (3).

(3) A: ...(1.5) kukey mwe-ya?
that.NM what-IE
'what is that?'
B: ...ai,
'well,'
A: ...(2.0) [wethe suphleyi?] ←
'water spray (moisturizer)?'
B: [suphyeyi.]
'spray (moisturizer).'

In (3), A and B are talking about a small accident that happened to B, i.e., breaking a cosmetics container. A produces an utterance with a *wh*-question, seeking an answer to the question. However, B does not provide an answer immediately after the question: First, she produces a reactive token, and then a pause. Then, A provides a possible candidate answer for her own question, in the form of a full NP with rising intonation, which results in a single, independent full NPRI turn. As this excerpt shows, full NPRI turns occur in question-answer sequences as possible candidate answers for the question.

5. Functions/Social Actions of NPRIs in Conversation

As we have seen, full NPRIs turns are frequently used as instances of repetition of the immediately preceding turns. Examination of the present data shows there are 30 instances of NPRIs that repeat all or part of what has been said in the immediately preceding turn. Here, let us consider the functions of full NPRI turns resulting from repeating prior turns in more detail.

First, one of the most prominent functions of NPRIs that occur as instances of repetition in the second-turn position is seeking confirmation from the addressee. In this case, the full NP turn can be a full or partial repetition of the previous turn, which is often called a recapitulatory echo question (Quirk et al. 1985). This type of NPRI is used to seek confirmation from another speaker, as shown in Excerpt (4).

(4) J: ... kumyenun, cengswu oppa encey naoci-yo.
then Jungsoo Brother when come-HON
'Then, when is Brother Jungsoo coming?'
Y: ...moley.
'the day after tomorrow.'
J: mo[ley]? ← A
'the day after tomorrow.'

Y: [wa] wa.
come come
'He's coming, coming.'
J: a kkwasa-ey osi-nun ke-yey-yo?
oh dept.:office-to come-ATTR thing-be-HON
'Oh, will he come to the department office?'
Y: ung, way.
'Yeah, why?'
J: nayil moley? ← B
'The day after tomorrow?'
Y: ung.
'Yeah.'

In (4), the full NPRI turns marked A and B are repetitions of Y's preceding turn, produced in the form of an NP. In (4), when J produces a *wh*-question, Y provides an answer to it. However, J repeats what Y has said in the prior turn, in the form of a full NPRI turn, as a way of confirming what has been said. After that, J produces another question to verify whether the referent is coming to the department office. Then Y provides an affirmative answer to the question, adding a *wh*-question, seeking confirmation. However, J produces another full NPRI turn to seek confirmation from the addressee one more time. As shown above, in traditional grammar, this type of full NP turn is called a recapitulatory echo question. When this kind of full NPRI turn is considered in terms of the function it performs in its interactional context, the full NP turn is used to seek confirmation from the previous speaker. This observation shows that the confirmation process can be seen as an action of negotiation between speakers, and that such a social action of seeking and providing confirmation shapes the forms of turns and grammar.

Second, full NPRI turns, as repeats in the second-turn position, are used to initiate repair, in the sense that NPRI turns are used to ask for clarification of something that the addressee has misunderstood or has difficulty understanding (Schegloff, Sacks, and Jefferson 1977, Schegloff 1979, and Fox, Hayashi, and Jasperson 1996, among others). Examination of the present data shows that the occurrence of full NPRI turns is closely related to repair, including nine instances out of the total 53 tokens. This shows that full NPRI turns, which repeat all or part of the immediately preceding turn, frequently function as next turn repair initiators (NTRIs), as shown in (5).

(5) P: ..yey, onul cincca ciin-i op-nita.
yeah, today really Ciin-NM come-HON
'Yeah, today Jean is coming, really.'
S: ...ciin-ika? ← A
Jean-NM
'Jean?'
P: ..onul-pwuthe op-nita,
today-from come-HON
..cihui tongsayng
Jihee's sister.
'She will come today, Jihee's sister.'
S: cihui tongsaying-i-yo ← B
Jihee Sister-NM-HON
'Jihee's sister?'
P: yey=.
'Yes.'

In (5), two teachers are talking about two sisters who are students at their college-preparation academy. When P informs S of one student's plan to attend the academy, S repeats part of the immediately preceding turn. Such an action of repetition functions as a repair initiator, and the repetition displays S's trouble in identifying the student referred to. In this context, P first repeats his previous utterance and provides additional information as a way of solving the trouble. In (5), repair is occasioned by a repair initiator in the turn immediately following the trouble-source turn that includes a repairable element. In this case, the repair is initiated by someone other than the speaker of the trouble-source turn, indicating his or her problem in understanding or hearing. This excerpt shows that a full NPRI turn functions as a repair initiator, which in (5) results in a successful outcome to the effort at repair.

Third, another function of single full NPRI turns found in question-answer sequences, particularly in *wh*-question-answer sequences, is providing candidate answers when the next speaker does not possess definite and clear information requested by the current speaker. The question-answer sequence is one of the most frequently used types of adjacency pair in talk-in-interaction. Examination of the present data shows that single full NPRI turns in question-answer sequences are found in six out of the total of 53 cases of *wh*-questions.

(6) B: ...kuntey mwe ceke mwe-ya pang- pang-
by:the;way what that what-is proof- proof-
'By the way, well, what is that? Proof-, proof-?'
A: ..pangumcangchi? ←
'sound-proof facilities?'
B: e.
'Yeah.'

In (6), when Speaker B raises a question, A provides an answer in the form of a full NP, which serves as a potential answer to the information requested by the first speaker. In this case, the first speaker uses a *wh*-question as a way of getting information from the addressee. *Wh*-questions, often called information questions, are used mainly to seek information from the addressee. So, the form of the answer provided by the addressee often varies according to the status of information. The principal function of using a *wh*-question is to get information which the current speaker neither possesses nor shares with the next speaker. Thus, the information provided in the answer by the next speaker is new, and this new information is expressed in the form of a full NP. However, it is not always the case that the addressee possesses the information requested by the speaker. In such a case, the addressee cannot provide it. The next speaker, who does not have definite information about the referent, informs the first speaker that he lacks the information requested. Then, he provides only probable information in his guess, justifying his action of not providing the information requested. In such a situation, the addressee often provides a candidate answer in the form of a full NPRI turn.

Fourth, full NPRI turns used as candidate answers or try markers perform the action of seeking clarification in the contexts when prior turns contain elliptical or pronominal elements. In the process of communicating with each other, the first speaker often produces turns with an ellipsis of grammatical elements or with pronominal elements, assuming that the first speaker shares information with the second speaker. But, sometimes, it happens that the second speaker does not sufficiently share the information with the first speaker. In such a context, the second speaker uses a full NPRI turn as a way of asking for clarification from the first speaker.

(7) M: ..nay-ka maynal tayhakkyo-ttay,
I-NM everyday college-times
..kulen kes-man ccohatanye-ss-ketun.
such thing-only chase-PST-RETRO:IE
'When I was at college, I always did only such a thing.'
S: (0.7) kulen ke, ..kangcoi tutnun-ke? ←
(0.7) such thing ..class attending-thing
'Such a thing, attending (English) classes?'
M: ..ung.
'yeah.'

In (7), participants in the conversation are talking about attending English classes at school. When M talks about her experience at college, she uses the pronominal element *kelen kes* 'such a thing', assuming that the next speaker would know what she is talking about. However, the next speaker has a problem identifying what M is talking about. So, she repeats the pronominal element and produces a full NPRI turn as a candidate referent for the pronominal element. Then, M provides confirmation of the referent. As this excerpt shows, use of full NPRI turns performs the social action of seeking clarification of the trouble in the immediately preceding turns.

6. Summary and Conclusions

This research has explored the question of when full NPRI turns function as single, independent TCUs in conversation. In traditional grammar, single full NPRI turns have been treated as a type of echo question or declarative question. This research, however, has shown that full NPRI turns cannot be properly described and explained simply as echo questions and declarative questions, and attempts to characterize single NPRI turns in their sequential and interactional contexts.

To characterize single full NPRI turns in terms of interaction between speaker and hearer, we first discussed the context of this research, considering prior work on the interaction between conversation and grammar. We reviewed certain research that deals with the properties of NPs in conversation, such as Ono and Thompson (1994), Matsumoto (1997), and Ono et al. (1998). This review has shown that Ono et al.'s claim that one of the main functions of NPRIs in conversation is to get ratification from other interactants is a limited and partial answer to the question of when full NPRI turns are used in conversation.

Examination of the present data has shown that single NPRI turns are used mostly in the following contexts: (i) repetition of immediately preceding turns when repair or confirmation is needed, (ii) a candidate answer or a try marker immediately after a turn that contains elliptical or pronominal elements, and (iii) a candidate answer in question-answer sequences, particularly to *wh*-questions.

In the second part, this research has explored the functions or social actions that single NPRI turns perform in their sequential and interactional contexts, based on observation of the contexts in which full NPRI turns occur. First, examination of the present data has shown that instances of partial or full repetition of immediately preceding turns are closely related to the functions of seeking confirmation from the next speaker and initiating repair. The research has shown that full NPRI turns used as echo questions perform the social action of seeking confirmation from the addressee. It also has shown that full NPRI turns, which serve as repair initiators, are used to perform the social action of initiating repair when the next speaker has problems/difficulties in hearing or understanding what has been said by another speaker. Second, the function of single full NPRI turns used in *wh*-question-answer sequences is to provide candidate answers when the next speaker does not possess definite and clear information requested by the current speaker. In this regard, the use of single NPRI turns can be said to perform the social action of negotiating between speaker and hearer the delivery of information that the addressee possesses. Third, another function of full NPRI turns used as candidate answers or try markers is performing the action of seeking clarification of elliptical or pronominal elements in the prior turns.

In sum, this research has shown that full NPRI turns cannot be adequately described merely as echo utterances or declarative questions. Rather, it has shown that single full NPRI turns should be explored and characterized in those sequential and interactional contexts in which the full NPRI turns occur. It also has shown that the forms and functions of TCUs are determined by negotiation between speaker and hearer in talk-in-interaction in the process of performing social actions. This research on the functions of single NPRI turns has shown that there are structural and interactional constraints on the occurrence of full NP turns in conversation. Consequently, it has contributed to a better understanding of the interaction between conversation and grammar.

References

Du Bois, J., S. Schuetze-Coburn, D. Paolino, and S. Cumming. 1993. Outline of Discourse Transcription. *Talking Data: Transcription and Coding Methods for Language Research*, eds. J. Edwards and M. Lampert, 221-260. Hillsdale, NJ: Lawrence Erlbaum.

Ford, C., B. Fox, and S. A. Thompson. 1996. Practices in the Construction of Turns: The 'TCU' Revisited. *Pragmatics* 6: 427-454.

Ford, C., and S. A. Thompson. 1996. Interactional Units in Conversation: Syntactic, Intonational, and Pragmatic Resources for the Management of Turns. *Interaction and Grammar*, eds. E. Ochs, E. Schegloff, and S. A. Thompson, 134-184. Cambridge: Cambridge University Press.

Fox, B., M. Hayashi, and R. Jasperson. 1996. Resources and Repair: A Cross-linguistic Study of Syntax and Repair. *Interaction and Grammar*, ed. E. Ochs, E. Schegloff, and S. A. Thompson, 185-237. Cambridge: Cambridge University Press.

Freed, A. 1994. The Form and Function of Questions in Informal Dyadic Conversation. *Journal of Pragmatics* 21: 621-44.

Goodwin, C. 1981. *Conversational Organization: Interaction between Speakers and Hearers*. New York: Academic Press.

Kim, H. 2002. Full Noun Phrases as Turn-constructional Units in English Conversation. *Tamhwa-wa Inci (Discourse and Cognition)* 9: 21-50.

Matsumoto, K. 1997. NPs in Japanese Conversation. *Pragmatics* 7: 163-181.

Ochs, E., E. Schegloff, and S. A. Thompson. 1996. *Interaction and Grammar*. Cambridge: Cambridge University Press.

Ono, T., and S. A. Thompson. 1994. Unattached NPs in English Conversation. *Berkeley Linguistics Society* 20: 402-419.

Ono, T., and S. A. Thompson. 1995. What can Conversation Tell us about Syntax? *Alternative Linguistics: Descriptive and Theoretical Modes*, ed. P. Davis, 213-271. Amsterdam/Philadelphia: John Benjamins.

Ono, T., E. Yoshida, and M. Banno. 1998. It Takes Two to Dance: The Interactional Determinants of NP Intonation Units with a Marked Rising Intonation (*hangimonkei*) in Japanese Conversation. *Japanese/Korean Linguistics* 7: 95-103. Stanford: CSLI.

Quirk, R., S. Greenbaum, G. Leech, and J. Svartvik. 1985. *A Comprehensive Grammar of the English Language*. London: Longman.

Sacks, H., E. Schegloff and G. Jefferson. 1974. A Simplest Systematics for the Organization of Turn-taking Conversation. *Language* 50: 696-735.

Schegloff, E. 1979. The Relevance of Repair to Syntax-for-Conversation. *Syntax and Semantics Vol. 12, Discourse and Syntax,* ed. T. Givon, 261-286. New York: Academic Press.

Schegloff, E. 1996. Turn Organization: One Intersection of Grammar and Interaction. *Interaction and Grammar*, ed. E. Ochs, E. Schegloff, and S. A. Thompson, 52-133. Cambridge: Cambridge University Press.

Schegloff, E., H. Sacks, and G. Jefferson. 1977. The Preference for Self-correction in the Organization of Repair in Conversation. *Language* 53: 361-382.

Tanaka, H. 1999. *Turn-taking in Japanese Conversation: A Study in Grammar and Interaction*. Amsterdam/Philadelphia: John Benjamins.

Weber, E. 1993. *Varieties of Questions in English Conversation*. Amsterdam/Philadelphia: John Benjamins.

When Best Friends Do Not Use Their Own Home Language

CHUNHUA MA
Michigan State University

1. Introduction

Previous studies of bilingual and bidialectal language practices (e.g. Blom and Gumperz, 1972; Di Pietro, 1977; Auer, 1984; Poplack, 1987; Heller, 1988; Scotton, 1988; Nishimura, 1992; Yoon, 1996) have shown that many different factors motivate code choices. This paper examines Korean-Chinese bilinguals' language choice and argues that, when an honorific language (Korean) and a nonhonorific language (Chinese) come into contact, interpersonal relationships that are overtly signaled in the grammatical system of the honorific language play an important role.

Among studies of typologically unrelated languages such as Japanese-English and Korean-English, only a few (e.g., Yoon 1998) have explored the correlation between interpersonal relationships and code choice when the structure of the code itself reflects such relationships.

I will first show how Korean and Chinese are organized with respect to deferential forms and the relationship of such forms to the concepts of power and solidarity and then I will explore how a formal feature associated with honorific language use provides an impetus for language choice. I will also show how this particular situation leads to an unusual language choice — the use of the 'nonhome' language to signal more solidary relationships.

2. Background

2.1. Different Features of Korean and Chinese

This study focuses on a typological difference between Korean and Chinese — obligatory linguistic forms that encode the social status of and relations between participants. Korean is a typical honorific language; its speakers are required to adjust their lexical and morphological choices according to such variables as status, age, sex, level of intimacy, and situational formality as these variables change. According to Hijirida and Sohn's (1986) study of cross-cultural patterns of the deference systems of English, Japanese, and Korean, age is the most sensitive social variable in Korean, and therefore that is the variable I will principally address here.

Korean does not have a second person deferential pronoun like the well-known V forms of many European languages. The neutral second person pronoun is rather restricted in its usage — typically either by adults to children or between very intimate friends in informal contexts. In other cases, nominal substitutes (e.g. first name + *si, onni* 'older sister', *sacang-nim* 'company president') are employed extensively as the second person direct address polite or deferential forms.

Chinese, however, is a typical nonhonorific language. The same utterance can be addressed to almost anyone — friends, spouse, children, boss, strangers. Although there are two second person pronominal forms — *ni* (plain) and *nin* (polite), the use of *nin* indicates interpersonal distance between speaker and addressee and is restricted to addressing someone who has much higher status, is much older, or is met for the first time. Using *nin* only adds politeness, however, and impoliteness or inappropriateness is not signaled by avoiding it. *Ni* is almost the default choice for second person direct address in Chinese.

I hypothesize that bilingual speakers will strategically manipulate these two different systems to implement the deference norms of the culture and that they will show different patterns of language choice based in part on these second person usage options as the interpersonal relationships of interlocutors vary. To test this hypothesis, I will examine two Korean-Chinese bilingual speakers' different code choice behaviors when they talk to an age-superior and an age-peer.

2.2. Power and Solidarity

In their study of diachronic and synchronic variation in second person pronominal usage in European languages, Brown and Gilman (1960) provide an account based on solidarity and power. Many European languages, such as German, French, and Spanish, have two forms of the second person pronoun: a *V* form and a *T* form. *V* forms are 'formal' or 'polite' (*Sie*, *Vous*, *Usted*,) and *T* forms are 'familiar' (*du*, *tous*, *tu*). At least historically, interlocutors' practice in pronominal selection was primarily power-generated:

the interlocutor with greater power used the *T* form to address others of less power and received the *V* form from them. When the interlocutors were in an equal power relationship, solidarity was considered. A solidary relationship between power equals gave rise to the use of the *T* form, but a less solidary relationship required selection of the *V* form. I believe the system I will describe is still primarily power-based and that age is the primary indicator of the power hierarchy.

If we transfer the notion of a 'formal' *V* form and a 'familiar' *T* form to a language contact situation in which speakers have access to one system with and one without honorifics, a pattern parallel to that of the older European system emerges. I represent this parallelism in Figure 1 and assume, as in the older European system, that 'power' is the dominating concern and that 'solidarity' is secondary. In this figure '=' indicates that there is an equal probability for either code to be used (at least with regard to the variables under consideration here); a '>' or '<' indicates that there is a greater or lesser chance, respectively, that one code will be chosen, and combinations of the two symbols (e.g., '>=' or '<=') indicate a somewhat greater or lesser chance, respectively.

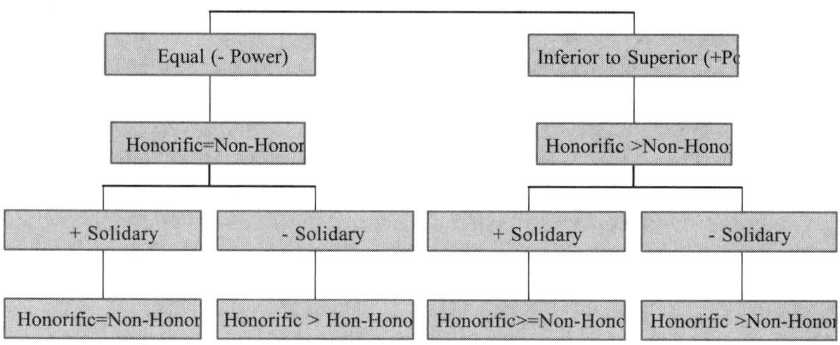

Figure 1: Power/solidarity relations in an honorific/nonhonorific language situation

Hypothetically, then, when inferiors address superiors, following the right side of Figure 1, deference or formality is observed; therefore, the language with the honorific system is preferred, as shown in the second level. If the conversation takes place between speakers who are solidary (third level, left branch), however, there is a greater likelihood for honorific code choice (fourth level); but if the speakers are in a nonsolidary relationship (third level, right branch), the language with the honorific system will be the code most frequently chosen by the speakers (fourth level, right branch). On the other hand, turning to the left side of Figure 1, if the conversation is carried out between equals, interlocutors have more freedom to choose either code (second level), and a more solidary relationship (third level, left branch) continues to allow more evenly distributed language choice (fourth level, left branch). Nonsolidary interactions between equals, however, show a slight preference for the honorific system (fourth level, right branch).

In this study, I adopt the findings of Hijirida and Sohn (1986), which emphasize age difference as the primary variable in the Korean deferential system. I equate it with 'power' and examine the correlation between age and code choice. I also discuss the role of solidarity when the power relationship remains fixed. I will carry out this investigation focusing on the three relationships shown in Figure 2.

Inferiors → Superiors + Power (age) - Solidarity	**Inferiors → Superiors** + Power (age) + Solidarity
Equals - Power (age) + Solidarity	

Figure 2. Power & solidarity relationships of the interlocutors in this study

2.3. The Speech Community

The data for this study come from informal conversations audio-recorded in a Korean/Chinese bilingual community, Yanji, a small city in the northeast part of China. Yanji is the capital of Yanbian — a Korean autonomous region. The population is approximately forty percent Korean and sixty percent other ethnic groups, mainly Han Chinese. In Yanji, the Korean language and writing system are widely used alongside Chinese, and both languages are used in official documents, announcements of government meetings, business and commerce, and written communications among technicians and workers.

Similarly, students are given the option of being educated and tested in their ethnic language. In Korean schools, Korean is the main language of instruction, and Chinese is taught as a subject. Since Korean students learn Chinese from elementary school, however, and have considerable influence from the media, which is mainly in Chinese, most students who go to Korean schools speak Chinese fluently. On the other hand, even those Korean students educated in Chinese schools can speak fluent Korean, due mainly to the fact that Korean is their mother tongue, which they spoke before entering elementary school, and it continues to function as the main tool for communication in the family, particularly with the older generations.

With regard to language practice, switching between Korean and Chinese is quite common in casual interactions between bilingual speakers but not in such public settings as TV shows, job interviews, and formal speech.

3. Data

Data for this study was collected in the winter of 2000. A three-hour conversation was recorded at the apartment of the researcher's sister, with three people: C (the researcher), X (C's best friend), and J (C's sister). This data offers an example of a three-way interpersonal relationship between interlocutors, while keeping other variables constant — in-group membership, degree of formality, social status, sex, and Chinese school background; this last factor implies the same language proficiency level for all three. The interpersonal relationship of the interlocutors in this study is shown below:

X→J relationship: [+power, -solidarity]
C→J relationship: [+power, +solidarity]
C↔X relationship: [-power, +solidarity]

Their balanced bilinguality is further supported by the data as shown in their overall language distribution during the conversation: Speaker X uses Chinese for 47% of her talk and Korean for 53%, while speaker C uses Chinese for 57% of her talk, and Korean for 43%.

All transcribed utterances were broken into utterance units ('U-UNIT'). Such a unit is a stretch of uninterrupted talk by one speaker that has grammatical and/or intonational limits; that is, a U-UNIT is a clausal, phrasal, or even lexical unit bounded by some sort of intonational indication of its completeness. Monolingual U-UNITs were identified as Korean or Chinese L-UNITs. For intrasentential codeswitches (i.e., switching within U-UNITs), material in each language is coded as a subunit ('L-UNIT').

For each unit and subunit, overt second person direct address references were indicated. Speakers and addressees were also identified in the coding. In the discourse samples, Korean is always given in italics, Chinese in plain type.

4. Results and Discussion

The total number of L-UNITs elicited from speaker X was 1453, out of which 410 were addressed to J and 1014 to C; the L-UNITs from speaker C totaled 1446; 412 to J and 981 to X, as shown in Table 2 and 3.

4.1. Code Choice

Table 2 and Figure 3 show the different language choices of speaker X as addressee identity changes. Speaker X uses significantly more Korean L-UNITs when she is talking to J, a superior, but more Chinese when the addressee is C, her friend of equal status. A similar pattern is shown for Speaker C's language choice in Table 3 and Figure 4. Korean is preferred when the addressee is older, and Chinese for conversation between peers. Both speakers' code choices are statistically significant when the addressee is used as the independent variable.

	Chinese	Korean	Total
Addressee C	549	465	1014
Addressee J	117	293	410

Table 2: Speaker X's code choice by addressee

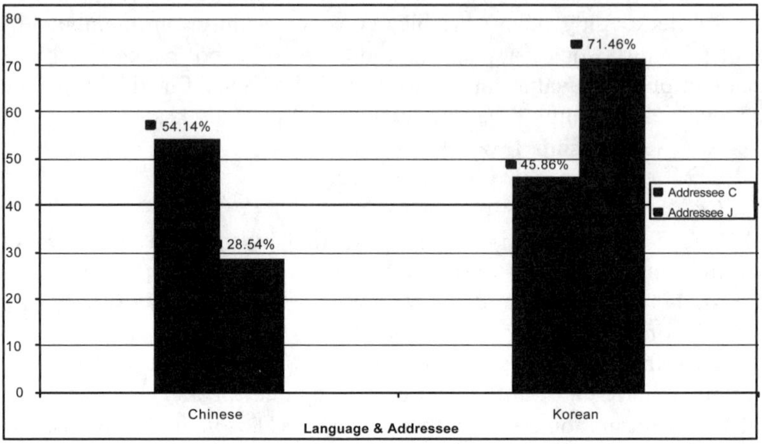

Figure 3. Speaker X's code choice by addressee. Chi-Square=.75, p=.000

	Chinese	Korean	Total
Addressee X	595	386	981
Addressee J	196	216	412

Table 3: Speaker C's code choice

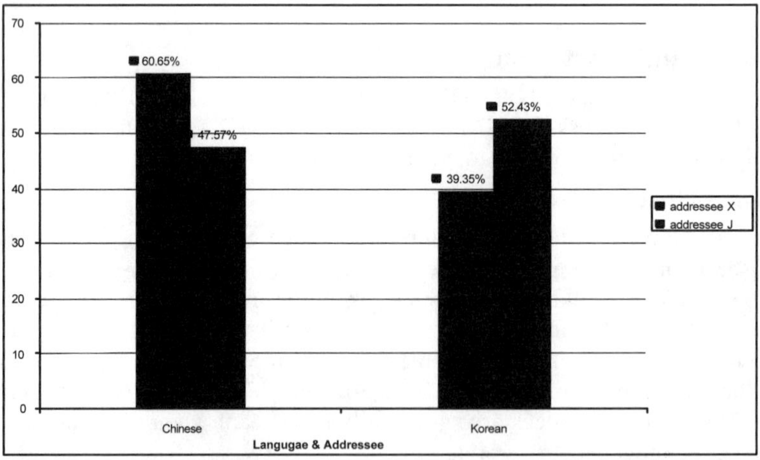

Figure 4. Speaker C's code choice by addressee. Chi-Square=.19, p=.000

Although Chinese is often used in conversations between casual acquaintances, this strategy may be regarded as impolite if the interlocutors are fully competent bilinguals, especially if their power relationship is asymmetrical. This general language choice finding suggests that Korean-Chinese bilinguals get around this situation by conducting their conversations with their superiors more in Korean than in Chinese. When no such social restrictions need to be observed, their speech pattern is more or less equally distributed between Korean and Chinese. I believe the clue to such choice lies in the second person address forms of Korean and Chinese.

4.2. Second Person Direct Address

In what follows, I will analyze the use of second person direct address forms, since that is the linguistic factor which is most closely related to the European T-V alternation discussed in Brown and Gilman (1960) and to the specific feature of the honorific – nonhonorific contrast I am investigating. Here I include under the general cover term 'second person direct address usage' both second person pronouns (Chinese only) and such direct address nominals as *onni* (Korean 'older sister'). The frequency of second person direct address usage by language as well as by each individual speaker is shown in Table 4.

	Chinese	Korean
Speaker X	10.43% (72/618)	6.03%(46/717)
Speaker C	6.34% (39/576)	13.72% (114/717)

Table 4: Frequency of 2nd person direct address in all L-UNITs by X and C

This table indicates that, in both Korean and Chinese, second person direct address usage is quite minimal. For Speaker X, only 72 out of 618 Chinese and 46 out of 717 Korean L-UNITs contain second person direct address forms. For Speaker C, 114 out of 717 Chinese and 39 out of 576 Korean L-UNITs contain second person direct address forms. This low ratio can be explained by the fact that both Korean and Chinese are *pro-drop* languages. Although this disproportion limits the number of tokens I can examine, I will next show how second person direct address usage correlates with the relationships between interlocutors.

	Chinese	Korean	Total
Addressee C	63	23	86
Addressee J	6	23	29

Table 5: Speaker X's second person direct address usage

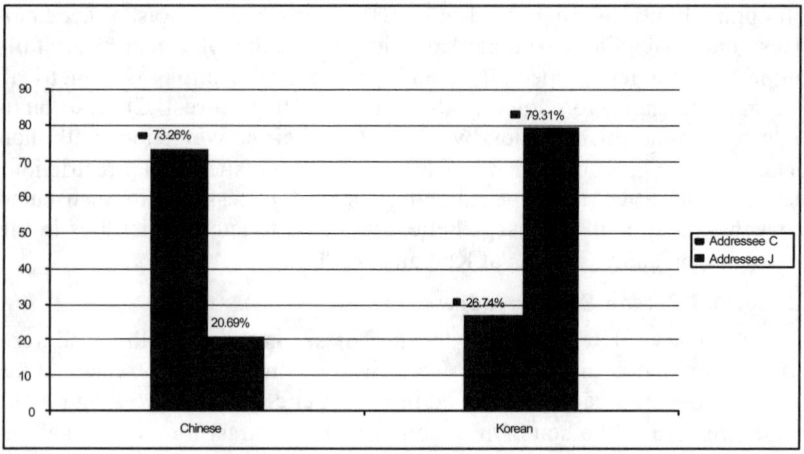

Figure 5: Speaker X's 2nd person direct address. Chi-Square=.23, p=.000

	Chinese	Korean	Total
Addressee X	92	19	111
Addressee J	20	20	40

Table 6: Speaker C's 2nd person direct address usage

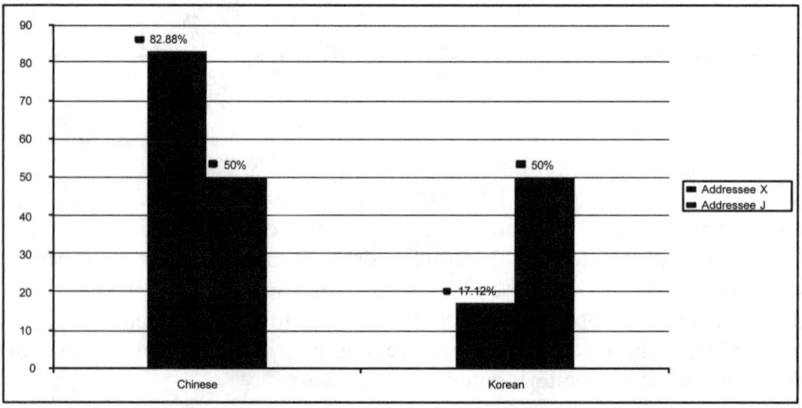

Figure 6: Speaker C's 2nd person direct address. Chi-Square=.15, p=.000

Figure 5 shows that Speaker X uses strikingly more Korean second person direct address forms (79.31%) when she addresses J and many fewer (26.74%) with C. Figure 6 indicates these proportions for Speaker C's speech — exactly 50% with J and only 17.12% with X. The result is quite similar to that shown in Figure 3 and 4. The two speakers' second person direct address usage shows a parallel pattern to their overall code choice:

Korean forms are preferred when the interaction is between an age-inferior and an age-superior — X to J or C to J.

In peer interaction between X and C, more Chinese second person direct address forms are used. In fact, Chinese second person direct address forms are used more than twice as often as Korean ones. Apparently, Korean-Chinese bilingual speakers minimize their usage of Chinese second person pronouns when they talk to someone who is older (i.e., more 'powerful'), while no such restriction limits them when the conversation is between two equals.

Recall that in Korean speech there is no such thing as an honorific second person pronoun; a nominal substitute is adopted to address someone who is superior, while in Chinese, a simple second person pronoun can be used to address almost anyone. When they have these two totally different systems available simultaneously, Korean-Chinese bilinguals use Chinese *ni* quite reservedly, even though its usage by no means suggests blunt or rude behavior in monolingual Chinese speech.

4.3. Different Behavior of X and C

Although the individual speakers' code choice shows a consistent pattern of using more Korean when talking to a superior and more Chinese with an equal, a comparison between the two speakers' behavior when they talk to J shows that the difference between them is also statistically significant.

	Chinese	Korean	Total
Speaker X	117	293	410
Speaker C	196	216	412

Table 7: Comparison of X and C addressing J

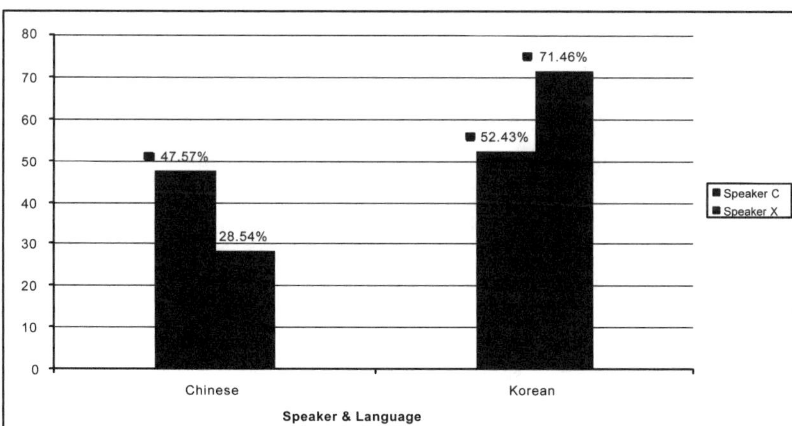

Figure 7. X and C's language choice addressing J. Chi-Square=.31, p=.000

	Chinese	Korean	Total
Speaker X	6	23	29
Speaker C	20	20	40

Table 8: C and X's different pronominal use to J

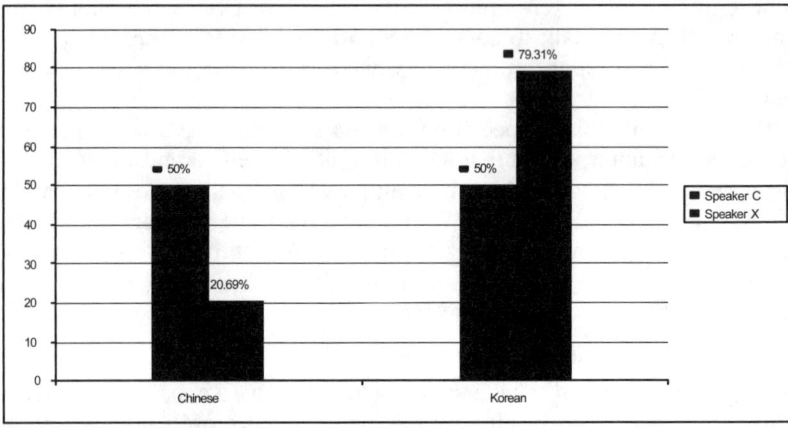

Figure 8: X and C's 2nd person direct address to J.Chi-Square=4.97, p=.025

Table 7 and Figure 7 indicate that, when addressing J, Speaker X produces considerably more Korean utterances than C. A similar pattern is shown in their second person direct address usage (Table 8 and Figure 8). Apparently, Korean-Chinese bilinguals' language selection is power-generated (by age), but, when the power variable remains constant, the dimension of solidarity emerges. As biological sisters, C & J share much more intimacy than X & J; therefore, when C is talking to her sister, she will be more inclined to make choices that reflect that greater solidarity; X, in addressing J, is more likely to deviate more from the forms that one might expect for the expression of solidarity.

This result is somewhat parallel to the findings of Yoon's (1996) case study of group membership and code choices among Korean-English bilingual speakers. Linguistically coded human relationships in Korean serve better as an outgroup code because 'the relationship between outgroup members is mobile, and therefore constant awareness of one's place in relation to the other is needed to maintain the appropriate social relationship' (402). English is a better ingroup code since there is no need to reinforce the difference between interlocutors. Here one might denote outgroup as [-solidarity] and ingroup [+solidarity]. Both Yoon's and my study suggest that we should not assume that the home language is always or perhaps even the usual ingroup or solidary code among bilingual speakers, for, in some cases, structural properties (i.e. honorific forms) of the languages involved give rise to a rather unusual language choice — a nonhome language is preferred to signal more solidary relationships.

5. Conclusion

This paper has attempted to explore the linguistic factors that influence bilingual code choice when honorific and nonhonorific languages are involved. By examining Korean-Chinese bilingual speakers' code choice overall and in light of their second person direct address usage, I have shown that status (or 'power') differences, here the age difference in particular, play an important role. Addressing a superior promotes Korean language use, while interaction between equals shows no such preference. Furthermore, the study reveals how the solidarity factor correlates with individual speakers' code choices. While power relationships remain constant, the more intimate the relationship is, the more freedom speakers have to use either language — honorific or nonhonorific. Conversely, a less solidary relationship triggers the use of Korean — a language with overt grammaticalization to reinforce subtle differences in human relationships and thereby express deference.

I conclude that, in addition to the many factors that have been proposed in the bilingual language choice literature, structural properties of the language are also motivating elements for codeswitches. An honorific language, even if it is the home language of the interlocutors, may be more suited to unequal power relationships, however they are calculated in a given language. In that context, a nonhonorific language may take on the role of expressing solidarity. This study encourages researchers in bilingual codeswitching to investigate the internal linguistic characteristics of the contact languages for a more complete understanding of bilingual language practice. Future studies involving honorific/nonhonorific language pairs, such as Korean-English, Japanese-English, Japanese-Chinese, etc., may shed more light on our understanding of bilingual speakers' language practices.

References

Auer, P. 1984. *Bilingual Conversation.* Amsterdam: John Benjamins Publishing Company.

Blom, J. P. & J. J. Gumperz. 1972. Social Meaning in Linguistic Structure: Code-switching in Norway. *Directions in Sociolinguistics,* ed. J. Gumperz & D. Hymes, 407-434. New York: Holt, Rinehart and Winston.

Brown, R. & A. Gilman. 1960. The Pronouns of Power and Solidarity. *Style in Language*, ed. T. Sebeok, 253-276. Cambridge, MA: MIT press.

Di Pietro, R. 1977. Code-switching as a Verbal Strategy among Bilinguals. *Current Themes in Linguistics: Bilingualism, Experimental Linguistics, and Language Typologies.* ed. F. Eckman, 3-13. Washington, DC: Hemisphere Publishing Corporation.

Heller, M. 1988. Introduction. *Codeswitching: Anthropological and Sociolinguistic Perspectives,* ed. M. Heller, 1-24. Berlin: Mouton de Gruyter.

Hijirida, K. & H. M. Sohn. 1986. Cross-Cultural Patterns of Honorifics and Sociolinguistic Sensitivity to Honorific Variables: Evidence from English, Japanese, and Korean. *Papers in Linguistics* 19(3): 365-401.

Nishimura, M. 1992. Language Choice and In-Group Identity among Canadian Niseis. *Journal of Asian Pacific Communication* 3(1): 97-113.

Poplack, S. 1987. Contrasting Patterns of Code-switching in Two Communities. *Aspects of Multilingualism: Proceedings from the Fourth Nordic Symposium on Bilingualism*, ed. E. Wande, et al, 51-77. Sweden: Uppsala.

Scotton, C. 1988. Code-switching as Indexical of Social Negotiation. *Codeswitching: Anthropological and Sociolinguistic Perspectives*, ed. M. Heller, 1-24. Berlin: Mouton de Gruyter.

Yoon, K. K. 1996. A Case Study of Fluent Korean-English Bilingual Speakers: Group Membership and Code Choices. *Journal of Pragmatics* 25: 395-407.

Expressive Function of Japanese Adnominal Demonstrative *Konna/Sonna/Anna*

KEIKO NARUOKA
Japan Women's University

1. Introduction

Demonstratives have been studied from various perspectives in many languages. Japanese demonstratives are no exception. Previous studies on the Japanese demonstrative usually have the following tendencies: First, the majority of studies on Japanese demonstratives aim to reveal the differences in usage among three types of demonstrative – *ko-*, *so-* and *a-* – in order to build a theory of demonstratives (e.g. Horiguchi 1978, Kamio 1990, Kinsui and Takubo 1990, Kuno 1973, Kuroda 1979, Sakuma 1983). Because of this aim, the analysis is often based on the researcher's introspection and pays little attention to actual use in discourse. Second, since previous studies have been conducted for the purpose of finding an abstract framework for demonstratives, they tend to look exclusively at the 'typical' forms, i.e. the pronominal *kore/sore/are* (this/that/that) and the adnominal *kono/sono/ano* (this/that/that + NP). Scholars often disregard the variations in demonstratives despite the fact that the Japanese demonstrative system is lexically complex and has many variations in terms of parts of speech as well as what is referred to (pronominal forms for location *koko/soko/asoko* (this/that/that place), and for direction in formal usage *kochira/sochira/achira* and informal usage *kocchi/socchi/acchi* (this/that/that way); adnominal forms for characteristics of an object *konna/sonna/anna* (this/that/that kind of); and adverbial forms *koo/soo/aa* (in this/ that/that manner)). The third point applies not only to studies of the Japanese demonstrative but also demonstratives in other languages. Most studies examine the function of demonstratives that points to an object in a speech situation or discourse ('referential function'). Demonstratives have been regarded as a linguistic form for this function, and researchers have not taken into account any other functions.

This study, on the other hand, examines demonstratives from a different perspective as compared to previous studies, analyzing a form that has not been discussed yet, using conversational data, and aiming to examine the functional differences among the variations. The ultimate objectives underlying this study are 1) understanding the basis of the whole complex system of Japanese demonstratives through examining the use and function of demonstrative variation, and 2) revealing the roles of the demonstrative in human interaction. Especially, this study attempts to comprehend demonstratives not just as deictic terms but as forms that have dynamic functions in interaction. For these objectives, we will adopt a new methodology in studying the demonstrative. The object of the analysis is the adnominal demonstrative '*konna/sonna/anna*.' This form is described in Japanese grammar as the form used for referring to characteristics of an object, equivalent to the English 'this/that kind of.' As for data, we pay much attention to naturally occurring conversational data. In the conversational data, the form *konna/ sonna/anna* is not always used as grammar books describe. In addition, although this form is not considered typical, its frequency in conversation is relatively high. Lastly, our aim is not to examine the differences among the three types (*ko*-, *so*- and *a*-) but to show the differences among variations: How the form *konna/sonna/anna* is used differently from other forms, such as *kore/sore/are* and *kono/sono/ano*. In the course of finding different usage among the variations, we look at functions beyond the referential function of this form. This study particularly shows the usage that expresses the speaker's emotion and attitude. We call this usage the 'expressive function' in this study.

2. Expressive Function of Demonstratives

The 'expressive function' of demonstratives, showing the speaker's emotion and attitude, is mentioned in various studies (e.g. 'social deixis' Fillmore 1982, 'emotional deixis' Lakoff 1974, 'empathetic deixis' Lyons 1977). However, these studies introduce the function without any in-depth discussion except in the work of Lakoff (1974). Lakoff argues that the English 'this/these' and 'that/those' sometimes express the speaker's emotional sharedness and solidarity. The use of 'that' in 'That Henry Kissinger sure knows his way around Hollywood! (1974: 352)' establishes emotional solidarity between the speaker and the addressee by implying that both participants in the conversation share the same view toward the subject of the discussion.

Using Lakoff's (1974) work as a model, the Japanese *a*-type demonstrative is discussed by Kitagawa (1979) and Ono (1994). They argue that Japanese *a*-type demonstratives have the same effect as the English emotional deictic 'that' and express a sense of sharing the same view. These studies show that the Japanese demonstrative serves the expressive function, but they touch upon this function in the course of explaining the differences in usage among *ko-*, *so-* and *a-* (i.e. the same kind of treatment as in the previous studies mentioned in Section 1). In this study, we will show that close examination of the expressive function can illustrate its importance in the use of demonstratives. Also, this study will show, through an analysis of *konna/sonna/anna*, that the expressive function is not just for *a*-type demonstratives, but can be seen in other types as well.

3. Data

The data used in this study are from naturally occurring informal conversations. My colleagues and I collected and transcribed three and a half hours of recorded conversations. These include eight sets of conversations among family members, relatives, and friends. Additionally, there are two hours of conversation taken from the published corpus *Josei no Kotoba Shokubahen* (Women's Language in the Workplace) and *Dansei no Kotoba Shokubahen* (Men's Language in the Workplace) (Gendai Nihongo Kenkyu-kai 1999, 2002). The conversations are each ten minuteslong, with twelve settings in total. As the corpus titles show, these conversations were taken from workplaces and schools. But in order to limit the data to informal speech, conversations among coworkers during breaks at the office are used.

4. Expressive Functions of *Konna/Sonna/Anna*

Based on analysis of the conversational data, *konna/sonna/anna* are categorized into three usages. Table 1 indicates the number and percentage of each usage in the five and a half hours of conversational data. The first category is 'referential.' Referential usage is the same as described in Japanese grammars: referring to characteristics of an object. As can be seen in Table 1, this usage is very limited in the data. The second category is 'expressive and referential.' This usage appears most frequently in my data. It expresses the speaker's emotion and at the same time, indicates a referent. The emotions expressed with the form are 'negative emotion' and 'surprise.' The final category is only seen in the use of *sonna*. The usage does not seem to have any clear referent and it is used like an interjection, often with negative emotion. When we deal with the expressiveness of a linguistic form, it is necessary to examine not just the utterance, but also the larger discourse in conversation. As we will see, the examples discussed in this study are rather long, which enables us to see the emotional state of the speaker clearly.

	Referential	Expressive + Referential	Interjection	Total
konna	2 (5.00%)	38 (95.00%)	0 (0.00%)	40 (100.00%)
sonna	3 (3.03%)	79 (79.80%)	17 (17.17%)	99 (100.00%)
anna	3 (25.00%)	9 (75.00%)	0 (0.00%)	12 (100.00%)

Table 1. Number and percentage of three usages of *konna/sonna/anna* in 5.5 hours of conversational data

The qualitative analysis in the following sections focuses on 'expressive and referential' and 'interjection' usages. The analysis is based mainly on *konna* and *sonna*, only because they occur more frequently than *anna*. However, we do not intend to compare internal differences among the three types (*ko-*, *so-*, and *a-*). The low frequency of *anna* reveals an interesting point: As mentioned in Section 2, previous studies on the expressive function have so far been limited to *a*-type demonstratives. In contrast, the expressive function is also found in *ko-* and *so*-types in this study.

4.1. *Konna/Sonna/Anna* in 'Expressive and Referential' Usage

In our conversational data, the emotions expressed by the forms *konna/sonna/anna* are usually negative, while some instances express surprise. We will first look at the examples expressing negative emotion, then at an example expressing surprise. These emotions are not always directed toward the referent of the demonstrative. They can be directed toward an action or situation that involves the referent, toward the interlocutor's utterance as a whole, or toward the interlocutor.

Negative emotion toward the interlocutor is expressed by the use of *sonna* in example (1). K and J, close female friends, have been talking about writing letters to their professors. K is saying that she writes informal rather than formal letters to her professors.

(1)

1. K: *E= atashi= kekkoo nanka, erai ojii-chan no sensei toka de*[*mo*],
   'Well, even to a respectable elderly (grandfatherly) professor,
   I usually...'
2. J: [*Un*].
   'Uh-huh.'

3. K: *Futuuni tegami kaichau.*
   '...write an informal letter.'
4. J: .. *Nto?*
   'Really?'
5. K: *Un.*
   'Yeah.'
6. J: *A=,* <Q *ma=, wakamono dakara shoonai na=* Q> *nante kanji de?*
   'Oh, you think the professor will say something like, "Oh well, it can't be helped, she is too young to know (that she shouldn't write an informal letter)"?'
7. K: ... *Konaida Doraemon no hagaki ni, !chi=chai ji de ippai kaite* <@ *dashita kara*@> [@@@.]
   'The other day, I wrote a message on a Doraemon (cartoon character) postcard with very very small letters and sent it...'
8. J: [*Dashita no?*]
   'Did you really send it?'
9. : *Ojii-chan ni?*
   'To the elderly professor?'
10. **: [*Yomenai* *tte* *sonna-no* @@].**
    cannot read QT *sonna*-NOM
    'He will never be able to read that! (because the letters are too small)'
11. K: [@@@].

In lines 8 and 9, J asks with surprise whether K really sent the elderly professor a postcard with a cute cartoon character and written in small letters. Then, J criticizes K in line 10, saying the professor will not be able to read such small letters. The demonstrative *sonna-no* in line 10 refers to the message K wrote on the postcard, and at the same time, J's negative emotion toward K is apparently expressed. Although J criticizes K for what she did, we can see that J and K consider the story to be funny, judging from their laughter toward the end of the discourse.

Example (1) exhibits two characteristics in the use of *sonna*. First, *sonna* is used with the nominalizer *-no*. *Konna*/*sonna*/*anna* is often used with the nominalizer *-no* or *-mono* (*-mon*) in my data. The nominalized form *sonna-no* and *sonna-mono* (*-mon*) is sometimes used as an alternative form of the pronominal demonstrative *sore* (that) (this point will be discussed in example (4)). Second, the utterance in line 10 exhibits non-canonical word order. Japanese clausal word order is subject-predicate, but in this utterance, the verb '*yomenai* (cannot read)' is followed by the subject '*sonna-no*.' Ono and Suzuki (1992) illustrate several types of Japanese non-canonical word order and the motivations for using them. One of these types is the 'emotive type,' and they argue that most of the predicates express the speaker's feeling or attitude, and that post-predicate elements are often demonstratives. Thus, the non-canonical word order emphasizes the speaker's emotion together with the choice of demonstrative forms.

The next example clearly illustrates the functional differences between demonstrative variations of the same type (*konna* and *kono*). Examples (2) and (3) are from dinner conversation among family members: father, mother and their daughter, who is in her mid 20s. In the following excerpt, the family is having soup that the mother has cooked. The daughter has tasted it and found it disgusting, and the mother is explaining why the soup tastes different from usual.

(2)
1. Daughter: .. <LO *Aa= nani kore* LO>. (while tasting the soup)
   'Yuck, what is this?!?'
2. Mother: @@.
3. Daughter: *Naani kore?*
   'What is this?'
4. Mother: *Toogan.*
   'It's wax gourd (soup).'
5. **Daughter: *Toogan tte konna henna aji shita?***
   wax gourd QT *konna* strange taste did
   'Does wax gourd (soup) taste this strange?'
6. Mother: *Un, sorya kyoo wa hora moo tonikaku yasai ga= tten de,*
   'Well, I just wanted to use all the vegetables today anyway.'
7. **: *Toogan suupu futsuu wa kono aji ni shinai kedo.***
   wax gourd soup usually T *kono*(this) taste IO do not but
   'We don't usually cook wax gourd soup like this though.'
8. Father: *Toogan suupu ni wa ninjin nanka hairanai n da yo futuu.*
   'We don't usually put carrots in wax gourd soup.'

This example shows that the two people, who have different attitudes toward the referent, use different variations of the demonstrative. The daughter, who feels that the soup is disgusting, utters '*konna henna aji* (konna strange taste)' for the soup in line 5. On the contrary, the mother, who cooked the soup, says '*kono aji* (this taste).' The difference comes from different reactions to the soup. The daughter doesn't think it is tasty, while the mother thinks it isn't bad or at least does not express a negative reaction.

Next, we will see an example that indicates the negative connotation of *konna* at the level of consciousness. The father has finished his meal and is moving out of the dining room. The daughter, who is trying to record the conversation, asks her father to stay at the dinner table longer, but the father claims that he wants to watch a baseball game on TV.

(3)

1. Father: *Gossosama=.*
 'I'm finished! (Thanks for the dinner)'
2. Daughter: *!A=.*
 'Wait!'
3. Father: *Nan da yo.*
 'What?'
4. Daughter: *Ma, suwanna yo @@.*
 'Well, let's sit down.'
5. Father: *Kore* (tape-recorder) *no tame nan da yo, koitsu.*
 'She says it for this (tape-recorder).'
6. Daughter: @@@.
7. Father: *!Dakara ore ippai nomoo janaika tte itta n da yo omae.*
 'I told you that I'd better have a drink during the meal.'
8. Daughter: <WH *Ii jan betsuni ichinichijuu hima nandakara kongurai tukiatta tte*. WH>
 'You have nothing to do all day long, so why can't you stay for a while for me…'
9. Father: *Kooshien de Hanshin ga kusen shiten no.*
 'The Hanshin Tigers (baseball team) are having a close game at Kooshien Stadium.'

10. Daughter: **<LO *Konna jikan ni yatten no?* LO>**
konna time IO doing NOM
'Are they playing a baseball game this late at night?'

11. Father: ***Konna jikan tt yatteru sa*, [*X*-].**
konna time QT doing IP
''This late at night?' Of course they are!'

12. Daughter: [*Na*]*itaa yatten no?*
 'Are they having a night game?'
13. Father: *Naitaa da yo mochiron.*
 'Of course they are having a night game.'
14. : *Kono jiki naitaa ni kimatten no moo.*
 'They always have night games at this time of the year.'

In line 10, the daughter asks her father whether they are really having a night game using '*konna jikan* (*konna* time).' From the choice of *konna* and her low pitched voice, it can be surmised that she is suspicious about her father's comment, possibly suspicious that her father just wants to move out of the dining room to avoid being recorded.

This example shows that the addressee notices the speaker's negative emotion in her use of *konna*. In line 11, the father reacts to the daughter's word choice by quoting her words '*konna jikan*.' This quotation indicates that the father realizes that the daughter is suspicious of his reason for wanting to leave the dining room. The father afterwards even explains to the daughter that it is common knowledge that there are night games at this time of year.

Konna/sonna/anna sometimes express the speaker's surprise, although the frequency is lower than negative feelings. The following excerpt is from a conversation between close female friends, talking about making New Year's cards.

(4)

1. J: *Atashi inku-jetto yoo no ne, .. Nengajoo?*
   'I… postcards for an inkjet printer...'
2. K: *Un.*
   'Uh-huh.'
3. J: *Kaitai-, .. katta kedo=, are moo sugu urikireta.*
   'I want-I wanted to buy the postcards, but they sold out quickly.'
4. K: *A soo nano?*
   'Oh really?'
5. J: *Un.*
   'Yeah.'
6. K: [*He=*].
   'Really.'
7. J: [XXX] *Minna pasokon de tsukuru jan?*
   'Many people make New Year's cards with their computer, right?'
8. **K: *Sonna-no* aru n da=.**
   ***sonna*-NOM exist NOM COP**
   '(I didn't know) there was such a thing.'
9. J: *U=n.*
   'Yeah.'
10. **K: *Sore=* e-, futsuuni yuubinkyoku ga uridashite-,**
    ***sore*(that) uh regularly post office S put on sale**
    'Are those sold at the post office like regular postcards?'
11. J: *Soo soo, onaji nedan, shikamo.*
    'Yeah, and they are even the same price (as regular postcards).'

In line 8, K utters '*sonna-no*' to refer to postcards for printing out with an inkjet printer. The usage in this existential sentence implies the speaker's surprise that she has never heard of this product.

It also illustrates that the speaker can use different forms of the demonstrative to refer to the same object in a short discourse. Speaker K uses the adnominal demonstrative *sonna* plus *-no* to refer to the postcards in line 8. But in line 10, she uses the pronominal demonstrative *sore* (that) to indicate the postcards when asking for more information about them. The use of *sore* instead of *sonna-no* could be interpreted to mean that K has already understood the existence of the product, and is not surprised anymore. This instance indicates that the nominalized form *sonna-no* can be an alternative form of *sore*, and the choice depends on the speaker's emotional state.

4.2. *Sonna* as 'Interjection'

Sonna is not always used as an adnominal demonstrative as in '*sonna* + NP,' but sometimes as an interjection. The form can occur at the beginning of the utterance as in example (5). A and C are coworkers, talking about trips. C, who often goes on trips, is planning another trip and A expresses her envy.

(5)

1. C: *Doo shiyokka na=.*
   'What am I going to do (about the trip)?'
2. A: *Ii na=.*
   'I envy you (because you are planning another trip).'
3. C: *Ikunai desu yo.*
   'It's not so good really.'
4. A: *Nani ga.*
   'Why?'
5. **C: *<u>Sonna</u> chanto kaisha ni kiteru hoo ga ii desu yo=.***
   ***sonna* regularly office to coming way S better COP IP**
   'I think it's better to come to the office as usual.'
6. A: *Ii jan.*
   'I still envy you.'
7. C: *Soo ka na=.*
   'I don't know about that.'

In line 5, C might be being humble or trying to avoid too much envy, but is clearly opposing A. At the beginning of this utterance, C inserts *sonna*. This *sonna* is not followed by a noun phrase. Moreover, it does not seem to have any specific referent.

As in this example, the interjection *sonna* can be used when the speaker reacts to what the other person has said, often when she denies her interlocutor's utterance. A demonstrative is often used to link what the speaker indicates and a referent that has already appeared in discourse. Even though there is no clear referent, adding *sonna* seems to have the function of linking her utterance with what the interlocutor has said. Thus, *sonna* in a sense maintains one of the features of the demonstrative when used as an interjection.

5. Conclusion

In this study, we have shown that the variations of the demonstrative *konna/sonna/anna* have a strong expressive function in addition to a referential function. Purely referential usage, which is described in grammars, is limited in actual conversation. In fact, most uses of *konna/sonna/anna* express the speaker's emotion and attitude (see Table 1). Lakoff's (1974) 'emotional deixis "this/that"' has an expressive function when the form appears in a certain structure or environment. However, the present study further claims that *konna/sonna/anna* itself has a connotation of expressiveness. Of course, other factors, such as intonation, the adjective attached to the expression, and sentence structure are involved in expressing the speaker's emotion and attitude. But uses such as example (3) support our claim: The speaker in (3) shows his understanding of the negative feeling of the interlocutor conveyed by her choice of the demonstrative *konna*. Moreover, we have shown that *sonna*, which has a strongly expressive nature and occurs frequently, is used as an interjection. The interjection *sonna* has the effect of reacting to what the interlocutor has said. Thus, the interjection, to some extent, maintains one of the features of the demonstrative in that it links what the speaker indicates to a previously introduced referent.

We also have shown that speakers choose not only among *ko-*, *so-* and *a-*, but also among all the variations of the demonstrative forms in actual conversation. In selecting demonstrative forms from among the variations, we have seen that speakers' emotion or attitude is one of the factors. Two of the speakers in example (2) use different forms (*konna* and *kono*) to refer to the same object because they have different attitudes toward the referent. In (4), the same speaker uses different forms (*sonna-no* and *sore*) to refer to the same object depending on her feeling. Thus, when we consider choice among variations, the speaker's emotion or attitude becomes one of the important factors in addition to grammatical categories (e.g. pronominal or adnominal) and what the form refers to (e.g. the object itself or the characteristics of the object).

An interesting question remains: Why does the form *konna/sonna/anna* have a strong expressive function compared to other forms such as *kono/sono/ano* or *kore/sore/are*? The key may lie in its 'referential' function, i.e. that of referring to the characteristics of an object, as opposed to *kono/sono/ano* and *kore/sore/are*, which refer directly to an object itself.[1] Suzuki (1998) discusses how the pejorative connotation present in such Japanese particles as *nanka* or *nante* is evoked by the implication of lack of specification. In the same manner, the indirectness of *konna/sonna/anna* brings

[1] I would like to thank Professor Satoshi Kinsui for his valuable comments on this point.

about the expressive connotation, and the context of the speech plays a crucial role in interpreting the connotation, as Suzuki (1998) points out.

For several years, a number of linguistic forms and phenomena have been reexamined using such methods as Discourse Analysis. These studies have revealed crucial functions of forms and phenomena that have been neglected. Importantly, newly discovered functions are often indispensable aspects of human interaction. The present study focuses on demonstratives, which are considered a rather functional element in grammar, and which have been well studied already. But as we have seen, this analysis reveals the function of expressing the speaker's emotion and attitude, which is fundamental to human interaction. We believe that application of the same research perspective to other linguistic forms can lead to a real picture of the 'language' that people practice, rather than to an abstract representation of language.

Symbols for Discourse Transcription

[words]: Overlap, =: Lengthening, ...: Pause, X: Indecipherable syllable, !: Higher pitch on a word, @: Laughter, <@ words @>: Laugh quality, <Q words Q>: Quotation quality, <LO words LO>: Lowered pitch level, <WH words WH>: Whispered

Abbreviations

COP: Copula, IO: Indirect object marker, IP: Interactional particle, NOM: Nominalizer, QT: Quotative marker, S: Subject marker, T: Theme marker

References

Fillmore, C. J. 1982. Towards a Descriptive Framework for Spacial Deixis. *Speech, Place, and Action: Studies in Deixis and Related Topics*, eds. R. Jarvella and W. Klein, 31-59. New York: Wiley.

Gendai Nihongo Kenkyu-kai. ed. 1999. *Josei no Kotoba Shokubahen*. Tokyo: Hitsuji Shobo.

Gendai Nihongo Kenkyu-kai, ed. 2002. *Dansei no Kotoba Shokubahen*. Tokyo: Hitsuji Shobo.

Horiguchi, K. 1978. Shijishi no Hyoogensei. *Nihongo Nihonbunka* 8: 23-44.

Kamio, A. 1990. *Joohoo no Nawabari Riron: Gengo no Kinooteki Bunseki*. Tokyo: Taishukan.

Kinsui, S., and Takubo, Y. 1990. Danwa Kanri Riron kara mita Nihongo no Shijishi. *Ninchi Kagaku no Hatten*, ed. Nihon Ninchi Kagaku-kai, 85-115. Tokyo: Kodansha.

Kitagawa, C. 1979. A Note on *Sono* and *Ano*. *Explorations in Linguistics: Papers in Honor of Kazuko Inoue*, eds. G. Bedell, E. Kobayashi and M. Muraki, 232-243. Tokyo: Kenkyusha.

Kuno, S. 1973. *The Structure of the Japanese Language*. Cambridge, MA: MIT Press.

Kuroda, S. 1979. (Ko)-so-a ni tsuite. *Eigo to Nihongo to: Hayashi Eiichi Kyooju Kanreki Kinen Ronbunshuu*, 41-59. Tokyo: Kuroshio Shuppan.

Lakoff, R. 1974. Remarks on *This* and *That*. *CLS* 10: 345-356.

Lyons, J. 1977. *Semantics*.vol. 2. Cambridge: Cambridge University Press.
Ono, K. 1994. Territories of Information and Japanese Demonstratives. *Journal of the Association of Teachers of Japanese* 28: 131-155.
Ono, T., and Suzuki, R. 1992. Word Order Variability in Japanese Conversation: Motivations and Grammaticization. *Text* 12: 429-445.
Sakuma, K. 1983. *Geidai Nihongo no Hyoogen to Gohoo*. Tokyo: Kuroshio Shuppan.
Suzuki, S. 1998. Pejorative Connotation: A Case of Japanese. *Discourse Markers: Descriptions and Theory*, eds. A. H. Jucker and Y. Ziv, 261-276. Amsterdam/ Philadelphia: John Benjamins.

Culture and Interactional Styles: The Interpretation of Reactive Tokens in Japanese Conversations

SHIGEKO OKAMOTO AND SHIE SATO
California State University, Fresno and Massey University

1. Introduction[1]

It is often said that interactional style is culture-specific. Each culture is believed to have its preferred styles of social interaction, which may differ from those in other cultures. We are familiar with characterizations such as 'American Indians are taciturn' and 'Japanese are polite'. Studies have also shown that in inter-cultural communication misunderstandings may occur due to the participants' differing expectations about what is an appropriate interactional style for a given context (e.g. Gumperz 1982; Yamada 1992; Tannen 1993). While previous research has made it evident

[1]This study is an extension of Sato and Okamoto (1999). We thank those who helped us with the data collection, in particular, Take Izumi, Misako Kure, Hatsue Sato, and those who participated in recording the conversations. We also thank Noriko Akatsuka, Naomi H. McGloin, and Karen Mistry for their valuable comments.

that interactional style needs to be examined in its cultural context, the focus on cultural uniqueness and cultural differences may encourage over-generalizations and contribute to reproducing cultural stereotypes.

This study reexamines the relation of culture to interactional style using Japanese as a case in point. Japanese interactional style is commonly characterized as a reflection of the Japanese culture, which is said to sharply differ from the Western culture. Compared to the 'West', which emphasizes individualism, Japanese are assumed to be more concerned with relational harmony, interdependence, and hierarchy (e.g. Reischauer and Jansen 1995). Japanese interactional styles are commonly thought to reflect these cultural concerns in that people are polite, harmonious, cooperative, non-confrontational, empathetic, etc. (e.g. Gudykunst and Nishida 1986; Tsujimura 1987; Watanabe 1993; Maynard 1997). Analyzing the use of Reactive Tokens (hereafter, RTs) in Japanese conversations, this paper considers to what extent linguistic norms, as reflections of Japanese cultural values, affect the speech styles of real people interacting in specific social contexts.

2. Method

The data consist of audio-taped informal conversations. As summarized in Table 1, there are four sets of two dyadic conversations--one between a mother and her daughter (hereafter, M-D conversation), and the other between female close friends (hereafter, F-F conversation). In each set, one speaker (the daughter in the M-D conversation) participated in both conversations. Note that Conversation 4 is the same as Conversation 8.

	Conversations	Participant 1	Participant 2
Set A	Conversation 1	Aiko, 17 years old	Aiko's mother, 47 years old
	Conversation 2	Aiko	Miki, Aiko's friend, 17 years old
Set B	Conversation 3	Mari, 22 years old	Mari's mother, 52 years old
	Conversation 4	Mari	Natsu, Mari's friend, 22 years old
Set C	Conversation 5	Tomoe, 23 years old	Tomoe's mother, 56 years old
	Conversation 6	Tomoe	Tomoe's friend, 23 years old
Set D	Conversation 7	Natsu, 22 years old	Natsu's mother, early 50s
	Conversation 8	Natsu	Mari, Natsu's friend, 22 years old

Table 1: Participants in the eight conversations examined

The lengths of the conversations varied from twenty minutes to one hour. The speakers recorded their own conversations, sitting face to face; conversational topics were self-selected. All conversations were transcribed, although only the first fifteen-minute segment of each conversation was used for the quantitative analysis.[2]

3. Types of Reactive Tokens

Although there are many linguistic devices that are said to be used to make Japanese interactional style harmonious, polite, and empathetic (e.g. honorifics, backchannels, indirect speech), the present study focuses on the use of RTs, including backchannels. Compared to speakers of English, Japanese are said to use backchannels, or *aizuchi*, more frequently to express interactional support and involvement in the conversation (Maynard 1989, 1997; Matsuda 1988; Mizutani 1988; White 1989). For example, Hirokawa (1995: 380) suggests that the active listener participation by the use of *aizuchi* reflects 'the other-oriented, listening-oriented interactional approach' in Japanese and it functions 'to exhibit their conversational cooperation, support, and a way of building and maintaining interpersonal harmony'.

Clancy, Thompson, Suzuki, and Tao (1996), on the other hand, compared the use of RTs in English, Japanese, and Mandarin face-to-face conversations among friends, and found that generally Japanese and English speakers used RTs 'more than three times as frequently as Mandarin speakers' (378). This similarity between English and Japanese may partly derive from the fact that the RTs Clancy et al. examined included not only backchannels, but also other types of expressions. Clancy et al. define RT as 'a short utterance produced by an interlocutor who is playing a listener's role during the other interlocutor's speakership' (355) and identify the following five types of RTs: (1) Backchannel (a non-lexical vocalic form, serving as a 'continuer', display of interest, or claim of understanding--e.g. *un* 'yeah'); (2) Reactive Expression (a short non-floor taking lexical phrase or word--e.g. *hontoo* 'really'); (3) Repetition (a portion of the speech of the primary speaker repeated by the non-primary speaker); (4) Collaborative Finish (an utterance made by the non-primary speaker to finish a previous speaker's utterance); and (5) Resumptive Opener (a non-lexical element which is used at turn-initial points).

While the overall frequency of RT use was similar in English and Japanese conversations, Clancy et al. found considerable differences in the types of RTs used, including a large difference in the use of Backchannels (68.3% in Japanese and 37.9% in English). In the present study we draw

---

[2]The transcription conventions used in this study are as follows: [overlapping talk; ? rising intonation; . falling/utterance-final intonation; , continuing intonation; (.) micro-pause; (0.0) length of pause/silence in tenths of a second; ( ) non-linguistic activity or change in pitch/volume.

on the classification of RTs given by Clancy et al., although we do not include Resumptive Openers since they involve taking a full turn.

4. The Use of Reactive Tokens in the Present Data

Table 2 shows the frequency of different types of Reactive Tokens used by both speakers in a fifteen-minute segment of each of the eight conversations. As we can see, although there are differences among the four sets of conversations, generally RTs were used much more frequently in the F-F conversations than in the M-D conversations.

		Backchannels	Reactive Expressions	Repetitions	Collaborative Finishes	Total
Set A	C1	57 (85%)	10 (15%)	0 (0%)	0 (0%)	67
	C2	104 (71%)	40 (27%)	0 (0%)	3 (2%)	147
Set B	C3	6 (67%)	3 (33%)	0 (0%)	0 (0%)	9
	C4	179 (95%)	4 (2%)	5 (3%)	1 (1%)	189
Set C	C5	25 (74%)	9 (27%)	0 (0%)	0 (0%)	34
	C6	77 (68%)	27 (24%)	4 (4%)	5 (4%)	113
Set D	C7	13 (72%)	5 (28%)	0 (0%)	0 (0%)	18
	C8	179 (95%)	4 (2%)	5 (3%)	1 (1%)	189

Table 2: Frequency of RT tokens by type

Our data also show that the same speaker changes the amount of RTs depending on the situation. Table 3 shows the frequency of RTs used by the daughters in the two conversations in each set of conversations.

		Backchannels	Reactive Expressions	Repetitions	Collaborative Finishes	Total
Aiko	C1	16 (80%)	4 (20%)	0 (0%)	0 (0%)	20
	C2	82 (74%)	26 (23%)	0 (0%)	3 (3%)	111
Mari	C3	0 (0%)	0 (0%)	0 (0%)	0 (0%)	0
	C4	69 (96%)	2 (3%)	1 (1%)	0 (0%)	72
Tomoe	C5	4 (80%)	1 (20%)	0 (0%)	0 (0%)	5
	C6	49 (67%)	19 (26%)	2 (3%)	3 (4%)	73
Natsu	C7	8 (100%)	0 (0%)	0 (0%)	0 (0%)	8
	C8	110 (94%)	2 (2%)	4 (3%)	1 (1%)	117

Table 3: RT tokens by type for four speakers

Examples (1) and (2)--typical of all the pairs--illustrate how one speaker (Aiko) changes her RT use in the M-D and F-F conversations.

(1) Set A Conversation 1 (talking about the postcards which M purchased)

1 Mother: *Tenkeeteki na ukiyoe?*
'Typical Ukiyoe?'
2 (3.0)
3 Mother: *Kore dooshite kattaka tte yuuto,*
'Let me tell you why I bought this.'
4 (0.3)
5 Mother: *Watashi ga shigoto shiteru kaisha,*
'The company I work for"
6 *Ko kore.*
'This.'
7 *Mieru?*
'Can you see?'
8 *Moshikashitara mieru kamo wakaran.*
'Maybe you can see it.'
9 *Dooshite ka tte yuuto koko ni daimaru ga aru yaro?*
'The reason I'm asking you is because, see this Daimaru (building) over here?'
10 (0.5)
11 Mother: *Hora.*
'See?'
12 (0.9)
13 Aiko: *Un.*
'Yeah.'

(2) Set A Conversation 2 (Aiko's friend, talking about a male classmate that she always meets at their private cram school.)

1 Friend: *A, moo kinoo wa na-*
'Oh, you know yesterday'
2 Aiko: *Un.*
'Uh huh.'
3 Friend: *Atashi na- sono mukaiatteru kimoi otokonoko ga na-*
'The unpleasant-looking guy sitting right in front of me, you know'
4 Aiko: *Un.*
'Uh huh.'
5 Friend: *Ano- kojinjuku na, chitchai kora mo onnen.*
'There are also small kids in that private cram school.'

6 Aiko: *Un.*
'Uh huh.'
7 Friend: *Shoogakusee kurai no ko [toka,*
'Like elementary school kids.'
8 Aiko: *[Un.*
'Uh huh.'
9 Friend: *De watashi itsumo na- [koshitsu ni na?*
'And I normally, in an individual room'
10 Aiko: *[Un.*
'Uh huh.'
11 Friend: *Hutari hutari suware… hutari shika orehen heya ni na?*
'Two people, two people can sit … in a room where only two will fit, right?'
12 Aiko: *Un.*
'Uh huh.'
13 Friend: *Itsumo onne yan ka.*
'(he 's) always there, right?'

In Example (1) Aiko uses only one RT at the end of the excerpt, although there are eight Intonation Units (IUs) produced by M in prior discourse. In Example (2), the same speaker uses 6 RTs--i.e. after every IU of her friend's utterance. Moreover, in Example (1) four utterances of the primary speaker, Mother, were followed by a silence (lines 2, 4, 10, and 12) and in line 13 Aiko utters a RT after a silence. In contrast, in Example (2) every RT made by Aiko either immediately follows or overlaps with her friend's utterance.

What accounts for these differences? We cannot attribute them to a difference in formality. The two kinds of conversations examined here are both informal conversations, which is indicated by the fact that no participant uses honorifics to each other, while using many other informal expressions (e.g. *un* 'yeah, uh-huh' instead of *hai* 'yes'; interactional particles such as *yo* and *sa*). However, as shown above, RT use is very different in the two kinds of conversation. Below we consider the reasons for this difference.

First, long narrative-like utterances occur more frequently in the F-F conversations than in the M-D conversations; in the former the speakers also tend to stay on the same topic longer than in the latter, as seen in Example (2), which lasts 80 IUs (not shown in (2)) talking about the same topic; see also Example (4) below). In the M-D conversations, utterances tend to be short and have specific purposes, such as making a request and asking a question; the conversational topic also shifts frequently. Accordingly, there are fewer places to use RTs, as illustrated in Example (3).

(3) Set B Conversation 3 (M-D, talking about New Year's cards in the beginning of the conversation)

1 Mother: *80 mai kaita no. Kita no wa 50 mai kurai.*
'I wrote 80 cards. Those that I received were about 50.'
2 Mari: *50 mai mo kita no?*
'You received as many as 50?'
3 Mother: *50 mai kiteru yo.*
'I received 50.'
4 (8.0)
5 Mother: *Kono terebi nanji made?*
'How long is this TV show going to last?'
6 Mari: *Wakannai. 12 ji han gurai ma[de*
'I don't know. Until about 12:30 (a.m.)'
7 Mother: *[12 ji ha-n?*
'12:30?'
8 Mari: *Datte 12 ji han kara atashi miru yo.*
'But I'll watch another show from 12:30.'
9 Mother: *Nani o miru no?*
'What are you going to watch?'
10 Mari: *Inamura Junichi.*
'Inamura Junichi.'
11 Mother: *N? Inamura, [att*
'Huh? Inamura...'
12 Mari: *[Inamura ne.*
'It is Inamura.'
13 Mother: *Jaa eega ni natta yatsu? N?*
'The one which came out as a movie?'
14 Mari: *Nani itte n no?*
'What are you saying?'
15 Mother: *Eega o miru no?*
'So, are you going to watch a movie?'
16 Mari: *Eega o miru no, are da yo, ano, ano hora sazan ooru staazu [no Kuwata*
'I'm going to watch a movie. That one, you know, the one by Kuwata in Southern All Stars.'
17 Mother: *[Aaa Kuwata no ka.*
'Oh, the one by Kuwata.'
18 (2.2)
19 Mother: *Ashi, ashita wa soija yotee wa doosuru?*
'What are we going to do tomorrow then?'

In Example (3) the conversation topic changes in lines 5 and 19. In each case, there is a silence before the topic change and a new topic is introduced abruptly without any warning like *tokorode* 'by the way'. Further, most utterances are brief information-seeking questions, as in lines 9 and 15.

Secondly, in the F-F conversations the (primary) speakers tend to use a greater amount of expressions that are likely to induce RTs--expressions, such as certain interactional particles (e.g *ne* or *na* 'right?', *sa* 'you know'), tag-questions (e.g. *ja nai* or *jan* 'isn't it?', *desho*(*o*) 'right?'), interjections (e.g. *hora* 'look'), and a rising intonation. This is illustrated in Example (4).

(4) Set B Conversation 4 (Mari, talking about her commuting to work)

1 Mari: *Soo sungoi atashi* ***hora*** *ie tooi* ***jan****?*
'Yeah, you know my house is really far.'
2 Friend: *Aan.*
'Yeah.'
3 Mari: *De nijikan gurai kakatte,*
'It takes about 2 hours, and'
[michi no are ni yotte ***sa hora***
'It depends on how much traffic there is, you know.'
4 Friend: *[Un.*
'Yeah.'
5 (0.2)
6 Mari: *Okureru toki mo [aru n da, [demo sore o* ***sa****,*
'There are times when I get there late, but'
7 Friend: *[Un.* *[Un.*
'Yeah. Yeah.'
8 Mari: *Shikatanai [tto omoo* ***ja nai****?*
'Don't you think it can't be helped?'
9 Friend: *[Un.*
'Yeah.'

In this short excerpt, there are six tokens of RT-inducing expressions (bolded) in the primary speaker's utterances. (See also Example (2), where the primary speaker, Aiko's friend, uses the particle *na* 'right?' seven times.) The use of such RT-inducing expressions is limited in the M-D conversations; even when relatively long utterances are made, the primary speaker often does not use such expressions. In Example (1), for instance, Aiko's mother did not use RT-inducing expressions in lines 1, 3, 5, and 6, although she could have used them, as indicated by the bolded expressions in parentheses in (1a).[3]

(1a) Set A Conversation 1 (talking about the postcards which M purchased)

1 Mother: *Tenkeeteki na ukiyoe* **(*ne*).**
'Typical Ukiyoe?'
2 (3.0)
3 Mother: *Kore* **(*ne*)** *dooshite kattaka tte yuuto* **(*ne*),**
'Let me tell you why I bought this.'
4 (0.3)
5 Mother: *Watashi ga shigoto shiteru kaisha* **(*de ne*),**
'The company I work for"
6 *Ko kore* **(*ne*).**
'This.'

5. Interpretation of the Presence and Absence of RTs

What does the absence or infrequent usage of RTs in the M-D conversations mean? Does it imply, for example, that the speakers are unusually uncooperative? In contrast, does the frequent use of RTs in the F-F conversations indicate that the speakers are supportive and cooperative?

As mentioned earlier, Clancy et al. (1996) found that the use of RTs was strikingly low in Mandarin conversations, as compared to both English and Japanese conversations. The infrequent use of RTs by Mandarin speakers, however, does not seem to mean that they are being uncooperative and not concerned about engaging in a harmonious conversation, since all conversations are 'ordinary, non-argumentative conversations among friends' (357). Clancy et al. argue that 'it is important to keep in mind that culture-specific interpretations of the same phenomenon often vary radically' (381), and that for Mandarin speakers, avoidance of backchanneling is interpreted as a sign of 'respect for the primary speaker's right to formulate and produce their talk undisturbed,' while for Japanese listeners, it may be interpreted as 'uncooperative and lacking in empathy' (382). Clancy et al. (ibid.) then note that this difference between Japanese and Mandarin may derive from different, culture-specific, politeness strategies, such as Brown and Levinson's (1987) positive and negative politeness.

---

[3]Note also that although the number was limited, there were some cases in which relatively long narrative-like utterances accompanied by RT-inducing expressions appeared in the M-D conversations. But even in such cases the secondary speaker tended to use few RTs.

While the notion that the interpretation of a linguistic form is relative to the cultural context is important to keep in mind, the analyses of our data suggest that this interpretive relativity is applicable not only to different cultures, but also to different situations within a single culture. For example, the lack of RTs in the M-D conversations in our data does not seem to index negative politeness, as in the Mandarin conversations among friends. Family members are normally in a most intimate relationship, a context in which the speakers can be most spontaneous and need not be reserved toward each other. However, this does not necessarily mean that family members in our data are being uncooperative and rude by avoiding RTs or positive politeness. Rather, it is possible that in family conversations, the frequent use of RTs is not generally expected and hence the infrequent use of RTs may not be interpreted as rude, but rather serves as a sign of intimacy. Thus, if an excessive amount of RTs is used in such a context, it may be perceived as unusual, insincere, or even rude; it may also signal a change in the nature of the relationship. On the other hand, friends (in our data) may be expected to use RTs relatively frequently, or to actively express positive politeness, in order to establish and reinforce solidarity between them.

The interpretation of the presence or absence of RTs is but one example of the potential ambiguity of social meanings. The interpretation of honorifics offers another example. Depending on the context, the use of honorifics may be considered polite or impolite (due to distancing). Likewise, the nonuse of honorifics may be perceived as rude or as friendly (Okamoto 1999). These examples suggest that we must take into consideration situational variability within a culture in the interpretation of the same linguistic form, since different situations evoke different norms and expectations.[4]

6. Conclusion

While many studies have noted that RTs or backchannels are used frequently in Japanese as a reflection of cultural concerns for harmony and interdependence, our analysis indicates that Japanese speakers may not always use RTs frequently. Our comparison of the M-D and F-F conversations has revealed that speakers use significantly fewer RTs in the former than in the latter. One possible reason for this difference is the type of utterances used; that is, compared to the M-D conversations, the F-F con-

---

[4]Note that we do not mean to claim that a particular situation--e.g. a family relationship or friendship--directly determines the use of linguistic forms like RTs. Even if the same kind of situation is involved, there may be variation due to a variety of reasons, including differences in individual speakers' attitudes toward the use of particular linguistic forms.

versations included more utterances that encourage the use of RTs, such as long narrative-like utterances and RT-inducing expressions. It is also possible that depending on the situation, speakers are not expected to use RTs frequently, and that RTs do not always function in the same way across contexts. This variability is suggested by the contrastive use of RTs between the M-D and F-F conversations in our data, as well as that between the Japanese and Mandarin conversations among friends observed by Clancy et al. (1996). Our analysis demonstrates the importance of considering not only the cultural variability, but also the situational variability in the norms and expectations for interactional styles, and hence in the interpretation of the same linguistic forms. Thus the presence or absence of certain linguistic features, such as RTs, cannot be straightforwardly regarded as constituting a harmonious (or disharmonious) interaction independently of the context.

Clearly, further research is called for to investigate variations in interactional styles within a single culture. Such research requires investigations of conversations carried out in diverse social contexts, including not only casual conversations, but also conversations in different genres (see, for example, Saft, in press).[5] We hope our study serves as a first step toward reexamining the complex relationship between culture and interactional styles.

References

Brown, P. and S. C. Levinson. 1987. *Politeness: Some universals in language usage*. Cambridge: Cambridge University Press.

Clancy, P. M., S. A. Thompson, R. Suzuki, and H. Tao. 1996. The Conversational Use of Reactive Tokens in English, Japanese, and Mandarin. *Journal of Pragmatics* 26: 355-387.

Gudykunst, W. B. and T. Nishida. 1986. Attributional Confidence in Low- and High-Context Cultures. *Human Communication Research* 12: 525-549.

Gumperz, J. 1982. *Discourse Strategies*. Cambridge: Cambridge University Press.

Hirokawa, K. 1995. *The Expressions of Culture in the Conversational Styles of Japanese and Americans*. Doctoral dissertation, University of Michigan.

Matsuda, Y. 1988. Taiwa no Nihon-go Kyooiku-Gaku: Aizuchi ni Kanren Shite (Teaching of Japanese Dialogue: With Reference to Backchannels). *Nihongo-gaku* (Japanese Linguistics) 7: 59-66.

[5]For example, employing a Conversation Analytic approach, Saft (forthcoming) examines the use of *aizuchi* in a political discussion program on television and argues that *aizuchi* may have versatile functions, such as serving as resources for organizing talk in a particular genre, or more specifically, for getting access to the floor.

Maynard, S. 1997. *Japanese Communication: Language and Thought in Context.* Honolulu: University of Hawaii Press.

Maynard, S. 1989. *Japanese Conversation: Self-Contextualization through Structure and Interactional Management.* Norwood, NJ: Ablex.

Mizutani, N. 1988. Aizuchi-ron (On Backchannels). *Nihongo-gaku* (Japanese Linguistics) 7(12): 4-11.

Okamoto, S. 1999. Situated Politeness: Manipulating Honorific and Non-Honorific Expressions in Japanese Conversations. *Pragmatics* 8: 51-74.

Reischauer, E. O. and M. B. Jansen. 1995. *The Japanese Today: Change and Continuity.* Cambridge, MA: Belknap Press of Harvard University Press.

Saft, S. In press. Exploring Aizuchi as Resources in Japanese Social Interaction: The Case of a Political Discussion Program. *Journal of Pragmatics.*

Sato, S. and S. Okamoto. 1999. Reexamination of Japanese "Cooperative" Communication Style. *Pragmatics in 1998: Selected Papers from the 6th International Pragmatics Conference*, ed. J. Verschueren, 518-527. Antwerp: International Pragmatics Association.

Tannen, D. 1993. The Relativity of Linguistic Strategies: Rethinking Power and Solidarity in Gender and Dominance. *Gender and Conversational Interaction*, ed. D. Tannen, 165-188. Oxford: Oxford University Press.

Tsujimura, A. 1987. Some Characteristics of the Japanese Way of Communication. *Communication Theory from Eastern and Western Perspectives*, ed. D. L. Kincaid, 115-126. New York: Academic Press.

Yamada, H. 1992. *American and Japanese Business Discourse: A Comparison of Interactional Styles.* Norwood, NJ: Ablex.

Watanabe, S. 1993. Cultural Differences in Framing: American and Japanese Group Discussions. *Framing in Discourse*, ed. D. Tannen, 197-209. Oxford: Oxford University Press.

White, S. 1989. Back-channels across Cultures: A Study of Americans and Japanese. *Language in Society* 18:59-77.

Index

Japanese and Korean Linguistics at CSLI Publications

15 volumes of *Japanese/Korean Linguistics* have been published since 1990 with over 400 articles. All volumes remain in print and a cumulative table of contents for the entire series may be found at

http://cslipublications.stanford.edu/ja-ko-contents/jako-collective-toc.html

where articles are grouped by the following subject categories:

Phonetics and Phonology
Syntax and Morphology
Semantics
Pragmatics, Discourse and Conversation
Psycholinguistics and Cognition
L1 and L2 Acquisition
Historical Linguistics, Language Change and Grammaticalization
Sociolinguistics and Language Use

For more information on other volumes in this series, please visit

http://cslipublications.stanford.edu/site/JAKO.html

Japanese/Korean Linguistics, Vol. 15	Naomi Hanaoka McGloin and Junko Mori, editors
Japanese/Korean Linguistics, Vol. 14	Timothy J. Vance and Kimberly Jones, editors
Japanese/Korean Linguistics, Vol. 13	Mutsuko Endo Hudson, Sun-Ah Jun, Peter Sells, Patricia M. Clancy, Shoichi Iwasaki and Sung-Ock Sohn, editors
Japanese/Korean Linguistics, Vol. 12	William McClure, editor
Japanese/Korean Linguistics, Vol. 11	Patricia M. Clancy, editor
Japanese/Korean Linguistics, Vol. 10	Noriko Akatsuka, Susan Strauss, and Bernard Comrie, editors
Japanese/Korean Linguistics, Vol. 9	Mineharu Nakayama and Charles J. Quinn, Jr., editors
Japanese/Korean Linguistics, Vol. 8	David James Silva, editor
Japanese/Korean Linguistics, Vol. 7	Noriko Akatsuka, Hajime Hoji, Shoichi Iwasaki, Sung-Ock Sohn, and Susan Strauss, editors
Japanese/Korean Linguistics, Vol. 6	Ho-min Sohn and John Haig, editors
Japanese/Korean Linguistics, Vol. 5	Noriko Akatsuka, Shoichi Iwasaki, and Susan Strauss, editors

Japanese/Korean Linguistics, Vol. 4	Noriko Akatsuka, editor
Japanese/Korean Linguistics, Vol. 3	Soonja Choi, editor
Japanese/Korean Linguistics, Vol. 2	Patricia M. Clancy, editor
Japanese/Korean Linguistics, Vol. 1	Hajime Hoji, editor